# 32/64-Bit 80x86 Assembly Language Architecture

## James C. Leiterman

Wordware Publishing, Inc.

**Library of Congress Cataloging-in-Publication Data**

Leiterman, James (James C.)
　32/64-bit 80x86 assembly language architecture / by James C. Leiterman.
　　p.　cm.
　Includes index.
　ISBN-13: 978-1-59822-002-5
　ISBN-10: 1-59822-002-0 (pbk.)
　1. Computer architecture.　2. Assembler language (Computer program language)　I. Title.
　QA76.9.A73L47 2005
　004.2'2--dc22　　　　　　　　　　　　　　2005013995
　　　　　　　　　　　　　　　　　　　　　CIP

ISBN-13: 978-1-59822-002-5
ISBN-10: 1-59822-002-0
10 9 8 7 6 5 4 3 2 1
0506

All inquiries for volume purchases of this book should be addressed to Wordware
Publishing, Inc., at the above address. Telephone inquiries may be made by calling:

(972) 423-0090

# Contents

# Preface

(or, So Why Did He Write Yet Another Book?)

Yet another book? Well, actually I am merely just one of the other ex-Atari employees who was a member of Alan Kay's group, Atari Corporate Research, and has published books.

For those of you who have been following my eventful career, you already know that this is actually my third published book.

Just to bring you up to date, my first book was titled *The Death and Rebirth of the x86 Assembly Language Programmer* and was originally written between July 1997 and June 1998. It also went under the title of *x86 Assembly Language Optimization in Computer Games.* Its timing was perfect as SSE code named Katmai by Intel was just about to come out. I could not find a publisher willing to sign as they "could not sell their last 80x86 assembly language book," and so I put it aside and went back to school to work on my next degree at Oregon State University. (*Go Beavers!*)

Two years later I came up with a SIMD (vector) assembly language book idea. Having learned my lesson, I sold the idea to a publisher first (Wordware Publishing) and *Vector Game Math Processors* became my first published book. It probably should have included 80x86, Mips, and PowerPC in the title, as that would have helped to increase its sales. It seems most people stumble across it.

Everybody who read it and contacted me seemed to like it. It was more of a niche book as it primarily taught how to vectorize code to take advantage of the vector instruction sets of processors only recently introduced into offices and homes. These contain functionality that was once confined to the domain of the super computer. *Vector Game Math Processors* discusses pseudo vector code that actually emulated vector processors using generic optimized C, as well as heavy utilization of the following instruction sets:

- 80x86 (MMX, SSE(2), 3DNow! Professional)
- PowerPC and AltiVec

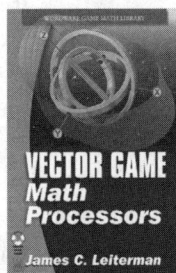

▥   MIPS (MIPS-3D, MIPS V, etc.)

While writing it I wrote a chapter on vertex shaders and sold the idea to my publisher. Thus my second book published was *Learn Vertex and Pixel Shader Programming with DirectX 9*.

And now we have come full circle, as this book is actually the completion of my original 80x86 book, *The Death*... But I digress. The title was too long and not really to the point. So now that book has been completed, updated, and designed to be the prequel to my vector book. And thank you for buying both (you did, did you not?) as you are reading one of them now!

The problem with writing "yet another book" is that one tends to use the best jokes or favorite stories in the first one. Well, I have so many from over the years, especially since I have eight kids (with the same wife), that I have saved some for this book. But relax, the worst stories are laying on the editing room floor in order to make this book more academic friendly.

One (almost) last item. Keep an eye out for my not-so-technical book, *Programming Pyrite — The Fool's Gold of Programming Video Games*. It is meant not to be a programming book, but a book about the trials and tribulations of becoming a video game programmer. It is meant to be a satirical peek into this world, and is based on my experiences as well as the good and bad stories that I have encountered over the years.

▮   ▮   ▮

I wish to thank those who have contributed information, hints, testing time, etc., for this book. Paul Stapley for some recommendations and technical overview recommendations; Peter Jefferies and John Swiderski for some code sample testing; Ken Mayfield for some 3D computer art donations; John Romero for his technical check and tip recommendations; and some of those others that I have neglected to mention here for their contributions.

And most of all to my wife for not balking too much after she thought I had finished writing for good after finishing my second published book and then noticed within a couple weeks that I was working on this book. "Revising your vector book for a second edition?" Of course she did not seem to notice (or mention) the purchases of new

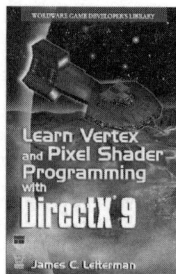

motherboards and processors as they were hidden inside my nice super quiet Sonata computer equipment.

I finally wish to thank Wes Beckwith from Wordware Publishing, Inc., for seeing the niche that this book would fill and convincing his company to publish yet another of my books.

So get up from that floor or chair in the bookstore in which you are currently reading this book; you know you will need this book for work or school. Besides, I filled it with so much stuff you might as well stop copying the stuff into that little notebook, grab a second copy for use at home, walk over to that check stand, and buy them both. Tell your friends how great the book is so they will buy a copy too! Insist to your employer that the technical book library needs a few copies as well. This book is a tutorial and a reference manual.

My eight children and my outnumbered domestic engineering wife will be thankful that we will be able to afford school clothes as well as Christmas presents this year! Unlike the title of Steve Martin's remake of the movie that kids are *Cheaper by the Dozen*, they are not! They eat us out of house and home! (Fortunately for me, my kids are *typically* not quite as rambunctious as his!)

To check for any updates or code supplements to any of my books, check out my web site at http://www.leiterman.com/books.html.

Send any questions or comments to books@leiterman.com.

■  ■  ■

My brother Ranger Robert Leiterman is a writer of mystery related nature books that cover diverse topics such as natural resources, as well as his Big Foot Mystery series. Buy his books too! Especially buy them if you are a game designer and interested in cryptozoology or natural resources or just have kids. If it were not for his sending me his books to help proofread, I probably would not have started writing my own books as well.

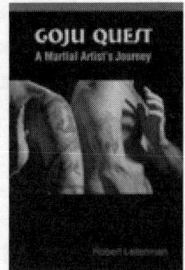

Watch out for books from Thomas, yet another of my brothers who has joined the Leiterman brothers' book writing club. That leaves my three remaining brothers yet to join!

(Now if we can only get our kids to read our books! Something about needing more pictures or not being so technical....)

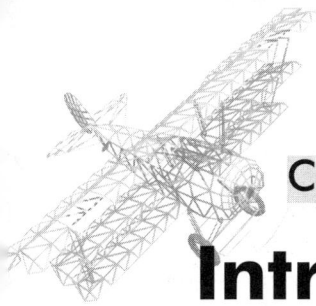

# Chapter 1

# Introduction

When the processor manufacturer Intel is mentioned, two 64-bit processors come to mind: EM64T and the Itanium. For AMD: the AMD64. Non-80x86 manufacturers discovered years ago that competing against an established desktop market is difficult to impossible. The key to successful market injection is being able to run a large quantity of pre-existing applications. Intel and AMD have built their business upon this by periodically creating superset instruction sets for their 80x86 processors so that pre-existing software still runs on the new equipment and new software can be written for the new equipment.

The technology has been forked into two 64-bit paths. One uses the Itanium-based platform with a new 64-bit primary instruction set that belongs to the IA-64 family. The other is a superset to the IA-32, referred to as the Extended Memory 64 Technology (EM64T). Newer P4 and Xeon processors are of this alternate type.

This book targets the AMD32/64, IA-32, and EM64T processor technology. It is not written for the Itanium series. (Look for a future book to cover the Itanium processor.) The EM64T supports a new superset instruction set, SSE-3, and 64-bit extensions to the IA-32 general-purpose instruction set. It also allows 64-bit operating systems such as Windows XP Professional x64 and Windows Server 2003 x64 editions to run both 64-bit and 32-bit software on the same machine.

This book can be used for both 32-bit and 64-bit instruction sets, but there is an operating system application dependency that needs to be followed.

| Operating System | App (32-bit) IA-32 | App (64-bit) AMD64/EM64T |
|---|---|---|
| Win9X (32-bit) | X | |
| WinXP (32-bit) | X | |
| Win2K (32-bit) | X | |
| Win2003 (32-bit) | X | |
| XP – X64 (64-bit) | X | X |
| Win Server 2003 X64 | X | X |

The 80x86 processor has joined the domain of the super computer since the introduction of the SIMD (single instruction multiple data) such as Intel's Pentium III used in the Xbox, and all other x86s including the Pentium IV and AMD's 3DNow! extension instructions used in PCs. And now they are available in 64 bit. Both fixed-point (inclusive of integer) and floating-point math are being used by the computer, video gaming, and embedded worlds in assembly and vector-based operations.

3D graphic rendering hardware has been going through major increases in the numbers of polygons that can be handled by using geometry engines as part of their rendering hardware to accelerate the speed of mathematical calculations. There is also the recent introduction of the programmable vertex and pixel shaders built into newer video cards that use this same vector functionality. (This is another type of assembly language programming. For more information on shaders read my book *Learn Vertex and Pixel Shader Programming with DirectX 9*.) These work well for rendering polygons with textures, depth ordering Z-buffers or W-buffers, and translucency controlled alpha channels with lighting, perspective correction, etc., at relatively high rates of speed. The problem is that the burden of all the other 3D processing, culling, transformations, rotations, etc., are put on the computer's central processing unit (CPU), which is needed for artificial intelligence (AI), terrain following, landscape management, property management, sound, etc. Fortunately for most programmers, a continuous growth market of middle-ware providers is developing key building blocks such as the Unreal 3D rendering libraries and physics packages such as Havok. Whether you are looking to become employed by these companies and generate this technology or merely one who wishes to use these libraries, you should keep in mind that the introduction of new hardware technology has created a surplus of CPU processor power that can now be used to fulfill aspects of your programming projects as well as develop new technologies. All of this creates openings for programmers needing to write assembly language, whether using a scalar or parallel architecture.

There are perhaps only two reasons for writing code in assembly language: writing low-level kernels in operating systems and writing high-speed optimized critical code. A vector processor can be given sequences and arrays of calculations to perform to enhance the performance above that of scalar operations that high-level compilers typically generate during a compile.

**Hint:** Check out the following web site for additional information, code, links, etc., related to this book: http://www.leiterman.com/books.html.

There are exceptions to this as some vector compilers do exist but as of yet have not been adopted into the mainstream marketplace. These are well worth investigating if you are in need of high-level C code that takes advantages of SIMD instruction sets.

One other item to keep in mind is that if you understand this information, it may be easier for you to get a job in the game or embedded software development industry. This is because you will have enhanced your programming foundation and possibly have a leg up on your competition. Even if you rarely program in 80x86 assembly language, peeking at the disassembly output of your high-level compiler while debugging your application can give you insight into code bloat due to your coding methodology and you will better be able to resolve some of the weird bugs you encounter in your applications.

**Goal:** A better understanding of 80x86 assembly.

I know how a number of you like technical books to be like a resource bible, but I hate for assembly books (no matter how detailed) to be arranged in that fashion, because:

1. It takes me too long to find what I am looking for!
2. They almost always put me to sleep!

This book is not arranged like a bible, but it contains the same information. By using the instruction mnemonic lookup in Appendix B, it becomes an abstracted bible. It is instead arranged in chapters of functionality. If you want that bible-like alpha-sorted organization, just look at the index or Appendix B of this book, scan for the instruction you are looking for, and turn to the page.

**Info:** Appendix B is the master instruction index listing and what processors support it.

I program multiple processors in assembly and occasionally have to reach for a book to look up the correct mnemonic. Quite often my own books! Manufacturers almost always seem to camouflage those needed instructions. As an example, mnemonics shifting versus rotating can be located all over the place in a book. For example, in the 80x86, {psllw, pslld, psllq, …, shld, shr, shrd} are mild cases due to the closeness of their spellings, but for Boolean bit logic, {and … or, pand … xor} are all over the place in an alphabetical arrangement. When grouped in chapters of functionality, however, one merely turns to the chapter related to what functionality is required and then leafs through the pages. For these examples, merely turn to Chapter 4, "Bit Mangling" or Chapter 5, "Bit Wrangling." Okay, okay, so I had a little fun with the chapter titles, but there is no having to wade through pages of extra information trying to find what you are looking for. In addition (not meant to be a pun), there are practical examples near the descriptions as well as in Chapter 19, which are even more helpful in jogging your memory as to an instruction's usage. Even the companion code for this book uses this same orientation.

The examples are for the 80x86. I tried to minimize printed computer code as much as possible so that the pages of the book do not turn into a mere source code listing! Hopefully I did not overtrim and make it seem confusing. If that occurs, merely open your source code editor or integrated development environment (IDE) to the chapter and project in the accompanying code related to that point in the book you are trying to understand. By the way, if you find a discrepancy between the code and the book, you should favor the code as the code in the book was cut and pasted from elements of code that could be lost during the editing process.

The book is also written in a friendly style so as to occasionally be amusing and thus help you in remembering the information over a longer period of time. What good is a technical book that is purely mathematical in nature, difficult to extract any information from, and just puts you (I mean me) to sleep? You would most likely have to reread the information again once you woke up! The idea is that you should be able to sit down in a comfortable setting and read the book cover to cover to get a global overview. (My favorite place to read is in a lawn chair on the back patio with a wireless laptop.) Then go back to your computer and, using the book as a tool, implement what you need or cut and paste into your code. *But use at your own risk!* You should use this book as an appendix to more in-depth technical information to gain an understanding of that information.

An attempt was made to layer the information so you would be able to master the information at your skill level. In regard to cutting and pasting: You will find portions of this book also occur inside one of my other published books: *Vector Game Math Processors*. There is a degree of overlap, but this book is to be considered the prequel and a foundation for that book. Any duplication of information between the two has been enhanced in this book as it is now almost three years later and the technology has been extended.

The code is broken down by platform, chapter, and project, but most of the code has not been optimized. This is explained later but briefly, optimized code is difficult to read and understand. For that reason, I tried to keep this book as clear and as readable as possible. Code optimizers such as Intel's VTune program are available for purposes of optimization.

This book, as mentioned, is divided into chapters of functionality. It is related to the use of learning to write 80x86 assembly language for games, or embedded and scientific applications. (Except for writing a binary-coded decimal (BCD) package, there is not a big need for assembly language in pure business applications.) Now graphically or statistically oriented, that is another matter. With that in mind, you will learn from this book:

- Adapted coding standards that this book recommends
- Bit manipulations and movement
- Converting data from one form into another
- Addition/subtraction (integer/floating-point/BCD)
- Multiplication/division (integer/floating-point)
- Special functions
- (Some) trigonometric functionality
- Branching and branchless coding
- Some vector foundations
- Debugging

It is very important to write functions in a high-level language such as C code before rewriting in assembly. Do not write code destined for assembly code using the C++ programming language because you will have to untangle it later. Assembly language is designed for low-level development and C++ for high-level object-oriented development using inheritance, name mangling, and other levels of abstraction, which makes the code harder to simplify. There is of course no reason why you would not wrap your assembly code with C++ functions or

libraries. But I strongly recommend you debug your assembly language function before locking it away in a static or dynamic library, as debugging it will become harder. This allows the algorithm to be debugged and mathematical patterns to be identified before writing the algorithm. In addition, the results of both algorithms can be compared to verify that they are identical and thus the assembly code is functioning as expected.

**Tip:** Sometimes examining compiler output can give insight into writing optimized code. (That means peeking at the disassembly view while debugging your application.)

# Conventions Used in This Book

## Companion Code

This book is accompanied by downloadable code available from www.wordware.com/files/8086 and www.leiterman.com/books.html. Each chapter with related sample code will have a table similar to the following:

**Workbench Files:** \Bench\\*x86*\chap02\\*project*\\*platform*

|  | project | platform |
|---|---|---|
| **Ram Test** | **\ramtest\** | \vc6 |
| **ram** | **\ram\** | \vc.net |

Substituting the data elements in a column into the "Workbench Files:" path will establish a path as to where a related project is stored.

The idea of the code is to be a usable sample of assembly code that has been split open to display its internals for observation and learning. Each module has its own initialization routine to set up function prototype pointers. These are used to vector to the appropriate function designed to be executed by a specific instruction set. This is mainly for the PC as the Xbox only uses a single PIII processor. The correct functions best suited for that processor are assigned to the pointers. If you are one of those (unusual) people running two or more processors in a multiprocessor computer, and they are not identical, then I am sorry! A few motherboards still support this scenario. The good news is that the samples are single threaded so you should theoretically be okay.

One other item: There are many flavors of processors and although the basis of each function call was a cut-and-paste from other functions,

the core functionality of the function was not. So there may be some debris where certain comments are not exactly correct; forgive me. There is a lot of code to have to wade through and keep in sync with the different models of 80x86 processors. It has been primarily borrowed from my vector book.

## Image Patterning

The images in this book show flow control and sometimes have a split in the middle. These types of images are typically 128-bit SSE, but in cases where the 64-bit MMX has identical functionality, the right side of the split is used to represent the 64-bit sub-set bits 0...63.

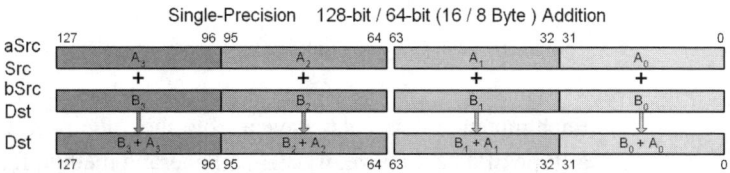

Sometimes the sub-pattern is not appropriate and so it will be shown separately.

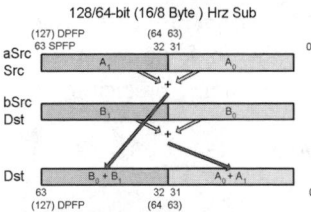

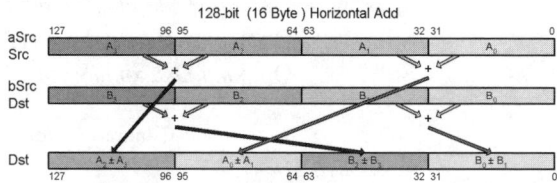

Some of these instructions support not only 4× single-precision floating-point (SSE) and 2× single-precision floating-point (MMX), but also 2× double-precision floating-point (SSE2). It just so happens that the patterns for MMX and SSE2 match. So refer to the MMX pattern when working with double-precision floating-point.

## Processor Legend

Each mnemonic will indicate a version of processor that supports it.

|  | Intel |  |  |  | AMD |
|---|---|---|---|---|---|
| P | Pentium |  | K6 | K6 |
| PII | Pentium II (MMX) |  | 3D! | 3DNow! |
| SSE | SSE (Katmai NI) |  | 3Mx+ | 3DNow! and MMX Ext. |
| SSE2 | SSE2 |  | A64 | AMD64 |
| SSE3 | SSE3 (Prescott NI) |  |  |  |
| E64T | 64-bit Memory |  |  |  |

| Mnemonic | P | PII | K6 | 3D! | 3Mx+ | SSE | SSE2 | A64 | SSE3 | E64T |
|---|---|---|---|---|---|---|---|---|---|---|
| INC | ✓ | ✓ | ✓ | ✓ | ✓ | ✓ | ✓ | 32 | ✓ | 32 |
| SYSRET |  |  | ✓ | ✓ | ✓ |  |  | ✓ |  | 64 |

| ✓ | Mnemonic supported |
|---|---|
| 32 | 32-bit support only |
| 64 | 64-bit support only |

Each mnemonic will also have a table showing its organization as well as type of data, bit size of data, and operand method for each processor supported.

|  | Op *rmDst, rSrc(8/16/32/64)* | Signed |  |
|---|---|---|---|
|  | Op *rDst, rmSrc(8/16/32/64)* |  |  |
| MMX | Op *mmxDst, mmxSrc/m64* | Signed | 64 |
| 3DNow! | Op *mmxDst, mmxSrc/m64* | Signed | 64 |
| SSE | Op *xmmDst, xmmSrc/m128* | Single-precision | 128 |
| SSE2 | Op *xmmDst, xmmSrc/m128* | Single-precision | 128 |

| *rDst* | General-purpose register — {8-, 16-, 32-, 64-bit} |
|---|---|
| *rSrc{8/16/32/64}* |  |
| *m32, m64, m128* | 32-, 64-, 128-bit memory access |
| *rmDst* | General-purpose register and/or memory |
| *mmxDst, mmxSrc* | MMX registers |
| *xmmDst, xmmSrc* | XMM registers |

**Note:** When general-purpose registers specify 64 bit, such as rDst, rmSrc{8/16/32/64}, then that is *only* available when running in 64-bit mode. Contrarily, 64-bit data is available for MMX and SSE instruction sets.

Some operators take zero, one, two, or three arguments. Unlike some non-80x86 processors, *sourceB* is the same as the *destination*. The 80x86 uses a D += A methodology. When the SIMD operator is being explained, both arguments will be used, such as "The Op instruction operates upon the sources *aSrc* (*xmmSrc*) and *bSrc* (*xmmDst*), and the result is stored in the destination *Dst* (*xmmDst*)." In some cases *operand* is used instead of *source* and/or *destination*, especially when the instruction has no destination. SSE registers (*xmm*) are favored over MMX (*mmx*) registers in explanations. 32-bit general-purpose registers are favored over 8/16/64-bit registers as that is the default size for both 32-bit and 64-bit processors.

The following list describes the data types given above.

- **Unsigned** — Unsigned integer
- **Signed** — Signed integer
- **[Un]signed** — Sign neutral, thus integer can be either signed or unsigned
- **Single-Precision** — Single-precision floating-point
- **Double-Precision** — Double-precision floating-point
- **Extended-Precision** — Double extended-precision floating-point
- **DPFP → INT32** — (Conversion) double-precision floating-point to signed 32-bit integer

**Note:** Technically an integer that is considered signless, meaning without sign (sign neutral), is called either signless in languages such as in Pascal or [un]signed.

Normally, however, there is typically no third case because if it is not signed, then it is unsigned. In regard to this book, however, I needed this third case to represent that a value could be either signed or unsigned, thus [un]signed is utilized.

## Notes, Tips, and Hints

A Hint is an indicator of something to watch for and take notice. It is typically something that can be helpful in the development of code, such as the following:

**Hint:** Not all processors handle the same set of parallel instructions. Located throughout this book are emulation code samples to help explain functionality and alleviate any missing operators, or give you as a developer ideas for implementing your own algorithm on a computer.

The No 64-bit icon indicates that a particular instruction is not supported in 64-bit mode. It looks like the following:

**No 64-bit:** Due to remapping of the REX prefix in 64-bit mode, this instruction can no longer access a register directly.

The No App (Sys Only) icon indicates that a particular instruction is only accessible from Real Mode or Privilege Level 0.

**No App (Sys Only):** This is only accessible from Real Mode or Privilege Level 0.

# Pseudo Vec

A pseudo vector declaration will have an associated C language macro or functions to emulate the functionality of a SIMD operator.

The source code contains various sets of code for the different processors. Almost none of the functions actually return a value; instead the results of the equation are assigned to a pointer specified by the first (and sometimes second) function parameters. They will always be arranged in an order similar to the following:

```
void vmp_functionPlatform(argDest, argSourceA, argSourceB)
```

For the generic C code, the term "Generic" will be embedded as in the following:

```
void vmp_FAddGeneric(float *pfD,              // Dest
                  float fA, float fB)          // SrcA

void vmp_QVecAddGeneric(vmp3DQVector * const pvD,   // Dest
                  const vmp3DQVector * const pvA,   // SrcA
                  const vmp3DQVector * const pvB)   // SrcB
```

The important item to note is the actual parameter, {pvD, pvA, pvB} in the above example. The "F" in FAdd represents a scalar single-precision float.

*Table 1-1: Float data type declaration*

| "F" in vmp_**F**Add | Scalar single-precision float |
|---|---|
| "Vec" in vmp_**Vec**Add | Single-precision (3) float vector |
| "QVec" in vmp_**QVec**Add | Single-precision (4) float vector |
| "DVec" in vmp_**DVec**Add | Double-precision (4) float vector |

*Table 1-2: Data size of an element*

| | |
|---|---|
| "v" as in p**v**D | 128-bit vector typically (SP float) |
| "b" as in p**b**D | 8-bit [Un]signed packed |
| "h" as in p**h**D | 16-bit [Un]signed packed |
| "w" as in p**w**D | 32-bit [Un]signed packed |
| "d" as in p**d**D | 64-bit [Un]signed packed |

Really complicated, don't you think? Of course when you selectively cut and paste some of this library code into your functions and change them just enough to make them your own, you will most probably be using your own conventions and not mine. Whatever works for you!

## Pseudo Vec (x86) (3DNow!) (3DNow!+) (MMX) (MMX+) (SSE) (SSE2) (SSE3)

Declarations that are followed by a processor label specify alternate assembly code specifically for use by that processor to emulate an operation.

## Graphics 101 (x86) (3DNow!) (MMX)

An algorithm typically found in graphics programming; the 101 is a play on a university beginning class number. This is a graphics algorithm implementation for the specified processor instruction set.

## Algebraic Law

| | | |
|---|---|---|
| Identity | n1 = 1n = n | n+0 = 0 + n = n |

This item is self-explanatory. Algebraic laws are used in this book as well as other books related to mathematics. The first time one of the laws is encountered it will be defined similarly to this as a reminder to the rules of algebra learned back in school.

The following are some of the symbols used throughout this book.

| | | | |
|---|---|---|---|
| ± | Signed | ≈ | Approximately |
| + | Unsigned | ? | Comparison |
| ∧ | AND | ¬ | NOT |
| ∨ | OR | ⊕ | XOR |
| Δ | Delta (difference) | ≡ | Equivalent |

| | | |
|---|---|---|
| [ ] | Inclusive | [–128, 128) |
| ( ) | Exclusive | Range: –128 ≤ N < 128 |

# I-VU-Q

The I-VU-Q abbreviation represents the answer to an interview question that has been encountered and its solution.

I have thrown interview questions and their answers into this book that have come up from time to time during my interviews over the years. Hopefully they will help you when you have to handle a programming test, as it seems that some of those same questions are continuously passed around from company to company.

If you wish to read my diatribe related to programming tests, either buy my vector book or one of my new books to be published, such as *Programming Pyrite — The Fool's Gold of Programming Video Games!*

■ ■ ■

So let us begin! But wait! During the development of this book (or any of my books) I frequent bookstores and examine similar books to see what were good and bad features, what they did to make their books more complete, etc. I was just about to send this book to the publisher when a new book came out. I rushed over to check out a copy. I picked it up, saw the reduced price, leafed through it, smiled, and returned it to the shelf. For 80x86 processors, do not buy a book published prior to 2001 unless you are truly a beginner and are trying to learn basic foundations. Even if the book was just published, look at it carefully and compare it to others. All the post-MMX instructions came out from 2001 to the present. These later instructions are really the interesting ones. Some of those early instructions are not even available on the latest processors, so you would learn something that would not even be valid. I have seen some of these books not only discuss but document all the interrupt function methods including video interrupt 10h, DOS interrupt 21h, printer interrupts, or some of the other interrupts long since retired with the release of Win95. (That was around 1995, was it not?) Those were DOS commands (pre-32-bit Windows!). (Okay, I admit I did a tad, but only enough to explain the functionality of the INT instruction.) Organizations of CD or disk drive sectors was important back then as well but not now unless you are writing your own kernel drivers for the manufacturer. The point is, you will not find filler such as that in this book.

At the time of this writing this book was the most complete book in terms of instruction sets that I could find. Besides, books with large page counts are hard to just kick back with feet on the desk and read.

Your hands get cramps just trying to hold the book in a comfortable position.

This book does not come with a CD, but the source code used in this book is downloadable from both www.wordware.com/files/8086 and www.leiterman.com/books.html.

Now we are ready to begin!

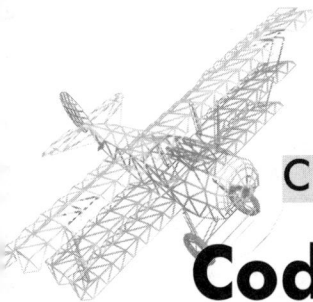

# Chapter 2

# Coding Standards

I am not going to bore you to death with coding standards, as there are a multitude of books on the subject already and that is mostly not what this book is about. To become a better programmer, however, you should adopt and rigidly follow a set of coding standards.

I just said I was not going to bore you with coding standards, as this book is about assembly language programming, and this chapter is titled "Coding Standards"? What does one have to do with the other? One actually supports the other. You should have a proper development environment before attempting to write any assembly code in an attempt to make that development project better. If you have read this chapter in my vector book, you can skip to the next chapter, but I would recommend reading it anyway as a refresher. It also contains a bit more information than what was in the vector book.

The source code for this book use terms such as const and assert, as well as naming conventions, which should be a standard that you adopt for your own style of programming, if you have not already. The following coding methods cost very little, only a little extra time to drop them into your code, but they will save you time in the long run, especially when dealing with general-purpose or SIMD assembly code. You can think of them as a couple extra tools for your software development toolbox. They primarily entail the use of const and assert as well as memory alignment. It should be noted that due to page count limitations, they are mostly only used in the first few functions in print and then infrequently. This is not an indicator that they are not needed, only that I did not want the pages in the book to appear to be too verbose in printed computer code. You will find that those equivalent functions will be fully loaded with the use of const and the appropriate assertions.

**Workbench Files:** \Bench\\*x86*\chap02\\*project*\\*platform*

|  | *project* | *platform* |
|---|---|---|
| **Ram Test** | **\ramtest\** | \vc6 |
| **ram** | **\ram\** | \vc.net |

# Constants

To put it simply, the const can essentially be thought of as a write protection of sorts.

```
void voodoo(const Foo * const pInfo);
```

In this example the contents of the data structure (first const) and the
pointer to the structure (second const) cannot be altered. This function
merely reads information contained within that structure and does not
alter it or its pointer in any fashion. The const guarantees it! Of course
that does not stop the programmer from casting the pointer to a
const-less pointer and then modifying the data. *But that would be bad!*

The placement of the second const protecting the pointer is very
specific, but the placement of the first const is a little more liberal. It can
occur before or after the data type declaration such as in the following:

```
void voodoo(const Foo     * const pInfo);
void voodoo(    Foo const * const pInfo);
```

**Tip:** When working with C++ all data members — private, protected or public — can be protected with the inclusion of an
appended const to the prototype and declaration.

```
class foo
{
private:
        int a;

public:
        int b;

    void voodoo(const byte * const pFoo) const;
};


void foo::voodoo(const byte * const pFoo) const
{
//  *pFoo = 'a';  // The (first) const protects data!
//   pFoo++;      // The (second) const protects pointer!
//   a = b = 5;   // The (third) const protects data members!
}
```

# Data Alignment

Processors work most efficiently with data that is properly aligned. In the case of the SSE or better instruction set, there is not one 128-bit load but two. Processors have been designed for efficient operations so internally the data is not loaded misaligned, it is loaded 128-bit aligned, but in the case of the SSE, it is corrected by shifting two halves of two 128-bit loads to adjust for the requested 128 bits of data. This misalignment is very inefficient and time consuming! This means that instead of loading only the needed 16 bytes, 32 bytes were loaded by the processor.

The first item on the agenda is the alignment of data values. Pointers are typically 4-byte on a 32-bit processor; 64-bit requires 8-byte; 128-bit requires 16-byte.

```
#define ALIGN2(len)  (((len) + 1) & ~1)    // round up to 2 items
#define ALIGN4(len)  (((len) + 3) & ~3)    // round up to 4 items
#define ALIGN8(len)  (((len) + 7) & ~7)    // round up to 8 items
#define ALIGN16(len) (((len) + 15) & ~15)  // round up to 16 items
```

These can easily be used to align bytes (or implied ×8 bits). So to align to 16 bytes:

```
nWidth = ALIGN16(nWidth);  // 128-bit alignment!
```

Some of you may note that the basic equation of these macros:

```
(A, X)     (((A) + (X)) & ~(X))
```

relies on a byte count of $2^N$ so that a logical AND can be taken to advantage and could possibly be replaced with:

```
(A, X)     ((A) % ((X) + 1))
```

and be easier to read, but that would be giving too much credit to the C compiler as some will do a division for the modulus and some will see the binary mask and take advantage with a mere logical AND operation. Even though this latter code is clearer, it may not be compiled as fast code. If you are not sure what your compiler does, then merely set a breakpoint at a macro, then either expand the macro or display mixed C and assembly code. The division or logical AND will be right near where your instruction pointer (IP) is pointing to your position within the code.

A macro using this alternate method would be:

```
#define ALIGN(len, bytes)(((len) + ((bytes)-1)) % (bytes))
```

This is a little obscure and typically unknown by non-console developers, but CD sector size alignment is needed for all files destined to be loaded directly from a CD or DVD as they are typically loaded by number of sectors rather than number of bytes and this is typically 2048 or 2336 bytes in size. All these require some sort of alignment correction jig.

```
    // round up 1 CD sector
#define ALIGN2048(len) (((len) + 2047) & ~2047)
```

Sometimes CD sectors are not 2048 byte but 2336. Since this is not $2^N$, a modulus (%) must be used since simple bit masking will not work.

```
#define ALIGN2336(len) (((len) + 2335) % 2336)
```

The correction is as simple as:

```
void *foo(uint nReqSize)
{
    uint nSize;
    nSize = ALIGN16(nReqSize);
  :
  :     // Insert your other code here!
}
```

**Tip:**   There is a simple trick to see if your value is $2^N$.

```
A ∧ (A − 1) ? 0
```

Subtracting a value of 1 before a logical AND would skew the bits. If only one bit is set, then the result of the AND would be 0. If more than one bit is set, the result would be non-zero.

The requested size is stretched to the appropriate sized block. This really comes in handy when building dedicated relational databases in tools for use in games.

**Goal:**   Ensure properly aligned data.

I have had several incidents over the years with compilers and misaligned data. Calls to the new function or the C function malloc() returned memory on a 4-byte alignment but when working with 64-bit MMX or some 128-bit SSE instructions there would be unaligned memory stall problems. Some instructions cause a misalignment exception error, while others just cause memory stalls. The 80x86 is more forgiving than other processors as its memory accesses can be misaligned without a penalty, but there are SIMD instructions that require proper memory alignment or an exception will occur. Thus it is always best to ensure memory is *always* properly aligned. The PowerPC and MIPS processors require that memory be properly aligned. For cross-platform portability, it is very important to ensure that your data is properly aligned at all times whether you know your application will be ported or not.

The 80x86 has an alignment check flag in the CR0 register that can be enabled to verify all memory is aligned properly. (Use with caution unless you are writing your own board support package.)

The first half of the remedy is easy. Just make sure your vectors are a data type with a block size set to 16 bytes and that your compiler is set to 16-byte alignment and not 1-byte aligned or the default, even if using 64-bit MMX-based instructions. The smart move is to ensure that all data structures are padded so they will still be aligned properly even if the compiler alignment gets set to 1 byte. This will make your life easier, especially if code is ever ported to other platforms, especially UNIX. This is a safety factor. Normally one would manually pack the data elements by their size to ensure proper alignment and insert (future) pad bytes where appropriate, but by adjusting the alignment in the compiler you can ensure that the ported applications using different compilers will export proper data files and network messages.

Notice the "Struct member alignment" field in the following property page for Project Settings in Visual Studio version 6 and Visual C++ .NET. The default is 8 bytes, which is denoted by the asterisk, but 16 bytes is required for vector programming.

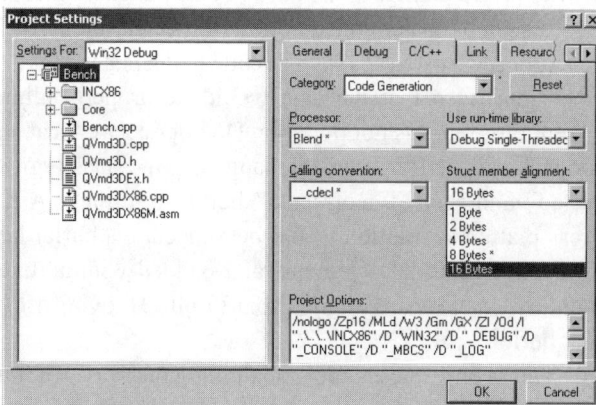

*Figure 2-1: Visual C++ (version 6) memory alignment property page*

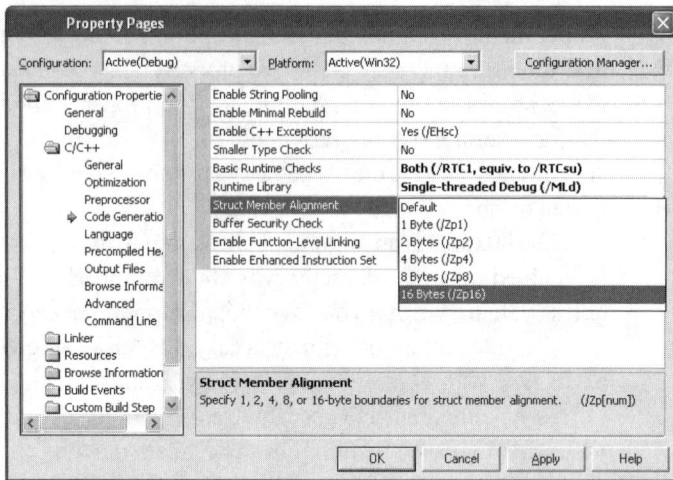

*Figure 2-2: Visual C++ .NET (version 7) memory alignment property page*

You should get into the habit of always setting your memory alignment to 16 for any new project. It will help your application even if it uses scalar and no SIMD-based instructions.

# Stacks and Vectors

*Never, never, never* pass packed data on the stack as a data argument; always pass a pointer to the packed data instead. Ignoring any possible issues such as faster consumption of a stack, the need for more stack space, or security issues such as code being pushed onto the stack, there is no guarantee that the data would be properly aligned. There are exceptions, but it is not portable. Do not declare local stack arguments for packed data. If in assembly language, the stack register can be "corrected" and then "uncorrected" before returning. A better (portable cross-platform) solution would be to declare a buffer large enough for 16-byte aligned data elements and padded with an extra 12 bytes of memory. Vectors are aligned to 128-bit (16-byte) data blocks within that buffer.

This is only one example of aligning memory. Adding fixed sizes to allow for modulus 16 to the buffer will correct the alignment and will improve processing speed as well.

I realize that padding or aligning memory to 16 bytes initially appears to be crude, but it delivers the functionality you require through the use of pointers, and it is cross-platform compatible.

# 3D Vector (Floating-Point)

| Z | Y | X |
|---|---|---|

```
typedef struct vmp3DVector
{
  float x;
  float y;
  float z;
} vmp3DVector;

  // Three 96-bit vectors aligned to 128 bits each, thus four floats each
  // so 3 × 4 = 12 bytes, but add three extra floats (+3) to handle a
  // possible misaligned offset of {4, 8, 12}. Once the first is
  // aligned, all other 4-byte blocks will be aligned as well!

float vecbuf[(3 *4)+3];  // enough space for 3 full vectors.
vmp3DVector *pvA, *pvB, *pvD;

  // Force proper alignment

pvA = (vmp3DVector*) ALIGN16((int)(vecbuf));   // Force
pvB = (vmp3DVector*) ALIGN16((int)(pvA+1));    // +4 float
pvD = (vmp3DVector*) ALIGN16((int)(pvB+1));    // +4 float
```

Of course if you are dealing with quad vectors, then align the first one. All the others, which are the same data type and are already 16 bytes in size, will automatically be aligned.

# 3D Quad Vector (Floating-Point)

| W | Z | Y | X |
|---|---|---|---|

```
typedef struct vmp3DQVector
{
  float x;
  float y;
  float z;
  float w;
} vmp3DQVector;

vmp3DQVector *pvC, *pvE, *pvF;
```

```
    // Force proper alignment

pvC = (vmp3DQVector*) ALIGN16((int)(vecbuf));
pvE = pvC+1;
pvF = pvE+1;
```

The same applies for 4×4 matrices. The following is just a quick and dirty demonstration of *aligned* three-element vector data structures.

```
    // Copy vectors to aligned memory
pvA->x=vA.x;   pvA->y=vA.y;   pvA->z=vA.z;
pvB->x=vB.x;   pvB->y=vB.y;   pvB->z=vB.z;

vmp_SIMDEntry();      // x86 FPU/MMX switching

    // if (most likely) non-aligned memory
vmp_CrossProduct0(&vD, &vA, &vB);

    // if (guaranteed) aligned memory
vmp_CrossProduct(pvD, pvA, pvB);

vmp_SIMDExit();       //x86 FPU/MMX switching
```

Note the convention of the appended zero used by vmp_CrossProduct0 and vmp_CrossProduct. The zero denotes that the function is not guaranteed to be aligned to (n mod 16) with a zero remainder.

Another item to keep in mind is that a vector is 12 bytes in length (as it is made up of three floats, and a float is four bytes in size), but it is being read/written as 16 bytes on a processor with a 128-bit data width. The extra 4-byte float must be preserved. If the trick of 128-bit memory allocation is utilized, then an out of bounds error will not occur since the data is being advanced in 16-byte blocks. This fourth float is scratch data and as such is not harmful. (No past end of buffer access!)

There are always exceptions to the rule and that occurs here as well. The compiler for the AltiVec instruction set for Motorola typically found in Macintosh PowerPC computers uses the following local argument stack declaration:

```
void Foo(void)
{
  vector float vD, vA, vB;
}
```

**Trivia:**  The PowerPC's AltiVec SIMD instructions never have an alignment exception as the four lower address bits, $A_{0...3}$, are always forced to zero. So if your memory is misaligned, your data will not be. But it definitely will not be where you expected it!

The following vector declaration automatically aligns the data to a 16-byte alignment. The GNU C compiler (GCC) can generate the following definition:

```
typedef float FVECTOR[4] \
                        __attribute__((aligned (16)));

void Foo(void)
{
  FVECTOR vD, vA, vB;
}
```

I am sorry to say that there is only one method for the 16-byte aligned stack frame of data within the Visual C++ environment for the 80x86-based Win32 environment, but unfortunately this only works with Visual C++ .NET (version 7.0) or higher, or with version 6 and a processor pack. The following is a snippet from a DirectX header file d3dx8math.h:

```
#if _MSC_VER >= 1300    // Visual C++ ver. 7
#define _ALIGN_16 __declspec(align(16))
#else
#define _ALIGN_16       // Earlier compiler may not understand
#endif                  // this; do nothing.
```

So that the following could be used:

```
vmp3DVector vA;
  __declspec(align(16)) vmp3DVector vB;
  _ALIGN_16 vmp3DVector vC;
```

The alignment of vA cannot be guaranteed, but vB and vC are aligned on a 16-byte boundary. Codeplay's Vector C and Intel's C++ compilers also support this declaration.

There is, however, the Macro Assembler (MASM), which has the following:

```
align 16
```

followed by a 16-byte aligned data declaration for Real4 (float).

```
vHalf Real4  0.5,0.5,0.5,0.5
```

Another item that can easily be implemented from within assembly language is a stack correction for 16-byte memory alignment. The stack pointer works by moving down through memory while adding items to the stack, so by using a secondary stack frame pointer the stack can be corrected.

```
push ebx
mov ebx,esp             ; ebx references passed arguments
```

```
and esp,0ffffff0h      ; 16-byte align

; Insert your code   reference by [esp-x]

mov esp,ebx
pop ebx
```

| xxx0 | |
|------|--|
| xxxc | ⅂ |
| xxx8 | ⅂ |
| xxx4 | ⅂ |
| xxx0 | ↵ |
| xxxc | |

The line of assembly {and esp} actually snaps the stack pointer down the stack to a 16-byte boundary; thus the next local stack argument will be 16-byte aligned, e.g., [esp-16], [esp-32], etc.

# Compiler Data

Within the recent Visual C++ and Intel compilers SIMD functionality has been incorporated, such as the allocation of registers and aligned stack memory.

| Definition | Description |
|------------|-------------|
| __m64 | (64-bit) memory for MMX |
| __m128 | (128-bit) memory for single-precision floating-point |
| __m128d | (128-bit) memory for double-precision floating-point |
| __m128i | (128-bit) memory for streaming integer SSE2 |

These align stack memory through a mask.

```
__m128 ta, tb;

push     ebx
mov      ebx,esp
and      esp,0FFFFFFF0h   ; 16-byte alignment

movaps   xmm0,xmmword ptr [esp-20h]  ; tb
movaps   xmm1,xmmword ptr [esp-10h]  ; ta
```

Using this same implementation, a bit of magic using unions can be utilized:

```
#define MY_FLT_ARY    100

union
{
    __m128 t[ MYFLT_ARY/4 ];
    float ary[ MYFLT_ARY ];
};
```

The __m128 aligns the stack memory, which the float takes advantage of since it is the same size, and maps to the same location compliments of the nameless union declaration.

There are other methodologies, but these should get you rolling for now.

**Tip:** Use assertions in your code to trap errors early in the development process.

# Assertions

Assembly code can get confusing enough without having to debug it just to find that misaligned memory was the problem. Thus, a code development tool used within the source code for this book is the use of an assertion. Typically, the top of your file should include the following header file declaration:

```
#include    <assert.h>
```

Sorry to bore those of you who religiously use these! An assertion is essentially a test for a "not true thus false" condition. That is, if the condition is false, then an assertion will occur whereby the instruction pointer is halted at the offending line of code. This is very similar to the following:

```
if (!(3==a))                    // assert(3==a)
{
    // System Break
    DebugBreak();               // Win32, Xbox
}
```

As mentioned, the condition *must* fail to halt the code. Here we wanted the variable *a* to be assigned the value of 3 to be successful; otherwise it would halt the system. There are many philosophies on the subject about assertions. In my case, I believe in four types of assertions:

- Fatal – Debug
- Fatal – Release
- Non-fatal – Debug
- Non-fatal – Release

A Fatal – Debug is a programmer error. This is something that should *never, ever, ever* occur, such as passing a NULL, the address of a pointer, an obviously bad pointer, an out-of-range argument to a function, or a misaligned vector or matrix. It halts the debug version of the code and forces the programmer to fix it right away. This is the one assertion that should occur most of the time in your debug code while it is being developed, but never in the shipped code.

A Fatal – Release is an unrecoverable error in a shipped version of the application. The computer is totally out of memory so there is not even enough memory to display an error message. Catastrophic error. This should preferably *never* be used. There are even ways in an application to stop the application logic, jettison memory, and put up your "Sorry, I am dead! Call your Customer Support Person" screen. You do not want your customers to ever get the Blue Screen of Death! (Windows users know what I am talking about!)

These last two — Non-fatal – Debug and Non-fatal – Release — are recoverable errors. That is, they are errors that can be worked around without killing the application. These errors are typically not able to load a resource from the media, missing or contaminated file, missing sound resources, etc. Your application can be crippled in such a way to allow it to progress. Resources such as art can use placeholders when are can't be loaded and allocated. Sounds that aren't loaded don't get played. The idea is to try to keep the application running. Even during development of the application you may want to alert the developer that table sizes do not match the number of defined indexes for that table. That sort of thing. The idea is to not kill the running application but to annoy the programmer enough to get him to fix the problem. I like that so much I am going to state that again!

**Tip:** The idea of non-fatal assertions is to not kill the running application but to annoy the programmer enough to get him to fix the problem.

On a personal note: Please do not get annoyed and then turn off the assertions at the source instead of fixing the real problem. (I once worked with a programmer who did just that! It caused lots of Homer

Simpson type errors to creep into the code that would have been caught immediately otherwise. DOH!) On the other hand, a non-technical supervisor once threatened to chop off my fingers because the assertions in the code to catch errors were doing just that and thus breaking the build! A better method is to spend a couple minutes now catching the errors early in the development cycle rather than a long time during crunch mode at the tail end of the project trying to track them down, or never knowing about them until after the product has shipped.

For purposes of this book, only a debug assertion will be utilized. In essence this means if an application were to be defined as a debug model, then the assertion would exist in the code, making the code run a little slower but considerably safer. In a release model, it is stubbed out, thus does not exist, and your code will magically run a bit faster. In the code for this book you will find the following assertions in use for the generic assertion ASSERT():

*Listing 2-1: Assertion type definitions*

```
#ifdef USE_ASSERT    // Active assertions

#define ASSERT(arg1)          assert((arg1))
#define ASSERT_PTR(arg1)      assert(NULL!=(arg1))
#define ASSERT_PTR4(arg1)     assert((NULL!=(arg1)) \
                              && (0==(((long)(arg1))&3)))
#define ASSERT_PTR8(arg1)     assert((NULL!=(arg1)) \
                              && (0==(((long)(arg1))&7)))
#define ASSERT_PTR16(arg1)    assert((NULL!=(arg1)) \
                              && (0==(((long)(arg1))&15)))
#define ASSERT_FNEG(arg1)     assert(0.0f<=(arg1));
#define ASSERT_FZERO(arg1)    assert(0.0f!=(arg1));
#define ASSERT_NEG(arg1)      assert(0<=(arg1));
#define ASSERT_ZERO(arg1)     assert(0!=(arg1));

#else        // Assertions stubbed to nothing
             // (empty macro)
#define ASSERT(arg1)
#define ASSERT_PTR(arg1)
#define ASSERT_PTR4(arg1)
#define ASSERT_PTR8(arg1)
#define ASSERT_PTR16(arg1)
#define ASSERT_FNEG(arg1)
#define ASSERT_FZERO(arg1)
#define ASSERT_NEG(arg1)
#define ASSERT_ZERO(arg1)
#endif
```

You would merely insert your custom assertion.

```
uint nActor = 5;
ASSERT(nActor < MAX_ACTOR);
```

The pointer assertion ASSERT_PTR4() does two things: The first is to guarantee that the pointer is not assigned to NULL. The second is that memory pointers must or should be (depending on the processor and exception settings) referencing memory that is at least 4-byte aligned so that pointer alignment is checked for. Even if only referencing strings, it should be recognized that if they are at least 4-byte aligned, algorithms can be made more efficient when dealing with those string components in parallel.

```
void *pApe;
ASSERT_PTR4(pApe);
```

This is a good way to ensure that integers and single-precision floating-point values are properly aligned.

The pointer assertion ASSERT_PTR16() is virtually the same, except that it guarantees that the pointer is not NULL and is referencing data on a 16-byte alignment, which is necessary for vector math processing. This is what this part of the book is all about!

```
ASSERT_PTR16(pApe);


;        Assert if 32-bit pointer is n=NULL or not 16-byte aligned.
;
ASSERT_PTR16    MACRO    arg1
ifdef USE_ASSERT
        test    arg1,0FFFFFFFFh     ; Not NULL? then...
        jnz     $+3                 ; ...Hop over interrupt

        int     3                   ; Break (OOPS)

        test    arg1,0000000Fh      ; Is zero aligned...
        jz      $+3                 ; ...Hop over interrupt

        int     3                   ; Break (OOPS)
endif
endm
```

Different processors have different behaviors, which could become a camouflage problem. Asserting on a non-aligned 16-byte data reference finds these problems fast. These last two deal with assertions of values of zero or negative single-precision floating-point numbers.

```
float f;
ASSERT_FNEG(f);      // Assert if a negative
ASSERT_FZERO(f);     // Assert if absolute zero
```

One last assertion topic would be the utilization of strings with variable arguments within your assertions as an additional type of assertion. The trick here though is that assertion macros do not like variable arguments, so you would need something in the assertion name to represent the number of string arguments, such as the following:

```
ASSERT1(a == b, "So BOOM because %u", nDucks);
```

# Memory Systems

Another code development tool is to do a memory allocation check for any compiled code to verify that the memory manager is indeed allocating properly aligned memory for the superset single instruction multiple data (SIMD) instruction sets. You can test this by executing a simple algorithm such as the following one.

## RamTest Memory Alignment Test

*Listing 2-2: ...\chap02\ramTest\Bench.cpp*

```
#define RAM_TBL_SIZE        4096

int main(int argc, char *argv[])
{
  unsigned int n, nCnt, bSet, bTst, bMsk, a, b;
  void *pTbl[RAM_TBL_SIZE];

    // Allocate a series of incr. size blocks

    for (n=0; n<RAM_TBL_SIZE; n++)
    {
//pTbl[n]=(byte *) malloc(n+1);
      pTbl[n]= new byte[n+1];
      if (NULL==pTbl[n])
      {
        cout << "low memory. (continuing)..." << endl;
        break;
      }
    }
    nCnt = n;              // # of entries allocated

    // Test memory for alignments

    bSet = 16;             // Preset to 128-bit (128÷16)
    bTst = bSet - 1;
    bMsk = ~bTst;

    for (n=0; n<nCnt; n++)
    {
      a = (unsigned int) pTbl[n];
      do                   // round up to 'bSet' bits
      {
```

```
          b = (a + bTst) & bMsk;
          if (a==b)
          {
            break;              // okay
          }
                                // Unaligned...
          bSet >>= 1;           // reduce by a bit
          bTst = bSet - 1;
          bMsk = ~0 ^ bTst;
        } while(1);
    }

      // Release all of memory to clean up

    for (n=0; n<nCnt; n++)
    {
      byte *pRaw;
      pRaw = pTbl[n];
      pTbl[n] = NULL;

      delete [] pRaw;
  //free(pTbl[n]);
    }

    cout << "Ram Alignment is set to " << bSet;
    cout << " bytes (" << (bSet<<3) << " bits).\n";
    cout << flush;
    return 0;
}
```

Please note that it loops up to 4096 times, slowly increasing the size of the allocation just in case the memory manager issues properly aligned memory for a short period of time before allocating any that might be skewed. Also, you will most likely get a memory low message but that is okay; you are only allocating about 8 MB or so. If everything is fine, there will be a match between your processor and the following table.

Table 2-1: SIMD instruction set with data width in bits and bytes

| SIMD Instruction Set (Data Width) | Bits | Bytes |
|---|---|---|
| AMD 3D Now! | 64 | 8 |
| AMD 3D Now! Extensions | 64 | 8 |
| AMD 3D Now! MMX Extensions | 64 | 8 |
| AMD 3D Now! Professional | 64/128 | 8/16 |
| MMX | 64 | 8 |
| SSE | 128 | 16 |
| SSE2 | 128 | 16 |
| SSE3 | 128 | 16 |

If there is a mismatch, then you have an alignment error problem. This can be rectified by using memory allocation code similar to that in Listing 2-4. This function is designed to wrap the standard function call to malloc() or new[]. Do not forget to add the assertion as a good programming practice.

# Memory Header

The following header is hidden at the true base of memory allocated by our function. Basically, memory is slightly overallocated. The malloc function is in essence routed to the correct core allocation function.

---

*Listing 2-3: ...\chap02\ram\ram.cpp*

```
typedef struct RamHeadType
{
  uint32  nReqSize;    // Requested size
  uint32  extra[3];    // Padding to help align to 16 byte
} RamHead;
```

# Allocate Memory (Malloc Wrapper)

*Listing 2-4: ...\chap02\ram\ram.cpp*

```
void * ramAlloc(uint nReqSize)
{
  byte *pMem;
  RamHead *pHead;
  uint nSize;

  ASSERT_ZERO(nReqSize);

    // Force to 16-byte block + room for header

  nSize = ALIGN16(nReqSize) + sizeof(RamHead);

//pMem = (byte*)malloc(nSize);
  pMem = new byte[ nSize ];
  pHead = (RamHead *)pMem;

  if (NULL==pMem)
  {                        // Allocation error
  }
  else
  {                        // Save Req Size
    pHead->nReqSize = nReqSize + sizeof(RamHead);
    pHead->extra[0] = 1;
    pHead->extra[1] = 2;
    pHead->extra[2] = 3;
```

```
        // Align by adj header +4 to +16 bytes

    pMem = (byte *) ALIGN16(((uint)pMem) + sizeof(uint32));
    }
    return (void*)pMem;
}
```

How this functions is that it aligns the amount of memory requested to the nearest 16-byte boundary. This will assist in maintaining memory to a 16-byte block size. An additional 16 bytes are allocated as the header. This is useful for two reasons:

■ The memory passed to the calling function can be forced to the proper alignment.

■ A side benefit of storing the requested size is that size adjustments similar to a realloc() can be issued and the calling function does not have to know what the current size is when releasing that memory back to the pool.

Hidden in the beginning of the allocated memory is a header where the requested size is stored in the first 32-bit word and the other three words are set to the values of {1, 2, 3}. The pointer is then advanced to a 16-byte alignment and passed to the calling function.

When releasing memory back to the system, the returned pointer needs to be unadjusted back to the true base address; otherwise a memory exception will occur. The following function wraps the release function free().

This may seem wasteful, but the base address of the memory being allocated by new or malloc is unknown. With current malloc libraries it tends to be 4- or 8-byte aligned, so there is a need to allocate for a worst case.

## Release Memory (Free Wrapper)

*Listing 2-5: ...\chap02\ram\ram.cpp*

```
void ramFree(const void * const pRaw)
{
    uint32 *pMem;
    byte   *pbMem;

    ASSERT_PTR4(pRaw);
    ASSERT_PTR(*pRaw);

    pMem = (uint32 *)pRaw;
    if (*(--pMem)< sizeof(RamHead))
    {
```

```
     pMem -= *pMem;
   }
     // pMem original (unadjusted) pointer
   pbMem = (byte *)pMem;
// free(pbMem);
   delete [] pbMem;
}
```

The memory release occurs by decrementing the word pointer by one 4-byte word. If that location contains a value between one and three, the pointer is decremented by that value so that it then points at the size information when cast to a RamHead pointer. This is the true memory base position and the pointer that gets returned to the system function free().

For C++ fans, the new and delete operators can be overloaded to this insulating memory module. I also recommend one final item: The memory allocation and release functions should require a pointer to be passed. This will allow the release function to nullify the pointer, and in future enhancements each pointer could be considered the "owner" of the memory and thus adjusted for any garbage collection algorithms instituted for a heap compaction in a flat memory environment.

## Allocate Memory

A pointer is passed as ppMem and set.

Listing 2-6: ...\chap02\ram\ram.cpp

```
bool ramGet(byte ** const ppMem, uint nReqSize)
{
  ASSERT_PTR4(ppMem);

  *ppMem = (byte *) ramAlloc(nReqSize);
  return (NULL!=*ppMem) ? true : false;
}
```

## Allocate (Cleared) Memory

Listing 2-7: ...\chap02\ram\ram.cpp

```
bool ramGetClr(byte **const ppMem, uint nReqSize)
{
  bool ret;

  ASSERT_PTR4(ppMem);

  ret = false;
  *ppMem = (byte *)ramAlloc(nReqSize);
```

```
if (NULL!=*ppMem)
{
  ramZero(*ppMem, nReqSize);
  ret = true;
}

return ret;
}
```

## Free Memory — Pointer Is Set to NULL

*Listing 2-8: ...\chap02\ram\ram.cpp*

```
void ramRelease(byte ** const ppMem)
{
  ASSERT_PTR4(ppMem);

  ramFree(*ppMem);
  *ppMem = NULL;
}
```

# Exercises

1. What is an assertion?
2. How many assertion types does the author recommend? What are they and what do they do?
3. Create another memory allocation scheme with code to allocate and release that memory for allocation of any size, but still be properly aligned.
4. What should one do when allocating memory for a file load to guarantee that no memory access by a processor could accidentally get a memory exception for accessing past the end of allocated memory without special handling?
5. If a raw ASCII text file were loaded into memory, how would it be loaded and what is the easiest method of treating it as just one large string?
6. Give your explanation as to how the calling conventions function.

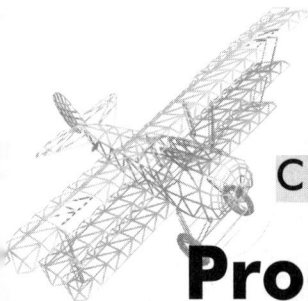

# Chapter 3

# Processor Differential Insight

This chapter discusses the similarities and differences between the various 80x86 processors from the manufacturers AMD and Intel.

**Workbench Files:** \Bench\\*x86*\chap03\\*project*\\*platform*

|  | *project* | *platform* |
|---|---|---|
| **CPU ID** | **\cpuid\** | \vc6 |
|  |  | \vc.net |

## Processor Overview

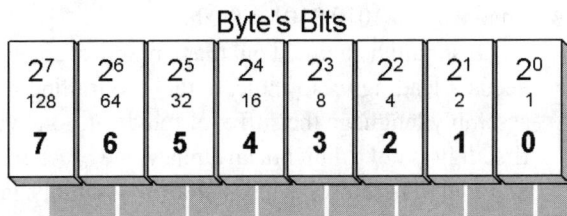

Byte's Bits

| $2^7$ | $2^6$ | $2^5$ | $2^4$ | $2^3$ | $2^2$ | $2^1$ | $2^0$ |
|---|---|---|---|---|---|---|---|
| 128 | 64 | 32 | 16 | 8 | 4 | 2 | 1 |
| **7** | **6** | **5** | **4** | **3** | **2** | **1** | **0** |

There are a large variety of computers with different processors and different word sizes but there is one constant, the byte. Memory in a computer is represented as a series of bytes and each of these bytes is made up of eight bits. This allows an unsigned value ranging from 0...255 or a signed value ranging from –128...0...127 to be stored in each byte. These eight bits can store one ASCII character A...Z. These bytes can be used together to form larger data structures such as a 16-bit short, 32-bit int, 64-bit long, etc.

In a higher level language such as C this is typically represented by a hex value. For example, 123 decimal is: 64+32+16+8+2+1.

| $2^7$<br>128 | $2^6$<br>64 | $2^5$<br>32 | $2^4$<br>16 | $2^3$<br>8 | $2^2$<br>4 | $2^1$<br>2 | $2^0$<br>1 |
|---|---|---|---|---|---|---|---|
| 0 | I | I | I | I | 0 | I | I |

So binary 01111011 broken into nibbles (4-bit chunks) 0111 1011 is 7B hex. I did it for you here, but you really should already know how to do decimal-to-hex and hex-to-decimal conversions. In the C programming language this is represented by 0x7B. In an assembler such as MASM this can be represented in a variety of ways:

```
mov eax, 123          ; Decimal
mov eax, 7bh          ; Hex
mov eax, 01111011b    ; Binary
```

Let's try that again but with a slightly bigger number in which the most significant bit (MSB) gets set.

| $2^7$<br>128 | $2^6$<br>64 | $2^5$<br>32 | $2^4$<br>16 | $2^3$<br>8 | $2^2$<br>4 | $2^1$<br>2 | $2^0$<br>1 |
|---|---|---|---|---|---|---|---|
| I | 0 | I | 0 | 0 | I | 0 | I |

This maps to 1010 0101 = 0a5h.

It should be pointed out that a number represented in hex in C only needs a leading 0x to indicate that the trailing digits are hex code. In assembly language the suffix of h indicates the value is hex. But if the first digit is not a digit but an alpha value of A…F, then a leading zero is required. Therefore, a hex value in assembly language must *always* begin with a digit even if it is zero. Letters indicate the word about to be processed by the assembler is a label and not a value! Hex letters A…F can be mixed and matched upper- and/or lowercase; capitalization does not matter.

We are using the value of 0a5h = **1**0100101B. The B represents binary and the MSB indicated in bold is a 1. If this were an unsigned value ranging from 0…255, then 0a5h would resolve to 128+32+4+1 = 165 decimal. Numbers without prefixes or suffixes are in decimal. But what if this were a negative number? 0a5h is a decimal value of –91. How did we do that? Well, we needed something called a two's complement. This is a one's complement followed by an addition of +1.

Since the MSB is set and this is a signed number ranging from –128 to 127, then first NOT (meaning flip) all the bits in the number.

| $2^7$ | $2^6$ | $2^5$ | $2^4$ | $2^3$ | $2^2$ | $2^1$ | $2^0$ |
| 128 | 64 | 32 | 16 | 8 | 4 | 2 | 1 |
|---|---|---|---|---|---|---|---|
| 1 | 0 | 1 | 0 | 0 | 1 | 0 | 1 |
| 0 | 1 | 0 | 1 | 1 | 0 | 1 | 0 |

The bit sequence of 0101 1010 gives us 5Ah. (Just a coincidence; I chose the 5 and A on purpose since they are complements of each other! Now add 1 to that: 5Ah + 1 = 5Bh = 01011011B = 64+16+8+2+1 = 91. Since we performed the two's complement we also stick the negative sign (–) back on it: – (91), thus –91. Again, this should be review for you but I want to make sure you understand signed versus unsigned values and how to handle one or the other.

**Note:**　To help alleviate any confusion between this book and my vector book, this one was written for multiple processors. Both books share a generic calling convention and a standard naming convention for data types: (b)yte 8-bit, (h)alf-word 16-bit, (w)ord 32-bit, (d)word 64-bit, and (q)word 128-bit.

They are used for function declarations to maintain compatibility between books as well as processor types.

Even though the 80x86 does not use a half-word declaration, I forced it to do so for easier understanding of the vector book. This book is strictly about 80x86 assembly language, and its letter encoding is directly connected to data types and instructions, so the specific 80x86 convention will be used here: (b)yte 8-bit, (w)ord 16-bit, (d)word 32-bit, (q)word 64-bit, and (dq)word 128-bit.

Please keep this in mind if you are switching back and forth between the two books!

**History:**　The declaration of "word" has a bit of a history. When the 8086 processor was first produced it had 16-bit registers. At that time a word was considered the width of the data, so a word became the definition for a 16-bit value. Other processors had a data width of 32 bits, so a word was used to represent 32 bits. With the release of the 80386, the word was already embedded in the 80x86 assembly code to represent 16 bits, and all code would have to be modified accordingly, so 32 bits came to be known as double words. And so a schism of bit widths related to the definition of a word came to be. In high-level languages such as C an integer (int) was used to represent a word. Since it was not directly tied to an absolute data width, it expanded with time. With the 8086 an int and a short were 16 bits, but with 32-bit processors the int came to represent 32-bit data, while the short still represents 16-bit data.

Table 3-1: 80x86 data types

| C type | | procType | Bytes | Bits |
|---|---|---|---|---|
| char | b | byte | 1 | 8 |
| short | w | word | 2 | 16 |
| int | d | dword | 4 | 32 |
| long | q | qword | 8 | 64 |
| SSE, SSE2 (128-bit) | | | | |
| long long | dq | dqword | 16 | 128 |

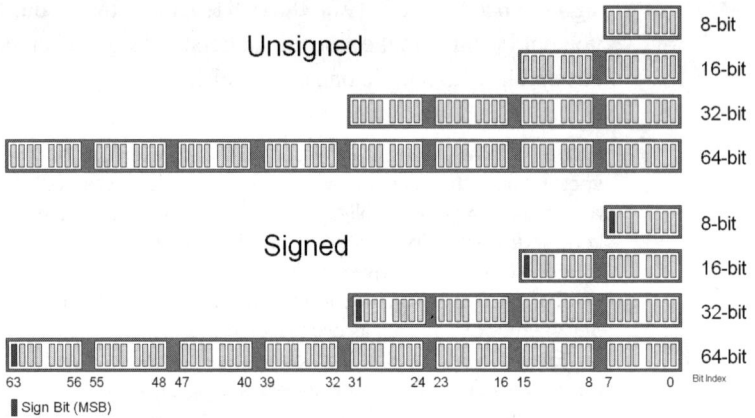

Figure 3-1: Unsigned/signed data types

# History

A quick history lesson. The 80x86 family started with the 8088 and 8086 (16-bit) processors. These were 16-bit processors as the general-purpose register was 16 bits in size. The 8088, however, had an 8-bit databus. The general-purpose registers had two addressable components, i.e., AX, with the upper 8 bits as AH and the lower 8 bits as AL. Along came the 80186 and 80286. With these came the first foundations of segment:offset addressing. These had a 16-bit segment and a 16-bit offset, which were used to generate a 20-bit address. Thus, there were 12 bits of overlap between the two registers. The segment was used to address a 16-byte block within 1 MB of memory.

$$BaseAddress = (Segment \times 16) + offset$$

The 80386 was the first 32-bit processor to break the 1 MB memory barrier. Additional instructions were added, and the segment:offset registers became selector:offsets. There then became a differentiation between Real Mode using 16-bit addressing and Protected Mode, which used the new 32-bit technology. Then the processor clone wars started between manufacturers. The 80486 came along with additional instructions. The Pentium series came next with the introduction of multimedia instructions known as SIMD with the MMX registers. There were different flavors, different instructions — it was very convoluted and confusing. AMD introduced 3DNow! This is about when the book you are now reading was started. Then came Katmai by Intel, now known as the SSE new instruction set. AMD countered, Intel countered, back and forth. Other manufacturers either sunk at battle or pushed onto the shores of an embedded island. Then the technology was forked by Intel (but we are ignoring the Itanium series in this book). Somewhere along the way AMD and Intel each came out with 64-bit processors and seem to have reached a tentative truce.

Incidentally, the FPU (floating-point unit) was an optional second coprocessor originally known as the 8087 and subsequently the 80187, 80287, 80387, and then the 80487. Back then, floating-point was emulated in software as an alternative if no hardware was present. The FPU grew up with the CPU and eventually become an internal component of the 80486DX CPU. The 80486SX still had to rely upon a coprocessor.

**History:**   Rumor or fact? There are lots of stories of processors, faulty FPU chips, math bugs, etc. One story has to do with the 80486SX. Rumor has it that if the Intel 80486DX's FPU failed testing or cheaper SX processors were in short supply, then connections to the FPU were zapped within the 80486DX to transform it into an 80486SX processor. (*Rumor or fact?*)

This is as deep into Real Mode as this book is going to get. If you need additional information, please investigate specific documentation from the 80x86 processor manufacturer for your embedded application as Real Mode is fading into obscurity. The same applies to the need for selector manipulation as it can get pretty complicated, but this is only needed by operating system programmers for pre-64 bit processors, and that is not what this book is about. It is written to help those programmers but primarily written for application developers for 32- and 64-bit operating systems. System-level programming pretty much requires its own book about this size.

Many interesting things occurred during the introduction of the Protected and Private Modes. C compilers had to be selected for various code vs. data models.

| Model | Code | Data |
|-------|------|------|
| Huge | 32-bit | 32-bit |
| Small | 32-bit | 16-bit |
| Large | 16-bit | 32-bit |
| Tiny | 16-bit | 16-bit |

# The 64-Bit Processor

Here is a little tidbit before jumping into the details. The 64-bit processor has three operating modes:

- 64-bit Mode: 64-bit code/data running under a 64-bit OS
- Compatibility Mode: 32-bit code/data running under a 64-bit OS
- Legacy Mode: 32-bit code/data running under a 32-bit OS

These various operating modes give a nice upgrade methodology as well as extend the life of a large portion of pre-existing software as it has the ability to run under the new hardware and operating systems. Additional instructions and hardware have been added to the 32-bit hardware base to enhance its functionality while moving forward into the 64-bit world. I am not going to hype the technology here, as the manufacturers are doing a pretty good job themselves. My job with this book is to help you learn to program in assembly code for 32/64-bit processors. If you are already up to speed with 32-bit, it will help with your transition to the 64-bit machine. At the time of writing this book the new 64-bit operating systems were XP 64 and Linux 64.

At this point you are probably wondering to yourself, "My, this is a small section on the topic for 64-bit processors. Wasn't 64-bit 80x86 in the title?" From this book's point of view its only interest is the hardware capabilities of the instruction set and that means software, not the infrastructure of the hardware. But keep in mind that in 64-bit mode the data size becomes $2^{64}$.

**Tip:** $2^{64}$ bits are used to store a pretty big number.
   A 32-bit unsigned number is 0...4,294,967,295. That is approximately 4.2 GB.
   A 64-bit unsigned number is 0...18,446,744,073,709,551,615. That is approximately 18.4 exabytes.
   Add computer memory and video memory to get your computer's maximum limit of memory. 64-bit is much higher than 32-bit and should be enough for a couple years of expansion.

That is almost too big most of the time.

```
for (uint i = 0; i < 7; i++)
```

For example, in this C for-loop snippet three bits were needed to represent the loop, thus 61 bits are wasted! (Well, not really, but you may begin to see my point.) The advantage to registers that are 64 bits in size is not only can you store a value twice as big as a 32-bit register, but you can address memory that is twice the size. That drastically increases the amount of memory your application can access. Applications can be *much bigger*! Which means that you can put larger memory sticks into your computers so your computer can run even hotter. (*That meant heat, not necessarily speed!*) For network applications that is good. But what the chip manufacturers realized is that sometimes those extra bits for size were needed for size of data but mostly not. So this is where things get cool: The default is 32-bit data! The processor stack, however, is still 64 bits.

   The topic of 64-bit mode is spread throughout this book. Almost every instruction has a difference when used while in 64-bit mode. Some have been invalidated and thus do not exist anymore. Some have been renamed to help differentiate between 32-bit and 64-bit modes. The one thing to keep in mind is that most use a new 64-bit data addressing scheme involving a REX prefix, which will be discussed later in this chapter. The neat thing is some scalar operations that used to be done with MMX registers can now be done with the general-purpose registers. Instructions that used MMX registers such as PAND, POR, or XOR can now be done alternatively, using 64-bit general-purpose registers in 64-bit mode, thus minimizing the use of MMX registers and alleviating their associated dependency issues.

   The goal is to preferably use XMM (SSE) registers or general-purpose registers instead.

   So do not feel swizzled! 64 bit is discussed throughout this book!

# 80x86 Registers

The Intel 80x86 processor family has internal storage that is referred to as registers. These have been organized into seven groups: general-purpose data registers, segment registers, status registers, control registers, FPU registers used by the FPU (floating-point unit), MMX registers, and XMM registers. Please note that the FPU and MMX registers share storage area and thus are mutually exclusive (only one of them can be used at a time). Each has its own set of functionality.

The following registers and their ranges are for dealing with the SIMD instruction sets directly. They do not include system registers.

*Table 3-2: SIMD instruction with register names and bit widths*

| SIMD Instruction Set | Regs | IA-32 | EM64T | Bits |
|---|---|---|---|---|
| MMX | mm# | (0...7) | (0...7) | 64 |
| 3DNow! | mm# | (0...7) | (0...7) | 64 |
| 3DNow! Extensions (3DNow!+) | mm# | (0...7) | (0...7) | 64 |
| 3DNow! MMX Extensions (MMX+) | mm# | (0...7) | (0...7) | 64 |
| SSE | xmm# | (0...7) | (8...15) | 128 |
| SSE2 | xmm# | (0...7) | (8...15) | 128 |
| SSE3 | xmm# | (0...7) | (8...15) | 128 |

## General-Purpose Registers

The general-purpose registers are organized into two groups of eight registers: The RAX, RBX, RCX, and RDX general registers each have an 8-, 16-, 32-, and 64-bit form, as well as the index registers RSI and RDI, and the stack pointers RBP and RSP. The second set of eight are new registers R8...R15. The instruction pointer RIP has a 16-, 32-, and 64-bit form depending on which mode the processor is running in.

**64-bit**    **No 64-bit:**   There is a special case where the AH, BH, CH, and DH are not accessible when the REX prefix is used. REX is used for all extended 64-bit registers as well as SIL, DIL, BPL, and SPL register access.

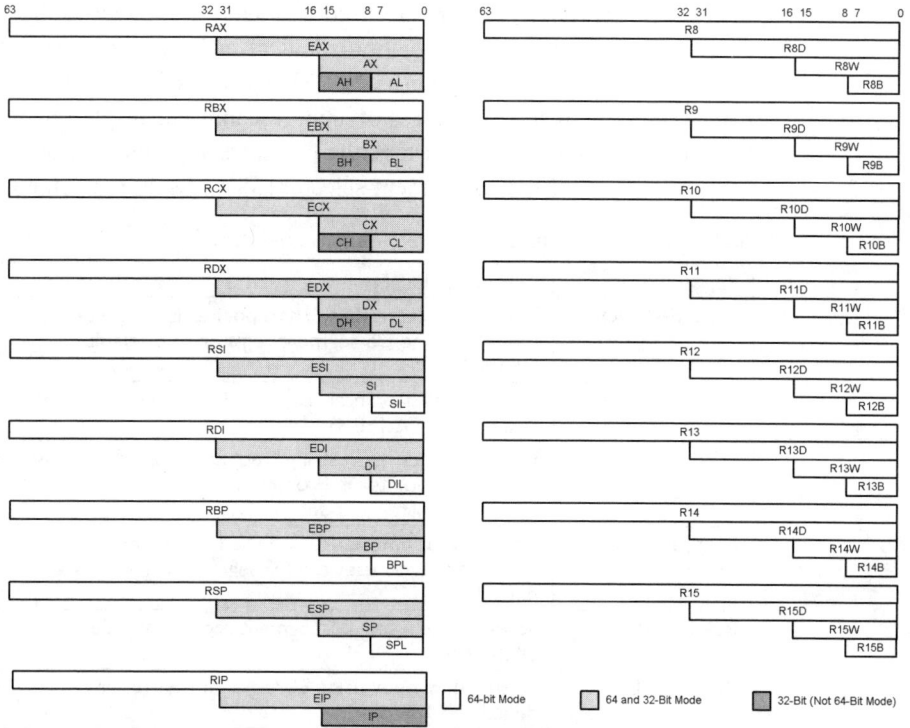

Figure 3-2: 64/32/16-bit general-purpose 80x86 registers

Table 3-3: 64-bit mode registers

| 64 | RAX | RBX | RCX | RDX | RSI | RDI | RBP | RSP | RIP |
|----|-----|-----|-----|-----|-----|-----|-----|-----|-----|
| 32 | EAX | EBX | ECX | EDX | ESI | EDI | EBP | ESP | |
| 16 | AX | BX | CX | DX | SI | DI | BP | SP | |
| 8 | AL | BL | CL | DL | SIL | DIL | BPL | SPL | |

| 64 | R8 | R9 | R10 | R11 | R12 | R13 | R14 | R15 |
|----|-----|-----|------|------|------|------|------|------|
| 32 | R8D | R9D | R10D | R11D | R12D | R13D | R14D | R15D |
| 16 | R8W | R9W | R10W | R11W | R12W | R13W | R14W | R15W |
| 8 | R8B | R9B | R10B | R11B | R12B | R13B | R14B | R15B |

Table 3-4: 32-bit (Protected/Real Mode) registers

| 32 | EAX | EBX | ECX | EDX | ESI | EDI | EBP | ESP | EIP |
|----|-----|-----|-----|-----|-----|-----|-----|-----|-----|
| 16 | AX | BX | CX | DX | SI | DI | BP | SP | IP |
| 8 | AL | BL | CL | DL | | | | | |
| | AH | BH | CH | DH | | | | | |

The general-purpose registers are used as memory pointers, address calculations (displacement w/scaling), logical bit, and mathematical operations. There is an exception as the RSP register is the stack pointer and has limitations such as it does not support scaling and displacement. In relation to the segment registers, the 64-bit stack pointer is used in conjunction with the stack segment-selector (SS) register as a default.

*Table 3-5: 64-, 32-, and 16-bit general-purpose registers*

| Register | Extra Functionality |
| --- | --- |
| RAX, EAX, AX | The accumulator. If used as a pointer in Protected Mode uses the DS segment register as a default. DS:[EAX] |
| RBX, EBX, BX | Used as a data pointer using the DS segment register as a default. DS:[EBX] |
| RCX, ECX, CX | Used as a counter in string (rep) and loop operations. If used as a pointer in Protected Mode uses the DS segment register as a default. DS:[ECX] |
| RDX, EDX, DX | Input/output port address. If used as a pointer in Protected Mode uses the DS segment register as a default. DS:[EDX] |
| RSI, ESI, SI | Source index using DS segment register as a default. DS:[ESI] |
| RDI, EDI, DI | Destination index using ES segment register as a default. ES:[EDI] |
| RBP, EBP, BP | Pointer to data on the stack (very similar to ESP); uses the SS segment register as a default. SS:[EBP] |
| RSP, ESP, SP | Stack pointer used the SS segment register as a default. SS:[ESP] |
| RIP, EIP, IP | Instruction pointer. CS:[EIP] |

Note: The "R" prefix of these registers only became available with the 64-bit versions of the processor. The "E" prefix of these registers became available with the introduction of the 32-bit 386 processor. Prior to that, only 16-bit registers were supported.

Regardless of which mode you were in, you could access either 32-bit or 16-bit registers. But this was with the introduction of a pre-op code. If in 32 bit, you accessed 32-bit registers. In 16 bit, you accessed 16-bit registers. But if you needed to access the alternate type, then a hidden leading prefix was embedded in the binary output:

(**66h**) operand-size prefix
(**67h**) address-size prefix

So from 32-bit code…

```
    mov eax,3
66h mov ax,3
```

...from 16-bit code...

```
66h mov eax,3
    mov ax,3
```

This covers all the 32-bit processors. So now that I have complicated things for you with some history, let us examine the new REX prefix.

# REX

The prefix REX is not an instruction, it is an invisible prefix. It is similar to the operand-size and address-size prefix that the assembler and compilers inject into the code when switching before a 16-bit and 32-bit access method. With the new 64-bit instructions it has been extended again.

**Note:**   When the processor is running in 64-bit mode the data is 32 bit. A REX prefix of **40h...48h** is embedded when using 64-bit data access. After all, a 64-bit number is a *very big number* and thus not needed that often. Sign extending a 32-bit number when needed is more code efficient.

With the introduction of 64-bit processors a new invisible prefix is used: REX (**40h...4Fh**). So if this new processor is running in 64-bit mode the previous rules still apply, but to access the 64-bit data a REX opcode is injected:

```
66h mov ax,3
    mov eax,3
REX mov rax,3
```

**No 64-bit:**   You cannot use 64-bit data while running in 32-bit mode or inc/dec register instructions in 64-bit mode and here is why: The opcodes 40h...4Fh are mapped to register increment and decrement instructions in a 32-bit mode environment! Thus, in 32-bit mode only the 32-bit data and instruction sets can be accessed. REX does not exist. In 64-bit mode, 32-bit and 64-bit data can be accessed, but the inc/dec instructions are no longer available for direct use by a register.

Table 3-6: Mappings of inc/dec instructions that use the opcode 40h-4Fh in compatibility or legacy 32-bit mode.

| | | | | |
|---|---|---|---|---|
| 40h | inc EAX | | 48h | dec EAX |
| 41h | inc ECX | | 49h | dec ECX |
| 42h | inc EDX | | 4ah | dec EDX |
| 43h | inc EBX | | 4bh | dec EBX |
| 44h | inc ESP | | 4ch | dec ESP |
| 45h | inc EBP | | 4dh | dec EBP |
| 46h | inc ESI | | 4eh | dec ESI |
| 47h | inc EDI | | 4fh | dec EDI |

Table 3-7: Mappings of opcode 40h-4Fh in 64-bit mode

| 7 | 6 | 5 | 4 | 3 | 2 | 1 | 0 |
|---|---|---|---|---|---|---|---|
| 0 | 1 | 0 | 0 | W | R | X | C |

W   0 = Default operand size, 1 = 64-bit operand size
R   Extension of mod r/m register field
X   Extension of the SIB index field
C   Extension of the mod r/m field, SIB base field,
    or opcode reg. field

The instruction format is a grouping of a prefix that is optional, opcode, mod r/m, sib, displacement, and data. This book does not get into the nitty-gritty of how an instruction, registers, and/or memory references map into an actual opcode. But the bit mapping for the mod r/m is as follows:

Table 3-8: Mappings of mod r/m code. 32-bit is the default. Substitute 16/64-bit for 32-bit form where needed, such as 00-001 DS:[ECX], DS:[CX], [RCX].

| MOD | R/M | | MOD | R/M | |
|---|---|---|---|---|---|
| 00 | 000 | DS:[EAX] | 01 | 000 | DS:[EAX+d8] |
| 00 | 001 | DS:[ECX] | 01 | 001 | DS:[ECX+d8] |
| 00 | 010 | DS:[EDX] | 01 | 010 | DS:[EDX+d8] |
| 00 | 011 | DS:[EBX] | 01 | 011 | DS:[EBX+d8] |
| 00 | 100 | s-i-b | 01 | 100 | s-i-b |
| 00 | 101 | DS:d32 | 01 | 101 | SS:[EBP+d8] |
| 00 | 110 | DS:[ESI] | 01 | 110 | DS:[ESI+d8] |
| 00 | 111 | DS:[EDI] | 01 | 111 | DS:[EDI+d8] |

| MOD | R/M | | MOD | R/M | |
|---|---|---|---|---|---|
| 10 | 000 | DS:[EAX+d32] | 11 | 000 | AL AX EAX RAX |
| 10 | 001 | DS:[ECX+d32] | 11 | 001 | CL CX ECX RCX |
| 10 | 010 | DS:[EDX+d32] | 11 | 010 | DL DX EDX RDX |

| MOD | R/M | |
|-----|-----|-----|
| 10 | 011 | DS:[EBX+d32] |
| 10 | 100 | s-i-b |
| 10 | 101 | SS:[EBP+d32] |
| 10 | 110 | DS:[ESI+d32] |
| 10 | 111 | DS:[EDI+d32] |

| MOD | R/M | |
|-----|-----|-----|
| 11 | 011 | BL BX EBX RBX |
| 11 | 100 | AH SP ESP RSP SPL |
| 11 | 101 | CH BP EBP RBP BPL |
| 11 | 110 | DH SI ESI RSI SIL |
| 11 | 111 | BH DI EDI RDI DIL |

There are other mappings but this is sufficient. The reason this book does not get too deep into details is that you are probably not writing assemblers or compilers. If you were, then you mostly would not need this book except as a reference. It is just one of those interesting tidbits but unnecessary for assembly language programming or debugging. "s-i-b" represents (scale-index-base) byte.

# Segment/Selector Registers

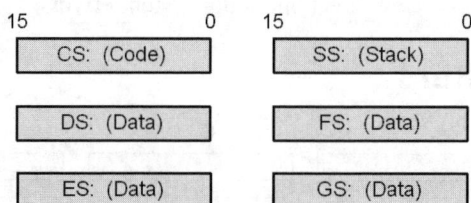

*Figure 3-3: Segment-selector registers*

In Protected Mode these registers are referred to as "selectors" and in Real Mode "segment registers." In Real Mode they are used in conjunction with an index register to calculate a memory address. As they are functionally the same, in this section "segment" will mean both. They are sometimes referred to as segment-selectors.

| 15...0 | Description |
|--------|-------------|
| CS | Code segment |
| DS | Data segment |
| ES | Extra (data) segment |
| FS | Data segment |
| GS | Data segment |
| SS | Stack segment |

Note: The FS and GS were not available prior to the 386 processor.

When modifying any segment-selector register you must first save a copy of its stored value and restore it before exiting your function or your program will go "BOOM!" (That is a technical term!) Well, it will not explode as it will just cause the process to crash, but it will sure seem like it exploded. (Ask any assembly language programmer!)

If you are writing a Win32 type application, then typically all the segment-selectors are used in the execution of your code but are usually not denoted in your code as the defaults will be used. The FS and GS are used in your assembly code typically only in device drivers. This is the case of a flat memory model and the DS and ES are set to the same base address in memory. This section essentially becomes a no-brainer! You can completely ignore the segment registers since the DS, ES, and SS are set to the same segment and the indexing registers have used one or the other segment register as a default.

If you are writing an Extended DOS or other OS-based application, then you will typically use most or all of the segment-selector registers, especially in your low-level operating system drivers.

## MMX Registers

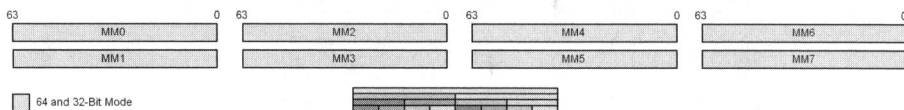

*Figure 3-4: MMX registers*

There are eight 64-bit MMX registers (MM0, MM1, MM2, MM3, MM4, MM5, MM6, MM7). These are 64-bit registers that can deal with a single 64-bit number, or two 32-bit, four 16-bit, or eight 8-bit packed values. In the 3DNow! instruction set they used for both integers and floating-point value pairs. These registers were introduced with the Pentium Pro series processors. There are no flags to set or read but based upon the instruction the individual packed data values are treated individually to effectively replicate a desired instruction.

# XMM Registers

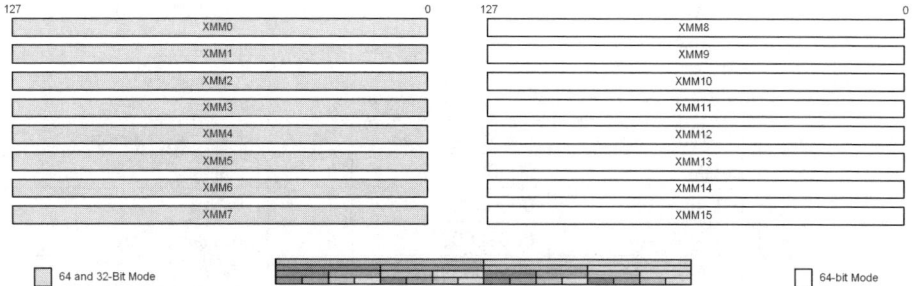

Figure 3-5: XMM registers

There are eight 128-bit SSE registers (XMM0, XMM1, XMM2, XMM3, XMM4, XMM5, XMM6, XMM7) for pre 64-bit and eight additional registers (XMM8, XMM9, XMM10, XMM11, XMM12, XMM13, XMM14, XMM15) for 64-bit or larger data processors. These are 128-bit registers that can deal with two single 64-bit, four 32-bit, eight 16-bit, or sixteen 8-bit packed values, whether they be integer or single/double-precision floating-point. These registers were introduced with the PIII series processors. There are no flags to set or read, but based upon the instruction the individual packed data values are treated individually to effectively replicate a desired instruction. The functionality of the 64-bit MMX registers was migrated to the 128-bit SSE registers, thus doubling the size but without the burden of the FPU vs. MMX data type switching. Whenever possible, these should be used instead of MMX.

# CPU Status Registers (EFLAGS/64-Bit RFLAGS)

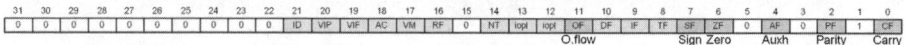

Figure 3-6: EFLAGS register

Each 80x86 processor has standard status flags stored in an EFLAGS/RFLAGS register, which indicate various conditions of the processor. In 64-bit mode the EFLAGS register is referred to as the 64-bit register

RFLAGS, with the upper bits set to zero. As this book is written mainly for the application programmer there are only a few EFLAGS that you need to know initially. All the EFLAGS are defined in Chapter 18 but for now:

Table 3-9: RFLAG/EFLAG(s) and bit encoding

| EFLAG | Code | Bit | Flag Descriptions |
|---|---|---|---|
| EFLAGS_CF | 00000001h | 0 | Carry |
| EFLAGS_PF | 00000004h | 2 | Parity |
| EFLAGS_AF | 00000010h | 4 | Auxiliary Carry |
| EFLAGS_ZF | 00000040h | 6 | Zero |
| EFLAGS_SF | 00000080h | 7 | Sign |
| EFLAGS_OF | 00000800h | 11 | Overflow |

In this book you will find the following table with each general-purpose instruction description indicating the flags that it sets. Those flags are in reality the individual bits found in the EFLAGS register.

| Flags | O.flow | Sign | Zero | Aux | Parity | Carry |
|---|---|---|---|---|---|---|
| | - | - | - | - | - | - |

# LAHF — Load AH Flags

| Mnemonic | P | PII | K6 | 3D! | 3Mx+ | SSE | SSE2 | A64 | SSE3 | E64T |
|---|---|---|---|---|---|---|---|---|---|---|
| LAHF | ✓ | ✓ | ✓ | ✓ | ✓ | ✓ | ✓ | 32 | ✓ | 32 |

    lahf

The LAHF instruction loads the lower 8 bits of the EFLAGS register into the AH register. This only loads the standard conditional flags used by the Jcc and SETcc instructions. The complement to this instruction is SAHF.

| Bit | 7 | 6 | 5 | 4 | 3 | 2 | 1 | 0 |
|---|---|---|---|---|---|---|---|---|
| Flag | SF | ZF | 0 | AF | 0 | PF | 1 | CF |

For more detailed information about EFLAGS, see Chapter 18.

| Flags | O.flow | Sign | Zero | Aux | Parity | Carry |
|---|---|---|---|---|---|---|
| | - | - | - | - | - | - |

Flags: None are affected by this opcode.

This instruction can get you a copy of all the conditional flags in one step without having to use the stack. It should be remembered that only bits $\{0, 2, 4, 6, 7\}$ are usable and $\{1, 3, 5\}$ are reserved and not usable.

**64-bit**  **No 64-bit:**  This instruction is not supported in 64-bit mode! To get the flags into register AL use instead:

```
PUSHFQ        ; Push RFLAGS
POP    RAX    ; Pop into RAX
```

# SAHF — Save AH Flags

| Mnemonic | P | PII | K6 | 3D! | 3Mx+ | SSE | SSE2 | A64 | SSE3 | E64T |
|----------|---|-----|----|-----|------|-----|------|-----|------|------|
| SAHF | ✓ | ✓ | ✓ | ✓ | ✓ | ✓ | ✓ | 32 | ✓ | 32 |

sahf

The SAHF instruction saves the AH register to the lower 8 bits of the EFLAGS register. This only sets the standard conditional flags used by the Jcc, SETcc, and other instructions. The complement to this instruction is LAHF.

For more detailed information about EFLAGS, see the instruction LAHF and Chapter 18.

| **Flags** | O.flow | Sign | Zero | Aux | Parity | Carry |
|-----------|--------|------|------|-----|--------|-------|
| | - | X | X | X | X | X |

Flags: All flags except overflow are affected by this opcode.

This can set all the conditional flags in one step without having to use the stack. It should be remembered that only bits $\{0, 2, 4, 6, 7\}$ are usable and $\{1, 3, 5\}$ are reserved and not usable.

**64-bit**  **No 64-bit:**  This instruction is not supported in 64-bit mode!

# PUSHF/PUSHFD — Push EFLAGS onto Stack

# PUSHFQ — Push RFLAGS onto Stack

| Mnemonic | P | PII | K6 | 3D! | 3Mx+ | SSE | SSE2 | A64 | SSE3 | E64T |
|----------|---|-----|----|-----|------|-----|------|-----|------|------|
| PUSHF | ✓ | ✓ | ✓ | ✓ | ✓ | ✓ | ✓ | ✓ | ✓ | ✓ |
| PUSHFD | ✓ | ✓ | ✓ | ✓ | ✓ | ✓ | ✓ | 32 | ✓ | 32 |
| PUSHFQ | | | | | | | | 64 | | 64 |

| pushf | 16 |
| pushfd | 32 |
| pushfq | 64 |

The PUSHF instruction pushes the lower 16 bits of the EFLAGS register and the PUSHFD instruction pushes the entire 32 bits of the EFLAGS register. PUSHFQ replaces PUSHFD, but it pushes all 64 bits of RFLAGS (the extended EFLAGS). They are the WORD, DWORD, and QWORD forms of the same instruction. (They all map to the same opcode.)

| **Flags** | O.flow | Sign | Zero | Aux | Parity | Carry |
|-----------|--------|------|------|-----|--------|-------|
| - | - | - | - | - | - | - |

Flags: None are affected by this opcode.

**64-bit**

**No 64-bit:** The PUSHFD instruction is not supported in 64-bit mode. It has been replaced with PUSHFQ.

To get the EFLAGS, one only needs to push it onto the stack and then pop it off into a general-purpose register!

```
pushfd          ; push EFLAGS register
pop     eax     ; pop those flags into EAX
```

# POPF/POPFD — Pop EFLAGS from Stack

# POPFQ — Pop RFLAGS from Stack

| Mnemonic | P | PII | K6 | 3D! | 3Mx+ | SSE | SSE2 | A64 | SSE3 | E64T |
|----------|---|-----|----|----|------|-----|------|-----|------|------|
| POPF | ✓ | ✓ | ✓ | ✓ | ✓ | ✓ | ✓ | ✓ | ✓ | ✓ |
| POPFD | ✓ | ✓ | ✓ | ✓ | ✓ | ✓ | ✓ | 32 | ✓ | 32 |
| POPFQ | | | | | | | | 64 | | 64 |

| popf | 16 |
| popfd | 32 |
| popfq | 64 |

The POPF instruction pops the stack value into the lower 16 bits of the EFLAGS register, and the POPFD instruction pops the entire 32 bits off the stack into the EFLAGS register. In 64-bit mode POPFQ replaces the POPFD instruction and pops all 64 bits of RFLAGS. They are the WORD, DWORD, and QWORD forms of the same instruction. This instruction is the complement to PUSHF and PUSHFD.

| Flags | O.flow | Sign | Zero | Aux | Parity | Carry |
|-------|--------|------|------|-----|--------|-------|
|       | X      | X    | X    | X   | X      | X     |

Flags: All flags are affected by this opcode.

**No 64-bit:** The POPFD instruction is not supported in 64-bit mode. It has been replaced with POPFQ.

Some of the EFLAGS bits can be individually modified by using the PUSHF/PUSHFD and POPF/POPFD CPU instructions. They pop the flags onto the stack, at which point you pop them into a general-purpose register, manipulate the bits, push the register value back onto the stack, and then pop it back into the EFLAGS. This same trick is used to detect CPU capability (see Chapter 16). The same applies to RFLAGS in conjunction with PUSHFQ and POPFQ.

```
pushfd                        ; push EFLAGS register
pop      eax                  ; pop those flags into EAX
xor      eax,EFLAGS_ID        ; flip ID bit#21 in EFLAGS
push     eax                  ; push modified flags on stack
popfd                         ; pop flags back into EFLAGS
```

During an interrupt call, the EFLAGS are automatically stored on the stack with the return address so that when the interrupt returns, the register status can be restored to exactly the way it was when the interrupt occurred. The same thing happens in a multithreaded environment. When a thread is preempted so that another thread can be executed for a while, the processor status related to that thread is saved and restored accordingly. This is hidden from the application programmer and so does not need to be worried about. Just keep in the back of your mind that it is taken care of for you.

# CLC — Clear (Reset) Carry Flag

| Mnemonic | P | PII | K6 | 3D! | 3Mx+ | SSE | SSE2 | A64 | SSE3 | E64T |
|----------|---|-----|----|----|------|-----|------|-----|------|------|
| CLC      | ✓ | ✓   | ✓  | ✓  | ✓    | ✓   | ✓    | ✓   | ✓    | ✓    |

clc

This general-purpose instruction clears (resets) the Carry flag.

| Flags | O.flow | Sign | Zero | Aux | Parity | Carry |
|-------|--------|------|------|-----|--------|-------|
|       | -      | -    | -    | -   | -      | 0     |

## STC — Set Carry Flag

| Mnemonic | P | PII | K6 | 3D! | 3Mx+ | SSE | SSE2 | A64 | SSE3 | E64T |
|----------|---|-----|----|----|------|-----|------|-----|------|------|
| STC | ✓ | ✓ | ✓ | ✓ | ✓ | ✓ | ✓ | ✓ | ✓ | ✓ |

stc

This general-purpose instruction sets the Carry flag.

| Flags | O.flow | Sign | Zero | Aux | Parity | Carry |
|-------|--------|------|------|-----|--------|-------|
| | - | - | - | - | - | I |

## CMC — Complement Carry Flag

| Mnemonic | P | PII | K6 | 3D! | 3Mx+ | SSE | SSE2 | A64 | SSE3 | E64T |
|----------|---|-----|----|----|------|-----|------|-----|------|------|
| CMC | ✓ | ✓ | ✓ | ✓ | ✓ | ✓ | ✓ | ✓ | ✓ | ✓ |

cmc

This general-purpose instruction complements the Carry flag.

c = c′

| Flags | O.flow | Sign | Zero | Aux | Parity | Carry |
|-------|--------|------|------|-----|--------|-------|
| | - | - | - | - | - | X |

```
Carry = (Carry == 0) ? 1 : 0;
```

# NOP — No Operation

| Mnemonic | P | PII | K6 | 3D! | 3Mx+ | SSE | SSE2 | A64 | SSE3 | E64T |
|----------|---|-----|----|----|------|-----|------|-----|------|------|
| NOP | ✓ | ✓ | ✓ | ✓ | ✓ | ✓ | ✓ | ✓ | ✓ | ✓ |

nop

The NOP is a no-operation instruction. It uses up one instruction byte and changes no flags. It is typically used for code alignment by one byte or a time delay.

Other instructions can be used for nop's of N bytes:

```
1    NOP
1    XCHG EAX,EAX
3    LEA EAX, {8 disp}
6    LEA EAX, {32 disp}
```

# Floating-Point 101

Remember that this is not rocket science, and thus minor deviations will occur in the formulas since, for example, a single-precision float is only 32 bits in size. For higher precision, 64-bit double-precision or 80-bit double extended-precision floating-point should be used instead. These floating-point numbers are based upon a similarity to the IEEE 754 standards specification. Unfortunately the 80-bit version is only available in a scalar form on the 80x86's FPU and the 64-bit *packed* double-precision is only available on the SSE2 processor.

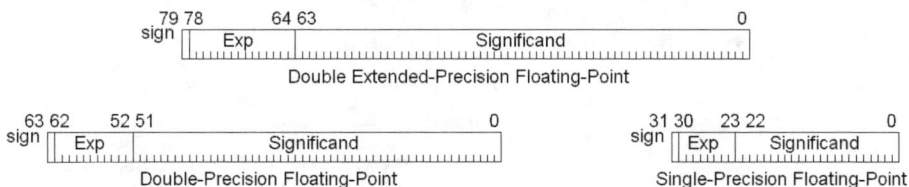

*Figure 3-7: Floating-point bit configurations*

Most programmers only know a floating-point value from using a declaration such as float, double, real4, or real8, etc. They know that there is a sign bit that if set indicates the value is negative and if clear indicates the value is positive. That is typically about the limit of the programmer's knowledge, as floating-point is typically treated as a black box and they typically do not need to dig into it further.

For this book you will be required to understand a little bit more and that will be discussed in Chapter 8.

# Processor Data Type Encoding

The 80x86 processor is the most complicated of all the processors due to its life span and constant upgrades and enhancements since its introduction to the marketplace on August 12, 1980. If the 1983 Charlie Chaplin promoter of the IBM personal computer with its 8088 were to see it now he would be proud and astonished at all the architectural changes that have occurred to it over the years.

For a processor to survive it must either be enhanced to meet the demands of technology, find a second life in an embedded marketplace, or die. Intel and AMD have done just that (not the die part), but unfortunately in the process, the technology has forked and so there are now a multitude of flavors of the original 80x86 processor core in existence. In addition, AMD has merged the technologies of the 3DNow! extensions and SSE(2) and formed the 3DNow! Professional instruction sets.

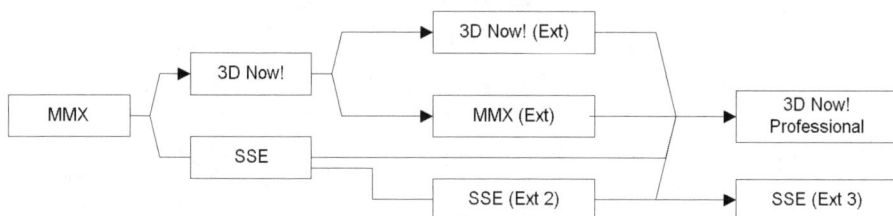

Figure 3-8: Flavor tree of x86 processors

The point is that now there are several 80x86 SIMD feature sets and not all processors have them all. So the first step is to resolve this. Intel initially did so by developing an instruction with the mnemonic CPUID along with a set of sample processor detection code. AMD adopted the same instruction with their set of sample code. As the technology forked further, each company's sample CPUID code emphasized its own processors so programmers have had to merge both companies' code a bit, although AMD's was more diverse. To make it even more complicated, AMD put out 3DNow! Professional. This is a hybrid of all the 80x86 instruction sets of the AMD and Intel technologies, except the SSE (Extensions 3) (at least at the time this book was written). Because of the confusion factor, this book's goal is to try to make it easier to understand.

In Chapter 16 the CPUID instruction is explained. This is a very complicated instruction, but it is wrapped with a function call used by this book that fills in a structure and builds an ASCII string describing the capabilities of a computer in code. It or something similar to it should be used to decide whether a certain set of instructions is usable on a particular computer. Since you are most likely learning this subject material, then you are most likely using one or two computers to test this code and thus know the processor type already. Just to be sure you are running the correct instructions on the correct machine there is a CPUID testing logic included with most of the test applications to run the appropriate set of code. If you wish to learn more about this, please skip ahead to Chapter 16.

```
void CpuDetect(CpuInfo * const pInfo);
```

Briefly, the CPU detection code checks for the processor type and its capability and sets flags accordingly. The initialization function attaches function pointers to appropriate code compatible with that processor type and then it is just a matter of the application calling a generic function pointer, which gets routed to the appropriate code.

When you write your code, try to use SSE instructions whenever possible for scalar as well as vector processing. When possible use the instructions that perform quick estimations as they are designed for higher speed calculations despite their lower accuracy. In that way you will always have the best performance for your code, even on newer machines released after you ship your code.

The 80x86 processor has a dual mode in relationship to its MMX and FPU registers. In these particular cases whenever there is a need to switch back and forth, the appropriate instruction needs to be called. In addition, there is a difference between the AMD instruction FEMMS and the Intel instruction EMMS. (These will be discussed in Chapter 8.) When writing code, use instructions that favor using the SSE instructions as the (F)EMMS instructions are only needed if switching between MMX and FPU.

# EMMS — Enter/Leave MMX State

| Mnemonic | P | PII | K6 | 3D! | 3Mx+ | SSE | SSE2 | A64 | SSE3 | E64T |
|----------|---|-----|----|----|------|-----|------|-----|------|------|
| EMMS     |   | ✓   | ✓  | ✓  | ✓    | ✓   | ✓    | ✓   | ✓    | ✓    |

emms

# FEMMS — Enter/Leave MMX State

| Mnemonic | P | PII | K6 | 3D! | 3Mx+ | SSE | SSE2 | A64 | SSE3 | E64T |
|----------|---|-----|----|----|------|-----|------|-----|------|------|
| FEMMS    |   |     |    | ✓  | ✓    |     |      | ✓   |      |      |

3DNow!    femms

> **Tip:** Note that if your floating-point code gets erratic and appears to have unexpected QNAN or infinity or illegal values, then look for a usage of an FPU or MMX instruction while the other mode was thought to be in effect. It is probably because you are missing an (F)EMMS instruction to flip modes.

The point is that whatever mechanism you put into place — switch-case statements, lookup tables, etc. — you want to have the best (fastest) set of code available for that processor. The trick, however, is not to use up valuable memory supporting all those combinations. Fortunately, consoles such as Xbox are fixed targets, which can assist you in being more selective. In fact, you can get away with absolute function calls rather than function pointers, but that would really be up to you! It all depends upon how you implement your cross-platform capabilities. The code samples use a platform-specific file to connect the dots so to speak, so it can be abstracted out easily to a platform-specific implementation. Of course, if using direct calls you would want to have two flavors of function prototypes in the header files: those set up to be function pointer based and those set up as standard function prototypes.

# Destination/Source Orientations

Another difference between platforms has to do with the format of the assembly instructions. Depending on the processor there are typically two orientations.

Some non-80x86 processors allow the destination register to not be a source register. Thus, Register D = Register A + Register B. Or D = D + A. In C programming this is a form similar to:

```
D = A + B
D = D + A
```

The 80x86 processor family requires the destination to be one of the sources. In C programming this is similar to:

```
D += A
D = D + A
```

| Proc: x86 — MMX, SSE, SSE2, 3DNow!, etc. |
| --- |
| mnemonic *destination, source* |
| paddb xmm1, xmm2 |

# Big/Little-Endian

One very important processor specification to be aware of is the endian orientation. This drastically affects how byte ordering affects data orientation. Depending on the processor and its manufacturer, data structures larger than a byte are typically arranged in one of two orientations:

■ Little-endian

■ Big-endian

One interesting aspect is that for either little or big endian, the 8-bit byte both have an identical bit ordering of bits $\{0...7\}$. The MIPS processors (as a default) and the 80x86 are little-endian, but the Motorola 68000 and the PowerPC RISC microprocessor are big-endian.

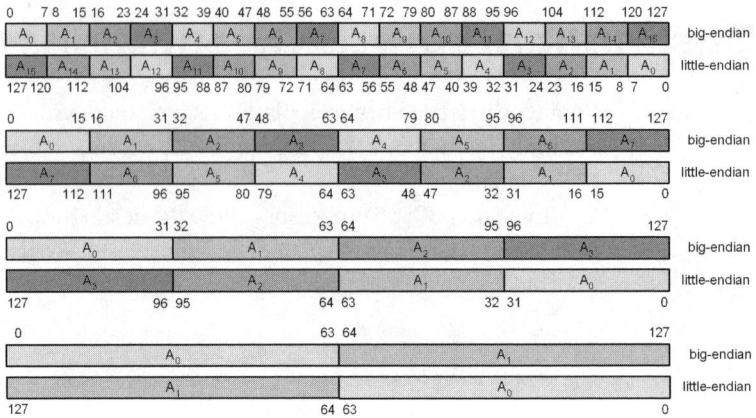

*Figure 3-9: Data conversions*

Little-endian is linear just like memory, so every more significant byte would be the next (incremental) addressed one in memory. For the size of a data word in big-endian, every more significant byte would be the previous (decremental) addressed one in memory.

In big-endian the most significant byte is first in memory and it progresses down to the least significant byte; the cycle repeats for the next block. In the following diagram, the data in memory is blocked into groups of 128 bits (16 bytes).

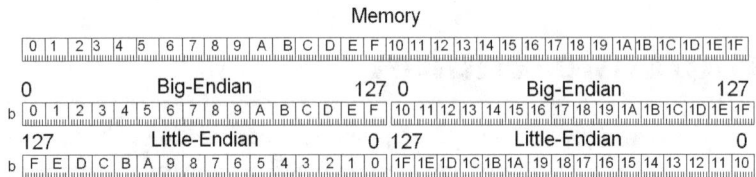

*Figure 3-10: Big-endian and little-endian byte orientations in relation to memory*

The Intel 80x86 processor is a little-endian based processor. That is, the memory is laid out in a linear fashion so the first byte contains the LSB (least significant bit). For example, as Figure 3-11 shows, a dword has the lower bits (7…0) in the first byte (#0) and bits (31…24) in the fourth byte (#3). This pattern is repeated over and over.

In the C programming language, use the following shift to the left by one for a 32-bit data word (int).

```
a = a << 1;
```

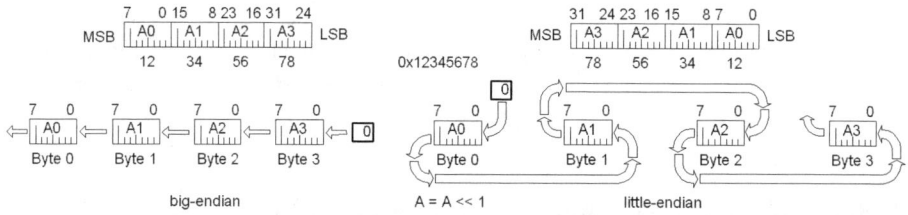

*Figure 3-11: Visible connections between individual bytes and the left shift of a 32-bit data element*

Dealing with endian orientation can sometimes be confusing, especially if you primarily work in little-endian and then need to convert data to the form of big-endian. This makes perfect visual sense for big-endian because the fourth byte contains the least significant bit (LSB) and data is shifted to the left toward the most significant bit (MSB). For little-endian the same shift in C magnifies the value by a factor of two for each bit but visually it makes no sense because the LSB is on the left. By using a mirrored reflection it then becomes clear.

At this point this should be enough conversation about endian orientation of memory until you get to Chapter 6, "Data Conversions," where this is discussed more thoroughly.

# Alignment Quickie

In the following little-endian ordered data snippet, you will find an example of the most common data types. The actual hex value is on the right and the byte arrangement in memory is on the left.

```
0000 12                 Ape   db    12h          ; (byte)
0001 34 12              Bat   dw    1234h        ; (word)
0003 78 56 34 12        Cat   dd    12345678h    ; (dword)
0007 F0 DE BC 9A
     78 56 34 12        Dog   dq    123456789ABCDEF0h ; (qword)
```

Note that the data should be properly aligned to their data type, so a slight rearrangement of the previous data snippet is in order. You should note the previous odd addressing versus the following aligned addressing:

```
0000 f0 DE BC 9A
     78 56 34 12        Dog   dq    123456789ABCDEF0h ; (qword)
0008 78 56 34 12        Cat   dd    12345678h    ; (dword)
000C 34 12              Bat   dw    1234h        ; (word)
000E 12                 Ape   db    12h          ; (byte)
```

You will note by the base address on the far left that the data has been reordered to ensure that all elements of a data type are properly aligned for their data type. Eight-byte values are aligned on 8-byte boundaries, 4-byte on 4-byte boundaries, etc.

# (Un)aligned Memory Access

As discussed in the previous chapter, it is very important to have proper data alignment on all data. There are however, times when this is not possible; in those cases the data would still need to be accessed quickly, so before we get into the heavy-duty instructions that can be handled, let us look at a method of handing the pre- and postpreparation of the data for them.

**ASM 101:** MOV (Move) means to COPY.

## MOV/MOVQ — Move Data

MOV *destination, source*

| Mnemonic | P | PII | K6 | 3D! | 3Mx+ | SSE | SSE2 | A64 | SSE3 | E64T |
|---|---|---|---|---|---|---|---|---|---|---|
| LDDQU | | | | | | | | | ✓ | ✓ |
| MOV | ✓ | ✓ | ✓ | ✓ | ✓ | ✓ | ✓ | ✓ | ✓ | ✓ |
| MOVAPD | | | | | | | ✓ | ✓ | ✓ | ✓ |
| MOVAPS | | | | | | ✓ | ✓ | ✓ | ✓ | ✓ |
| MOVD | ✓ | ✓ | ✓ | ✓ | ✓ | ✓ | ✓ | ✓ | ✓ | ✓ |
| MOVDQA | | | | | | | ✓ | ✓ | ✓ | ✓ |
| MOVDQU | | | | | | | ✓ | ✓ | ✓ | ✓ |
| MOVQ | | ✓ | ✓ | ✓ | ✓ | ✓ | ✓ | ✓ | ✓ |
| MOVUPD | | | | | | | ✓ | ✓ | ✓ | ✓ |
| MOVUPS | | | | | | ✓ | ✓ | ✓ | ✓ | ✓ |

## Move (Unaligned)

```
mov    rmDst(8/16/32/64), #(8/16/32)    [Un]signed
mov    rmDst, rSrc(8/16/32/64)
mov    rDst, rmSrc(8/16/32/64)
```

*System Level Functionality*

|       |        |                           |                  |     |
|-------|--------|---------------------------|------------------|-----|
|       | mov    | *srDst, rmSrc(16/32)*     |                  |     |
|       | mov    | *rmDst, srSrc(16/32)*     |                  |     |
| MMX   | movd   | *mmxDst, mmxSrc/m64*      | [Un]signed       | 64  |
| "     | movq   | *mmxDst, mmxSrc/m64*      | "                |     |
| SSE   | movups | *xmmDst, xmmSrc/m128*     | Single-precision | 128 |
| "     | movups | *xmmDst/m128, xmmSrc*     | "                |     |
| SSE2  | movdqu | *xmmDst, xmmSrc/m128*     | [Un]signed       | 128 |
| "     | movdqu | *xmmDst/m128, xmmSrc*     | "                |     |
| "     | movupd | *xmmDst, xmmSrc/m128*     | Double-precision |     |
| "     | movupd | *xmmDst/m128, xmmSrc*     | "                |     |
| 3DNow!| movq   | *mmxDst, mmxSrc/m64*      | Single-precision | 64  |
|       | lddqu  | *xmmDst, mSrc(128)*       | [Un]signed       | 128 |

# Move (Aligned)

|       |                               |                  |     |
|-------|-------------------------------|------------------|-----|
| SSE   | movaps *xmmDst, xmmSrc/m128*   | Single-precision | 128 |
| "     | movaps *xmmDst/m128, xmmSrc*   | "                |     |
| SSE2  | movdqa *xmmDst, xmmSrc/m128*   | [Un]signed       | 128 |
| "     | movdqa *xmmDst/m128, xmmSrc*   | "                |     |
| "     | movapd *xmmDst, xmmSrc/m128*   | Double-precision |     |

The instructions do not really move data; rather it "copies" 8-, 16-, 32-, 64-, or 128-bit values from register to register, register to memory, memory to register, and immediate to register or memory, but almost never memory to memory.

| **Flags** | O.flow | Sign | Zero | Aux | Parity | Carry |
|-----------|--------|------|------|-----|--------|-------|
|           | -      | -    | -    | -   | -      | -     |

Flags: None are altered by this opcode.

**No 64-bit:** Please note that 64-bit data is *not* supported by general-purpose instructions in non-64-bit mode. 64-bit data is supported by MMX and SSE registers in 32-bit mode.

You will note that these are either a specified floating-point value or a signless "[Un]signed" integer. As the data is being copied, whether or not it is signed has no meaning!

**ASM 101:** Sorry to do this to those of you who are more experienced, but I need to embellish further for those new to the subject matter. I of course do not need to remind you to skip ahead at any time!

**MOV** — Copy a (32-bit) double-word value from one location to another. From a 32-bit (4 bytes) general-purpose register to a general-purpose register:

```
mov   eax,ebx          // Copy INT32 from register to register
```

From memory to a general-purpose register, or from a general-purpose register back to memory:

```
mov   eax,mem32        // Copy INT32 from memory to register
mov   mem32,ecx        // Copy INT32 from register to memory
```

**MOVQ** — Copy a (64-bit) quad-word value from one location to another. From 64-bit (8 bytes) memory to an MMX register, or from a MMX register back to memory:

```
movq   mm0,mem64        // Read INT64 from memory
movq   mem64,mm0        // Write INT64 to memory
```

For the MMX and SSE the MMX registers can only manipulate integer values. Any kind of data can be loaded but it is treated as an integer whether in reality it is a floating-point value or not. The 3DNow! instruction set, however, does not differentiate.

```
movq   mm0,mem64        // Read SPFP from memory
movq   mem64,mm0        // Write SPFP to memory
```

**MOVDQU** — Move an unaligned double-quad word value from memory to 128-bit memory and vice versa:

```
movdqu   xmm0,mem128     // Read INT from unaligned memory
movdqu   mem128,xmm0     // Write INT to unaligned memory
```

**MOVDQA** — Move an aligned double-quad word value from memory to 128-bit memory and vice versa:

```
movdqa   xmm0,mem128     // Read INT from aligned memory
movdqa   mem128,xmm0     // Write INT to aligned memory
```

**MOVUPS** — Move an unaligned single-precision floating-point value from memory to 128-bit memory and vice versa:

```
movups   xmm0,mem128     // Read SPFP from unaligned memory
movups   mem128,xmm0     // Write SPFP to unaligned memory
```

**MOVAPS** — Move an aligned single-precision floating-point value from memory to 128-bit memory and vice versa:

```
movaps  xmm0,mem128    // Read SPFP from aligned memory
movaps  mem128,xmm0    // Write SPFP to aligned memory
```

**MOVUPD** — Move an unaligned double-precision floating-point value from memory to 128-bit memory and vice versa:

```
movupd  xmm0,mem128    // Read DPFP from unaligned memory
movupd  mem128,xmm0    // Write DPFP to unaligned memory
```

**MOVAPD** — Move an aligned double-precision floating-point value from memory to 128-bit memory and vice versa:

```
movapd  xmm0,mem128    // Read DPFP from aligned memory
movapd  mem128,xmm0    // Write DPFP to aligned memory
```

Keep in mind that the 3DNow! floating-point uses the same MMX registers as the integer instructions and thus this same MOVQ instruction.

## Misaligned SSE(2) (128-bit)

For SSE and SSE2, things get a little bit more complicated. The XMM registers are used by the SSE and SSE2 instructions and are used primarily for single-precision scalar or vector floating-point for SSE and both double-precision and 128-bit integer for the SSE2 instructions; they are not interchangeable. There are different memory movement instructions depending on whether or not the memory is aligned. There are other memory load/save instructions other than these, but these are the ones of interest to us in this book.

## Aligned SSE(2) (128-bit)

The functionality for aligned is exactly the same as for unaligned except for one difference. The aligned functions are designed for speed but the memory access must be properly aligned. If the access is misaligned, a processor exception will occur. (The processor execution stops abruptly; aka: Boom!) The penalty for the optimal feature of speed! These instructions were labeled earlier with the declaration "Move an Aligned."

**Note:**  The move instructions in this chapter only demonstrate a same size source:destination move. See Chapter 6 for movements in which source and destination are not the same size.

Data can be moved around using all sorts of methods: immediate to register, immediate to memory, register to memory, memory to register, and register to register, but data cannot be copied from memory to memory, from register to immediate, from memory to immediate, or from immediate to segment register.

Let's begin with immediate values. These are values in C such as A=5. The (5) is an immediate value.

```
foo     dd      0           ; a 4-byte memory location
```

Copy an immediate value directly into memory:

```
mov     foo,71077345        ; Move directly
```

Or copy the immediate value into a register and then to memory:

```
mov     eax,71077345        ; Get the value in decimal
mov     foo,eax             ; Then set it
```

Or copy it indirectly to memory:

```
mov     eax,71077345        ; Get the value in decimal
mov     ebx,offset foo      ; Get the address for foo
mov     [ebx],eax           ; Save the value at the address
```

In all of these examples foo now contains the specified value. All instructions use this sort of *destination, source* methodology, and I hope you understand that as I am now going to reduce verbosity a tad.

Out of curiosity, how many of you recognized 71077345 as the old calculator trick of "Shell Oil" upside down? :) (Okay, okay, a little calculator humor!)

# XCHG — Exchange (Swap) Data

XCHG *destination, source*

| Mnemonic | P | PII | K6 | 3D! | 3Mx+ | SSE | SSE2 | A64 | SSE3 | E64T |
|----------|---|-----|----|----|------|-----|------|-----|------|------|
| XCHG | ✓ | ✓ | ✓ | ✓ | ✓ | ✓ | ✓ | ✓ | ✓ | ✓ |

```
xchg    rmDst, rSrc(8/16/32/64)   [Un]signed
xchg    rDst, rmSrc(8/16/32/64)
```

8-, 16-, 32-, or 64-bit data can be exchanged between registers of the same size or between memory and a register of the same size. Note that 64-bit exchange is only in 64-bit mode.

# System Level Functionality

The move instruction has a system level functionality where segment/
selector registers can be loaded or set.

**64-bit**   **No 64-bit:** If you are developing 64-bit applications you should
skip over this section, as the CS, DS, ES, and SS selectors are nullified
and thus ignored. The FS and GS are left in reserve for use.

If you are developing 32-bit applications the system registers are
known as selectors. In Win32 the CS, DS, and ES selectors are typically
set to the same block of memory and need not be modified.

If you are developing in Real Mode, aka 16-bit applications, then
these system registers are known as segment registers. In the Real Mode
environment *sreg* represents the segment register supporting a 16-bit
offset addressing up to a maximum of 65,536 x 16 bytes. In a Protected
Mode environment the selector register indexes a 32-bit address using
virtual memory. Application programmers do not need to worry about
this. In the DOS and Extended DOS Protected Mode environments the
ES is typically set to the same value as the DS, and the FS and GS are
used to address extraneous memory blocks such as a video graphics
adapter (VGA).

Real Mode — An example of an old monochrome write access:

```
monosel dw      0b000h

        xor     edi,edi
        mov     es,monosel

        mov     es:[di],ax
        add     di,4
```

Protected Mode — An example of an old monochrome write access:

```
monoadr dd      0b0000h
monosel dw      013fh

        mov     edi,monoadr
        mov     fs,monosel

        mov     fs:[edi],eax
        add     edi,4
```

# Indirect Memory Addressing

Memory can be referenced directly using an absolute address like this:

```
mov eax,MonkeyBrainSoup
```

or with some displacement. The assembler resolves the address with the offset for a new address:

```
mov eax,MonkeyBrainSoup+8
```

This is still an absolute address. The address is simply adjusted and the new address is encoded into the code. If MonkeyBrainSoup were in data memory at location 1000h, then adding the displacement merely would encode the address as 10008h. A structure is referenced in the same way.

```
vmp3DVector STRUCT
        x        REAL4 ? ;float  ?
        y        REAL4 ? ;float  ?
        z        REAL4 ? ;float  ?
vmp3DVector ends

MyPos     vmp3Dvector    <1.0, 2.0, 3.0>
```

So addressing this static structure directly:

```
mov eax.MyPos.x
mov ecx.MyPos.y
mov edx.MyPos.z
```

really maps to:

```
mov eax,DWORD PTR MyPos+0
mov ecx,DWORD PTR MyPos+4
mov edx,DWORD PTR MyPos+8
```

We could address this indirectly by setting ebx to the base address:

```
mov ebx,offset MyPos

mov eax,(vmp3Dvector PTR[ebx]).x
mov ecx,(vmp3Dvector PTR[ebx]).y
mov edx,(vmp3Dvector PTR[ebx]).z
```

Or how about as an array of floats as shown below? Note that 0*4, 1*4, and 2*4 are not addressing multipliers. They are base address multipliers. To truly be a multiplier a register has to be the prefix argument, such as EDX*8 or EAX*2, etc. What the following really says is the base address of $0 \times 1 = 0$ or $1 \times 4 = 4$ or $2 \times 4 = 8$ + the value in ebx = the adjusted base address.

```
mov   eax,[ebx+0*4]
mov   ecx,[ebx+1*4]
mov   edx,[ebx+2*4]
```

Or an indexed element of the array:

```
mov   eax,1           ; Using eax as the element index
mov   ecx,[ebx+eax*4] ; 4 byte float
```

Those were just some examples, as almost any register can be used alone, in a pair addition, with an optional base address and/or scale factor of {2, 4, or 8}, but note that there are some limitations in regard to the ESP register. For address memory the equivalent scaling factor is needed: int16=×2, int32=×4, int64=×8. During code reviews of other programmers' assembly code I have seen single registers with and without scaling but rarely multiple register addition; instead there is usually some discrete logic to calculate a base address. (That is a waste of CPU time when hardware can resolve some of the addressing for you!)

In regard to the following mapping mechanisms I have read a lot of books and they usually have some minimal reference or simple tables made to show multiple register referencing.

*Table 3-10: 64-bit memory reference (64-bit Mode)*

| Displacement | | Base | | Index | | Scale |
|---|---|---|---|---|---|---|
| None | | RAX | | None | | |
| 8-bit | | RBX | | RAX | | 1 |
| 16-bit | + | RCX | + | RBX | * | 2 |
| 32-bit | | RDX | | RCX | | 3 |
| 64-bit | | RSP | | RDX | | 4 |
| | | RBP | | RBP | | |
| | | RSI | | RSI | | |
| | | RDI | | RDI | | |

*Table 3-11: 32-bit memory reference (Protected Mode)*

| Displacement | | Base | | Index | | Scale |
|---|---|---|---|---|---|---|
| | | EAX | | None | | |
| | | EBX | | EAX | | |
| None | | ECX | | EBX | | 1 |
| 8-bit | + | EDX | + | ECX | * | 2 |
| 16-bit | | ESP | | EDX | | 3 |
| 32-bit | | EBP | | EBP | | 4 |
| | | ESI | | ESI | | |
| | | EDI | | EDI | | |

*Table 3-12: 16-bit memory reference (Real Mode)*

| Displacement | | Base | | Index | | Scale |
|---|---|---|---|---|---|---|
| None<br>8-bit<br>16-bit | + | AX<br>BX<br>CX<br>DX<br>SP<br>BP<br>SI<br>DI | + | None<br>AX<br>BX<br>CX<br>DX<br>BP<br>SI<br>DI | * | 1<br>2<br>3<br>4 |

I have never seen them in a verbose table such as that in Appendix C. Even the data books direct from the chip manufacturers seem to be lacking in this information, and so here it is. Seeing it should help you remember and then entice you to use them.

## uint32 OddTable[ ]

| 0 | 1 | 2 | 3 | 4 | 5 | 6 | 7 | 8 | 9 | 10 | 11 | 12 | 13 | 14 | 15 |
|---|---|---|---|---|---|---|---|---|---|----|----|----|----|----|----|
| 1 | 3 | 5 | 7 | 11 | 13 | 17 | 19 | 23 | 29 | 31 | 37 | 41 | 43 | 47 | 53 |

```
ebx = 0  edx = 1
mov eax, OddTable                ; = 1
mov eax, OddTable[ebx]           ; = 1
mov ecx, OddTable[eax * 4]       ; = 11
mov ebx, OddTable[ebx + ecx]     ; = 37
mov ebx, OddTable[ecx + edx * 4] ; = 53
mov esi, offset OddTable
mov eax, [esi + ebx * 4]
```

Since the table is 32-bit (4 byte) a multiplier of ×4 can be used to reference the correct array cell. If the table were 16-bit, the multiplier would be ×2, 64-bit then ×8.

The same kind of memory reference used to access an element in a memory table or array can also be used to access a jump or call vector.

# LEA — Load Effective Address

LEA *destination, source*

| Mnemonic | P | PII | K6 | 3D! | 3Mx+ | SSE | SSE2 | A64 | SSE3 | E64T |
|---|---|---|---|---|---|---|---|---|---|---|
| LEA | ✓ | ✓ | ✓ | ✓ | ✓ | ✓ | ✓ | ✓ | ✓ | ✓ |

```
lea   rDst16, mSrc(16/32)        Unsigned
lea   rDst32, mSrc(16/32)
lea   rDst64, mSrc16
```

This instruction calculates the effective address of the source argument and stores it in the destination. It can be used as multi-register math:

```
mov ebx,2
mov ecx,3
lea eax, [10+ebx+ecx]   ; eax = 10+2+3 = 15
```

...or a little more indirectly:

```
lea eax, [10+ebx+ecx*8] ; eax = 10+2+3×8 = 36
```

# Translation Table

An alternate method of lookup simply uses the 8-bit AL register in conjunction with an indirect memory reference for a 256-byte table lookup.

## XLAT/XLATB — Translation Table Lookup

| Mnemonic | P | PII | K6 | 3D! | 3Mx+ | SSE | SSE2 | A64 | SSE3 | E64T |
|----------|---|-----|-----|-----|------|-----|------|-----|------|------|
| XLAT | ✓ | ✓ | ✓ | ✓ | ✓ | ✓ | ✓ | ✓ | ✓ | ✓ |
| XLATB | ✓ | ✓ | ✓ | ✓ | ✓ | ✓ | ✓ | ✓ | ✓ | ✓ |

```
xlat      mSrc8                    [Un]signed
xlatb
```

This general-purpose instruction does a table lookup by adding the AL register to the DS:[eBX] address and copies the selected memory location to the AL register. It is equivalent to the following:

```
mov   al,[rbx+al]       ; 64-bit Mode
mov   al,ds:[ebx+al]    ; Protected Mode (32-bit)
mov   al,ds:[bx+al]     ; Real Mode (16-bit)
```

| Flags | O.flow | Sign | Zero | Aux | Parity | Carry |
|-------|--------|------|------|-----|--------|-------|
|       | - | - | - | - | - | - |

Flags: None are altered by this opcode.

If you are building your own logging mechanism for your application and you are not using C where you could use a function similar to:

```
printf("0x%x", dw);
```

then you will probably want to use the following binary to hex text print algorithm. Or at least some form of it! Okay, I am already breaking rules of precedence where I am using instructions before they are discussed. But bear with me!

```
HexTbl: db      "0123456789ABCDEF"

;       void HexDmp32(uint32 dw);

HexDmp32 proc   near
         push   ebp
         mov    ebp,esp

         push   ebx

         mov    edx,[ebp+arg1]     ; 32 bits of data

         mov    ebx,offset HexTbl
         mov    ecx,8              ; # of hex letters

$L1:     rol    edx,4              ; MSB ... LSB
         mov    eax,edx
         and    eax,0000000fh      ; mask a nibble
         xlatb                     ; Translate nibble into hex

         call   ChrOut             ; Draw the letter

         dec    ecx
         jnz    $L1                ; Loop for 8 letters

         pop    ebx
         pop    ebp
         ret
HexDmp32 endp
```

Let's try using an XLATB in a nonsensical state machine mechanism.

```
; Traverse the state mechanism

State:  db     3, 4, 5, 1, 2, 0ffh

        lea    ebx,State
        mov    al,0

$L1:    xlatb                      ; al = [ebx+al]
        cmp    al,0ffh
        jne    $L1

; at $L1 the AL register will become {3, 1, 4, 2, 5, 0ffh}
```

# String Instructions

The following instruction groups LODS, STOS, and MOVS are string functions, which are discussed shortly. An extra instruction REP is used to repeatedly execute a list of data types for a count indicated by the looping count register (CX/ECX/RCX). The register is dependent upon the data-bit mode (16/32/64-bit).

There are additional string instructions not discussed in this chapter. CMPS and SCAS are discussed in Chapter 9, "Comparison." The INS and OUTS instructions are discussed in Chapter 17, "PC I/O." These should be used very carefully. There are alternatives that use register pairing and other methods of optimization. With older processors these were the optimal method of data manipulation but with the newer processors that is not so much the case any more. Loop counters need to be large values to be effective.

*Table 3-13: String function and associated index register(s)*

| Mnemonic | ESI | EDI |
|----------|-----|-----|
| CMPSx | ✓ | ✓ |
| INSx | | ✓ |
| LODSx | ✓ | |
| MOVSx | ✓ | ✓ |
| OUTSx | ✓ | |
| SCASx | | ✓ |
| STOSx | | ✓ |

## LODSB/LODSW/LODSD/LODSQ — Load String

| Mnemonic | P | PII | K6 | 3D! | 3Mx+ | SSE | SSE2 | A64 | SSE3 | E64T |
|----------|---|-----|----|-----|------|-----|------|-----|------|------|
| LODSx | ✓ | ✓ | ✓ | ✓ | ✓ | ✓ | ✓ | ✓ | ✓ | ✓ |
| LODSQ | | | | | | | | 64 | | 64 |

```
lods{b/w/d/q}              [Un]signed
lods    mDst{8/16/32/64}
```

This instruction reads the contents of memory and loads it into the AL, AX, EAX, or RAX register. It belongs to the group of string functions but it really has nothing to do with text strings in the C sense. It has to do with loading strings of memory, which are contiguous bytes of memory. These functions are equivalent to:

32-bit mode

| lodsb | lodsw | lodsd | lodsq |
|---|---|---|---|
| mov al,ds:[esi]<br>inc esi | mov ax,ds:[esi]<br>add esi,2 | mov eax,ds:[esi]<br>add esi,4 | |

64-bit mode

| lodsb | lodsw | lodsd | lodsq |
|---|---|---|---|
| mov al,[rsi]<br>inc esi | mov ax,[rsi]<br>add esi,2 | mov eax,[rsi]<br>add esi,4 | mov rax,[rsi]<br>add rsi,8 |

# REP LODSx

A single read operation can be performed or a repeat sequence specified by a REP prefix word and a count specified in the RCX register in 64-bit mode, the ECX register in Protected Mode, or the CX register in Real Mode.

```
rep lodsd
L3: mov eax,ds:[esi]
    add esi,4
    dec ecx
    jne L3
```

```
rep lodsw
L3: mov ax,ds:[si]
    add si,2
    dec cx
    jne L3
```

The LOOP instruction could be used instead of DEC and JNE but do not do so, as it is considered complex and actually costs CPU cycles on more advanced model processors. It takes a very special application indeed that does nothing but read a series of bytes into the destination register without processing them. The only result is that only the last data read is remembered! And the source index ESI would point to the next available memory location.

| Flags | O.flow | Sign | Zero | Aux | Parity | Carry |
|---|---|---|---|---|---|---|
| | - | - | - | - | - | - |

Flags: None are altered by this opcode.

# STOSB/STOSW/STOSD/STOSQ — Save String

STOSx

| Mnemonic | P | PII | K6 | 3D! | 3Mx+ | SSE | SSE2 | A64 | SSE3 | E64T |
|----------|---|-----|----|-----|------|-----|------|-----|------|------|
| STOSx | ✓ | ✓ | ✓ | ✓ | ✓ | ✓ | ✓ | ✓ | ✓ | ✓ |
| STOSQ | | | | | | | | 64 | | 64 |

stos{b/w/d/q}          [Un]signed
stos    mDst{8/16/32/64}

This instruction writes the contents of the AL, AX, EAX, or RAX register to memory. It belongs to the group of string functions but it really has nothing to do with text strings in the C sense. It has to do with strings of memory. Those single write operations can be performed or a repeat sequence specified by a REP prefix word and a count specified in the RCX register in 64-bit mode, the ECX register in Protected Mode, or the CX register in Real Mode. Those are contiguous bytes of memory. These functions are equivalent to:

32-bit mode

| stosb | stosw | stosd | stosq |
|-------|-------|-------|-------|
| mov es:[edi],al<br>inc edi | mov es:[edi],ax<br>add edi,2 | mov es:[edi],eax<br>add edi,4 | |

64-bit mode

| stosb | stosw | stosd | stosq |
|-------|-------|-------|-------|
| mov [rdi],al<br>inc edi | mov [rdi],ax<br>add edi,2 | mov [rdi],eax<br>add edi,4 | mov [rdi],rax<br>add rdi,8 |

# REP/REPE/REPZ/REPNE/REPNZ — Repeat String

| Mnemonic | P | PII | K6 | 3D! | 3Mx+ | SSE | SSE2 | A64 | SSE3 | E64T |
|----------|---|-----|----|-----|------|-----|------|-----|------|------|
| REP | ✓ | ✓ | ✓ | ✓ | ✓ | ✓ | ✓ | ✓ | ✓ | ✓ |
| REPE | ✓ | ✓ | ✓ | ✓ | ✓ | ✓ | ✓ | ✓ | ✓ | ✓ |
| REPNE | ✓ | ✓ | ✓ | ✓ | ✓ | ✓ | ✓ | ✓ | ✓ | ✓ |
| REPNZ | ✓ | ✓ | ✓ | ✓ | ✓ | ✓ | ✓ | ✓ | ✓ | ✓ |
| REPZ | ✓ | ✓ | ✓ | ✓ | ✓ | ✓ | ✓ | ✓ | ✓ | ✓ |

```
rep  ins   m(8/16/32), dx
rep  outs  dx, m(8/16/32)
rep  movs  mDst, mSrc(8/16/32/64)
rep  stos  mSrc(8/16/32/64)
rep  lods  mDst, al
rep  lods  mDst, ax
rep  lods  mDst, eax
rep  lods  mDst, rax

repe cmps  mDst, mSrc(8/16/32/64)
repe scas  mSrc(8/16/32/64)
```

## REP STOSx

```
rep stosd
─────────────────────
L3: mov ds:[esi],eax
    add esi,4
    dec ecx
    jne L3
```

| Flags | O.flow | Sign | Zero | Aux | Parity | Carry |
|-------|--------|------|------|-----|--------|-------|
|       | -      | -    | -    | -   | -      | -     |

Flags: None are altered by this opcode.

This function is great for setting a block of memory with a particular value such as for clearing large blocks of memory.

## MOVSB/MOVSW/MOVSD/MOVSQ — Move String

MOVSx

| Mnemonic | P | PII | K6 | 3D! | 3Mx+ | SSE | SSE2 | A64 | SSE3 | E64T |
|----------|---|-----|-----|-----|------|-----|------|-----|------|------|
| MOVSx    | ✓ | ✓   | ✓   | ✓   | ✓    | ✓   | ✓    | ✓   | ✓    | ✓    |
| MOVSQ    |   |     |     |     |      |     |      | 64  |      | 64   |

movs{b/w/d/q}                    [Un]signed
movs    mDst, mSrc{8/16/32/64}

This instruction copies the contents of memory addressed by the DS:[SI], DS:[ESI], or [RSI] source register pair to the ES:[DI], ES:[EDI], or [RDI] destination register pair. It is similar to using both the LODSB/W/D/Q and STOSB/W/D/Q functions except that the AL/AX/EAX/RAX registers are not used. It belongs to the group of string functions, but it really has nothing to do with text strings in the C sense; it has to do with moving strings of memory. This is the only

memory-to-memory move. The strings are contiguous bytes of memory. These functions are equivalent to:

32-bit mode

| movsb | movsw | movsd | movsq |
|---|---|---|---|
| mov al,ds:[esi]<br>mov es:[edi],al<br>inc esi<br>inc edi | mov ax,ds:[esi]<br>mov es:[edi],ax<br>add esi,2<br>add edi,2 | mov eax,ds:[esi]<br>mov es:[edi],eax<br>add esi,4<br>add edi,4 | |

# REP MOVSx

A single move operation can be performed or a repeat sequence specified by a REP prefix word and a count specified in the ECX register in Protected Mode or CX in Real Mode.

```
rep movsd

L3: mov eax,ds:[esi]
    add esi,4
    mov es:[edi],eax
    inc edi,4
    dec ecx
    jne L3
```

| Flags | O.flow | Sign | Zero | Aux | Parity | Carry |
|---|---|---|---|---|---|---|
| | - | - | - | - | - | - |

Flags: None are altered by this opcode.

# CLD/STD — Clear/Set Direction Flag

| Mnemonic | P | PII | K6 | 3D! | 3Mx+ | SSE | SSE2 | A64 | SSE3 | E64T |
|---|---|---|---|---|---|---|---|---|---|---|
| CLD | ✓ | ✓ | ✓ | ✓ | ✓ | ✓ | ✓ | ✓ | ✓ | ✓ |
| STD | ✓ | ✓ | ✓ | ✓ | ✓ | ✓ | ✓ | ✓ | ✓ | ✓ |

```
cld
std
```

The direction flag is only used by the string instructions to indicate whether the RSI/RDI, ESI/EDI, and SI/DI registers are advanced in a forward or reverse direction. CLD is the norm, where the advance is in a forward (n+1) direction. STD indicates a reverse (n–1) direction.

| Flags | O.flow | Sign | Zero | Aux | Parity | Carry |
|-------|--------|------|------|-----|--------|-------|
|       | -      | -    | -    | -   | -      | -     |

Flags: None are affected by this opcode.

**Note:** You should avoid the STD instruction as any memory access in a reverse direction is less efficient than in a forward direction, due to memory access cache intelligence built into the processors. It is, however, sometimes necessary to do so for reverse scanning algorithms but should be avoided whenever possible.

# Special (Non-Temporal) Memory Instructions

To understand these special memory instructions better one first needs to understand some terms:

**Temporal data** — Memory that requires multiple accesses and therefore is loaded into a cache (as a default) for normal access.

**Non-temporal hint** — An indicator to the processor that memory only requires a single access (one shot). This would be similar to copying a block of memory or performing a calculation, but the result is not going to be needed for a while so there is no need to write it into the cache; thus the memory access has no need to read and load cache, and therefore the code can be faster!

For more information, see Chapter 18, "System," for more information related to the cache.

## MOVNTx — Copy Using Non-Temporal Hint

| Mnemonic | P | PII | K6 | 3D! | 3Mx+ | SSE | SSE2 | A64 | SSE3 | E64T |
|----------|---|-----|----|-----|------|-----|------|-----|------|------|
| MOVNTDQ  |   |     |    |     |      |     | ✓    | ✓   | ✓    | ✓    |
| MOVNTI   |   |     |    |     |      |     | ✓    | ✓   | ✓    | ✓    |
| MOVNTQ   |   |     |    | ✓   |      | ✓   | ✓    | ✓   | ✓    | ✓    |

| SSE   | movntdq | mDst128, xmmSrc | [Un]signed | 128 |
| SSE   | movntq  | mDst64, mmxSrc  | [Un]signed | 64  |
| SSE3  | movnti  | mDst32, rSrc32  |            | 128 |
| EM64T | movnti  | mDst64, rSrc64  | [Un]signed | 128 |

The MOVNTDQ instruction copies 128 bits of (non-floating-point) data from xmmSrc to mDst128 using a non-temporal hint.

The MOVNTQ instruction copies 64 bits of (non-floating-point) data from mmxSrc to mDst64 using a non-temporal hint.

The MOVNTI instruction copies 32 bits of (non-floating-point) data from xmmSrc to mDst32 using a non-temporal hint. In 64-bit mode, 64 bits of (non-floating-point) data is copied from a 64-bit general-purpose register rSrc64 to memory destination mDst64 using a non-temporal hint.

**Hint:** These instructions generate a *non-temporal hint* to the processor (indicating one-shot data) that it can bypass the cache, which can make them faster than a standard copy to memory instruction. Standard compilers do not support these instructions, which is yet another reason to write some of your code in assembly.

## MOVNTPS — Copy 4×SPFP Using Non-Temporal Hint

| Mnemonic | P | PII | K6 | 3D! | 3Mx+ | SSE | SSE2 | A64 | SSE3 | E64T |
|----------|---|-----|----|----|------|-----|------|-----|------|------|
| MOVNTPS  |   |     |    |    |      | ✓   | ✓    | ✓   | ✓    | ✓    |

SSE        movntps *mDst128*, *xmmSrc*        Single-precision 128

The MOVNTPS instruction copies 128 bits of four (packed single-precision floating-point) elements from xmmSrc to mDst128 using a non-temporal hint.

## MOVNTPD — Copy 2×DPFP Using Non-Temporal Hint

| Mnemonic | P | PII | K6 | 3D! | 3Mx+ | SSE | SSE2 | A64 | SSE3 | E64T |
|----------|---|-----|----|----|------|-----|------|-----|------|------|
| MOVNTPD  |   |     |    |    |      |     | ✓    | ✓   | ✓    | ✓    |

SSE2        movntpd *mDst128*, *xmmSrc*        Double-precision 128

The MOVNTPD instruction copies 128 bits of two (packed double-precision floating-point) elements from xmmSrc to mDst128 using a non-temporal hint.

## MASKMOVQ/MASKMOVDQU — Copy Selected Bytes

| Mnemonic | P | PII | K6 | 3D! | 3Mx+ | SSE | SSE2 | A64 | SSE3 | E64T |
|---|---|---|---|---|---|---|---|---|---|---|
| MASKMOVQ | | | | | ✓ | ✓ | ✓ | ✓ | ✓ | ✓ |
| MASKMOVDQU | | | | | | | ✓ | ✓ | ✓ | ✓ |

| | | |
|---|---|---|
| maskmovq | *mmxSrcA, mmxSrcB* | 64 |
| maskmovdqu | *xmmSrcA, xmmSrcB* | 128 |

This instruction copies up to 128/64 bits of memory from xmmSrcA (mmxSrcA) to DS:[EDI] depending on the MSB of each correlating byte in the mask indicated in xmmSrcB (mmxSrcB). If an 8-bit mask element of SrcB has its bit set, then that same correlated 8-bit element of SrcA is copied to the destination memory.

This instruction generates a *non-temporal hint* to the processor (indicating one-shot data) that it can bypass the cache!

Note that for the MMX instruction MASKMOVQ, the CPU forces a transition from x87 to MMX mode.

# Exercises

```
0x12, 0x56, 0x89, 0x23, 0xEF, 0x89, 0x28, 0xC3
0xE2, 0xFF, 0x04, 0x23, 0x49, 0x41, 0x74, 0x3F
0x56, 0x89, 0xAA, 0xB2, 0xC7, 0x38, 0x28, 0x2A
0x28, 0x28, 0x42, 0x73, 0x82, 0xDE, 0xF3, 0x28
```

1. Show 128-bit data for SSE in proper endian order, for 8-bit, 16-bit, 32-bit, and 64-bit block sizes.

2. 128 bits = four single-precision floats. How wide would the next generation processor have to be for quad vector double-precision? Write a memory handler for this new hypothetical type processor.

3. Future super matrix processors will be able to number-crunch entire matrices at a time. How wide would the data path be? Write an alignment macro for that width. Hint: There are two primary solutions!

4. Earlier in this chapter the function HexDmp32() demonstrated a 32-bit (8 ASCII byte) hex dump. Write a slightly different function that prints a string of 8-bit bytes in hex of a specified count.

```
void HexDmp(byte *pData, uint nCount);
```

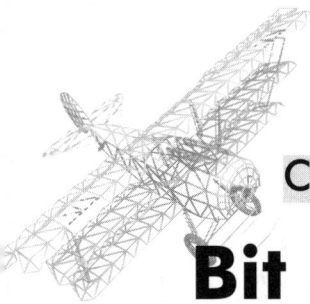

# Chapter 4

# Bit Mangling

For about seven years my family and I lived in the California Sierras. During that time I developed a passion for rustic mountain living as well as most environmental associations related to the mountains and the Old West: snow, historic mining towns, coaches and wagons, treasure hunting, narrow gauge railroads, wildland fire fighting, and other miscellaneous rural benefits. Now that I have milled that Old West imagery into your mind "ore" bored you to death, you can continue reading what I fondly refer to as the mangling of bits. This is one of my favorite sections, because with their use, I typically devise speedier methods for use in the manipulation of data. I label this "thinking out of the box," sometimes referred to as "Thar's gold in them thar bits!"

Bit mangling relates to the individual twiddling of bits using Boolean logic such as NOT, AND, OR, XOR, or some combination thereof. Each bit is individually isolated so no bit affects any adjacent bit encapsulated by the register. In vector mathematical operations, groups of bits are isolated so that an operation on one vector group does not affect another. Boolean operations are similar but on an individual bit basis. Each group in this case is a group of one bit; thus, an operation to a single bit does not affect an adjacent bit. This is why there are no vector type Boolean operations. There are operations that do, however, use 32/64-bit general-purpose registers, 64-bit MMX registers, and 128-bit SSE2 registers for Boolean operations so as to manipulate more bits simultaneously in parallel.

**Hint:** In a manner of speaking, all processors that support Boolean operations on pairs of bits have a degree of SIMD support.

These are heavily used by algorithms utilizing vectors, which is why they are in this book. Included in this chapter are the electronic symbols for each logical operation. Typically, I use my own books for reference, and from time to time I have found that drawing logic circuits using digital logic symbols actually makes more complex Boolean logic algorithms easier for me to simplify. Maybe it will work the same for you.

Any processor professing to contain a multimedia, SIMD, packed, parallel, or vector instruction set will contain almost all of the following instructions in one form or another. Parallel instructions typically do not have a Carry flag as found in some of the older scalar based instruction sets using general-purpose registers, such as the 80x86. They tend to lose overflows through the shifting out of bits, wraparound of data, or saturation. Another item to note is that not all the displayed diagrams are used by all the various 80x86 processors defined. Over the years the functionality has been enhanced, so older processors will not have the same abilities as the newer processors.

It must be reiterated that you watch the alignment of your data objects in memory very closely. It takes extra overhead to adjust the memory into an aligned state and it is a lot more efficient to ensure that they are aligned in the first place. Your code will be smaller and faster! This will be made obvious by the sample code included in this chapter.

You will find in this chapter and throughout this book sections titled "Pseudo Vec." As processors are enhanced, new superset functionality is given to them such as SIMD operations. Some of you, however, are still programming for older processors and need the newer functionality, while some of you require a more in-depth understanding of vector operations. The "Pseudo Vec" sections are for you!

**Workbench Files:** \Bench\x86\chap04\\*project*\\*platform*

|                   | *project*   | *platform*   |
|-------------------|-------------|--------------|
| **Boolean Logic** | **\pbool\** | \vc6         |
|                   |             | \vc.net      |

# Boolean Logical AND

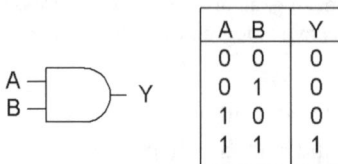

| A | B | Y |
|---|---|---|
| 0 | 0 | 0 |
| 0 | 1 | 0 |
| 1 | 0 | 0 |
| 1 | 1 | 1 |

| Mnemonic | P | PII | K6 | 3D! | 3Mx+ | SSE | SSE2 | A64 | SSE3 | E64T |
|----------|---|-----|-----|-----|------|-----|------|-----|------|------|
| AND | ✓ | ✓ | ✓ | ✓ | ✓ | ✓ | ✓ | ✓ | ✓ | ✓ |
| ANDPD | | | | | | | ✓ | ✓ | ✓ | ✓ |
| ADDPS | | | | | | ✓ | ✓ | ✓ | ✓ | ✓ |
| PAND | | ✓ | ✓ | ✓ | ✓ | ✓ | ✓ | ✓ | ✓ | ✓ |

|     | and | *rmDst(8/16/32/64), #(8/16/32)* | [Un]signed | |
|-----|-----|------|------|---|
|     | and | *rmDst, rSrc(8/16/32/64)* | | |
|     | and | *rDst, rmSrc(8/16/32/64)* | | |
| MMX | pand | *mmxDst, mmxSrc/m64* | [Un]signed | 64 |
| SSE | andps | *xmmDst, xmmSrc/m128* | Single-precision | 128 |
| SSE2 | pand | *xmmDst, xmmSrc/m128* | [Un]signed | 128 |
| " | andpd | *xmmDst, xmmSrc/m128* | Double-precision | 128 |

An AND operation means that one would need both A *and* B to be true to have a true result. The AND general-purpose instruction logically AND's the 8-, 16-, 32-, or 64-bit source with the destination and stores the result in the destination. An 8-bit source value can be sign extended to a 16-, 32-, or 64-bit value. A 32-bit source value can be sign extended to a 64-bit destination. The source can be an immediate value, a register, or memory. The destination is a register or memory. A memory-to-memory operation is invalid!

| **Flags** | O.flow | Sign | Zero | Aux | Parity | Carry |
|-----------|--------|------|------|-----|--------|-------|
| | 0 | X | X | - | X | 0 |

Flags: With the AND general-purpose instruction, the Carry and Overflow flags are cleared. The Zero flag is set if all destination bits are 0, thus *destination* = 0. The Sign flag reflects the state of the MSB.

The following 32-bit example demonstrates this:

```
        mov     eax,00000a5a5h
        mov     edx,000000ff0h
        and     eax,edx

B       00000000000000001010010110100101b   00000a5a5h
A       00000000000000000000111111110000b   000000ff0h
A∧B     00000000000000000000010110100000b   0000005a0h
```

This is typically used for masking operations as in jump vectors:

```
        and     ebx,0000111b       ; Mask for 0...7 =8 vectors
        jmp     VecTbl[ebx*4]      ; Jump using the vector
```

The multimedia extension instruction is a parallel operation that uses a Boolean AND operation upon each of the corresponding 64 or 128 bits.

The source A and B are aSrc (xmmSrc) and bSrc (xmmDst), and the result is stored in the destination Dst (xmmDst). The instruction may be labeled as packed, parallel, or vector but each bit is in reality isolated from each other so there is no need for a data bit block arrangement. No flags are set.

```
msk      dd      00000ffffffff0000h
dat      dd      00000a5a50000ff11h

         mov     esi,offset dat   ; Data pointer
         mov     ebx,offset msk   ; Mask pointer

         movq    mm7,[esi]        ; Get 64 bits of data
         pand    mm7,[ebx]        ; AND it with the mask data
         movq    [edi],mm7        ; Save the masked data
```

For the SSE instruction, the ANDPS is a bitwise AND of four packed single-precision floating-point values with a bit mask.

For the SSE2 instruction, the ANDPD is a bitwise AND of two packed double-precision floating-point values with a bit mask.

These floating-point related instructions will be discussed in Chapter 8, "Floating-Point Anyone?"

# Pseudo Vec

The following C code demonstrates the simulated vector functionality of a logical AND upon a 128-bit vector. The code sample logical AND's the four packed 32-bit values from vector $A$ and $B$, to effectively AND all 128 bits and then stores the result in vector $D$. Note that the function stores the result pointed to by the first function argument.

### Logical Packed AND D=(A∧B)

Listing 4-1: ...\chap04\pbool\PBool.cpp

```
void vmp_pand(void *pvD, void *pvA, void *pvB)
{
  uint32 *pD, *pA, *pB;

  ASSERT_PTR16(pvD);
  ASSERT_PTR16(pvA);
  ASSERT_PTR16(pvB);

  pD=(uint32*) pvD;
  pA=(uint32*) pvA;
  pB=(uint32*) pvB;
  *(pD+0) = *(pA+0) & *(pB+0);
  *(pD+1) = *(pA+1) & *(pB+1);
```

```
    *(pD+2) = *(pA+2) & *(pB+2);
    *(pD+3) = *(pA+3) & *(pB+3);
}
```

The assertion macro ASSERT_PTR4 could have been used instead since memory alignment for generic code only needs to be aligned to four bytes to support a 32-bit value, but the ASSERT_PTR16 was used instead to ensure 16-byte vector data alignment

## vmp_pand (x86) 32-bit

This first code snippet has been constructed to take advantage of instruction pipelining and uses a general-purpose 80x86 assembly language logical AND. Please note the code indicated in bold. By substituting alternative mnemonics, such as the Boolean logic instructions ANDC, OR, and XOR that have not been discussed yet, in place of AND, the code encapsulation (code snippets) can be mostly reused.

Listing 4-2: ...\chap04\pbool\PBoolx86M.asm

```
mov  eax,pvA        ; A (Source) Vector
mov  ebx,pvB        ; B (Source) Vector
mov  edx,pvD        ; D (Destination) Vector
```

The previous MOV instructions are common to the following code samples and thus not replicated in those samples, but they need to be recognized as loading general-purpose registers in preparation for those samples.

```
mov  ebp,[eax+0]    ; Read A lower 64 bits
mov  esi,[eax+4]
mov  ecx,[ebx+0]    ;    "  B  "        "
mov  edi,[ebx+4]
and  ebp,ecx        ; AND bits (31...0)
and  esi,edi        ; AND bits (63...32)
mov  [edx+0],ebp    ; Write lower 64 bits
mov  [edx+4],esi

mov  ebp,[eax+8]    ; Read A upper 64 bits
mov  esi,[eax+12]
mov  ecx,[ebx+8]    ;    "  B  "        "
mov  edi,[ebx+12]
and  ebp,ecx        ; AND bits (95...64)
and  esi,edi        ; AND bits (127...96)
mov  [edx+8],ebp    ; Write upper 64 bits
mov  [edx+12],esi
```

An optimization worth noting is the interlacing of the general-purpose registers into pairs to minimize dependencies.

## vmp_pand (x86) 64-bit

If in 64-bit mode, you can directly AND 64 bits of memory without using MMX registers.

**Listing 4-3:** ...\chap04\pbool\PBoolx86M.asm

```
mov   rax,pvA         ; A (Source) Vector
mov   rbx,pvB         ; B (Source) Vector
mov   rdx,pvD         ; D (Destination) Vector


mov   r8,[rax+0]      ; Read A lower 64 bits
mov   r9,[rax+8]      ; Read A upper 64 bits
mov   r10,[rbx+0]     ; Read B lower 64 bits
mov   r11,[rbx+8]     ; Read B upper 64 bits
and   r8,r10          ; AND bits (63...0)
and   r9,r11          ; AND bits (127...64)
mov   [rdx+0],r8      ; Write lower 64 bits
mov   [rdx+8],r9      ; Write upper 64 bits
```

## vmp_pand (MMX)

In the following examples the burden is placed upon 64- or 128-bit registers, so the 32-bit general-purpose registers are only used for memory access. With the MMX instructions, only 64 bits can be manipulated at a time so the data is handled as upper and lower 64-bit pairs. It also helps minimize processor stalls due to register dependencies.

**Listing 4-4:** ...\chap04\pbool\PBoolx86M.asm

```
movq  mm0,[ebx+0]     ; Read B lower 64 bits
movq  mm1,[ebx+8]     ;    "  B upper    "
movq  mm2,[eax+0]     ; Read A lower 64 bits
movq  mm3,[eax+8]     ;    "  A upper    "

pand  mm0,mm2         ; AND lower 64 bits
pand  mm1,mm3         ; AND upper 64 bits

movq  [edx+0],mm0     ; Write D lower 64 bits
movq  [edx+8],mm1     ;    "      upper    "
```

## vmp_pand (SSE2) Aligned Memory

For full 128-bit handling on an 80x86 processor it becomes necessary to require a minimum of a Pentium 4 with the SSE2 instruction set. The following SSE2 example is a better solution as compared to the MMX version. Despite the register dependency stall that is in this specific example, there is no FPU/MMX conflict; thus there is an avoidance of the MMX registers, all 128 bits are handled simultaneously, and the code size is smaller. There is a little problem of memory alignment with

SSE and SSE2, so two versions of the function will be needed if strict memory alignment procedures are not followed.

*Listing 4-5: ...\chap04\pbool\PBoolx86M.asm*

```
movdqa   xmm0,[ebx]   ; Read B Aligned 128 bits
movdqa   xmm1,[eax]   ; Read A

pand     xmm0,xmm1    ; AND 128 bits

movdqa   [edx],xmm0   ; Write D Aligned 128 bits
```

Note the use of MOVDQA (aligned) used previously and MOVDQU (unaligned) used in the following examples. The code is virtually identical for both examples, except that if the data is misaligned and if the MOVDQA instruction is utilized, an exception will occur. If memory alignment cannot be guaranteed, the following (slightly slower version) should be used instead.

## vmp_pand (SSE2) Unaligned Memory

*Listing 4-6: ...\chap04\pbool\PBoolx86M.asm*

```
movdqu   xmm0,[ebx]   ; Read B non-aligned 128 bits
movdqu   xmm1,[eax]   ; Read A

pand     xmm0,xmm1    ; AND 128 bits

movdqu   [edx],xmm0   ; Write D non-aligned 128 bits
```

I was not trying to pull the wool over your eyes or anything. The really nice feature for the SSE and SSE2 instructions is that for both aligned and unaligned data, the code is virtually identical except for the method of access. The only trick is to make sure it is properly aligned before using MOVDQA. If in doubt, use the instruction MOVDQU; otherwise an exception will occur upon that misaligned access.

You may now be thinking, but why bother using MOVDA? Why not just use MOVDQU all the time?

The answer? Your code will run slower, and that is contrary to the reason for writing your code in assembly or using vector instructions!

# Boolean Logical OR

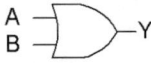

| A | B | Y |
|---|---|---|
| 0 | 0 | 0 |
| 0 | 1 | 1 |
| 1 | 0 | 1 |
| 1 | 1 | 1 |

| Mnemonic | P | PII | K6 | 3D! | 3Mx+ | SSE | SSE2 | A64 | SSE3 | E64T |
|---|---|---|---|---|---|---|---|---|---|---|
| OR | ✓ | ✓ | ✓ | ✓ | ✓ | ✓ | ✓ | ✓ | ✓ | ✓ |
| ORPD | | | | | | | ✓ | ✓ | ✓ | ✓ |
| ORPS | | | | | | ✓ | ✓ | ✓ | ✓ | ✓ |
| POR | | ✓ | ✓ | ✓ | ✓ | ✓ | ✓ | ✓ | ✓ | ✓ |

|  | or | rmDst(8/16/32/64), #(8/16/32) [Un]signed | | |
|---|---|---|---|---|
| | or | rmDst, rSrc(8/16/32/64) | | |
| | or | rDst, rmSrc(8/16/32/64) | | |
| MMX | por | mmxDst, mmxSrc/m64 | [Un]signed | 64 |
| SSE | orps | xmmDst, xmmSrc/m128 | Single-precision FP | 128 |
| SSE2 | por | xmmDst, xmmSrc/m128 | [Un]signed | 128 |
| " | orpd | xmmDst, xmmSrc/m128 | Double-precision FP | 128 |

An OR operation means that one would need either A *or* B to be true to have a true result. The OR general-purpose instruction logically OR's the 8-, 16-, 32-, or 64-bit source with the destination and stores the result in the destination. An 8-bit source value can be sign extended to 16-, 32-, or 64-bit value. A 32-bit source value can be sign extended to a 64-bit destination.

The source can be an immediate value, register, or memory. The destination is a register or memory. A memory-to-memory operation is invalid!

| Flags | O.flow | Sign | Zero | Aux | Parity | Carry |
|---|---|---|---|---|---|---|
| | 0 | X | X | - | X | 0 |

Flags: With the OR general-purpose instruction, the Carry and Overflow flags are cleared. The Zero flag is set if all destination bits are 0, thus *destination* = 0. The Sign flag reflects the state of the MSB.

The following 32-bit example demonstrates this:

```
mov     eax,00000a5a5h
mov     edx,000000ff0h
or      eax,edx
```

| | | |
|---|---|---|
| B | 00000000000000001010010110100101b | 0a5a5h |
| A | 00000000000000000000111111110000b | 00ff0h |
| A∨B | 00000000000000001010111111110101b | 0aff5h |

This multimedia extension instruction is a parallel operation that uses a Boolean OR operation upon each of the corresponding 64 or 128 bits. The source *A* and *B* are *aSrc (xmmSrc)* OR *bSrc (xmmDst)*, and the result is stored in the destination *Dst (xmmDst)*. The instruction may be labeled as packed, parallel, or vector, but each bit is in reality isolated from each other so there is no need for a data bit block arrangement. The following 32-bit example demonstrates that.

For the SSE instruction, the ORPS is a bitwise OR of four packed single-precision floating-point values with a bit mask.

For the SSE2 instruction, the ORPD is a bitwise OR of two packed double-precision floating-point values with a bit mask.

These floating-point related instructions will be discussed in Chapter 8, "Floating-Point Anyone?"

# Pseudo Vec

The following C code demonstrates the functionality of a logical OR upon a 128-bit vector. The code sample logical OR's the four blocks of 32-bit values from vector A and B 32 bits at a time four times to effectively OR all 128 bits, and then stores the result in vector D. Note that the function stores the result pointed to by the first function argument.

### Logical Packed OR D=(A∨B)

Listing 4-7: ...\chap04\pbool\PBool.cpp

```
void vmp_por(void *pvD, void *pvA, void *pvB)
{
    uint32 *pD, *pA, *pB;

    pD=(uint32*) pvD;
    pA=(uint32*) pvA;
    pB=(uint32*) pvB;
    *(pD+0) = *(pA+0) | *(pB+0);    // {31...0}
    *(pD+1) = *(pA+1) | *(pB+1);    // {63...32}
    *(pD+2) = *(pA+2) | *(pB+2);    // {95...64}
    *(pD+3) = *(pA+3) | *(pB+3);    // {127...96}
}
```

See the code snippets from the previously discussed instruction AND, then substitute the instruction {|, *or*, *por*} for the {&, *and*, *pand*} accordingly.

# Boolean Logical XOR (Exclusive OR)

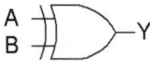

| A | B | Y |
|---|---|---|
| 0 | 0 | 0 |
| 0 | 1 | 1 |
| 1 | 0 | 1 |
| 1 | 1 | 0 |

| Mnemonic | P | PII | K6 | 3D! | 3Mx+ | SSE | SSE2 | A64 | SSE3 | E64T |
|---|---|---|---|---|---|---|---|---|---|---|
| PXOR | | ✓ | ✓ | ✓ | ✓ | ✓ | ✓ | ✓ | ✓ | ✓ |
| XOR | ✓ | ✓ | ✓ | ✓ | ✓ | ✓ | ✓ | ✓ | ✓ | ✓ |
| XORPD | | | | | | | ✓ | ✓ | ✓ | ✓ |
| XORPS | | | | | | ✓ | ✓ | ✓ | ✓ | ✓ |

```
      xor    rmDst(8/16/32/64), #(8/16/32) [Un]signed
      xor    rmDst, rSrc(8/16/32/64)
      xor    rDst, rmSrc(8/16/32/64)
MMX   pxor   mmxDst, mmxSrc/m64        [Un]signed          64
SSE   xorps  xmmDst, xmmSrc/m128       Single-precision FP 128
SSE2  pxor   xmmDst, xmmSrc/m128       [Un]signed          128
 "    xorpd  xmmDst, xmmSrc/m128       Double-precision FP 128
```

An XOR operation means that one would need either A *or* B to be true but *not* both to have a true result. The XOR general-purpose instruction logically AND's the 8-, 16-, 32-, or 64-bit source with the destination and stores the result in the destination. An 8-bit source value can be sign extended to a 16-, 32-, or 64-bit value. A 32-bit source value can be sign extended to a 64-bit destination. The source can be an immediate value, a register, or memory. The destination is a register or memory. A memory-to-memory operation is invalid.

| Flags | O.flow | Sign | Zero | Aux | Parity | Carry |
|-------|--------|------|------|-----|--------|-------|
|       | 0      | X    | X    | -   | X      | 0     |

Flags: With the XOR general-purpose instruction, the Carry and Overflow flags are cleared. The Zero flag is set if all destination bits are 0, thus *destination* = 0. The Sign flag reflects the state of the MSB.

The best method to clear a register is to exclusive or (XOR) it with itself. The newer processors have incorporated optimization logic that encodes that since there are no dependencies upon a read operation when the source and the destination are the same (as the end result is cleared bits), and so merely writes all bits with zero.

The following 32-bit example demonstrates this:

```
mov     eax,00000a5a5h
mov     edx,000000ff0h
xor     eax,edx
```

```
B       00000000000000010100101101001011b    0a5a5h
A       00000000000000000000111111110000b    00ff0h
A⊕B     00000000000000010101010010101011b    0aa55h
```

This is typically used for the flipping of selected bits.

This multimedia extension instruction is a parallel operation that uses a Boolean XOR operation upon each of the corresponding 64 or 128 bits. The source *A* and *B* are *aSrc (xmmSrc)* XOR *bSrc (xmmDst)*, and the result is stored in the destination *Dst (xmmDst)*. The instruction may be labeled as packed, parallel, or vector, but each bit is in reality isolated from each other so there is no need for a data bit block arrangement.

For the SSE instruction, XORPS is a bitwise XOR of four packed single-precision floating-point values with a bit mask.

For the SSE2 instruction, XORPD is a bitwise XOR of two packed double-precision floating-point values with a bit mask.

These floating-point related instructions will be discussed in Chapter 8, "Floating-Point Anyone?"

## Pseudo Vec

The following C code demonstrates the functionality of a logical XOR upon a 128-bit vector. The code sample logical XOR's the four blocks of 32-bit elements from vector *A* and *B* to effectively XOR all 128 bits and then stores the result in vector *D*. Note that the function stores the result referenced by the first function parameter pointer.

### Logical Packed XOR D=(A⊕B)

| Listing 4-8: ...\chap04\pbool\PBool.cpp |
|---|

```
void vmp_pxor(void *pvD, void *pvA, void *pvB)
{
  uint32 *pD, *pA, *pB;

  pD=(uint32*) pvD;
  pA=(uint32*) pvA;
  pB=(uint32*) pvB;
  *(pD+0) = *(pA+0) ^ *(pB+0);    // {31...0}
  *(pD+1) = *(pA+1) ^ *(pB+1);    // {63...32}
  *(pD+2) = *(pA+2) ^ *(pB+2);    // {95...64}
  *(pD+3) = *(pA+3) ^ *(pB+3);    // {127...96}
}
```

See the code snippets from the previously discussed instruction AND, then substitute the instruction {^, *xor*, *pxor*} for the {&, *and*, *pand*} accordingly.

Another use for this operation is as a Boolean NOT (one's complement) operator. By using an input *A* and setting *B* permanently to a logical one, an inverse bit is achieved. Note the following table where zero becomes one and one becomes zero.

| A ⊕ B |   | Y |
|---|---|---|
| 0 | 1 | 1 |
| 1 | 1 | 0 |

Figure 4-1: Example of using a logical XOR with a logical true bit to achieve the equivalent of a logical NOT condition.

As can be seen, input A and output Y are the exact opposite. Keep in mind that Boolean logic is bit based and bit isolated so that adjacent bits do not affect each other.

# NOT — One's Complement Negation

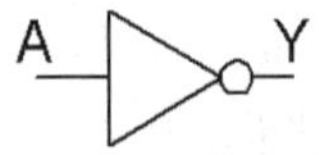

| A | Y |
|---|---|
| 0 | 1 |
| 1 | 0 |

| Mnemonic | P | PII | K6 | 3D! | 3Mx+ | SSE | SSE2 | A64 | SSE3 | E64T |
|---|---|---|---|---|---|---|---|---|---|---|
| NOT | ✓ | ✓ | ✓ | ✓ | ✓ | ✓ | ✓ | ✓ | ✓ | ✓ |

not    *rmDst(8/16/32/64)*          [Un]signed

This instruction logically inverts the bits of the destination. All ones become zeros, and all zeros become ones.

| Flags | O.flow | Sign | Zero | Aux | Parity | Carry |
|-------|--------|------|------|-----|--------|-------|
|       | -      | -    | -    | -   | -      | -     |

Flags: None are affected by this opcode.

```
            mov     eax,00000a5a5h
            not     eax
; NOT 00000000000000000101001011010010b     00000a5a5h
;     11111111111111110101101001011010b     0ffff5a5ah
```

And guess what you get when you flip it again?

```
; NOT 11111111111111110101101001011010b     0ffff5a5ah
;     00000000000000000101001011010010b     00000a5a5h
```

The original value! Flip-flop.

# NEG — Two's Complement Negation

| Mnemonic | P | PII | K6 | 3D! | 3Mx+ | SSE | SSE2 | A64 | SSE3 | E64T |
|----------|---|-----|----|----|------|-----|------|-----|------|------|
| NEG      | ✓ | ✓   | ✓  | ✓  | ✓    | ✓   | ✓    | ✓   | ✓    | ✓    |

neg    *rmDst(8/16/32/64)* [Un]signed

This instruction logically inverts the sign of the number.

| Flags | O.flow | Sign | Zero | Aux | Parity | Carry |
|-------|--------|------|------|-----|--------|-------|
|       | X      | X    | X    | X   | X      | X     |

Flags: Carry is cleared if the destination is 0; else it is set. The other bits are set accordingly from its results.

```
            mov     eax,00000a5a5h
            neg     eax
;     00000000000000000101001011010010b     00000a5a5h (42405)
;     11111111111111110101101001011011b     0ffff5a5bh (-42405)
```

🔍 **Hint:** For a NEG (two's complement negation), use an XOR followed by an increment.

```
        00000000000000000101001011010010b     00000a5a5h (42405)
NOT 11111111111111110101101001011010b     0ffff5a5ah (-42406)
INC 11111111111111110101101001011011b     0ffff5a5bh (-42405)
```

Another use for an XOR is in an implementation for a negation (two's complement). As a refresher, a subtraction is a two's complement followed by an addition. By inverting all bits, a one's complement is achieved. The next step for the two's complement is by an increment (addition of one) of this value. This is followed by the addition, which effectively results in the subtraction.

This operation is the result of a Boolean NOT (one's complement) operator that was just discussed, followed by an increment or an addition by one. Of course, this is not as slick as a reverse subtraction where...

```
-A = A ISUB 0    thus    -A = 0 - A
```

but not all processors support that. Keep in mind though, that when dealing with pipelining your code, a two-step operation may be more helpful than a single step.

## ToolBox Snippet — The Butterfly Switch

An interesting use for a logical XOR is as a butterfly switch to allow for branchless coding. Branchless code is discussed in Chapter 11, but this is a good time to take a break and twiddle some bits. Normal coding that uses branching is typically taught using something as follows:

```
#define FLIP  -30
#define FLOP   47

  if (FLIP == nf)
  {
    nf = FLOP;
  }
  else
  {
    nf = FLIP;
  }
```

...or...

```
nf = (FLIP == nf) ? FLOP : FLIP;
```

No matter which way you coded it, it is the same, identical code. This is fine and dandy, but the branching and especially a possible misprediction of a branch takes time and there are two branches to contend with. If in a flip, it flops, and if in a flop, it flips. Of course, instead of two branches such as the previous code snippet, it could always be coded for one branch such as follows:

```
nf = FLIP;
if (FLIP == nf)
```

```
{
  nf = FLOP;
}
```

The code, if not a FLIP as in the previous code snippet, branches around and continues on, but again, there could be a misprediction.

A misprediction is as it sounds. A more advanced CPU will predict that at an if-then conditional, it will take the branch and do the conditional or branch around, thus the if-then-else. The problem is that the CPU gains efficiency by predicting that it is correct because it is preloading memory and, in some cases, executing instructions that are further down in the code. The punishment comes that if it predicted wrong, that memory has to be thrown away and the results of the calculations it processed ahead of time disposed of. Then it needs to continue processing down the correct path. Either way, this is very time consuming, and so alternative (branchless) methods need to be devised if possible.

My favorite solution is a branchless result so there is no misprediction and the appropriate value can be selected with a butterfly switch. Let's examine these two values more closely:

```
FLOP    =    47   =   0x002F   =   0000000000101111b
FLIP    =   -30   =   0xFFE2   =   1111111111100010b
```

…and calculate the logical XOR of those two values:

```
FLIPPY =   -51   =   0xFFCD   =   1111111111001101b
```

So if in our code initialization we preset a value:

```
nf = FLOP;
```

…and in place of the branching code the following snippet is used instead:

```
xor   nf,nf,FLIPPY    // FLIP/FLOP
```

…then each time the code is executed it will flip to the alternate value.

FLIP FLOP FLIP FLOP FLIP FLOP FLIP, etc.

```
     FLIP      1111111111100010b  0xFFE2  -30
⊕  FLIPPY    1111111111001101b  0xFFCD
     FLOP      0000000000101111b  0x002F   47
⊕  FLIPPY    1111111111001101b  0xFFCD
     FLIP      1111111111100010b  0xFFE2  -30
```

Pretty cool, huh! And the best part is the actual code is a single instruction, not a group of instructions to process a branch and decide whether to branch or not! The code runs a lot faster, and it's smaller. This also works with non-definitions as well. Initialize with the following:

```
nf = valueA;          // First value
iFlipVal = nf ^ valueB; // Butterfly key
```

...and then select the value with the following:

```
nf = nf ^ iFlipVal;
```

... and it works great in a parallel configuration. Different butterflies to control different elements, all in parallel.

If anything, at least this book is informative!

# I-VU-Q

I know this is not x86 related, but what instruction is thought to be missing from the VU coprocessor on the PS2?

The XOR!!!

This seems to be a popular interview question, as I have encountered it numerous times. Yes, I know, I digress. The 80x86 supports the XOR instruction as was discussed, but this is good practice for the other Boolean instructions that have been touched on in this chapter.

After interviewers ask this question, they then sometimes want to know how to write equivalent code. Funny thing is that they do not seem to remember the answer themselves. I will hastily draw out the following truth table from left to right, and then draw the circuit for good measure. (That is, if I am not too tired and frustrated from having to answer programming questions all day long!)

| A B | Y | A∨B | (A∧B)' | ∧ |
|-----|---|-----|--------|---|
| 0 0 | 0 | 0 | 1 | 0 |
| 0 1 | 1 | 1 | 1 | 1 |
| 1 0 | 1 | 1 | 1 | 1 |
| 1 1 | 0 | 1 | 0 | 0 |

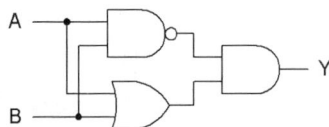

Figure 4-2: A four-gate (OR, NOT-AND, AND) solution to achieve an equivalent result of a logical XOR

I will then hesitate for a second and then announce, "But wait!" This takes four logical operations — an OR, AND, NOT, then AND. So instead let's make this a bit smaller. If ANDC type functionality is used (which has not been discussed yet)...

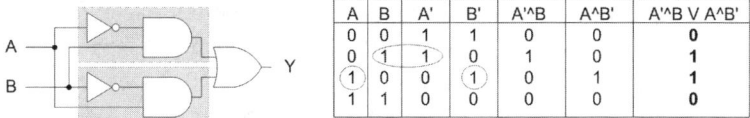

| A | B | A' | B' | A'^B | A^B' | A'^B V A^B' |
|---|---|----|----|------|------|-------------|
| 0 | 0 | 1  | 1  | 0    | 0    | **0**       |
| 0 | 1 | 1  | 0  | 1    | 0    | **1**       |
| 1 | 0 | 0  | 1  | 0    | 1    | **1**       |
| 1 | 1 | 0  | 0  | 0    | 0    | **0**       |

*Figure 4-3: A two-gate (ANDC, OR) solution to achieve an equivalent result of a logical XOR*

…notice the swapped inputs and the gate functionality similar to a logical AND, then the outputs are logical OR gated together. So now it is down to two!

But wait. What if there were no NOT, NOR, XOR, or ANDC instruction? At this point, if you replicate what is being presented here at your interview as a response to the question, you will either come off sounding like a really smart guy or a prima donna, depending on how you do it. So you then announce, "But wait! There is no NOT or ANDC, so how do we do it!" (Keep in mind there is a NOT and an ANDC on the 80x86.) "Ever hear of a half-adder?" It has the same result as that of an XOR except that it also contains a carry, and that is where the problem resides. That carry bit is contaminating an adjacent bit.

*Table 4-1: A half-adder solution. By ignoring the carry, a logical XOR will result.*

| A + B | Carry | Y |
|-------|-------|---|
| 0   0 | 0     | **0** |
| 0   1 | 0     | **1** |
| 1   0 | 0     | **1** |
| 1   1 | 1     | **0** |

So if the bits are stripped into an odd-even arrangement, the $A$ and $B$ (odd bits) are summed, then masked with the 1010 bit mask pattern. The $A$ and $B$ (even bits) are summed, then masked with the 0101 even bit mask pattern. The results of the odd and even are logical OR'd with each other; effectively a logical XOR is simulated. Let's examine some 16-bit data:

```
        oeoeoeoeoeoeoeoe
B       1010010110100101b   0a5a5h
A       0000111111110000b   00ff0h
A⊕B     1010101001010101b   0aa55h
```

So effectively all the odd bits are separated from the even bits. Odd bits are stored in a {o0o0…o0o0} bit pattern while the even bits are stored in a {0e0e…0e0e} bit pattern. So by a logical AND with the odd {10} and even {01} binary masks, an un-interlaced form is generated. This allows the odd and even bits to be handled separately, and the overflow from any operation is stored in the adjacent (next higher) bit. This means any carry will be ignored when the odd and even results are blended back together. The carry results will be removed using the same odd or even mask. Notice the bits indicated in bold are the usable result from the AND.

| | | | |
|---|---|---|---|
| | B | 1010010110100101b | 0a5a5h |
| Even ∧ | B | 0101010101010101b | 05555h (Mask) |
| Even's | B | 0000010100000101b | 00505h |
| | | | |
| | B | 1010010110100101b | 0a5a5h |
| Odd ∧ | B | 1010101010101010b | 0aaaah (Mask) |
| Odd's | B | 1010000010100000b | 0a0a0h |
| | | | |
| | A | 0000111111110000b | 00ff0h |
| Even ∧ | A | 0101010101010101b | 05555h (Mask) |
| Even's | A | 0000010101010000b | 00550h |
| | | | |
| | A | 0000111111110000b | 00ff0h |
| Odd ∧ | A | 1010101010101010b | 0aaaah (Mask) |
| Odd's | A | 0000101010100000b | 00aa0h |

Now the even and odd values of *A* and *B* are summed up separately. Note that we only care about the resulting bits in bold and not the others, as those are the individual carries, which are stripped by the logical AND of the original mask.

| | | | |
|---|---|---|---|
| Even's | B | 0000010100000101b | 00505h |
| Even's | A + | 0000010101010000b | 00550h |
| | | 0000101001010101b | 00a55h |
| Even | ∧ | 0101010101010101b | 05555h (Mask) |
| Even | A⊕B | 0000000001010101b | 00055h |
| | | | |
| Odd's | B | 1010000010100000b | 0a0a0h |
| Odd's | A + | 0000101010100000b | 00aa0h |
| | | 1010101101000000b | 0ab40h |
| Odd | ∧ | 1010101010101010b | 0aaaah (Mask) |
| Odd | A⊕B | 1010101000000000b | 0aa00h |

Now logical OR the even bits and odd bits back together for the inter-laced XOR result.

| | | | |
|---|---|---|---|
| Even | A⊕B | 0000000001010101b | 00055h |
| Odd ∨ | A⊕B | 1010101000000000b | **0aa00h** |
| | A⊕B | 1010101001010101b | 0aa55h |

And when compared to the expected results of a "real" XOR:

| | | | |
|---|---|---|---|
| | A⊕B | 1010101001010101b | 0aa55h |

...exactly the same. Okay, okay, a lot more operations, but just another technique for your repertoire. But now that you have special insight into the problem, here is the start of solving this equation for yourself!

You did not think that I would be giving you all the answers, did you?

**Hint:**  There is one more method available to do a logical NOT. A subtraction is a two's complement as it is a bit flip (one's complement) followed by an increment (two's complement), and then an addition. If the result of a subtraction from zero is decremented, you effectively get a NOT (one's complement)!    $A'=(0-A)-1$
Does this give you any ideas?

# Boolean Logical ANDC

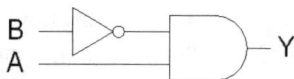

| A | B | B' | Y |
|---|---|----|---|
| 0 | 0 | 1  | 0 |
| 0 | 1 | 0  | 0 |
| 1 | 0 | 1  | 1 |
| 1 | 1 | 0  | 0 |

| Mnemonic | P | PII | K6 | 3D! | 3Mx+ | SSE | SSE2 | A64 | SSE3 | E64T |
|----------|---|-----|----|----|------|-----|------|-----|------|------|
| ANDNPD   |   |     |    |    |      |     | ✓    | ✓   | ✓    | ✓    |
| ANDNPS   |   |     |    |    |      | ✓   | ✓    | ✓   | ✓    | ✓    |
| PANDN    |   | ✓   | ✓  | ✓  | ✓    | ✓   | ✓    | ✓   | ✓    | ✓    |

MMX    pandn    *mmxDst, mmxSrc/m64*      [Un]signed              64
SSE     andnps   *xmmDst, xmmSrc/m128*   Single-precision FP  128
SSE2   pandn    *xmmDst, xmmSrc/m128*   [Un]signed             128
  "       andnpd  *xmmDst, xmmSrc/m128*   Double-precision FP 128

This instruction is a one's complement of *B* logical AND with *A*.

    Dst=Src∧(¬Dst')

This multimedia extension instruction is a parallel operation that uses a Boolean NOT AND operation upon each of the corresponding 64 or 128 bits. The source *A* and *B* are *aSrc (xmmSrc)* and a one's complement of *bSrc (xmmDst)*, and the result is stored in the destination *Dst (xmmDst)*. The instruction may be labeled as packed, parallel, or vector, but each bit is in reality isolated from each other so there is no need for a data bit block arrangement. The following 32-bit example demonstrates this.

```
B          00000000000000001010010110100101b   00000a5a5h
¬B NOT     11111111111111110101101001011010b   0ffff5a5ah
A      ∧   00000000000000000000111111110000b   000000ff0h
A∧(¬B)     00000000000000000000101001010000b   000000a50h
```

For the SSE instruction, ANDNPS is a bitwise NOT AND of four packed single-precision floating-point values with a bit mask.

For the SSE2 instruction, ANDNPD is a bitwise NOT AND of two packed double-precision floating-point values with a bit mask.

These floating-point related instructions will be discussed in Chapter 8, "Floating-Point Anyone?"

# Pseudo Vec

The following C code demonstrates the functionality of a logical ANDC upon a 128-bit vector. The code sample logical NOT's the bits from vector $B$, then AND's these bits with vector $A$, 32 bits at a time, four times, to effectively ANDC all 128 bits, and then stores the result in vector $D$. Note that the function stores the result referenced by the first function parameter pointer.

## Logical Packed ANDC D=(A∧B′)

Listing 4-9: ...\chap04\pbool\PBool.cpp

```cpp
void vmp_pandc(void *pvD, void *pvA, void *pvB)
{
  uint32 *pD, *pA, *pB;

  pD=(uint32*) pvD;
  pA=(uint32*) pvA;
  pB=(uint32*) pvB;

  *(pD+0) = (0xffffffff ^ *(pB+0)) & *(pA+0);
  *(pD+1) = (0xffffffff ^ *(pB+1)) & *(pA+1);
  *(pD+2) = (0xffffffff ^ *(pB+2)) & *(pA+2);
  *(pD+3) = (0xffffffff ^ *(pB+3)) & *(pA+3);
}
```

See the code snippets from the instruction AND, then substitute the instruction {pandn} for the {pand} accordingly.

# Exercises

1. What is a half-adder?
2. Make a NOT gate using
   a) an XOR gate
   b) a NAND gate
   c) a NOR gate.
3. Write a software algorithm for the following equation.
   $$D=(-1-(A \land B)) \land (A \lor B)$$
   What does the equation do?
4. Draw an XOR circuit using only OR gates and AND gates, and a subtraction.
5. Make a 128-bit XOR using only bitwise OR and bitwise AND, and a subtraction.
6. Write code to change the value of tri-state data. Note the series of states is a repeating pattern $\{0, 1, 2, 0, 1, 2, ...\}$. The starting state is State #0.

| State | 0 | 1 | 2 | 0... |
|-------|------|------|------|------|
| Value | 0x34 | 0x8A | 0xE5 | 0x34 |

Extra credit:

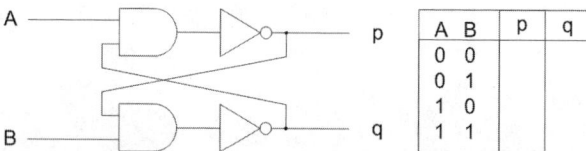

| A B | p | q |
|-----|---|---|
| 0 0 |   |   |
| 0 1 |   |   |
| 1 0 |   |   |
| 1 1 |   |   |

This cross-coupled SR flip-flop will be more familiar to those of you with electronics experience. Using A=0 and B=0 as the starting state, finish the logic table.

How does this circuit function? What are the behaviors of $p$ and $q$ if the data inputs of $A$ and $B$ are changed to a new state? Try all 12 possibilities. How would you code it?

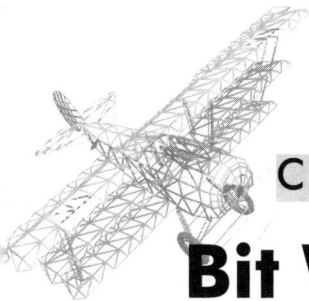

# Chapter 5

# Bit Wrangling

Think of this chapter as a continuation of the previous chapter, "Bit Mangling."

This chapter deals with bit wrangling and thus the movement of bits. They can be shifted into oblivion, rotated, and watched going around and around. As Bugs Bunny would say, "Dizzing, ain't it!"

Bit wrangling actually occurs with the rotation and logical and arithmetic shifting of bits within each parallel bit range of packed bits. Just as in the scalar point of view of a similar general-purpose CPU instruction, the bits can be used for masking, base two multiplication and division, and other functionality.

It must be reiterated that you watch the alignment of your data objects in memory very closely. It takes extra overhead to adjust the memory into an aligned state, and it is a lot more efficient to ensure that they are aligned in the first place. Your code will be smaller and faster! This will be made obvious by the sample code included in this chapter.

**Workbench Files:** \Bench\\*x86*\chap05\\*project*\\*platform*

|  | *project* | *platform* |
| --- | --- | --- |
| **Shift/Rotations** | **\prot\** | \vc6 |
|  |  | \vc.net |

# Logical Left Shifting

It is recommended that you use an addition instead of a shift on newer processors for optimization.

```
A + A  = 2A = A << 1
2A + 2A = 4A = A << 2
```

# SHL/SAL – Shift (Logical/Arithmetic) Left

SHL *destination, count*

| Mnemonic | P | PII | K6 | 3D! | 3Mx+ | SSE | SSE2 | A64 | SSE3 | E64T |
|----------|---|-----|----|----|------|-----|------|-----|------|------|
| SAL | ✓ | ✓ | ✓ | ✓ | ✓ | ✓ | ✓ | ✓ | ✓ | ✓ |
| SHL | ✓ | ✓ | ✓ | ✓ | ✓ | ✓ | ✓ | ✓ | ✓ | ✓ |

shl   *rmDst(8/16/32/64), 1*          [Un]signed
shl   *rmDst(8/16/32/64), #($2^n-1$)*
shl   *rmDst(8/16/32/64), cl*

This instruction is a multiplier ($2^n$) by shifting the destination to the left and shifting the most significant bit (MSB) into the carry. The previous content of the carry is shifted out and lost, and a 0 is shifted into the least significant bit (LSB). The count indicating the number of bits to shift is invalid if greater than or equal to width of data ($2^n$). If shifted enough times, the data will be emptied, being set to all zeroes. If *count* = 0, then there is no shift and thus the destination and flags are not changed. Shift Logical Left and Shift Arithmetic Left are the same identical instruction.

| Flags | O.flow | Sign | Zero | Aux | Parity | Carry |
|-------|--------|------|------|-----|--------|-------|
|       | X | X | X | - | X | X |

Flags: Carry = last bit shifted out, Zero = 1 if all destination bits are 0, thus *destination* = 0. If using the shift by 1, then Overflow = 0 if Carry = MSB.

```
datd  dd    32
datw  dw    16
datb  db    8

      mov   dx,1010010110100101b  ;0a5a5h  carry=0
      mov   cl,2          ; ×4 = 2²

      shl   datd,4        ; datd = 512 = 32 × 16 = 32 × (2⁴)
      shl   dx,1          ; dx = dx × 2
; dx = 0100101101001010b  04b4ah  carry=1
      shl   eax,cl        ; eax = eax × 4
```

With Pentium processors a multiply is pretty quick, but for a 486 processor or older it was sometimes necessary and faster to do shifting and adding to compensate. For example, a video display with a resolution of 640x480x8-bit would need to calculate an actual screen (memory pointer) related to an X and Y coordinate.

```
mov     ecx,X
mov     edx,Y
mov     edi,edx
shl     edi,2           ; 4x
add     edi,edx         ; 5x = (4x+x)
shl     edi,7           ; 640x = (5x)×(128)
add     edi,ecx         ; edi = memory index
mov     es:[edi],al     ; Write a byte pixel
```

# SHLD — Shift (Logical) Left (Double)

SHLD *destination, count*

| Mnemonic | P | PII | K6 | 3D! | 3Mx+ | SSE | SSE2 | A64 | SSE3 | E64T |
|---|---|---|---|---|---|---|---|---|---|---|
| SHLD | ✓ | ✓ | ✓ | ✓ | ✓ | ✓ | ✓ | ✓ | ✓ | ✓ |

shld   *rmDst(16/32/64), rSrc(16/32/64), #($2^n-1$)*   [Un]signed
shld   *rmDst(16/32/64), rSrc(16/32/64), cl*

This instruction shifts the upper half of an unsigned 64-bit integer by $2^n$, which shifts the source to the left into the destination to the left and shifts the most significant bit (MSB) into the carry. The previous content of the carry is shifted out and lost. (It should be noted that in reality the source is not altered, only the destination.) The count indicating the number of bits to shift is invalid if it is greater than or equal to width of data ($2^n$). If you exceed the operand size, the result in destination is undefined. If *count* = 0, then there is no shift and the destination and flags are not changed.

| Flags | O.flow | Sign | Zero | Aux | Parity | Carry |
|---|---|---|---|---|---|---|
|  | X | X | X | - | X | X |

Flags: Carry = last bit shifted out, Zero = I if all destination bits are 0, thus *destination* = 0. If using the shift by I, then Overflow = I if a sign change occurred; else it is 0.

```
datd    dd    32
datw    dw    16
datb    db    8

        mov   ax,0001001000110100b  01234h
        mov   dx,1010010110100101b  0a5a5h
        mov   cl,4

        shld  dx,ax,4
        shl   ax,4
        ; dx = 0101101001010001b  05a51h  carry=0
```

# PSLLx — Parallel Shift Left (Logical)

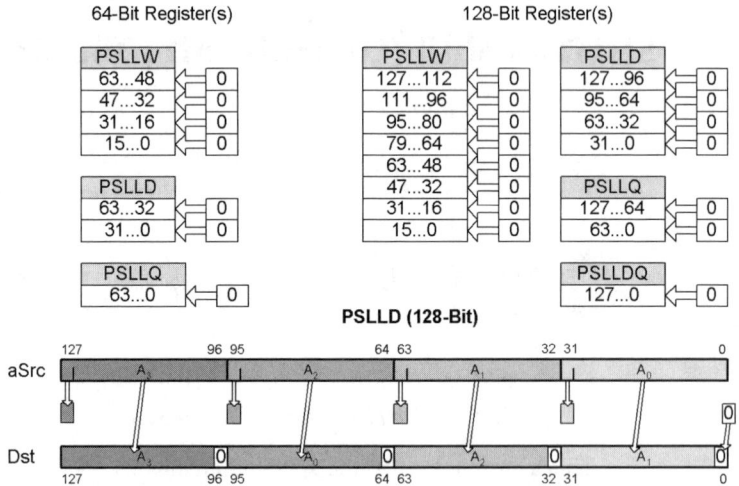

*Figure 5-1: Miscellaneous examples of data types being shifted to the left by one bit*

| Mnemonic | P | PII | K6 | 3D! | 3Mx+ | SSE | SSE2 | A64 | SSE3 | E64T |
|---|---|---|---|---|---|---|---|---|---|---|
| PSLLx | | ✓ | ✓ | ✓ | ✓ | ✓ | ✓ | ✓ | ✓ | ✓ |
| PSLLDQ | | | | | | | ✓ | ✓ | ✓ | ✓ |

| | | | | |
|---|---|---|---|---|
| MMX | psll(w/d/q) | *mmxDst, count(#/mmx/m64)* | [Un]signed | 64 |
| SSE2 | psll(w/d/q) | *xmmDst, count(#/xmm/m128)* | [Un]signed | 128 |
| " | pslldq | *xmmDst, count(#)* | [Un]signed | 128 |

These multimedia and SIMD extension instructions are parallel operations that logically left shift each of the data bit blocks, by a *count* of bits. Depending upon the processor and the instruction, block sizes of 16, 32, 64, or 128 bits can be shifted by the specified *count*.

This is a multiplier ($2^n$) by shifting a 0 into the LSB of each packed value of the source *aSrc (xmmSrc)* and causing all bits to be shifted to the left and the MSB of each packed value being lost. The result is stored in the destination *Dst (xmmDst)*. There is no Carry flag to save the bit. If the *count* indicating the number of bits to shift is more than packed bits – 1 — 15 for (**W**ords), 31 for (**D**ouble words), 63 for (**Q**uad words), or 127 for (Double Quad words) — then the destination will be typically set to a value of zero. This is most effective when used in an integer math function where multiple numbers need to be multiplied by $2^n$ concurrently.

## Pseudo Vec

Although logical left, right, or arithmetic shifting is supported by almost all processors, parallel shifting is not. The same parallel effect can be simulated in those particular cases of non-SIMD supporting processors. The following C code demonstrates it by concurrently shifting four packed 8-bit values to the left. All 32 bits are shifted to the left in unison but as the remaining bits become corrupted by the adjacent byte, a logical AND using a mask in the table lookup forces those vacated bits to zero.

```
#define eMASKFE 0xfefefefe        // Mask FE

uint32 val;

val = (val << 1) & eMASKFE;
```

As you saw in the previous example, an absolute shift value is the most simplistic way to go, as it is merely a matter of shifting the *n* number of bits and masking with the appropriate value.

```
11111111    11111111
11111110    01111111
11111100    00111111
11111000    00011111
11110000    00001111
11100000    00000111
11000000    00000011
10000000    00000001
```

*Table 5-1: An 8-bit mask for stripping bits in conjunction with shifting data (0…7) bits to the left or to the right*

| 8-bit Shift | 0 | 1 | 2 | 3 | 4 | 5 | 6 | 7 |
|---|---|---|---|---|---|---|---|---|
| Left | FF | FE | FC | F8 | F0 | E0 | C0 | 80 |
| Right | FF | 7F | 3F | 1F | 0F | 07 | 03 | 01 |

If the shift factor is unknown, then the algorithm required, such as the following, becomes more complicated as a table lookup is needed for the masking value.

```
uint32 llMaskBD[] = {  // Left Shift 32-bit 4×8-bit mask
    0xffffffff, 0xfefefefe, 0xfcfcfcfc, 0xf8f8f8f8,
    0xf0f0f0f0, 0xe0e0e0e0, 0xc0c0c0c0, 0x80808080 };
```

```
uint32 rrMaskBD[] = {  // Right Shift 32-bit 4×8-bit mask
    0xffffffff, 0x7f7f7f7f, 0x3f3f3f3f, 0x1f1f1f1f,
    0x0f0f0f0f, 0x07070707, 0x03030303, 0x01010101 };
```

Since packed 8-bit logical shift is not supported, let us first examine a block of four 8-bit bytes being shifted simultaneously. Similar to the processors, the shift count needs to be truncated to a value of n–1, thus 0…7 in this particular case. Different processors have different results (especially with the various C compilers due to being a feature of the C language). For example, on some compilers a shift of an 8-bit byte by a value of nine would result in a zero, on some a one, and some, if directly transposing to assembly instructions, would tend to ignore the extraneous bits. For the 8-bit value only the three least significant bits would be used, for a shift value of {0…7}. A shift by nine would be effectively a shift by one since a value of nine in Boolean (1001b) would have its upper bits ignored (1001b) and so only the lower three bits (001b) would be used as a shift count; thus it becomes a value of one.

This also helps to prevent an out of bounds memory reference in regard to the mask lookup. The value is then shifted by the adjusted *count*, and then logical AND'd with the mask. This effectively processes all four values simultaneously as mentioned!

## Packed Shift Left Logical 16×8-bit by n:{0...7}

*Listing 5-1: …\chap05\prot\PRot.cpp*

```
void vmp_psllB(uint8 * pbD, uint8 * pbA, uint count)
{
  uint32 msk, *pD, *pA;

  pD=(uint32*) pvD;
  pA=(uint32*) pvA;
```

```
    msk = llMaskBD[count];
    count &= (8-1);          // Clip count to data bit size -1

    *(pD+0) = (*(pA+0) & msk) << count;
    *(pD+1) = (*(pA+1) & msk) << count;
    *(pD+2) = (*(pA+2) & msk) << count;
    *(pD+3) = (*(pA+3) & msk) << count;
}
```

# Pseudo Vec (x86)

The following is an example needed for the x86 processor because it supports packed 16, 32, and 64 bits, but not a packed 8-bit logical shift. This uses a similar table of masks for the zero bit fill as viewed previously.

```
llMaskBQ dq 0ffffffffffffffffh, 0fefefefefefefefeh,
         dq 0fcfcfcfcfcfcfcfch, 0f8f8f8f8f8f8f8f8h,
         dq 0f0f0f0f0f0f0f0f0h, 0e0e0e0e0e0e0e0e0h,
         dq 0c0c0c0c0c0c0c0c0h, 08080808080808080h,
```

As an MMX register is only 64 bits, the 128-bit value is handled using register pairs. This is actually faster and easier than these 128-bit C pseudocode samples.

## vmp_psllB (MMX) 16×8-bit Vector

Listing 5-2: ...\chap05\prot\psllX86M.asm

```
    mov    ecx,dword ptr count  ; # of bits to shift
    mov    edx,pbD
    mov    eax,pbA
    and    ecx,8-1              ; Clip count to 0...7 bits

    movq   mm0,[eax+0]          ; Read data
    movq   mm1,[eax+8]
    movd   mm2,ecx              ; mm0=64 bits mm1=64 bits
                                ; mm2=# of bits to shift
    psllq  mm0,mm2              ; val << count
    psllq  mm1,mm2
    pand   mm0,llMaskBQ[ecx*8]  ; Strip lower bits
    pand   mm1,llMaskBQ[ecx*8]

    movq   [edx+0],mm0          ; Write data
    movq   [edx+8],mm1
```

Of course with this instruction, if only a shift by one is needed, the AND and PSLLQ can be replaced with only a PADDB. The MMX and SSE2 instructions support a byte add, and (A<<1) is equivalent to (A+A)!

So replace this:

```
psllq mm0,1                    ; val << 1
psllq mm1,1
pand  mm0,llMaskBQ[1*8]        ; Strip lower bit
pand  mm1,llMaskBQ[1*8]
```

...with this:

```
paddb mm0,mm0
paddb mm1,mm1
```

One last thing to note is the actual operation. There is no difference between a pre-mask vs. a post-mask. Only the mask!

```
((A&7F)<<1)              is equivalent to          ((A<<1)&FE)

     AAAAAAAA BBBBBBBB                        AAAAAAAA BBBBBBBB C
   & 01111111 01111111        << 1           _____.
     0AAAAAAA 0BBBBBBB                        A AAAAAAAB BBBBBBBC
<< 1 _____                       & 0 11111110 11111110
     AAAAAAA0 BBBBBBB0                         AAAAAAA0 BBBBBBB0
```

If you compare the left and right trace, you should see that they have the same result.

# Logical Right Shifting

## SHR — Shift (Logical) Right

SHR *destination*, *count*

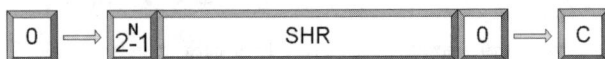

| Mnemonic | P | PII | K6 | 3D! | 3Mx+ | SSE | SSE2 | A64 | SSE3 | E64T |
|---|---|---|---|---|---|---|---|---|---|---|
| SHR | ✓ | ✓ | ✓ | ✓ | ✓ | ✓ | ✓ | ✓ | ✓ | ✓ |

| | | |
|---|---|---|
| shr | *rmDst(8/16/32/64), 1* | [Un]signed |
| shr | *rmDst(8/16/32/64), #($2^n-1$)* | |
| shr | *rmDst(8/16/32/64), cl* | |

This instruction is an unsigned divide by $2^n$ that shifts the destination to the right and shifts the least significant bit (LSB) into the carry. The previous content of the carry is shifted out and lost, and a 0 is shifted into the most significant bit (MSB). The *count* indicating the number of bits to shift is invalid if greater than or equal to the width of data ($2^n$). If you

shift enough times, you will empty the data, setting it to all 0's. If *count* = 0, then there is no shift and the destination and flags are not changed.

| Flags | O.flow | Sign | Zero | Aux | Parity | Carry |
|-------|--------|------|------|-----|--------|-------|
|       | X      | X    | X    | -   | X      | X     |

Flags: Carry = last bit shifted out, Zero = 1 if all *destination* bits are 0, thus *destination* = 0. If using the shift by 1, then Overflow is set to 0; else Overflow is set to the starting MSB.

```
datd    dd      32
datw    dw      16
datb    db      8

        mov     dx,1010010110100101b  ;0a5a5h  carry=0
        mov     cl,2          ;  ×4 = 2²

        shr     datd,4        ; datd = 2 = 32 ÷ 16 = 32 ÷ (2⁴)
        shr     dx,1          ; dx = dx × 2
                              ; dx = 0101001011010010b  052d2h  carry=1
        shr     eax,cl        ; eax = eax ÷ 4
```

This is typically used as a divisor for use in masking for table lookups such as:

```
        mov     eax,nWidth  ; # of bytes to alter
        shr     eax,3       ; divide by (2³)=(n÷8)
                            ; At this point eax is # of 64-bit #'s
```

# SHRD — Shift (Logical) Right (Double)

SHRD *destination, source, count*

| Mnemonic | P | PII | K6 | 3D! | 3Mx+ | SSE | SSE2 | A64 | SSE3 | E64T |
|----------|---|-----|-----|-----|------|-----|------|-----|------|------|
| SHRD     | ✓ | ✓   | ✓   | ✓   | ✓    | ✓   | ✓    | ✓   | ✓    | ✓    |

shrd    *rmDst(16/32), rSrc(16/32), #(2ⁿ–1)* [Un]signed
shrd    *rmDst(16/32), rSrc(16/32), cl*

This instruction is the lower half of an unsigned 64-bit integer divide by $2^n$ that shifts the *source* to the right into the *destination* to the right and shifts the least significant bit (LSB) into the carry. The previous content of the carry is shifted out and lost. (It should be noted that in reality the source is not altered, only the destination.) The *count* indicating the number of bits to shift is invalid if it is greater than or equal to the width of data $(2^n)$. If *count* = 0, then there is no shift, and the destination and flags are not changed.

| Flags | O.flow | Sign | Zero | Aux | Parity | Carry |
|-------|--------|------|------|-----|--------|-------|
| | X | X | X | - | X | X |

Flags: Carry = last bit shifted out, Zero = 1 if all *destination* bits are 0, thus *destination* = 0. If using the shift by 1, then Overflow = 1 if a sign change occurred; else it is 0.

```
datd    dd      32
datw    dw      16
datb    db      8

        mov     ax,0001001000110100b   01234h
        mov     dx,1010010110100101b   0a5a5h
        mov     cl,4

        shrd    dx,ax,4   ; lower bits
        shr     ax,4      ; upper bits
                          ; dx = 0100101001011010b   04a5ah   carry=0
```

# PSRLx — Parallel Shift Right (Logical)

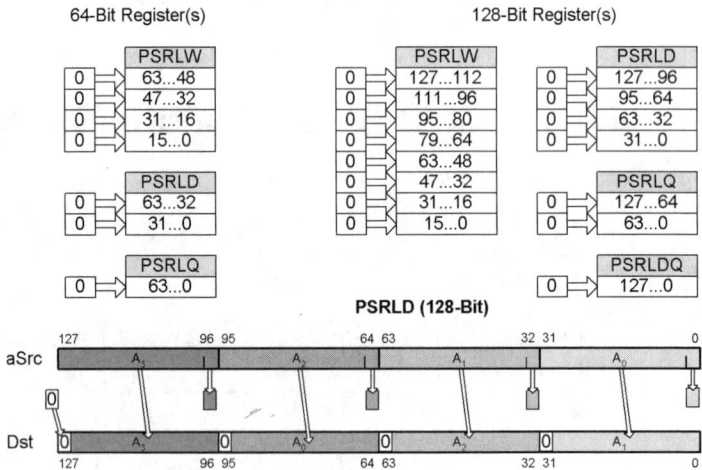

Figure 5-2: Miscellaneous examples of data types being logical shifted to the right by one bit

| Mnemonic | P | PII | K6 | 3D! | 3Mx+ | SSE | SSE2 | A64 | SSE3 | E64T |
|---|---|---|---|---|---|---|---|---|---|---|
| PSRLx | | ✓ | ✓ | ✓ | ✓ | ✓ | ✓ | ✓ | ✓ | ✓ |
| PSRLDQ | | | | | | | ✓ | ✓ | ✓ | ✓ |

MMX    psrl(w/d/q) *mmxDst, count(#/mmx/m64)*    [Un]signed    64
SSE2   psrl(w/d/q) *xmmDst, count(#/xmm/m128)*   [Un]signed    128
"      psrldq     *xmmDst, count(#)*             [Un]signed    128

These multimedia and SIMD extension instructions are parallel operations that logically right shift each of the data bit blocks by a *count* of bits. Depending on the processor and the instruction, block sizes of 16, 32, 64, or 128 bits can be shifted by the specified *count*.

This is a divisor ($2^n$) of *unsigned* values by shifting a 0 into the MSB of each packed value of the source *aSrc (xmmSrc)*, which cause all bits to be shifted to the right and the LSB of each packed value being lost; the result is stored in the destination *Dst (xmmDst)*. There is no Carry flag to save the bit. If the *count* indicating the number of bits to shift is more than packed bits – 1 — 15 for (**W**ords), 31 for (**D**ouble words), 63 for (**Q**uad words), or 127 for (Double Quad words) — then the destination will be typically set to a value of zero. This is most effective when used in an integer math function where multiple unsigned numbers need to be divided by $2^n$ concurrently.

# Pseudo Vec

The C code simulating the functionality is almost identical to the *Parallel Shift (Logical) Left* instruction, previously discussed in this chapter, except in this case a different mask and a shift to the right are used instead. This should look very similar to you as previously reviewed in SLL; only the bold areas should be different!

## Packed Shift Right Logical 16×8-bit by n:{0...7}

```
Listing 5-3: ...\chap05\prot\PRot.cpp

void vmp_psrlB(uint8 * pbD, uint8 * pbA, uint count)
{
  uint32 msk, *pD, *pA;

  pD=(uint32*) pvD;
  pA=(uint32*) pvA;

  count &= (8-1);        // Clip count to data bit size-1
  msk = 11MaskBD[count];

  *(pD+0) = (*(pA+0) & msk) >> count;
```

```
    *(pD+1) = (*(pA+1) & msk) >> count;
    *(pD+2) = (*(pA+2) & msk) >> count;
    *(pD+3) = (*(pA+3) & msk) >> count;
}
```

There are similarities between left and right logical shifting for the various processor instructions. The function shell code is very similar as lower versus upper bits are masked. The bits are shifted to the left versus to the right. In assembly code, one merely needs to substitute the correct instruction for the same functionality. In simulated C code, the correct mask needs to be chosen. Those instructions, along with their complement, are reflected in the following table.

Table 5-2: Instruction substitution table to convert a previous SLL (Shift Left Logical) instruction into a SRL (Shift Right Logical), as well as masks and their complement

| Instructions | | Masks | |
|---|---|---|---|
| **SLL** | **SRL** | **SLL** | **SRL** |
| psllq | psrlq | rrMaskBQ | llMaskBQ |
| psllw | psrlw | | |
| pslld | psrld | llMaskBO | rrMaskBO |

# Arithmetic Right Shifting

## SAR — Shift (Arithmetic) Right

SAR *destination, count*

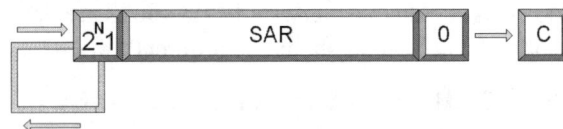

| Mnemonic | P | PII | K6 | 3D! | 3Mx+ | SSE | SSE2 | A64 | SSE3 | E64T |
|---|---|---|---|---|---|---|---|---|---|---|
| SAR | ✓ | ✓ | ✓ | ✓ | ✓ | ✓ | ✓ | ✓ | ✓ | ✓ |

sar   *rmDst(8/16/32/64), 1*       [Un]signed
sar   *rmDst(8/16/32/64), #(2$^n$–1)*
sar   *rmDst(8/16/32/64), cl*

This instruction is a signed divide by $2^n$ that shifts the destination to the right and shifts the least significant bit (LSB) into the carry. The previous content of the carry is shifted out and lost, and a 0 is shifted into the most significant bit (MSB). The *count* indicating the number of bits to shift is invalid if it is greater than or equal to the width of data ($2^n$). If you shift enough times you will empty the data, setting it to all 0's. If *count* = 0, then there is no shift and the destination and flags are not changed.

| Flags | O.flow | Sign | Zero | Aux | Parity | Carry |
|---|---|---|---|---|---|---|
| | X | X | X | - | X | X |

Flags: Carry = last bit shifted out, Zero = 1 if all *destination* bits are 0, thus *destination* = 0. If using the shift by 1, then Overflow is cleared to 0; else the Overflow is undefined.

```
datd    dd      32
datw    dw      16
datb    db      8

        mov     dx,1010010110100101b  ;0a5a5h  carry=0
        mov     cl,2          ;  x4 = 2²

        sar     datd,4        ; datd = 2 = 32 ÷ 16 = 32 ÷ (2⁴)
        sar     dx,1          ; dx = dx × 2
                              ; dx = 1101001011010010b  0d2d2h  carry=1 Z=0 OF=0
        sar     eax,cl        ; eax = eax ÷ 4
```

This instruction is typically used as a signed divisor. Its use of the "sticky" MSB is great for use in generating masks. As an arithmetic shift retains the MSB while data is being shifted down, this "retained" bit is stuck. Thus, it sticks in position!

By using:

```
        sar     eax,31
```

a negative value sets EAX with all bits set to 1 and a positive value sets all 0's. With the use of masking bit logic, some algorithms could run faster due to not needing to branch. Investigate Chapter 11, "Branchless," for more information.

# PSRAx — Packed Shift Right (Arithmetic)

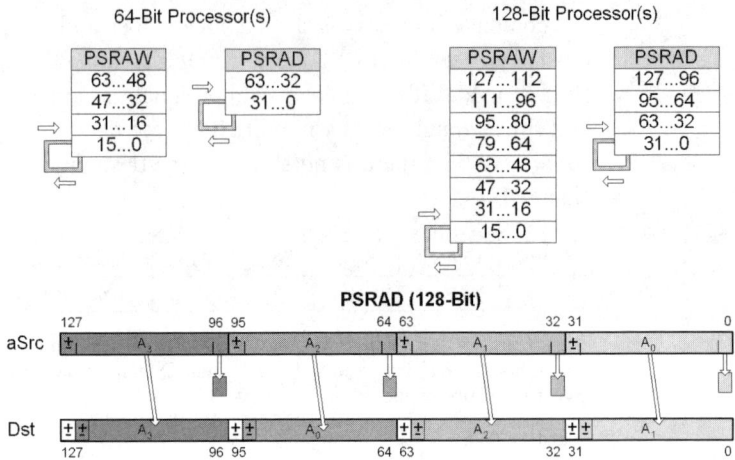

64-Bit Processor(s)                    128-Bit Processor(s)

| PSRAW |
|-------|
| 63...48 |
| 47...32 |
| 31...16 |
| 15...0 |

| PSRAD |
|-------|
| 63...32 |
| 31...0 |

| PSRAW |
|-------|
| 127...112 |
| 111...96 |
| 95...80 |
| 79...64 |
| 63...48 |
| 47...32 |
| 31...16 |
| 15...0 |

| PSRAD |
|-------|
| 127...96 |
| 95...64 |
| 63...32 |
| 31...0 |

**PSRAD (128-Bit)**

Figure 5-3: Miscellaneous examples of data types being arithmetically shifted to the right by one bit

| Mnemonic | P | PII | K6 | 3D! | 3Mx+ | SSE | SSE2 | A64 | SSE3 | E64T |
|----------|---|-----|----|----|------|-----|------|-----|------|------|
| PSRAx |   | ✓ | ✓ | ✓ | ✓ | ✓ | ✓ | ✓ | ✓ | ✓ |

MMX    psra(w/d) *mmxDst, count(#/mmx/m64)*    Signed    64
SSE2   psra(w/d) *xmmDst, count(#/xmm/m128)*    Signed    128

These multimedia and SIMD extension instructions are parallel operations that arithmetically right shift each of the data bit blocks by a *count* of bits. Depending on the processor and the instruction, block sizes of 16 or 32 bits can be shifted by the specified *count*.

This is a divisor ($2^n$) by shifting the MSB, a "sticky" bit, of each signed packed value of the source *aSrc (xmmSrc)*, causing all bits to be shifted to the right and the LSB of each packed value being lost; the result is stored in the destination *Dst (xmmDst)*. There is typically no Carry flag to save the bit. If the *count* indicating the number of bits to shift is more than (packed bits – 1) — 15 for (**W**ords) or 31 for (**D**Words) — then the destination will be typically set to the same value as the MSB, a value of zero. This is most effective when used in an integer math function where multiple signed numbers need to be divided by $2^n$ concurrently.

## Pseudo Vec

Pseudo vectors do not work well with this instruction due to the nature of the sticky bit. The technique demonstrated in a previous section of this chapter related to left shift discussed emulated vector processing by shifting followed by a logical AND, but it does not work with this instruction. If you really wish to investigate this further, my *Vector Game Math Processors* book has more information.

# Rotate Left (or n-Right)

A multimedia extension instruction for a parallel rotation does not exist at this time. To rotate data is a process of shifting up the lower bits, shifting down the upper bits, masking, and blending by the specified count. It is recommended to only rotate by one instead of an immediate or by another register.

## ROL — Rotate Left

ROL *destination, count*

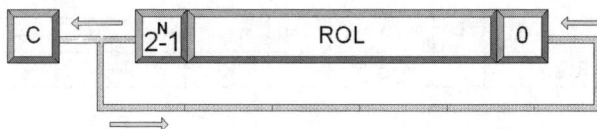

| Mnemonic | P | PII | K6 | 3D! | 3Mx+ | SSE | SSE2 | A64 | SSE3 | E64T |
|----------|---|-----|----|-----|------|-----|------|-----|------|------|
| ROL | ✓ | ✓ | ✓ | ✓ | ✓ | ✓ | ✓ | ✓ | ✓ | ✓ |

    rol   *rmDst(8/16/32/64), 1*       [Un]signed
    rol   *rmDst(8/16/32/64), #($2^n-1$)*
    rol   *rmDst(8/16/32/64), cl*

This instruction shifts the *destination* to the left and the most significant bit (MSB) is rotated into the carry and the least significant bit (LSB). The previous content of the carry is lost. This is like a wagon wheel with the bits going counterclockwise around and around shooting off bits like sparks. The *count* indicating the number of bits to rotate is invalid if it is greater than or equal to the width of data ($2^n$). If *count* = 0, then there is no shift and the destination and flags are not changed.

| Flags | O.flow | Sign | Zero | Aux | Parity | Carry |
|-------|--------|------|------|-----|--------|-------|
|       | X      | X    | X    | -   | X      | X     |

Flags: Carry = last bit rotated out of MSB, Zero = 1 if all *destination* bits are 0, thus *destination* = 0. If using a *count* of 1, then Overflow = the exclusive OR of the two MSBs before the rotate. (This is the same as the Carry XOR MSB after the rotate!) If the rotation is greater than 1, Overflow is undefined.

```
datd    dd    32
datw    dw    16
datb    db    8

        mov   dx,1010010110100101b  0a5a5h  carry=0

        rol   dx,1
              ; dx = 0100101101001011b  04b4bh  carry=1 OF=1
```

# RCL — Rotate Carry Left

RCL *destination, count*

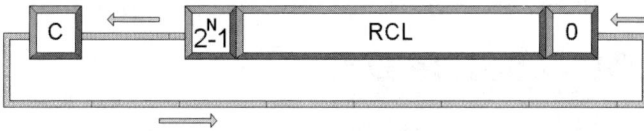

| Mnemonic | P | PII | K6 | 3D! | 3Mx+ | SSE | SSE2 | A64 | SSE3 | E64T |
|----------|---|-----|----|----|------|-----|------|-----|------|------|
| RCL      | ✓ | ✓   | ✓  | ✓  | ✓    | ✓   | ✓    | ✓   | ✓    | ✓    |

rcl    *rmDst(8/16/32/64), 1*          [Un]signed
rcl    *rmDst(8/16/32/64), #($2^n$–1)*
rcl    *rmDst(8/16/32/64), cl*

This instruction shifts the destination to the left, rotates the most significant bit (MSB) into the carry, and rotates the previous contents of the carry into the least significant bit (LSB). This is like a wagon wheel with an extra spoke. The *count* indicating the number of bits to rotate is invalid if it is greater than or equal to the width of data ($2^n$). If *count* = 0, then there is no shift and the destination and flags are not changed.

| Flags | O.flow | Sign | Zero | Aux | Parity | Carry |
|-------|--------|------|------|-----|--------|-------|
|       | X      | X    | X    | -   | X      | X     |

Flags: Carry = last bit rotated out, Zero = 1 if all *destination* bits are 0, thus *destination* = 0. If using a *count* of 1, then Overflow = the exclusive OR of the two MSBs before the rotate. (This is the same as the Carry XOR MSB after the rotate!) If the rotation is greater than 1, Overflow is undefined.

```
datd    dd      32
datw    dw      16
datb    db      8


        mov     dx,1010010110100101b  0a5a5h  carry=0

        rcl     dx,1
                ; dx = 0100101101001010b  04b45h  carry=1 Z=0 OF=1
```

This is effective for the shifting of monochrome data or masking planes, effectively making an image appear to move to the right.

```
; actual nibble mask    f00000000000ffff00e300080ff00ef7
Msk:    dd      00000000fh,0ffff0000h,080003e00h,07fe00ff0h


$Beg:   mov     esi,offset Msk+(16-4)
        add     edi,16-4
        mov     ecx,3-1                  ; 4 arguments

        mov     eax,[esi]
        shl     eax,1
        mov     [edi],eax

$L1:    mov     eax,[esi]
        rcl     eax,1
        mov     [edi],eax
        sub     edi,4
        sub     esi,4
        dec     ecx
        jne     $L1
```

# Rotate Right

## ROR — Rotate Right

ROR *destination, count*

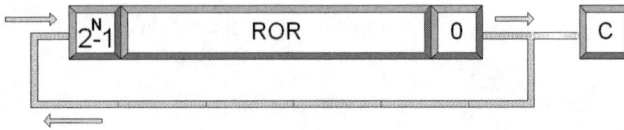

| Mnemonic | P | PII | K6 | 3D! | 3Mx+ | SSE | SSE2 | A64 | SSE3 | E64T |
|----------|---|-----|----|----|------|-----|------|-----|------|------|
| ROR | ✓ | ✓ | ✓ | ✓ | ✓ | ✓ | ✓ | ✓ | ✓ | ✓ |

ror  *rmDst(8/16/32/64), 1*        [Un]signed
ror  *rmDst(8/16/32/64), #(2ⁿ–1)*
ror  *rmDst(8/16/32/64), cl*

This instruction shifts the *destination* to the right and rotates the least significant bit (LSB) into the carry and the most significant bit (MSB). The previous content of the carry is lost. This is similar to a wagon wheel with the bits going clockwise around and around shooting off bits like sparks. The *count* indicating the number of bits to rotate is invalid if it is greater than or equal to the width of the data ($2^n$). If *count* = 0, then there is no shift and the destination and flags are not changed.

| Flags | O.flow | Sign | Zero | Aux | Parity | Carry |
|-------|--------|------|------|-----|--------|-------|
| | X | X | X | - | X | X |

Flags: Carry = last bit rotated out, Zero = 1 if all *destination* bits are 0; thus *destination* = 0. If using a *count* of 1, then Overflow = the exclusive OR of the two MSBs after the rotate. If the rotation is greater than 1, Overflow is undefined.

```
datd    dd      32
datw    dw      16
datb    db      8

        mov     dx,1010010110100101b  0a5a5h  carry=0

        ror     dx,1
        ; dx = 1101001011010010b  0d2d2h  carry=1 Z=0 OF=0
```

# RCR — Rotate Carry Right

RCR *destination, count*

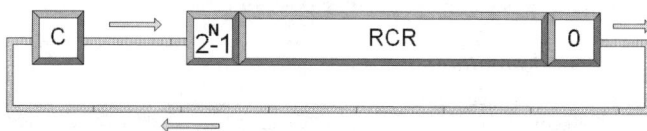

| Mnemonic | P | PII | K6 | 3D! | 3Mx+ | SSE | SSE2 | A64 | SSE3 | E64T |
|---|---|---|---|---|---|---|---|---|---|---|
| RCR | ✓ | ✓ | ✓ | ✓ | ✓ | ✓ | ✓ | ✓ | ✓ | ✓ |

rcr    *rmDst(8/16/32/64), 1*          [Un]signed
rcr    *rmDst(8/16/32/64), #(2^n–1)*
rcr    *rmDst(8/16/32/64), cl*

This instruction shifts the *destination* to the right and rotates the least significant bit (LSB) into the carry. The previous content of the carry is rotated into the most significant bit (MSB). This is like a wagon wheel with an extra spoke. The *count* indicating the number of bits to rotate is invalid if it is greater than or equal to the width of the data ($2^n$). If *count* = 0, then there is no shift and the destination and flags are not changed.

| **Flags** | O.flow | Sign | Zero | Aux | Parity | Carry |
|---|---|---|---|---|---|---|
| | X | X | X | - | X | X |

Flags: Carry = last bit rotated out, Zero = 1 if all *destination* bits are 0; thus *destination* = 0. If using a *count* of 1, then Overflow = the exclusive OR of the two MSBs after the rotate. If rotation is greater than 1, Overflow is undefined.

```
datd    dd      32
datw    dw      16
datb    db      8

        mov     dx,1010010110100101b  0a5a5h  carry=0

        rcr     dx,1
                ; dx = 0100101101001010b  0d2d2h  carry=1 Z=0 OF=1
```

# Bit Scanning

## BSF — Bit Scan Forward

BSF *destination, source*

| Mnemonic | P | PII | K6 | 3D! | 3Mx+ | SSE | SSE2 | A64 | SSE3 | E64T |
|----------|---|-----|----|----|------|-----|------|-----|------|------|
| BSF | ✓ | ✓ | ✓ | ✓ | ✓ | ✓ | ✓ | ✓ | ✓ | ✓ |

bsf   *rDst, rmSrc(16/32/64)*      [Un]signed

This instruction scans the *source* for the least significant bit (LSB); if found, it sets the *destination* to the index (0…n). If the *source* is set to 0, the *destination* is undefined.

| **Flags** | O.flow | Sign | Zero | Aux | Parity | Carry |
|-----------|--------|------|------|-----|--------|-------|
| | - | - | X | - | - | - |

Flags: If the source is zero, then the Zero flag is set to 1; else it is set to 0.

```
                          ; ebx = some value
        mov    ecx,0      ; Preset to zero in case ebx is 0.
        mov    ebx,eax
        bsf    ecx,ebx    ; ecx contains the bit setting
        shr    ebx,cl     ; Down shift the data
```

**Note:** Preset the BSF destination to zero if the source is not guaranteed to be not zero (unless you plan to branch if zero).

## BSR — Bit Scan Reverse

BSR *destination, source*

| Mnemonic | P | PII | K6 | 3D! | 3Mx+ | SSE | SSE2 | A64 | SSE3 | E64T |
|----------|---|-----|----|----|------|-----|------|-----|------|------|
| BSR | ✓ | ✓ | ✓ | ✓ | ✓ | ✓ | ✓ | ✓ | ✓ | ✓ |

bsr   *rDst, rmSrc(16/32/64)*      [Un]signed

This instruction scans the *source* for the most significant bit (MSB); if found, it sets the *destination* to the index (0..n). If the *source* is set to 0, the *destination* is undefined.

| Flags | O.flow | Sign | Zero | Aux | Parity | Carry |
|-------|--------|------|------|-----|--------|-------|
|       | -      | -    | X    | -   | -      | -     |

Flags: If the source is zero, then the Zero flag is set to 1; else it is set to 0.

# ToolBox Snippet — Get Bit Count

Here is an obvious use for an 80x86 instruction versus generic C code. In various compression and data packing methods, it is sometimes necessary to find out the maximum number of bits needed to store a value from a list of values, such as how many bits it takes to compress a piece of data. For example, if we take a histogram of all the colors in a bitmap and the highest count is 53 colors $(53 - 1 = 52)$ (034h) (110100b), then it would take 6 bits to store it:

$$2^6=64 \quad 2^5=32 \quad 64 \geq 53 > 32 \quad \text{so too big for } 2^5 \text{ bits.}$$

The following calculates the number of bits needed to store an unsigned value.

```
uint CountBits(uint val)
{
     uint nCnt;

#if 01
               // Use this! VERY MUCH FASTER than a bit scanner!
               // Reverse scan for MSB
          __asm {
          mov    eax,0              // Set to zero, in case val is zero.
                 bsr    eax,val     // N...0      Bit index
                 inc    eax         // N+1...1    # of bits
                 mov    nCnt,eax
          };
#else
     uint nBit = 0x80000000;
     nCnt = 32;

     while ((nCnt > 1) && (0 == (nBit & val)))
     {
          nCnt--;
          nBit >>= 1;
     }
#endif

     return nCnt;
```

So if you had numerous numbers to crunch, which of the code snippet algorithms just shown would you rather utilize? A couple instructions of assembly in the upper conditional code or looping up to 31 times maximum for each 32-bit integer value as shown in the lower conditional code?

# Graphics 101 — Palette Bits

There is a problem when writing graphics-based applications for Win32. If graphics is 256 color, then the palette is a table lookup. If 24- or 32-bit true color, then the RGB bit orientation is standardized, but if in 16-bit hi-color, then you have a problem. There is no standard, however, although there seem to be two orientations: {5:5:5} and {5:6:5}. But which does that card you are trying to run your application on really use? Direct Draw solved this problem, as you can request the bit and mask information, but what if you are writing a Windows application running under GDI, or a DOS application, or whatever? If your source art is 256 color, you would need to create a conversion table to match your graphics mode. If you have Targa art files that are {5:5:5} and the graphics card is {5:6:5}, you would need to detect this and compensate for it. You will have to paste this code section into your own C code. So, my apologies to those only interested in pure assembly.

---

**Tip:**    These days there is typically not a good reason for pure assembly code. It is a waste of programming resources.

Sorry if I am offending any of you speed freaks. I personally happen to like to squeeze every last drop of clock cycle out of my CPU, but development projects are about balance: code size vs. code speed. Project budget vs. time constraints. There are also portability issues, but these are usually resolved through abstraction where function pointers are used to vector to generic C or custom assembler based upon processor requirements.

```
// Color Masking information

typedef struct RGBInfoType
{
    uint RedMask;
    uint GreenMask;
    uint BlueMask;
    uint RedShift;
    uint GreenShift;
    uint BlueShift;
    uint zRedShift;
    uint zGreenShift;
    uint zBlueShift;
} RGBInfo;
```

```
// If a fixed palette then get 16/24/32-bit color masking information.

// hDC = (HDC) DC to window
// wgInfo = (BITMAPINFOHEADER)
// nDepth = BitsPerPixel;

HBITMAP hBitmap;
byte *pBMap;
RGBInfo info;

hBitmap = CreateDIBSection(hDC, (BITMAPINFO *) &wgInfo,
            DIB_PAL_COLORS, (VOID **) &pBMap,
            (HANDLE) NULL, (DWORD) NULL);
if (hBitmap != NULL)
{
    HBRUSH hBrush;
    RECT rect;

    rect.left = rect.top = 0;
    rect.right = rect.bottom = 2;

        // Test for Red Mask bits
    hBrush = CreateSolidBrush(0x000000ff); // 0x00bbggrr
    FillRect(hDC, &rect, hBrush);
    info.RedMask = *(DWORD *)(pBMap);

        // Test for Green Mask bits
    hBrush = CreateSolidBrush(0x0000ff00); // 0x00bbggrr
    FillRect(hDC, &rect, hBrush);
    info.GreenMask = *(DWORD *)(pBMap);

        // Test for Blue Mask bits
    hBrush = CreateSolidBrush(0x00ff0000); // 0x00bbggrr
    FillRect(hDC, &rect, hBrush);
    info.BlueMask = *(DWORD *)(pBMap);

        // Now analyze
    gfxGetColorMasks(nDepth, &info);
}
```

Now we come to the fun part. Normally we would only call these function pairs once during program initialization, so it does not need to be very fast. However, the BSF and BSR instructions are two that do not translate well to C code. They would need a slowpoke bit-shifting loop, so I thought it would be a good example and a function that you would be able to use in your own graphic applications.

```
; Color masking information

RGBInfo STRUCT 4
    RedMask    dd    0        ; Red color mask
    GreenMask  dd    0        ; Green color mask
```

```
        BlueMask    dd    0        ; Blue color mask
; These bits are used to shift the bits into position
        RedShft     dd    0        ; Red shift bits up
        GreenShft   dd    0        ; Green shift bits up
        BlueShft    dd    0        ; Blue shift bits up
; These bits are used to reduce the bits needed
        zRedShft    dd    0        ; Red shift bits down
        zGreenShft  dd    0        ; Green shift bits down
        zBlueShft   dd    0        ; Blue shift bits down
RGBInfo     ENDS


;  Get fixed palette color mask information

;bool gfxGetColorMasks(uint nDepth, RGBInfo *pInfo)

        public  gfxGetColorMasks
gfxGetColorMasks proc near
        push    ebp
        mov     ebp,esp

        mov     eax,[ebp+arg1]    ; nDepth - Get pixel depth
        push    esi
        shr     eax,3             ; n÷8
        push    ebx
        mov     ebx,RGBMsks[eax*4] ; Get Premask
        mov     esi,[ebp+arg2]    ; pInfo - Get (RGBInfo *)
        test    ebx,ebx
        jz      $Xit              ; false (failure)

        ; Save masks. Get position of first and last
        ; bits in mask for each color!

        ; Green bits
        mov     eax,(RGBInfo PTR [esi]).GreenMask
        and     eax,ebx               ; AND with mask
        mov     (RGBInfo PTR [esi]).GreenMask,eax
        bsf     ecx,eax               ; get LSB set to 1
        bsr     edx,eax               ; get MSB set to 1
        mov     (RGBInfo PTR [esi]).GreenShft,ecx
        sub     edx,ecx
        add     edx,-7
        neg     edx
        mov     (RGBInfo PTR [esi]).zGreenShft,edx

        ;Blue bits
        mov     eax,(RGBInfo PTR [esi]).BlueMask
        and     eax,ebx
        mov     (RGBInfo PTR [esi]).BlueMask,eax
        bsf     ecx,eax               ; get LSB set to 1
        bsr     edx,eax               ; get MSB set to 1
        mov     (RGBInfo PTR [esi]).BlueShft,ecx
        sub     edx,ecx
        add     edx,-7
        neg     edx
```

```
mov      (RGBInfo PTR [esi]).zBlueShft,edx

;Red bits
mov      eax,(RGBInfo PTR [esi]).RedMask
and      eax,ebx
mov      (RGBInfo PTR [esi]).RedMask,eax
bsf      ecx,eax            ; get LSB set to 1
bsr      edx,eax            ; get MSB set to 1
mov      (RGBInfo PTR [esi]).RedShft,ecx
sub      edx,ecx
add      edx,-7
neg      edx
mov      (RGBInfo PTR [esi]).zRedShft,edx

mov      eax,1              ; true (success)

$Xit: pop     ebx
      pop     esi
      pop     ebp
      ret                        ; Return eax
gfxGetColorMasks endp
```

# Exercises

1.  With a 32-bit data element size, what is the result of a logical right shifting of the following data by 34 bits? With an arithmetic right shift? With a logical left shift?

    0xB83DE7820

2.  Write a function to count the number of bits to contain a *signed* value.

3.  Write a packed 16× 8-bit SAR, using pseudo vector code.

4.  Write a packed 16× 8-bit SAR, using SIMD instructions.

5.  Write a packed ROL using SIMD.

    a)  8-bit

    b)  16-bit

    c)  32-bit

6.  Write a packed ROR using SIMD.

    a)  8-bit

    b)  16-bit

    c)  32-bit

# Chapter 6

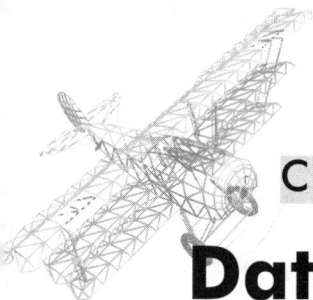

# Data Conversion

## Data Interlacing, Exchanging, Unpacking, and Merging

Data must sometimes be interlaced to get it into a form that can be easily handled. By understanding how to interlace and de-interlace data, a most productive solution can be found for solving an expression.

The instructions in this chapter are easier to understand through visualization, and each processor has its set of instructions that it handles, but here is where data swizzling can easily be confusing: converting data from the output of one instruction and used as the input of another.

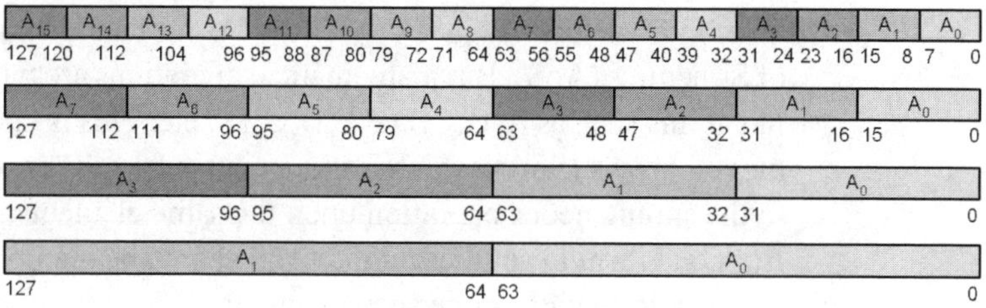


*Figure 6-1: Little-endian data conversion*

As a guide to assist you in remembering big- versus little-endian orientations, the following are the placement of bytes within the 64-bit data diagrams used in this chapter. Keep in mind that each 64-bit block is a repeat of the previous block.

Little-Endian

```
0x88,0x99,0xaa,0xbb,0xcc,0xdd,0xee,0xff  (8-bit)
  0x9988,   0xbbaa,   0xddcc,   0xffee   (16-bit)
     0xaab9988,          0xffeeddcc      (32-bit)
```

## Big-Endian

```
0x88,0x99,0xaa,0xbb,0xcc,0xdd,0xee,0xff  (8-bit)
  0x8899,   0xaabb,   0xccdd,   0xeeff   (16-bit)
    0x8899aabb,            0xccddeeff    (32-bit)
```

The one thing to remember here is that the data elements are isolated from each other. The $A_n$ placement of each element is related to its position. For example, when related to a quad vector:

$$A_0 : A_x, \quad A_1 : A_y, \quad A_2 : A_z, \quad \text{and } A_3 : A_w.$$

So that means that $A_w\, A_z\, A_y\, A_x$ are visually on the far right just like $A_3$ $A_2\, A_1\, A_0$ for little-endian, and $A_x, A_y, A_z, A_w$ are on the far left just like $A_0, A_1, A_2, A_3$ for big-endian.

As long as you get the element positions correct for your processor, then the data flow represented by the arrows in the diagrams will be correct.

**Note:** The bit indicators on the diagrams in this section are in *little-endian* byte order.

Quite often, data needs to be migrated from one form to another, and a single instruction may not be sufficient. For instance, a matrix is made up of four vectors: $A_{xyzw}, B_{xyzw}, C_{xyzw}, D_{xyzw}$. This is known as an Array of Structures (AoS). But mathematical operations are typically between like terms such as $A_xB_xC_xD_x$, $A_yB_yC_yD_y$, etc. This is known as a Structure of Arrays (SoA), which is more matrix friendly (and efficient) due to the simultaneous operation upon the same elements. To get the data from one form to another requires the data to be manipulated.

The following is one such example.

Array of Structures (AoS)

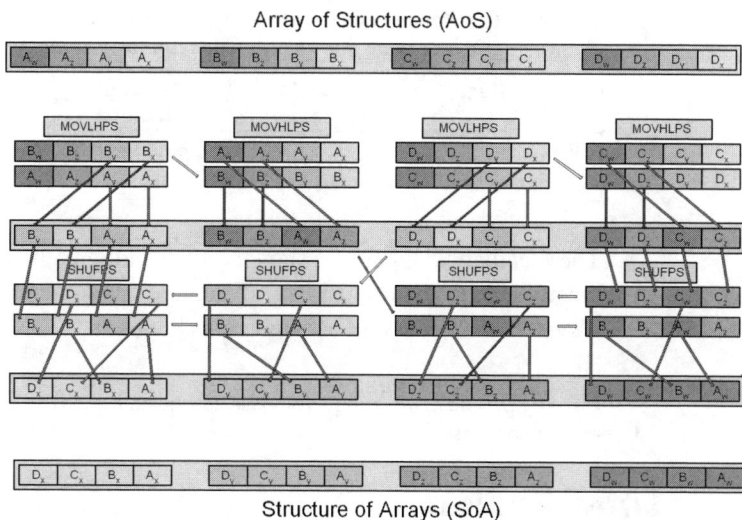

Structure of Arrays (SoA)

*Figure 6-2: AoS to SoA SIMD conversion*

# Byte Swapping

Before exploring various methods of converting data, let us first examine the method most often needed: The endian conversion! The handling of big- and little-endian was initially discussed in Chapter 3 but let us re-examine.

If your application is designed to be multiplatform, then having multiple endian declarations might make your life easier. Having Endian16(), Endian32(), Endian64(), and Endian128() conversion functions are one thing, but having extra declarations such as BigEndian64() versus LittleEndian64() that map to either a stub macro or an Endian64 converter will save you some time. The data file being read will be in a known endian orientation. The target platform knows what it needs, so if the big-endian label is used if the source data is known to be big-endian and vice versa for little-endian, then the use of that declaration will resolve any confusion. This will work for any platform!

*Table 6-1: Correlation between little- and big-endian orientation and whether a byte swap or a stub function is implemented*

| Source Data | Big-Endian Machine | Little-Endian Machine |
|---|---|---|
| BigEndian( ) | -stub- | Byte swap |
| LittleEndian( ) | Byte swap | -stub- |

These endian wrappers are shown only for little-endian as this book is mostly meant for little-endian. If you are truly interested, my *Vector Game Math Processors* book contains both sets.

**Hint:** Use descriptive big- versus little-endian macros to simplify endian conversion.

# Little-Endian

#define VMP_LITTLE_ENDIAN

This is oversimplifying it and there are better methods such as the BSWAP instruction on the 80x86, but this is a generic method for cross-platform portability.

*Listing 6-1: Generic 32-bit endian conversion*

```
int32 VMP_ENDIAN32(int32 val)
{
  uint8 buf[4];

  buf[ 0 ]=*(((uint8*)&val)+3);   // = [3]
  buf[ 1 ]=*(((uint8*)&val)+2);   // = [2]
  buf[ 2 ]=*(((uint8*)&val)+1);   // = [1]
  buf[ 3 ]=*(((uint8*)&val)+0);   // = [0]
  return *(int32*)buf;
}
```

*Listing 6-2: Generic 16-bit endian conversion*

```
int16 VMP_ENDIAN16(int16 val)
{
  uint8 buf[2];

  buf[ 0 ]=*(((uint8*)&val)+1);   // = [1]
  buf[ 1 ]=*(((uint8*)&val)+0);   // = [0]
  return *(int16*)buf;
}
```

The typecasting camouflages it a bit, but it is merely a byte read-write with inverse offsets. I will leave the actual endian implementation up to you! Just remember that it is preferable to have the tools handle your endian conversion so that a game application does not have to. And since tools exercise the same data over and over for the length of a project, you might as well make them as efficient as possible.

For cross-platform compatibility I refer to the following as a little pretzel logic. It looks a little twisted, but if you dig a little deeper it becomes what it is — slicker 'n snail snot!

# (Big/Little)-Endian to (Big/Little)-Endian Data Relationship Macros

*Listing 6-3: KariType.h*

```
#ifdef VMP_LITTLE_ENDIAN    // Little-endian processor

        // Big-endian data on little-endian processor
    #define VMP_BIG_ENDIAN32        VMP_ENDIAN32
    #define VMP_BIG_ENDIAN16        VMP_ENDIAN16

        // Little-endian data on little-endian processor
    #define VMP_LITTLE_ENDIAN32                 // stub
    #define VMP_LITTLE_ENDIAN16                 // stub

#endif
```

Note that same endian to same endian assignment merely stubs out the macro, so no conversion is needed or implemented. One only needs to know what byte order the data is in and what order is needed, and use the appropriate macro. It will then be cross-platform compatible to *all* other platforms as long as the endian flag is set properly for that platform.

Neat, huh? No extra #ifdef cluttering up the code!

# BSWAP — Byte Swap

BSWAP *destination*

| Mnemonic | P | PII | K6 | 3D! | 3Mx+ | SSE | SSE2 | A64 | SSE3 | E64T |
|----------|---|-----|----|-----|------|-----|------|-----|------|------|
| BSWAP | ✓ | ✓ | ✓ | ✓ | ✓ | ✓ | ✓ | ✓ | ✓ | ✓ |

bswap    *rDst(32/64)*     [Un]signed

This general-purpose instruction does a big/little-endian conversion. It reverses the byte order of a 32-bit or 64-bit register.

| | D31-D24 | D23-D16 | D15-D8 | D7-D0 |
|---|---|---|---|---|
| BEFORE | D | C | B | A |
| AFTER | A | B | C | D |

```
bswap eax
```

This is used in the conversion of communications messages from big-endian platforms such as Unix or Macintosh, or file formats such as TIFF, MIDI, etc.

| Flags | O.flow | Sign | Zero | Aux | Parity | Carry |
|---|---|---|---|---|---|---|
| | - | - | - | - | - | - |

Flags: None are altered by this opcode.

The C code equivalent is slow, especially when compared to the speed of a BSWAP instruction. I normally do not believe in in-line assembly as it makes code less portable to other platforms, but here is one of my rare exceptions. Note that compiling C with optimization set for speed should truly embed the Endian32 function into your code like a macro.

*Listing 6-4: BSWAP-based 32-bit endian conversion*

```
int32 VMP_ENDIAN32(int32 val)
{
    _asm {
        mov     eax,val
        bswap   eax
        mov     val,eax
    };

    return val;
}
```

For those of you working with an embedded 8086…80386 processor, a 16-bit endian conversion can be accomplished with a ROR, which would have the same effect as an XCHG; however, it is more efficient depending on the processor manufacturer and model.

When using that same technique for 32-bit endian conversion, it should be noted that the ROR will cause a stall performing an operation with the EAX register after the write to the AX. So use the BSWAP on the Pentiums!

|         | **Best** | **Worst**                           |
|---------|----------|-------------------------------------|
|         | bswap    | ror ax,8<br>ror eax,16<br>ror ax,8 |
| P bytes | 2        | 11                                  |
| R bytes | 3        | 10                                  |

---

*Listing 6-5: 32-bit mode : 64-bit endian conversion*

```
mov     eax,[ebx+4]     ; Bits 32...63
mov     edx,[ebx+0]     ; Bits 0...31
bswap   eax             ; Upper bits
bswap   edx             ; Lower bits
ret                     ; edx:eax
```

---

*Listing 6-6: 64-bit mode : 64-bit endian conversion*

```
bswap   rax             ; Convert all 8 bytes.
```

# PSWAPD — Packed Swap Double Word

pswapd *destination, source*  (2×32-bit)  (2×SPFP)

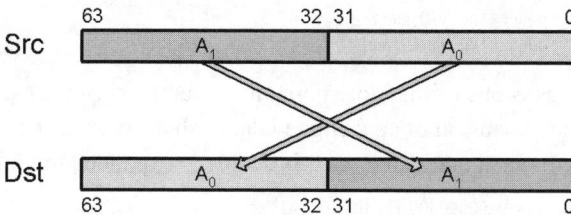

| Mnemonic | P | PII | K6 | 3D! | 3Mx+ | SSE | SSE2 | A64 | SSE3 | E64T |
|----------|---|-----|-----|-----|------|-----|------|-----|------|------|
| PSWAPD   |   |     |     |     | ✓    |     |      | ✓   |      |      |

3DNow!+  pswapd *mmxDst, mmxSrc/m64*    [Un]signed      64
                                        Single-precision

```
pswapd mm0,mm1
```

If this functionality is needed, it can be emulated with the following:

```
movq        mm0,mm1     ; y x
punpckldq   mm1,mm1     ; x x
punpckhdq   mm0,mm1     ; x y
```

# Data Interlacing

## PUNPCKLBW — Parallel Extend Lower from Byte

punpcklbw *destination*, *source*  (8×8-bit)  (16×8-bit)

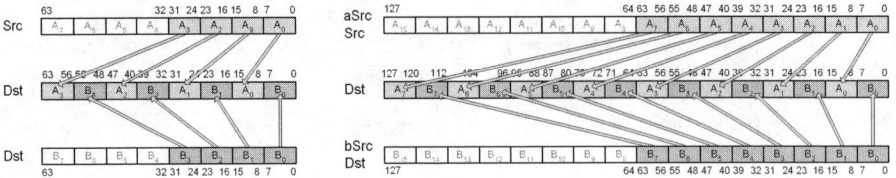

| Mnemonic | P | PII | K6 | 3D! | 3Mx+ | SSE | SSE2 | A64 | SSE3 | E64T |
|----------|---|-----|-----|-----|------|-----|------|-----|------|------|
| PUNPCKLBW | | ✓ | ✓ | ✓ | ✓ | ✓ | ✓ | ✓ | ✓ | ✓ |

MMX   punpcklbw *mmxDst, mmxSrc/m64*    [Un]signed    64

SSE2   punpcklbw *xmmDst, xmmSrc/m128*  [Un]signed  128

```
punpcklbw mm0,mm1
punpcklbw xmm0,xmm1
```

This is one of the more popular instructions as it is extremely useful in the expansion of an unsigned data value. By interlacing a value of zero with an actual value, an 8-bit value is expanded to 16 bits.

```
A = 0x00000000    B = 0x44332211

D = 00  44  00  33  00  22  00  11
    0044    0033    0022    0011

punpcklbw  mm0,mm0 ; {w w z z y y x x}  ← {u t s r w z y x}
```

# PUNPCKHBW — Parallel Extend Upper from Byte

punpckhbw *destination*, *source*  (8×8-bit)  (16×8-bit)

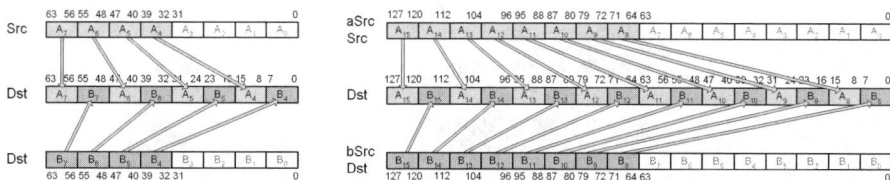

| Mnemonic | P | PII | K6 | 3D! | 3Mx+ | SSE | SSE2 | A64 | SSE3 | E64T |
|----------|---|-----|----|----|------|-----|------|-----|------|------|
| PUNPCKHBW | | ✓ | ✓ | ✓ | ✓ | ✓ | ✓ | ✓ | ✓ | ✓ |

| MMX | punpckhbw *mmxDst, mmxSrc/m64* | [Un]signed | 64 |
| SSE2 | punpckhbw *xmmDst, xmmSrc/m128* | [Un]signed | 128 |

```
punpckhbw mm0,mm1
punpckhbw xmm0,xmm1

fooa    qword 0ffffa5a55a5a0000h
foob    qword 08000003f007f00ffh

        movq    mm7,fooa
        movq    mm6,foob
        punpckhbw mm7,mm6

; 80 00 00 3f 00 7f 00 ff   ff ff a5 a5 5a 5a 00 00
;                became
;  80 ff 00 ff 00 a5 3f a5

punpckhbw  mm0,mm0 ; {u u t t s s r r}   ←   {u t s r w z y x}
```

# PUNPCKLWD — Parallel Extend Lower from 16-Bit

punpcklwd *destination*, *source*  (4×16-bit)  (8×16-bit)

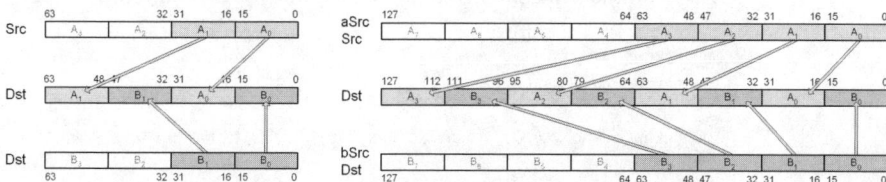

| Mnemonic | P | PII | K6 | 3D! | 3Mx+ | SSE | SSE2 | A64 | SSE3 | E64T |
|----------|---|-----|----|----|------|-----|------|-----|------|------|
| PUNPCKLWD | | ✓ | ✓ | ✓ | ✓ | ✓ | ✓ | ✓ | ✓ | ✓ |

MMX   punpcklwd *mmxDst, mmxSrc/m64*   [Un]signed   64
SSE2   punpcklwd *xmmDst, xmmSrc/m128*   [Un]signed   128

```
punpcklwd mm0,mm1
punpcklwd xmm0,xmm1

fooa    qword Offffa5a55a5a0000h
foob    qword 08000003f007f00ffh

        movq    mm7,fooa
        movq    mm6,foob
        punpcklwd mm7,mm6

; 8000 003f 007f 00ff   ffff a5a5 5a5a 0000
;                 became
;   007f 5a5a 00ff 0000

punpcklwd  xmm0,xmm0 ; {w w z z y y x x}  ← {u t s r w z y x}
```

# PUNPCKHWD — Parallel Extend Upper from 16-Bit

punpckhwd *destination, source*  (4×16-bit)  (8×16-bit)

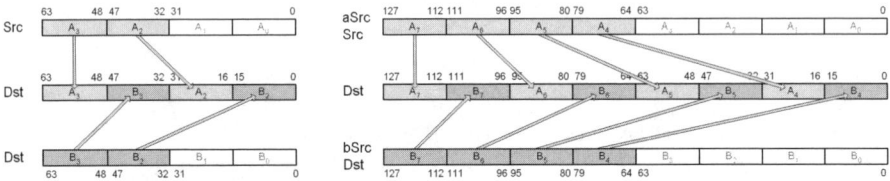

| Mnemonic | P | PII | K6 | 3D! | 3Mx+ | SSE | SSE2 | A64 | SSE3 | E64T |
|----------|---|-----|----|----|------|-----|------|-----|------|------|
| PUNPCKHWD | | ✓ | ✓ | ✓ | ✓ | ✓ | ✓ | ✓ | ✓ | ✓ |

MMX   punpckhwd *mmxDst, mmxSrc/m64*   [Un]signed   64
SSE2   punpckhwd *xmmDst, xmmSrc/m128*   [Un]signed   128

```
punpckhwd mm0,mm1
punpckhwd xmm0,xmm1

punpckhwd  xmm0,xmm0 ; {u u t t s s r r}  ← {u t s r w z y x}
```

# PUNPCKLDQ — Parallel Extend Lower from 32-Bit

## Also: (Unpack and Interleave Low Packed SPFP)

punpckldq *destination, source* (2×32-bit) (4×32-bit)

unpcklps *destination, source* (4×SPFP)

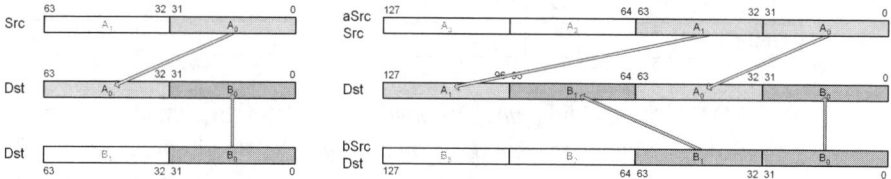

| Mnemonic | P | PII | K6 | 3D! | 3Mx+ | SSE | SSE2 | A64 | SSE3 | E64T |
|---|---|---|---|---|---|---|---|---|---|---|
| PUNPCKLDQ | | ✓ | ✓ | ✓ | ✓ | ✓ | ✓ | ✓ | ✓ | ✓ |
| UNPCKLPS | | | | | | ✓ | ✓ | ✓ | ✓ | ✓ |

| | | | | |
|---|---|---|---|---|
| MMX | punpckldq *mmxDst, mmxSrc/m64* | [Un]signed | 64 |
| SSE | unpcklps *xmmDst, xmmSrc/m128* | Single-precision | 128 |
| SSE2 | punpckldq *xmmDst, xmmSrc/m128* | [Un]signed | 128 |

```
punpckldq mm0,mm1
unpcklps  xmm0,xmm1
punpckldq xmm0,xmm1
```

If a "splat" functionality is needed, it can be emulated with the following:

```
punpckldq mm0,mm0    ; 64-bit    {x x}    A =    {y x}
punpckldq xmm0,xmm0  ; 128-bit {y y x x}  A = {w z y x}
```

# PUNPCKHDQ — Parallel Extend Upper from 32-Bit

## ALSO: (Unpack and Interleave High Packed SPFP)

punpckhdq *destination, source* (2×32-bit) (4×32-bit)

unpckhps *destination, source* (4×SPFP)

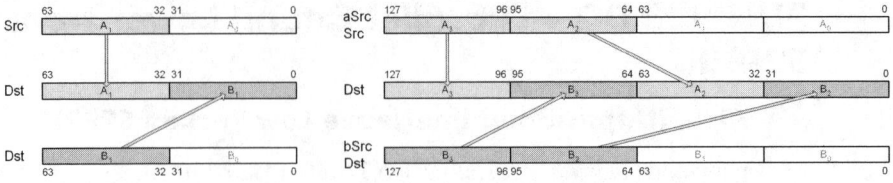

| Mnemonic | P | PII | K6 | 3D! | 3Mx+ | SSE | SSE2 | A64 | SSE3 | E64T |
|----------|---|-----|-----|-----|------|-----|------|-----|------|------|
| PUNPCKHDQ | | ✓ | ✓ | ✓ | ✓ | ✓ | ✓ | ✓ | ✓ | ✓ |
| UNPCKHPS | | | | | | ✓ | ✓ | ✓ | ✓ | ✓ |

| | | | | |
|---|---|---|---|---|
| MMX | punpckhdq *mmxDst, mmxSrc/m64* | [Un]signed | 64 |
| SSE | unpckhps *xmmDst, xmmSrc/m128* | Single-precision | 128 |
| SSE2 | punpckhdq *xmmDst, xmmSrc/m128* | [Un]signed | 128 |

```
punpckhdq  mm0,mm1
unpckhps   xmm0,xmm1
punpckhdq  xmm0,xmm1
```

```
fooa    qword 0ffffa5a55a5a0000h
foob    qword 08000003f007f00ffh


        movq    mm7,fooa
        movq    mm6,foob
        punpckhdq mm7,mm6
```

```
; 8000003f 007f00ff   ffffa5a5 5a5a0000
;               becomes
;           007f00ff   5a5a0000
```

If a "splat" functionality is needed, it can be emulated with the following:

```
punpckhdq  mm0,mm0    ; 64-bit    {y y}    ←    {y x}
punpckhdq  xmm0,xmm0  ; 128-bit {w w z z}  ← {w z y x}
```

# MOVSS — Move Scalar (SPFP)

movss *destination, source*

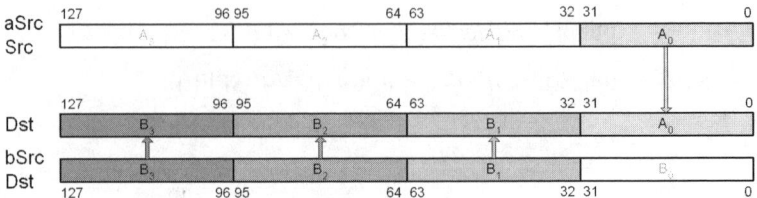

| Mnemonic | P | PII | K6 | 3D! | 3Mx+ | SSE | SSE2 | A64 | SSE3 | E64T |
|----------|---|-----|-----|-----|------|-----|------|-----|------|------|
| MOVSS    |   |     |     |     |      | ✓   | ✓    | ✓   | ✓    | ✓    |

SSE    movss *xmmDst, xmmSrc/m32*     Single-precision   128
"      movss *xmmDst/m32, xmmSrc*

This SSE instruction copies the least significant single-precision float-ing-point scalar value from 32-bit memory *aSrc* and copies it to destination *Dst*. Source and destination can be XMM register, XMM to 32-bit memory, or 32-bit memory to XMM scalar copy.

# MOVQ2DQ — Move Scalar (1×32-Bit) MMX to XMM

movq2dq *destination, source*

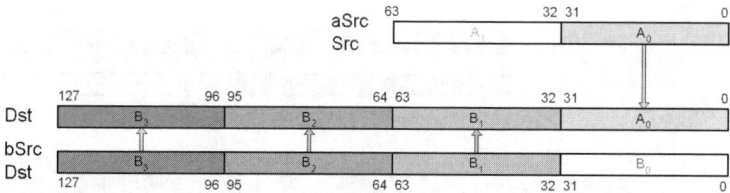

| Mnemonic | P | PII | K6 | 3D! | 3Mx+ | SSE | SSE2 | A64 | SSE3 | E64T |
|----------|---|-----|-----|-----|------|-----|------|-----|------|------|
| MOVQ2DQ  |   |     |     |     |      |     | ✓    | ✓   | ✓    | ✓    |

SSE    movq2dq *xmmDst, mmxSrc(mmx/m32)*   [Un]signed   128

This SSE instruction copies the least significant 32-bit unsigned scalar value from MMX or 32-bit memory *aSrc* and copies it to XMM destina-tion *Dst*. Other elements remain unchanged.

# MOVDQ2Q — Move Scalar (1×32-bit) XMM to MMX

movdq2q *destination, source*

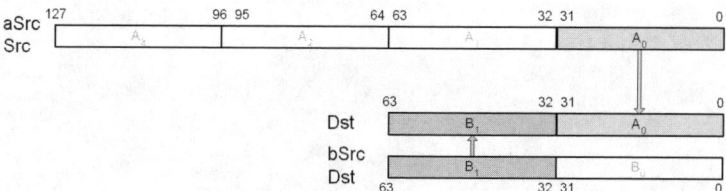

| Mnemonic | P | PII | K6 | 3D! | 3Mx+ | SSE | SSE2 | A64 | SSE3 | E64T |
|----------|---|-----|----|----|------|-----|------|-----|------|------|
| MOVDQ2Q |   |     |    |    |      |     | ✓    | ✓   | ✓    | ✓    |

SSE     movdq2q *mmxDst, (xmmSrc/m32)*     [Un]signed     128

This SSE instruction copies the least significant 32-bit unsigned scalar value from XMM or 32-bit memory *aSrc* to the least significant 32-bit element of the MMX destination *Dst*. The other element of *Dst* remains unchanged.

# MOVLPS — Move Low Packed (2×SPFP)

movlps *destination, source*

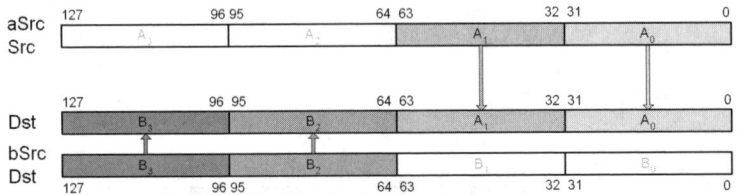

| Mnemonic | P | PII | K6 | 3D! | 3Mx+ | SSE | SSE2 | A64 | SSE3 | E64T |
|----------|---|-----|----|----|------|-----|------|-----|------|------|
| MOVLPS |   |     |    |    |      | ✓   | ✓    | ✓   | ✓    | ✓    |

SSE     movlps *xmmDst, mSrc64*     Single-precision     128
"       movlps *mDst64, xmmSrc*

This SSE instruction copies the two least significant single-precision floating-point values from XMM source register or 32-bit memory *aSrc* to the two least significant single-precision floating-point elements of the XMM destination *Dst*. The other elements of *Dst* remain unchanged.

# MOVHPS — Move High Packed (2×SPFP)

movhps *destination, source*

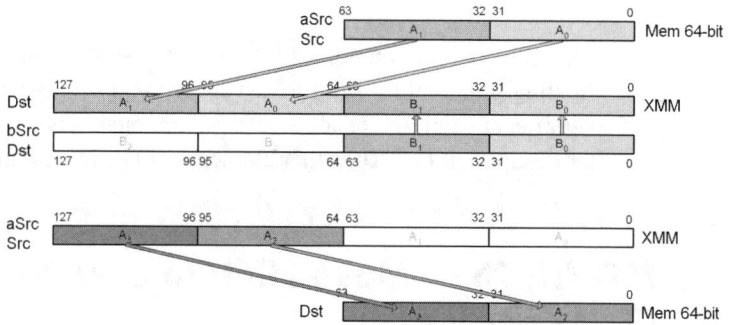

| Mnemonic | P | PII | K6 | 3D! | 3Mx+ | SSE | SSE2 | A64 | SSE3 | E64T |
|----------|---|-----|----|----|------|-----|------|-----|------|------|
| MOVHPS   |   |     |    |    |      | ✓   | ✓    | ✓   | ✓    | ✓    |

| SSE | movhps *xmmDst, m64* | Single-precision | 128 |
|-----|----------------------|------------------|-----|
| "   | movhps *m64, xmmSrc* |                  |     |

When the source is memory, this SSE instruction copies the two single-precision floating-point values from 64-bit memory *aSrc* and copies them to the two most significant single-precision floating-point elements within an XMM register specified by *Dst*. When *aSrc* is an XMM register, the two most significant single-precision floating-point values are copied to 64-bit memory *Dst*.

# MOVLHPS — Move Low to High Packed (2×SPFP)

movlhps *destination, source*

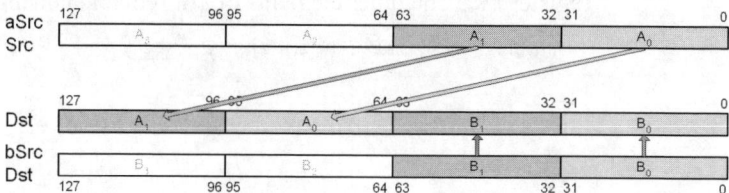

| Mnemonic | P | PII | K6 | 3D! | 3Mx+ | SSE | SSE2 | A64 | SSE3 | E64T |
|----------|---|-----|----|-----|------|-----|------|-----|------|------|
| MOVLHPS  |   |     |    |     |      | ✓   | ✓    | ✓   | ✓    | ✓    |

SSE    movlhps *xmmDst, xmmSrc*    Single-precision    128

This SSE instruction copies the two least significant single-precision floating-point values from XMM source register *aSrc* to the two most significant single-precision floating-point elements of the XMM register destination *Dst*. The other elements of *Dst* remain unchanged.

```
movlhps  xmm0,xmm0  ; {y x y x}  ←  {w z y x}
```

# MOVHLPS — Move High to Low Packed (2×SPFP)

movhlps *destination, source*

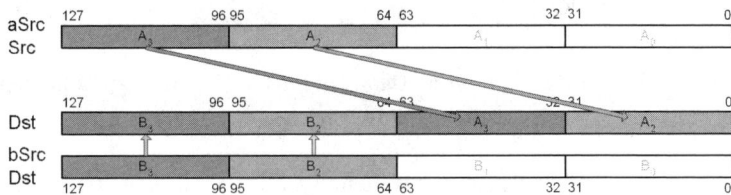

| Mnemonic | P | PII | K6 | 3D! | 3Mx+ | SSE | SSE2 | A64 | SSE3 | E64T |
|----------|---|-----|----|-----|------|-----|------|-----|------|------|
| MOVHLPS  |   |     |    |     |      | ✓   | ✓    | ✓   | ✓    | ✓    |

SSE    movhlps *xmmDst, xmmSrc*    Single-precision    128

This SSE instruction copies the two most significant single-precision floating-point values from the XMM register *aSrc* to the two least significant single-precision floating-point elements of destination XMM register *Dst*. The other elements of *Dst* remain unchanged.

```
movhlps  xmm0,xmm0  ; {w z w z}  ←  {w z y x}
```

# MOVSD — Move Scalar (1×DPFP)

movsd *destination, source*

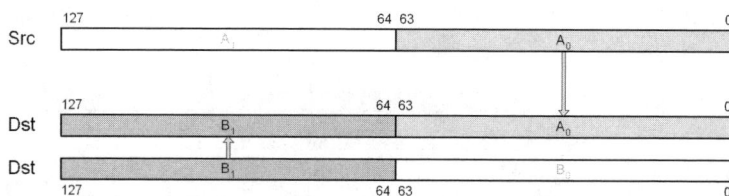

| Mnemonic | P | PII | K6 | 3D! | 3Mx+ | SSE | SSE2 | A64 | SSE3 | E64T |
|----------|---|-----|-----|-----|------|-----|------|-----|------|------|
| MOVSD    |   |     |    |     |      |     | ✓    | ✓   | ✓    | ✓    |

SSE2   movsd *xmmDst, xmmSrc/m64*    Double-precision    128
  "    movsd *xmmDst/m64, xmmSrc*

When the source is memory, this SSE2 instruction copies the double-precision floating-point value from 64-bit memory *aSrc* and copies it to the least significant double-precision floating-point element of the XMM destination register specified by *Dst*. The upper double-precision floating-point value is unchanged. When *aSrc* is an XMM register, the lower double-precision floating-point value is copied to 64-bit memory.

**Note:**   This MOVSD instruction should not be confused with the string instruction MOVSD. This instruction uses XMM registers, not general-purpose registers, and does not work with the REP prefix.

# MOVLPD — Move Low Packed (1×DPFP)

movlpd *destination, source*

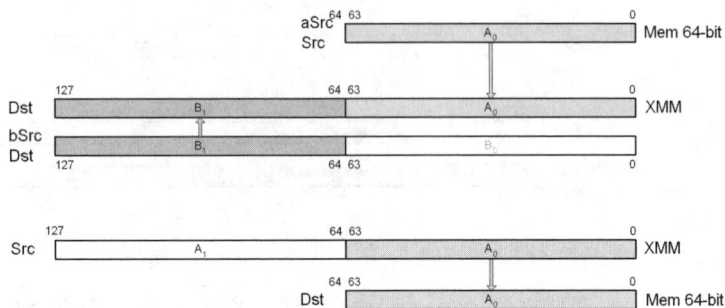

| Mnemonic | P | PII | K6 | 3D! | 3Mx+ | SSE | SSE2 | A64 | SSE3 | E64T |
|----------|---|-----|----|----|------|-----|------|-----|------|------|
| MOVLPD   |   |     |    |    |      |     | ✓    | ✓   | ✓    | ✓    |
| MOVSD    |   |     |    |    |      |     | ✓    | ✓   | ✓    | ✓    |

| | | | |
|---|---|---|---|
| SSE2 | movsd *xmmDst, mSrc64* | Double-precision | 128 |
| " | movsd *mSrc64, xmmSrc* | | |
| " | movlpd *xmmDst, mSrc64* | | |
| " | movlpd *mSrc64, xmmSrc* | | |

The MOVLPD instruction copies the double-precision floating-point value from 64-bit memory *aSrc* to the lower 64 bits of the XMM register or from the lower 64 bits of the XMM register to 64-bit memory. The upper double-precision floating-point value in the XMM register is unchanged when the destination is the XMM register.

**Note:** The MOVLPD and MOVSD instructions appear to be functionally identical. However, the MOVSD can optionally move XMM to XMM, while the MOVLPD cannot!

# MOVHPD — Move High Packed (1×DPFP)

movhpd *destination, source*

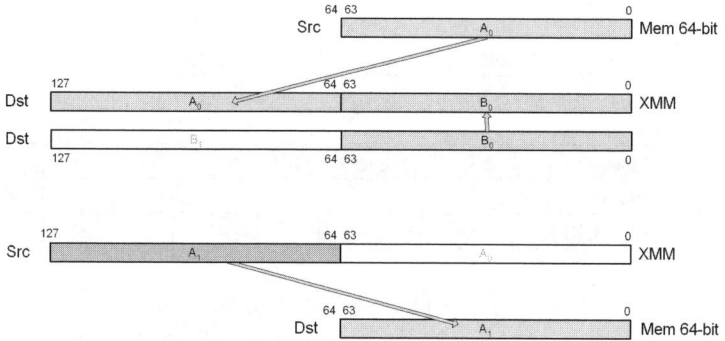

| Mnemonic | P | PII | K6 | 3D! | 3Mx+ | SSE | SSE2 | A64 | SSE3 | E64T |
|----------|---|-----|----|----|------|-----|------|-----|------|------|
| MOVHPD   |   |     |    |     |      |     | ✓    | ✓   | ✓    | ✓    |

| SSE2 | movhpd *xmmDst, m64* | Double-precision | 128 |
|------|---------------------|------------------|-----|
| "    | movhpd *m64, xmmSrc* |                  |     |

The MOVHPD instruction copies the double-precision floating-point value from 64-bit memory *aSrc* to the upper 64 bits of the XMM register or from the upper 64 bits of the XMM register to 64-bit memory. The upper double-precision floating-point value in the XMM register is unchanged when the destination is the XMM register.

# PUNPCKLQDQ — Parallel Copy Lower (2×64-Bit)

## Also: (Unpack and Interleave Low Packed Double-Precision Floating-Point Values)

punpcklqdq *destination, source*

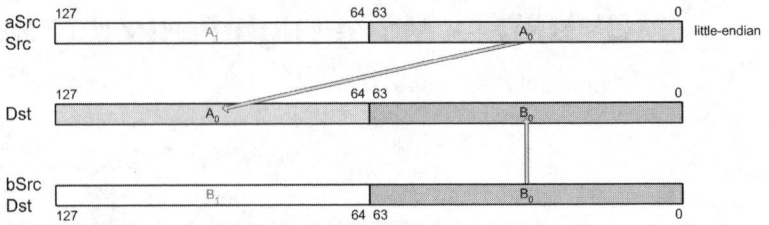

| Mnemonic | P | PII | K6 | 3D! | 3Mx+ | SSE | SSE2 | A64 | SSE3 | E64T |
|---|---|---|---|---|---|---|---|---|---|---|
| PUNPCKLQDQ |  |  |  |  |  |  | ✓ | ✓ | ✓ | ✓ |
| UNPCKLPD |  |  |  |  |  |  | ✓ | ✓ | ✓ | ✓ |

SSE2   punpcklqdq *xmmDst, xmmSrc/m128* [Un]signed       128
  "       unpcklpd   *xmmDst, xmmSrc/m128* Double-precision  128

```
punpcklqdq  xmm0,xmm1
unpcklpd    xmm0,xmm1

punpcklqdq  xmm0,xmm0 ; {x x}   ←   {y x}
```

# PUNPCKHQDQ — Parallel Copy Upper (2×64-Bit)

## Also: (Unpack and Interleave High Packed Double-Precision Floating-Point Values)

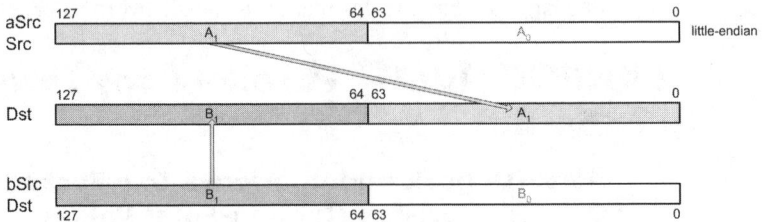

punpckhqdq *destination, source*

| Mnemonic | P | PII | K6 | 3D! | 3Mx+ | SSE | SSE2 | A64 | SSE3 | E64T |
|---|---|---|---|---|---|---|---|---|---|---|
| PUNPCKHQDQ |  |  |  |  |  |  | ✓ | ✓ | ✓ | ✓ |
| UNPCKHPD |  |  |  |  |  |  | ✓ | ✓ | ✓ | ✓ |

SSE2    punpckhqdq *xmmDst, xmmSrc/m128* [Un]signed        128
"       unpckhpd    *xmmDst, xmmSrc/m128* Double-precision  128

```
punpckhqdq  xmm0,xmm1
unpckhpd    xmm0,xmm1

punpckhqdq  xmm0,xmm0 ; {y y}   ←   {y x}
```

# Swizzle, Shuffle, and Splat

The various manufacturers refer to the swapping of data values by different terms: swizzle, shuffle, splat, etc. Some of these replicate a data value into two or more destination locations. In a few hybrid cases the functions use a defined distribution or a custom-defined interlacing of source arguments such as was discussed in the previous section.

The splat functionally is similar to a bug hitting the windshield of an automobile at 70 mph.

A bit sequence is used to indicate which source elements are mapped to which destination elements.

## PINSRW — Shuffle (1×16-Bit) to (4×16-Bit)

pinsrw *destination, source, #*

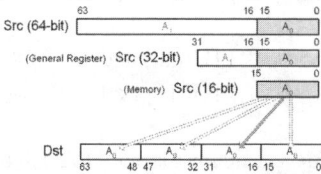

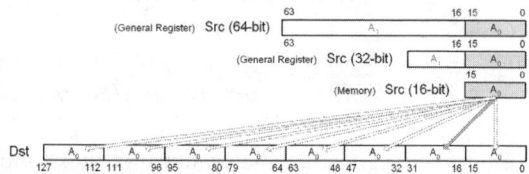

| Mnemonic | P | PII | K6 | 3D! | 3Mx+ | SSE | SSE2 | A64 | SSE3 | E64T |
|----------|---|-----|----|----|------|-----|------|-----|------|------|
| PINSRW   |   |     |    |    | ✓    | ✓   | ✓    | ✓   | ✓    | ✓    |

MMX+    pinsrw *mmxDst, r32, #*    [Un]signed    64
"       pinsrw *mmxDst, m16, #*    "             "
SSE2    pinsrw *xmmDst, r64, #*    "             128
"       pinsrw *xmmDst, m32, #*    "             "

For 64-bit data there exist four output elements and so an immediate value of 0...3; thus two bits are needed to identify which element is the destination. The two least significant bits of the index are masked to only allow a selectable value of 0...3. With 128-bit data there exist eight output elements and therefore a value of 0...7; thus three bits are used to select the destination.

```
pinsrw mm0,eax,01b ; 1   {3...0}
```

The lower 16 bits of the general-purpose register are assigned to one of the four destination 16-bit values selected by the index.

# PSHUFW — Shuffle Packed Words (4×16-Bit)

pshufw *destination, source,* #

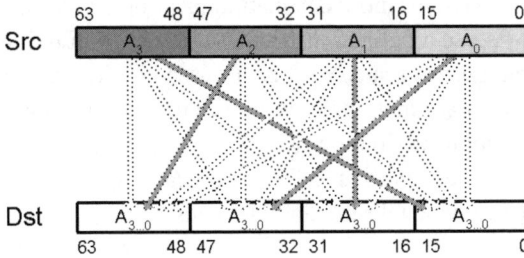

| Mnemonic | P | PII | K6 | 3D! | 3Mx+ | SSE | SSE2 | A64 | SSE3 | E64T |
|----------|---|-----|-----|-----|------|-----|------|-----|------|------|
| PSHUFW | | | | | ✓ | ✓ | ✓ | ✓ | ✓ | ✓ |

| | | | | | |
|------|------|------|------|------|------|
| MMX+ | pshufw *mmxDst, (mmxSrc/m64),* # | | [Un]signed | | 64 |
| SSE | pshufw *mmxDst, (mmxSrc/m64),* # | | [Un]signed | | 64 |

The immediate value indicates which source index is mapped to each of the destination elements. The immediate value is a single 8-bit byte; with four possible source elements needing two bits each, that leaves a maximum of four remappable elements. There are $4\times4\times4\times4 = 4^4 = 256$ possible patterns.

```
pshufw mm0,mm1,10000111b ; 2 0 1 3
```

## PSHUFLW — Shuffle Packed Low Words (4×16-Bit)

pshuflw *destination, source,* #

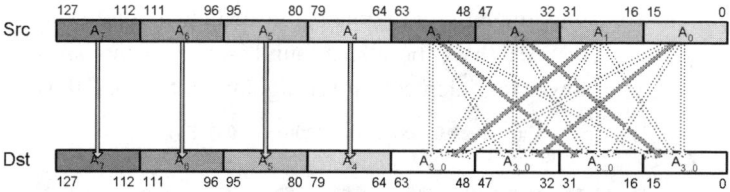

| Mnemonic | P | PII | K6 | 3D! | 3Mx+ | SSE | SSE2 | A64 | SSE3 | E64T |
|---|---|---|---|---|---|---|---|---|---|---|
| PSHUFLW | | | | | | | ✓ | ✓ | ✓ | ✓ |

SSE2    pshuflw *xmmDst, (xmmSrc/m128),* #    [Un]signed    128

The immediate value indicates which source index is mapped to each of the destination elements. The immediate value is a single 8-bit byte; with four possible source elements needing two bits each, that leaves a maximum of four remappable elements. This is similar in functionality to PSHUFW; the lower four 16-bit elements are remappable but the upper four elements are straight mappings and thus a direct copy.

```
pshuflw xmm0,xmm1,01001110b ; 1 0 3 2
```

## PSHUFHW — Shuffle Packed High Words (4×16-Bit)

pshufhw *destination, source,* #

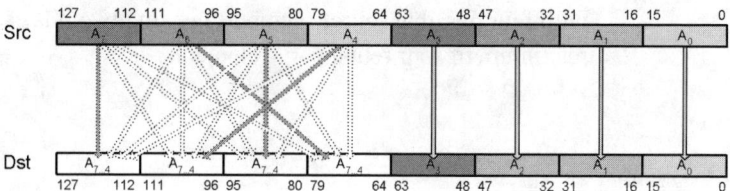

| Mnemonic | P | PII | K6 | 3D! | 3Mx+ | SSE | SSE2 | A64 | SSE3 | E64T |
|---|---|---|---|---|---|---|---|---|---|---|
| PSHUFHW | | | | | | | ✓ | ✓ | ✓ | ✓ |

SSE2    pshufhw *xmmDst, (xmmSrc/m128)*, #  [Un]signed    128

The immediate value indicates which source index is mapped to each of the destination elements. The immediate value is a single 8-bit byte, and with four possible source elements needing two bits each, that leaves a maximum of four remappable elements. This is similar in functionality to PSHUFW; the upper four 16-bit elements are remappable but the lower four elements are straight mappings and thus a direct copy.

```
pshufhw xmm0,xmm1,11000110b ; 3 0 1 2
```

# PSHUFD — Shuffle Packed Double Words (4×32-Bit)

pshufd *destination, source,* #

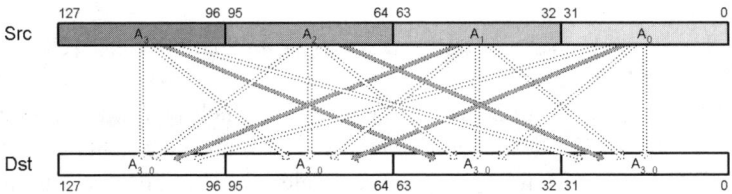

| Mnemonic | P | PII | K6 | 3D! | 3Mx+ | SSE | SSE2 | A64 | SSE3 | E64T |
|----------|---|-----|-----|------|-------|------|------|------|------|------|
| PSHUFD   |   |     |     |      |       |      | ✓    | ✓    | ✓    | ✓    |

SSE2    pshufd *xmmDst, (xmmSrc/m128)*, #    [Un]signed    128

```
pshufd xmm0,xmm1,01001110b ; 1 0 3 2
```

The immediate value indicates which source index is mapped to each of the destination elements. The immediate value is a single 8-bit byte, and with four possible source elements needing two bits each, that leaves a maximum of four remappable elements.

# SHUFPS — Shuffle Packed SPFP Values (4×SPFP)

shufps *destination*, *source*, #

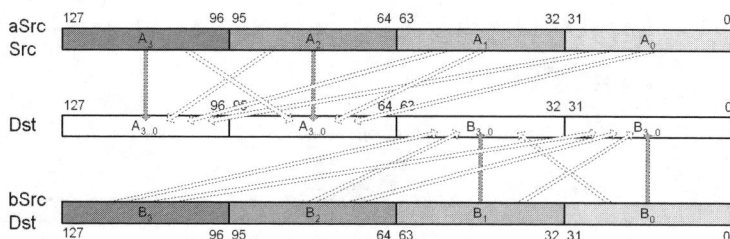

| Mnemonic | P | PII | K6 | 3D! | 3Mx+ | SSE | SSE2 | A64 | SSE3 | E64T |
|----------|---|-----|----|-----|------|-----|------|-----|------|------|
| SHUFPS   |   |     |    |     |      | ✓   | ✓    | ✓   | ✓    | ✓    |

SSE    shufps *xmmDst*, *(xmmSrc/m128)*, #    Single-precision    128

The immediate value is split between where the two lowest elements are selectable from the destination and the two highest elements of the destination are selectable from the source. The immediate value is a single 8-bit byte; with four possible source elements needing two bits each, that leaves a maximum of four remappable elements.

```
shufps xmm0,xmm1,11100100b  ; 3 2 1 0    {3...0}
```

# MOVSLDUP — Splat Packed Even SPFP to (4×SPFP)

movsldup *destination*, *source*

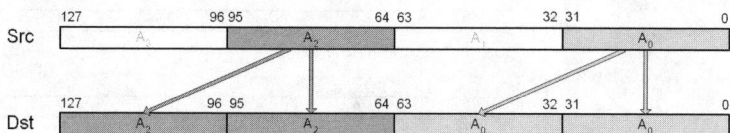

| Mnemonic | P | PII | K6 | 3D! | 3Mx+ | SSE | SSE2 | A64 | SSE3 | E64T |
|----------|---|-----|----|-----|------|-----|------|-----|------|------|
| MOVSLDUP |   |     |    |     |      |     |      |     | ✓    | ✓    |

SSE3    movsldup *xmmDst*, *(xmmSrc/m32)*    Single-precision    128

The even single-precision floating-point elements from the source are replicated so element #0 is copied to the two lower destination elements and the source element #2 is copied to the upper two destination elements.

# MOVSHDUP — Splat Packed Odd SPFP to (4×SPFP)

movshdup *destination, source*

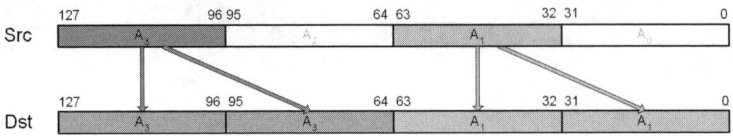

| Mnemonic | P | PII | K6 | 3D! | 3Mx+ | SSE | SSE2 | A64 | SSE3 | E64T |
|---|---|---|---|---|---|---|---|---|---|---|
| MOVSHDUP | | | | | | | | | ✓ | ✓ |

SSE3    movshdup *xmmDst, (xmmSrc/m32)*    Single-precision    128

The odd single-precision floating-point elements from the source are replicated so element #1 is copied to the two lower destination elements and the source element #3 is copied to the upper two destination elements.

# MOVDDUP — Splat Lower DPFP to Packed (2×DPFP)

movddup *destination, source*

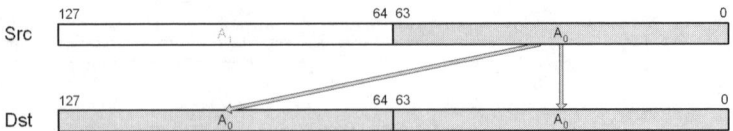

| Mnemonic | P | PII | K6 | 3D! | 3Mx+ | SSE | SSE2 | A64 | SSE3 | E64T |
|---|---|---|---|---|---|---|---|---|---|---|
| MOVDDUP | | | | | | | | | ✓ | ✓ |

SSE3    movddup *xmmDst, (xmmSrc/m32)*    Double-precision    128

The lower double-precision floating-point element from the source is replicated and copied to the lower and upper double-precision floating-point elements.

## SHUFPD — Shuffle Packed DPFP (2×64-Bit)

shufpd *destination*, *source*, #

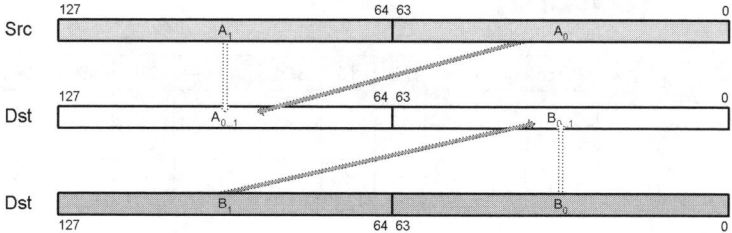

| Mnemonic | P | PII | K6 | 3D! | 3Mx+ | SSE | SSE2 | A64 | SSE3 | E64T |
|----------|---|-----|----|-----|------|-----|------|-----|------|------|
| SHUFPD   |   |     |    |     |      |     | ✓    | ✓   | ✓    | ✓    |

SSE2    shufpd *xmmDst, (xmmSrc/m128)*, #   Double-precision    128

```
shufpd xmm0,xmm1,01b ; 0 1   {1...0}
```

Four possibilities:  {x x}  {x y}  {y x}  {y y} ← {y x}

# Data Bit Expansion

The important item to remember is that with regular data expansion, the enlarging of the data size from a lower bit count to a higher bit count of an unsigned number only requires a 128-bit value of zero. This needs to be interlaced with the value and when the bit size is doubled, a zero is in effect, moved into the upper bits. When working with signed values, instructions such as those that follow are needed so that the sign bit is replicated into the upper bits. Note the size differential in the following diagrams. A data element is being doubled in size: to word from byte or dword from word. Also, a possible change in sign may occur, which is denoted with a from/to (±).

# CBW Convert Signed AL (Byte) to AX (Word)

# CWDE Convert Signed AX (Word) to EAX (DWord)

# CDQE Convert Signed EAX (DWord) to RAX (QWord)

| Mnemonic | P | PII | K6 | 3D! | 3Mx+ | SSE | SSE2 | A64 | SSE3 | E64T |
|----------|---|-----|----|----|------|-----|------|-----|------|------|
| CBW | ✓ | ✓ | ✓ | ✓ | ✓ | ✓ | ✓ | ✓ | ✓ | ✓ |
| CDQE | | | | | | | | ✓ | | ✓ |
| CWDE | ✓ | ✓ | ✓ | ✓ | ✓ | ✓ | ✓ | ✓ | ✓ | ✓ |

| | | |
|------|--------|----|
| cbw | Signed | 16 |
| cwde | Signed | 32 |
| cdqe | Signed | 64 |

The CBW general-purpose instruction converts the (7+1)-bit signed value in the AL register to a (15+1)-bit signed value in the AX register.

The CWDE general-purpose instruction converts the (15+1)-bit signed value in the AX register to the (31+1)-bit signed value in the EAX register.

The CDQE general-purpose instruction converts the (31+1)-bit signed value in the EAX register to the (63+1)-bit signed value in the RAX register.

| Flags | O.flow | Sign | Zero | Aux | Parity | Carry |
|-------|--------|------|------|-----|--------|-------|
| | - | - | - | - | - | - |

Flags: None are altered by this opcode.

**Conversion of signed 8-bit to 16-bit**

To convert a signed value of [–128...0...127] to a 16-bit value. This only works with the AL to AX register, and is most efficient if the data value originated in the AL; if not, then the MOVSX is best.

| | Best | | | | Worst |
|---|---|---|---|---|---|
| | cbw | movsx eax,al | movsx ax,al | ror eax,8<br>sar eax,24 | ror ax,8<br>sar ax,8 |
| P bytes | 2 | 3 | 4 | 6 | 8 |
| R bytes | 1 | 4 | 3 | 6 | 6 |

### Conversion of signed 16-bit to 32-bit

To convert a signed value of [–32768…0…32767] to a 32-bit value.

| | Best | | | Worst |
|---|---|---|---|---|
| | cwde | movsx eax,ax | shl eax,16<br>sar eax,16 | ror eax,16<br>sar eax,16 |
| P bytes | 1 | 3 | 6 | 6 |
| R bytes | 1 | 4 | 6 | 6 |

# MOVSX/MOVSXD — Move with Sign Extension

MOVSX *destination, source*

| Mnemonic | P | PII | K6 | 3D! | 3Mx+ | SSE | SSE2 | A64 | SSE3 | E64T |
|---|---|---|---|---|---|---|---|---|---|---|
| MOVSX | ✓ | ✓ | ✓ | ✓ | ✓ | ✓ | ✓ | ✓ | ✓ | ✓ |
| MOVSXD | | | | | | | | 64 | | 64 |

> movsx   *rDst16, rmSrc8*     Signed
> movsx   *rDst32, rmSrc(8/16)*
> movsx   *rDst64, rmSrc(8/16)*
> movsxd *rDst64, rmSrc32*

These general-purpose instructions are very similar to CBW and CWDE except that they are a lot more versatile in which other registers can be sign extended to the same or a different register instead of just the AL or AX. A (7+1)-bit signed value can be converted to a (15+1)-bit or (31+1)-bit signed value. A (15+1)-bit signed value is converted into a (31+1)-bit signed value.

| Flags | O.flow | Sign | Zero | Aux | Parity | Carry |
|---|---|---|---|---|---|---|
| | - | - | - | - | - | - |

Flags: None are altered by this opcode.

### Conversion of signed 8-bit to 16-bit

To convert a signed value of [−128...0...127] to a 16-bit value. If working with AX,AL then use the CBW instruction as it is more efficient. I recommend using 32-bit form, as it is the best.

| | Best | (+Best+) | | Worst |
|---|---|---|---|---|
| | movsx ax,bl | movsx eax,bl | mov eax,ebx<br>shl eax,24<br>sar eax,24 | mov ax,bx<br>shl ax,8<br>sar ax,8 |
| P bytes | 4 | 3 | 8 | 11 |
| R bytes | 3 | 4 | 11 | 8 |

### Conversion of signed 8-bit to 32-bit

| | Best | | Worst |
|---|---|---|---|
| | movsx eax,bl | mov eax,ebx<br>shl eax,24<br>sar eax,24 | mov al,bl<br>(stall)<br>shl eax,24<br>sar eax,24 |
| P bytes | 3 | 8 | 10 |
| R bytes | 4 | 11 | 8 |

### Conversion of signed 16-bit to 32-bit

| | Best | | Worst |
|---|---|---|---|
| | movsx eax,bx | mov eax,ebx<br>shl eax,16<br>sar eax,16 | mov ax,bx<br>(stall)<br>shl eax,16<br>sar eax,16 |
| P bytes | 3 | 8 | 9 |
| R bytes | 4 | 11 | 10 |

# MOVZX — Move with Zero Extension

MOVZX *destination, source*

| Mnemonic | P | PII | K6 | 3D! | 3Mx+ | SSE | SSE2 | A64 | SSE3 | E64T |
|---|---|---|---|---|---|---|---|---|---|---|
| MOVZX | ✓ | ✓ | ✓ | ✓ | ✓ | ✓ | ✓ | ✓ | ✓ | ✓ |

movzx   *rDst16, rmSrc8*        Unsigned
movzx   *rDst32, rmSrc(8/16)*
movzx   *rDst64, rmSrc(8/32)*

This instruction converts an unsigned value into a larger unsigned value. An 8-bit unsigned value can be converted to a 16-bit or 32-bit unsigned value. A 16-bit unsigned value is converted into a 32-bit unsigned value.

| Flags | O.flow | Sign | Zero | Aux | Parity | Carry |
|-------|--------|------|------|-----|--------|-------|
|       | -      | -    | -    | -   | -      | -     |

Flags: None are altered by this opcode.

### Conversion of same unsigned 8- to 16-bit register (no move)

To convert an unsigned number (0...255) to a 16-bit.

|         | **Best**      | **(+Best+)**   |                | **Worst**        |
|---------|---------------|----------------|----------------|------------------|
|         | movzx ax,al   | movzx eax,al   | and ax,00ffh   | and eax,000ffh   |
| P bytes | 4             | 3              | 4              | 5                |
| R bytes | 3             | 4              | 3              | 6                |

### Conversion of same unsigned 8- to 32-bit register (no move)

To convert an unsigned number (0...255) to a 32-bit.

|         | **Best**      | **Worst**        |
|---------|---------------|------------------|
|         | movzx eax,al  | and eax,000ffh   |
| P bytes | 3             | 5                |
| R bytes | 4             | 6                |

### Conversion of unsigned 8-bit to 16-bit

To convert an unsigned value of (0...255) to a 16-bit value. I recommend using the 8- to 32-bit form.

|         | **Best**      |                           |                           | **Worst**                 |
|---------|---------------|---------------------------|---------------------------|---------------------------|
|         | movzx ax,bl   | xor ax,ax<br>mov al,bl    | sub ax,ax<br>mov al,bl    | mov ax,bx<br>and ax,0ffh  |
| P bytes | 4             | 5                         | 5                         | 7                         |
| R bytes | 3             | 4                         | 4                         | 5                         |

### Conversion of unsigned 8-bit to 32-bit

|         | **Best**      |                             |                             | **Worst**                       |
|---------|---------------|-----------------------------|-----------------------------|---------------------------------|
|         | movzx eax,bl  | xor eax,eax<br>mov al,bl    | sub eax,eax<br>mov al,bl    | mov eax,ebx<br>and eax,0ffh     |
| P bytes | 3             | 4                           | 4                           | 7                               |
| R bytes | 4             | 5                           | 5                           | 9                               |

### Conversion of unsigned 16-bit to 32-bit

|         | **Best**     |                          | **Worst**                      |
|---------|--------------|--------------------------|--------------------------------|
|         | movzx eax,bx | xor eax,eax<br>mov ax,bx | mov eax,ebx<br>and eax,0ffffh  |
| P bytes | 3            | 5                        | 7                              |
| R bytes | 4            | 5                        | 9                              |

# CWD — Convert Signed AX (Word) to DX:AX

# CDQ — Convert Signed EAX (DWord) to EDX:EAX

# CQO — Convert Signed RAX (QWord) to RDX:RAX

| Mnemonic | P | PII | K6 | 3D! | 3Mx+ | SSE | SSE2 | A64 | SSE3 | E64T |
|----------|---|-----|----|-----|------|-----|------|-----|------|------|
| CWD      | ✓ | ✓   | ✓  | ✓   | ✓    | ✓   | ✓    | ✓   | ✓    | ✓    |
| CDQ      | ✓ | ✓   | ✓  | ✓   | ✓    | ✓   | ✓    | ✓   | ✓    | ✓    |
| CQO      |   |     |    |     |      |     |      | 64  |      | 64   |

| cwd | Signed |
| cdq | Signed |
| cqo | Signed |

The general-purpose CWD, CDQ, and CQO instructions are typically used for preparation of a number before a division. The integer division requires:

AX or DX:AX or EDX:EAX or RDX:RAX

You would get the same result by multiplying two numbers together.

| Flags | O.flow | Sign | Zero | Aux | Parity | Carry |
|-------|--------|------|------|-----|--------|-------|
|       | -      | -    | -    | -   | -      | -     |

Flags: None are altered by this opcode.

|         | **Best** |                              | **Worst**                  |
|---------|----------|------------------------------|----------------------------|
|         | cwd      | mov edx,eax<br>sar dx,16     | mov dx,ax<br>sar dx,16     |
| P bytes | 2        | 6                            | 7                          |
| R bytes | 1        | 6                            | 5                          |

|         | **Best** | **Worst**                                |
|---------|----------|------------------------------------------|
|         | cdq      | mov edx,eax<br>sar edx,31<br>sar edx,1   |
| P bytes | 1        | 7                                        |
| R bytes | 2        | 10                                       |

# PEXTRW — Extract (4×16-bit) into Integer to (1×16)

pextrw *destination, source, #*

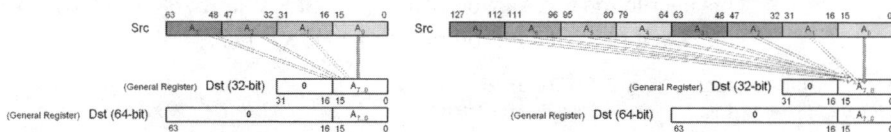

| Mnemonic | P | PII | K6 | 3D! | 3Mx+ | SSE | SSE2 | A64 | SSE3 | E64T |
|----------|---|-----|----|-----|------|-----|------|-----|------|------|
| PEXTRW   |   |     |    |     | ✓    | ✓   | ✓    | ✓   | ✓    | ✓    |

MMX    pextrw *r(32/64), mmxSrc, #*        [Un]signed        64
SSE    pextrw *r(32/64), xmmSrc, #*

```
pextrw eax,mm1,00b ; {3...0}
```

One of the four 16-bit values is assigned to the lower 16 bits of the general-purpose register and zero extended into the upper 16 bits for the 32-bit register, or 48 bits for the 64-bit register.

One of the eight 16-bit values is assigned to the lower 16 bits of the general-purpose register and zero extended into the upper 16 bits for the 32-bit register, or 48 bits for the 64-bit register.

# Data Bit Reduction (with Saturation)

## PACKSSWB — Packed Signed int16 to int8 with Saturation

packsswb *destination, source*

| Mnemonic | P | PII | K6 | 3D! | 3Mx+ | SSE | SSE2 | A64 | SSE3 | E64T |
|----------|---|-----|----|-----|------|-----|------|-----|------|------|
| PACKSSWB |   | ✓ | ✓ | ✓ | ✓ | ✓ | ✓ | ✓ | ✓ | ✓ |

| MMX | packsswb mmxDst, mmxSrc/m64 | Signed | 64 |
| SSE2 | packsswb xmmDst, xmmSrc/m128 | Signed | 128 |

```
packsswb mm0,mm1
packsswb xmm0,xmm1
```

This instruction takes a word value in the range {–32768 … 32767} and saturates it to a signed 8-bit range of {–128…127}.

```
fooa    qword 0ffffa5a55a5a0000h
foob    qword 08000003f007f00ffh

        movq    mm7,fooa
        movq    mm6,foob
        packsswb mm7,mm6

; 8000 003f 007f 00ff   ffff a5a5 5a5a 0000
;                 became
; 80   3f   7f   7f      ff   80   7f   00
```

## PACKUSWB — Packed uint16 to uint8 with Saturation

packuswb *destination, source*

| Mnemonic | P | PII | K6 | 3D! | 3Mx+ | SSE | SSE2 | A64 | SSE3 | E64T |
|----------|---|-----|----|-----|------|-----|------|-----|------|------|
| PACKUSWB |   | ✓ | ✓ | ✓ | ✓ | ✓ | ✓ | ✓ | ✓ | ✓ |

| | | | |
|---|---|---|---|
| MMX | packuswb *mmxDst, mmxSrc/m64* | [Un]signed | 64 |
| SSE2 | packuswb *xmmDst, xmmSrc/m128* | [Un]signed | 128 |

```
packuswb mm0,mm1
```

This instruction uses the same diagram as the 64-bit form of the PACKSSWB instruction but saturates an unsigned word with a range of {–32768…32767} to an unsigned 8-bit range of {0…255}.

```
packuswb xmm0,xmm1
```

The following instruction uses the same diagram as the 128-bit form of the PACKSSWB instruction but saturates an unsigned word with a range of {–32768…32767} to an unsigned 8-bit range of {0…255}.

```
fooa    qword 0ffffa5a55a5a0000h
foob    qword 08000003f007f00ffh

        movq    mm7,fooa
        movq    mm6,foob
        packuswb mm7,mm6

; 8000 003f 007f 00ff   ffff a5a5 5a5a 0000
;                became
; 00   3f   7f   ff     00   00   ff   00
```

# PACKSSDW — Packed int32 to int16 with Saturation

packssdw *destination, source*

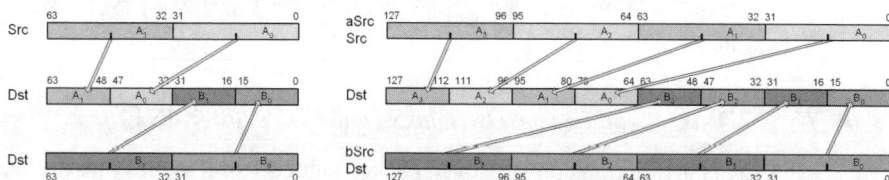

| Mnemonic | P | PII | K6 | 3D! | 3Mx+ | SSE | SSE2 | A64 | SSE3 | E64T |
|---|---|---|---|---|---|---|---|---|---|---|
| PACKSSDW | | ✓ | ✓ | ✓ | ✓ | ✓ | ✓ | ✓ | ✓ | ✓ |

| | | | |
|---|---|---|---|
| MMX | packssdw *mmxDst, mmxSrc/m64* | Signed | 64 |
| SSE2 | packssdw *xmmDst, xmmSrc/m128* | Signed | 128 |

```
packssdw mm0,mm1
packssdw xmm0,xmm1
```

This instruction takes a 32-bit signed value in the range {–2147483648 ... 2147483647} and saturates it to a signed 16-bit range of {–32768... 32767}.

```
fooa    qword 0ffffa5a55a5a0000h
foob    qword 08000003f007f00ffh

        movq    mm7,fooa
        movq    mm6,foob
        packssdw mm7,mm6

; 8000003f 007f00ff   ffffa5a5 5a5a0000
;                became
;  8000    7fff        a5a5     7fff
```

# Data Conversion (Integer : Float, Float : Integer, Float : Float)

## PI2FW — Convert Packed Even int16 to SPFP

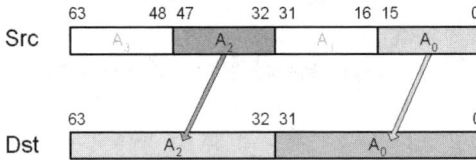

| Mnemonic | P | PII | K6 | 3D! | 3Mx+ | SSE | SSE2 | A64 | SSE3 | E64T |
|----------|---|-----|----|----|------|-----|------|-----|------|------|
| PI2FW    |   |     |    |    | ✓    |     |      | ✓   |      |      |

3DMx+    pi2fw *mmxDst, mmxSrc/m64*    SPFP ← INT16    64

This instruction converts even packed signed 16-bit values into packed single-precision floating-point values and stores the result in the destination *mmxDst*.

# CVTDQ2PS — Convert Packed int32 to SPFP

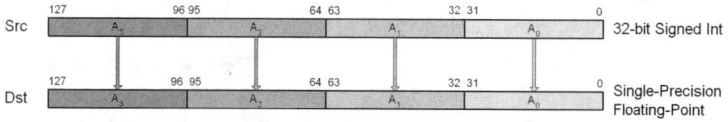

| Mnemonic | P | PII | K6 | 3D! | 3Mx+ | SSE | SSE2 | A64 | SSE3 | E64T |
|---|---|---|---|---|---|---|---|---|---|---|
| CVTDQ2PS | | | | | | | ✓ | ✓ | ✓ | ✓ |

SSE    cvtdq2ps *xmmDst, xmmSrc/m128*    SPFP ← INT32    128

This instruction converts a packed 32-bit signed integer from *source* xmm to xmm single-precision floating-point *destination*.

# CVTPS2DQ — Convert Packed SPFP to int32

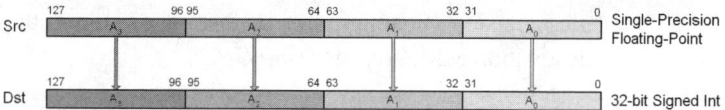

| Mnemonic | P | PII | K6 | 3D! | 3Mx+ | SSE | SSE2 | A64 | SSE3 | E64T |
|---|---|---|---|---|---|---|---|---|---|---|
| CVTPS2DQ | | | | | | | ✓ | ✓ | ✓ | ✓ |
| CVTTPS2DQ | | | | | | | ✓ | ✓ | ✓ | ✓ |

SSE    cvtps2dq *xmmDst, xmmSrc/m128*    INT32 ← SPFP    128

This converts a packed single-precision floating-point *source* xmm to xmm 32-bit signed *destination*.

SSE    cvttps2dq *xmmDst, xmmSrc/m128*    INT32 ← SPFP    128

This converts a packed single-precision floating-point with truncation *source* xmm to xmm 32-bit signed *destination*.

# CVTPI2PS — Convert Lo Packed int32 to SPFP

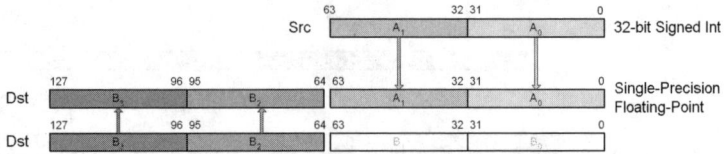

| Mnemonic | P | PII | K6 | 3D! | 3Mx+ | SSE | SSE2 | A64 | SSE3 | E64T |
|---|---|---|---|---|---|---|---|---|---|---|
| CVTPI2PS | | | | | | ✓ | ✓ | ✓ | ✓ | ✓ |
| PI2FD | | | | ✓ | ✓ | | | ✓ | | |

| SSE | cvtpi2ps *xmmDst, xmmSrc/m64* | SPFP ← INT32 | 128 |
|---|---|---|---|
| 3DNow! | pi2fd *mmxDst, mmxSrc/m64* | SPFP ← INT32 | 64 |

This instruction converts packed signed 32-bit values into packed single-precision floating-point values and stores the result in the destination MMX register *mmxDst*.

# CVTPS2PI — Convert Lo Packed SPFP to int32

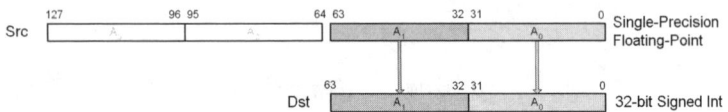

| Mnemonic | P | PII | K6 | 3D! | 3Mx+ | SSE | SSE2 | A64 | SSE3 | E64T |
|---|---|---|---|---|---|---|---|---|---|---|
| CVTPS2PI | | | | | | ✓ | ✓ | ✓ | ✓ | ✓ |
| CVTTPS2PI | | | | | | ✓ | ✓ | ✓ | ✓ | ✓ |
| PF2ID | | | | ✓ | | | | ✓ | | |
| PF2IW | | | | | ✓ | | | ✓ | | |

| SSE | cvtps2pi *xmmDst, xmmSrc/m64* | INT32 ← SPFP | 128 |
|---|---|---|---|
| SSE | cvttps2pi *mmxDst, mmxSrc/m64* | INT32 ← SPFP | 128 |

(the same but with truncation)

| 3DNow! | pf2id *mmxDst, mmxSrc/m64* | INT32 ← SPFP | 64 |
|---|---|---|---|

This instruction converts packed single-precision values in source *mmxSrc* to signed (saturated) 32-bit values and stores the result in the destination *mmxDst*.

3DMx+   pf2iw *mmxDst, mmxSrc/m64* INT32 ← INT16 ← DPFP 64

This instruction converts packed single-precision values in source *mmxSrc* to signed (saturated) 16-bit values [–32768, 32767], then sign extends to 32 bits and stores the result in the destination *mmxDst*.

# CVTSI2SS — Convert Scalar int32 to SPFP

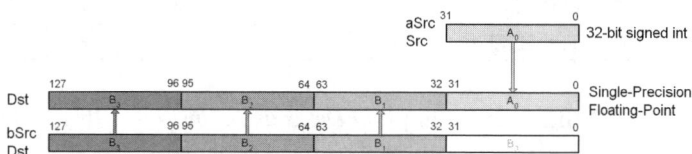

| Mnemonic | P | PII | K6 | 3D! | 3Mx+ | SSE | SSE2 | A64 | SSE3 | E64T |
|----------|---|-----|----|----|------|-----|------|-----|------|------|
| CVTSI2SS |   |     |    |    |      | ✓   | ✓    | ✓   | ✓    | ✓    |

SSE     cvtsi2ss *xmmDst, r/m32*       SPFP ← INT32        128

# CVTDQ2PD — Convert Even Packed int32 to DPFP

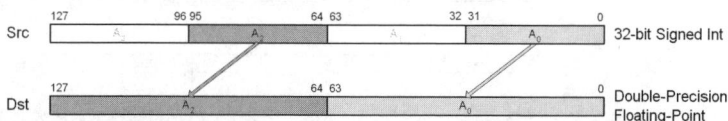

| Mnemonic | P | PII | K6 | 3D! | 3Mx+ | SSE | SSE2 | A64 | SSE3 | E64T |
|----------|---|-----|----|----|------|-----|------|-----|------|------|
| CVTDQ2PD |   |     |    |    |      |     | ✓    | ✓   | ✓    | ✓    |

SSE2     cvtdq2pd *xmmDst, xmmSrc/m64*   SPFP ← INT32    128

This instruction converts a packed even signed 32-bit integer value from *source* xmm to *destination* xmm double-precision floating-point.

# CVTPD2DQ — Convert Packed DPFP to Even int32

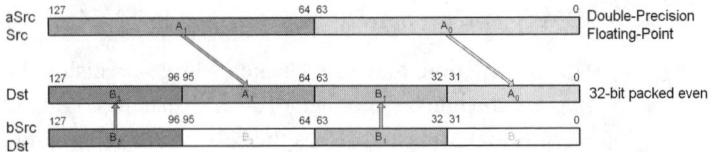

| Mnemonic | P | PII | K6 | 3D! | 3Mx+ | SSE | SSE2 | A64 | SSE3 | E64T |
|----------|---|-----|-----|-----|------|-----|------|-----|------|------|
| CVTPD2DQ | | | | | | | ✓ | ✓ | ✓ | ✓ |
| CVTTPD2DQ | | | | | | | ✓ | ✓ | ✓ | ✓ |

SSE2    cvtpd2dq *xmmDst, xmmSrc/m128*    INT32 ← DPFP    128

This converts a packed double-precision floating-point from *source* xmm to *destination* even packed 32-bit signed integer.

SSE2    cvttpd2dq *xmmDst, xmmSrc/m128*    INT32 ← DPFP    128

(the same but with truncation)

# CVTPD2PS — Convert Packed DPFP to Lo SPFP

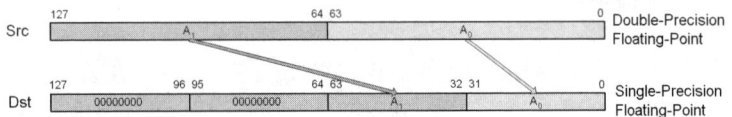

| Mnemonic | P | PII | K6 | 3D! | 3Mx+ | SSE | SSE2 | A64 | SSE3 | E64T |
|----------|---|-----|-----|-----|------|-----|------|-----|------|------|
| CVTPD2PS | | | | | | | ✓ | ✓ | ✓ | ✓ |

SSE2    cvtpd2ps *xmmDst, xmmSrc/m128*    SPFP ← DPFP    128

This converts a packed double-precision floating-point from *source* xmm to *destination* xmm packed single-precision floating-point.

# CVTPS2PD — Convert Lo Packed SPFP to DPFP

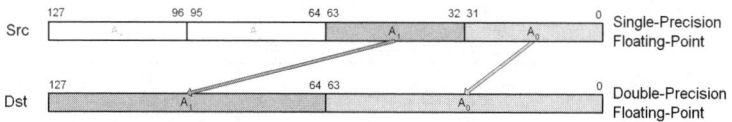

| Mnemonic | P | PII | K6 | 3D! | 3Mx+ | SSE | SSE2 | A64 | SSE3 | E64T |
|----------|---|-----|-----|-----|------|-----|------|-----|------|------|
| CVTPS2PD |   |     |     |     |      |     | ✓    | ✓   | ✓    | ✓    |

SSE2    cvtps2pd *xmmDst, xmmSrc/m64*    DPFP ← SPFP    128

This converts a lower packed single-precision floating-point xmm *source* to xmm double-precision *destination*.

# CVTPD2PI — Convert Packed DPFP to int32

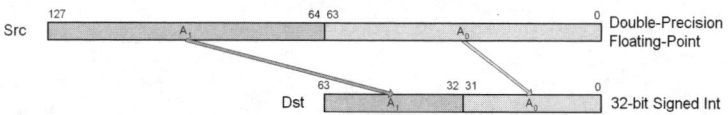

| Mnemonic | P | PII | K6 | 3D! | 3Mx+ | SSE | SSE2 | A64 | SSE3 | E64T |
|----------|---|-----|-----|-----|------|-----|------|-----|------|------|
| CVTPD2PI |   |     |     |     |      |     | ✓    | ✓   | ✓    | ✓    |
| CVTTPD2PI |  |     |     |     |      |     | ✓    | ✓   | ✓    | ✓    |

SSE2    cvtpd2pi *mmxDst, xmmSrc/m128*    INT32 ← DPFP    64

This converts a packed double-precision floating-point from *source* xmm to *destination* mmx register.

SSE2    cvttpd2pi *mmxDst, xmmSrc/m128*    INT32 ← DPFP    64

This converts a packed double-precision floating-point with truncation from *source* xmm to *destination* mmx register.

# CVTPI2PD — Convert Packed int32 to DPFP

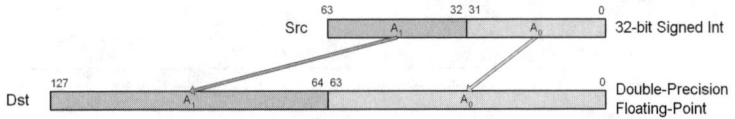

| Mnemonic | P | PII | K6 | 3D! | 3Mx+ | SSE | SSE2 | A64 | SSE3 | E64T |
|----------|---|-----|-----|-----|------|-----|------|-----|------|------|
| CVTPI2PD |   |     |     |     |      |     | ✓    | ✓   | ✓    | ✓    |

SSE2    cvtpi2pd *xmmDst, xmmSrc/m64*        SPFP ← INT32    128

This converts a packed 32-bit signed integer *source* mmx to double-precision floating-point xmm *destination*.

# CVTSS2SI — Convert Scalar SPFP to int32/64

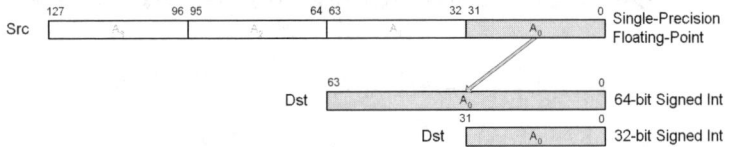

| Mnemonic | P | PII | K6 | 3D! | 3Mx+ | SSE | SSE2 | A64 | SSE3 | E64T |
|----------|---|-----|-----|-----|------|-----|------|-----|------|------|
| CVTSS2SI |   |     |     |     |      | ✓   | ✓    | ✓   | ✓    | ✓    |
| CVTTSS2SI |  |     |     |     |      | ✓   | ✓    | ✓   | ✓    | ✓    |

| SSE | cvtss2si *r32, xmmSrc/m32* | INT32 ← SPFP | 32 |
|-----|----------------------------|--------------|----|
| "   | cvtss2si *r64, xmmSrc/m32* | INT64 ← SPFP | 64 |
| "   | cvttss2si *r32, xmmSrc/m32* | INT32 ← SPFP | 32 |
| "   | cvttss2si *r64, xmmSrc/m32* | INT64 ← SPFP | 64 |

(the same but with truncation)

# CVTSD2SI — Convert Scalar DPFP to Int

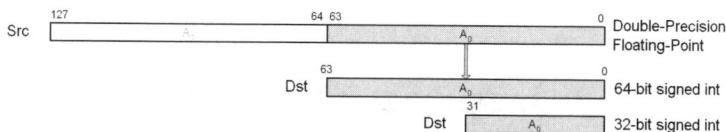

| Mnemonic | P | PII | K6 | 3D! | 3Mx+ | SSE | SSE2 | A64 | SSE3 | E64T |
|----------|---|-----|----|----|------|-----|------|-----|------|------|
| CVTSD2SI |   |     |    |    |      |     | ✓ | ✓ | ✓ | ✓ |
| CVTTSD2SI |   |     |    |    |      |     | ✓ | ✓ | ✓ | ✓ |

| SSE2 | cvtsd2si *r64, xmmSrc/m64* | INT64 ← DPFP | 64 |
|------|---------------------------|--------------|-----|
| " | cvtsd2si *r32, xmmSrc/m64* | INT32 ← DPFP | 32 |
| " | cvttsd2si *r32, xmmSrc/m64* | INT32 ← DPFP | 32 |
| " | cvttsd2si *r64, xmmSrc/m64* | INT64 ← DPFP | 64 |

(the same but with truncation)

# CVTSI2SD — Convert Scalar Int to DPFP

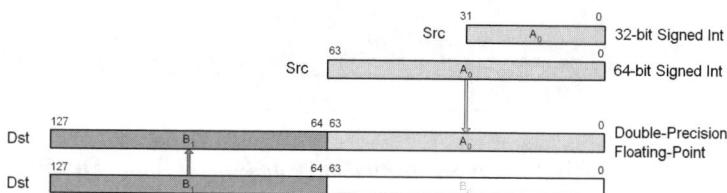

| Mnemonic | P | PII | K6 | 3D! | 3Mx+ | SSE | SSE2 | A64 | SSE3 | E64T |
|----------|---|-----|----|----|------|-----|------|-----|------|------|
| CVTSI2SD |   |     |    |    |      |     | ✓ | ✓ | ✓ | ✓ |

| SSE2 | cvtsi2sd *xmmDst, rmSrc64* | DPFP ← INT64 | 128 |
|------|---------------------------|--------------|------|
| " | cvtsi2sd *xmmDst, rmSrc32* | DPFP ← INT32 | 128 |

## CVTSD2SS — Convert Scalar DPFP to SPFP

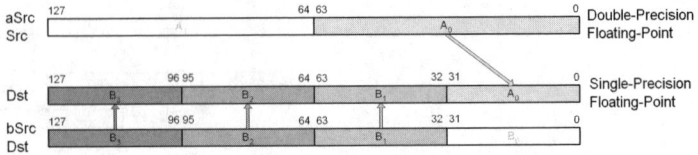

| Mnemonic | P | PII | K6 | 3D! | 3Mx+ | SSE | SSE2 | A64 | SSE3 | E64T |
|----------|---|-----|-----|-----|------|-----|------|-----|------|------|
| CVTSD2SS |   |     |     |     |      |     | ✓    | ✓   | ✓    | ✓    |

SSE2    cvtsd2ss *xmmDst, xmmSrc/m64*        SPFP ← DPFP        128

## CVTSS2SD — Convert Scalar SPFP to DPFP

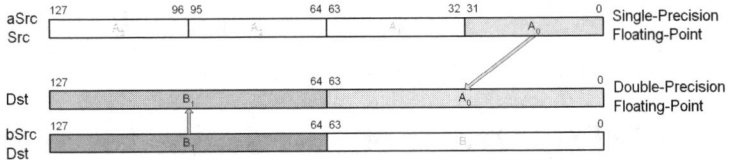

| Mnemonic | P | PII | K6 | 3D! | 3Mx+ | SSE | SSE2 | A64 | SSE3 | E64T |
|----------|---|-----|-----|-----|------|-----|------|-----|------|------|
| CVTSS2SD |   |     |     |     |      |     | ✓    | ✓   | ✓    | ✓    |

SSE2    cvtss2sd *xmmDst, xmmSrc/m32*        DPFP ← SPFP        128

# Exercises

1. Write code for your favorite processor to convert an image 256 pixels wide by 256 pixels high from 32-bit RGB data to 24-bit RGB.

2. Same as problem #1 but convert to 5:6:5-bit RGB (5 bits red, 6 bits green, 5 bits blue).

3. Convert from packed 5:5:5 RGB to 32-bit RGB.

4. For {SSE2} what instruction is needed to convert from a 16-bit signed number to 32-bit? Unsigned?

5. For {SSE2} write code snippets to pack four 128-bit vectors from packed 32-bit to packed 8-bit.

6.  Write a function to convert a 128-bit vector of 32-bit packed integers from big-endian to little-endian and vice versa.

7.  Same as problem #6 but 32-bit single-precision floating-point values.

8.  Same as problem #6 but 64-bit double-precision floating-point values.

9.  The beginning of this chapter shows a diagram for an AoS to SoA. Write it using
    a) 3DNow!
    b) SSE
    c) SSE2

10. The beginning of this chapter shows a diagram for an AoS to SoA. Write the reverse from SoA to AoS using
    a) 3DNow!
    b) SSE
    c) SSE2

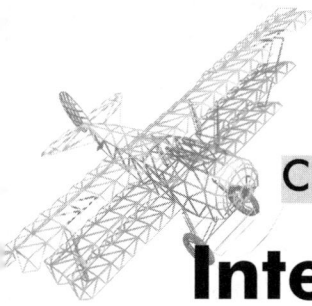

# Chapter 7

# Integer Math

This chapter involves math related to whole numbers that you learned in grade school: the processes of addition and subtraction. There you learned about the number line in which numbers just go on forever in positive and negative directions. In computers, as the numbers increase in a positive or negative amount they actually approach a limit (the end of their finite space). Upon reaching the end of the world (Flat Earth Society), they overflow and wrap to the opposite end of the number line (quantum physics, or was that string theory?) Well, anyway, your integer range of numbers is limited by the size of the data used to store them.

**Workbench Files:** \Bench\x86\chap07\*project*\*platform*

|  | *project* | *platform* |
|---|---|---|
| **Boolean Logic** | \pas\ | \vc6 |
|  |  | \vc.net |

## General Integer Math

We learned negation with the NEG instruction in Chapter 4, "Bit Mangling," and binary multiplication ($2^N$) and division using bit shifting in Chapter 5, "Bit Wrangling."

We can add 8-, 16-, 32-, and 64-bit numbers, and 4-bit if you include BCD (binary-coded decimal) discussed later in Chapter 15.

**No 64-bit:** The general-purpose BCD instructions are not available in 64-bit mode!

The EFLAGS Overflow, Sign, Zero, Auxiliary Carry, Parity, and Carry are all altered when using the general-purpose instructions.

| Overflow | Whether the numbers overflow the binary limit of the destination operand |
|---|---|
| Sign | Set to the resulting value of the MSB (most significant bit) |
| Zero | Set if the result is a value of zero |
| Aux. Carry | Set as a result of a carry of the low-order nibble |
| Parity | Set to 1 if the bits add up to an even number; 0 if not |
| Carry | Any mathematical carry results of the mathematical operation |

# ADD — Add

# ADC — Add with Carry

ADD *destination, source*

| Mnemonic | P | PII | K6 | 3D! | 3Mx+ | SSE | SSE2 | A64 | SSE3 | E64T |
|---|---|---|---|---|---|---|---|---|---|---|
| ADC | ✓ | ✓ | ✓ | ✓ | ✓ | ✓ | ✓ | ✓ | ✓ | ✓ |
| ADD | ✓ | ✓ | ✓ | ✓ | ✓ | ✓ | ✓ | ✓ | ✓ | ✓ |

add    *rmDst(8/16/32/64), #(8/16/32)*    Signed
add    *rmDst, rSrc(8/16/32/64)*
add    *rDst, rmSrc(8/16/32/64)*

The ADD general-purpose instruction logically sums the 8-, 16-, 32-, or 64-bit *source* to the *destination,* saves the result in *destination*, and sets the flags accordingly. An 8-bit source immediate value can be sign extended to 16-, 32-, or 64-bit value. A 32-bit source immediate value can be sign extended to a 64-bit *destination*.

$d = a + b$    $d = b$   so   $d = a + d = d + a$    $d \mathrel{+}= a$

**Algebraic Law:** | Commutative Law of Addition | $a + b = b + a$ |

adc    *rmDst(8/16/32/64), #(8/16/32)*    Signed
adc    *rmDst, rSrc(8/16/32/64)*
adc    *rDst, rmSrc(8/16/32/64)*

The ADC general-purpose instruction does exactly the same operation but with one difference. The carry value of 0 or 1 is added to the ending result: $d = a + b + (carry)$

| Flags | O.flow | Sign | Zero | Aux | Parity | Carry |
|-------|--------|------|------|-----|--------|-------|
|       | X      | X    | X    | X   | X      | X     |

Flags: The flags are set as a result of the addition operation.

```
mov     al,0efh          1 1
add     al,01ah           EF
mov     bx,1234h        + 1A
add     bx,5678h         109
mov     eax,00000a5a5h
add     eax,000000ff0h
```

When adding a series of numbers one typically uses the non-carry ADD first, followed by ADC for each additional calculation, taking into account the resulting Carry flag.

```
a = a  +   b    +  c   +  d   + e
a = a  ADD b  ADC c  ADC d  ADC e

        mov     eax,0000a5a5h
        add     eax,00000ff0h
        adc     eax,0000ff00h
        adc     eax,000ff000h
        adc     eax,00ff0000h

; Add two 64 #'s     ecx:ebx + edx:eax
        add     ebx,eax     ; Carry results from lower 32 bits.
        adc     ecx,edx     ; Add upper 32 bits + carry

; or when using a 64-bit processor
        add     rbx,rax     ; 64 bits
; and then add with carry for a 128-bit summation.
        adc     rcx,rdx
```

Sums for really big numbers can be calculated in this way. Need a number 8000 bits long? You can do it in assembly by continuously adding the carry of previous arithmetic operations onto a current operation.

# INC — Increment by 1

| Mnemonic | P | PII | K6 | 3D! | 3Mx+ | SSE | SSE2 | A64 | SSE3 | E64T |
|----------|---|-----|----|-----|------|-----|------|-----|------|------|
| INC | ✓ | ✓ | ✓ | ✓ | ✓ | ✓ | ✓ | 32 | ✓ | 32 |

inc    *rmDst(8/16/32/64)*    (Un)signed

The INC general-purpose instruction is very similar to the ADD instruction, adding a value of 1 to the 8-, 16-, 32-, or 64-bit *destination*. The result is saved in the *destination*: $d = a + 1$.

| Flags | O.flow | Sign | Zero | Aux | Parity | Carry |
|-------|--------|------|------|-----|--------|-------|
|       | X      | X    | X    | X   | X      | -     |

Flags: The flags are set as a result of the addition operation. Note that the Carry flag is unaffected.

It is recommended that an ADD instruction be used instead of an INC since flag dependencies can cause stalling due to previous writes to the EFLAG registers.

**64-bit**   **No 64-bit:**   Due to remapping of the REX prefix in 64-bit mode, this instruction can no longer access a register directly:

```
inc  eax
```

Use this instead:

```
add eax,1
```

Various forms of indirect memory reference, such as the following, are still allowed:

```
inc [eax]
inc [eax+ebx*4]
```

This applies to all the general-purpose registers.

```
mov     al,0efh
inc     al

mov     bx,1234h
inc     bx

mov     eax,00000a5a5h
inc     eax
```

$$
\begin{array}{r}
1 \\
\mathrm{EF} \\
+\quad 1 \\
\hline
\mathrm{F0}
\end{array}
$$

**Note:** There is no Carry flag set for this instruction. If a carry is needed, use ADD reg/mem, 1.

**Tip:** The 80x86 is one of the few processors that can perform an operation upon a memory location, not necessarily only in a register. An instruction cannot be preempted by another thread or process in the middle of its execution. It must complete its execution first!

## Thread-Safe Increment

```
#ifdef _M_IX86
#define  QUICK_INCREMENT(v) __asm inc v;
#else
#define  QUICK_INCREMENT(v) \
    EnterMutex()    \
    v++;            \
    ExitMutex()
#endif
```

# XADD — Exchange and Add

XADD *destination, source*

| Mnemonic | P | PII | K6 | 3D! | 3Mx+ | SSE | SSE2 | A64 | SSE3 | E64T |
|----------|---|-----|-----|-----|------|-----|------|-----|------|------|
| XADD | ✓ | ✓ | ✓ | ✓ | ✓ | ✓ | ✓ | ✓ | ✓ | ✓ |

xadd   *rmDst, rSrc(8/16/32/64)*   Signed

The XADD general-purpose instruction first exchanges the values in the *source* general-purpose register and *destination* just like the XCHG instruction and then logically sums the 8-, 16-, 32-, or 64-bit *source* to the *destination,* saves the result in *destination*, and sets the flags accordingly.

This instruction is rarely used except in the case where a register exchange needs to take place so as to preserve the old value. This is equivalent to four separate instructions:

|              | edx = D | eax = A | ebx = tmp |
|--------------|---------|---------|-----------|
|              | OLD     | NEW     |           |
| mov ebx,eax  | OLD     | NEW     | NEW       |
| mov eax,edx  | OLD     | OLD     | NEW       |
| mov edx,ebx  | NEW     | OLD     | NEW       |
| add edx,eax  | NEW+OLD | OLD     |           |
|              | NEW+OLD | OLD     |           |

...or two instructions by using the XCHG instruction.

|  | edx = D | eax = A |
|---|---|---|
|  | OLD | NEW |
| xchg edx,eax | NEW | OLD |
| add  edx,eax | NEW+OLD | OLD |
|  | NEW+OLD | OLD |

As you can see, the old value is preserved in the source register, and the destination memory gets the sum of the new and old values.

| Flags | O.flow | Sign | Zero | Aux | Parity | Carry |
|---|---|---|---|---|---|---|
|  | X | X | X | X | X | X |

Flags: The flags are set as a result of the addition operation.

# SUB — Subtract

# SBB — Subtract with Borrow

SUB *destination, source*

| Mnemonic | P | PII | K6 | 3D! | 3Mx+ | SSE | SSE2 | A64 | SSE3 | E64T |
|---|---|---|---|---|---|---|---|---|---|---|
| SUB | ✓ | ✓ | ✓ | ✓ | ✓ | ✓ | ✓ | ✓ | ✓ | ✓ |
| SBB | ✓ | ✓ | ✓ | ✓ | ✓ | ✓ | ✓ | ✓ | ✓ | ✓ |

sub    *rmDst(8/16/32/64), #(8/16/32)*    Signed
sub    *rmDst, rSrc(8/16/32/64)*
sub    *rDst, rmSrc(8/16/32/64)*

The SUB general-purpose instruction logically subtracts the 8-, 16-, 32-, or 64-bit *source* from the *destination,* saves the result in *destination,* and sets the flags accordingly. An 8-bit immediate source value can be sign extended to 16-, 32-, or 64-bit value. A 32-bit immediate source value can be sign extended to a 64-bit *destination*: $d = b - a$.

sbb    *rmDst(8/16/32/64), #(8/16/32)*    Signed
sbb    *rmDst, rSrc(8/16/32/64)*
sbb    *rDst, rmSrc(8/16/32/64)*

The SBB general-purpose instruction does exactly the same thing but with one difference: The Carry flag is referred to as the borrow flag with a value of 0 or 1, which is subtracted from the ending result.

$6d = b - a - (Carry)$

| Flags | O.flow | Sign | Zero | Aux | Parity | Carry |
|-------|--------|------|------|-----|--------|-------|
|       | X      | X    | X    | X   | X      | X     |

Flags: The flags are set as a result of the subtraction operation. When carry is set (1) it indicates a borrow is needed.

```
mov    al,0efh
sub    al,01ah
```

$$\begin{array}{r} EF \\ -\ 1A \\ \hline D5 \end{array}$$

When subtracting a series of numbers one typically uses SUB for the first subtraction, followed by SBB for each additional subtraction, taking into account the Carry flag, which indicates a borrow is required from the next calculation.

```
a = a – b – c – d – e
a = a SUB b SBB c SBB d SBB e
```

```
mov    eax,0000a5a5h
sub    eax,00000ff0h
sbb    eax,0000ff00h
sbb    eax,000ff000h
sbb    eax,00ff0000h
```

# DEC — Decrement by 1

| Mnemonic | P | PII | K6 | 3D! | 3Mx+ | SSE | SSE2 | A64 | SSE3 | E64T |
|----------|---|-----|-----|-----|------|-----|------|-----|------|------|
| DEC      | ✓ | ✓   | ✓   | ✓   | ✓    | ✓   | ✓    | 32  | ✓    | 32   |

dec    *rmDst(8/16/32/64)*    (Un)signed

The DEC general-purpose instruction is very similar to the SUB instruction, subtracting a value of 1 from the 8-, 16-, 32-, or 64-bit *destination*. The result is saved in the *destination*: d = a – 1.

| Flags | O.flow | Sign | Zero | Aux | Parity | Carry |
|-------|--------|------|------|-----|--------|-------|
|       | X      | X    | X    | X   | X      | -     |

Flags: The flags are set as a result of the subtraction operation. Note that the carry is unaffected.

It is recommended that a SUB instruction be used instead of a DEC since flag dependencies can cause stalling due to previous writes to the EFLAG registers.

64-bit **No 64-bit:**  Due to remapping of the REX prefix in 64-bit mode, this instruction can no longer access a register directly:

```
dec   eax
```

Use this instead:

```
sub eax,1
```

The various forms of indirect memory reference, such as the following, are still allowed:

```
dec [eax]
dec tbl[ebx+ecx*2]
```

This applies to all the general-purpose registers.

```
mov     al,0efh
dec     al
```

$$
\begin{array}{r}
1 \\
EF \\
-\ \ 1 \\
\hline
EE
\end{array}
$$

## Thread-Safe Decrement

```
#ifdef _M_IX86
#define  QUICK_DECREMENT(v) __asm dec v;
#else
#define  QUICK_DECREMENT(v) \
    EnterMutex()   \
    v--;           \
    ExitMutex()
#endif
```

**Hint:**  A problem sometimes appears in programming, especially in video games with really high score rollovers. A value is incremented and needs to be saturated at $2^N-1$, such as $2^8-1$ is 255. Some programmers assume the maximum value will never be reached and thus allow it to be incremented too much, risking that the value will roll over to zero.

Some programmers will have code such as follows:

```
      inc al
      jnz $L1      ; Jump if not saturated!
      dec al
$L1:
```

But that introduces some branching and misprediction. (Branch misprediction will be discussed in a later chapter.) A branchless code methodology can be alternatively utilized where the state of the Carry flag is taken to advantage. Remember, the INC does not affect the Carry flag but the ADD instruction does.

```
add al,1
sbb al,0
```

Instead of using an increment, a non-carry addition is used. A normal advancement of one to a value ranging from [0, 255) has a carry of zero, but upon 255+1, a carry is generated. Immediately subtracting a zero with no carry has no effect. But subtracting a zero with a carry takes that one increment back off. Normally $d = a + 1 - 0_c$, then upon rollover $d = a + 1 - 1_c$. In essence, a saturation is created. This same logic can be applied for $2^{16}$, $2^{32}$, or $2^{64}$, whatever your data size is. The code is smaller and much faster.

Contrarily, a down count to the floor value of zero can be implemented utilizing this same rollback method:

```
sub al,1
adc al,0
```

The number is decremented until the floor is reached, thus initiating a borrow, and then the borrow is summed back in. Normally, $d = a - 1 + 0_c$, then upon rollover, $d = a - 1 + 1_c$.

# Packed Addition and Subtraction

At this point the focus turns to the integer addition and subtraction of numbers in parallel. With the general-purpose instructions of a processor, normal calculations of addition and subtraction take place one at a time as scalar operations. These can instead be pipelined so that multiple integer calculations can occur simultaneously, but when performing large numbers of similar type calculations there is a bottleneck of processor calculation time. By using vector calculations, multiple like calculations can be performed simultaneously. The only trick here is to remember the key phrase "multiple *like* calculations."

If, for example, four pairs of 32-bit words are being calculated simultaneously such as in the following addition:

$$
\begin{array}{cccc}
47 & 53 & 38 & 87 \\
+\ 23 & +\ 74 & +\ 39 & +\ 16 \\
\hline
70 & 127 & 77 & 103 \\
\end{array}
$$

...or subtraction:

| 47 | 53 | 38 | 87 |
|---|---|---|---|
| − 23 | − 74 | − 39 | − 16 |
| 24 | − 21 | −1 | 71 |

...the point is that the calculations all need to use the same operator. There is an exception, but this is too early to discuss it. There are workarounds, such as if only a couple of expressions need a calculated adjustment while others do not, then adding or subtracting a zero would keep their result neutral.

| 47 | 53 | 38 | 87 |
|---|---|---|---|
| + 23 | + 0 | + 39 | + 0 |
| 70 | 53 | 77 | 87 |

Remember your algebraic law:

**Algebraic Law**: | Additive Identity | $n + 0 = 0 + n = n$ |

It is in essence a wasted calculation, but its use as a placeholder helps make SIMD instructions easier to use.

**Algebraic Law**: | Additive Inverse | $a - b = a + (-b)$ |

The other little item to remember is that subtraction is merely the addition of a value's additive inverse:

$$a - b = a + (-b)$$

# PADDB/PADDW/PADDD/PADDQ Integer Addition

PADDx *destination, source*

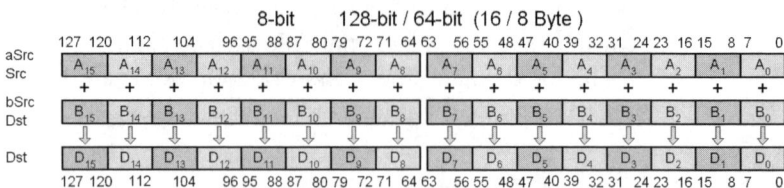

8-bit    128-bit / 64-bit (16 / 8 Byte )

$$d_{(0...n-1)} = a_{(0...n-1)} + b_{(0...n-1)} \quad n = \{16, 8, 4, 2\}$$

| Mnemonic | P | PII | K6 | 3D! | 3Mx+ | SSE | SSE2 | A64 | SSE3 | E64T |
|---|---|---|---|---|---|---|---|---|---|---|
| PADDx | | ✓ | ✓ | ✓ | ✓ | ✓ | ✓ | ✓ | ✓ | ✓ |
| PADDQ | | | | | | | ✓ | ✓ | ✓ | ✓ |

MMX    padd(b/w/d/q) *mmxDst, mmxSrc/m64*    [Un]signed    64
SSE2    padd(b/w/d/q) *xmmDst, xmmSrc/m128*    [Un]signed    128

The PADDx instruction is a parallel operation that uses an adder on each of the source bit blocks *aSrc (xmmSrc)* and *bSrc (xmmDst)* and stores the result in the destination *Dst (xmmDst)*.

The instructions may be labeled as packed, parallel, or vector, but each *block of bits* is in reality isolated from each other. The following is a 32-bit example consisting of four *unsigned* 8-bit values:

| 31...24 | 23...16 | 15...8 | 7...0 | 31...0 |
|---|---|---|---|---|
| 95 | 231 | 131 | 187 | 0x5F E7 83 BB |
| + 85 | + 37 | + 103 | + 11 | + 0x55 25 67 0B |
| (0xB4) 180 | (0x0C) 12 | (0xEA) 234 | (0xC6) 198 | 0xB4 0C EA C6 |

...and four *signed* 8-bit values:

| 31...24 | 23...16 | 15...8 | 7...0 | 31...0 |
|---|---|---|---|---|
| 95 | − 25 | − 125 | − 69 | 0x5F E7 83 BB |
| + 85 | + 37 | + 103 | + 11 | + 0x55 25 67 0B |
| (0xB4) 180 | (0x0C) 12 | (0xEA) − 22 | (0xC6) − 58 | 0xB4 0C EA C6 |

Regardless of the decimal representation of unsigned or signed, the hex values of the two examples remains the same, which is the reason for these being [Un]signed, thus sign neutral.

Notice in the following additions of 7-bit signed values that with the limit range of −64...63 the worst case of negative and positive limit values results with no overflow.

```
  11000000b  C0 (−64)       00111111b  3F (63)
+ 11000000b  C0 (−64)     + 00111111b  3F (63)
  80000000b  80 (−128)      11111110b  7E (126)
```

Of course, positive and negative signed values could also be intermixed without an overflow. For a 7-bit unsigned value, 0...127, there would be no overflow.

```
  11000000b  C0 (−64)       01111111b  7F (127)
+ 00111111b  3F  (63)     + 01111111b  7F (127)
  11111111b  FF  (−1)       11111110b  FE (254)
```

The eighth unused bit is in reality used as a buffer to prevent any overflow to a ninth bit.

# Vector {8/16/32/64}-Bit Int Addition with Saturation

$$d_{(0...n-1)} = \text{Max}(\text{Min}(a_{(0...n-1)} + b_{(0...n-1)}, \text{HI\_LIMIT}), \text{LO\_LIMIT}) \quad _{n=\{16, 8, 4, 2\}}$$

| Mnemonic | P | PII | K6 | 3D! | 3Mx+ | SSE | SSE2 | A64 | SSE3 | E64T |
|----------|---|-----|----|----|------|-----|------|-----|------|------|
| PADDSx | ✓ | ✓ | ✓ | ✓ | ✓ | ✓ | ✓ | ✓ | ✓ | ✓ |
| PADDUSx | ✓ | ✓ | ✓ | ✓ | ✓ | ✓ | ✓ | ✓ | ✓ | ✓ |

| | | | | |
|---|---|---|---|---|
| MMX | paddus(b/w) *mmxDst, mmxSrc/m64* | Unsigned | 64 | |
| " | padds(b/w) *mmxDst, mmxSrc/m64* | Signed | | |
| SSE2 | paddus(b/w) *xmmDst, xmmSrc/m128* | Unsigned | 128 | |
| " | padds(b/w) *xmmDst, xmmSrc/m128* | Signed | | |

The PADDSx (signed) and PADDUSx (unsigned) instructions are a parallel operation that uses an adder on each of the source bit block registers *aSrc (xmmSrc)* and *bSrc (xmmDst)* and stores the result in the destination *Dst (xmmDst)* using saturation logic to prevent any possible wraparound.

Each calculation limits the value to the extents of the related data type so that if the limit is exceeded, it is clipped inclusively to that limit. This is handled differently whether it is signed or unsigned, as they both use different limit values. Effectively, the result of the summation is compared to the upper limit with a Min expression and compared to the lower limit with a Max expression. Notice in the previous section that when two signed 8-bit values of 0x7F (127) are summed, a value of 0xFE (254) results but is clipped to the maximum value of 0x7f (127).

The same applies if, for example, two values of 0x80 (–128) are summed, resulting in –256 but clipped to the minimum value of 0x80 (–128).

The instructions may be labeled as packed, parallel, or vector but each block of bits is in reality isolated from each other.

| 31...24 | 23...16 | 15...8 | 7...0 | 31...0 |
|---|---|---|---|---|
| 95 | 120 | –125 | –69 | 0x5F 78 83 BB |
| + 85 | + 37 | + –32 | + 11 | + 0x55 25 E0 0B |
| (0x7F) 127 | (0x7F) 127 | (0x80) –128 | (0xC6) –58 | 0x7F 7F 80 C6 |

A sample use of this instruction would be for sound mixing where two sound waves are mixed into a single wave for output. The saturation point keeps the amplitude of the wave from wrapping from a positive or high level into a negative or low one, thus creating a pulse encoded harmonic, or distortion.

For saturation, the limits are different for the data size as well as for signed and unsigned.

|  | 8-bit | 16-bit |
|---|---|---|
| signed | –128...127 | –32768...32767 |
| unsigned | 0...255 | 0...65535 |

## PSUBB/PSUBW/PSUBD/PSUBQ Integer Subtraction

PSUBx *destination, source*  $D\mathrel{-}= A$

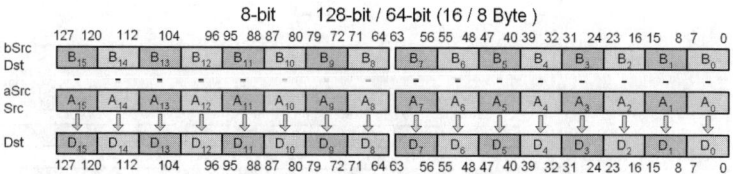

$$d_{(0...n-1)} = b_{(0...n-1)} - a_{(0...n-1)} \quad n=\{16, 8, 4, 2\}$$

| Mnemonic | P | PII | K6 | 3D! | 3Mx+ | SSE | SSE2 | A64 | SSE3 | E64T |
|----------|---|-----|-----|-----|------|-----|------|-----|------|------|
| PSUBx | | ✓ | ✓ | ✓ | ✓ | ✓ | ✓ | ✓ | ✓ | ✓ |
| PSUBQ | | | | | | | ✓ | ✓ | ✓ | ✓ |

MMX   psub(b/w/d/q) *mmxDst, mmxSrc/m64*   [Un]signed   64
SSE2   psub(b/w/d/q) *xmmDst, xmmSrc/m128*   [Un]signed   128

This vector instruction is a parallel operation that subtracts each of the source bit blocks *aSrc (xmmSrc)* from *bSrc (xmmDst)* and stores the result in the destination *Dst (xmmDst)*.

> **Note:** Be careful here! The register and operator ordering is as follows:
>
> $xmmDst_{(31...0)} = xmmDst_{(31...0)} - xmmSrc_{(31...0)}$   D = D – A

| 31...24 | 23...16 | 15...8 | 7...0 | 31...0 |
|---------|---------|--------|-------|--------|
| −126 | 91 | −56 | −96 | 0x82 5B C8 A0 |
| − 12 | − 122 | − −57 | − 114 | − 0x0C 7A C7 72 |
| (0x76) 118 | (0xE1) −31 | (0x01) 1 | (0x2E) 46 | 0x76 E1 01 2E |

# Vector {8/16/32/64}-Bit Integer Subtraction with Saturation

PSUBSx *destination, source*    $D -= A$

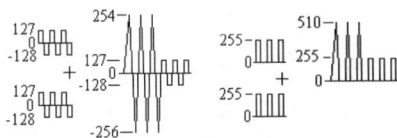

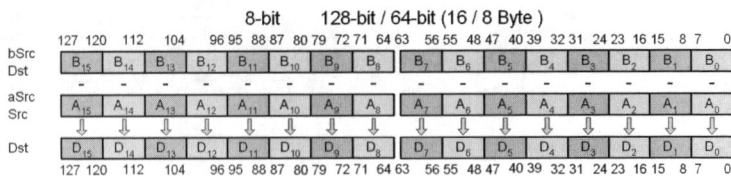

8-bit    128-bit / 64-bit (16 / 8 Byte )

$$d_{(0...n-1)} = Max(Min(b_{(0...n-1)} - a_{(0...n-1)}, HI\_LIMIT), LO\_LIMIT)$$   n={16, 8, 4, 2}

| Mnemonic | P | PII | K6 | 3D! | 3Mx+ | SSE | SSE2 | A64 | SSE3 | E64T |
|----------|---|-----|----|----|------|-----|------|-----|------|------|
| PSUBSx   |   | ✓ | ✓ | ✓ | ✓ | ✓ | ✓ | ✓ | ✓ | ✓ |
| PSUBUSx  |   | ✓ | ✓ | ✓ | ✓ | ✓ | ✓ | ✓ | ✓ | ✓ |

| | | | |
|---|---|---|---|
| MMX | psubus(b/w) *mmxDst, mmxSrc/m64* | Unsigned | 64 |
| | psubs(b/w) *mmxDst, mmxSrc/m64* | Signed | |
| SSE2 | psubus(b/w) *xmmDst, xmmSrc/m128* | Unsigned | 128 |
| | psubs(b/w) *xmmDst, xmmSrc/m128* | Signed | |

This vector instruction is a parallel operation that subtracts each of the source bit blocks *aSrc (xmmSrc)* from *bSrc (xmmDst)* and stores the result in the destination *Dst (xmmDst)*.

| 31...24 | 23...16 | 15...8 | 7...0 | 31...0 |
|---------|---------|--------|-------|--------|
| −126 | 91 | −56 | −96 | 0x82 5B C8 A0 |
| − 12 | − 122 | − −57 | − 114 | − 0x0C 7A C7 72 |
| (0x80) −128 | (0xE1) −31 | (0x01) 1 | (0x80) −128 | 0x76 E1 01 80 |

# Vector Addition and Subtraction (Fixed Point)

For most of the number crunching in your games or tools you will most likely use single-precision floating-point. For artificial intelligence (AI) and other high-precision calculations, you may wish to use the higher precision double-precision, but it only exists in scalar form on the FPU, except for the case of the SSE2 or above, so functionality must be emulated in a sequential fashion whenever possible. But even with the higher precision, there is still a bit of an accuracy problem.

An alternative would be to use integer calculations in a fixed-point format of zero or more places. If the data size is large enough to contain the number, then there is no precision loss!

## Pseudo Vec

These can get pretty verbose, as for fixed-point (integer) addition there would be support for 8-, 16-, and 32-bit data elements within a 128-bit vector and these would be signed and unsigned, with and without saturation. The interesting thing about adding signed and unsigned numbers, other than the carry or borrow, is that the resulting value will be exactly the same and thus the same equation can be used. This can be viewed in the following 8-bit example:

| Unsigned | Hex | Signed |
|---:|---:|---:|
| 95 | 05Fh | 95 |
| + 240 | + 0F0h | + −16 |
| 335 | C=1 04Fh | C=0 79 |
| C=1 79 | C=1 (79) | C=0 79 |

Notice that the resulting bits from the 8-bit calculation are all the same. Only the carry is different and the resulting bits are only interpreted as being signed or unsigned.

# Pseudo Vec (x86)

Now let's examine these functions closer. MMX and SSE2 have the biggest payoff, as 3DNow! and SSE are primarily for floating-point support.

```
mov   ebx,pbB       ; Vector B
mov   eax,pbA       ; Vector A
mov   edx,pbD       ; Vector Destination
```

The following is a 16×8-bit addition but substituting a PSUBB for the PADDB will transform it into a subtraction.

## vmp_paddB (MMX) 16×8-Bit

Listing 7-1: ...\chap07\pas\PAddX86M.asm

```
movq   mm0,[ebx+0]    ; Read B Data {B₇...B₀}
movq   mm1,[ebx+8]    ;              {B_F...B₈}
movq   mm2,[eax+0]    ; Read A Data {A₇...A₀}
movq   mm3,[eax+8]    ;              {A_F...A₈}

paddb  mm0,mm2        ; lower 64 bits {A₇+B₇ ... A₀+B₀}
paddb  mm1,mm3        ; upper 64 bits {A_F+B_F ... A₈+B₈}

movq   [edx+0],mm0
movq   [edx+8],mm1
```

For SSE, it is essentially the same function wrapper, keeping in mind aligned memory MOVDQA versus non-aligned memory MOVDQU.

## vmp_paddB (SSE2) 16×8-Bit

Listing 7-2: ...\chap07\pas\PAddX86M.asm

```
movdqa  xmm0,[ebx]    ; Read B Data {B_F...B₀}
movdqa  xmm1,[eax]    ; Read A Data {A_F...A₀}
paddb   xmm0,xmm1     ; {vA+vB} 128 bits {A_F+B_F ... A₀+B₀}
movdqa  [edx],xmm0    ; Write D Data
```

The following is a master substitution table for change of functionality, addition versus subtraction (inclusive/exclusive of saturation).

|         | Add   | Sub   | Add    | Sub    | Add     | Sub     |
|---------|-------|-------|--------|--------|---------|---------|
| 8-bit   | paddb | psubb | paddsb | psubsb | paddusb | psubusb |
| 16-bit  | paddw | psubw | paddsw | psubsw | paddusw | psubusw |
| 32-bit  | paddd | psubd |        |        |         |         |
| 64-bit  | paddq | psubq |        |        |         |         |

# Averages

$$VD[] = (vA[] + vB[] + 1) \div 2;$$

## PAVGB/PAVGUSB — N×8-Bit [Un]signed Integer Average

| Mnemonic | P | PII | K6 | 3D! | 3Mx+ | SSE | SSE2 | A64 | SSE3 | E64T |
|----------|---|-----|----|-----|------|-----|------|-----|------|------|
| PAVGB    |   |     |    |     | ✓    | ✓   | ✓    | ✓   | ✓    | ✓    |
| PAVGUSB  |   |     |    | ✓   | ✓    |     |      | ✓   |      |      |

| 3DNow! | pavgusb *mmxDst, mmxSrc/m64* | Unsigned | 64 |
|--------|------------------------------|----------|-----|
| MMX+   | pavgb  *mmxDst, mmxSrc/m64*  | Unsigned | 64 |
| SSE    | pavgb  *mmxDst, mmxSrc/m64*  | Unsigned | 64 |
| SSE2   | pavgb  *xmmDst, xmmSrc/m128* | Unsigned | 128 |

This SIMD instruction is a 64 (128)-bit parallel operation that sums the eight (16) individual 8-bit source integer bit blocks *aSrc* (*xmmSrc*) and *bSrc* (*xmmDst*), adds one, then divides by two and returns the lower 8 bits with the result being stored in the destination *Dst* (*xmmDst*).

**(64-bit) 8×8-bit**

$$Dst_{(7...0)} = ( aSrc_{(7...0)} + 1 + bSrc_{(7...0)} ) >> 1$$
$$Dst_{(15...8)} = ( aSrc_{(15...8)} + 1 + bSrc_{(15...8)} ) >> 1$$
$$Dst_{(23...16)} = ( aSrc_{(23...16)} + 1 + bSrc_{(23...16)} ) >> 1$$
$$Dst_{(31...24)} = ( aSrc_{(31...24)} + 1 + bSrc_{(31...24)} ) >> 1$$
$$Dst_{(39...32)} = ( aSrc_{(39...32)} + 1 + bSrc_{(39...32)} ) >> 1$$
$$Dst_{(47...40)} = ( aSrc_{(47...40)} + 1 + bSrc_{(47...40)} ) >> 1$$
$$Dst_{(55...48)} = ( aSrc_{(55...48)} + 1 + bSrc_{(55...48)} ) >> 1$$
$$Dst_{(63...56)} = ( aSrc_{(63...56)} + 1 + bSrc_{(63...56)} ) >> 1$$

$$Dst_{(71...64)} = (aSrc_{(71...64)} + 1 + bSrc_{(71...64)}) >> 1$$
$$Dst_{(79...72)} = (aSrc_{(79...72)} + 1 + bSrc_{(79...72)}) >> 1$$
$$Dst_{(87...80)} = (aSrc_{(87...80)} + 1 + bSrc_{(87...80)}) >> 1$$
$$Dst_{(95...88)} = (aSrc_{(95...88)} + 1 + bSrc_{(95...88)}) >> 1$$
$$Dst_{(103...96)} = (aSrc_{(103...96)} + 1 + bSrc_{(103...96)}) >> 1$$
$$Dst_{(111...104)} = (aSrc_{(111...104)} + 1 + bSrc_{(111...104)}) >> 1$$
$$Dst_{(119...112)} = (aSrc_{(119...112)} + 1 + bSrc_{(119...112)}) >> 1$$
$$Dst_{(127...120)} = (aSrc_{(127...120)} + 1 + bSrc_{(127...120)}) >> 1$$

(128-bit) **16×8-bit**

**Tip:** These two instructions are remnants from the processor wars. They have two different mnemonics with two different opcodes, but they have the same functionality. PAVGB was added to the AMD instruction set, which matched the SSE instruction PAVGB but had the same functionality as AMD's PAVGUSB. If the target is 3DNow! and MMX extensions or better, use the instruction PAVGB.

# PAVGW — N×16-Bit [Un]signed Integer Average

| Mnemonic | P | PII | K6 | 3D! | 3Mx+ | SSE | SSE2 | A64 | SSE3 | E64T |
|----------|---|-----|----|-----|------|-----|------|-----|------|------|
| PAVGW    |   |     |    |     | ✓    | ✓   | ✓    | ✓   | ✓    | ✓    |

| MMX+ | pavgw *mmxDst, mmxSrc/m64* | Unsigned | 64 |
| SSE | pavgw *mmxDst, mmxSrc/m64* | Unsigned | 64 |
| SSE2 | pavgw *xmmDst, xmmSrc/m128* | Unsigned | 128 |

This SIMD instruction is a 64 (128)-bit parallel operation that sums the four (eight) individual 16-bit source integer bit blocks *aSrc (xmmSrc)* and *bSrc (xmmDst)*, adds one, then divides by two and returns the lower 16 bits with the result being stored in the destination *Dst (xmmDst)*.

(64-bit) **4×16-bit**

$$Dst_{(15...0)} = (aSrc_{(15...0)} + 1 + bSrc_{(15...0)}) >> 1$$
$$Dst_{(31...16)} = (aSrc_{(31...16)} + 1 + bSrc_{(31...16)}) >> 1$$
$$Dst_{(47...32)} = (aSrc_{(47...32)} + 1 + bSrc_{(47...32)}) >> 1$$
$$Dst_{(63...48)} = (aSrc_{(63...48)} + 1 + bSrc_{(63...48)}) >> 1$$
$$Dst_{(79...64)} = (aSrc_{(79...64)} + 1 + bSrc_{(79...64)}) >> 1$$
$$Dst_{(95...80)} = (aSrc_{(95...80)} + 1 + bSrc_{(95...80)}) >> 1$$
$$Dst_{(111...96)} = (aSrc_{(111...96)} + 1 + bSrc_{(111...96)}) >> 1$$
$$Dst_{(127...112)} = (aSrc_{(127...112)} + 1 + bSrc_{(127...112)}) >> 1$$

(128-bit) **8×16-bit**

# Sum of Absolute Differences

The simplified form of this parallel instruction individually calculates the differences of each of the packed bits, then sums the absolute value for all of them, and returns the result in the destination.

VD[0] = | vA[0] – vB[0] | + ... + | vA[n–1] – vB[n–1] |;

## PSADBW — N×8-Bit Sum of Absolute Differences

| Mnemonic | P | PII | K6 | 3D! | 3Mx+ | SSE | SSE2 | A64 | SSE3 | E64T |
|---|---|---|---|---|---|---|---|---|---|---|
| PSADBW | | | | | ✓ | ✓ | ✓ | ✓ | ✓ | ✓ |

| | | | |
|---|---|---|---|
| MMX+ | psadbw *mmxDst, mmxSrc/m64* | Unsigned | 64 |
| SSE | psadbw *mmxDst, mmxSrc/m64* | Unsigned | 64 |
| SSE2 | psadbw *xmmDst, xmmSrc/m128* | Unsigned | 128 |

### 8×8-Bit Sum of Absolute Differences

```
Dst(15...0) = abs(Src(7...0) - Dst(7...0)) + abs(Src(15...8) -
        Dst(15...8))
    + abs(Src(23...16) - Dst(23...16)) + abs(Src(31...24) - Dst(31...24))
    + abs(Src(39...32) - Dst(39...32)) + abs(Src(47...40) - Dst(47...40))
    + abs(Src(55...48) - Dst(55...48)) + abs(Src(63...56) - Dst(63...56))
Dst(63...16) = 0;
```

### 16×8-Bit Sum of Absolute Differences

```
Dst(31...16) = abs(Src(71...64) - Dst(71...64)) + abs(Src(79...72) -
        Dst(79...72))
    + abs(Src(87...80) - Dst(87...80)) + abs(Src(95...88) - Dst(95...88))
    + abs(Src(103...96) - Dst(103...96)) + abs(Src(111...104) -
        Dst(111...104))
    + abs(Src(119...112) - Dst(119...112)) + abs(Src(127...120) -
        Dst(127...120))
Dst(127...32) = 0
```

# Integer Multiplication

Integer data is expanded upon the calculation of a product between two operands, and thus two operands are needed to store the result. Depending on whether the source values are small enough, the operand receiving the upper bits of the result may be ignored as it always contains a predictable amount.

## MUL — Unsigned Muliplication (Scalar)

MUL *operand*

| Mnemonic | P | PII | K6 | 3D! | 3Mx+ | SSE | SSE2 | A64 | SSE3 | E64T |
|----------|---|-----|-----|-----|------|-----|------|-----|------|------|
| MUL | ✓ | ✓ | ✓ | ✓ | ✓ | ✓ | ✓ | ✓ | ✓ | ✓ |

mul     *rmDst(8/16/32/64)*     (Un)signed

The MUL general-purpose instruction multiplies the unsigned 8-, 16-, 32-, or 64-bit *operand* by the unsigned AL/AX/EAX/RAX register, saves the result based upon the bit size of the operand as indicated in the table below, and sets the flags accordingly.

|  | 8-bit | 16-bit | 32-bit | 64-bit |
|-----------|----------|----------|------------|------------|
| operation | AL × BL | AX × BX | EAX × EBX | RAX × RBX |
| result | AX | DX:AX | EDX:EAX | RDX:RAX |

| **Flags** | O.flow | Sign | Zero | Aux | Parity | Carry |
|-----------|--------|------|------|-----|--------|-------|
|  | X | - | - | - | - | X |

Flags: If the upper half of the resulting bits are 0, then the Overflow and Carry bits are set to 0; else they are set to 1. The other flags are undefined.

A square operation ($x^2$) is actually pretty simple!

```
mov     rax,7
mul     rax          ; rdx:rax = rax × rax
```

## IMUL — Signed Multiplication (Scalar)

IMUL *operand*
IMUL *operand1, operand2*
IMUL *operand1, operand2, operand3*

| Mnemonic | P | PII | K6 | 3D! | 3Mx+ | SSE | SSE2 | A64 | SSE3 | E64T |
|----------|---|-----|-----|-----|------|-----|------|-----|------|------|
| IMUL | ✓ | ✓ | ✓ | ✓ | ✓ | ✓ | ✓ | ✓ | ✓ | ✓ |

imul *rmDst(8/16/32/64)*                      Signed
imul *rDst(16/32/64), rmSrc(16/32/64)*
imul *rDst(8/16/32/64), #(8/16/32)*
imul *rDst(16/32/64), rmSrc(16/32/64), #(8/16/32)*

The IMUL general-purpose instruction has three forms based upon the number of operands.

■ One Operand — Similar to that of the MUL instruction but deals with signed numbers. That is, it multiplies the 8-, 16-, 32-, or 64-bit signed *operand* by the unsigned AL/AX/EAX/RAX register, saves the result based upon the bit size of the operand as indicated in the table below, and sets the flags accordingly.

■ Two Operands — Used for multiplication of 16-, 32-, or 64-bit signed numbers in *operand1* with the value in *operand2* and stores the result in *operand1*. Unlike MUL, AX/EAX/RAX is not used unless it is one of the two operands. If *operand2* is an immediate value, then it is sign extended to match *operand1*.

■ Three Operands — Used for multiplication of 16-, 32-, or 64-bit signed numbers in *operand2* with the sign extended immediate value in *operand3*. The result is stored in *operand1*. Unlike MUL, AX/EAX/RAX is not used unless it is one of the three operands.

|  | 8-bit | 16-bit | 32-bit | 64-bit |
|--------|-------|--------|--------|--------|
| result | AX | DX:AX | EDX:EAX | RDX:RAX |

| Flags | O.flow | Sign | Zero | Aux | Parity | Carry |
|-------|--------|------|------|-----|--------|-------|
|  | X | - | - | - | - | X |

Flags: If the upper half of the resulting bits are 0 then the Overflow and Carry bits are set to 0, else they are set to 1. The other flags are undefined.

**Hint:** This instruction is designed for signed values, but the register receiving the lower set of bits of the calculated result will contain an identical value whether the source numbers were signed or unsigned.

# Packed Integer Multiplication

Packed integer multiplication is one of the mathematical equations that you will tend to use in your SIMD application either as fixed-point or just parallel integer processing. This works out nicely when it is necessary to increase the magnitude of a series of integers. The problem here comes up because fixed-point multiplication is not like floating-point multiplication. In floating-point, there is a precision loss with each calculation since a numerical value is stored in an exponential form. With fixed-point, there is no precision loss, which is great but leads to another problem. When two integers are used in a summation, the most significant bits are carried into an additional (n+1) bit. With a multiplication of two integers, the resulting storage required is (n+n=2n) bits. This poses a problem of how to deal with the resulting solution. Since the data size increases, there are multiple solutions to contain the result of the calculation.

| HI( int16×int16 ) | HI( uint16×uint16 ) | LO( int16×int16 ) |
|---|---|---|
| pmulhw | pmulhuw | pmullw |

- Store upper bits.
- Store lower bits.
- Store upper/lower bits into two vectors.
- Store even n bit elements into 2n bit elements.
- Store odd n bit elements into 2n bit elements.

## PMULLW — N×16-Bit Parallel Multiplication (Lower)

PMULLW *destination, source*

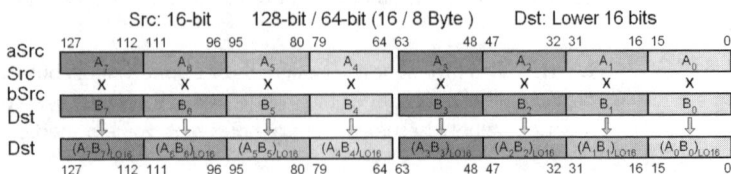

| Mnemonic | P | PII | K6 | 3D! | 3Mx+ | SSE | SSE2 | A64 | SSE3 | E64T |
|----------|---|-----|-----|-----|------|-----|------|-----|------|------|
| PMULLW   |   | ✓ | ✓ | ✓ | ✓ | ✓ | ✓ | ✓ | ✓ | ✓ |

| | | | | |
|------|------|------|------|------|
| MMX | pmullw *mmxDst, mmxSrc/m64* | [Un]signed | 64 |
| MMX+ | pmullw *mmxDst, mmxSrc/m64* | [Un]signed | 64 |
| SSE2 | pmullw *xmmDst, xmmSrc/m128* | [Un]signed | 128 |

These vector instructions use a 64 (128)-bit data path and so four (eight) operations occur in parallel. The product is calculated using each of the 16-bit half-words of the multiplicand *mmxSrc (xmmSrc)* and the 16-bit half-words of the multiplier *mmxDst (xmmDst)* for each 16-bit block, and stores the lower 16 bits of each of the results in the original 16-bit half-words of the destination *mmxDst (xmmDst)*.

**(64-bit) 4×16-bit**

$$Dst_{(15...0)} = LOWER16(\ Dst_{(15...0)} \times Src_{(15...0)}\ )$$
$$Dst_{(31...16)} = LOWER16(\ Dst_{(31...16)} \times Src_{(31...16)}\ )$$
$$Dst_{(47...32)} = LOWER16(\ Dst_{(47...32)} \times Src_{(47...32)}\ )$$
$$Dst_{(63...48)} = LOWER16(\ Dst_{(63...48)} \times Src_{(63...48)}\ )$$
$$Dst_{(79...64)} = LOWER16(\ Dst_{(79...64)} \times Src_{(79...64)}\ )$$
$$Dst_{(95...80)} = LOWER16(\ Dst_{(95...80)} \times Src_{(95...80)}\ )$$
$$Dst_{(111...96)} = LOWER16(\ Dst_{(111...96)} \times Src_{(111...96)}\ )$$
$$Dst_{(127...112)} = LOWER16(\ Dst_{(127...112)} \times Src_{(127...112)}\ )$$

**(128-bit) 8×16-bit**

| D63...D48 | D47...D32 | D31...D16 | D15...D0 |
|-----------|-----------|-----------|----------|
| 5678h | 5678h | 5678h | 5678h |
| ×0012h | ×0023h | ×0034h | ×0056h |
| 00061470h | 000bd268h | 00119060h | 001d0c50h |
| 1470h | d268h | 9060h | 0c50h |
| 1470h | 0d268h | 9060h | 0c50h |

**Hint:** When multiplying two integers of n bit size together, regardless of their values being signed or unsigned, the lower n bits of the base result will be the same so this instruction is considered sign neutral and thus [un]signed.

# PMULHW/PMULHUW — N×16-Bit Parallel Multiplication (Upper)

PMULHW *destination, source*

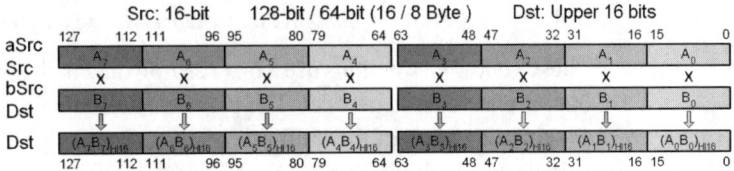

| Mnemonic | P | PII | K6 | 3D! | 3Mx+ | SSE | SSE2 | A64 | SSE3 | E64T |
|----------|---|-----|----|----|------|-----|------|-----|------|------|
| PMULHUW  |   |     |    |    | ✓    | ✓   | ✓    | ✓   | ✓    | ✓    |
| PMULHW   | ✓ | ✓   | ✓  | ✓  | ✓    | ✓   | ✓    | ✓   | ✓    | ✓    |

| MMX  | pmulhuw | *mmxDst, mmxSrc/m64*   | Unsigned | 64  |
|------|---------|------------------------|----------|-----|
|      | pmulhw  | *mmxDst, mmxSrc/m64*   | Signed   |     |
| MMX+ | pmulhuw | *mmxDst, mmxSrc/m64*   | Unsigned | 64  |
| SSE2 | pmulhuw | *xmmDst, xmmSrc/m128*  | Unsigned | 128 |
|      | pmulhw  | *xmmDst, xmmSrc/m128*  | Signed   |     |

These vector instructions use a 64 (128)-bit data path and so four (eight) operations occur in parallel. The product is calculated using each of the 16-bit half-word of the multiplicand *mmxSrc (xmmSrc)* and the 16-bit half-word of the multiplier *mmxDst (xmmDst)* for each 16-bit block, and stores the upper 16 bits of each of the results in the original 16-bit half-words of the destination *mmxDst (xmmDst)*.

(64-bit) **4×16-bit**

$$Dst_{(15...0)} = UPPER16( Dst_{(15...0)} \times Src_{(15...0)} )$$
$$Dst_{(31...16)} = UPPER16( Dst_{(31...16)} \times Src_{(31...16)} )$$
$$Dst_{(47...32)} = UPPER16( Dst_{(47...32)} \times Src_{(47...32)} )$$
$$Dst_{(63...48)} = UPPER16( Dst_{(63...48)} \times Src_{(63...48)} )$$
$$Dst_{(79...64)} = UPPER16( Dst_{(79...64)} \times Src_{(79...64)} )$$
$$Dst_{(95...80)} = UPPER16( Dst_{(95...80)} \times Src_{(95...80)} )$$
$$Dst_{(111...96)} = UPPER16( Dst_{(111...96)} \times Src_{(111...96)} )$$
$$Dst_{(127...112)} = UPPER16( Dst_{(127...112)} \times Src_{(127...112)} )$$

(128-bit) **8×16-bit**

| 63...48 | 47...32 | 31...16 | 15...0 | 63...0 |
|---------|---------|---------|--------|--------|
| 8374 | 373 | 9382 | 2043 | 20B6 0175 24A6 07FB |
| × 54 | × 38 | × 5 | × 7 | × 0036 0026 0005 0007 |
| 452196 | 14174 | 46910 | 14301 | E664 375E B73E 37DD |

| D63...D48 | D47...D32 | D31...D16 | D15...D0 |
|-----------|-----------|-----------|----------|
| 5678h | 5678h | 5678h | 5678h |
| ×0012h | ×0023h | ×0034h | ×0056h |
| 00061470h | 000bd268h | 00119060h | 001d0c50h |
| 0006    h | 000b    h | 0011    h | 001d    h |
| 0006h | 000bh | 0011h | 001dh |

# PMULHRW — Signed 4×16-Bit Multiplication with Rounding (Upper)

PMULHRW *destination, source*

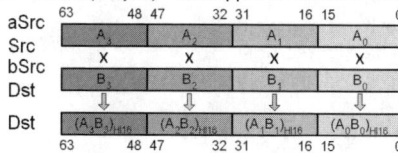

| Mnemonic | P | PII | K6 | 3D! | 3Mx+ | SSE | SSE2 | A64 | SSE3 | E64T |
|----------|---|-----|-----|-----|------|-----|------|-----|------|------|
| PMULHRW | | | | ✓ | ✓ | | | ✓ | | |

3DNow!    pmulhrw *mmxDst, mmxSrc/m64*      Signed          64

This vector instruction uses a 64-bit data path and so four operations occur in parallel. The product is calculated using each of the unsigned 16-bit half-words of the multiplicand *mmxDst* and the 16-bit half-word of the multiplier *mmxSrc* for each 16-bit block, sums 00008000 hex to the 32-bit product, and stores the resulting upper 16 bits in the destination *mmxDst (xmmDst)*.

$$Dst_{(15...0)} = UPPER16((Dst_{(15...0)} \times Src_{(15...0)}) + 0x8000)$$
$$Dst_{(31...16)} = UPPER16((Dst_{(31...16)} \times Src_{(31...16)}) + 0x8000)$$
$$Dst_{(47...32)} = UPPER16((Dst_{(47...32)} \times Src_{(47...32)}) + 0x8000)$$
$$Dst_{(63...48)} = UPPER16((Dst_{(63...48)} \times Src_{(63...48)}) + 0x8000)$$

| D63...D48 | D47...D32 | D31...D16 | D15...D0 |
|---|---|---|---|
| 5678h | 5678h | 5678h | 5678h |
| ×0012h | ×0023h | ×0034h | ×0056h |
| 00061470h | 000bd268h | 00119060h | 001d0c50h |
| +00008000h | +00008000h | +00008000h | +00008000h |
| 00069470h | 000c5268h | 00121060h | 001d8c50h |
| 0006    h | 000c    h | 0012    h | 001d    h |
| 0006h | 800bh | 0012h | 001dh |

# Pseudo Vec (x86)

An interesting thing about the SSE instruction set is that it is primarily designed for floating-point operations. The MMX instruction set handles most of the packed integer processing except the case of unsigned 16-bit multiplication. This was not resolved until a later release of extensions for the MMX by AMD and the SSE by Intel, but this is only 64 bits. Intel came back with the SSE2 instruction set with a complete set of packed instructions for supporting 128 bits.

```
mov    ebx,phB    ; Vector B
mov    eax,phA    ; Vector A
mov    edx,phD    ; Vector Destination
```

## (MMX Mul Low) 4×16-Bit

The instruction PMULLW is the [un]signed multiplication storing the *lower* 16 bits; PMULHW is the *signed* multiplication storing the *upper* 16 bits; and PMULHUW is the *unsigned* multiplication storing the *upper* 16 bits. The following function is designed to return only 16 bits of the resulting product, and selection of the appropriate instruction will return that value. Using the following code shell but with the PMULLW instruction calculates the lower bits, while PMULHW calculates the upper bits. PMULHW calculates the upper signed bits and PMULHUW the upper unsigned bits. The following code is designed for use with the 64-bit MMX register and is used in pairs for 128-bit support.

*Listing 7-3: ...\chap7\pmd\PMulX86M.asm*

```
movq    mm0,[ebx+0]    ; Read B Data {3...0}
movq    mm1,[ebx+8]    ;              {7...4}
movq    mm2,[eax+0]    ; Read A Data {3...0}
movq    mm3,[eax+8]    ;              {7...4}

pmullw  mm0,mm2
pmullw  mm1,mm3
```

```
movq  [edx+0],mm0 ; Write D ??? 16 bits {3...0}
movq  [edx+8],mm1 ;  (upper or lower)   {7...4}
```

To return 16 high signed integer bits, use PMULH instead of PMULLW.

```
pmulhw mm0,mm2    ; SIGNED HIGH {3...0}
pmulhw mm1,mm3    ;            {7...4}
```

To return 16 unsigned high integer bits, use PMULHUW instead of PMULLW.

```
pmulhuw mm0,mm2   ; UNSIGNED HIGH {3...0}
pmulhuw mm1,mm3   ;              {7...4}
```

### (SSE2 Mul Low) 8×16-Bit

With the release of the SSE2 instruction set, Intel handles 128 bits simultaneously using the XMM registers. These same instructions can be used with 128-bit data.

**Listing 7-4: ...\chap7\pmd\PMulX86M.asm**

```
movdqa xmm0,[ebx] ; Read B Data  {7...0}
movdqa xmm1,[eax] ; Read A Data  {7...0}
pmullw xmm0,xmm1
movdqa [edx],xmm0 ; Write D lower 16 bits {7...0}
```

# PMULUDQ — Unsigned N×32-Bit Multiply Even

PMULUDQ *destination, source*

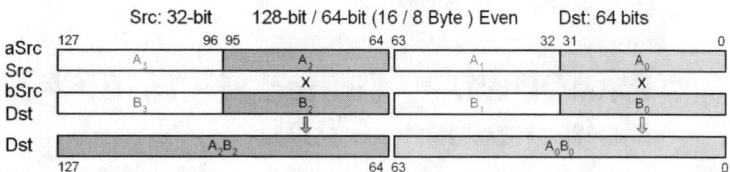

| Mnemonic | P | PII | K6 | 3D! | 3Mx+ | SSE | SSE2 | A64 | SSE3 | E64T |
|----------|---|-----|----|----|------|-----|------|-----|------|------|
| PMULUDQ  |   |     |    |    |      |     | ✓    | ✓   | ✓    | ✓    |

SSE2    pmuludq *mmxDst, mmxSrc/m64*      Unsigned    64
        pmuludq *xmmDst, xmmSrc/m128*     Unsigned    128

This vector instruction calculates the product of the (even) lower 32 bits of each set of 64 (128) bits of the multiplicand *aSrc (xmmSrc)* and the lower 32 bits of the multiplier *bSrc (xmmDst)* for each 64 (128)-bit block, and stores each full 64 (128)-bit integer result in the destination *Dst (xmmDst)*.

(64-bit) **1× 32-bit**

$$Dst_{(63...0)} = Dst_{(31...0)} \times Src_{(31...0)}$$

$$Dst_{(127...64)} = Dst_{(95...64)} \times Src_{(95...64)}$$

(128-bit) **2× 32-bit**

In the following 64-bit table, the upper 32 bits {63...32} of *mmxSrc* and *mmxDst* are ignored. Note that this is not a SIMD reference but included for reference.

| 31...0 | 63...0 |
|---|---|
| 3287565 | 0000000000322A0D |
| × 593 | × 0000000000000251 |
| 1949526045 | 000000007433681D |

In the following 128-bit table, the upper odd pairs of 32 bits {127...96, 63...32} of *xmmDst* and *xmmSrc* are ignored.

| 95...64 | 31...0 | 127...0 |
|---|---|---|
| 85490485 | 3287565 | 0000000005187B350000000000322A0D |
| × 9394 | × 593 | × 00000000000024B20000000000000251 |
| 803097616090 | 1949526045 | 000000BAFC591EDA000000007433681D |
| (0xBAFC591EDA) | (0x7433681D) | |

# PMADDWD — Signed N×16-Bit Parallel Multiplication — ADD

PMADDWD *destination, source*

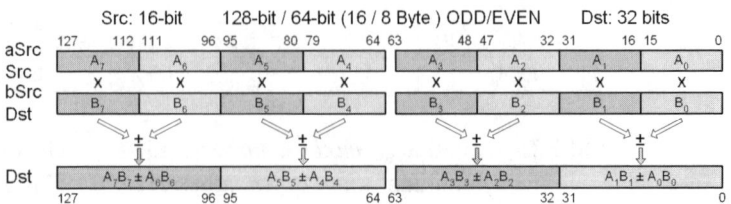

# IDIV — Signed Division

IDIV *operand*

| Mnemonic | P | PII | K6 | 3D! | 3Mx+ | SSE | SSE2 | A64 | SSE3 | E64T |
|----------|---|-----|-----|-----|------|-----|------|-----|------|------|
| IDIV | ✓ | ✓ | ✓ | ✓ | ✓ | ✓ | ✓ | ✓ | ✓ | ✓ |

idiv    *rmDst(8/16/32/64)*    Signed

The IDIV general-purpose instruction divides the signed 16-, 32-, 64-, or 128-bit AX, DX:AX, EDX:EAX, RDX:RAX pair into the 8-, 16-, 32-, or 64-bit *operand* and saves the result based upon the bit size of the operand as indicated in the table below and sets the flags accordingly.

|  | 8-bit | 16-bit | 32-bit | 64-bit |
|-----------|-------|--------|---------|---------|
| Dividend | AX | DX:AX | EDX:EAX | RDX:RAX |
| Divisor | idiv bl | idiv bx | idiv ebx | idiv rbx |
| Quotient | AL | AX | EAX | RAX |
| Remainder | AH | DX | EDX | RDX |

| Flags | O.flow | Sign | Zero | Aux | Parity | Carry |
|-------|--------|------|------|-----|--------|-------|
|  | - | - | - | - | - | - |

Flags: All the flags are undefined.

The sign of the remainder always matches the sign of the divisor. An overflow is indicated by a Divide Error Exception instead of the Overflow flag.

# Exercises

1. Write a code snippet to saturate an unsigned 8-bit incrementing count at a value of 99.

2. The result of the summation of two integers increases the size of the source by one bit (the carry). How many bits are needed from the product of two 32-bit values?

3. What are different output methods to store the various results of a product of two integers?

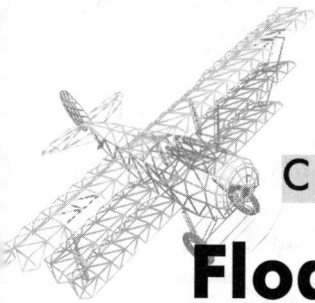

# Chapter 8

# Floating-Point Anyone?

If you are interested in programming the FPU (floating-point unit) in assembly, you are either bored or deeply disturbed. My apologies to those few of you writing compilers or low-level operating system kernels who actually need to know how to do this! Then again, you may just be curious. Other books tend to stick this topic in the section beginning with "F," or somewhere buried in the back in an appendix, and maybe 1% of the readers actually even glance at it. Some people have been known to tape those pages together or just rip them out of their book (not my book) altogether. If C/C++ is good enough for you to handle your floating-point math, then just skip this section.

**Wait!:** There are a couple items you REALLY NEED TO KNOW! Stuff not in the standard runtime C libraries. Something to make your code just a *bit faster and better*!

My gosh! You're still reading this? You must be indeed interested in floating-point math. So we will chat about a couple items but we are not going to go into very much detail — only enough to take advantage of some enhanced functionality.

These are the three methods available to use for floating-point calculation: 3DNow!, SSE, and SSE2 packed instructions; run-time C libraries; and of course, ye old floating-point coprocessor known as the FPU (floating-point unit), for which most whom program it directly have a love/hate relationship. This book should help you get over that, at least in part.

It is strongly recommended that if you only have generic floating-point programming in mind (whether it be single-precision floating-point or double-precision floating-point), then just use your higher level language such as C/C++ instead. It will be much easier and any optimization will be merely that of intermixing general-purpose instructions with floating-point instructions.

Working with the SIMD instructions for floating-point support is much easier than working with the FPU, but the FPU has some helpful features. Fortunately, most of the hard work of directly programming the FPU has been done for you already and is available in libraries such as the runtime library for the C programming language. The FPU has so many nuances that it could take a several hundred-page book to understand all the feature sets, controls, exception handling, etc. This chapter is going to describe how floating-point works in general and paint some broad strokes as to how to use the FPU, especially the few instructions that can be of use but are not utilized by off-the-shelf libraries. If you indeed want to do in-depth programming I suggest you download the various technical manuals and application notes from the manufacturer.

**Workbench Files:** \Bench\x86\chap08\*project*\*platform*

|  | *project* | *platform* |
|---|---|---|
| **Boolean Logic** | **\fas\** | \vc6 |
|  |  | \vc.net |

# The Floating-Point Number

Before digging very deeply let us first examine the floating-point number and its sub-components.

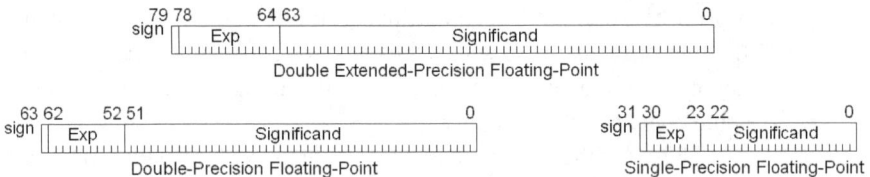

Figure 8-1: Floating-point formats

The FPU supports three sizes of floating-point numbers, as shown below.

| Data Size | C reference | Assembler | Bytes |
|---|---|---|---|
| Single-Precision | (float) | REAL4 | 4 |
| Double-Precision | (double) | REAL8 | 8 |
| Double Extended-Precision | --- | REAL10 | 10 |

You are probably familiar with the single- and double-precision but not the double extended-precision. Did you know that when you do a floating-point calculation that the data is actually expanded into the 10-byte (80-bit) form — double extended-precision floating-point — as it is pushed on the FPU stack?

6.28318530717958623

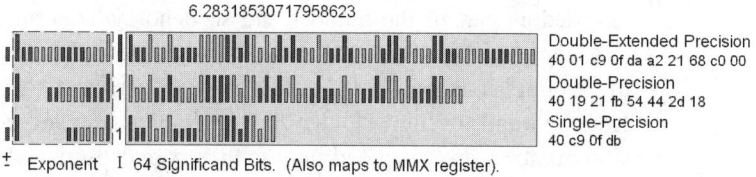

Double-Extended Precision
40 01 c9 0f da a2 21 68 c0 00
Double-Precision
40 19 21 fb 54 44 2d 18
Single-Precision
40 c9 0f db

± Exponent  I 64 Significand Bits. (Also maps to MMX register).

*Figure 8-2: Floating-point bit expansion*

The larger the number of bits used to store the number, the higher the precision of that number.

| Component | SPFP | DPFP | DEPFP |
|---|---|---|---|
| Sign | 1 | 1 | 1 |
| Exponent | 8 | 11 | 15 |
| Integer | 0 | 0 | 1 |
| Significand | 23 | 52 | 63 |
| Total | 32 | 64 | 80 |

The exponent is a base-2 power representation stored as a binary integer. The significand (mantissa) really consists of two components: a J-bit and a binary fraction.

For the single-precision value, there is a hidden integer bit (1.) leading the 23 bits of the mantissa, thus making it a 24-bit significand. The exponent is 8 bits, thus having a bias value of 127. The magnitude of the supported range of numbers is $2\times10^{-38}$ to $2\times10^{38}$.

For double-precision values, there is a hidden integer bit (1.) leading the 52 bits of the mantissa, thus making it a 53-bit significand. The exponent is 11 bits, thus having a bias value of 1023. The magnitude of the supported range of numbers is $2.23\times10^{-308}$ to $1.8\times10^{308}$.

For the 80-bit version, the extra bits are primarily for protection against precision loss from rounding and over/underflows. The leading integer bit (1.) is the 64th bit of the significand. The exponent is 15 bits, thus having a bias value of 32767. The magnitude of the supported range of numbers is $3.3\times10^{-4932}$ to $1.21\times10^{4932}$.

The product of the exponent and significand result in the floating-point value.

A zero exists in two forms (±0): positive zero (+0) and negative zero (−0). Both of these are valid indications of zero. (The sign is ignored!)

For double-precision and single-precision floating-point numbers, the integer bit is always set to one. (It just is not part of the 64 or 32 bits used to encode the number.) For double extended-precision the bit is encoded as part of the number and so denormalized numbers apply. These are very small non-zero numbers represented with an exponent of zero and thus very close to the value of zero and considered tiny. Keep in mind for the FPU that the single-precision and double-precision numbers are expanded into double extended-precision where the integer bit is one of the 80 bits and thus denormalized numbers exist for the calculations. Upon saving the single- or double-precision floating-point number back to memory the bit is stripped out as an imaginary bit, which is set!

Programmers are also usually aware that floats cannot be divided by zero or process a square root of negative because an exception error would occur.

Table 8-1: Single-precision floating-point number representations. ± Sign bit. $x^e$ Exponent. Note: The integer bit of (1) 1.### is implied for single-precision and double-precision numbers.

| ± | $x^e$ | Significand | | NaN (Not a Number) |
|---|---|---|---|---|
| 0 | 255 | 1.1xxx… | 0 11111111 1xxxxxxxx… 7FC00000-7FFFFFFFh | QNaN |
| 0 | 255 | 1.0xxx… | 0 11111111 0xxxxxxx…1 7F800001h-7FBFFFFFh | SNaN |
| 0 | 255 | 1.000… | 0 11111111 000… 7f800000h | + ∞ |
| 0 | 1…254 | 1.xxx | 0 11111110 xxxxxx… 00000001h-7F7FFFFFh | + Normalized Finite |
| 0 | 0 | 0.xxx | (Not SPFP) | + Denormalized (Tiny) |
| 0 | 0 | 0 | 00000000h | + Positive Zero |
| 1 | 0 | 0 | 80000000h | − Negative Zero |
| 1 | 0 | 0.xxx | 1000 0000 0 xxx 80000001h-807FFFFFh | − Denormalized (Tiny) |
| 1 | 1…254 | 1.xxx | 1 11111110 xxxxxx… FF000000h-FF7FFFFFh | − Normalized Finite |
| 1 | 255 | 1.000… | 1 11111111 000… FF800000h | − ∞ |
| 1 | 255 | 1.0xxx… | FF800001h-FFBFFFFFh | SNaN |
| 1 | 255 | 1.1xxx… | FFC00000h-FFFFFFFFh | QNaN |

There are two types of NaNs (non-numbers): The *quiet* NaNs known as QNaNs and the *signalling* NaNs known as SNaNs.

■    QNaN

The QNaN has the most significant fraction bit set and is a valid value to use in most floating-point instructions even though it is not a number. A QNaN is an *unordered* number due to not being a real floating-point value.

■    SNaN

The SNaN has the most significant fraction bit reset (clear) and typically signals an invalid exception when used with floating-point instructions. SNaN values are never generated by the result of a floating-point operation. They are only operands supplied by software algorithms. A SNaN is an *unordered* number due to not being a real floating-point value.

■    NaN

The NaN (Not A Number) is a number that is either a QNaN or SNaN.

■    Unordered

An unordered number is a number that is valid or a QNaN. (It is not SNaN.)

■    Ordered

An ordered number is a valid number that is not NaN (neither QNaN nor SNaN).

*Table 8-2: Single-precision floating-point to hex equivalent*

| Value | Hex | Sign Exp Sig. |
|-------|-----|---------------|
| −1.0 | 0xBF800000 | 1  7F  000000 |
| 0.0 | 0x00000000 | 0  00  000000 |
| 0.0000001 | 0x33D6BF95 | 0  67  56BF95 |
| 1.0 | 0x3F800000 | 0  7F  000000 |
| 2.0 | 0x40000000 | 0  80  000000 |
| 3.0 | 0x40400000 | 0  80  800000 |
| 4.0 | 0x40800000 | 0  81  000000 |

Table 8-3: Double-precision floating-point to hex equivalent

| Value | Hex |
|---|---|
| −1.0 | 0xBFF00000 00000000 |
| 0.0 | 0x00000000 00000000 |
| 1.0 | 0x3FF00000 00000000 |

Table 8-4: Double extended-precision floating-point to hex equivalent

| Value | Hex |
|---|---|
| −1.0 | 0xBFFF8000 00000000 |
| 0.0 | 0x00000000 00000000 |
| 1.0 | 0x3FFF8000 00000000 |

# FPU Registers

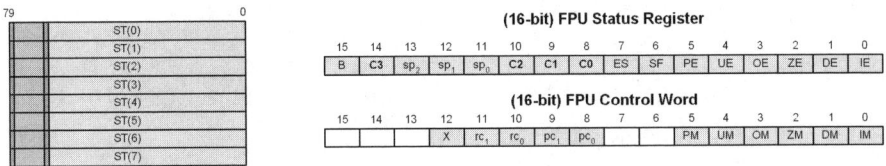

**(16-bit) FPU Status Register**

| 15 | 14 | 13 | 12 | 11 | 10 | 9 | 8 | 7 | 6 | 5 | 4 | 3 | 2 | 1 | 0 |
|---|---|---|---|---|---|---|---|---|---|---|---|---|---|---|---|
| B | C3 | $sp_2$ | $sp_1$ | $sp_0$ | C2 | C1 | C0 | ES | SF | PE | UE | OE | ZE | DE | IE |

**(16-bit) FPU Control Word**

| 15 | 14 | 13 | 12 | 11 | 10 | 9 | 8 | 7 | 6 | 5 | 4 | 3 | 2 | 1 | 0 |
|---|---|---|---|---|---|---|---|---|---|---|---|---|---|---|---|
| | | | X | $rc_1$ | $rc_0$ | $pc_1$ | $pc_0$ | | | PM | UM | OM | ZM | DM | IM |

Figure 8-3: FPU registers

The floating-point unit has eight data registers, {ST(0), ST(1), ST(2), ST(3), ST(4), ST(5), ST(6), ST(7)}, and Status, Control Word, Tag Word, IP, Data Pointer, and Op Code Registers.

Table 8-5: (16-bit) FPU status register

| Def. | Code | Bit | Description |
|---|---|---|---|
| FPU_IE | 00001h | 0 | Invalid operation (exception) |
| FPU_DE | 00002h | 1 | Denormalized operand (exception) |
| FPU_ZE | 00004h | 2 | Zero divide (exception) |
| FPU_OE | 00008h | 3 | Overflow (exception) |
| FPU_UE | 00010h | 4 | Underflow (exception) |
| FPU_PE | 00020h | 5 | Precision (exception) |
| FPU_SF | 00040h | 6 | Stack fault |
| FPU_ES | 00080h | 7 | Error summary status |
| FPU_C0 | 00100h | 8 | (C0) Condition Code Bit#0 |
| FPU_C1 | 00200h | 9 | (C1) Condition Code Bit#1 |
| FPU_C2 | 00400h | 10 | (C2) Condition Code Bit#2 |
| | | 11-13 | Top of stack pointer |
| FPU_C3 | 04000h | 14 | (C3) Condition Code Bit#3 |
| FPU_B | 08000h | 15 | FPU busy bit |

The FPU has condition code bits contained within the status register. These bits match 1:1 with the EFLAGS of the CPU. They can be copied to the AX register using the FSTSW AX instruction followed by a SAHF instruction to place them into the EFLAGS register.

| A ? B | C3 (Zero) | C2 (Parity) | C1 (Oflow) | C0 (Carry) |
|---|---|---|---|---|
| Unordered | x | x | x | 1 |

Table 8-6: (16-bit) FPU control word

| Def. | Code | Bit | Description |
|---|---|---|---|
| FPU_IM | 00001h | 0 | Invalid operation |
| FPU_DM | 00002h | 1 | Denormalized operand |
| FPU_ZM | 00004h | 2 | Zero divide |
| FPU_OM | 00008h | 3 | Overflow |
| FPU_UM | 00010h | 4 | Underflow |
| FPU_PM | 00020h | 5 | Precision |
| FPU_PC | 00300h | 8,9 | Precision control |
| FPU_RC | 00c00h | 10,11 | Rounding control |
| FPU_X | 01000h | 12 | Infinity control |

Now would be a good time to talk about FPU exceptions. The FPU uses exceptions for invalid operations in a manner similar to how the CPU uses exceptions.

Table 8-7: FPU exceptions

| Mnemonic | C/C++ | Description |
|---|---|---|
| #IA | | Invalid arithmetic operation |
| #IS | #IND | Stack overflow or underflow |
| #D | #QNAN | Denormal/un-normal operand |
| #O | | _FPE_OVERFLOW — Numerical overflow in result |
| #P | | Precision loss |
| #U | | _FPE_UNDERFLOW — Numerical underflow in result |
| #Z | #INF | _FPE_ZERODIVIDE — Divide by zero |

Most of the single- and double-precision floating-point functionality is covered by the C runtime math library, which can be accessed in the file: #include <math.h>.

# Loading/Storing Numbers and the FPU Stack

## FLD — Floating-Point Load

| Mnemonic | P | PII | K6 | 3D! | 3Mx+ | SSE | SSE2 | A64 | SSE3 | E64T |
|----------|---|-----|----|-----|------|-----|------|-----|------|------|
| FLD | ✓ | ✓ | ✓ | ✓ | ✓ | ✓ | ✓ | ✓ | ✓ | ✓ |

| FPU | fld *source* | Single-precision | 32 |
|-----|--------------|------------------|----|
|     |              | Double-precision | 64 |
|     |              | Extended-precision | 80 |

The floating-point load instruction loads the value in memory, expands it to an 80-bit double extended-precision floating-point form, and pushes it on the stack, thereby making it addressable by the FPU as register ST(0).

```
float a;
double b;

__asm {
      fld    a   ; Load SPFP 32-bit to 80-bit
      fld    b   ; Load DPFP 64-bit to 80-bit
      fadd
};
```

The CPU handles integer addition through a simple process of
$D = A + B$
…which is in reality:

```
 add    edx,ebx   ; D = D + B
```

The FPU, however, has its registers as entries on a stack. Thus, values are pushed on a stack and an operation is performed upon the values stored at the top of the stack.

A standard calculator operates as:

| l | + | 2 | = |
|---|---|---|---|

The FPU behaves like an RPN (Reverse Polish Notation) calculator. Arguments are "pushed" on the stack and then the operation is performed.

| l | 2 | + |
|---|---|---|

And in the case of the FPU:

| I.0 | 2.0 | FADD |
|-----|-----|------|

There are eight floating-point data registers, which are treated like a circular stack. The stack pointer ST(0) references the register number that is at the top of the stack.

| ST(0) | 2.0 |
|-------|-----|
| ST(I) | I.0 |
| ST(2) |     |
| ST(3) |     |
| ST(4) |     |
| ST(5) |     |
| ST(6) |     |
| ST(7) |     |

As values are loaded they are pushed onto the top of the stack, and the other items on the stack are pushed down, leaving the new item addressed as ST(0) and the other items addressed as ST(1)...ST(7). A maximum of eight values can be pushed on the FPU stack, as the ninth item generates an FPU error: #IS aka: 1#IND "Stack overflow or underflow."

If the stack had only one or no arguments pushed, the operation would have generated a stack underflow due to the missing argument.

As mentioned, ST(0) references the top of the stack but the stack is really a rotating queue. Let us examine a simple addition operation again but step by step: $1 + 2 + 5$ thus $1\ 2 + 5 +$.

```
a = 1; b = 2; c = 5;

        fld    a
        fld    b
        fadd
        fld    c
        fadd
        fst    d           ; Save float to memory.
```

|        | 1.0 | 2.0 | FADD | 5.0 | FADD | FST |
|--------|-----|-----|------|-----|------|-----|
| ST(0)  | 1.0 | 2.0 | 3.0  | 5.0 | 8.0  | 8.0 |
| ST(1)  |     | 1.0 |      | 3.0 |      |     |
| ST(2)  |     |     |      |     |      |     |
| ST(3)  |     |     |      |     |      |     |
| ST(4)  |     |     |      |     |      |     |
| ST(5)  |     |     |      |     |      |     |
| ST(6)  |     |     |      |     |      |     |
| ST(7)  |     |     | 2.0  |     | 5.0  | 5.0 |

First, the value of 1 was loaded and thus pushed onto the stack. Then, the value of 2 was loaded and thus pushed onto the stack.

The FADD operation actually caused the stack to unwind. The 2.0 was retrieved from ST(0), and the stack was rolled back one slot, then summed with the new ST(0) value 1.0 and the result written back to ST(0). The effect is the result was stored for the next operation, but the old ST(0) was rolled into ST(7) and the other slots rolled down by one. If a new value is loaded and processed, the same kind of operation occurs. Notice the activity of ST(0) and ST(7).

Now let us try that again but this time: 1 + 2 + 5 thus 1 2 5 + +.

```
fld   a
fld   b
fld   c
fadd
fadd
fst   d              ; Save float to memory.
```

|        | 1.0 | 2.0 | 5.0 | FADD | FADD | FST |
|--------|-----|-----|-----|------|------|-----|
| ST(0)  | 1.0 | 2.0 | 5.0 | 7.0  | 8.0  | 8.0 |
| ST(1)  |     | 1.0 | 2.0 | 1.0  |      |     |
| ST(2)  |     |     | 1.0 |      |      |     |
| ST(3)  |     |     |     |      |      |     |
| ST(4)  |     |     |     |      |      |     |
| ST(5)  |     |     |     |      |      |     |
| ST(6)  |     |     |     |      | 5.0  | 5.0 |
| ST(7)  |     |     |     | 5.0  | 7.0  | 7.0 |

All three values are pushed on the stack and they are popped as the stack gets rolled and processed. Upon completion of the floating-point operation, the value is exported in one of the forms while being popped off the stack and put back into system memory.

Be careful when mixing your operators due to rules of precedence:

$$A + B \times C \quad \text{is} \quad A + (B \times C) \quad \text{thus} \quad A\ B\ C \times +$$

**Warning!** There seems to be some confusion or encoding errors in some of the macro assemblers in regard to the "P" suffix. If you try to assemble your code and get an error on one of the FPU instructions, try the alternative (with or without P).

# FST/FSTP — FPU Floating-Point Save

| Mnemonic | P | PII | K6 | 3D! | 3Mx+ | SSE | SSE2 | A64 | SSE3 | E64T |
|----------|---|-----|----|----|------|-----|------|-----|------|------|
| FST | ✓ | ✓ | ✓ | ✓ | ✓ | ✓ | ✓ | ✓ | ✓ | ✓ |
| FSTP | ✓ | ✓ | ✓ | ✓ | ✓ | ✓ | ✓ | ✓ | ✓ | ✓ |

| FPU | fst | *source* | Single-precision | 32 |
|-----|-----|----------|------------------|----|
| | | | Double-precision | 64 |
| | | | Extended-precision | 80 |

The FST instruction copies the truncated integer from ST(0) to 16/32/64-bit memory and leaves the FPU stack intact.

The FSTP instruction is similar to FST, but it pops the value off the FPU stack.

# FILD — FPU Integer Load

| Mnemonic | P | PII | K6 | 3D! | 3Mx+ | SSE | SSE2 | A64 | SSE3 | E64T |
|----------|---|-----|----|----|------|-----|------|-----|------|------|
| FILD | ✓ | ✓ | ✓ | ✓ | ✓ | ✓ | ✓ | ✓ | ✓ | ✓ |

| FPU | fild | *mSrc(16/32/64)* | Signed | 80 |
|-----|------|------------------|--------|----|

The integer load instruction loads the 16/32/64-bit integer in the 80-bit double extended-precision floating-point value.

# FIST/FISTP/FISTTP — FPU Integer Save

| Mnemonic | P | PII | K6 | 3D! | 3Mx+ | SSE | SSE2 | A64 | SSE3 | E64T |
|----------|---|-----|----|----|------|-----|------|-----|------|------|
| FIST | ✓ | ✓ | ✓ | ✓ | ✓ | ✓ | ✓ | ✓ | ✓ | ✓ |
| FISTP | ✓ | ✓ | ✓ | ✓ | ✓ | ✓ | ✓ | ✓ | ✓ | ✓ |
| FISTTP | | | | | | | | | ✓ | ✓ |

FPU     fist   *mSrc(16/32/64)*          Signed          80
        fistp  *mSrc(16/32/64)*

The FIST instruction copies the integer from ST(0) to 16/32/64-bit memory. The FISTP instruction does the same, only it pops the value off the FPU stack.

SSE3-FPU   fisttp *mDst{16/32/64}*      Signed          80

The FISTTP instruction is similar to FISTP, but it copies the truncated integer from ST(0) to 16/32/64-bit memory and it pops the value off the FPU stack. This instruction was introduced with SSE3.

# FPU Constants

Some FPU values are predefined constants that get loaded into stack register ST(0) and as such do not need to be loaded from memory.

| Mnemonic | P | PII | K6 | 3D! | 3Mx+ | SSE | SSE2 | A64 | SSE3 | E64T |
|----------|---|-----|----|----|------|-----|------|-----|------|------|
| FLD1 | ✓ | ✓ | ✓ | ✓ | ✓ | ✓ | ✓ | ✓ | ✓ | ✓ |
| FLDL2E | ✓ | ✓ | ✓ | ✓ | ✓ | ✓ | ✓ | ✓ | ✓ | ✓ |
| FLDL2T | ✓ | ✓ | ✓ | ✓ | ✓ | ✓ | ✓ | ✓ | ✓ | ✓ |
| FLDLG2 | ✓ | ✓ | ✓ | ✓ | ✓ | ✓ | ✓ | ✓ | ✓ | ✓ |
| FLDLN2 | ✓ | ✓ | ✓ | ✓ | ✓ | ✓ | ✓ | ✓ | ✓ | ✓ |
| FLDPI | ✓ | ✓ | ✓ | ✓ | ✓ | ✓ | ✓ | ✓ | ✓ | ✓ |
| FLDZ | ✓ | ✓ | ✓ | ✓ | ✓ | ✓ | ✓ | ✓ | ✓ | ✓ |

*Table 8-8: FPU constants*

| $\mu$P | Mnemonic | Description | Bits |
|--------|----------|-------------|------|
| FPU | **FLDZ** | +0.0 | 80 |
| FPU | **FLD1** | +1.0 | 80 |
| FPU | **FLDPI** | $\pi$ (PI) 3.1415926535897932 | 80 |
| FPU | **FLDL2T** | $\log_2 10$  3.3221 $= 1/0.3010$  $2^{3.3221} = 10$ | 80 |
| FPU | **FLDL2E** | $\log_2 e$ | 80 |
| FPU | **FLDLG2** | $\log_{10}2$  0.3010   $10^{0.3010} = 2$ | 80 |
| FPU | **FLDLN2** | $\log_e 2$ | 80 |

# FXCH

| Mnemonic | P | PII | K6 | 3D! | 3Mx+ | SSE | SSE2 | A64 | SSE3 | E64T |
|----------|---|-----|----|----|------|-----|------|-----|------|------|
| FXCH | ✓ | ✓ | ✓ | ✓ | ✓ | ✓ | ✓ | ✓ | ✓ | ✓ |

FPU        fxch                    Extended-precision              80
           fxch st(i)

The FXCH instruction can be used to exchange any of the stack registers {ST(1) … ST(7)} with stack register ST(0). The default (with no parameter) is ST(1) and ST(0). The stack exchange value must be valid before the exchange to be valid after the swap.

Since floats and doubles are pretty much handled for you there is no real need to pick them apart as scalar libraries have been written for you by compiler manufacturers. If you want to use the double extended-precision, then you have a lot of work that you will need to do since standard C compilers do not tend to support it and thus you need to do the math yourself using FPU instructions.

# FINCSTP — FPU Increment Stack Pointer

| Mnemonic | P | PII | K6 | 3D! | 3Mx+ | SSE | SSE2 | A64 | SSE3 | E64T |
|---|---|---|---|---|---|---|---|---|---|---|
| FINCSTP | ✓ | ✓ | ✓ | ✓ | ✓ | ✓ | ✓ | ✓ | ✓ | ✓ |

FPU        fincstp

The FINCSTP instruction effectively rolls the stack. The value indexed by ST(0) becomes ST(7), but the data does not become invalidated. A valid stack argument in ST(0) gets rolled to ST(7). As the data is still valid, it is still eligible for exchange with the FXCHG instruction.

# FDECSTP — FPU Decrement Stack Pointer

| Mnemonic | P | PII | K6 | 3D! | 3Mx+ | SSE | SSE2 | A64 | SSE3 | E64T |
|---|---|---|---|---|---|---|---|---|---|---|
| FDECSTP | ✓ | ✓ | ✓ | ✓ | ✓ | ✓ | ✓ | ✓ | ✓ | ✓ |

FPU        fdecstp

The FDECSTP instruction effectively rolls the stack. The value indexed by ST(0) becomes ST(1) and ST(7) becomes ST(0), but the data retains its valid/invalid state. A valid stack argument in ST(0) gets rolled to ST(1). As the data is still valid, it is still eligible for exchange with the FXCHG instruction.

# FWAIT/WAIT

| Mnemonic | P | PII | K6 | 3D! | 3Mx+ | SSE | SSE2 | A64 | SSE3 | E64T |
|---|---|---|---|---|---|---|---|---|---|---|
| FWAIT | ✓ | ✓ | ✓ | ✓ | ✓ | ✓ | ✓ | ✓ | ✓ | ✓ |
| WAIT | ✓ | ✓ | ✓ | ✓ | ✓ | ✓ | ✓ | ✓ | ✓ | ✓ |

FPU       fwait
 "        wait

The FWAIT instruction is used to wait for the FPU (floating-point unit) operation to complete. Without it, an operation that is in effect can be preempted by a new floating-point calculation pushed on the FPU stack.

# EMMS/FEMMS

Whenever MMX and FPU instructions are both used within the same thread there must be a switch-over by the CPU calling the EMMS instruction. The 3DNow! instruction set has the fast instruction FEMMS. Having to switch back and forth is time consuming and a burden on the CPU, so whenever possible the instructions should be grouped by type or kept in separate threads.

| Mnemonic | P | PII | K6 | 3D! | 3Mx+ | SSE | SSE2 | A64 | SSE3 | E64T |
|---|---|---|---|---|---|---|---|---|---|---|
| EMMS | | ✓ | ✓ | ✓ | ✓ | ✓ | ✓ | ✓ | ✓ | ✓ |
| FEMMS | | | | ✓ | ✓ | | | ✓ | | |

# FNOP

| Mnemonic | P | PII | K6 | 3D! | 3Mx+ | SSE | SSE2 | A64 | SSE3 | E64T |
|---|---|---|---|---|---|---|---|---|---|---|
| FNOP | ✓ | ✓ | ✓ | ✓ | ✓ | ✓ | ✓ | ✓ | ✓ | ✓ |

FPU       fnop

The FNOP instruction has no operation. Idle!

# General Math Instructions

## FCHS — FPU Two's Complement
## ST(0) = – ST(0)

| Mnemonic | P | PII | K6 | 3D! | 3Mx+ | SSE | SSE2 | A64 | SSE3 | E64T |
|----------|---|-----|----|----|------|-----|------|-----|------|------|
| FCHS | ✓ | ✓ | ✓ | ✓ | ✓ | ✓ | ✓ | ✓ | ✓ | ✓ |

FPU       fchs            Extended-precision           80

This instruction performs a one's complement on the sign bit in ST(0). This effectively two's complements the value in the ST(0) register.

A = – A

```
fldpi          ; ST(0) =  π  (PI)  3.1415926535897932
fchs           ; ST(0) = – π
```

## FABS — FPU Absolute Value ST(0) = |ST(0)|

| Mnemonic | P | PII | K6 | 3D! | 3Mx+ | SSE | SSE2 | A64 | SSE3 | E64T |
|----------|---|-----|----|----|------|-----|------|-----|------|------|
| FABS | ✓ | ✓ | ✓ | ✓ | ✓ | ✓ | ✓ | ✓ | ✓ | ✓ |

FPU       fabs            Extended-precision           80

This instruction clears (resets) the sign bit in ST(0).

A = |A|

```
fld1           ; ST(0) = 1.0
fchs           ; ST(0) = –1.0
fabs           ; ST(0) = 1.0
```

## FADD/FADDP/FIADD — FPU Addition
## D = ST(0) + A

| Mnemonic | P | PII | K6 | 3D! | 3Mx+ | SSE | SSE2 | A64 | SSE3 | E64T |
|----------|---|-----|----|----|------|-----|------|-----|------|------|
| FADD | ✓ | ✓ | ✓ | ✓ | ✓ | ✓ | ✓ | ✓ | ✓ | ✓ |
| FADDP | ✓ | ✓ | ✓ | ✓ | ✓ | ✓ | ✓ | ✓ | ✓ | ✓ |
| FIADD | ✓ | ✓ | ✓ | ✓ | ✓ | ✓ | ✓ | ✓ | ✓ | ✓ |

FPU    faddp                  Extended-precision        80
"       fadd   *mSrc(32/64)*

```
"       fadd    st(0)Dst, st(i)Src
"       fadd    st(i)Dst, st(0)Src
"       faddp   st(i)Dst, st(0)Src
"       fiadd   mSrc(32/64)              Signed
```

The FADD instruction performs a summation of the source to the destination and stores the result in the destination. If no destination is specified, the default is ST(0).

FADDP performs the same operation, but it pops ST(0) off the stack and pushes the result back onto the stack at ST(0).

The FIADD instruction performs the same operation as FADD except the source value is a 16/32-bit integer.

```
fs      REAL4   2.0
fldpi           ; ST(0) = π (PI) 3.1415926535897932
fldpi
faddp           ; ST(0) = 2π = π+π

fadd    fs
```

# FSUB/FSUBP/FISUB — FPU Subtraction
# D = ST(0) – A

| Mnemonic | P | PII | K6 | 3D! | 3Mx+ | SSE | SSE2 | A64 | SSE3 | E64T |
|----------|---|-----|----|----|------|-----|------|-----|------|------|
| FSUB | ✓ | ✓ | ✓ | ✓ | ✓ | ✓ | ✓ | ✓ | ✓ | ✓ |
| FSUBP | ✓ | ✓ | ✓ | ✓ | ✓ | ✓ | ✓ | ✓ | ✓ | ✓ |
| FISUB | ✓ | ✓ | ✓ | ✓ | ✓ | ✓ | ✓ | ✓ | ✓ | ✓ |

```
FPU     fsubp                   Extended-precision      80
"       fsub    mSrc(32/64)
"       fsub    st(0)Dst, st(i)Src
"       fsub    st(i)Dst, st(0)Src
"       fsubp   st(i)Dst, st(0)Src
"       fisub   mSrc(32/64)      Signed
```

The FSUB instruction subtracts the source from the destination and stores the result in the destination. If no destination is specified, the default is ST(0).

FSUBP performs the same operation, but it pops ST(0) off the stack and stores the result in ST(0).

The FISUB instruction performs the same operation as FSUB except the source value is a 16/32-bit integer.

## FSUBR/FSUBRP/FISUBR — FPU Reverse Subtraction D = A – ST(0)

| Mnemonic | P | PII | K6 | 3D! | 3Mx+ | SSE | SSE2 | A64 | SSE3 | E64T |
|----------|---|-----|----|----|------|-----|------|-----|------|------|
| FSUBR | ✓ | ✓ | ✓ | ✓ | ✓ | ✓ | ✓ | ✓ | ✓ | ✓ |
| FSUBRP | ✓ | ✓ | ✓ | ✓ | ✓ | ✓ | ✓ | ✓ | ✓ | ✓ |
| FISUBR | ✓ | ✓ | ✓ | ✓ | ✓ | ✓ | ✓ | ✓ | ✓ | ✓ |

| FPU | fsubrp | | Extended-precision | 80 |
|-----|--------|--|--------------------|----|
| " | fsubr | *mSrc(32/64)* | | |
| " | fsubr | *st(0)Dst, st(i)Src* | | |
| " | fsubr | *st(i)Dst, st(0)Src* | | |
| " | fsubrp | *st(i)Dst, st(0)Src* | | |
| " | fisubr | *mSrc(32/64)* | Signed | |

The FSUBR instruction is a reverse subtraction where the destination is subtracted from the source and the result is stored in the destination. If no destination is specified, the default is ST(0).

Instead of D = (B) + (– A), the expression D = (– B) + A is used.

FSUBRP performs the same operation, but it pops ST(0) off the stack and stores the result in ST(0).

The FISUBR instruction performs the same operation as FSUBR except the source value is a 16/32-bit integer.

## FMUL/FMULP/FIMUL — FPU Multiplication D = ST(0) × A

| Mnemonic | P | PII | K6 | 3D! | 3Mx+ | SSE | SSE2 | A64 | SSE3 | E64T |
|----------|---|-----|----|----|------|-----|------|-----|------|------|
| FMUL | ✓ | ✓ | ✓ | ✓ | ✓ | ✓ | ✓ | ✓ | ✓ | ✓ |
| FMULP | ✓ | ✓ | ✓ | ✓ | ✓ | ✓ | ✓ | ✓ | ✓ | ✓ |
| FIMUL | ✓ | ✓ | ✓ | ✓ | ✓ | ✓ | ✓ | ✓ | ✓ | ✓ |

| FPU | fmulp | | Extended-precision | 80 |
|-----|-------|--|--------------------|----|
| " | fmul | *mSrc(32/64)* | | |
| " | fmul | *st(0)Dst, st(i)Src* | | |
| " | fmul | *st(i)Dst, st(0)Src* | | |
| " | fmulp | *st(i)Dst, st(0)Src* | | |
| " | fimul | *mSrc(32/64)* | Signed | |

The FMUL instruction calculates the product of the source and the destination and stores the result in the destination. If no destination is specified, the default is ST(0).

FMULP performs the same operation, but it pops ST(0) off the stack and stores the result in ST(0).

The FIMUL instruction performs the same operation as FMUL except the source value is a 16/32-bit integer.

## FDIV/FDIVP/FIDIV — FPU Division
## D = Dst ÷ Src

| Mnemonic | P | PII | K6 | 3D! | 3Mx+ | SSE | SSE2 | A64 | SSE3 | E64T |
|---|---|---|---|---|---|---|---|---|---|---|
| FDIV | ✓ | ✓ | ✓ | ✓ | ✓ | ✓ | ✓ | ✓ | ✓ | ✓ |
| FDIVP | ✓ | ✓ | ✓ | ✓ | ✓ | ✓ | ✓ | ✓ | ✓ | ✓ |
| FIDIV | ✓ | ✓ | ✓ | ✓ | ✓ | ✓ | ✓ | ✓ | ✓ | ✓ |

| FPU | fdivp |  | Extended-precision | 80 |
|---|---|---|---|---|
| " | fdiv | mSrc(32/64) | | |
| " | fdiv | st(0)Dst, st(i)Src | | |
| " | fdiv | st(i)Dst, st(0)Src | | |
| " | fdivp | st(i)Dst, st(0)Src | | |
| " | fidiv | mSrc(32/64) | Signed | |

The FDIV instruction calculates the dividend of the destination quotient and source divisor and stores the result in the destination. If no destination is specified, the default is ST(0).

FDIVP performs the same operation, but it pops ST(0) off the stack and stores the result in ST(0).

The FIDIV instruction performs the same operation as FDIV except the source value is a 16/32-bit integer.

## FDIVR/FDIVRP/FIDIVR — FPU Reverse
## Division D = Src ÷ Dst

| Mnemonic | P | PII | K6 | 3D! | 3Mx+ | SSE | SSE2 | A64 | SSE3 | E64T |
|---|---|---|---|---|---|---|---|---|---|---|
| FDIVR | ✓ | ✓ | ✓ | ✓ | ✓ | ✓ | ✓ | ✓ | ✓ | ✓ |
| FDIVRP | ✓ | ✓ | ✓ | ✓ | ✓ | ✓ | ✓ | ✓ | ✓ | ✓ |
| FIDIVR | ✓ | ✓ | ✓ | ✓ | ✓ | ✓ | ✓ | ✓ | ✓ | ✓ |

| FPU | fdivrp |  | Extended-precision | 80 |
| " | fdivr | *mSrc(32/64)* |  |  |
| " | fdivr | *st(0)Dst, st(i)Src* |  |  |
| " | fdivr | *st(i)Dst, st(0)Src* |  |  |
| " | fdivrp | *st(i)Dst, st(0)Src* |  |  |
| " | fidivr | *mSrc(32/64)* | Signed |  |

The FDIVR instruction calculates the dividend of the source quotient and destination divisor and stores the result in the destination. If no destination is specified, the default is ST(0).

FDIVRP performs the same operation, but it pops ST(0) off the stack and stores the result in ST(0).

The FIDIVR instruction performs the same operation as FDIVR except the source value is a 16/32-bit integer.

# FPREM — FPU Partial Remainder

| Mnemonic | P | PII | K6 | 3D! | 3Mx+ | SSE | SSE2 | A64 | SSE3 | E64T |
|---|---|---|---|---|---|---|---|---|---|---|
| FPREM | ✓ | ✓ | ✓ | ✓ | ✓ | ✓ | ✓ | ✓ | ✓ | ✓ |

FPU     fprem                    Extended-precision     80

This instruction returns the remainder from dividing the dividend ST(0) by the divisor ST(1) and stores the result in ST(0). This instruction is the equivalent of a modulus:

$$ST(0) = ST(0) \bmod ST(1)$$

# FPREM1 — FPU Partial Remainder

| Mnemonic | P | PII | K6 | 3D! | 3Mx+ | SSE | SSE2 | A64 | SSE3 | E64T |
|---|---|---|---|---|---|---|---|---|---|---|
| FPREM1 | ✓ | ✓ | ✓ | ✓ | ✓ | ✓ | ✓ | ✓ | ✓ | ✓ |

FPU     fprem1                   Extended-precision     80

This instruction is similar to the instruction FPREM but returns the IEEE remainder from dividing the dividend ST(0) by the divisor ST(1) and stores the result in ST(0). This instruction is the equivalent of a modulus:

$$ST(0) = ST(0) \bmod ST(1)$$

## FRNDINT — FPU Round to Integer

| Mnemonic | P | PII | K6 | 3D! | 3Mx+ | SSE | SSE2 | A64 | SSE3 | E64T |
|----------|---|-----|-----|-----|------|-----|------|-----|------|------|
| FRNDINT  | ✓ | ✓   | ✓   | ✓   | ✓    | ✓   | ✓    | ✓   | ✓    | ✓    |

FPU    frndint                    Extended-precision      80

# Advanced Math Instructions

## FSQRT — FPU ST(0) Square Root

| Mnemonic | P | PII | K6 | 3D! | 3Mx+ | SSE | SSE2 | A64 | SSE3 | E64T |
|----------|---|-----|-----|-----|------|-----|------|-----|------|------|
| FSQRT    | ✓ | ✓   | ✓   | ✓   | ✓    | ✓   | ✓    | ✓   | ✓    | ✓    |

FPU    fsqrt                      Extended-precision      80

The FSQRT instruction pops the ST(0) off the stack, performs a square root operation, then pushes the result back on the stack.

## FSCALE — FPU Scale ST(0) = ST(0) << ST(1)

| Mnemonic | P | PII | K6 | 3D! | 3Mx+ | SSE | SSE2 | A64 | SSE3 | E64T |
|----------|---|-----|-----|-----|------|-----|------|-----|------|------|
| FSCALE   | ✓ | ✓   | ✓   | ✓   | ✓    | ✓   | ✓    | ✓   | ✓    | ✓    |

FPU    fscale                     Extended-precision      80

The FSCALE instruction effectively shifts ST(0) by the amount set in ST(1). This is equivalent to $D = D \times 2^A$.

## F2XM1 — FPU ST(0) = $2^{ST(0)} - 1$

| Mnemonic | P | PII | K6 | 3D! | 3Mx+ | SSE | SSE2 | A64 | SSE3 | E64T |
|----------|---|-----|-----|-----|------|-----|------|-----|------|------|
| F2XM1    | ✓ | ✓   | ✓   | ✓   | ✓    | ✓   | ✓    | ✓   | ✓    | ✓    |

FPU    f2xm1                      Extended-precision      80

The F2XM1 instruction calculates $2^X - 1$, where the source x is ST(0) and the result is stored in ST(0).

# FYL2X — FPU ST(0) = y log₂x

| Mnemonic | P | PII | K6 | 3D! | 3Mx+ | SSE | SSE2 | A64 | SSE3 | E64T |
|----------|---|-----|----|----|------|-----|------|-----|------|------|
| FYL2X | ✓ | ✓ | ✓ | ✓ | ✓ | ✓ | ✓ | ✓ | ✓ | ✓ |

FPU    fyl2x                    Extended-precision        80

The FYL2X instruction calculates $y \log_2 x$, where the source y is ST(1), the source x is ST(0), and the result is stored in ST(0). The operand x must be > 0.

# FYL2XP1 — FPU ST(0) = y log₂(x+1)

| Mnemonic | P | PII | K6 | 3D! | 3Mx+ | SSE | SSE2 | A64 | SSE3 | E64T |
|----------|---|-----|----|----|------|-----|------|-----|------|------|
| FYL2XP1 | ✓ | ✓ | ✓ | ✓ | ✓ | ✓ | ✓ | ✓ | ✓ | ✓ |

FPU    fyl2xp1                    Extended-precision        80

The FYL2XP1 instruction calculates $y \log_2(x+1)$, where the source y is ST(1), the source x is ST(0), and the result is stored in ST(0). The operand x must be within the range $-(1 - (\sqrt{2}/2)) \dots (1 - (\sqrt{2}/2))$.

# FXTRACT — FPU Extract Exponent and Significand

| Mnemonic | P | PII | K6 | 3D! | 3Mx+ | SSE | SSE2 | A64 | SSE3 | E64T |
|----------|---|-----|----|----|------|-----|------|-----|------|------|
| FXTRACT | ✓ | ✓ | ✓ | ✓ | ✓ | ✓ | ✓ | ✓ | ✓ | ✓ |

FPU    fxtract                    Extended-precision        80

This instruction pops the ST(0) value off the stack, separates the exponent and significand, and pushes the exponent on the stack. The significand is then set with the 3FFFh exponent and pushed on the stack.

# Floating-Point Comparison

Do not expect the resulting values from different calculations to be identical. For example, 2.0 x 9.0 is about 18.0, and 180.0 ÷ 10.0 is about 18.0, but the two 18.0 values are not guaranteed to be identical.

$$2.0 \times 9.0 \approx 180.0 \div 10.0$$

Let us examine a range of values $10^n$ and compare a displacement of ±0.001 versus ±0.0000001.

Table 8-9: Note the single-precision loss between the ±0.001 displacement as the number of digits goes up in the base number. As the base number gets larger, fewer decimal places of precision can be supported. The hexadecimal numbers in bold are where the precision was totally lost.

| Base number | −0.001 | +0.0 | +0.001 |
|---|---|---|---|
| 1.0 | 0x3F7FBE77 | 0x3F800000 | 0x3F8020C5 |
| 10.0 | 0x411FFBE7 | 0x41200000 | 0x41200419 |
| 100.0 | 0x42C7FF7D | 0x42C80000 | 0x42C80083 |
| 1000.0 | 0x4479FFF0 | 0x447A0000 | 0x447A0010 |
| 10000.0 | 0x461C3FFF | 0x461C4000 | 0x461C4001 |
| 100000.0 | **0x47C35000** | **0x47C35000** | **0x47C35000** |
| 1000000.0 | **0x49742400** | **0x49742400** | **0x49742400** |
| 10000000.0 | **0x4B189680** | **0x4B189680** | **0x4B189680** |
| 100000000.0 | **0x4CBEBC20** | **0x4CBEBC20** | **0x4CBEBC20** |

Table 8-10: This is a similar single-precision table except the displacement is between ±0.0000001. Note the larger number of hexadecimal numbers in bold indicating a loss of precision.

| Base number | −0.0000001 | +0.0 | +0.0000001 |
|---|---|---|---|
| 1.0 | 0x3F7FFFFE | 0x3F800000 | 0x3F800001 |
| 10.0 | **0x41200000** | **0x41200000** | **0x41200000** |
| 100.0 | **0x42C80000** | **0x42C80000** | **0x42C80000** |
| 1000.0 | **0x447A0000** | **0x447A0000** | **0x447A0000** |
| 10000.0 | **0x461C4000** | **0x461C4000** | **0x461C4000** |
| 100000.0 | **0x47C35000** | **0x47C35000** | **0x47C35000** |
| 1000000.0 | **0x49742400** | **0x49742400** | **0x49742400** |
| 10000000.0 | **0x4B189680** | **0x4B189680** | **0x4B189680** |
| 100000000.0 | **0x4CBEBC20** | **0x4CBEBC20** | **0x4CBEBC20** |

Okay, one more table for more clarity.

Table 8-11: Note that accuracy of the precision of the numbers diminishes as the number of digits increases.

| Base number | +0.001 | +0.002 | +0.003 |
|---|---|---|---|
| 1.0 | 0x3F8020C5 | 0x3F804189 | 0x3F80624E |
| 10.0 | 0x41200419 | 0x41200831 | 0x41200C4A |
| 100.0 | 0x42C80083 | 0x42C80106 | 0x42C80189 |
| 1000.0 | 0x447A0010 | 0x447A0021 | 0x447A0031 |
| 10000.0 | 0x461C4001 | 0x461C4002 | 0x461C4003 |
| 100000.0 | **0x47C35000** | **0x47C35000** | **0x47C35000** |
| 1000000.0 | **0x49742400** | **0x49742400** | **0x49742400** |

What this means is that smaller numbers such as those that are normalized and have a numerical range from −1.0 to 1.0 allow for higher precision values, but those with larger values are inaccurate and thus not very precise. For example, the distance between 1.001 and 1.002, 1.002 and 1.003, etc. is about 0x20c4 (8,388). This means that about 8,387 numbers exist between those two samples. A number with a higher digit count such as 1000.001 or 1000.002 support about 0x11 (17), so only about 16 numbers exist between those two numbers. And a number around 1000000 identifies 1000000.001 and 1000000.002 as the same number. This makes for comparisons of floating-point numbers with nearly the same value very tricky. This is one of the reasons why floating-point numbers are not used for currency as they tend to lose pennies. Binary-coded decimal (BCD) and fixed-point (integer) are used instead.

So when working with normalized numbers {−1.0 … 1.0}, a comparison algorithm with a precision slop factor (accuracy) of around 0.0000001 should be utilized. When working with estimated results, a much smaller value should be used. The following function returns a Boolean true : false value to indicate that the two values are close enough to be considered the same value. Normally you would not compare two floating-point values except to see if one is greater than the other for purposes of clipping. You almost never use a comparison of the same value as shown here. It is only used in this book for purposes of comparing the results of C code to assembly code to see if you are getting results from your algorithms in the range of what you expected.

> *Listing 8-1: vmp_IsFEqual() — Compares two single-precision floating-point values and determines if they are equivalent based upon the precision factor or if one is less than or greater than the other.*

```
bool vmp_IsFEqual(float fA, float fB, float fPrec)
{
    // The same so very big similar numbers or very small
    // accurate numbers.
  if (fA == fB) return true;

    // Try with a little precision slop!
  return (((fA-fPrec)<=fB) && (fB<=(fA+fPrec)));
}
```

Making the call for single-precision floating-point numbers is easy:

```
#define SINGLE_PRECISION 0.0000001f

if (!vmp_IsFEqual(f, f2, SINGLE_PRECISION))
```

For a fast algorithm that uses estimation for division or square roots, then merely reduces the precision to something less accurate:

```
#define FAST_PRECISION   0.001f
```

This book will discuss these fast estimate algorithms in later chapters. For vector comparisons, this book uses the following code:

> *Listing 8-2: Compare two {XYZ} vectors using a specified precision factor.*

```
bool vmp_IsVEqual(const vmp3DVector * const pvA,
     const vmp3DVector * const pvB, float fPrec)
{
  ASSERT_PTR4(pvA);  // See explanation of assert macros
  ASSERT_PTR4(pvB);  // later in this chapter!

  if (  !vmp_IsFEqual(pvA->x, pvB->x, fPrec)
      || !vmp_IsFEqual(pvA->y, pvB->y, fPrec)
      || !vmp_IsFEqual(pvA->z, pvB->z, fPrec))
  {
    return false;
  }

  return true;
}
```

When dealing with quad vectors (vmp3DQVector) an alternative function is called:

---

*Listing 8-3: Compare two {XYZW} vectors using a specified precision factor.*

```
bool vmp_IsQVEqual(const vmp3DQVector *const pvA,
                   const vmp3DQVector *const pvB,
                   float fPrec)
```

...and a fourth element {.w} is tested:

```
|| !vmp_IsFEqual(pvA->w, pvB->w, fPrec)
```

---

# FTST — FPU Test If Zero

| Mnemonic | P | PII | K6 | 3D! | 3Mx+ | SSE | SSE2 | A64 | SSE3 | E64T |
|---|---|---|---|---|---|---|---|---|---|---|
| FTST | ✓ | ✓ | ✓ | ✓ | ✓ | ✓ | ✓ | ✓ | ✓ | ✓ |

FPU    ftst                           Extended-precision       80

This instruction compares 0.0 with the value in FPU register ST(0) and sets the FPU code flags {C0, C2, and C3} with the results. (The state of the sign bit is ignored, allowing 0.0 = ±0.0.) If register ST(0) contains NaN an unordered condition is set.

| A ? B | C3 (Zero) | C2 (Parity) | C1 (Oflow) | C0 (Carry) |
|---|---|---|---|---|
| Unordered | 1 | 1 | 0 | 1 |
| 0.0 = ST(0) | 1 | 0 | 0 | 0 |
| 0.0 > ST(0) | 0 | 0 | 0 | 1 |
| 0.0 < ST(0) | 0 | 0 | 0 | 0 |

Flags: The condition flag C0 is cleared.

# FCOM/FCOMP/FCOMPP — FPU Unordered CMP FP

| Mnemonic | P | PII | K6 | 3D! | 3Mx+ | SSE | SSE2 | A64 | SSE3 | E64T |
|---|---|---|---|---|---|---|---|---|---|---|
| FCOM | ✓ | ✓ | ✓ | ✓ | ✓ | ✓ | ✓ | ✓ | ✓ | ✓ |
| FCOMP | ✓ | ✓ | ✓ | ✓ | ✓ | ✓ | ✓ | ✓ | ✓ | ✓ |
| FCOMPP | ✓ | ✓ | ✓ | ✓ | ✓ | ✓ | ✓ | ✓ | ✓ | ✓ |

FPU    fcom    *mSrc(32/64)*      Extended-precision     80
        fcom    *st(i)*
        fcom
        fcomp  *mSrc(32/64)*
        fcomp  *st(i)*

fcomp
fcompp

This *ordered* instruction compares the value of ST(0) with ST(i) or 32/64-bit memory and sets the condition flags. If no source operand is specified, ST(1) is used as a default. This instruction has the same functionality as FUCOM, but exceptions occur for operands with NaN. QNaN or SNaN values both set an unordered condition but generate an exception. The FCOMP instruction pops ST(0) off the stack, while FCOMPP pops ST(0) and ST(1) off the stack. (The state of the sign bit is ignored if zero, allowing 0.0 = ±0.0.)

| A ? B | C3 (Zero) | C2 (Parity) | C1 (Oflow) | C0 (Carry) |
|---|---|---|---|---|
| Unordered | 1 | 1 | – | 1 |
| 0.0 = ST(0) | 1 | 0 | – | 0 |
| 0.0 > ST(0) | 0 | 0 | – | 1 |
| 0.0 < ST(0) | 0 | 0 | – | 0 |

Flags: The condition flag C1 remains unchanged.

## FUCOM/FUCOMP/FUCOMPP — FPU Unordered CMP FP

| Mnemonic | P | PII | K6 | 3D! | 3Mx+ | SSE | SSE2 | A64 | SSE3 | E64T |
|---|---|---|---|---|---|---|---|---|---|---|
| FUCOM | ✓ | ✓ | ✓ | ✓ | ✓ | ✓ | ✓ | ✓ | ✓ | ✓ |
| FUCOMP | ✓ | ✓ | ✓ | ✓ | ✓ | ✓ | ✓ | ✓ | ✓ | ✓ |
| FUCOMPP | ✓ | ✓ | ✓ | ✓ | ✓ | ✓ | ✓ | ✓ | ✓ | ✓ |

FPU    fucom    *st(i)*          Extended-precision          80
       fucom
       fucomp   *st(i)*
       fucomp
       fucompp

This *unordered* instruction compares the value of ST(0) with ST(i) and sets the condition flags. If no source operand is specified, ST(1) is used as a default. This instruction has the same functionality as FCOM, but exceptions only occur for operands with SNaN. A QNaN or SNaN sets the condition to unordered but the QNaN value is valid in comparisons. The FUCOMP instruction pops ST(0) off the stack, while FUCOMPP pops ST(0) and ST(1) off the stack. (The state of the sign bit is ignored if zero, allowing 0.0 = ±0.0.)

| A ? B | C3 (Zero) | C2 (Parity) | C1 (Oflow) | C0 (Carry) |
|---|---|---|---|---|
| Unordered | 1 | 1 | – | 1 |
| 0.0 = ST(0) | 1 | 0 | – | 0 |
| 0.0 > ST(0) | 0 | 0 | – | 1 |
| 0.0 < ST(0) | 0 | 0 | – | 0 |

Flags: The condition flag C1 remains unchanged.

## FCOMI/FCOMIP/FUCOMI/FUCOMIP — FPU A ? B and EFLAGS

| Mnemonic | P | PII | K6 | 3D! | 3Mx+ | SSE | SSE2 | A64 | SSE3 | E64T |
|---|---|---|---|---|---|---|---|---|---|---|
| FCOMI | ✓ | ✓ | ✓ | ✓ | ✓ | ✓ | ✓ | ✓ | ✓ | ✓ |
| FCOMIP | ✓ | ✓ | ✓ | ✓ | ✓ | ✓ | ✓ | ✓ | ✓ | ✓ |
| FUCOMI | ✓ | ✓ | ✓ | ✓ | ✓ | ✓ | ✓ | ✓ | ✓ | ✓ |
| FUCOMIP | ✓ | ✓ | ✓ | ✓ | ✓ | ✓ | ✓ | ✓ | ✓ | ✓ |

FPU     fcomi     *st, st(i)*           Extended-precision
            fcomip     *st, st(i)*
            fucomi     *st, st(i)*
            fucomip     *st, st(i)*

The FCOMI and FCOMIP instructions have identical functionality to the FCOM and FCOMP instructions, except that the EFLAGS are set instead of the FPU conditional flags.

    The FUCOMI and FUCOMIP instructions have identical functionality to the FUCOM and FUCOMP instructions, except that the EFLAGS are set instead of the FPU conditional flags.

| **Flags** | O.flow | Sign | Zero | Aux | Parity | Carry |
|---|---|---|---|---|---|---|
| | 0 | - | X | - | X | X |

Flags: The flags are set as a result of the addition operation.

## FICOM/FICOMP — FPU A ? B

| Mnemonic | P | PII | K6 | 3D! | 3Mx+ | SSE | SSE2 | A64 | SSE3 | E64T |
|---|---|---|---|---|---|---|---|---|---|---|
| FICOM | ✓ | ✓ | ✓ | ✓ | ✓ | ✓ | ✓ | ✓ | ✓ | ✓ |
| FICOMP | ✓ | ✓ | ✓ | ✓ | ✓ | ✓ | ✓ | ✓ | ✓ | ✓ |

FPU    ficom    *mSrc(16/32)*         Extended-precision        80
       ficomp   *mSrc(16/32)*

This *unordered* instruction loads the 16/32-bit integer from memory, converts it to double extended-precision floating-point, compares it to the value in the ST(0) register and sets the condition flags. A QNaN or SNaN value sets the condition to unordered, but the QNaN value is valid in comparisons and a SNaN generates an exception. The FICOMP instruction pops ST(0) off the stack. (The state of the sign bit is ignored if zero, allowing 0.0 = ±0.0.)

| A ? B | C3 (Zero) | C2 (Parity) | C1 (Oflow) | C0 (Carry) |
|---|---|---|---|---|
| Unordered | I | I | – | I |
| 0.0 = ST(0) | I | 0 | – | 0 |
| 0.0 > ST(0) | 0 | 0 | – | I |
| 0.0 < ST(0) | 0 | 0 | – | 0 |

Flags: The condition flag C1 remains unchanged.

# FCMOVcc — FPU Conditional Move

| Mnemonic | P | PII | K6 | 3D! | 3Mx+ | SSE | SSE2 | A64 | SSE3 | E64T |
|---|---|---|---|---|---|---|---|---|---|---|
| FCMOVx | ✓ | ✓ | ✓ | ✓ | ✓ | ✓ | ✓ | ✓ | ✓ | ✓ |

FPU    fcmovb     *st(0), st(i)*      Extended-precision        80
 "     fcmove     *st(0), st(i)*            "                    "
 "     fcmovbe    *st(0), st(i)*            "                    "
 "     fcmovu     *st(0), st(i)*            "                    "
 "     fcmovnb    *st(0), st(i)*            "                    "
 "     fcmovne    *st(0), st(i)*            "                    "
 "     fcmovnbe   *st(0), st(i)*            "                    "
 "     fcmovnu    *st(0), st(i)*            "                    "

The EFLAGS are examined and the FPU moves the value from ST(i) to ST(0) if the condition is met.

Left and right columns are complemented instructions. **If conditional set...**

| FCMOVNBE | If above. ZF=0, CF=0 | | FCMOVBE | If Below or Equal. ZF=1, CF=1 |
|---|---|---|---|---|
| | op1 > op2 | | | op1 ≤ op2 |
| FCMOVNB | If above or equal. CF=0 | | FCMOVB | If below. CF=1 |
| | op1 ≥ op2 | | | op1 < op2 |
| FCMOVE | Set if equal. ZF=1 | | FCMOVNE | Set if not equal. ZF=0 |
| | op1 = op2 | | | op1 ≠ op2 |
| FCMOVU | If parity. PF=1 | | FCMOVNU | If not parity. PF=0 |
| | If parity even. | | | If parity odd. |

| A ? B | C3 (Zero) | C2 (Parity) | C1 (Oflow) | C0 (Carry) |
|---|---|---|---|---|
| Unordered | – | – | 0 | – |

Flags: The condition flags C0, C2, and C3 remain unchanged. C0 is cleared if stack underflow occurred.

# FXAM — FPU Examine

| Mnemonic | P | PII | K6 | 3D! | 3Mx+ | SSE | SSE2 | A64 | SSE3 | E64T |
|---|---|---|---|---|---|---|---|---|---|---|
| FXAM | ✓ | ✓ | ✓ | ✓ | ✓ | ✓ | ✓ | ✓ | ✓ | ✓ |

FPU    fxam

This instruction sets the conditional flags to reflect the value in ST(0).

| ST(0) State | C3 | C2 | C1(±) | C0 |
|---|---|---|---|---|
| Denormal | 1 | 1 | x | 0 |
| Empty | 1 | 0 | x | 1 |
| 0 | 1 | 0 | x | 0 |
| ∞ | 0 | 1 | x | 1 |
| Normal finite | 0 | 1 | x | 0 |
| NaN | 0 | 0 | x | 1 |
| Unsupported | 0 | 0 | x | 0 |

Flags: The condition flag C1 reflects the sign bit of ST(0).

# FPU BCD (Binary-Coded Decimal)

One other feature of the FPU that can be taken advantage of is the BCD capability. BCD can be loaded, calculations performed, and data written back out. It allows for 18 4-bit BCD digits plus a sign bit within a number to be processed simultaneously. Due to precision loss, a number represented by BCD and utilizing BCD math is the safest method of representing monetary values (money) without losing pennies. This will be discussed in Chapter 15, "Binary-Coded Decimal."

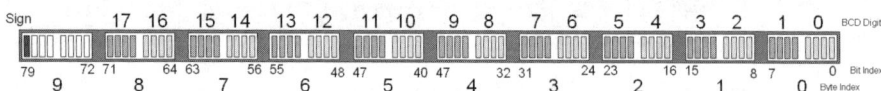

Figure 8-4: Ten-byte BCD data storage. The MSB in the far left byte (byte #9) is the sign bit and the rightmost eight bytes (#8...0) contain the BCD value pairs. The 18th BCD digit resides in the upper nibble of byte #8 and the first BCD digit resides in the lower nibble of byte #0.

## FBLD — FPU (BCD Load)

| Mnemonic | P | PII | K6 | 3D! | 3Mx+ | SSE | SSE2 | A64 | SSE3 | E64T |
|----------|---|-----|-----|------|-------|------|------|------|------|------|
| FBLD | ✓ | ✓ | ✓ | ✓ | ✓ | ✓ | ✓ | ✓ | ✓ | ✓ |

FPU    fbld  *source*      BCD      80

The binary-coded decimal (BCD) load instruction loads the 80-bit value in memory, expands it to an 80-bit double extended-precision floating-point form, and pushes it on the stack, thereby making it addressable by the FPU as register ST(0).

```
TBYTE bcd
REAL8 f
fbld  tbyte ptr bcd   ; Load (10 byte) BCD
fstp  f               ; Write 64-bit double-precision
```

For more detail see Chapter 15.

## FBSTP — FPU (BCD Save and Pop ST(0))

| Mnemonic | P | PII | K6 | 3D! | 3Mx+ | SSE | SSE2 | A64 | SSE3 | E64T |
|----------|---|-----|-----|------|-------|------|------|------|------|------|
| FBSTP | ✓ | ✓ | ✓ | ✓ | ✓ | ✓ | ✓ | ✓ | ✓ | ✓ |

FPU    fbstp  *destination*      BCD      80

The binary-coded decimal (BCD) save instruction reads the 80-bit value in register ST(0) and pops it off the stack, then saves to memory. For more detail see Chapter 15.

# FPU Trigonometry

## FPTAN — FPU Partial Tangent

| Mnemonic | P | PII | K6 | 3D! | 3Mx+ | SSE | SSE2 | A64 | SSE3 | E64T |
|----------|---|-----|-----|-----|------|-----|------|-----|------|------|
| FPTAN | ✓ | ✓ | ✓ | ✓ | ✓ | ✓ | ✓ | ✓ | ✓ | ✓ |

FPU     fptan                         Extended-precision        80

The partial tangent of the source radians in ST(0) is calculated, then stored in ST(0).

$$ST(0) = \tan(ST(0))$$

## FPATAN — FPU Partial Arctangent

| Mnemonic | P | PII | K6 | 3D! | 3Mx+ | SSE | SSE2 | A64 | SSE3 | E64T |
|----------|---|-----|-----|-----|------|-----|------|-----|------|------|
| FPATAN | ✓ | ✓ | ✓ | ✓ | ✓ | ✓ | ✓ | ✓ | ✓ | ✓ |

FPU     fpatan                        Extended-precision        80

The value of the divisor ST(0) is divided into the quotient ST(1), and the resulting value is stored into the unwound stack into ST(0).

$$ST(0) = \arctan(ST(1) \div ST(0))$$

## FSINCOS — Sine and Cosine

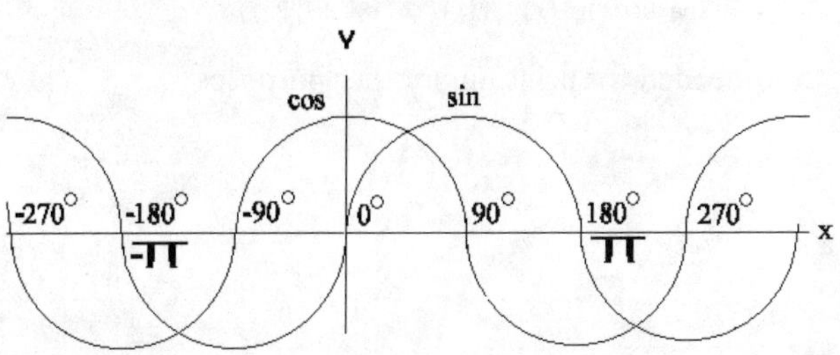

Figure 8-5: Sine-cosine waves

$$\sin \theta = \frac{\text{opposite side}}{\text{hypotenuse}} \qquad\qquad \cos \theta = \frac{\text{adjacent side}}{\text{hypotenuse}}$$

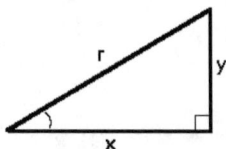

*Figure 8-6: Sine and cosine trigonometric relationships*

$$\sin \theta = \frac{y}{r} \qquad y = r \sin \theta \qquad r = \frac{y}{\sin \theta}$$

$$\cos \theta = \frac{x}{r} \qquad x = r \cos \theta \qquad r = \frac{x}{\cos \theta}$$

*Equation 8-1: Sine and Cosine*

The standard C math library contains these functions:

```
float cos(float x);        double cos(double x);
float sin(float x);        double sin(double x);
```

You should already be familiar with the fact that the angle is not passed into those functions in degrees but instead in radians. If you recall, π (PI) is equivalent to 180° and 2π to 360°. By using the following macro, an angle in degrees can be converted to radians:

```
#define PI          3.141592f
#define DEG2RAD(x)  ((x) * (PI/180.0F))
```

…and used in the calculations. It can then be converted from radians back to degrees:

```
#define RAD2DEG(x)  ((x) * (180.0f/PI))
```

…if needed for printing or other purposes.

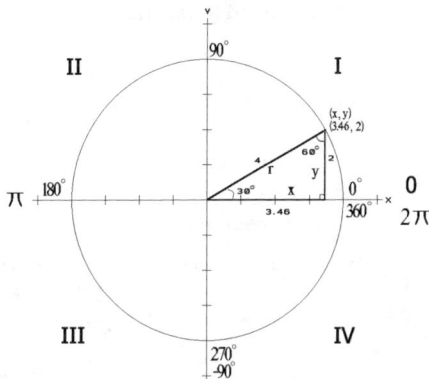

*Figure 8-7: 2D rotation angle*

For a simple 2D rotation the use is merely:

```
x = cos(fRadian);
y = sin(fRadian);
```

There is one thing that has always bothered me about these two functions: When a cosine is needed, a sine is typically needed as well, and that one is in reality 90 degrees out of phase of the other, which means that they share similar algorithms. As the following equation shows, subtracting an angle from 90 degrees results in the alternate angle. So, for example, a sin(30°) is equal to the cos(60°). As the angles of a triangle always add up to 180 degrees, that would mean that the two angles are really not that far from each other, and mathematical operations to find one of the angles can be slightly adapted to find the other angle without having to do twice the work.

$$\sin(90° - \theta) = \cos\theta$$

*Equation 8-2: Angular relationship sine to cosine.*

But I find something really interesting. In Intel's wisdom they not only support the sine and cosine on their FPU (floating-point unit) but they also support the combination sine-cosine, which returns both results. What I find amazing is that very few programmers actually take advantage of it! In addition, I am upon occasion called in to review other programmer's code and I quite consistently have to recommend calling the sine and cosine functions only once in their matrix algorithms.

**Left-Handed Rotations**

$$\begin{bmatrix} 1 & 0 & 0 & 0 \\ 0 & \cos\theta & \sin\theta & 0 \\ 0 & -\sin\theta & \cos\theta & 0 \\ 0 & 0 & 0 & 1 \end{bmatrix} \quad \begin{bmatrix} \cos\theta & 0 & -\sin\theta & 0 \\ 0 & 1 & 0 & 0 \\ \sin\theta & 0 & \cos\theta & 0 \\ 0 & 0 & 0 & 1 \end{bmatrix} \quad \begin{bmatrix} \cos\theta & \sin\theta & 0 & 0 \\ -\sin\theta & \cos\theta & 0 & 0 \\ 0 & 0 & 1 & 0 \\ 0 & 0 & 0 & 1 \end{bmatrix}$$

Rotate X · · · · · · · · · · · · · Rotate Y · · · · · · · · · · · · · Rotate Z

**Right-Handed Rotations**

$$\begin{bmatrix} 1 & 0 & 0 & 0 \\ 0 & \cos\theta & -\sin\theta & 0 \\ 0 & \sin\theta & \cos\theta & 0 \\ 0 & 0 & 0 & 1 \end{bmatrix} \quad \begin{bmatrix} \cos\theta & 0 & \sin\theta & 0 \\ 0 & 1 & 0 & 0 \\ -\sin\theta & 0 & \cos\theta & 0 \\ 0 & 0 & 0 & 1 \end{bmatrix} \quad \begin{bmatrix} \cos\theta & -\sin\theta & 0 & 0 \\ \sin\theta & \cos\theta & 0 & 0 \\ 0 & 0 & 1 & 0 \\ 0 & 0 & 0 & 1 \end{bmatrix}$$

Rotate X · · · · · · · · · · · · · Rotate Y · · · · · · · · · · · · · Rotate Z

*Figure 8-8: Left/right-handed rotation matrices*

A 3D rotational matrix for an axis will use two identical cosines, a sine, and a negative sine, but why do I keep seeing these functions each called twice? I see code such as follows for a left-handed rotate X:

```
Mx[1][2] = sin(fRadian);
Mx[2][2] = cos(fRadian);
Mx[1][1] = cos(fRadian);
Mx[2][1] = −sin(fRadian);
```

…or the just slightly better:

```
Mx[1][2] =             sin(fRadian);
Mx[2][2] = Mx[1][1] = cos(fRadian);
Mx[2][1] =            −sin(fRadian);
```

…and then you wonder why your code runs so slow! Instead, your code should be more like:

```
Mx[1][2] =             sin(fRadian);
Mx[2][2] = Mx[1][1] =  cos(fRadian);
Mx[2][1] = −Mx[1][2]; //−sin
```

…or better yet, if you are using an x86 processor use its combination sine/cosine instruction! When I work on legacy projects involving trigonometry I quite often find that I need to drop the following code snippet into the application:

```
sincos(&fSin, &fCos, fRadian);
Mx[1][2] =             fSin;
Mx[2][2] = Mx[1][1] =  fCos;
Mx[2][1] = −fSin;
```

The reason will soon become evident!

## Pseudo Vec

Similar to the other functions in this book, the sine and cosine functions have been wrapped for extra portability and for alternate specialty function replacements. One for single-precision floating-point and another for double-precision floating-point:

```
Listing 8-4: ...\chap8\ vtrig3d\VTrig3D.cpp

void sincosf(float * const pfSin,
             float * const pfCos, float fRads)
{
  *pfSin = sinf(fRads);
  *pfCos = cosf(fRads);
}
.
.
.
void sincos(double * const pfSin,
            double * const pfCos, double fRads)
{
  *pfSin = sin(fRads);
  *pfCos = cos(fRads);
}
```

## Pseudo Vec (x86)

Early Microsoft math libraries did not include this functionality, which is understandable as the C programming language was born in the land of UNIX and was brought forth to the x86 DOS world by other companies and eventually by Microsoft. I believe the absence of a library function for a combination sine-cosine was merely an oversight. It has recently been introduced in third-party libraries and in different forms.

### AMD-SDK

```
void _sincos(float, float *);
void a_sincos(void);             // mm0 -> mm0 (cos|sin)
__m64 _m_sincos(__m64);          // mm0 -> mm0 (cos|sin)
```

### 3DSMax-SDK

```
inline void SinCos(float angle, float *sine, float *cosine)
```

I did a wildcard search on my computer for header files within various SDKs and this is all that turned up with all the compilers I work with. Apparently, most programmers up until now either did not understand the issue or did not have the ability to write FPU code! Let's fix that right now.

First, stub your cross-platform C function for sincos(). No matter the platform, you should always use something similar.

We will soon build an equivalent function using the FPU found in every 80x86 processor since the 80486, and available as an optional coprocessor before that.

# FSIN — FPU Sine

| Mnemonic | P | PII | K6 | 3D! | 3Mx+ | SSE | SSE2 | A64 | SSE3 | E64T |
|---|---|---|---|---|---|---|---|---|---|---|
| FSIN | ✓ | ✓ | ✓ | ✓ | ✓ | ✓ | ✓ | ✓ | ✓ | ✓ |

FPU    fsin                          Extended-precision     80

The sine of the source radians in ST(0) is calculated and the result is stored in ST(0). See the table for the FSINCOS instruction for source versus destination details.

```
float sinf(float rad);
double sin(double rad);
```

# FCOS — FPU Cosine

| Mnemonic | P | PII | K6 | 3D! | 3Mx+ | SSE | SSE2 | A64 | SSE3 | E64T |
|---|---|---|---|---|---|---|---|---|---|---|
| FCOS | ✓ | ✓ | ✓ | ✓ | ✓ | ✓ | ✓ | ✓ | ✓ | ✓ |

FPU    fcos                         Extended-precision     80

The cosine of the source radians in ST(0), is calculated and the result is stored in ST(0). See the table for the FSINCOS instruction for source versus destination details.

```
float cosf(float rad);
double cos(double rad);
```

# FSINCOS — FPU Sine and Cosine

| Mnemonic | P | PII | K6 | 3D! | 3Mx+ | SSE | SSE2 | A64 | SSE3 | E64T |
|---|---|---|---|---|---|---|---|---|---|---|
| FSINCOS | ✓ | ✓ | ✓ | ✓ | ✓ | ✓ | ✓ | ✓ | ✓ | ✓ |

FPU    fsincos                   Extended-precision     80

The FSINCOS instruction calculates the sine and cosine simultaneously for a single-precision floating-point radian in ST(0) and stores the result in ST(0). It's slower than calling just sine or cosine, but faster than calling them both consecutively.

**Note:** The value used for radians must be a proper floating-point normalized value between $[-\pi, \pi]$. If valid but out of range, a precision loss will occur.

| Radians (Src) | Destination | |
|---|---|---|
| ST(0) | ST(1) Cos | ST(0) Sin |
| NaN | NaN | NaN |
| $+\infty$ | <Invalid> | <Invalid> |
| +Finite | $[-1, 1]$  $[-\pi, \pi]$ | $[-1, 1]$  $[-\pi, \pi]$ |
| +0 | +1 | +0 |
| −0 | +1 | −0 |
| − Finite | $[-1, 1]$  $[-\pi, \pi]$ | $[-1, 1]$  $[-\pi, \pi]$ |
| − $\infty$ | <Invalid> | <Invalid> |

If the source radians are outside the allowed range of $[-2^{63}, 2^{63}]$, the value can be reduced within range by N mod $(2\pi)$.

*Listing 8-5: ...\chap8\vtrig3d\VTrig3DX86.asm*

```
void sincosf(float *pfSin, float *pfCos, float r)
{
#if 01
    __asm {
        fld    r            ; Load radians from memory

        fwait               ; Wait for FPU to be idle
        fsincos             ; ST(0)=cos ST(1)=sin

        mov    eax,pfSin
        mov    ecx,pfCos

        fwait               ; Wait for FPU to be idle

        fstp   [ecx]        ; ST(0)=cos ST(1)=sin
        fstp   [eax]        ; sin
        };
#else
        *pfSin = sinf(r);
        *pfCos = cosf(r);
#endif
}
```

## vmp_SinCos (3DNow!)

AMD has a really nice solution for their 3DNow! functionality. It resolves the sine and cosine simultaneously using the MMX register set. Their algorithm is actually pretty cool, as what they do is ratio $\pi$ (3.14159) to a value of 4. The value of {–3.14159 … 3.14159} is effectively scaled to a value of {–4.0 … 4.0}, which in essence makes $\pi$ radians a base 2 number and thus integer math is used in conjunction with parallel floating-point math and MMX registers. Signs are tracked to encode the quadrant of the circle in which the angle resides. Since a circle is actually made up of eight quadrants (investigate the Bresenham DDA algorithm for circle plotting), then only the modulus 45° angle needs to be resolved. Using this methodology, several cos/sin functions could be processed simultaneously.

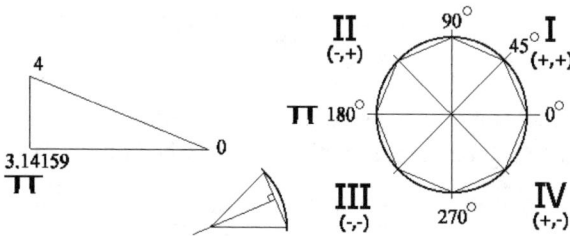

*Figure 8-9: The relationship of a circle with its quadrants and associated sizes*

The code can be downloaded from the AMD web site (www.amd.com) and is contained within their Software Development Kit (SDK) – AMD Library Reference.

Cut and paste it into your own code. If using Direct3D, it is automatically called if you are using a processor supporting the 3DNow! instruction set; there is also an SSE version. It is a lot more efficient than having to do an FPU/MMX switch, especially as sine and cosine are processed simultaneously in parallel.

I am not telling you to reverse-engineer the DirectX library, as that would be wrong and illegal, but by setting a break point on the DirectX library function call and upon getting the break, set your view to assembly code and step into the code. You can cut and paste a copy of that code to a text editor, allowing you to edit and analyze how it works. Remember, there is more than one algorithm residing in the library as well.

# FPU System Instructions

The following are FPU instructions used for system administration purposes. A typical application will not need to use these. These have been left here instead of moving them to Chapter 18, "System," just to keep the FPU documentation grouped together.

## FINIT/FNINIT — FPU Init

| Mnemonic | P | PII | K6 | 3D! | 3Mx+ | SSE | SSE2 | A64 | SSE3 | E64T |
|----------|---|-----|----|----|------|-----|------|-----|------|------|
| FINIT | ✓ | ✓ | ✓ | ✓ | ✓ | ✓ | ✓ | ✓ | ✓ | ✓ |
| FNINIT | ✓ | ✓ | ✓ | ✓ | ✓ | ✓ | ✓ | ✓ | ✓ | ✓ |

FPU    finit
        fninit

The FINIT instruction checks for pending unmasked floating-point exceptions, then initializes the FPU.

The FNINIT instruction initializes the FPU without any pending checks.

## FCLEX/FNCLEX — FPU Clear Exceptions

| Mnemonic | P | PII | K6 | 3D! | 3Mx+ | SSE | SSE2 | A64 | SSE3 | E64T |
|----------|---|-----|----|----|------|-----|------|-----|------|------|
| FCLEX | ✓ | ✓ | ✓ | ✓ | ✓ | ✓ | ✓ | ✓ | ✓ | ✓ |
| FNCLEX | ✓ | ✓ | ✓ | ✓ | ✓ | ✓ | ✓ | ✓ | ✓ | ✓ |

FPU    fclex
        fnclex

The FCLEX instruction checks for pending unmasked floating-point exceptions, then clears the exception flags.

The FNCLEX instruction clears the exception flags without any pending checks.

| | C3 (Zero) | C2 (Parity) | C1 (Oflow) | C0 (Carry) |
|---|-----------|-------------|------------|------------|
| | – | – | – | – |

Flags: The condition of flags {C0, C1, C2, C3} remain unchanged; however, the other FPU flags (PE, UE, OE, ZE, DE, IE, ES, SF, and B) are cleared.

## FFREE — FPU Free FP Register

| Mnemonic | P | PII | K6 | 3D! | 3Mx+ | SSE | SSE2 | A64 | SSE3 | E64T |
|---|---|---|---|---|---|---|---|---|---|---|
| FFREE | ✓ | ✓ | ✓ | ✓ | ✓ | ✓ | ✓ | ✓ | ✓ | ✓ |

FPU    ffree  *st(i)*

This instruction sets the tag associated with ST(i) to an empty state.

## FSAVE/FNSAVE — FPU Save X87 FPU, MMX, SSE, SSE2

| Mnemonic | P | PII | K6 | 3D! | 3Mx+ | SSE | SSE2 | A64 | SSE3 | E64T |
|---|---|---|---|---|---|---|---|---|---|---|
| FSAVE | ✓ | ✓ | ✓ | ✓ | ✓ | ✓ | ✓ | ✓ | ✓ | ✓ |
| FNSAVE | ✓ | ✓ | ✓ | ✓ | ✓ | ✓ | ✓ | ✓ | ✓ | ✓ |

FPU    fsave    *mSrc(94/108)*
       fnsave   *mSrc(94/108)*

The FSAVE instruction checks for pending unmasked floating-point exceptions, saves the FPU state to 94/108-byte memory, and then reinitializes the FPU.

The FNSAVE instruction saves the FPU state to 94/108-byte memory, and then reinitializes the FPU.

The assembler typically inserts the FWAIT instruction before this instruction to ensure the FPU is ready (no instruction in process) to save.

(16-bit) Real Mode saves 94 bytes, and (32-bit) Protected Mode saves 108 bytes. The complement of this instruction is FRSTOR.

## FRSTOR — FPU Restore x87 State

| Mnemonic | P | PII | K6 | 3D! | 3Mx+ | SSE | SSE2 | A64 | SSE3 | E64T |
|---|---|---|---|---|---|---|---|---|---|---|
| FRSTOR | ✓ | ✓ | ✓ | ✓ | ✓ | ✓ | ✓ | ✓ | ✓ | ✓ |

FPU    frstor    *mSrc(94/108)*

This instruction loads the FPU state from 94/108-byte memory that was saved with the instruction FSAVE or FNSAVE.

## FXSAVE — FPU Save x87 FPU, MMX, SSE, SSE2, SSE3

| Mnemonic | P | PII | K6 | 3D! | 3Mx+ | SSE | SSE2 | A64 | SSE3 | E64T |
|----------|---|-----|----|----|------|-----|------|-----|------|------|
| FXSAVE   |   |     |    |     |      | ✓   | ✓    | ✓   | ✓    | ✓    |

FPU     fxsave     *mSrc(512)*

This instruction saves the registers {FPU, MMX, XMM, and MXCSR} to a 512-byte memory block. The complement of this instruction is FXRSTOR.

## FXRSTOR — FPU Restore x87 FPU, MMX, SSE, SSE2, SSE3

| Mnemonic | P | PII | K6 | 3D! | 3Mx+ | SSE | SSE2 | A64 | SSE3 | E64T |
|----------|---|-----|----|----|------|-----|------|-----|------|------|
| FXRSTOR  |   |     |    |     |      | ✓   | ✓    | ✓   | ✓    | ✓    |

FPU     fxrstor     *mSrc(512)*

This instruction loads registers from 512-byte memory saved with the FXSAVE instruction.

## FSTENV/FNSTENV — FPU Store x87 Environment

| Mnemonic | P | PII | K6 | 3D! | 3Mx+ | SSE | SSE2 | A64 | SSE3 | E64T |
|----------|---|-----|----|----|------|-----|------|-----|------|------|
| FSTENV   | ✓ | ✓   | ✓  | ✓   | ✓    | ✓   | ✓    | ✓   | ✓    | ✓    |
| FNSTENV  | ✓ | ✓   | ✓  | ✓   | ✓    | ✓   | ✓    | ✓   | ✓    | ✓    |

FPU     fstenv     *mSrc(14/28)*
        fnstenv    *mSrc(14/28)*

The FSTENV instruction checks for pending unmasked floating-point exceptions, then masks all exceptions and saves the FPU environment to 14/28-byte memory.

The FNSTENV instruction save the FPU environment to 14/28-byte memory, then masks all floating-point exceptions.

The assembler typically inserts the FWAIT instruction before this instruction to ensure the FPU is ready (no instruction in process) to save.

The data saved is the FPU control word, status word, tag word, instruction pointer, data pointer, and last opcode. (16-bit) Real Mode saves 14 bytes, and (32-bit) Protected Mode saves 28 bytes. The complement of this instruction is FLDENV.

# FLDENV — FPU Load x87 Environment

| Mnemonic | P | PII | K6 | 3D! | 3Mx+ | SSE | SSE2 | A64 | SSE3 | E64T |
|----------|---|-----|----|----|------|-----|------|-----|------|------|
| FLDENV | ✓ | ✓ | ✓ | ✓ | ✓ | ✓ | ✓ | ✓ | ✓ | ✓ |

FPU    fldenv    *mSrc(14/28)*

This instruction loads the environment from 14/28-byte memory that was saved with the instruction FSTENV or FNSTENV.

# FSTCW/FNSTCW — FPU Store x87 Control Word

| Mnemonic | P | PII | K6 | 3D! | 3Mx+ | SSE | SSE2 | A64 | SSE3 | E64T |
|----------|---|-----|----|----|------|-----|------|-----|------|------|
| FSTCW | ✓ | ✓ | ✓ | ✓ | ✓ | ✓ | ✓ | ✓ | ✓ | ✓ |
| FNSTCW | ✓ | ✓ | ✓ | ✓ | ✓ | ✓ | ✓ | ✓ | ✓ | ✓ |

FPU    fstcw    *mSrc(2)*
       fnstcw   *mSrc(2)*

The FSTCW instruction checks for pending unmasked floating-point exceptions, then saves the 16-bit FPU control word to memory.

The FNSTCW instruction saves the 16-bit FPU control word to memory.

The assembler typically inserts the FWAIT instruction before this instruction to ensure the FPU is ready (no instruction in process) to save.

The complement of this instruction is FLDCW.

# FLDCW — FPU Load x87 Control Word

| Mnemonic | P | PII | K6 | 3D! | 3Mx+ | SSE | SSE2 | A64 | SSE3 | E64T |
|----------|---|-----|----|----|------|-----|------|-----|------|------|
| FLDCW | ✓ | ✓ | ✓ | ✓ | ✓ | ✓ | ✓ | ✓ | ✓ | ✓ |

FPU    fldcw    *mSrc(2)*

This instruction loads the 16-bit FPU control word from memory that was saved with the instruction FSTCW or FNSTCW.

## FSTSW/FNSTSW — FPU Store x87 Status Word

| Mnemonic | P | PII | K6 | 3D! | 3Mx+ | SSE | SSE2 | A64 | SSE3 | E64T |
|----------|---|-----|----|----|------|-----|------|-----|------|------|
| FSTSW    | ✓ | ✓   | ✓  | ✓  | ✓    | ✓   | ✓    | ✓   | ✓    | ✓    |
| FNSTSW   | ✓ | ✓   | ✓  | ✓  | ✓    | ✓   | ✓    | ✓   | ✓    | ✓    |

```
FPU     fstsw     mSrc(2)
        fstsw     AX
        fnstsw    mSrc(2)
        fnstsw    AX
```

The FPU has condition code bits contained within the status register. These bits match 1:1 with the EFLAGS of the CPU. They can be copied to memory or the AX register using this instruction. They can then be copied to the EFLAGS register using the SAHF instruction.

```
fstsw   ax    ; Copy FPU condition bits to AX register.
sahf          ; Copy AH to EFLAGS.
```

# Validating (Invalid) Floating-Point

When a floating-point value becomes invalid due to overflows, etc., the easiest way to make it valid is stretch the value into a larger floating-point form, which becomes valid, and then store it back out as a valid form. Confusing?

The following is a code snippet that detects single-precision floating-point overflows. In this case, the value is radians.

```
OFLOW_FIXUP fRads    ; Overflow fixup
```

Listing 8-6: incx86\vmp3DX86M.inc

```
OFLOW_FIXUP    MACRO    arg1
    mov  eax,DWORD PTR arg1 ; 03F800000h = 1.0f  0BF800000h=-1.0
    and  eax,07F800000h
    cmp  eax,07F800000h      ;Check for an non-zero exponent!
    jne  $ok
```

```
    mov  eax,DWORD PTR arg1
    call FixupReal4
$ok:                        ; ST(0)= value
    endm
```

To fix the overflow of a single-precision floating-point value, it can be expanded to double extended-precision floating-point or double-precision floating-point, such as in the following code snippet.

*Listing 8-7: FixupReal4*

```
;   Fixup Real4 (float)
;        eax=bad float
; NOTE: ST(0) already contains the float!!!

FixupReal4 proc near
    fstp qword ptr [esp-8-10]       ; Save Real8 (double) & pop ST(0)

; Build a Real10

    mov  eax,[esp-8-10+4]           ; Hi
    or   eax,7FFF0000h              ; Set Real8 (Double)
    mov  dword ptr [esp-10+6],eax   ; 7FFFXXXX????????????

    mov  eax,[esp-8-10+4]           ; Real8 Hi
    mov  ecx,[esp-8-10+0]           ; Real8 Lo
    shld eax,ecx,11
    shl  ecx,11
    mov  dword ptr [esp-10+4],eax   ; 7FFFHHHHHHHHH????????
    mov  dword ptr [esp-10+0],ecx   ; FFFHHHHHHHHHLLLLLLLL
    fld  tbyte ptr [esp-10+0]       ; Load Real10

    ret                             ; ST(0)=value
FixupReal4 endp
```

# Exercises

1. Write a sincos function in assembly language similar to sincosf but using double-precision floating-point.

2. Write a floating-point equation A+B×C+D using RPN. Write it using FPU instructions.

3. Write a factorial program to solve for !15 using FPU instructions and taking advantage of the stack.

4. How much accuracy does the vmp_IsFEqual() function allow with a single-precision definition? Fast precision?

5. Does vmp_IsFEqual() accept a negative value for the third argument? Should there be an assertion? Why or why not?

6. In this chapter, vmp_IsVEqual() uses an ASSERT_PTR4(). What assertion would be used instead to force a 16-byte alignment?

7. Write C functions to support double-precision for:
   a) vmp_IsDEqual() scalar double-precision
   b) vmp_IsDVEqual() vector double-precision
   c) vmp_IsDQVEqual() quad vector double-precision

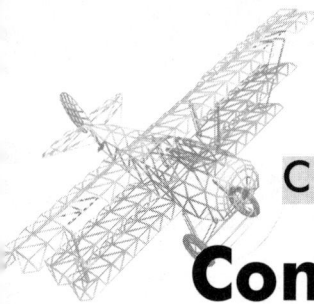

# Chapter 9

# Comparison

Comparisons are typically related to decision making. A C programmer is typically familiar with one of the following:

- An index into a table is calculated by deciding between multiple factors:

```
index = (a < b ) ? i : j;
```

- A comparison is used to decide which branch to take:

```
if (a < b )
{
    dothis();
}
else
{
    dothat();
}
```

In assembly code, comparisons actually take on multiple forms.

The general-purpose instructions set the EFLAGS/RFLAGS conditional flags to indicate their scalar result. Additional instructions would then utilize individual flags that are reset (cleared) or set, such as branching and bit shifting/rotation. The instructions utilizing packed data store the result of the comparison as packed Boolean values of 0=False and 1=True.

Since the logical AND operation has already been discussed, let us start with the TEST instruction, which has a similar functionality.

# TEST — Logical Compare  A ∧ B

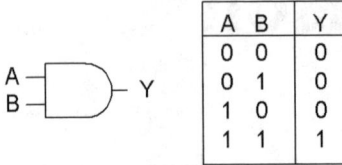

| A  B | Y |
|------|---|
| 0  0 | 0 |
| 0  1 | 0 |
| 1  0 | 0 |
| 1  1 | 1 |

TEST *operand1*, *operand2*

| Mnemonic | P | PII | K6 | 3D! | 3Mx+ | SSE | SSE2 | A64 | SSE3 | E64T |
|----------|---|-----|----|-----|------|-----|------|-----|------|------|
| TEST | ✓ | ✓ | ✓ | ✓ | ✓ | ✓ | ✓ | ✓ | ✓ | ✓ |

test    *rmDst(8/16/32/64)*, *#(8/16/32)*        [Un]signed

test    *rmDst, rSrc(8/16/32/64)*

The TEST general-purpose instruction logically AND's the 8-, 16-, 32-, or 64-bit *operand1* with the *operand2* and sets the flags accordingly, but there is no destination as the result is not stored. An AND operation means that you would need both A *and* B to be true to have a true result. The behavior of this instruction is identical to the AND instruction except that there is no saved result. A 32-bit source value can be sign extended to a 64-bit *destination*.

| **Flags** | O.flow | Sign | Zero | Aux | Parity | Carry |
|-----------|--------|------|------|-----|--------|-------|
| | 0 | X | X | - | X | 0 |

Flags: The Carry and Overflow flags are cleared. The Sign flag reflects the state of the MSB.

```
        mov     eax,00000a5a5h
        mov     edx,000000ff0h
        test    eax,edx
;       0000000000000000010100101101001101b  00000a5a5h
; AND   00000000000000000000000111111110000b  000000ff0h
```

**Tip:**   The best way to test for zero is to AND a value with itself with a TEST instruction; nothing is written, only data is read, and EFLAGS are set but no write cycles.

```
        test    ebx,ebx         ; cmp ebx,ebx
        jne     $L1
```

# Indexed Bit Testing

A selected bit can be tested for its state, manipulate the state of the bit upon that tested state, and return a result of the test.

## BT — Bit Test

BT *operand, index*

| Mnemonic | P | PII | K6 | 3D! | 3Mx+ | SSE | SSE2 | A64 | SSE3 | E64T |
|----------|---|-----|----|----|------|-----|------|-----|------|------|
| BT | ✓ | ✓ | ✓ | ✓ | ✓ | ✓ | ✓ | ✓ | ✓ | ✓ |

    bt    *rmDst(16/32/64), #(8)*      [Un]signed
    bt    *rmDst, rSrc(16/32/64)*

This general-purpose instruction tests the bit in the *operand*, using the index $\{0...2^N-1\}$, and returns the state of the bit in the Carry flag.

| Flags | O.flow | Sign | Zero | Aux | Parity | Carry |
|-------|--------|------|------|-----|--------|-------|
|  | - | - | - | - | - | X |

Flags: The Carry flag contains the value of the indexed bit.

```
foo:    dd      010110111011110111111011111101111b

        mov     ebx,0fedcba98h
                ;11111110110111001011101010011000b
        mov     eax,31

        bt      ebx,10    ; carry will equal 0
        bt      ebx,0     ; carry will equal 0
        bt      bx,7      ; carry will equal 1
        bt      ebx,eax   ; carry will equal 1

        bt      foo,eax   ; carry will equal 0
```

## BTC — Bit Test and Complement

BTC *destination, index*

| Mnemonic | P | PII | K6 | 3D! | 3Mx+ | SSE | SSE2 | A64 | SSE3 | E64T |
|----------|---|-----|----|----|------|-----|------|-----|------|------|
| BTC | ✓ | ✓ | ✓ | ✓ | ✓ | ✓ | ✓ | ✓ | ✓ | ✓ |

    btc    *rmDst(16/32/64), #(8)*      [Un]signed
    btc    *rmDst, rSrc(16/32/64)*

This general-purpose instruction tests the bit in the *destination*, using the *index* $\{0...2^N-1\}$, returns the state of the bit in the Carry flag, and then performs a one's complement, that is, it flips the indexed bit.

| Flags | O.flow | Sign | Zero | Aux | Parity | Carry |
|---|---|---|---|---|---|---|
| | - | - | - | - | - | X |

Flags: The Carry flag contains the value of the indexed bit before the complement.

```
        mov     ebx,0fedcba98h
                ;11111110110111001011101010011000b

        btc     ebx,10    ; carry will equal 0
; ebx is now   11111110110111001011110010011000b 0fedcbe98h
; note that bit#10 is flipped (complemented).

        btc     ebx,0     ; carry will equal 0
; ebx is now   11111110110111001011111010011001b 0fedcbe99h

        btc     bx,7      ; carry will equal 1
; ebx is now   11111110110111001011111000011001b 0fedcbe19h

        mov     eax,31
        btc     ebx,eax   ; carry will equal 1
; ebx is now   01111110110111001011111000011001b 07edcbe19h
```

# BTR — Bit Test and Reset (Clear)

BTR *destination, index*

| Mnemonic | P | PII | K6 | 3D! | 3Mx+ | SSE | SSE2 | A64 | SSE3 | E64T |
|---|---|---|---|---|---|---|---|---|---|---|
| BTR | ✓ | ✓ | ✓ | ✓ | ✓ | ✓ | ✓ | ✓ | ✓ | ✓ |

btr  *rmDst(16/32/64), #(8)*      [Un]signed
btr  *rmDst, rSrc(16/32/64)*

This general-purpose instruction tests the bit in the *destination*, using the *index* $\{0...2^N-1\}$, returns the state of the bit in the Carry flag, and then resets (clears) the indexed bit to 0.

| Flags | O.flow | Sign | Zero | Aux | Parity | Carry |
|---|---|---|---|---|---|---|
| | - | - | - | - | - | X |

Flags: The Carry flag contains the value of the indexed bit before it is altered.

```
        mov     ebx,0fedcba98h
                ;11111110110111001011101010011000b

        btr     ebx,10    ; carry will equal 0
; ebx is now    11111110110111001011101010011000b 0fedcba98h
; note that bit#10 is cleared.

        btr     ebx,0     ; carry will equal 0
; ebx is now    11111110110111001011101010011000b 0fedcba98h

        btr     bx,7      ; carry will equal 1
; ebx is now    11111110110111001011101000011000b 0fedcba18h

        mov     eax,31
        btr     ebx,eax   ; carry will equal 1
; ebx is now    01111110110111001011101000011000b 07edcba18h
```

# BTS — Bit Test and Set

BTS *destination, index*

| Mnemonic | P | PII | K6 | 3D! | 3Mx+ | SSE | SSE2 | A64 | SSE3 | E64T |
|----------|---|-----|-----|-----|------|-----|------|-----|------|------|
| BTS | ✓ | ✓ | ✓ | ✓ | ✓ | ✓ | ✓ | ✓ | ✓ | ✓ |

```
        bts     rmDst(16/32/64), #(8)         [Un]signed
        bts     rmDst, rSrc(16/32/64)
```

This general-purpose instruction tests the bit in the *destination*, using the *index* $\{0...2^N-1\}$, returns the state of the bit in the Carry flag, and then sets the bit to 1.

| **Flags** | O.flow | Sign | Zero | Aux | Parity | Carry |
|-----------|--------|------|------|-----|--------|-------|
|           | - | - | - | - | - | X |

Flags: The Carry flag contains the value of the indexed bit before it is altered.

```
        mov     ebx,0fedcba98h
                ;11111110110111001011101010011000b

        bts     ebx,10    ; carry will equal 0
; ebx is now    11111110110111001011111010011000b 0fedcbe98h
; note that bit#10 is set.

        bts     ebx,0     ; carry will equal 0
; ebx is now    11111110110111001011111010011001b 0fedcbe99h

        bts     bx,7      ; carry will equal 1
; ebx is now    11111110110111001011111010011001b 0fedcbe99h
```

```
        mov      eax,31
        bts      ebx,eax   ; carry will equal 1
    ; ebx is now 11111110110111001011111010011001b 0fedcbe99h
```

# SETcc — Set Byte on Condition

SET *destination*

| Mnemonic | P | PII | K6 | 3D! | 3Mx+ | SSE | SSE2 | A64 | SSE3 | E64T |
|----------|---|-----|----|----|------|-----|------|-----|------|------|
| SETcc | ✓ | ✓ | ✓ | ✓ | ✓ | ✓ | ✓ | ✓ | ✓ | ✓ |

setcc   *rmDst(8)*                    [Un]signed

This instruction sets the 8-bit *destination* to 1 (true) if the EFLAGS condition is met or 0 (false) if not. These flags are typically set to the result of the comparison of two values. These values can be equal (=) or not equal (≠). When the two values compared are signed versus unsigned and are not equal to each other, then the mathematical operations of {<, ≤, ≥, >} have different meanings. When the values are signed {±}, that means that values are less than (<), less than or equal to (≤), greater than or equal to (≥), or greater than (>) another. This utilizes the combination of the Zero and Carry flag states. When the values are unsigned, that means that values are below (<), below or equal to (≤), above or equal to (≥), or above (>) another. This utilizes the combination of the Zero and Sign flag states.

| Flags | O.flow | Sign | Zero | Aux | Parity | Carry |
|-------|--------|------|------|-----|--------|-------|
|       | - | - | - | - | - | - |

Flags: None are affected by this opcode. They are read-only for their flag states.

Left and right columns are complemented instructions. **Conditional Set if...**

| | | | | |
|---|---|---|---|---|
| SETA + | Set if above. ZF=0, CF=0 | | SETBE + | Set if below or equal. ZF=1, CF=1 |
| SETNBE | Set if not below or equal. | | SETNA | Set if not above. |
| SETAE + | Set if above or equal.  CF=0 | | SETB + | Set if below. CF=1 |
| SETNB | Set if not below. | | SETNAE | Set if not above or equal. |
| SETC | Set if carry. CF=1 | | SETNC | Set if no carry.  CF=0 |
| SETE | Set if equal.  ZF=1 | | SETNE | Set if not equal.  ZF=0 |
| SETZ | Set if zero. | | SETNZ | Set if not zero. |
| SETG ± | Set if greater. SF=OF. ZF=0. | | SETLE ± | Set if less or equal.  SF<>OF, ZF=1 |
| SETNLE | Set if not less or equal. | | SETNG | Set if not greater. |
| SETGE ± | Set if greater or equal. SF=OF | | SETL ± | Set if less. SF<>OF |
| SETNL | Set if not less. | | SETNGE | Set if not greater or equal. |
| SETO | Set if overflow. OF=1 | | SETNO | Set if not overflow.  OF=0 |
| SETP | Set if parity. PF=1 | | SETNP | Set if not parity.  PF=0 |
| SETPE | Set if parity even. | | SETPO | Set if parity odd. |
| SETS | Set if sign.  SF=1 | | SETNS | Set if no sign.  SF=0 |

One of the reasons for this instruction is to remove branches from our code such as follows:

```
        test    eax,ebx
        mov     eax,0
        jne     $L1                 ; Jump if not equal

        inc     eax
$L1:    ; eax =0 if false, 1 if true
```

It takes time to actually process the branch — prediction failure, prefetch load, etc. — but the same result can be achieved with the following:

```
        test    eax,ebx
        mov     eax,0
        sete    al
```

Some computer languages use the following to indicate a true or false condition:

```
typedef enum {
    FALSE = 0,
    TRUE = 1
} BOOL;
```

Others use something a little different:

```
typedef enum {
    false = 0,                    // All bits 0
    true = -1                     // All bits 1
} bool;
```

We can duplicate it by using an opposite SETcc instruction and then decrement. Let's modify the sample from above:

```
test    eax,ebx
mov     eax,0
setne   al          ; Note: the sete vs setne
dec     eax         ; 0 becomes 0ffffffffh (-1)
                    ; 1 becomes 000000000h (0)
```

# Comparing Operands and Setting EFLAGS

## CMP — Compare Two Operands

CMP *operand1, operand2*

| Mnemonic | P | PII | K6 | 3D! | 3Mx+ | SSE | SSE2 | A64 | SSE3 | E64T |
|----------|---|-----|-----|-----|------|-----|------|-----|------|------|
| CMP | ✓ | ✓ | ✓ | ✓ | ✓ | ✓ | ✓ | ✓ | ✓ | ✓ |

```
cmp    rmDst(8/16/32/64), #(8/16/32)    [Un]signed
cmp    rmDst, rSrc(8/16/32/64)
cmp    rDst, rmSrc(8/16/32/64)
```

This general-purpose instruction compares *operand1* with *operand2* by subtracting *operand2* from *operand1*. The flags are set as per a SUB (subtraction) instruction, but the end result is thrown away and not saved. An 8-bit source immediate value can be sign extended to 16-, 32-, or 64-bit value. A 32-bit immediate source value can be sign extended to a 64-bit destination.

| Flags | O.flow | Sign | Zero | Aux | Parity | Carry |
|-------|--------|------|------|-----|--------|-------|
| | X | X | X | X | X | X |

Flags: Based upon whether the operands were signed or unsigned the following table should be used to reflect the results.

| Comparison | (±) Signed | (+)Unsigned | ± | + |
|---|---|---|---|---|
| op1 > op2 | OF = SF, ZF=0 | ZF=0, CF=0 | Greater | Above |
| op1 ≥ op2 | OF = SF | CF=0 | GreaterEq | AboveEq |
| op1 = op2 | ZF = 1 | ZF=1 | Equal | Equal |
| op1 ≤ op2 | OF ≠ SF, ZF = 1 | ZF=1, CF=1 | LessEq | BelowEq |
| op1 < op2 | OF ≠ SF | CF=1 | Less | Below |

Comparisons are all about signage. Is the comparison signed or unsigned? The conditional response is based upon terminology: *greater-less* is signed, and *above-below* is unsigned.

```
foodd:   dd       0

         cmp      al,12h
         cmp      bx,1234h
         cmp      ecx,12345678h
         cmp      rdx,rax
         cmp      foodd,12345678h
```

# COMISS — Compare Scalar SPFP, Set EFLAGS

# COMISD — Compare Scalar DPFP, Set EFLAGS

| Mnemonic | P | PII | K6 | 3D! | 3Mx+ | SSE | SSE2 | A64 | SSE3 | E64T |
|---|---|---|---|---|---|---|---|---|---|---|
| COMISD | | | | | | | ✓ | ✓ | ✓ | ✓ |
| COMISS | | | | | | ✓ | ✓ | ✓ | ✓ | ✓ |

SSE     comiss *xmmA, xmmB/m32*     Single-precision     128
SSE2    comisd *xmmA, xmmB/m64*     Double-precision     128

These SSE-based instructions compare the ordered scalar operands of source *xmmA* and source *xmmB* to each other and set the general-purpose EFLAGS as to the result. The upper elements are ignored. Unlike UCOMISS or UCOMISD, QNaN or SNaN generate an exception. The COMISS instruction is used for single-precision floating-point, and COMISD is used for double-precision floating-point comparisons.

| A ? B | Zero | Parity | Carry |
|-------|------|--------|-------|
| Unordered | 1 | 1 | 1 |
| = | 1 | 0 | 0 |
| < | 0 | 0 | 1 |
| > | 0 | 0 | 0 |

Unordered results if either source operand is QNaN or SNaN. This is also referred to as NaN.

| Flags | O.flow | Sign | Zero | Aux | Parity | Carry |
|-------|--------|------|------|-----|--------|-------|
|  | 0 | 0 | X | 0 | X | X |

Flags: The ZF, PF, and CF are set based upon the comparison. All other flags are set to zero.

As usual, try to keep your source floating-point values valid, as an invalid source value of SNaN or QNaN generates a floating-point exception error.

# UCOMISS — Unordered Cmp Scalar SPFP, Set EFLAGS

# UCOMISD — Unordered Cmp Scalar DPFP, Set EFLAGS

| Mnemonic | P | PII | K6 | 3D! | 3Mx+ | SSE | SSE2 | A64 | SSE3 | E64T |
|----------|---|-----|----|----|------|-----|------|-----|------|------|
| UCOMISD |  |  |  |  |  |  | ✓ | ✓ | ✓ | ✓ |
| UCOMISS |  |  |  |  |  | ✓ | ✓ | ✓ | ✓ | ✓ |

SSE     ucomiss *xmmDst, xmmSrc/m32*  Single-precision   128
SSE2   ucomisd *xmmDst, xmmSrc/m64*  Double-precision  128

These SSE-based instructions compare the *unordered* scalar operands of source *xmmA* and source *xmmB* to each other and set the general-purpose EFLAGS as to the result. The upper elements are ignored.

| A ? B | Zero | Parity | Carry |
|-------|------|--------|-------|
| Unordered | 1 | 1 | 1 |
| = | 1 | 0 | 0 |
| < | 0 | 0 | 1 |
| > | 0 | 0 | 0 |

The results are unordered if either source operand is QNaN or SNaN. This is also referred to as NaN. Only an SNaN generates an exception, unlike the COMISS and COMISD instructions, which generate an exception on either.

| Flags | O.flow | Sign | Zero | Aux | Parity | Carry |
|---|---|---|---|---|---|---|
| | 0 | 0 | X | 0 | X | X |

Flags: The ZF, PF, and CF are set based upon the comparison. All other flags are set to zero.

As usual, try to keep your source floating-point values valid, as an invalid source value of SNaN generates a floating-point exception error.

# CMPSB/CMPSW/CMPSD/CMPSQ — Compare String Operands

CMPS *operand1*, *operand2*

| Mnemonic | P | PII | K6 | 3D! | 3Mx+ | SSE | SSE2 | A64 | SSE3 | E64T |
|---|---|---|---|---|---|---|---|---|---|---|
| CMPSx | ✓ | ✓ | ✓ | ✓ | ✓ | ✓ | ✓ | ✓ | ✓ | ✓ |
| CMPSQ | | | | | | | | | | ✓ |

cmps{b/w/d/q}                    [Un]signed
cmps   *mDst, mSrc(8/16/32/64)*

This general-purpose instruction compares the memory referenced by *operand1* with that referenced by *operand2* by subtraction similar to that of the CMP instruction. The end result is thrown away and not saved, but the flags are set. The CMPSB, CMPSW, and CMPSD instructions compare the memory referenced by ES:[EDI] with DS:[ESI] in Protected Mode or ES:[DI] with DS:[SI] in Real Mode. The (e)SI and (e)DI index registers are incremented automatically depending on how the direction flag is set. For 64-bit mode the (R)SI and (R)DI registers are used instead. If the direction flag is clear, they are incremented, or if set, they are decremented; this is the same as the STOSB and MOVSB instructions. Also, in 64-bit mode AH, BH, CH, and DH cannot be used with REX encoding.

When used in a loop, typically one of the repeat instructions will be used: REP, REPE, REPZ, REPNE, or REPNZ.

For optimized code this instruction should be considered to be a "complex" instruction and an alternative should be used instead!

| **Flags** | O.flow | Sign | Zero | Aux | Parity | Carry |
|-----------|--------|------|------|-----|--------|-------|
|           | X      | X    | X    | X   | X      | X     |

Flags: Based upon whether the operands were signed or unsigned the following table should be used to reflect the results.

| Comparison | (±) Signed | (+)Unsigned | ± | + |
|------------|------------|-------------|-----|-----|
| op1 > op2  | OF = SF, ZF=0 | ZF=0, CF=0 | Greater | Above |
| op1 ≥ op2  | OF = SF    | CF=0        | GreaterEq | AboveEq |
| op1 = op2  | ZF = 1     | ZF=1        | Equal | Equal |
| op1 ≤ op2  | OF ≠ SF, ZF = 1 | ZF=1, CF=1 | LessEq | BelowEq |
| op1 < op2  | OF ≠ SF    | CF=1        | Less | Below |

```
;    Loop for the entire count, flags will only reflect the
;    last comparison.
     mov      ecx,count
  rep cmpsb

;    Loop while strings match
     mov      ecx,count
  repe cmpsb                        ; Repeat while equal

     test     ecx,ecx
     je       $L1                   ; Jump if done

;    Found a mismatch
$L1:
```

# CMP — Packed Comparison

The two types of comparison are integers and floating-point values. Integers are compared to integers and floating-point values are compared to floating-point values.

**Hint:** SSE and SSE2 use an immediate value to determine the type of condition for single-precision and double-precision values.

# CMPPS/CMPSS/CMPPD/CMPSD — Floating-Point

| Mnemonic | P | PII | K6 | 3D! | 3Mx+ | SSE | SSE2 | A64 | SSE3 | E64T |
|----------|---|-----|----|-----|------|-----|------|-----|------|------|
| CMPPD    |   |     |    |     |      |     | ✓    | ✓   | ✓    | ✓    |
| CMPPS    |   |     |    |     |      | ✓   | ✓    | ✓   | ✓    | ✓    |
| CMPSD    |   |     |    |     |      |     | ✓    | ✓   | ✓    | ✓    |
| CMPSS    |   |     |    |     |      | ✓   | ✓    | ✓   | ✓    | ✓    |

| SSE  | cmpps *xmmDst, xmmSrc/m128*, # | Single-precision | 128 |
|------|-------------------------------|------------------|-----|
| "    | cmpss *xmmDst, r32*, #         | Single-precision scalar | |
| "    | cmpss x*mmDst, xmmSrc/m32*, #  |                  |     |
| SSE2 | cmppd *xmmDst, xmmSrc/m128*, # | Double-precision | 128 |
| "    | cmpsd *xmmDst, r64*, #         | Double-precision scalar | 128 |
| "    | cmpsd x*mmDst, xmmSrc/m64*, #  |                  |     |

The SSE-based CMPSS, CMPSD, CMPPS, and CMPPD instructions use an immediate value that specifies the method of compare.

*Table 9-1: SSE SPFP and DPFP immediate compare codes*

| 0 | 1 | 2 | 3    | 4 | 5 | 6 | 7   |
|---|---|---|------|---|---|---|-----|
| = | < | ≤ | ~ORD | ≠ | ≥ | > | ORD |

```
vD[] = (vA[] ? vB[] ) ? -1 : 0  // an element
```

| Flags | O.flow | Sign | Zero | Aux | Parity | Carry |
|-------|--------|------|------|-----|--------|-------|
|       | -      | -    | -    | -   | -      | -     |

Flags: No flags are affected for XMM instructions.

The resulting bits set in the XMM register of 0 or –1 map to zero or QnaN, which are usable floating-point numbers. These can be used in conjunction with the logical Boolean instructions to affect the result. These are discussed later in this chapter.

# Packed Compare if Equal to (=)

| Mnemonic | P | PII | K6 | 3D! | 3Mx+ | SSE | SSE2 | A64 | SSE3 | E64T |
|----------|---|-----|----|-----|------|-----|------|-----|------|------|
| PCMPEQx  |   | ✓   | ✓  | ✓   | ✓    | ✓   | ✓    | ✓   | ✓    | ✓    |
| PFCMPEQ  |   |     |    | ✓   | ✓    |     |      | ✓   |      |      |

| | | | |
|---|---|---|---|
| MMX | pcmpeq{b/w/d} *mmxDst, mmxSrc* | [Un]signed | 64 |
| 3DNow! | pfcmpeq *mmxDst, mmxSrc* | Single-precision | 64 |
| SSE | cmpps *xmmDst, xmmSrc/m128, 0* | Single-precision | 128 |
| " | cmpss *xmmDst, r32, 0* | Single-precision scalar | |
| | cmpss *xmmDst, xmmSrc/m32, #* | | |
| SSE2 | cmppd *xmmDst, xmmSrc/m128, 0* | Double-precision | 128 |
| " | cmpsd *xmmDst, r64, 0* | Double-precision scalar | |
| " | | | |
| | pcmpeq{b/w/d} *xmmDst, xmmSrc* | [Un]signed | |

## Packed Compare if Greater Than or Equal (≥)

| Mnemonic | P | PII | K6 | 3D! | 3Mx+ | SSE | SSE2 | A64 | SSE3 | E64T |
|---|---|---|---|---|---|---|---|---|---|---|
| PFCMPGE | | | | ✓ | ✓ | | | ✓ | | |

| | | | |
|---|---|---|---|
| 3DNow! | pfcmpge *mmxDst, mmxSrc* | Single-precision | 64 |
| SSE | cmpps *xmmDst, xmmSrc, 5* | Single-precision | 128 |
| " | cmpss *xmmDst, r32, 5* | Single-precision scalar | |
| SSE2 | cmppd *xmmDst, xmmSrc,* 5 | Double-precision | 128 |
| " | cmpsd *xmmDst, r64, 5* | Double-precision scalar | |

## Packed Compare if Greater Than (>)

| Mnemonic | P | PII | K6 | 3D! | 3Mx+ | SSE | SSE2 | A64 | SSE3 | E64T |
|---|---|---|---|---|---|---|---|---|---|---|
| PCMPGTx | | ✓ | ✓ | ✓ | ✓ | ✓ | ✓ | ✓ | ✓ | ✓ |
| PFCMPGT | | | | ✓ | ✓ | | | ✓ | | |

| | | | |
|---|---|---|---|
| MMX | pcmpgt{b/w/d} *mmxDst, mmxSrc* | Signed | 64 |
| 3DNow! | pfcmpgt *mmxDst, mmxSrc* | Single-precision | 64 |
| SSE | cmpps *xmmDst, xmmSrc, 6* | Single-precision | |
| | cmpss *xmmDst, r32, 6* | Single-precision scalar | 128 |
| SSE2 | cmppd *xmmDst, xmmSrc, 6* | Double-precision | 128 |
| | cmpsd *xmmDst, r64, 6* | Double-precision scalar | |
| | pcmpgt{b/w/d} *xmmDst, xmmSrc* | Signed | |

This SIMD instruction is a 64 (128)-bit parallel operation that compares the individual {eight 8-bit, four 16-bit, or two 32-bit} ({16 8-bit, eight 16-bit, or four 32-bit}) source elements. If *aSrc (xmmDst)*'s *meets the condition* to *bSrc (xmmSrc)*, then all bits will be set to ones in the destination *Dst (xmmDst)* for that element; if not, all bits will be clear (reset) for that element. This is equivalent to –1 or 0.

```
vD[] = (vA[] ? vB[] ) ? -1 : 0  // an element
```

| MMX | SSE | SSE2 | 3D Now | *3DMX+* |
|---|---|---|---|---|
| 8×8-bit | 4×SPFP | 16×8-bit | 2×SPFP | |
| 4×16-bit | 1×SPFP | 8×16-bit | | |
| 2×32-bit | | 4×32-bit | | |
| | | 4×DPFP | | |
| | | 1×DPFP | | |

PCMPEQB (eight 8-bit values)

| op1 = op2 | 63...56 | 55...48 | 47...40 | 39...32 | 31...24 | 23...16 | 15...8 | 7...0 |
|---|---|---|---|---|---|---|---|---|

PCMPEQW (four 16-bit values)

| op1 = op2 | 63...48 | 47...32 | 31...16 | 15...0 |
|---|---|---|---|---|

PCMPEQD (two 32-bit values)

| op1 = op2 | 63...32 | 31...0 |
|---|---|---|

**Hint:** The following table is a guide so that if you are either too tired to think or do not have the elementary foundations of comparisons down pat, each comparison and its complement is shown.

| LT - GE | | EQ - NE | | LE - GT | |
|---|---|---|---|---|---|
| < | ≥ | = | ≠ | ≤ | > |

```
dst:    qword   0a5a411220405f604h
src:    qword   0a5a41122050503f7h

        mov     esi,offset src
        mov     edi,offset dst
        movq    mm7,[edi]
        pcmpeqb mm7,[esi]

; dst  0a5h 0a4h 011h 022h 004h 005h 0f6h 004h
; src  0a5h 0a4h 011h 022h 005h 005h 003h 0f7h
;      0ffh 0ffh 0ffh 0ffh 000h 0ffh 000h 000h
; mm7  0ffffffff00ff0000h
```

```
        movq    mm7,[edi]
        pcmpeqw mm7,[esi]

; dst  0a5a4h 01122h 00405h 0f604h
; src  0a5a4h 01122h 00505h 003f7h
;      0ffffh 0ffffh 00000h 00000h
; mm7  0ffffffff00000000h


        movq    mm7,[edi]
        pcmpeqd mm7,[esi]

; dst  0a5a41122h 00405f604h
; src  0a5a41122h 0050503f7h
;      0ffffffffh 000000000h
; mm7  0ffffffff00000000h
```

This can also be used in a not-equal (≠) form by using a one's complement on the result. The complement form of the less-than or equal to (≤)
form can be the result as well.

# Extract Packed Sign Masks

These instructions extract the sign bit from each packed element and
generate a zero extended mask.

## PMOVMSKB — Extract Packed Byte (Sign) Mask

| Mnemonic | P | PII | K6 | 3D! | 3Mx+ | SSE | SSE2 | A64 | SSE3 | E64T |
|----------|---|-----|----|----|------|-----|------|-----|------|------|
| PMOVMSKB |   |     |    |    | ✓ | ✓ | ✓ | ✓ | ✓ | ✓ |

SSE    pmovmskb *r(32/64), mmxSrc*    [Un]signed    64
           pmovmskb *r(32/64), xmmSrc*              128

This instruction copies the MSB sign bit from each byte of the source
xmmA and copies them to the associated bit of the least significant bits
of the destination general-purpose register. For MMX, an 8-bit mask is
generated with the upper bits set to zero. For SSE, a 16-bit mask is generated with upper bits set to zero.

## MOVMSKPS — Extract Packed SPFP Sign Mask

## MOVMSKPD — Extract Packed DPFP Sign Mask

| Mnemonic | P | PII | K6 | 3D! | 3Mx+ | SSE | SSE2 | A64 | SSE3 | E64T |
|----------|---|-----|----|-----|------|-----|------|-----|------|------|
| MOVMSKPS |   |     |    |     |      | ✓   | ✓    | ✓   | ✓    | ✓    |
| MOVMSKPD |   |     |    |     |      |     | ✓    | ✓   | ✓    | ✓    |

| | |
|---|---|
| movmskps *r32, xmmSrc* | 32 |
| movmskps *r64, xmmSrc* | 64 |
| movmskpd *r32, xmmSrc* | 32 |
| movmskpd *r64, xmmSrc* | 64 |

The MOVMSKPS instruction copies the four sign bits of the single-precision floating-point elements {0...3} into the corresponding bit positions 0...3 and sets the upper bits to zero with the result stored in the 32/64-bit general-purpose register. The four bits result in a mapping of 16 possibilities of sign states.

The MOVMSKPD instruction copies the two sign bits of the double-precision floating-point elements {0...1} into the corresponding bit positions 0...1 and sets the upper bits to zero with the result stored in the 32/64-bit general-purpose register. The two bits result in a mapping of four possibilities.

# SCAS/SCASB/SCASW/SCASD/SCASQ — Scan String

| Mnemonic | P | PII | K6 | 3D! | 3Mx+ | SSE | SSE2 | A64 | SSE3 | E64T |
|----------|---|-----|----|-----|------|-----|------|-----|------|------|
| SCASx    | ✓ | ✓   | ✓  | ✓   | ✓    | ✓   | ✓    | ✓   | ✓    | ✓    |
| SCASQ    |   |     |    |     |      |     |      | 64  |      | 64   |

| | |
|---|---|
| scas{b/w/d/q} | [Un]signed |
| scas *mDst{8/16/32/64}* | |

This instruction scans the contents of memory and compares it (using a read-only subtraction) to the {AL, AX, EAX, RAX} register dependent upon {SCASB, SCASW, SCASD, SCASQ} and sets the flags accordingly. It belongs to the group of string functions but it really has nothing to do with text strings in the C sense. It has to do with loading strings of memory. Those are contiguous bytes of memory.

| **Flags** | O.flow | Sign | Zero | Aux | Parity | Carry |
|-----------|--------|------|------|-----|--------|-------|
|           | -      | -    | -    | -   | -      | -     |

Flags: All the flags reflect the result of the scan. When used in conjunction with a REP prefix the flags reflect the last SCAS operation.

These functions are equivalent to:

32-bit mode

| scasb | scasw | scasd | scasq |
|-------|-------|-------|-------|
| mov al,es:[edi] | mov ax,es:[edi] | mov eax,es:[edi] | |
| inc edi | add edi,2 | add edi,4 | |

64-bit mode

| scasb | scasw | scasd | scasq |
|-------|-------|-------|-------|
| mov al,[rdi] | mov ax,[rdi] | mov eax,[rdi] | mov rax,[rdi] |
| inc edi | add edi,2 | add edi,4 | add rdi,8 |

# REP SCASx

A single scan operation can be performed or a repeat sequence specified by a REP prefix word and a count specified in the RCX register in 64-bit mode, ECX register in Protected Mode, or CX in Real Mode.

```
rep scasd
L3: mov eax,es:[edi]
    add edi,4
    dec ecx
    jne L3
```

# CMOVcc — Conditional Move

CMOVcc *destination, source*

| Mnemonic | P | PII | K6 | 3D! | 3Mx+ | SSE | SSE2 | A64 | SSE3 | E64T |
|----------|---|-----|----|----|------|-----|------|-----|------|------|
| CMOVcc | ✓ | ✓ | | | | ✓ | ✓ | ✓ | ✓ | ✓ |

cmovcc    *rDst, rmSrc(16/32/64)*    [Un]signed

This general-purpose instruction moves the data from *source* to *destination* if the flags condition is met. See the following chart.

| **Flags** | O.flow | Sign | Zero | Aux | Parity | Carry |
|-----------|--------|------|------|-----|--------|-------|
| | - | - | - | - | - | - |

Flags: None are affected by this opcode. They are read-only for their flag states.

This instruction helps remove branching. Instead of:

```
    test eax,eax
    jne $L1

    mov eax,edx
$L1:
```

...you can use:

```
    test    eax,eax
    cmoveq eax,edx
```

Left and right columns are complemented instructions. **Conditional Move if...**

| CMOVA  + | if above. ZF=0, CF=0 | | CMOVBE + | if Below or Equal. ZF=1, CF=1 |
|----------|----------------------|---|----------|-------------------------------|
| CMOVNBE | if not below or equal. | | CMOVNA | if not above. |
| CMOVAE + | if above or equal.  CF=0 | | CMOVB  + | if below. CF=1 |
| CMOVNB | if not below. | | CMOVNAE | if not above or equal. |
| CMOVC | if carry.  CF=1 | | CMOVNC | if no carry.  CF=0 |
| CMOVE | if equal.  ZF=1 | | CMOVNE | if not equal.  ZF=0 |
| CMOVZ | if zero. | | CMOVNZ | if not zero. |
| CMOVG  ± | if greater. SF=OF. ZF=0. | | CMOVLE ± | if less or equal.  SF<>OF, ZF=1 |
| CMOVNLE | if not less or equal. | | CMOVNG | if not greater. |
| CMOVGE ± | if greater or equal. SF=OF | | CMOVL  ± | if less. SF<>OF |
| CMOVNL | if not less. | | CMOVNGE | if not greater or equal. |
| CMOVO | if overflow. OF=1 | | CMOVNO | if not overflow.  OF=0 |
| CMOVP | if parity. PF=1 | | CMOVNP | if not parity.  PF=0 |
| CMOVPE | if parity even. | | CMOVPO | if parity odd. |
| CMOVS | if sign.  SF=1 | | CMOVNS | if no sign.  SF=0 |

# CMPXCHG — Compare and Exchange

| Mnemonic | P | PII | K6 | 3D! | 3Mx+ | SSE | SSE2 | A64 | SSE3 | E64T |
|----------|---|-----|-----|-----|------|-----|------|-----|------|------|
| CMPXCHG | ✓ | ✓ | ✓ | ✓ | ✓ | ✓ | ✓ | ✓ | ✓ | ✓ |

cmpxchg  *rmDst8, rSrc8*        [Un]signed
cmpxchg  *rmDst16, rSrc16*
cmpxchg  *rmDst32, rSrc32*
cmpxchg  *rmDst64, rSrc64*

A secondary source {AL/AX/EAX/RAX} is used depending on the referenced bit size {8/16/32/64}. This instruction compares {AL/AX/EAX/RAX} with the value in the destination, and if equal the Zero flag is set and the source is copied into the destination. If not equal, the {AL/AX/EAX/RAX} register is loaded with the value in the destination.

| Flags | O.flow | Sign | Zero | Aux | Parity | Carry |
|-------|--------|------|------|-----|--------|-------|
|       | - | - | X | - | - | - |

Flags: Only the Zero flag is affected by this opcode.

```
if (EAX ? Dst)
    EAX = mDst    ; zero flag = 0
else
    mDst = mSrc   ; zero flag = 1
```

# CMPXCHG8B — Compare and Exchange 64 Bits

| Mnemonic | P | PII | K6 | 3D! | 3Mx+ | SSE | SSE2 | A64 | SSE3 | E64T |
|----------|---|-----|-----|-----|------|-----|------|-----|------|------|
| CMPXCHG8B | ✓ | ✓ | ✓ | ✓ | ✓ | ✓ | ✓ | ✓ | ✓ | ✓ |

cmpxchg8b  *rmDst64*            [Un]signed              64

This instruction compares the 64-bit value in EDX:EAX with the value in the destination *mDst*. If equal, the Zero flag is set and ECX:EBX is copied into the destination *mDst*. If not equal, EDX:EAX is loaded with the value in the destination *mDst*.

| Flags | O.flow | Sign | Zero | Aux | Parity | Carry |
|-------|--------|------|------|-----|--------|-------|
|       | -      | -    | X    | -   | -      | -     |

Flags: Only the Zero flag is affected by this opcode.

```
if (EDX:EAX ? rmDst)
    EDX:EAX = rmDst    ; zero flag = 0
else
    rmDst = ECX:EBX    ; zero flag = 1
```

# CMPXCHG16B — Compare and Exchange 128 Bits

| Mnemonic | P | PII | K6 | 3D! | 3Mx+ | SSE | SSE2 | A64 | SSE3 | E64T |
|----------|---|-----|----|----|------|-----|------|-----|------|------|
| CMPXCHG16B | | | | | | | | | | 64 |

cmpxchg16b *rmDst128*      [Un]signed      128

This instruction compares the 128-bit value in RDX:RAX with the value in the destination *mDst*. If equal, the Zero flag is set and RCX:RBX is copied into the destination *mDst*. If not equal, the RDX:RAX is loaded with the value in the destination *mDst*.

| Flags | O.flow | Sign | Zero | Aux | Parity | Carry |
|-------|--------|------|------|-----|--------|-------|
|       | -      | -    | X    | -   | -      | -     |

Flags: Only the Zero flag is affected by this opcode.

```
if (RDX:RAX ? rmDst)
    RDX:RAX = rmDst    ; zero flag = 0
else
    rmDst = RCX:RBX    ; zero flag = 1
```

# Boolean Operations upon Floating-Point Numbers

For the SSE there is no mixing and matching of types; however, any masking value can be used provided that each element mask is also a valid number. A full masking value of 0 versus −1 is allowed since they are valid numbers. 0 is zero and −1 (all bits set) is a QNaN floating-point value. So if ANDed with a floating-point value the value will either keep existing or become zero. A value with only the MSB set is also valid, such as 80000000h as (−0, 0) is a negative floating-point zero. But one should be careful as this could be used to complement the sign bit ($-A = -0.0 \oplus A$) and thus negate a number. $A = -A$, when used in an XOR operation.

There is an exception to this and that is the use of 3DNow! With this instruction set integers and floating-point values can be mixed and matched.

A quick preview of floating-point numbers illuminates the individual bits and their associations with their particular components.

By manipulating key bits the number can be affected. For example, for a 32-bit single-precision floating-point number the sign bit is bit #31 080000000h. So setting it (1) indicates the number is negative, and resetting it (0) indicates the number is positive. Other bit manipulations can be conceived by re-examining the bits described at the beginning of this chapter.

This coincidently happens to be an example of branchless code. It uses bit blending using masks generated by the results of the floating-point comparison $0 : -1$.

```
a = (a ≥ b ) ? c : d;
```

| 0 | 1 | 2 | 3 | 4 | 5 | 6 | 7 |
|---|---|---|---|---|---|---|---|
| = | < | ≤ | ~ORD | ≠ | ≥ | > | ORD |

```
cmpps  xmm0, xmm1, 5     ; (a ≥ b ) ? -1 : 0
movaps xmm7, xmm0        ; Copy the bit mask
andps  xmm0, xmm2        ; a = a ∧ c
andnps xmm7, xmm3        ; t = ¬a ∧ d
orps   xmm0, xmm7        ; a = a ∨ t
```

The register xmm0 contains either c or d, depending on the result of the comparison.

# ANDPS — Logical AND of Packed SPFP
# D = A ∧ B

# ANDPD — Logical AND of Packed DPFP

| A | B | Y |
|---|---|---|
| 0 | 0 | 0 |
| 0 | 1 | 0 |
| 1 | 0 | 0 |
| 1 | 1 | 1 |

| Mnemonic | P | PII | K6 | 3D! | 3Mx+ | SSE | SSE2 | A64 | SSE3 | E64T |
|----------|---|-----|----|----|------|-----|------|-----|------|------|
| ANDPD    |   |     |    |    |      |     | ✓    | ✓   | ✓    | ✓    |
| ANDPS    |   |     |    |    |      | ✓   | ✓    | ✓   | ✓    | ✓    |

| | | | | |
|--|--|--|--|--|
| SSE | andps | *xmmDst, xmmSrc/m128* | Single-precision | 128 |
| SSE2 | andpd | *xmmDst, xmmSrc/m128* | Double-precision | 128 |

This instruction ANDs packed bits in the form of a floating-point number with the single- or double-precision floating-point value.

# Pseudo Vec — (XMM) FABS — FP Absolute A = | A |

The floating-point absolute function is not directly supported using MMX or XMM registers so it must be simulated. As we've learned, the sign bit is merely the MSB of the occupied bits. This maps to a legitimate value of –0.0, thus a value of +0.0.

```
FNegMask REAL4 07ffffffh,07ffffffh,07ffffffh,07ffffffh

        ; A_w=|A_w|    A_z=|A_z|    A_y=|A_y|    A_x=|A_x|
andps  xmmA,FNegMask      ; SPFP
```

By masking all but the sign bit for a floating-point number, the positive form of that number can be retained:

$A_{xy} = | A_{xy} |$

# Pseudo Vec — (3DNow!) FABS — FP Absolute A = | A |

3DNow! supports floating-point and integer mixing and matching so the standard packed Boolean logical AND can be used.

```
        ; A_y=|A_y|    A_x=|A_x|
pand   mmxA,FNegMask      ; SPFP
```

## ORPS — Logical OR of Packed SPFP
## D = A ∨ B

## ORPD — Logical OR of Packed DPFP

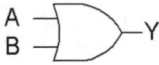

| A | B | Y |
|---|---|---|
| 0 | 0 | 0 |
| 0 | 1 | 1 |
| 1 | 0 | 1 |
| 1 | 1 | 1 |

| Mnemonic | P | PII | K6 | 3D! | 3Mx+ | SSE | SSE2 | A64 | SSE3 | E64T |
|----------|---|-----|----|----|------|-----|------|-----|------|------|
| ORPD | | | | | | | ✓ | ✓ | ✓ | ✓ |
| ORPS | | | | | | ✓ | ✓ | ✓ | ✓ | ✓ |

| SSE | orps | *xmmDst, xmmSrc/m128* | Single-precision | 128 |
|-----|------|------------------------|------------------|-----|
| SSE2 | orpd | *xmmDst, xmmSrc/m128* | Double-precision | 128 |

This instruction ORs packed bits in the form of a floating-point number with the single- or double-precision floating-point value. Typical masking values are 0 or –1.

## XORPS — Logical XOR of Packed SPFP
## D = A ⊕ B

## XORPD — Logical XOR of Packed DPFP

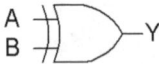

| A | B | Y |
|---|---|---|
| 0 | 0 | 0 |
| 0 | 1 | 1 |
| 1 | 0 | 1 |
| 1 | 1 | 0 |

| Mnemonic | P | PII | K6 | 3D! | 3Mx+ | SSE | SSE2 | A64 | SSE3 | E64T |
|----------|---|-----|----|----|------|-----|------|-----|------|------|
| XORPD | | | | | | | ✓ | ✓ | ✓ | ✓ |
| XORPS | | | | | | ✓ | ✓ | ✓ | ✓ | ✓ |

| SSE | xorps | *xmmDst, xmmSrc/m128* | Single-precision | 128 |
|-----|-------|------------------------|------------------|-----|
| SSE2 | xorpd | *xmmDst, xmmSrc/m128* | Double-precision | 128 |

This instruction XORs packed bits in the form of a floating-point number with the single- or double-precision floating-point value. Typical masking values are 0 or −1.

# Pseudo Vec — FCHS — FP Change Sign A = − A

The floating-point change sign (negation) is not directly supported using MMX or XMM registers so it must be simulated. One possibility is $A = 0 - A$, but that would require a register to be used to contain the zero. Alternatively, you could use $-A = A \times -1$.

As we've learned, the sign bit is merely the MSB of the occupied bits. This maps to a legitimate value of −0.0, thus a value of +0.0.

### Pseudo Vec (XMM)

```
FChsMask REAL4 080000000h,080000000h,080000000h,080000000h

        ; A_w= -A_w   A_z= -A_z  A_y= -A_y   A_x= -A_x
    xorps   xmm0,FChsMask    ; SPFP
```

By masking all bits but the sign bit for a floating-point number the sign will be flipped (one's complement) while that number can be retained.

$$A_{xyzw} = - A_{xyzw}$$

The SSE-based instructions differentiate between integers and floating-point values, and thus cannot be used for bit blending unless the source values are legitimate floating-point numbers. The 3DNow!-based instructions do not differentiate between integers or floating-point values so the two can be indiscriminately blended.

### Pseudo Vec — (3DNow!)

3DNow! supports floating-point and integer mixing and matching so the standard packed Boolean logical XOR can be used.

```
        ; A_y= -A_y   A_x= -A_x
    pxor    mmx0,FChsMask    ; SPFP
```

## ANDNPS — Logical ANDC of Packed SPFP
## D = A ∧ (¬B)

## ANDNPD — Logical ANDC of Packed DPFP

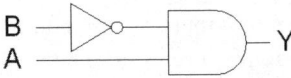

| A | B | B' | Y |
|---|---|---|---|
| 0 | 0 | 1 | 0 |
| 0 | 1 | 0 | 0 |
| 1 | 0 | 1 | 1 |
| 1 | 1 | 0 | 0 |

| Mnemonic | P | PII | K6 | 3D! | 3Mx+ | SSE | SSE2 | A64 | SSE3 | E64T |
|---|---|---|---|---|---|---|---|---|---|---|
| ANDNPD | | | | | | | ✓ | ✓ | ✓ | ✓ |
| ANDNPS | | | | | | ✓ | ✓ | ✓ | ✓ | ✓ |

SSE    andnps *xmmDst, xmmSrc/m128*    Single-precision    128
SSE2    andnpd *xmmDst, xmmSrc/m128*    Double-precision    128

This instruction ANDCs packed bits in the form of a floating-point number with the single- or double-precision floating-point value. The mask is inverted (bits flipped) and then logical ANDed with the other operand and the results stored.

# Min — Minimum

| MMX | SSE | SSE2 | 3D Now | 3DMX+ |
|---|---|---|---|---|
| | 8×8-bit | 16×8-bit | 2×SPFP | 8×8-bit |
| | 4×16-bit | 8×16-bit | | 4×16-bit |
| | 4×SPFP | 2×DPFP | | |
| | 1×SPFP | 1×DPFP | | |

The simplified form of this parallel instruction individually compares the integer or floating-point source arguments and returns the minimum value result in the destination.

```
vD[] = (vA[] < vB[] ) ? vA[] : vB[]   // an element
```

## Pseudo Vec

The previous C equation is a branching equation, which can cause a processor misprediction whether the branch is taken or not. A scalar operation could be done with branchless code such as follows:

```
                // r=(p < q) ? p : q;
  __inline MIN(int p, int q )
  {
      r = (p–q) >> INT_MAX_BITS;      // (–)=0xFFFFFFFF (+)=0x00000000
      return (p & r) | (q & (r^–1));  // keep lower of p or q
  }
```

The two values p and q are being compared so that the retained value is the smaller one. If p is less than q, subtraction (p–q) generates a negative value. The sign bit is then arithmetically shifted to the right the size of the data word, which would be a 31-bit shift and thus latching the MSB of 1 into all the bits. If $p = q$, then p–q is positive, the sign bit of zero would be latched into all the bits, thus generating a mask of all zeros. By bit blending with the mask and its inverse, the resulting value will be retained. For legacy processors that do not support this instruction it can be replicated in parallel using a packed arithmetic shift right or with a packed compare, if they are supported.

## N×8-Bit Integer Minimum

| Mnemonic | P | PII | K6 | 3D! | 3Mx+ | SSE | SSE2 | A64 | SSE3 | E64T |
|----------|---|-----|----|----|------|-----|------|-----|------|------|
| PMINUB   |   |     |    |    | ✓    | ✓   | ✓    | ✓   | ✓    | ✓    |

| | | | | |
|-----|--------|-----------------------|----------|-----|
| MMX+ | pminub | *mmxDst, mmxSrc/m64*   | Unsigned | 64  |
| SSE  | pminub | *mmxDst, mmxSrc/m64*   | Unsigned | 64  |
| SSE2 | pminub | *xmmDst, xmmSrc/m128*  | Unsigned | 128 |

This SIMD instruction is a 64 (128)-bit parallel operation that compares the eight (16) individual 8-bit source integer bit blocks *aSrc (xmmSrc)* and *bSrc (xmmDst)*, with the minimum value result being stored in the destination *Dst (xmmDst)*.

(64-bit) **8×8-bit**

$$Dst_{(7...0)} = ( aSrc_{(7...0)} < bSrc_{(7...0)} ) ? aSrc_{(7...0)} : bSrc_{(7...0)}$$
$$Dst_{(15...8)} = ( aSrc_{(15...8)} < bSrc_{(15...8)} ) ? aSrc_{(15...8)} : bSrc_{(15...8)}$$
$$Dst_{(23...16)} = ( aSrc_{(23...16)} < bSrc_{(23...16)} ) ? aSrc_{(23...16)} : bSrc_{(23...16)}$$
$$Dst_{(31...24)} = ( aSrc_{(31...24)} < bSrc_{(31...24)} ) ? aSrc_{(31...24)} : bSrc_{(31...24)}$$
$$Dst_{(39...32)} = ( aSrc_{(39...32)} < bSrc_{(39...32)} ) ? aSrc_{(39...32)} : bSrc_{(39...32)}$$
$$Dst_{(47...40)} = ( aSrc_{(47...40)} < bSrc_{(47...40)} ) ? aSrc_{(47...40)} : bSrc_{(47...40)}$$
$$Dst_{(55...48)} = ( aSrc_{(55...48)} < bSrc_{(55...48)} ) ? aSrc_{(55...48)} : bSrc_{(55...48)}$$
$$Dst_{(63...56)} = ( aSrc_{(63...56)} < bSrc_{(63...56)} ) ? aSrc_{(63...56)} : bSrc_{(63...56)}$$
$$Dst_{(71...64)} = ( aSrc_{(71...64)} < bSrc_{(71...64)} ) ? aSrc_{(71...64)} : bSrc_{(71...64)}$$
$$Dst_{(79...72)} = ( aSrc_{(79...72)} < bSrc_{(79...72)} ) ? aSrc_{(79...72)} : bSrc_{(79...72)}$$
$$Dst_{(87...80)} = ( aSrc_{(87...80)} < bSrc_{(87...80)} ) ? aSrc_{(87...80)} : bSrc_{(87...80)}$$
$$Dst_{(95...88)} = ( aSrc_{(95...88)} < bSrc_{(95...88)} ) ? aSrc_{(95...88)} : bSrc_{(95...88)}$$
$$Dst_{(103...96)} = ( aSrc_{(103...96)} < bSrc_{(103...96)} ) ? aSrc_{(103...96)} : bSrc_{(103...96)}$$
$$Dst_{(111...104)} = ( aSrc_{(111...104)} < bSrc_{(111...104)} ) ? aSrc_{(111...104)} : bSrc_{(111...104)}$$
$$Dst_{(119...112)} = ( aSrc_{(119...112)} < bSrc_{(119...112)} ) ? aSrc_{(119...112)} : bSrc_{(119...112)}$$
$$Dst_{(127...120)} = ( aSrc_{(127...120)} < bSrc_{(127...120)} ) ? aSrc_{(127...120)} : bSrc_{(127...120)}$$

(128-bit) **16×8-bit**

# N×16-Bit Integer Minimum

| Mnemonic | P | PII | K6 | 3D! | 3Mx+ | SSE | SSE2 | A64 | SSE3 | E64T |
|----------|---|-----|----|----|------|-----|------|-----|------|------|
| PMINSW   |   |     |    |    | ✓    | ✓   | ✓    | ✓   | ✓    | ✓    |

| MMX+ | pminsw | *mmxDst, mmxSrc/m64* | Signed | 64 |
| SSE  | pminsw | *mmxDst, mmxSrc/m64* | Signed | 64 |
| SSE2 | pminsw | *xmmDst, xmmSrc/m128* | Signed | 128 |

This SIMD instruction is a 64 (128)-bit parallel operation that compares the four (eight) individual 16-bit source integer bit blocks *aSrc (xmmSrc)* and *bSrc (xmmDst)*, with the minimum value result being stored in the destination *Dst (xmmDst)*.

(64-bit) **4×16-bit**

$$Dst_{(15...0)} = (aSrc_{(15...0)} < bSrc_{(15...0)})\ ?\ aSrc_{(15...0)} : bSrc_{(15...0)}$$
$$Dst_{(31...16)} = (aSrc_{(31...16)} < bSrc_{(31...16)})\ ?\ aSrc_{(31...16)} : bSrc_{(31...16)}$$
$$Dst_{(47...32)} = (aSrc_{(47...32)} < bSrc_{(47...32)})\ ?\ aSrc_{(47...32)} : bSrc_{(47...32)}$$
$$Dst_{(63...48)} = (aSrc_{(63...48)} < bSrc_{(63...48)})\ ?\ aSrc_{(63...48)} : bSrc_{(63...48)}$$
$$Dst_{(79...64)} = (aSrc_{(79...64)} < bSrc_{(79...64)})\ ?\ aSrc_{(79...64)} : bSrc_{(79...64)}$$
$$Dst_{(95...80)} = (aSrc_{(95...80)} < bSrc_{(95...80)})\ ?\ aSrc_{(95...80)} : bSrc_{(95...80)}$$
$$Dst_{(111...96)} = (aSrc_{(111...96)} < bSrc_{(111...96)})\ ?\ aSrc_{(111...96)} : bSrc_{(111...96)}$$
$$Dst_{(127...112)} = (aSrc_{(127...112)} < bSrc_{(127...112)})\ ?\ aSrc_{(127...112)} : bSrc_{(127...112)}$$

(128-bit) **8×16-bit**

# N×SPFP Minimum

| Mnemonic | P | PII | K6 | 3D! | 3Mx+ | SSE | SSE2 | A64 | SSE3 | E64T |
|---|---|---|---|---|---|---|---|---|---|---|
| PFMIN |  |  |  | ✓ | ✓ |  |  | ✓ |  |  |
| MINPS |  |  |  |  |  | ✓ | ✓ | ✓ | ✓ | ✓ |

3DNow! pfmin *mmxDst, mmxSrc/m64*  Single-precision  64
SSE   minps *xmmDst, xmmSrc/m128*  Single-precision  128

This SIMD instruction is a 64 (128)-bit parallel operation that compares the two (four) individual single-precision floating-point source bit blocks *aSrc (xmmSrc)* and *bSrc (xmmDst)*, with the minimum value result being stored in the destination *Dst (xmmDst)*.

(64-bit) **2×32-bit**

$$Dst_{(31...0)} = (aSrc_{(31...0)} < bSrc_{(31...0)})\ ?\ aSrc_{(31...0)} : bSrc_{(31...0)}$$
$$Dst_{(63...32)} = (aSrc_{(63...32)} < bSrc_{(63...32)})\ ?\ aSrc_{(63...32)} : bSrc_{(63...32)}$$
$$Dst_{(95...64)} = (aSrc_{(95...64)} < bSrc_{(95...64)})\ ?\ aSrc_{(95...64)} : bSrc_{(95...64)}$$
$$Dst_{(127...96)} = (aSrc_{(127...96)} < bSrc_{(127...96)})\ ?\ aSrc_{(127...96)} : bSrc_{(127...96)}$$

(128-bit) **4×32-bit**

# 1×SPFP Scalar Minimum

| Mnemonic | P | PII | K6 | 3D! | 3Mx+ | SSE | SSE2 | A64 | SSE3 | E64T |
|---|---|---|---|---|---|---|---|---|---|---|
| MINSS |  |  |  |  |  | ✓ | ✓ | ✓ | ✓ | ✓ |

SSE   minss *xmmDst, xmmSrc/m32*  Single-precision  128

This SIMD instruction is a 128-bit scalar operation that compares only the lowest bit block containing the scalar single-precision floating-point $aSrc$ ($xmmSrc$) and $bSrc$ ($xmmDst$), and stores the minimum value result in the lowest bit block at destination $Dst$ ($xmmDst$). The remaining floating-point bit blocks are left intact.

$Dst_{(31...0)} = (aSrc_{(31...0)} < bSrc_{(31...0)})$ ? $aSrc_{(31...0)}$ : $bSrc_{(31...0)}$
$Dst_{(127...32)}$ Remain the same.

# 2×DPFP Minimum

| Mnemonic | P | PII | K6 | 3D! | 3Mx+ | SSE | SSE2 | A64 | SSE3 | E64T |
|----------|---|-----|-----|-----|------|-----|------|-----|------|------|
| MINPD    |   |     |     |     |      |     | ✓    | ✓   | ✓    | ✓    |

SSE     minpd $xmmDst, xmmSrc/m128$     Double-precision     128

This SIMD instruction is a 128-bit parallel operation that compares the two individual double-precision floating-point source bit blocks $aSrc$ ($xmmSrc$) and $bSrc$ ($xmmDst$), with the minimum value result being stored in the destination $Dst$ ($xmmDst$).

**(128-bit) 2×64-bit**

$Dst_{(63...0)} = (aSrc_{(63...0)} < bSrc_{(63...0)})$ ? $aSrc_{(63...0)}$ : $bSrc_{(63...0)}$
$Dst_{(127...64)} = (aSrc_{(127...64)} < bSrc_{(127...64)})$ ? $aSrc_{(127...64)}$ : $bSrc_{(127...64)}$

# 1×DPFP Scalar Minimum

| Mnemonic | P | PII | K6 | 3D! | 3Mx+ | SSE | SSE2 | A64 | SSE3 | E64T |
|----------|---|-----|-----|-----|------|-----|------|-----|------|------|
| MINSD    |   |     |     |     |      |     | ✓    | ✓   | ✓    | ✓    |

SSE2     minsd $xmmDst, xmmSrc/m64$     Double-precision     128

This SIMD instruction is a 128-bit scalar operation that compares only the lower 64-bit block containing the scalar double-precision floating-point $aSrc$ ($xmmSrc$) and $bSrc$ ($xmmDst$), and stores the minimum value result in the lower bit block of the destination $Dst$ ($xmmDst$). The remaining upper 64-bit floating-point bit block is left intact.

$Dst_{(63...0)} = (aSrc_{(63...0)} < bSrc_{(63...0)})$ ? $aSrc_{(63...0)}$ : $bSrc_{(63...0)}$
$Dst_{(127...64)}$ Remain the same.

# Max — Maximum

| MMX | SSE | SSE2 | 3D Now | 3DMX+ |
|---|---|---|---|---|
| | 8×8-bit | 16×8-bit | 2×SPFP | 8×8-bit |
| | 4×16-bit | 8×16-bit | | 4×16-bit |
| | 4×SPFP | 2×DPFP | | |
| | 1×SPFP | 1×DPFP | | |

The simplified form of this parallel instruction individually compares the integer or floating-point source arguments and returns the maximum value result in the destination.

```
vD[] = (vA[] > vB[] ) ? vA[] : vB[]   // an element
```

## N×8-Bit Integer Maximum

| Mnemonic | P | PII | K6 | 3D! | 3Mx+ | SSE | SSE2 | A64 | SSE3 | E64T |
|---|---|---|---|---|---|---|---|---|---|---|
| PMAXUB | | | | | ✓ | ✓ | ✓ | ✓ | ✓ | ✓ |

MMX+ pmaxub *mmxDst, mmxSrc/m64*    Unsigned    64
SSE    pmaxub *mmxDst, mmxSrc/m64*    Unsigned    64
SSE2   pmaxub *xmmDst, xmmSrc/m128*   Unsigned   128

This SIMD instruction is a 64 (128)-bit parallel operation that compares the eight (16) individual 8-bit source integer bit blocks *aSrc (xmmSrc)* and *bSrc (xmmDst)*, with the maximum value result being stored in the destination *Dst (xmmDst)*.

**(64-bit) 8×8-bit**

$$Dst_{(7...0)} = ( aSrc_{(7...0)} > bSrc_{(7...0)} ) ? aSrc_{(7...0)} : bSrc_{(7...0)}$$
$$Dst_{(15...8)} = ( aSrc_{(15...8)} > bSrc_{(15...8)} ) ? aSrc_{(15...8)} : bSrc_{(15...8)}$$
$$Dst_{(23...16)} = ( aSrc_{(23...16)} > bSrc_{(23...16)} ) ? aSrc_{(23...16)} : bSrc_{(23...16)}$$
$$Dst_{(31...24)} = ( aSrc_{(31...24)} > bSrc_{(31...24)} ) ? aSrc_{(31...24)} : bSrc_{(31...24)}$$
$$Dst_{(39...32)} = ( aSrc_{(39...32)} > bSrc_{(39...32)} ) ? aSrc_{(39...32)} : bSrc_{(39...32)}$$
$$Dst_{(47...40)} = ( aSrc_{(47...40)} > bSrc_{(47...40)} ) ? aSrc_{(47...40)} : bSrc_{(47...40)}$$
$$Dst_{(55...48)} = ( aSrc_{(55...48)} > bSrc_{(55...48)} ) ? aSrc_{(55...48)} : bSrc_{(55...48)}$$
$$Dst_{(63...56)} = ( aSrc_{(63...56)} > bSrc_{(63...56)} ) ? aSrc_{(63...56)} : bSrc_{(63...56)}$$

$$Dst_{(71...64)} = ( aSrc_{(71...64)} > bSrc_{(71...64)} ) ? aSrc_{(71...64)} : bSrc_{(71...64)}$$
$$Dst_{(79...72)} = ( aSrc_{(79...72)} > bSrc_{(79...72)} ) ? aSrc_{(79...72)} : bSrc_{(79...72)}$$
$$Dst_{(87...80)} = ( aSrc_{(87...80)} > bSrc_{(87...80)} ) ? aSrc_{(87...80)} : bSrc_{(87...80)}$$
$$Dst_{(95...88)} = ( aSrc_{(95...88)} > bSrc_{(95...88)} ) ? aSrc_{(95...88)} : bSrc_{(95...88)}$$
$$Dst_{(103...96)} = ( aSrc_{(103...96)} > bSrc_{(103...96)} ) ? aSrc_{(103...96)} : bSrc_{(103...96)}$$
$$Dst_{(111...104)} = ( aSrc_{(111...104)} > bSrc_{(111...104)} ) ? aSrc_{(111...104)} : bSrc_{(111...104)}$$
$$Dst_{(119...112)} = ( aSrc_{(119...112)} > bSrc_{(119...112)} ) ? aSrc_{(119...112)} : bSrc_{(119...112)}$$
$$Dst_{(127...120)} = ( aSrc_{(127...120)} > bSrc_{(127...120)} ) ? aSrc_{(127...120)} : bSrc_{(127...120)}$$

(128-bit) **16×8-bit**

# N×16-Bit Integer Maximum

| Mnemonic | P | PII | K6 | 3D! | 3Mx+ | SSE | SSE2 | A64 | SSE3 | E64T |
|----------|---|-----|----|-----|------|-----|------|-----|------|------|
| PMAXSW   |   |     |    |     | ✓    | ✓   | ✓    | ✓   | ✓    | ✓    |

| | | | | |
|---|---|---|---|---|
| MMX+ | pmaxsw | *mmxDst, mmxSrc/m64* | Signed | 64 |
| SSE | pmaxsw | *mmxDst, mmxSrc/m64* | Signed | 64 |
| SSE2 | pmaxsw | *xmmDst, xmmSrc/m128* | Signed | 128 |

This SIMD instruction is a 64 (128)-bit parallel operation that compares the four (eight) individual 16-bit source integer bit blocks *aSrc (xmmSrc)* and *bSrc (xmmDst)*, with the maximum value result being stored in the destination *Dst (xmmDst)*.

(64-bit) **4×16-bit**

$$Dst_{(15...0)} = ( aSrc_{(15...0)} > bSrc_{(15...0)} ) ? aSrc_{(15...0)} : bSrc_{(15...0)}$$
$$Dst_{(31...16)} = ( aSrc_{(31...16)} > bSrc_{(31...16)} ) ? aSrc_{(31...16)} : bSrc_{(31...16)}$$
$$Dst_{(47...32)} = ( aSrc_{(47...32)} > bSrc_{(47...32)} ) ? aSrc_{(47...32)} : bSrc_{(47...32)}$$
$$Dst_{(63...48)} = ( aSrc_{(63...48)} > bSrc_{(63...48)} ) ? aSrc_{(63...48)} : bSrc_{(63...48)}$$
$$Dst_{(79...64)} = ( aSrc_{(79...64)} > bSrc_{(79...64)} ) ? aSrc_{(79...64)} : bSrc_{(79...64)}$$
$$Dst_{(95...80)} = ( aSrc_{(95...80)} > bSrc_{(95...80)} ) ? aSrc_{(95...80)} : bSrc_{(95...80)}$$
$$Dst_{(111...96)} = ( aSrc_{(111...96)} > bSrc_{(111...96)} ) ? aSrc_{(111...96)} : bSrc_{(111...96)}$$
$$Dst_{(127...112)} = ( aSrc_{(127...112)} > bSrc_{(127...112)} ) ? aSrc_{(127...112)} : bSrc_{(127...112)}$$

(128-bit) **8×16-bit**

# N×SPFP Maximum

| Mnemonic | P | PII | K6 | 3D! | 3Mx+ | SSE | SSE2 | A64 | SSE3 | E64T |
|----------|---|-----|-----|-----|------|-----|------|-----|------|------|
| MAXPS    |   |     |    |     |      | ✓   | ✓    | ✓   | ✓    | ✓    |
| PFMAX    |   |     |    | ✓   | ✓    |     |      | ✓   |      |      |

3DNow! pfmax  *mmxDst, mmxSrc/m64*  Single-precision  64
SSE    maxps  *xmmDst, xmmSrc/m128*  Single-precision  128

This SIMD instruction is a 64 (128)-bit parallel operation that compares the two (four) individual single-precision floating-point source bit blocks *aSrc (xmmSrc)* and *bSrc (xmmDst)*, with the maximum value result being stored in the destination *Dst (xmmDst)*.

(64-bit) **2×32-bit**

$$Dst_{(31...0)} = ( aSrc_{(31...0)} > bSrc_{(31...0)} ) \ ? \ aSrc_{(31...0)} : bSrc_{(31...0)}$$
$$Dst_{(63...32)} = ( aSrc_{(63...32)} > bSrc_{(63...32)} ) \ ? \ aSrc_{(63...32)} : bSrc_{(63...32)}$$
$$Dst_{(95...64)} = ( aSrc_{(95...64)} > bSrc_{(95...64)} ) \ ? \ aSrc_{(95...64)} : bSrc_{(95...64)}$$
$$Dst_{(127...96)} = ( aSrc_{(127...96)} > bSrc_{(127...96)} ) \ ? \ aSrc_{(127...96)} : bSrc_{(127...96)}$$

(128-bit) **4×32-bit**

# 1×SPFP Scalar Maximum

| Mnemonic | P | PII | K6 | 3D! | 3Mx+ | SSE | SSE2 | A64 | SSE3 | E64T |
|----------|---|-----|-----|-----|------|-----|------|-----|------|------|
| MAXSS    |   |     |    |     |      | ✓   | ✓    | ✓   | ✓    | ✓    |

SSE    maxss *xmmDst, xmmSrc/m32*    Single-precision    128

This SIMD instruction is a 128-bit scalar operation that compares only the lowest bit block containing the scalar single-precision floating-point *aSrc (xmmSrc)* and *bSrc (xmmDst)* and stores the maximum value result in the lowest bit block of the destination *Dst (xmmDst)*. The remaining floating-point bit blocks are left intact.

$$Dst_{(31...0)} = (aSrc_{(31...0)} > bSrc_{(31...0)} ) \ ? \ aSrc_{(31...0)} : bSrc_{(31...0)}$$
$Dst_{(127...32)}$ Remain the same.

# 2×DPFP Maximum

| Mnemonic | P | PII | K6 | 3D! | 3Mx+ | SSE | SSE2 | A64 | SSE3 | E64T |
|----------|---|-----|----|-----|------|-----|------|-----|------|------|
| MAXPD    |   |     |    |     |      |     | ✓    | ✓   | ✓    | ✓    |

SSE    maxpd *xmmDst, xmmSrc/m128*    Double-precision    128

This SIMD instruction is a 128-bit parallel operation that compares the two individual double-precision floating-point source bit blocks *aSrc (xmmSrc)* and *bSrc (xmmDst)*, with the maximum value result being stored in the destination *Dst (xmmDst)*.

(128-bit) **2×64-bit**

$$Dst_{(63...0)} = (aSrc_{(63...0)} > bSrc_{(63...0)}) ? aSrc_{(63...0)} : bSrc_{(63...0)}$$
$$Dst_{(127...64)} = (aSrc_{(127...64)} > bSrc_{(127...64)}) ? aSrc_{(127...64)} : bSrc_{(127...64)}$$

# 1×DPFP Scalar Maximum

| Mnemonic | P | PII | K6 | 3D! | 3Mx+ | SSE | SSE2 | A64 | SSE3 | E64T |
|----------|---|-----|----|-----|------|-----|------|-----|------|------|
| MAXSD    |   |     |    |     |      |     | ✓    | ✓   | ✓    | ✓    |

SSE2    maxsd *xmmDst, xmmSrc/m64*    Double-precision    128

This SIMD instruction is a 128-bit scalar operation that compares only the lower 64-bit block containing the scalar double-precision floating-point *aSrc (xmmSrc)* and *bSrc (xmmDst)*, and stores the maximum value result in the lower bit block of the destination *Dxt (xmmDst)*. The remaining upper 64-bit floating-point bit block is left intact.

$$Dst_{(63...0)} = (aSrc_{(63...0)} > bSrc_{(63...0)}) ? aSrc_{(63...0)} : bSrc_{(63...0)}$$
$Dst_{(127...64)}$ Remain the same.

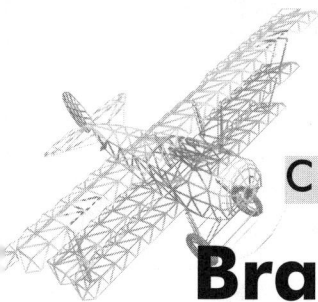

# Chapter 10

# Branching

The processor's instruction pointer is just that — a pointer to the instruction that is about to be executed. This register is the RIP in 64-bit, EIP in Protected Mode, and IP in Real Mode. It behaves very similarly to that of a CD player. You can only read one data stream at a time. To read elsewhere, you have to move the pointer to the new location to read. (A better visualization would be a record player with its needle that cannot skip around.)

The only way to read the value of the instruction pointer is to call a function with the CALL instruction and then read the value on the stack where you had been. There is no MOV EAX,EIP instruction.

There are four primary methods that can be used to change the position of the processor's instruction pointer: jump, call, interrupt, and return. You can jump a delta, near, or far distance; call and return near or far; interrupt; and return. These instructions tend to be the most confusing to an assembler, and the exact instruction that you think you are using sometimes is not.

**64-bit** **No 64-bit:** The concept of Real Mode memory does not exist in 64-bit mode, nor does 16-bit displacement as it is sign extended to 64 bits for the 64-bit instruction pointer (RIP).

# Jump Unconditionally

## JMP — Jump

JMP *destination*

| Mnemonic | P | PII | K6 | 3D! | 3Mx+ | SSE | SSE2 | A64 | SSE3 | E64T |
|----------|---|-----|----|----|------|-----|------|-----|------|------|
| JMP | ✓ | ✓ | ✓ | ✓ | ✓ | ✓ | ✓ | ✓ | ✓ | ✓ |

## Delta JMP

jmp    ± 8/16/32                    Relative Jump

### Protected Mode JMP (NEAR)

jmp    rm{16/32/64}                 Near

### Protected Mode JMP (FAR)

jmp    ptr16:32                     Far sel:addr
jmp    m16:32                       Near (Real Mode)
jmp    m16:64

### Real Mode JMP (NEAR)

jmp    rm16                         Near

### Real Mode JMP (FAR)

jmp    ptr16:16                     Far sel:addr
jmp    m16:16                       Near (Real Mode)        20

This is a general-purpose instruction used to jump to another location in memory. It can be a delta-based jump, or a near or far JMP. In a Real Mode environment the addresses are 16-bit based, supporting a segment size up to 65,536 bytes, and thus the segment and/or offset need to be 16-bit each. In a Protected Mode environment the addresses are 32-bit based with a 16-bit segment-selector register.

| Flags | O.flow | Sign | Zero | Aux | Parity | Carry |
|-------|--------|------|------|-----|--------|-------|
|       | -      | -    | -    | -   | -      | -     |

Flags: None are altered by this opcode.

# Delta JMP

The delta jump is in reality a hop in a signed direction. You will notice that the following JMP examples use an 8-bit signed destination value.

```
00000000  33 C0   FuncA:  xor   eax,eax
00000002  EB FC           jmp   FuncA   ; (–4 bytes)
00000004  EB 02           jmp   FuncB   ; (+2 bytes)
00000006  33 DB           xor   ebx,ebx
00000008  EB FE   FuncB:  jmp   FuncB   ; (–2 bytes) infinite loop
0000000A  EB 00           jmp   FuncC   ; (+0 bytes)
0000000C          FuncC:
```

An EB FF opcode pair obviously is not used as it jumps into the middle of the jump instruction. If the address being jumped to is out of range in a (−128) reverse direction or a (127) forward direction, then the assembler will automatically switch to the E9 opcode, which supports 32 bits of signed direction in Protected Mode and 16 bits of signed direction in Real Mode.

## Protected Mode JMP (NEAR)

This is a 32-bit value stored in a register, memory location, or 32-bit relative address.

```
NearAdrPtr  DWORD   offset NearJmp       ; Near pointer
            DWORD   offset OtherNearJmp  ; Near function
NearJmp proc    near
        ret
NearJmp endp

        jmp     NearJmp

        mov     ebx,offset NearJmp
        jmp     ebx

        mov     ebx,offset NearAdrPtr
        jmp     [ebx]

        xor     ebx,ebx
        jmp     NearAdrPtr[ebx]

        jmp     NearAdrPtr[ebx*4]
```

## Protected Mode JMP (FAR)

This is a 48-bit value stored in a register, memory location, or 48-bit relative address. As Win32, Extended DOS, or other Protected Mode flat memory environments are pretty much what is developed for today, the need for the FAR pointer is, for the most part, only in the domain of the operating system or device driver developer. (Note that there are exceptions!)

```
FarAdrPtr  FWORD   offset FarJmp        ; Far pointer
           FWORD   offset OtherFarJmp   ; Far function
FarJmp proc    far
       ret
FarJmp endp

       jmp     far ptr FarJmp
```

This will be discussed further in the section on the RET instruction, but if you jump to code with an RET in the logic flow you need to make sure that the RET is a near return type if the previous call instruction was near, or the RET is a far return type if the previous call instruction was far. It needs to match the call instruction. For example, if you are executing a code fragment in a NEAR type function such as NearJmp and you jump to a different set of code, you should never jump into a FAR type procedure as the RET instruction when executed will be of the wrong type. Instead of a 32-bit value being popped off the stack in a Protected Mode environment, a 48-bit value would be popped, thus disorienting the pointers and eventually causing the program to crash! Even though the assembly code uses the same spelling of RET in the NEAR and FAR procs, the NEAR is translated to 0C3h and the FAR is translated to 0CBh. These have different meanings! If you specifically need a far return, try using RETF.

A simple rule to remember is for each NEAR or FAR call, have the appropriate matching RET; this is typically automatically done for you by the assembler unless you start jumping around in the code.

```
NearAdrPtr  DWORD    offset NearJmp    ; Near pointer
            DWORD    offset OtherNearJmp

NearJmp proc    near
        ret
NearJmp endp
```

vs

```
FarJmp  proc    far
        ret
FarJmp  endp
```

See Appendix C for memory/register mapping.

The same kind of memory reference that is used to access a memory table or array can also be used to access a jump vector. Almost any register can be used alone, in a pair addition, or with an optional base address and/or scale factor of {2, 4, or 8}, but you will note that there are some limitations in regard to the ESP register.

## Real Mode — NEAR or FAR has Same Opcodes

## Protected Mode — NEAR or FAR has Same Opcodes

```
jmp ...
jmp NearAdrPtr[...]
```

| eax | ebx | ecx | edx | esp | ebp | esi | edi |
|-----|-----|-----|-----|-----|-----|-----|-----|
| ax  | bx  | cx  | dx  | sp  | bp  | si  | di  |

**Real Mode — NEAR or FAR has Same Opcodes**

**Protected Mode — NEAR or FAR has Same Opcodes**

```
jmp word ptr [...]
jmp dword ptr [...]
jmp fword ptr [...]
jmp NearAdrPtr[...]
```

# Jump Conditionally

## Jcc — Branching

Jcc *destination*

| Mnemonic | P | PII | K6 | 3D! | 3Mx+ | SSE | SSE2 | A64 | SSE3 | E64T |
|----------|---|-----|----|----|------|-----|------|-----|------|------|
| Jcc | ✓ | ✓ | ✓ | ✓ | ✓ | ✓ | ✓ | ✓ | ✓ | ✓ |

### Delta JMP

jcc    *disp{8/16/32}*              Near

All of the instructions in the following table are conditional jumps, sometimes referred to as branch instructions. The instruction pointer (RIP/EIP/IP) is redirected to the relative address if the associated conditions are met as a logical TRUE. If they fail, the pointer merely executes the next line of code. For a properly optimized program, these instructions need to be minimally used and well positioned within the code.

The 8086 and 286 processors only support 8-bit displacement, not 16- or 32-bit displacement. Protected Mode uses an 8-bit or 32-bit displacement. The displacement gets sign extended and the address stored in the instruction pointer gets adjusted. The default is an 8-bit displacement [–128, 127] unless the jump is out of range; in that case, the larger displacement will be used. The goal is to organize your code so that a minimal number of bytes are required for the conditional branching logic.

**64-bit**   **No 64-bit:**   The displacement of 16-bit is not supported in 64-bit mode!

*Table 10-1: Comparison types. The same value types are contained with an individual cell. Complement types (opposites) are across from each other.*

| | | | | | |
|---|---|---|---|---|---|
| JA<br>JNBE | + | Jump if above. ZF=0, CF=0<br>Jump if not below or equal. | JBE<br>JNA | + | Jump if Below or Equal. ZF=1,<br>CF=1<br>Jump if not above. |
| JAE<br>JNB | + | Jump if above or equal. CF=0<br>Jump if not below. | JB<br>JNAE | + | Jump if below. CF=1<br>Jump if not above or equal. |
| JC | | Jump if carry. CF=1 | JNC | | Jump if no carry. CF=0 |
| JE<br>JZ | | Jump if equal. ZF=1<br>Jump if zero. | JNE<br>JNZ | | Jump if not equal. ZF=0<br>Jump if not zero. |
| JG<br>JNLE | ± | Jump if greater. SF=OF. ZF=0.<br>Jump if not less or equal. | JLE<br>JNG | ± | Jump if less or equal. SF<>OF,<br>ZF=1<br>Jump if not greater. |
| JGE<br>JNL | ± | Jump if greater or equal. SF=OF<br>Jump if not less. | JL<br>JNGE | ± | Jump if less. SF<>OF<br>Jump if not greater or equal. |
| JO | | Jump of overflow. OF=1 | JNO | | Jump if not overflow. OF=0 |
| JP<br>JPE | | Jump if parity. PF=1<br>Jump if parity even. | JNP<br>JPO | | Jump if not parity. PF=0<br>Jump if parity odd. |
| JS | | Jump if sign. SF=1 | JNS | | Jump if no sign. SF=0 |

| Comparison | (±) Signed | (+)Unsigned | ± | + |
|---|---|---|---|---|
| op1 > op2 | OF = SF,<br>ZF = 0 | ZF = 0,<br>CF = 0 | Greater | Above |
| op1 ≥ op2 | OF = SF | CF = 0 | GreaterEq | AboveEq |
| op1 = op2 | ZF = 1 | ZF = 1 | Equal | Equal |
| op1 ≤ op2 | OF ≠ SF,<br>ZF = 1 | ZF = 1,<br>CF = 1 | LessEq | BelowEq |
| op1 < op2 | OF ≠ SF | CF = 1 | Less | Below |

| Flags | O.flow | Sign | Zero | Aux | Parity | Carry |
|---|---|---|---|---|---|---|
| | - | - | - | - | - | - |

Flags: None are altered by this opcode.

Back in the early processors using these instructions made it very easy to calculate loop timing, etc., but the newer model Pentium processors use prediction mechanisms to help keep your code flowing at a pretty good rate typically based upon decisions the last time through and a touch of black box magic. When designing your code you should try to architect it to take advantage of the predictor. Better yet, use something called branchless code. Try to use logic to circumvent the need for branching logic.

Current Pentium type processors use different prediction mechanisms to help make the code run at its fastest rate. A bad prediction can cost you cycles, making optimization using the Jcc instructions quite tricky. We are not going to discuss the older processors as most are not made anymore and discussing them here would be pretty much a waste of time, print, paper, and trees! Alas, those of you working with embedded processors are typically using exact models and manufacturers and will therefore be, for the most part, using their related data books.

**Warning:** Different processors have different methods of branch prediction for different manufacturers. The prefetch and other cache buffers increase in size, and processors get faster as newer models of the processor become available on the market. With this said, it should be pointed out that the material being discussed here is probably already dated.

# Branch Prediction

The most important optimization method for the 80x86 processors is using the branch prediction algorithm. These processors use what both Intel and AMD call a BTB (branch target buffer). This is essentially a history buffer of the behavior of the last n Jcc instructions. In a need for speed processors prefetch (preload) instruction code bytes before they are needed, translate them, and arrange them for processing within their multipipelines to be processed. When a relative or absolute jump or call occurs, that code is prefetched and prepared for processing. However, a problem comes up when a branch (Jcc) is encountered. Which way to go? Take the branch or flow through to the next instruction? Different solutions have been taken by different manufacturers. They have and use different sized BTBs, different prediction methodologies, different prefetch sizes, etc. This particular book is not about optimization but we will talk about the mechanism. The particulars depend on which manufacturer and which processor.

## Intel Branch Prediction

The Intel processor does its time sampling in cycles and uses a BTB as well as a prediction history. If a branch is taken, the branch is put into the BTB; if not taken (a flow through), the branch is not put into the BTB unless it was a false prediction. In other words, if executing instructions for the first time and none of the branches are taken, only flowed through, then they were all predicted correctly and thus are not put into the BTB. There is zero to no penalty for executing a branch instruction if the prediction was correct, but if wrong, there is a cycle penalty.

The instruction prefetch has four 32-byte buffers loaded sequentially (one at a time) until a branch is encountered, and then the BTB is used to predict a branch or not. If no predicted branch, the contiguous memory is loaded, but if a branch is predicted, the alternate prefetch buffer is loaded with the memory referenced by the branch. If the prediction was wrong, all the instruction pipelines are flushed and the prefetch mechanism begins again. So you should see the need to design your code to minimize the number of mispredictions. There is one other thing to be careful of and that has to do with two back-to-back Jcc instructions. If two Jcc instructions both have their last byte in the same 4-byte block, a misprediction can occur. This would only occur if the second branch has a displacement of 8 bits. Using a larger bit displacement, rearranging the code, or inserting a NOP instruction would solve the problem.

This method is bad as 14h and 16h are in the same 4-byte block {14h…17h}:

```
00000013   75 F8          jne    $Z1
00000015   74 07          jz     $Z2
```

The following is the best method to solve the problem, but only if your assembler lets you override an 8-bit displacement with a 32-bit one for Protected Mode, setting the last byte at 14h and 1ah. Note that in the following, the second code branch uses a 4-byte offset and not one byte. This is because it is outside the [−128, 127] range.

```
00000013   75 F8               jne    $Z1
00000015   0f 84 00000007      jz     near ptr $Z2
```

Here is a 16-bit displacement for Real Mode setting the last byte at 14h and 18h:

```
00000013   75 F8             jne    $Z1
00000015   0f 84 0007        jz     near ptr $Z2
```

Not that I am urging you to use the NOP instructions, but this one is an alternative as 14h and 18h are in different 4-byte blocks. The NOP pushes the second conditional branch address further down.

```
00000013   75 F8          jne    $Z1
00000015   90             nop
00000016   90             nop
00000017   74 07          jz     $Z2
```

Branches that are not already in the BTB use the static prediction logic as follows.

# Static Branch Prediction

### Back-Branch-Taken

The branch is predicted to be taken if a negative displacement, such as at the bottom of a loop. A flow through (branch not taken), would be a misprediction!

### Forward-Branch-Not-Taken

The branch is predicted *not* to be taken if a positive displacement such as a jump further down the code. The instruction pointer is expected to just flow through the branch instruction. A jump would be a misprediction.

```
$L1:    nop
        nop
        jne     $L1     ; ⅃  Back-Branch-Taken

        jz      $L2     ; ⅂  Forward-Branch-Not-Taken
        nop
$L2:    nop
```

### Branching Hints

A prefix of 3Eh (HT) is a hint to take the branch. A prefix of 2eh (HNT) is a hint not to take a branch (flow through). Only set if contrary to a static branch prediction. Sometimes there are no elements to test, so at the top of a function one might have an if conditional (size=0) empty test.

```
test ecx,ecx
db 3eh   ; Hint to take the branch
jz $L9

         ; Insert looping code here

$L9:
```

The default static prediction is to not branch as the jz is a forward-branch and the prediction logic does a flow through, but the 3eh says to override and take the branch as the length is typically expected to be zero most of the time.

# AMD Branch Prediction

The same rules for Intel apply here but with some minor changes. The AMD K6-2 chip uses a two-level 8192 entry branch prediction table. It is more effective to use only 8-bit displacements. Code with small loops should be aligned on 16-byte boundaries and code with loops that do not fit in the prefetch should be aligned on 32-byte boundaries. Small loops should be unrolled but large loops should not, due to inefficient use of the L1 instruction cache. A mispredicted branch is from one to four clocks. The penalty for a bad prediction if the branch is not in BTB is three clock cycles.

# Branch Optimization

Removing branches from your code such as unrolling loops makes it more efficient by removing the possibility of misprediction. This is discussed in more detail in the next chapter. One method is to use the SETcc instruction to set Boolean flags. Another method is to use CMOV or FCMOV instructions to copy data. These methods can sometimes be manipulated to duplicate the same effect you were trying to achieve with the Jcc instruction without any possible prediction failure that would cost cycles.

For example, the following is the signed integer absolute number function n = ABS(n), which uses a Jcc instruction.

```
        test    eax,eax     ; Test if negative
        jns     $Abs1       ; Jump if positive

        neg     eax         ; Invert number, two's complement

$Abs1:                      ; eax is positive
```

As an alternative, we can do this without a Jcc instruction:

```
        mov     ecx,eax
        sar     ecx,31      ; all 1's if neg, all 0's if pos
        xor     eax,ecx     ; At this point we are one's complement
        sub     eax,ecx     ; n-(-1)=n+1 = two's complement
```

So you see, we did an ABS() function without any Jcc instructions; just a sleight of hand using general-purpose instructions. Admittedly this technique will not work on everything, but it will help in your optimizations. In Chapter 11 we will go into more detail.

Destination addresses of a jump should be code aligned to take advantage of the instruction prefetch.

```
        align   16
```

Of course the Align statement must not be in the code flow, as unknown bytes are added to align the code, So it must always occur outside a function, thus after a JMP or RET statement. Another alignment type would be for fine-tuning on a byte-by-byte basis such as:

```
org      $+3
```

…which aligns by moving the origin pointer from the $ current location by three bytes, effectively adding three unknown bytes. Typically you will find it paired with an alignment to create a fixed alignment point. This prevents any alignment of a previous function affecting the alignment of a following function.

```
align  16
org      $+3
```

Inside the code flow you can add nondestructive instructions such as the following to help align your code. Your flags may be altered but not the registers.

```
    nop                    ; 1 byte
    mov     eax,eax    ; 2 bytes
66h mov     ax,ax      ; 3 bytes
```

Let's start by examining a C type strlen() function designed to find the number of bytes in a zero-terminated ASCII string:

```
uint strlen(char *p)
{
    uint cnt = 0;

    while (*p++)
        cnt++;

    return cnt;
}
```

Let's try that in assembly and align the code to a 16-byte boundary:

```
                              align 16

00000000  54              push  ebp
00000001  8B EC           mov   ebp,esp
00000003  8B 54 24 08     mov   edx,[ebp+arg1] ; String

00000007  B8 FFFFFFFF     mov   eax,-1

0000000C  40        $L1:  inc   eax
0000000D  8A 0A           mov   cl,[edx]        ; Get a character
0000000F  42              inc   edx
00000010  84 C9           test  cl,cl
```

```
00000012  75 F8              jnz    $L1            ; 0 terminator?

00000014  5D                 pop    ebp
00000015  C3                 ret                   ; return eax (length)
00000016
```

As you have probably noted, the entire function occupies 16h (22) bytes (000h..016h). It also has an efficiency problem. The 16-byte prefetch is first loaded with address 0000h...000fh, executes up to and including the "inc edx" and then reloads the prefetch with the next 16 bytes, address 0010h...001fh. The code then executes up to address 0013h and then the prefetch has to be reloaded with 0000h again. This continues over and over again until the zero terminator is encountered. Now if we tweak the alignment a tad we can contain this $L1 loop within one prefetch:

```
                             align 16
                             org  $+4

00000004  54                 push   ebp
00000005  8B EC              mov    ebp,esp
00000007  8B 54 24 08        mov    edx,[ebp+arg1] ; String

0000000B  B8 FFFFFFFF        mov    eax,-1

00000010  40         $L1:    inc    eax
00000011  8A 0A              mov    cl,[edx]       ; Get a character
00000013  42                 inc    edx
00000014  84 C9              test   cl,cl
00000016  75 F8              jnz    $L1            ; 0 terminator?

00000018  5D                 pop    ebp
00000019  C3                 ret                   ; return eax (length)
0000001A
```

You will now note that the beginning of the function actually starts on address 0004h, but the beginning of the loop is now aligned perfectly on a 16-byte boundary, allowing the entire loop to be contained with a single instruction prefetch load. This is a very old and simple alignment trick that is still usable on the newer processors.

# PAUSE — (Spin Loop Hint)

| Mnemonic | P | PII | K6 | 3D! | 3Mx+ | SSE | SSE2 | A64 | SSE3 | E64T |
|----------|---|-----|----|----|------|-----|------|-----|------|------|
| PAUSE | | | | | | | ✓ | ✓ | ✓ | ✓ |

pause

This was introduced with the P4. It indicates to the processor that this is a tight weight loop in one thread in a multithreaded application that is waiting for another thread. This is typically referred to as a spin loop. In essence, the processor is constantly testing and looping until a signal flag gets set.

```
$L1:    cmp     eax,bSignal
        jne     $L1                 ; I am *** BAD Code ***
```

**Tip:**  Tight loops are a burden on the processor in a single or multithreaded environment. Inserting the PAUSE instruction indicates to the processor to let the thread snooze a micro-bit so as to allow the other threads more time to run. This is also effective in helping to reduce current drawn by a processor and so can help it run a bit cooler.

```
        cmp     eax,bSignal
        je      $L2                 ; Already set so continue

$L1:    pause                       ; Snooze
        cmp     eax,bSignal
        jne     $L1                 ; Loop if not ready yet!
$L2:
```

The code byte for the PAUSE instruction maps to a NOP instruction on previous processors so invisible to them!

## I-VU-Q

"I would like you to write an insertion sort algorithm." Or "I would like you to write a function to convert a zero-terminated ASCII formatted string containing an upper/lowercase mix into just uppercase."

That is what the standard C runtime library function strupr() is for! The next time you are interviewing and they ask you to code the function strupr() but give you a minimal amount of information, smile, appear deep in thought, and then draw on that white board the following code in assembly. That will impress them! They will probably hire you.

The following is a sample string to uppercase conversion algorithm. It
is only partially optimized as a do loop is used instead of a while loop so
only one jump is utilized instead of two! It is also ASCII only as it has
not been modified for SJIS, WCHAR, or Unicode strings. Using char c
instead of char *p may or may not save you CPU cycles depending on
the optimization ability of your compiler.

```c
char *strupr(char *pStr)
{
    char *p;

    p = pStr;

    if (p != NULL)          // Test for NULL or assert()!
    {
        if (*p)             // If at least one character in string
        {
            do {            // do{} more efficient than while{}
                if (('a' <= *p) && (*p <= 'z'))
                {
                    *p -= 'a'-'A';   // 0x20;
                }

                ++p;
            } while (*p);   // Loop while characters
        }
    }

    return pStr;
}
```

Now try this in assembly. This can be done in one of two ways. If this
function is called a lot and needs to be very fast, a table lookup could be
used, as it would only cost a 256-byte enumeration table with indexes
61h to 7ah ("a" to "z") set to their uppercase equivalents.

```asm
struprtbl db    000h,001h,002h,003h,004h,005h,006h,007h,...
...etc
        xor     eax,eax

        mov     al,[edx]        ; Get a byte

$L1:    mov     al,struprtbl[eax]
        mov     [edx],al
        mov     al,[edx+1]      ; Get a byte
        inc     edx
        test    al,al
        jnz     $L1             ; Loop until a terminator
```

That code snippet is fine and dandy, but because there is a processor stall on line $L1, a technique learned earlier needs to be used. The following does just that and has no stall.

```
        mov     ebx,offset struprtbl
$L1:    xlatb
```

Obviously, using the memory alignment tricks learned in Chapter 2, "Coding Standards," in regard to the setting of memory, one could make this function fairly quick but a lot larger. But I leave that up to you.

The alternate method is using two comparisons similar to that used in the C code. The branch prediction within the CPU rewards you for a correct prediction and penalizes you for an incorrect one. If the English text string is examined it would be noted that it is mostly lowercase with some symbols and some uppercase. So if that is taken to advantage one can make this function pretty efficient.

Contrarily, writing the function strupr(), String Upper, the logic would want to skip around for symbols, uppercase, and extended ASCII and predict a flow through conversion for lowercase. In other words, skip below the conversion so the predictor will tend to be correct on a flow through.

```
;       strupr snippet
xyzzy   db      "Quick brown fox jumped!",0

        mov     al,[edx]    ; Get a character

$L1:    cmp     al,'a'
        jb      $L2         ; (1) Jump if symbols or uppercase
        cmp     al,'z'
        ja      $L2         ; (2) Jump if extended ASCII

        sub     al,20h      ; convert to uppercase
        mov     [edx],al    ; Save altered character

$L2:    inc     edx         ; Nothing to do, next!
        mov     al,[edx]    ; Get a character
        test    al,al
        jnz     $L1         ; 0 terminator?
```

That was pretty simple because I picked the simple one. The predictions for the JMP will succeed most of the time. Let's make things a little more interesting and try the complement function strlwr(), String Lower.

```
;       strlwr snippet

        mov    al,[edx]    ; Get a character

$L1:    cmp    al,'Z'
        ja     $L2         ; Jump if symbols or uppercase
        cmp    al,'A'
        jb     $L2         ; Jump if extended ASCII

        add    al,20h      ; convert to lowercase
        mov    [edx],al    ; Save altered character

$L2:    inc    edx         ; Nothing to do, next!
        mov    al,[edx]    ; Get a character
        test   al,al
        jnz    $L1         ; 0 terminator?
```

It is practically the same but definitely not very efficient as the branch predictor will fail more often. The following code is larger but more efficient.

```
;       strlwr snippet
;
        mov    al,[edx]

$L1:    cmp    al,'Z'
        jbe    $L4         ; Jump if symbol or uppercase

$L2:    inc    edx         ; Nothing to do; next!
        mov    al,[edx]    ; Get a character
        test   al,al
        jnz    $L1         ; 0 terminator?


;       Character is uppercase so we need to convert it!

$L3:    add    al,20h
        mov    [edx],al    ; Save altered character
        inc    edx         ; Advance string pointer!
        mov    al,[edx]    ; Get a character
        test   al,al
        jnz    $L1         ; 0 terminator?


; symbols or uppercase

$L4:    cmp    al,'A'
        jae    $L3         ; Jump up if uppercase

        inc    edx         ; Nothing to do; next!
        mov    al,[edx]    ; Get a character
        test   al,al
        jnz    $L1         ; 0 terminator?
```

In these examples it is basically known what the data would look like and this was taken to advantage so as to allow for the best data prediction, which could help the code run faster. Some types of data are hard to predict and those will require a little trial and error experimentation to get a handle on.

**Tip:** Branch predicting is not fortune-telling or soothsaying; it is pre-planning, data analysis, statistics, and a little dumb luck.

# JECXZ/JCXZ — Jump if ECX/CX Is Zero

JECXZ *destination*

JCXZ *destination*

JRCXZ *destination*

| Mnemonic | P | PII | K6 | 3D! | 3Mx+ | SSE | SSE2 | A64 | SSE3 | E64T |
|----------|---|-----|----|----|------|-----|------|-----|------|------|
| JCXZ | ✓ | ✓ | ✓ | ✓ | ✓ | ✓ | ✓ | 32 | ✓ | ✓ |
| JECXZ | ✓ | ✓ | ✓ | ✓ | ✓ | ✓ | ✓ | 32 | ✓ | ✓ |
| JRCXZ | | | | | | | | 64 | | ? |

```
jecxz   disp8
jcxz    disp8
jrcxz   disp8        ± 8-bit relative hop
```

This instruction jumps to the relative *destination* address if RCX/ECX/CX has a value of zero.

```
JCXZ    Jump if CX Zero
JECXZ   Jump if ECX zero
JRCXZ   Jump if RCX zero
```

| Flags | O.flow | Sign | Zero | Aux | Parity | Carry |
|-------|--------|------|------|-----|--------|-------|
| | - | - | - | - | - | - |

Flags: None are altered by this opcode.

| | jecxz $L1 | test ecx,ecx<br>jz    $L1 |
|---------|-----------|---------------------------|
| P bytes | 2 | 4 |
| R bytes | 3 | 5 |

|  | jcxz  $L1 | test  cx,cx<br>jz    $L1 |
|---|---|---|
| P bytes | 3 | 5 |
| R bytes | 2 | 4 |

This is pretty useful at the top of a function to detect a zero condition loaded from the stack. Note that the SETcc instruction does something very similar but this sample is to make JECXZ easier to understand.

```
        mov     ecx[ebp+arg1]   ; Get # of bytes
        jecxz   $xit            ; Jump if a value of 0
          :
          :
        mov     ecx,1           ; true

$xit:   mov     eax,ecx         ; false=0   true=1
        ret
```

# LOOPcc

LOOPZ *destination*

LOOPNZ *destination*

| Mnemonic | P | PII | K6 | 3D! | 3Mx+ | SSE | SSE2 | A64 | SSE3 | E64T |
|---|---|---|---|---|---|---|---|---|---|---|
| LOOPcc | ✓ | ✓ | ✓ | ✓ | ✓ | ✓ | ✓ | ✓ | ✓ | ✓ |

```
        loope   disp8       ± 8-bit relative hop
        loopz   disp8
        loopne  disp8
        loopnz  disp8
```

The LOOP instruction decrements the ECX/CX register. If not a value of zero, the instruction pointer jumps to the *destination* address. If it is zero, the instruction pointer merely advances to the next instruction.

The LOOPZ and LOOPE instructions decrement the ECX/CX register. If not a value of zero and the zero flag is set from a previous instruction, then the instruction pointer jumps to the *destination* address. If it is zero, the instruction pointer merely advances to the next instruction.

The LOOPNZ and LOOPNE instructions decrement the ECX/CX register. If not a value of zero and the zero flag is not set from a previous instruction, then the instruction pointer jumps to the *destination* address. If it is zero, the instruction pointer merely advances to the next instruction.

Left and right columns are complemented instructions.

| LOOPZ | Jump if above. ZF=0, CF=0 | | LOOPNZ | Jump if Below or Equal. ZF=1, CF=1 |
|---|---|---|---|---|
| LOOPE | Jump if not below or equal. | | LOOPNE | Jump if not above. |

| Flags | O.flow | Sign | Zero | Aux | Parity | Carry |
|---|---|---|---|---|---|---|
| | - | - | - | - | - | - |

Flags: None are altered by this opcode.

```
$L1:    add     esi,4
        test    [esi],al
        loopnz $L1
```

# LOOP

LOOP *destination*

| Mnemonic | P | PII | K6 | 3D! | 3Mx+ | SSE | SSE2 | A64 | SSE3 | E64T |
|---|---|---|---|---|---|---|---|---|---|---|
| LOOP | ✓ | ✓ | ✓ | ✓ | ✓ | ✓ | ✓ | ✓ | ✓ | ✓ |

loop   *disp8*        ± 8-bit relative hop

The following table is based upon using the LOOP instruction. You will note that this instruction was only effective for the original 80x86 processor. Since that time, its use is limited to the Cyrix processor. If writing generic code, do not use it! Write a macro to replace it; better yet, forget it exists! But if writing Cyrix-specific code, then use it by all means; it will save you a clock cycle.

| | loop $L1 | dec ecx / jz $L1 | dec cx / jz $L1 |
|---|---|---|---|
| P bytes | 2 | 3 | 4 |
| R bytes | 2 | 4 | 3 |

On the other hand, the LOOPZ and LOOPNZ instructions have an efficient CPU time. Even with the ability of processors to handle multiple instructions in multiple pipes, the LOOPZ and LOOPNZ instructions are the most efficient.

# Pancake Memory LIFO Queue

An alternative memory management scheme such as pancaking can be utilized. This is where a base (or sub-base) level is set and the next available memory pointer is merely advanced by the amount of memory needed. There is no memory-free function as memory is merely disposed of by resetting the memory available back to its original base (in essence, abandoning the memory), then merely making sure the base is on a 16-byte alignment. This is like a bottom based processor stack. A free memory pointer is preset to the bottom of the stack at the physical base level of that memory. As data is loaded into memory, the free pointer is moved higher up in memory. When it is decided it is time to release that memory, all allocated objects are instantly thrown away by merely resetting the free pointer to the base level again. Console games sometimes use this method to keep code space from having to deal with individual deallocations.

Obviously, since there is no need for reallocations, or freeing of memory, then there is no need for a header either.

There are other schemes. Just make sure your memory is 16-byte aligned. Now that any possible memory allocation alignment problems have been taken care of up front, it is time to move on to the good stuff.

# Stack

When one orders "all you can eat" pancakes, either a short stack or a tall stack is delivered to your table. If you have not finished eating the stack of pancakes and the server brings you more, you do not pick them all up and place them under your older pancakes; you have them placed on top of those already on your plate. So this would be considered a LIFO (last in, first out) system. Those new pancakes will be the first to be eaten, will they not?

Well, a computer stack is like that. Memory is typically allocated from the bottom up, and data in that memory is low address to high address oriented. The computer stack starts from the top of memory and works its way down, and hopefully the two ends do not meet or boom! That is why you have to watch recursive functions; if they "curse" too much, they run out of memory. We will go into a little more depth as we discuss the PUSH and POP instructions.

# PUSH — Push Value onto Stack

PUSH *operand*

| Mnemonic | P | PII | K6 | 3D! | 3Mx+ | SSE | SSE2 | A64 | SSE3 | E64T |
|----------|---|-----|----|----|------|-----|------|-----|------|------|
| PUSH | ✓ | ✓ | ✓ | ✓ | ✓ | ✓ | ✓ | ✓ | ✓ | ✓ |

> push  #{8/16/32/64}
> push  rm{16/32/64}
> push  sreg16

This instruction pushes an 8-, 16-, 32-, or 64-bit immediate value on the stack depending on the processor mode. A 16-, 32-, or 64-bit general-purpose register or memory value, or 16-bit segment register or memory value can also be pushed onto the stack. When operands are a different size than the CPU mode, the data size of the data is extended and the stack remains aligned. POP is the complement of this instruction.

| Flags | O.flow | Sign | Zero | Aux | Parity | Carry |
|-------|--------|------|------|-----|--------|-------|
|       | - | - | - | - | - | - |

Flags: None are affected by this opcode.

**64-bit** **No 64-bit:** In 64-bit mode, only the FS and GS segment-selectors can be pushed on the stack. 8/16/64-bit data can be pushed but not 32-bit.

# POP — Pop Value off Stack

POP *operand*

| Mnemonic | P | PII | K6 | 3D! | 3Mx+ | SSE | SSE2 | A64 | SSE3 | E64T |
|----------|---|-----|----|----|------|-----|------|-----|------|------|
| POP | ✓ | ✓ | ✓ | ✓ | ✓ | ✓ | ✓ | ✓ | ✓ | ✓ |

> pop  rm{16/32/64}
> pop  sreg16

This instruction pops a 16- or 32-bit register value or 16-bit segment register from the stack. PUSH is the complement of this instruction.

| Flags | O.flow | Sign | Zero | Aux | Parity | Carry |
|-------|--------|------|------|-----|--------|-------|
|       | - | - | - | - | - | - |

Flags: None are affected by this opcode.

**64-bit** **No 64-bit:** In 64-bit mode, only the FS and GS segment-selectors can be pushed on the stack. 8/16/64-bit data can be pushed but not 32-bit.

# PUSHA/PUSHAD — Push All General-Purpose Registers

| Mnemonic | P | PII | K6 | 3D! | 3Mx+ | SSE | SSE2 | A64 | SSE3 | E64T |
|----------|---|-----|-----|------|-------|------|-------|------|-------|------|
| PUSHA | ✓ | ✓ | ✓ | ✓ | ✓ | ✓ | ✓ | ✓ | ✓ | 32 |
| PUSHAD | ✓ | ✓ | ✓ | ✓ | ✓ | ✓ | ✓ | ✓ | ✓ | 32 |

```
pusha
pushad
```

The PUSHA and PUSHAD instructions use the same opcode, which pushes in order the following list of registers: EAX, ECX, EDX, EBX, ESP, EBP, ESI, and EDI if in Protected Mode or AX, CX, DX, BX, SP, BP, SI, and DI if in Real Mode. In Protected Mode PUSHAD should be used and in Real Mode PUSHA should be used. POPAD/POPA are the complement of this instruction. This is no 64-bit push!

| **Flags** | O.flow | Sign | Zero | Aux | Parity | Carry |
|-----------|--------|------|------|-----|--------|-------|
| | - | - | - | - | - | - |

Flags: None are affected by this opcode.

**64-bit** **No 64-bit:** The general-purpose instructions PUSHA and PUSHAD are not available in 64-bit mode.

The following are the equivalent functions and push order of the general-purpose registers.

| | pushad | push eax |
|---|--------|----------|
| | | push ecx |
| | | push edx |
| | | push ebx |
| | | push esp |
| | | push ebp |
| | | push esi |
| | | push edi |
| P bytes | 1 | 8 |
| R bytes | 2 | 16 |

| | pusha | push ax |
|---|-------|---------|
| | | push cx |
| | | push dx |
| | | push bx |
| | | push sp |
| | | push bp |
| | | push si |
| | | push di |
| | 1 | 16 |
| | 1 | 8 |

Intel recommends that you not use "complex" instructions and encourages you to use simple instructions instead.

# POPA/POPAD — Pop All General-Purpose Registers

| Mnemonic | P | PII | K6 | 3D! | 3Mx+ | SSE | SSE2 | A64 | SSE3 | E64T |
|---|---|---|---|---|---|---|---|---|---|---|
| POPA | ✓ | ✓ | ✓ | ✓ | ✓ | ✓ | ✓ | ✓ | ✓ | 32 |
| POPAD | ✓ | ✓ | ✓ | ✓ | ✓ | ✓ | ✓ | ✓ | ✓ | 32 |

```
popa
popad
```

The POPA and POPAD instructions use the same opcode, which pops in reverse order the results of the complement instruction PUSHA or PUSHAD. The following registers are popped from the stack in this order: EDI, ESI, EBP, ESP, EBX, EDX, ECX, and EAX if in Protected Mode or DI, SI, BP, SP, BX, DX, CX or AX if in Real Mode.

| Flags | O.flow | Sign | Zero | Aux | Parity | Carry |
|---|---|---|---|---|---|---|
| | - | - | - | - | - | - |

Flags: None are affected by this opcode.

**No 64-bit:** The general-purpose instructions POPA and POPAD are not available in 64-bit mode.

The following are the equivalent functions and pop order of the general-purpose registers.

| popad | |
|---|---|
| | pop edi |
| | pop esi |
| | pop ebp |
| | pop esp |
| | pop ebx |
| | pop edx |
| | pop ecx |
| | pop eax |

| popa | |
|---|---|
| | pop di |
| | pop si |
| | pop bp |
| | pop sp |
| | pop bx |
| | pop dx |
| | pop cx |
| | pop ax |

## PUSHFD/PUSHFQ and POPFD/POPFQ

See Chapter 3, "Processor Differential Insight."

## ENTER — Allocate Stack Frame for Procedure ARGS

ENTER *destination, source*

| Mnemonic | P | PII | K6 | 3D! | 3Mx+ | SSE | SSE2 | A64 | SSE3 | E64T |
|----------|---|-----|----|----|------|-----|------|-----|------|------|
| ENTER | ✓ | ✓ | ✓ | ✓ | ✓ | ✓ | ✓ | ✓ | ✓ | ✓ |

```
enter #(16), 0
enter #(16), 1
enter #(16), #(8)
```

This instruction allocates a stack frame for a procedure.

## LEAVE — Deallocate Stack Frame of Procedure ARGS

LEAVE *destination, source*

| Mnemonic | P | PII | K6 | 3D! | 3Mx+ | SSE | SSE2 | A64 | SSE3 | E64T |
|----------|---|-----|----|----|------|-----|------|-----|------|------|
| LEAVE | ✓ | ✓ | ✓ | ✓ | ✓ | ✓ | ✓ | ✓ | ✓ | ✓ |

```
leave
```

This instruction deallocates a stack frame for a procedure. The register pairings of SP and BP are dependent upon the mode running.

| 64-bit | 32-bit | 16-bit |
|--------|--------|--------|
| mov rsp,rbp | mov esp,ebp | mov sp,bp |
| pop rbp | pop ebp | pop bp |

# CALL Procedure (Function)

Now to discuss a totally different but related topic. These functions fall into one of two categories: the function and the procedure. Now as we all learned in school, a function returns a value and a procedure does not, but their code is typically written the same. The only real difference is that the calling code makes use of the EAX and/or EDX/EAX register(s) when the function returns.

| Function | Procedure |
|----------|-----------|
| $y = f(x)$ | $f(x)$ |

# CALL

CALL *destination*

| Mnemonic | P | PII | K6 | 3D! | 3Mx+ | SSE | SSE2 | A64 | SSE3 | E64T |
|----------|---|-----|-----|-----|------|-----|------|-----|------|------|
| CALL | ✓ | ✓ | ✓ | ✓ | ✓ | ✓ | ✓ | ✓ | ✓ | ✓ |

## Delta CALL

call   ± 16/32          Relative Jump

## Protected Mode CALL (NEAR)

call   rm{16/32/64}          Near

## Protected Mode CALL (FAR)

call   ptr16:32     Far sel:addr
call   m16:32       Near (Real Mode)
call   m16:64

## Real Mode CALL (FAR)

call   ptr16:16     Far sel:addr
call   m16:16       Near (Real Mode)          20

This is a general-purpose instruction used to call near or far code in another location in memory followed up by a RET or RETF instruction.

| Flags | O.flow | Sign | Zero | Aux | Parity | Carry |
|-------|--------|------|------|-----|--------|-------|
| | - | - | - | - | - | - |

Flags: None are altered by this opcode.

This instruction is very similar to the JMP instruction except that it puts a return address on the stack so when a matching RET or RETF instruction is encountered, it will return to the next instruction following the CALL.

## Protected Mode CALL (NEAR)

This is a 32-bit value stored in a register, memory location, or 32-bit relative address.

```
NearAdrPtr  DWORD   offset NearJmp        ; Near pointer
            DWORD   offset OtherNearJmp   ; Near function
NearJmp proc    near
        ret
NearJmp endp

        call    NearJmp

        mov     ebx,offset NearJmp
        call    ebx

        mov     ebx,offset NearAdrPtr
        call    [ebx]

        xor     eax,eax
        xor     ebx,ebx
        call    NearAdrPtr[ebx]

        call    NearAdrPtr[ebx*4]

        call    NearAdrPtr[eax+ebx*4]
```

## Protected Mode CALL (FAR)

This is a 48-bit value stored in a register, memory location, or 48-bit relative address. As Win32, Extended DOS, or other Protected Mode flat memory environments are pretty much what is developed for today, the need for the FAR pointer is, for the most part, only in the domain of the operating system or device driver developer. (Note that there are exceptions.)

```
FarAdrPtr   FWORD   offset FarJmp         ; Far pointer
            FWORD   offset OtherFarJmp    ; Far function
FarJmp  proc    far
        ret
FarJmp  endp

        call    far ptr FarJmp
```

The same kind of memory reference that is used to access a memory table or array can also be used to access a call vector. Almost any register or register pair can be used alone or in an addition equation with an optional base address and scale factor of {2, 4, or 8}, but you will note that there are some limitations in regard to the ESP register.

### Real Mode — NEAR or FAR has Same Opcodes

### Protected Mode — NEAR or FAR has Same Opcodes

```
call ...
call NearAdrPtr[...]
```

| eax | ebx | ecx | edx | esp | ebp | esi | edi |
|-----|-----|-----|-----|-----|-----|-----|-----|
| ax  | bx  | cx  | dx  | sp  | bp  | si  | di  |

### Real Mode — NEAR or FAR has Same Opcodes

### Protected Mode — NEAR or FAR has Same Opcodes

```
call word ptr [...]
call dword ptr [...]
call fword ptr [...]
call NearAdrPtr[...]
```

See Appendix C for the mapping tables.

# RET/RETF — Return

| Mnemonic | P | PII | K6 | 3D! | 3Mx+ | SSE | SSE2 | A64 | SSE3 | E64T |
|----------|---|-----|----|----|------|-----|------|-----|------|------|
| RET  | ✓ | ✓ | ✓ | ✓ | ✓ | ✓ | ✓ | ✓ | ✓ | ✓ |
| RETF | ✓ | ✓ | ✓ | ✓ | ✓ | ✓ | ✓ | ✓ | ✓ | ✓ |

```
ret                    Near
ret    #
retf                   Far
```

This is a general-purpose instruction used to return from a CALL instruction to a previous location in memory.

| Flags | O.flow | Sign | Zero | Aux | Parity | Carry |
|-------|--------|------|------|-----|--------|-------|
|       | -      | -    | -    | -   | -      | -     |

Flags: None are altered by this opcode.

The various calls given in the following table push onto the stack the listed number of bytes as a return address. When this instruction is encountered, that value is popped off the stack. The 0C3h opcode pops a NEAR call and the 0CBh opcode pops a FAR call. The actual number of bytes also depends on whether the processor is in Protected or Real Mode. The number of bytes of stack displacement can also be specified by 0C2h versus 0CAh.

| CALL | bytes on stack | RET opcode | Std/Fast Call Ret w/Stack Adj |
|------|----------------|------------|-------------------------------|
| Protected Mode Near | 4 | 0C3h | 0C2h, #{16} |
| Protected Mode Far | 6 | 0CBh | 0CAh, #{16} |
| Real Mode Near | 2 | 0C3h | 0C2h, #{16} |
| Real Mode Far | 4 | 0CBh | 0CAh, #{16} |

```
NearJmp proc    near
        ret
NearJmp endp

vs

FarJmp  proc    far
        retf
FarJmp  endp
```

Note that RETF is not really an instruction. With a procedural block marked as far, a RET instruction should automatically be encoded as a RET FAR. If your code has trouble at run time, peek at the assembly listing and verify the RET code byte is the correct one to match the call. Some macro assemblers allow the RETF reference to force a RET FAR.

# Calling Conventions (Stack Argument Methods)

Before we get too far along we should discuss the methods of passing arguments on a stack. In essence, a function call has to push arguments (if not a void function) onto the stack, push the current processor's instruction pointer (EIP or RIP) (the pointer to where the instruction being executed is) onto the stack, and perform a subroutine call. Use the stack yet again for any local data and then return to where it left off while unwinding the stack. There are three basic methods to this. From a high-level language such as C/C++ this is taken for granted, but from the low level of assembly language this has to be done carefully or the stack and program counter will be corrupted.

We are going to examine function calls using a 32-bit processor, as that is what most of you are currently using. Thus, each argument that gets pushed onto the stack is 4 bytes in size. An item such as a double-precision floating-point, which uses 8 bytes, is actually pushed as two halves — lower 4 bytes, upper 4 bytes. When the processor is in 64-bit mode, 8 bytes are pushed on the stack.

```
int hello(int a, int b)
{
    int c = a + b;
    return c;
}

int i = hello(1, 2);
```

# C Declaration (__CDECL)

The function call to hello is straightforward:

```
00401118  push    2
0040111A  push    1
0040111C  call    hello
00401121  add     esp,8
```

Once the instruction pointer (EIP) arrives at the first byte of the function hello, the stack will look similar to this:

| Register | Address (N...N+3) | HexValue | Description |
|---|---|---|---|
|  | 0012FF00h | 00000002 | Arg#2 |
|  | 0012FEFCh | 00000001 | Arg#1 |
| ESP= | 0012FEF8H | 00401121 | Return address |
|  | 0012FEF4H |  |  |

EIP=        004010D0                              hello()

The function hello looks similar to the following. I have left the addresses for each line of assembly for reference but they are not needed.

```
                                ; Set up stack frame
004010D0  push    ebp         ; Save old ebp
004010D1  mov     ebp,esp     ; Set local frame base
004010D3  sub     esp,4
```

Let us peek at the stack one more time and note the changes:

| Register | Address (N...N+3) | HexValue | Description |
|---|---|---|---|
| | 0012FF00h | 00000002 | Arg#2 |
| | 0012FEFCh | 00000001 | Arg#1 |
| | 0012FEF8H | 00401121 | Return address |
| EBP= | 0012FEF4H | ??? | (old EBP) |
| ESP= | 0012FEF0H | | Local arg 'c' |
| | 0012FEECH | | |

EIP=          004010E8                    hello()

The EBP register is used to remember where the ESP was last, and the ESP is moved lower in memory, leaving room for the local stack arguments and positioned for the next needed push.

```
                    ; Do the calculation   a+b
004010E8   mov        eax,dword ptr [ebp+8]
004010EB   add        eax,dword ptr [ebp+0Ch]
                    ; Restore stack frame
004010F1   mov        esp,ebp    ; Restore esp
004010F3   pop        ebp        ; Restore ebp
004010F4   ret                   ; Restore eip
```

So upon returning, anything lower than ESP in stack memory is essentially garbage, but the instruction pointer (EIP) is back to where it can continue in the code. But the stack pointer still needs to be corrected for the two arguments that were pushed.

```
00401118   push    2
0040111A   push    1
0040111C   call    hello
00401121   add     esp,8   ;2*sizeof(int)
```

They can either be popped:

```
pop    ecx
pop    ecx
```

...or, more simply, just adjust the stack pointer for two arguments, four bytes each:

```
add    esp,8
```

So in a C declaration (CDECL) type function call, the calling function corrects the stack pointer for the arguments it pushed. One other item to note is that immediate values {1, 2} were pushed on the stack. So the stack was used for the arguments and for the instruction pointer.

# Standard Declaration (__STDCALL)

Let us now examine the standard calling convention using this same code sample:

```
00401118  push   2
0040111A  push   1
0040111C  call   hello
```

You will note that there is no stack correction upon returning. This means that the function must handle the stack frame correction upon returning.

```
          ; Restore stack frame
004010F1  mov       esp,ebp   ; Restore esp
004010F3  pop       ebp       ; Restore ebp
004010F4  ret       8         ; Restore eip
```

In reality, the return instruction RET handles the stack correction by adjusting the return address by the number of bytes specified by the immediate value. In the previous snippet, it was adjusted by 8 bytes.

# Fast Call Declaration (__FASTCALL)

Let us now examine the fast calling convention using this same code sample. On a MIPS or PowerPC processor this is actually a very fast method of calling functions, but on an 80x86 it is not quite so fast. On those platforms there are 32 general-purpose registers of which a portion of them are used as stack arguments. As long as the number of arguments is reasonable the registers are used. When there are too many, the stack-like mechanism is used for the overage. On the 80x86 there are very few general-purpose instructions available in place of stack arguments for 16/32-bit mode. For example, under VC6 only two registers are available — ECX and EDX — at which point the stack is used for the additional arguments.

```
mov    edx,2    ; arg#2  Register used
mov    ecx,1    ; arg#1  Register used
call   hello
```

You will notice that the arguments were actually assigned to registers and the stack was only used to retain the program counter (EIP) for the function return. Since the values are already in registers, there is no need for the function to access them from the stack or copy them to a register.

When three arguments are used, however:

```
i = hello(1, 2, 3);

    push    3               ; arg#3  Stack used
    mov     edx,2           ; arg#2  Register used
    mov     ecx,1           ; arg#1  Register used
    call    hello
```

...the arguments that were pushed on the stack are stack corrected upon return by the function; this is the same as the fast call mechanism!

```
    mov     esp,ebp
    pop     ebp
    ret     4               ; One 4-byte arg to be popped.
```

It is very important to realize that both the calling routine and the function itself must be written using the same calling convention. These can all be used within a single application but can get very confusing as to which was used where, and so consistency is important or your code will fail.

# Interrupt Handling

## INT/INTO — Call Interrupt Procedure

| Mnemonic | P | PII | K6 | 3D! | 3Mx+ | SSE | SSE2 | A64 | SSE3 | E64T |
|----------|---|-----|----|----|------|-----|------|-----|------|------|
| INT      | ✓ | ✓   | ✓  | ✓  | ✓    | ✓   | ✓    | ✓   | ✓    | ✓    |
| INT n    | ✓ | ✓   | ✓  | ✓  | ✓    | ✓   | ✓    | ✓   | ✓    | ✓    |
| INTO     | ✓ | ✓   | ✓  | ✓  | ✓    | ✓   | ✓    | 32  | ✓    | 32   |

```
    int  #
    into
```

This is an operating system instruction typically used by an application to access a BIOS function. This is also referred to as a software interrupt. A hardware interrupt calls an interrupt procedure in response to servicing an IRQ (interrupt request). The base of the computer's memory is at memory location 0000:00000000h. At that base is a vector jump table. Multiplying 4 × the interrupt *number* will give you the offset to the entry that contains the address that will be vectored to.

| Flags | O.flow | Sign | Zero | Aux | Parity | Carry |
|-------|--------|------|------|-----|--------|-------|
|       | -      | -    | -    | -   | -      | -     |

Flags: None are altered by this opcode.

**No 64-bit:** The general-purpose instruction INTO is not available in 64-bit mode.

The interrupt function is typically written in one of two ways. If written to service a hardware interrupt, it services some predefined single task. If written to service a software interrupt, it is written as a function library where it takes values in registers and services them based upon the specialized functionality. On the 80x86 type personal computer the older DOS operating system typically required the application programmer to call the BIOS using the INT instruction to access all the peripherals such as keyboard, display card, mouse, communications port, printer port, timer, etc. Sometimes a peripheral would use more than one interrupt, one to support the BIOS (basic input/ouput system) library interface and one to handle the IRQs.

*Table 10-2: Device, interrupt, address, and IRQ mappings for PC*

| Device | Software INT | Hardware INT | 0000:???? Address | IRQ |
|--------|--------------|--------------|-------------------|-----|
| Debug (Break Point) | 3 | 3 | 000C-000Fh | 8 |
| Keyboard | 16h | 9 | 0058-005Bh | 1 |
|          |     |   | 0024-0027h |   |
| RS232 Com#2 | 14h | 0Bh | 0050-0053h | 3 |
|             |     |     | 002C-002Fh |   |
| RS232 Com#1 | 14h | 0Ch | 0050-0053h | 4 |
|             |     |     | 0030-0033h |   |
| Video | 10h | - | 0040-0043h | - |
| DOS (Primary Access) | 21h | | 0084-0087h | - |
| Mouse | 33h | - | 00CC-00CFh | - |

There are many more interrupts, which are too numerous to list. No matter how the interrupt is written, they all end exactly the same way, with the IRET instruction.

Win32 developers will find that calling the function DebugBreak() actually calls INT 3. This effectively stops the debugger at the position of the instruction pointer.

## IRET/IRETD/IRETQ — Interrupt Return

| Mnemonic | P | PII | K6 | 3D! | 3Mx+ | SSE | SSE2 | A64 | SSE3 | E64T |
|----------|---|-----|----|----|------|-----|------|-----|------|------|
| IRET | ✓ | ✓ | ✓ | ✓ | ✓ | ✓ | ✓ | ✓ | ✓ | ✓ |
| IRETD | ✓ | ✓ | ✓ | ✓ | ✓ | ✓ | ✓ | ✓ | ✓ | ✓ |
| IRETQ | | | | | | | | 64 | | 64 |

| | | |
|---|---|---|
| iret | [Un]Signed | 16 |
| iretd | [Un]Signed | 32 |
| iretq | [Un]Signed | 64 |

This is a general-purpose instruction used to return from an interrupt to a previous location in memory.

| Flags | O.flow | Sign | Zero | Aux | Parity | Carry |
|-------|--------|------|------|-----|--------|-------|
| | - | - | - | - | - | - |

Flags: None are altered by this opcode.

## CLI/STI — Clear (Reset)/Set Interrupt Flag

| Mnemonic | P | PII | K6 | 3D! | 3Mx+ | SSE | SSE2 | A64 | SSE3 | E64T |
|----------|---|-----|----|----|------|-----|------|-----|------|------|
| CLI | ✓ | ✓ | ✓ | ✓ | ✓ | ✓ | ✓ | ✓ | ✓ | ✓ |
| STI | ✓ | ✓ | ✓ | ✓ | ✓ | ✓ | ✓ | ✓ | ✓ | ✓ |

cli
sti

The STI instruction is used to set the interrupt flag, thus enabling (allowing) interrupts, and the CLI instruction is used to clear the interrupt flag, thus disabling (preventing) interrupts. It should be noted that NMI (non-maskable interrupts) and exceptions are not prevented.

| Flags | O.flow | Sign | Zero | Aux | Parity | Carry |
|-------|--------|------|------|-----|--------|-------|
| | - | - | - | - | - | - |

Flags: None are altered by this opcode.

When an interrupt is being serviced due to an elapsed timer, keyboard key pressed, communications received or sent, etc., the interrupt flag bit is automatically cleared to 0, thus preventing any other interrupts from interrupting (disturbing) the interrupt code already being run. The interrupt flag is automatically set to 1 upon the IRET instruction being executed.

```
IService proc   far
          push   eax

;                Insert your interrupt code here

          pop    eax
          iret
IService endp
```

If an interrupt is going to take some time to process and is not a quick in and out, a programmer will typically insert an STI instruction at the top of the interrupt to allow interrupts to occur. If at some point inter-rupt-critical hardware is being accessed, the CLI instruction will be called first to temporarily disable interrupts, the hardware will be accessed, and the STI instruction will be used to immediately allow interrupts again.

```
IService proc   far
          sti                 ; Enable Interrupts
          push   eax

;                Insert your interrupt code here

          pop    eax
          iret
IService endp
```

When interrupts are re-enabled inside an interrupt, there is a possibility that the event that instigated the interrupt can cause a new event requesting a new interrupt before the interrupt was done servicing the first interrupt. This interrupt "nesting" needs to be accounted for in your code through the use of a flag, etc., typically not allowing the body of the interrupt code to be executed by the second (nested) interrupt. It should return immediately. The body of the code, however, should take into account that interrupt nesting may have taken place and therefore should compensate for it. A simple directly manipulated flag can solve this problem. Something to keep in mind is that the only absolute is the code segment where the interrupt is! Data is unknown, so we actually store the data segment value in the code segment so we can access the application data.

```
IServCS   dw    0
IServCnt  dd    0

IService  proc  far
          test  cs:IServCnt,0
          jnz   $Nest           ; Jump if reinterant

          inc   cs:IServCnt     ; Set our flag
          sti                   ; Enable interrupts
          push  ds              ; Save data segment
          push  eax             ; Save any registers we'll use

          mov   ds,cs:IServCS   ; Get our real Data Segment

;               Insert your interrupt code here

          cli   ; Disable interrupts
;               Insert your interrupt-sensitive hardware code
          sti   ; Enable interrupts

;               Insert your other interrupt code here

          pop   eax             ; Restore registers
          pop   ds
          dec   cs:IServCnt

$Nest:    iret
IService  endp
```

You should note that the flag test occurred before the interrupt was
re-enabled. This was to ensure that another interrupt did not occur while
the possibility of nested interrupt was tested for. If application code
wants to *very* temporarily stop interrupts so it can set up interrupt-sensi-
tive hardware, all it needs to do is call the CLI instruction followed by a
STI instruction.

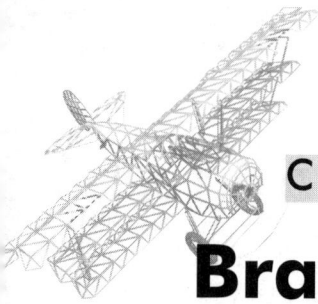

# Chapter 11
# Branchless

Okay, we learned how to branch in the last chapter. We also learned about some branchless coding methods such as the butterfly switch and value setting using bit blending. Now let's learn how to make decisions without branching. You have already learned instructions such as the bit test and set. Here you will be shown how to use masking logic to get the same result as one would with the use of branching. The first item to learn is that the MSB (negative bit #31) and Carry bits are your friends! Two values can be subtracted to obtain a positive or negative threshold, and then the resulting state of the MSB can be arithmetically shifted to create a mask of all ones or zeros. That mask can be used to mask or blend bits.

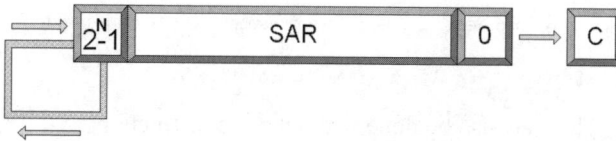

There is only one trick, however. The values need to be one bit less than the data size so as to take advantage of the MSB. Data could be shifted by the bit width of the data, but on some older embedded processors there are penalties for each shifted bit.

```
#define UINT_MAX_BITS   (sizeof(uint)  <<3)      // 32-bit value = 32
#define INT_MAX_BITS    ((sizeof(int)  <<3)-1)   // 32-bit value = 31
#define UCHAR_MAX_BITS  (sizeof(uchar) <<3)      // 8-bit value = 8
#define CHAR_MAX_BITS   ((sizeof(char) <<3)-1)   // 8-bit value = 7
```

# Function y=ABS(x) 'Absolute' D = | A |

Floating-point FABS was discussed in Chapter 8, "Floating-Point Anyone?" Here we will investigate packed integer-based floating-point. There is sometimes found in C code a macro definition similar to:

```
#define ABS(x) ((x) < 0 ? -(x) : (x))
```

But it can be easily replaced in C without the conditional test:

```
__inline int ABS(x)
{
    int y;
    y = x >> INT_MAX_BITS;
    return (x ^ y) - y;
}
```

In the previous chapter on branching, you found the following example of the signed integer absolute number function y = | x |, which uses a Jcc instruction.

```
        test eax,eax    ; Test if negative
        jns  $Abs       ; Jump if positive

        neg  eax        ; Invert number, two's complement

$Abs:                   ; eax is positive
```

This can also be done without a Jcc instruction:

```
    mov  ecx,eax
    sar  ecx,INT_MAX_BITS ; all one's if neg, else 0's
    xor  eax,ecx          ; At this point we're one's complement
    sub  eax,ecx          ; n-(-1)=n+1 = two's complement
```

Voilà, an ABS() function without any Jcc instructions. Just some sleight of hand using general-purpose instructions.

Let's look a little closer at how this works. Note that it will work on 8-, 16-, or 32-bit numbers in the same way. Below you will find an 8-bit negative number on the left and a positive 8-bit number on the right for a side-by-side comparison.

```
mov cl,al 10001010b 8Ah (-118)  mov dl,bl 01111011b 7Bh (123)
sar cl,7  11111111b FFh          sar dl,7  00000000b 00h
```

The SAR instruction shifts the MSB arithmetically into all the other bit positions, so a negative number becomes all FFs, and a positive number becomes all 00s. Now XOR those bits with their original XOR value. You learned in a previous chapter that 1⊕1=0 and 1⊕0=1.

```
; xor al,cl 01110101b 75h         xor bl,dl 01111011b 7Bh
```

A negative value would actually flip the original value's bits with a one's complement, and a positive value would keep the value intact. We then subtract the new value with that mask, which effectively adds a +1 or +0, thus a two's complement is performed, since n–(–1)=n+1 = two's complement.

```
; cl=        11111111b FFh        dl=        00000000b 00h
; sub al,cl 01110110b 76h (118)   sub bl,dl 01111011b 7Bh (123)
```

Pretty cool, huh! And no branching!

# Function y=MIN(p, q) 'Minimum'

In C code you may find a macro definition similar to:

```
#define MIN(p, q) ((p) < (q) ? (p) : (q))
```

But it can be easily replaced in C without the condition test:

```
__inline MIN(int p, int q)
{
    int r;
        // r=(p < q) ? p : q
    r = (p–q) >> INT_MAX_BITS;    // (–)=0xFFFFFFFF
                                   // (+)=0x00000000
    return (p & r) | (q & (r^–1)); // keep lower of p or q
}
```

Normally there would be a single branch test, but as you will note in the C example above and in the assembly below, there is no branch.

```
MIN PROC C PUBLIC p:DWORD, q:DWORD
    mov edx,p               ; edx = p
    mov ecx,q               ; ecx = q

        ; r=(p < q) ? p : q
        ; r = (p–q) >> INT_MAX_BITS;
        ; (–)=0xFFFFFFFF (+)=0x00000000
    mov eax,edx
    sub eax,ecx
    sar eax,INT_MAX_BITS    ; (int >> 31)

        ; return (p ∧ r) ∨ (q ∧ (¬r))
    and edx,eax             ; (p ∧ r)
    xor eax,–1              ; (¬)
    and eax,ecx             ; q ∧ (¬r)
    or  eax,edx
    ret                     ; result is in eax
MIN endp
```

This function is similar to the ABS() function above. The argument q is subtracted from p to force a negative value if p is less than q. Upon that negative result, a bit mask of all one's is created. By ANDing that mask with p, ANDing the inverse of that mask with q, and ORing the results, the minimum value is retrieved.

# Function y=MAX(p, q) 'Maximum'

The function MAX() would have a similar implementation except that p and q would be internally swapped as shown below.

```
MAX PROC C PUBLIC p:DWORD, q:DWORD
    mov edx,q            ; edx = q
    mov ecx,p            ; ecx = p

    ; r=(q < p) ? q : p
    ; r = (q-p) >> INT_MAX_BITS;
    ; (-)=0xFFFFFFFF (+)=0x00000000
    mov eax,edx
    sub eax,ecx
    sar eax,INT_MAX_BITS    ; (int >> 31)

    ; return (q ∧ r) ∨ (p ∧ (¬r))
    and edx,eax          ; (q ∧ r)
    xor eax,-1           ; (¬r)
    and eax,ecx          ; p ∧ (¬r)
    or  eax,edx
    ret                  ; result is in eax
MAX endp
```

There is also something to note in this code. This is a single MIN() function test. As such there is no branch, but there are dependency stalls. The EAX register is constantly being reassigned or operated upon and thus stalling any pipelining. The good news is that it is still faster than the branch. If a particular pair of arrays needed to have a similar operation performed, the code could be intermixed in such a way that pipelining could be used to advantage.

Then again, remember that job interview question in the previous chapter? It was related to writing a STRUPR() function. Let's try that again!

```
;       strupr snippet
xyzzy   db      "Quick brown fox jumped!",0

        mov   al,[edx]   ; Get a character
```

```
        if 0                    ; *** Old Branching Code ***

$L1: cmp   al,'a'
     jb    $L2                  ; (1) Jump if symbols or uppercase
     cmp   al,'z'
     ja    $L2                  ; (2) Jump if extended ASCII

     sub   al,20h               ; Convert to uppercase
     mov   [edx],al             ; Save altered character

$L2: inc   edx                  ; Nothing to do; next!
     mov   al,[edx]             ; Get a character
     test  al,al
     jnz   $L1                  ; 0 terminator?

        else                    ; *** New Branchless Code ***

$L1: mov   ah,al
     sub   ah,'a'
     sub   al,'z'+1
     shr   ah,2                 ; xx?xxxxxb  <'a'=0x20  else 0x00
     shr   al,2                 ; xx?xxxxxb  ≤ 'z'=0x20 else 0x00
     xor   ah,0ffh              ; Flip the bits
     and   ah,al                ; Blend the ~'a' and 'z' masks
     and   ah,020h              ; 00X00000b strip masking bit
     sub   [edx],ah             ; −00h or −20h adjustment to character
     inc   edx                  ; Nothing to do; next!

     mov   al,[edx]             ; Get the next character
     test  al,al
     jnz   $L1                  ; 0 terminator?
     endif
```

In the old branching code section you will notice the two branches, which can be costly in mispredictions. Statistically, there will be more lowercase than uppercase and symbols, and an even higher misprediction rate if Single-Byte Character System (SBCS) international characters are involved. The branchless code is not very optimized, but you will notice some pairing between the AL and AH registers processing the lower and upper limits of the inclusive character range of a to z. There are still some stalls near the bottom of the loop, but there are no prediction errors or CPU cycle hits from having to take a branch; thus, the new code is faster. By spending some optimization time intermixing the looping logic with the actual masking logic, the register dependencies can be reduced even further, allowing the code to run even faster.

```
$L1: mov   ah,al
     sub   al,'z'+1
     sub   ah,'a'
```

```
        shr   al,2        ; xx?xxxxxb ≤ 'z'=0x20 else 0x00
        shr   ah,2        ; xx?xxxxxb <'a'=0x20  else 0x00
        inc   edx         ; Nothing to do; next!
        not   ah          ; Flip the bit
;ah stall
        and   ah,al       ; Blend the ~'a' and 'z' masks
        mov   al,[edx]    ; Get the next character
        and   ah,020h     ; 00X00000b strip masking bit
;ah stall
        sub   [edx-1],ah  ; -00h or -20h adjustment to character

        test  al,al
        jnz   $L1         ; 0 terminator?
```

8-bit values can be mirrored, loaded into a 32-bit register, and then processed simultaneously, but there would be a significant stall in doing so. Experiment and give it a try anyway!

So now you are probably thinking, "That was silly, since it will probably never be needed!" Just remember that it just might be your next job interview test question. When writing code in optimized assembly, one has to initially decide whether it is worthwhile and an efficient use of time. I am sorry to say that string converters are typically not; however, the principles you learned here can be applied to both the C and assembly world of programming, making your code faster and more efficient, and earning the admiration of your fellow programming team, the recognition (or lack thereof) by your manager, and hopefully a better performance review and hefty pay hike! Or not!

# Graphics 101 — Quick 2D Distance

Quick 2D distance formulas are used for calculating waypoints in an isometric (flat) terrain-based computer world, artificial intelligence (AI) in path finding, and in (pre-) collision detection and other tasks, but these calculations need not be very accurate, only quick. Normally, to find a 2D distance one merely uses the Pythagorean theorem: $dx^2+dy^2=r^2$, hence $r=sqrt(dx^2+dy^2)$. You remember the hypotenuse of the triangle from a geometry lesson in school: the shortest line between two points. A 3D distance would use the equation $dx^2+dy^2+dz^2=r^2$. The problem is that the 2D version would require two multiplications, an addition, and a costly square root calculation. That would take too much time when a series of these calculations need to be performed. Since accuracy is not required, a formula such as the following could be used as an alternative. Note that this has a compiled code length of 127 bytes.

```
int Quick2DDist(int x1, int y1, int x2, int y2)
{
    int dx, dy;

    dx = (x2-x1) < 0 ? (x1-x2) : (x2-x1); // dx= | x2-x1 |
    dy = (y2-y1) < 0 ? (y1-y2) : (y2-y1); // dy= | y2-y1 |
    return((dx < dy) ? dy+(dx>>1) : dx+(dy>>1));
}
```

The equation returns a summation of the longest axis and half the shortest axis. It is fairly efficient but contains three conditional branches that can be removed and instead use masking logic to make it even faster. The ABS() function was discussed in detail earlier in this chapter. The new algorithm is a comparison with a substitution. So applying what we have learned about branchless coding we get this new function:

```
int Quick2DDist(int x1, int y1, int x2, int y2)
{
    int x, y, dx, dy;

        // dx=ABS(x2-x1);   dy=ABS(y2-y1);
    x = (x2-x1);
    y = (y2-y1);
    dx = x >> INT_MAX_BITS;
    dy = y >> INT_MAX_BITS;
    dx = (x ^ dx) - dx;
    dy = (y ^ dy) - dy;

        // return( (dx < dy) ? dy+(dx>>1) : dx+(dy>>1));
    x = dy + (dx >> 1);
    y = dx + (dy >> 1);
    dx = (dx-dy) >> INT_MAX_BITS;
    return (x & dx) | (y & (dx^-1));
}
```

Note that this function has a length of 133 bytes and is only slightly larger than the previous, but runs much faster. There is no branching, and it's been set up for pipelining although the compiler will optimize it in its own way. This would normally be good enough but if there is a need for more speed, then check out the following conversion of this optimized C code to assembly.

```
Quick2DDist PROC C PUBLIC x1:DWORD, y1:DWORD, x2:DWORD, y2:DWORD
    push ebx
        ; dx = |x2-x1|    dy = |y2-y1|
    mov  ecx,y2          ; y = (y2-y1)
    mov  ebx,x2          ; x = (x2-x1)
    sub  ecx,y1
    sub  ebx,x1
```

```
        ; dx = x >> INT_MAX_BITS;   dy = y >> INT_MAX_BITS
mov  edx,ecx
mov  eax,ebx
sar  edx,INT_MAX_BITS
sar  eax,INT_MAX_BITS

        ; dx = (x ⊕ dx) - dx;        dy = (y ⊕ dy) - dy
xor  ecx,edx            ; (y⊕dy)
xor  ebx,eax            ; (x⊕dx)
sub  ecx,edx            ; ecx=dy
sub  ebx,eax            ; ebx=dx

     ; return((dx < dy) ? dy+(dx>>1) : dx+(dy>>1));
mov  edx,ecx
mov  eax,ebx
shr  edx,1              ; (dy>>1)
shr  eax,1              ; (dx>>1)
add  edx,ebx           ; y = dx + (dy >> 1);

sub  ebx,ecx           ; r=(dx-dy)

add  eax,ecx           ; x = dy + (dx >> 1);

sar  ebx,INT_MAX_BITS ; r=(+)=00's or (-)=FF's
     ; ebx=r (dx mask)   eax=x edx=y

     ; ebx stall
     ; return (x ∧ r) ∨ (y ∧ (¬r))
mov  ecx,ebx           ; (r)
and  eax,ebx           ; (x ∧ r)
not  ecx               ; Flip mask
     ; ecx stall
and  edx,ecx           ; (y ∧ (¬r))
pop  ebx
or   eax,edx           ; eax = distance
ret
Quick2DDist endp
```

Note that this only requires half the length of either version of the C code as it is only 66 bytes in length. Since it was hand optimized assembly and not C, it is that much faster because of reduced code cache fetches and fewer stalls. Keep in mind that code written in assembly is not always smaller; in fact, it is typically larger, but this just demonstrates some hidden benefits. Again, you will note the blended instructions to support two pipelines, but unfortunately there are two remaining register stalls. By not using the proc macro, the POP EBP and POP EBX instructions can be moved up, removing one of the stalls. If you look carefully, the code is visually paired until you get about half-way down, at which point the logic gets a little foggy. That is because lower code was moved up to remove additional register stalls that would have occurred, and thus making the code less readable.

Again, please remember that you should rewrite your C code in an attempt to break it into simpler components, keeping in mind that it should be readable. Once this is proven to run, then work on the assembly code using this fresher C version as a template to follow. Use the Carry or one of the data bits such as the MSB to smear the bit pattern across the other bits as required. The alternative method would be to use the SET instruction to obtain a 0 or 1, then a decrement to get a −1 or 0 for a mask.

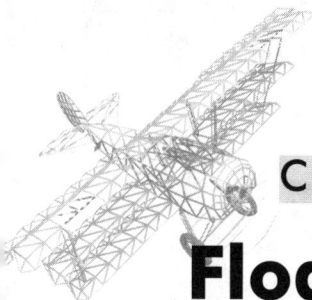

# Chapter 12

# Floating-Point Vector Addition and Subtraction

The topic of floating-point was discussed back in Chapter 8, "Floating-Point Anyone?" As the same methodologies of SIMD processing learned in Chapter 7, "Integer Math," apply for packed floating-point, it does not matter whether one is calculating the sum or the product. However, there is one exception. With integer addition, the data width increases by one bit. With integer multiplication, the data width increases by 2N bits. With floating-point, the number occupies the same number of bits. So with that said, let's jump right into packed floating-point addition.

The samples are actually three different types of examples: a standard single data element solution; a 3D value, typically an {XYZ} value; or a 4D value, {XYZW}. Integer or fixed point is important, but in terms of fast 3D processing, single-precision floating-point is of more interest.

**Workbench Files:** \Bench\x86\chap12\\*project*\\*platform*

| Add/Sub | *project* | *platform* |
|---------|-----------|------------|
| **3D Float** | \vas3d\ | \vc.net |
| **4vec Float** | \qvas3d\ | |

# Floating-Point Vector Addition and Subtraction

## Vector Floating-Point Addition

Single-Precision   128-bit / 64-bit (16 / 8 Byte ) Addition

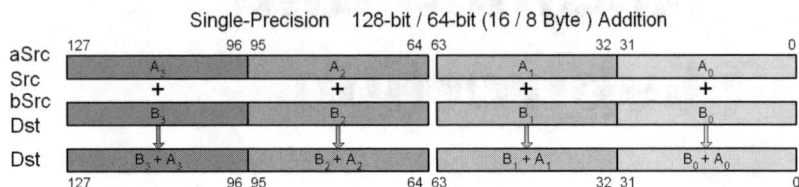

$$d_{(0 \ldots n-1)} = a_{(0 \ldots n-1)} + b_{(0 \ldots n-1)} \quad n = \{4, 2\}$$

| Mnemonic | P | PII | K6 | 3D! | 3Mx+ | SSE | SSE2 | A64 | SSE3 | E64T |
|----------|---|-----|----|----|------|-----|------|-----|------|------|
| ADDPD    |   |     |    |    |      |     | ✓    | ✓   | ✓    | ✓    |
| ADDPS    |   |     |    |    |      | ✓   | ✓    | ✓   | ✓    | ✓    |
| PFADD    |   |     |    | ✓  | ✓    |     |      | ✓   |      |      |

| | | | |
|---|---|---|---|
| 3DNow! | pfadd  *mmxDst, mmxSrc/mm64* | Single-precision | 64 |
| SSE    | addps  *xmmDst, xmmSrc/m128* | Single-precision | 128 |
| SSE2   | addpd  *xmmDst, xmmSrc/m128* | Double-precision | 128 |

This vector instruction is a parallel operation that uses an adder on each of the source floating-point blocks *aSrc (xmmSrc)* and *bSrc (xmmDst)* and stores the result in the destination *Dst (xmmDst)*.

The instructions may be labeled as packed, parallel, or vector, but each block of floating-point bits is in reality isolated from one another.

The following are 64/128-bit single- and double-precision summation samples.

### 64-bit single-precision floating-point

| 63...32 | 31...0 |
|---------|--------|
| 120.885 | −86.479 |
| + −120.622 | + 30.239 |
| 0.263 | −56.240 |

### 128-bit single-precision floating-point

| 127...96 | 95...64 | 63...32 | 31...0 |
|---|---|---|---|
| 56.929 | −20.193 | 120.885 | −86.479 |
| + −124.783 | + −49.245 | + −120.622 | + 30.239 |
| −67.854 | −69.438 | 0.263 | −56.240 |

### 128-bit double-precision floating-point

| 127...64 | 63...0 |
|---|---|
| −75.499 | 57.480 |
| + 124.073 | + −50.753 |
| 48.574 | 6.727 |

# Vector Floating-Point Addition with Scalar

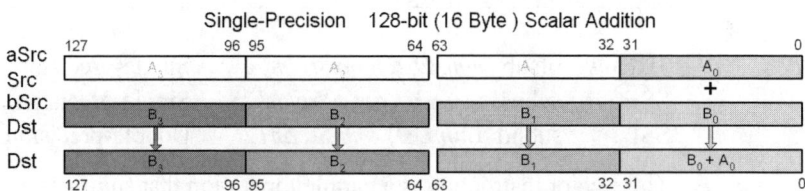

Single-Precision    128-bit (16 Byte ) Scalar Addition

$$d_{(0)} = a_{(0)} + b_{(0)}$$

| Mnemonic | P | PII | K6 | 3D! | 3Mx+ | SSE | SSE2 | A64 | SSE3 | E64T |
|---|---|---|---|---|---|---|---|---|---|---|
| ADDSD | | | | | | | ✓ | ✓ | ✓ | ✓ |
| ADDSS | | | | | | ✓ | ✓ | ✓ | ✓ | ✓ |

SSE    addss    *xmmDst, xmmSrc/m32*    Single-precision    128

SSE2    addsd    *xmmDst, xmmSrc/m64*    Double-precision    128

This vector instruction is a scalar operation that uses an adder with the source scalar *xmmSrc* and the source floating-point value in the least significant block within *xmmDst* and stores the result in the destination *xmmDst*. The upper float elements are unaffected.

# Vector Floating-Point Subtraction

Single-Precision    128-bit / 64-bit (16 / 8 Byte ) Subtraction

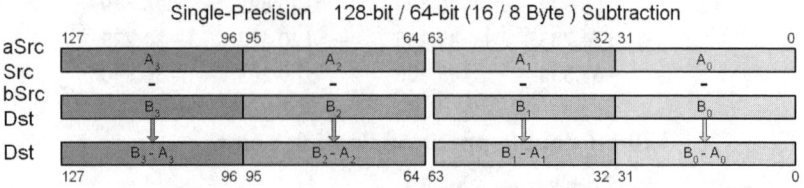

$$d_{(0\ldots n-1)} = b_{(0\ldots n-1)} - a_{(0\ldots n-1)} \quad n=\{4, 2\}$$

| Mnemonic | P | PII | K6 | 3D! | 3Mx+ | SSE | SSE2 | A64 | SSE3 | E64T |
|----------|---|-----|-----|-----|------|-----|------|-----|------|------|
| PFSUB    |   |     |    | ✓   | ✓    |     |      | ✓   |      |      |
| SUBPD    |   |     |    |     |      |     | ✓    | ✓   | ✓    | ✓    |
| SUBPS    |   |     |    |     |      | ✓   | ✓    | ✓   | ✓    | ✓    |

3DNow!  pfsub  *mmxDst, mmxSrc/m64*     Single-precision    64
SSE     subps  *xmmDst, xmmSrc/m128*    Single-precision    128
SSE2    subpd  *xmmDst, xmmSrc/m128*    Double-precision    128

This vector instruction is a parallel operation that subtracts each of the source floating-point blocks *aSrc (xmmSrc)* from *bSrc (xmmDst)* with the result stored in the destination *Dst (xmmDst)*.

**Note:** Be careful here as A − B ≠ B − A.

The register and operator ordering is as follows:

$$xmmDst_{(31\ldots0)} = xmmDst_{(31\ldots0)} - xmmSrc_{(31\ldots0)} \quad \text{D}-=\text{A}$$
$$Dst_{(31\ldots0)} = bSrc_{(31\ldots0)} - aSrc_{(31\ldots0)} \quad \text{D}=\text{B}-\text{A}$$

The instructions may be labeled as packed, parallel, or vector, but each block of floating-point bits is in reality isolated from one another.

### 64-bit single-precision floating-point

| 63...32 | 31...0 |
|---------|--------|
| −98.854 | 124.264 |
| − 50.315 | − 33.952 |
| −48.539 | 158.216 |

### 128-bit single-precision floating-point

| 127...96 | 95...64 | 63...32 | 31...0 |
|---|---|---|---|
| –64.185 | 108.856 | –98.854 | 124.264 |
| – 114.223 | – –117.045 | – 50.315 | – 33.952 |
| –178.408 | 225.901 | –48.539 | 158.216 |

### 128-bit double-precision floating-point

| 127...64 | 63...0 |
|---|---|
| –48.043 | 127.277 |
| – –106.051 | – –77.288 |
| 58.008 | 204.565 |

# Vector Floating-Point Subtraction with Scalar

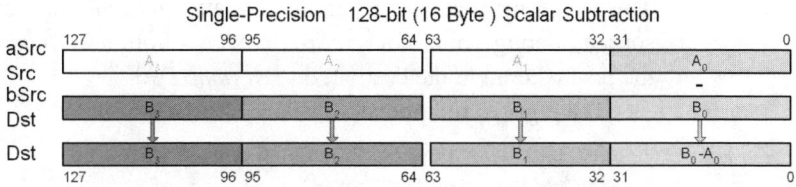

Single-Precision 128-bit (16 Byte ) Scalar Subtraction

$$d_{(0)} = b_{(0)} - a_{(0)}$$

| Mnemonic | P | PII | K6 | 3D! | 3Mx+ | SSE | SSE2 | A64 | SSE3 | E64T |
|---|---|---|---|---|---|---|---|---|---|---|
| SUBSD |  |  |  |  |  |  | ✓ | ✓ | ✓ | ✓ |
| SUBSS |  |  |  |  |  | ✓ | ✓ | ✓ | ✓ | ✓ |

SSE     subss *xmmDst, xmmSrc/m32*    Single-precision     128

SSE2    subsd *xmmDst, xmmSrc/m64*    Double-precision    128

This vector instruction is a scalar operation that subtracts the least significant source floating-point block of *xmmSrc* from the same block in *xmmDst* and stores the result in the destination *xmmDst*. The upper float elements are unaffected.

# Vector Floating-Point Reverse Subtraction

Single-Precision   64-bit ( 8 Byte ) Subtraction

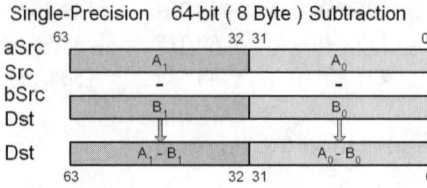

$$d_{(0...1)} = a_{(0...1)} - b_{(0...1)}$$

| Mnemonic | P | PII | K6 | 3D! | 3Mx+ | SSE | SSE2 | A64 | SSE3 | E64T |
|----------|---|-----|----|-----|------|-----|------|-----|------|------|
| PFSUBR   |   |     |    | ✓   | ✓    |     |      | ✓   |      |      |

3DNow!   pfsubr *mmxDst, mmxSrc/m64*   Single-Precision   64

This vector instruction is a parallel operation that subtracts each of the source floating-point blocks *bSrc (mmxDst)* from *aSrc (mmxSrc)* with the result stored in the destination *Dst (mmxDst)*.

The register and operator ordering is as follows:

$$mmxDst_{(31...0)} = mmxSrc_{(31...0)} - mmxDst_{(31...0)} \quad D = A - D$$
$$Dst_{(31...0)} = aSrc_{(31...0)} - bSrc_{(31...0)} \quad D = A - B$$

The instructions may be labeled as packed, parallel, or vector, but each block of floating-point bits is in reality isolated from one another.

A typical subtraction uses an equation similar to {a=a–b}, but what happens if the equation {a=b–a} is needed instead? This instruction solves that situation by limiting any special handling needed to exchange values between registers such as the following:

```
c[0]=a[0];          c[1]=a[1];

a[0]=b[0];          a[1]=b[1];

a[0]=a[0] – c[0];   a[1]=a[1] – c[1];

b[0]=c[0];          b[1]=c[1];
```

or

```
exchange(a, b)    A=b      B=a ← a=a  b=b
A = A – B         b=b–a    a=a
exchange(a, b)    a=(b–a) b=a ← b=(b–a)  a=a
```

# Pseudo Vec

By now you should be very aware that you should be using assertions in your code such as the ASSERT_PTR4 for normal pointers and ASSERT_PTR16 for pointers to vectors to ensure they are properly aligned in memory, so I will try not to bore you with it much anymore in print. You should also by now be aware of the penalties for dealing with out of alignment memory. Keep these in mind when writing your own code. There is also a limitation on the use of the term *const* to help make the printed code less wordy and more clear.

You will find that for purposes of cross-platform compatibility, these functions return no arguments. They are instead written as procedures where the first argument points to a buffer that the result is stored in. This is not written to make your life confusing. It is written this way because of one particular processor: the 80x86. Due to its MMX versus FPU usage an EMMS instruction must be called to reset that functionality as a clean slate, so only one of them can be used at a time. By not returning a value such as a float or array of floats, it minimizes the risk that the programmer might accidentally try to use the returned value while in the wrong mode. In this way the vmp_SIMDEntry() and vmp_SIMDExit() procedure calls are made to assist in switching between FPU and MMX mode of operation. Since most of you will be focused upon float and not integer or fixed-point vector math, that will be the focus, but the principles are the same!

The simple addition and subtraction of a single (scalar) float has been included here as a reference.

## Single-Precision Float Addition

Listing 12-1: ...\chap12\fas\Fas.cpp

```
void vmp_FAdd(float *pfD, float fA, float fB)
{
   *pfD = fA + fB;
}
```

## Single-Precision Float Subtraction

Listing 12-2: ...\chap12\fas\Fas.cpp

```
void vmp_FSub(float *pfD, float fA, float fB)
{
   *pfD = fA - fB;
}
```

The above are simple scalar addition and subtraction using single-precision floats. Now view the addition of two vectors containing a three-cell {XYZ} float.

## Single-Precision Vector Float Addition

*Listing 12-3: ...\chap12\vas3d\Vas3D.cpp*

```
void vmp_VecAdd(vmp3DVector * const pvD,
          const vmp3DVector * const pvA,
          const vmp3DVector * const pvB)
{
  pvD->x = pvA->x + pvB->x;
  pvD->y = pvA->y + pvB->y;
  pvD->z = pvA->z + pvB->z;
}
```

## Single-Precision Vector Float Subtraction

*Listing 12-4: ...\chap12\vas3d\Vas3D.cpp*

```
void vmp_VecSub(vmp3DVector * const pvD,
          const vmp3DVector * const pvA,
          const vmp3DVector * const pvB)
{
  pvD->x = pvA->x - pvB->x;
  pvD->y = pvA->y - pvB->y;
  pvD->z = pvA->z - pvB->z;
}
```

Now view the addition and subtraction of two vectors containing a four-cell (quad) {XYZW} single-precision float. For the sample cross-platform libraries there is a differentiation as a Vec is a standard 3D tri-elemental value, and a QVec is a full four-quad float vector. The Vec is more oriented to the AoS (Array of Structures) approach, and the QVec would work best in a SoA (Structure of Arrays). These concepts will be discussed later.

## Single-Precision Quad Vector Float Addition

*Listing 12-5: ...\chap12\qvas3d\QVas3D.cpp*

```
void vmp_QVecAdd(vmp3DQVector * const pvD,
          const vmp3DQVector * const pvA,
          const vmp3DQVector * const pvB)
{
  pvD->x = pvA->x + pvB->x;
  pvD->y = pvA->y + pvB->y;
  pvD->z = pvA->z + pvB->z;
  pvD->w = pvA->w + pvB->w;
}
```

### Single-Precision Quad Vector Float Subtraction

*Listing 12-6: ...\chap12\qvas3d\QVas3D.cpp*

```
void vmp_QVecSub(vmp3DQVector * const pvD,
         const vmp3DQVector * const pvA,
         const vmp3DQVector * const pvB)
{
  pvD->x = pvA->x - pvB->x;
  pvD->y = pvA->y - pvB->y;
  pvD->z = pvA->z - pvB->z;
  pvD->w = pvA->w - pvB->w;
}
```

# Pseudo Vec (x86)

Now examine these functions closer using x86 assembly. As MMX does not support floating-point, only 3DNow!, SSE, and above can be utilized. 3DNow! supports 64-bit so two loads must be handled simultaneously and two stores, but it is a simple matter of adding the two pairs of floats to each other. This example shows that three floats {XYZ} are being used and the fourth element {W} is being ignored.

```
mov   eax,vA   ; Vector A
mov   ebx,vB   ; Vector B
mov   edx,vD   ; Vector destination
```

### vmp_VecAdd   (3DNow!)

*Listing 12-7: ...\chap12\vas3d\Vas3DX86M.asm*

```
movq  mm0,[eax]                     ; vA.xy {Ay Ax}
movq  mm2,[ebx]                     ; vB.xy {By Bx}
movd  mm1,(vmp3DVector PTR [eax]).z ; {0 Az}
movd  mm3,(vmp3DVector PTR [ebx]).z ; {0 Bz}
pfadd mm0,mm2                       ; {Ay+By Ax+Bx}
pfadd mm1,mm3                       ; {0+0 Az+Bz}
movq  [edx],mm0                     ; {Ay+By Ax+Bx}
movd  (vmp3DVector PTR [edx]).z,mm1 ; {0 Az+Bz}
```

### vmp_VecSub   (3DNow!)

For subtraction, the functions are virtually identical to the addition functions, except for the exchanging of a PFSUB for the PFADD.

*Listing 12-8: ...\chap12\vas3d\Vas3DX86M.asm*

```
movq  mm0,[eax]                     ; vA.xy {Ay Ax}
movq  mm2,[ebx]                     ; vB.xy {By Bx}
movd  mm1,(vmp3DVector PTR [eax]).z ; {0 Az}
movd  mm3,(vmp3DVector PTR [ebx]).z ; {0 Bz}
pfsub mm0,mm2                       ; {Ay-By Ax-Bx}
```

```
pfsub  mm1,mm3                            ; {0-0  Az-Bz}
movq   [edx],mm0                          ; {Ay-By Ax-Bx}
movd   (vmp3DVector PTR [edx]).z,mm1      ; {0 Az-Bz}
```

## vmp_QVecAdd (3DNow!)

A quad vector access is not much different. Instead of loading a single float for each vector, a double float pair is loaded instead using a MOVQ instead of a MOVD.

### Listing 12-9: ...\chap12\vas3d\Vas3DX86M.asm

```
movq   mm0,[eax+0]            ; vA.xy {Ay Ax}
movq   mm2,[ebx+0]            ; vB.xy {By Bx}
movq   mm1,[eax+8]            ; vA.zw {Aw Az}
movq   mm3,[ebx+8]            ; vB.zw {Bw Bz}
pfadd  mm0,mm2                ; {Ay+By Ax+Bx}
pfadd  mm1,mm3                ; {Aw+Bw Az+Bz}
movq   [edx+0],mm0            ; {Ay+By Ax+Bx}
movq   [edx+8],mm1            ; {Aw+Bw Az+Bz}
```

## vmp_VecAdd (SSE) Unaligned

The SSE processor in the following code snippet can load 128 bits at a time, so the entire 96-bit vector can be loaded at once including an extra 32 bits. This introduces a problem of contamination when the 96-bit value is written to memory as 128 bits. The solution is to read those destination bits, preserve the upper 32 bits, and write the newly merged 128 bits. Keep in mind efficient memory organization and memory tail padding previously discussed in Chapter 4, "Bit Mangling." Data can be misaligned or aligned, but 128-bit alignment would be preferable.

You now need to review two SSE instructions: MOVAPS and MOVUPS. This was introduced in Chapter 3, "Processor Differential Insight."

■ MOVAPS — is for use in *aligned* memory access of single-precision floating-point values.

■ MOVUPS — is for use in *unaligned* memory access of single-precision floating-point values.

One other item that should be brought to light is the special handling required by vectors versus quad vectors. As previously discussed in Chapter 4, the vector is three single-precision floats 96 bits in size, but when accessed as a vector, 128 bits are accessed simultaneously. This means that those extra 32 bits must be preserved and not destroyed. Also, the data contained within it must not be expected to be a float; it should be garbage data to that particular expression but valid data to another expression, and thus must be treated as such. Therefore, the easiest method is to clear and then restore those bits. The following declarations work nicely as masks for bit blending just for that purpose:

```
himsk32 DWORD 000000000h, 000000000h, 000000000h,
                0FFFFFFFFh    ; Save upper 32 bits
lomsk96 DWORD 0FFFFFFFFh, 0FFFFFFFFh, 0FFFFFFFFh,
                000000000h    ; Save lower 96 bits
```

Also note that if bits are being preserved with a mask, then others are being cleared to zero. Of course it depends upon the endian type byte ordering of the platform but for x86 it is as listed!

Listing 12-10: ...\chap12\vas3d\Vas3DX86M.asm

```
movups  xmm2,[edx]              ; vD.xyzw {Dw Dz Dy Dx}
movups  xmm0,[ebx]              ; vB.xyzw {Bw Bz By Bx}
movups  xmm1,[eax]              ; vA.xyzw {Aw Az Ay Ax}
andps   xmm2,OWORD PTR himsk32  ; {Dw  0   0   0}
addps   xmm0,xmm1               ; {Aw+Bw Az+Bz Ay+By Ax+Bx}
andps   xmm0,OWORD PTR lomsk96  ; {0 Az+Bz Ay+By Ax+Bx}
orps    xmm0,xmm2               ; {Dw Az+Bz Ay+By Ax+Bx}
movups  [edx],xmm0              ; {Dw  Dz   Dy    Dx}
```

## vmp_VecAdd (SSE) Aligned

By replacing the MOVUPS marked in bold with MOVAPS the data *must* be properly aligned or an exception will occur, but the application will run more smoothly. This is where two versions of the function would work out nicely. One is for when data alignment is unknown, and the other is for when alignment is guaranteed.

Listing 12-11: ...\chap12\vas3d\Vas3DX86M.asm

```
movaps  xmm2,[edx]              ; vD.xyzw {Dw Dz Dy Dx}
movaps  xmm0,[ebx]              ; vB.xyzw {Bw Bz By Bx}
movaps  xmm1,[eax]              ; vA.xyzw {Aw Az Ay Ax}
andps   xmm2,OWORD PTR himsk32  ; {Dw  0   0   0}
addps   xmm0,xmm1               ; {Aw+Bw Az+Bz Ay+By Ax+Bx}
andps   xmm0,OWORD PTR lomsk96  ; {0 Az+Bz Ay+By Ax+Bx}
orps    xmm0,xmm2               ; {Dw Az+Bz Ay+By Ax+Bx}
movaps  [edx],xmm0              ; {Dw  Dz   Dy    Dx}
```

The code looks almost identical, so from this point forward, the book will only show the aligned code using MOVAPS.

## vmp_QVecAdd (SSE) Aligned

And for quad vectors, it is even easier as there is no masking of the fourth float {W}; just read, evaluate, and then write! Of course the function should have the instructions arranged for purposes of optimization but here they are left in a readable form.

*Listing 12-12: ...\chap12\qvas3d\QVas3DX86M.asm*

```
movaps  xmm1,[ebx]  ; {Bw Bz By Bx}
movaps  xmm0,[eax]  ; {Aw Az Ay Ax}
addps   xmm0,xmm1   ; {Aw+Bw Az+Bz Ay+By Ax+Bx}
movaps  [edx],xmm0  ; {Dw    Dz    Dy    Dx}
```

# Vector Scalar Addition and Subtraction

Scalar addition and subtraction of vectors are also a relative simple matter for vector math instructions to handle. Scalar math appears in one of two forms: either a single element processed within each vector, or one element is swizzled, shuffled, or splat (see Chapter 6, "Data Conversion") into each element position and applied to the other source vector. When this type instruction is not supported by a processor, the trick is to replicate the scalar so it appears as a second vector.

## Single-Precision Quad Vector Float Scalar Addition

*Listing 12-13: ...\chap12\vas3d\Vas3D.cpp*

```
void vmp_VecAddScalar(vmp3DVector * const pvD,
    const vmp3DVector * const pvA, float fScalar)
{
  pvD->x = pvA->x + fScalar;
  pvD->y = pvA->y + fScalar;
  pvD->z = pvA->z + fScalar;
}
```

## Single-Precision Quad Vector Float Scalar Subtraction

*Listing 12-14: ...\chap12\qvas3d\QVas3D.cpp*

```
void vmp_VecSubScalar(vmp3DVector * const pvD,
    const vmp3DVector * const pvA, float fScalar)
{
  pvD->x = pvA->x - fScalar;
  pvD->y = pvA->y - fScalar;
  pvD->z = pvA->z - fScalar;
}
```

Did that look strangely familiar? The big question now is, "How do we replicate a scalar to look like a vector since there tends not to be mirrored scalar math on processors?" Typically a processor will interpret a scalar calculation as the lowest (first) float being evaluated with a single *scalar* float. This is fine and dandy, but there are frequent times when a scalar needs to be replicated and summed to each element of a vector. So the next question is how do we do that?

With the 3DNow! instruction set it is easy. Since the processor is really a 64-bit half vector, the data is merely unpacked into the upper and lower 32 bits.

```
movd       mm2,fScalar    ; fScalar {0 s}
punpckldq  mm2,mm2        ; fScalar {s s}
```

Then it is just used twice, once with the upper 64 bits and then once with the lower 64 bits.

```
pfadd      mm0,mm2    ; {Ay+s  Ax+s}
pfadd      mm1,mm2    ; {Aw+s  Az+s}
```

With the SSE instruction set it is almost as easy. The data is shuffled into all 32-bit floats.

```
movss      xmm1,fScalar          ; {0 0 0 s}
shufps     xmm1,xmm1,00000000b   ; {s s s s}
```

Now the scalar is the same as the vector.

```
addps      xmm0,xmm1    ; {Aw+s Az+s Ay+s Ax+s}
```

Any questions?

# Special — FP Vector Addition and Subtraction

The addition and subtraction of simultaneous vectors are a relatively simple matter for vector math instructions to handle. SSE3 added simultaneous functionality, while older versions have to simulate it.

# Vector Floating-Point Addition and Subtraction

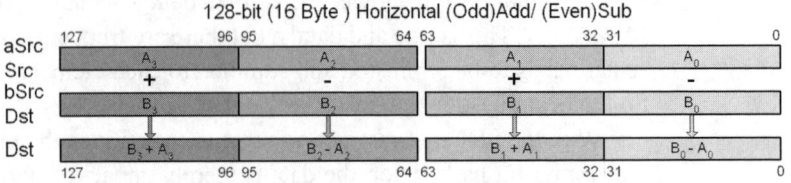

128-bit (16 Byte ) Horizontal (Odd)Add/ (Even)Sub

$$d_{(odd)} = b_{(odd)} + a_{(odd)} \quad d_{(even)} = b_{(even)} - a_{(even)}$$
$$d_{(3)} = b_{(3)} + a_{(3)} \quad d_{(2)} = b_{(2)} - a_{(2)} \quad d_{(1)} = b_{(1)} + a_{(1)} \quad d_{(0)} = b_{(0)} - a_{(0)}$$

| Mnemonic | P | PII | K6 | 3D! | 3Mx+ | SSE | SSE2 | A64 | SSE3 | E64T |
|----------|---|-----|----|----|------|-----|------|-----|------|------|
| ADDSUBPD |   |     |    |    |      |     |      |     | ✓ | ✓ |
| ADDSUBPS |   |     |    |    |      |     |      |     | ✓ | ✓ |

SSE3    addsubps    *xmmDst, xmmSrc/m128*    Single-precision    128
"       addsubpd    *xmmDst, xmmSrc/m128*    Double-precision    "

This vector instruction is a parallel operation that has an even subtraction and an odd addition of the source floating-point blocks. For the even elements, subtract *aSrc (xmmSrc)* from *bSrc (xmmDst)* with the result stored in the destination *Dst (xmmDst)*. For the odd elements, sum *aSrc (xmmSrc)* and *bSrc (xmmDst)* with the result stored in the destination *Dst (xmmDst)*.

# HADDPS/HADDPD/PFACC — Vector Floating-Point Horizontal Addition

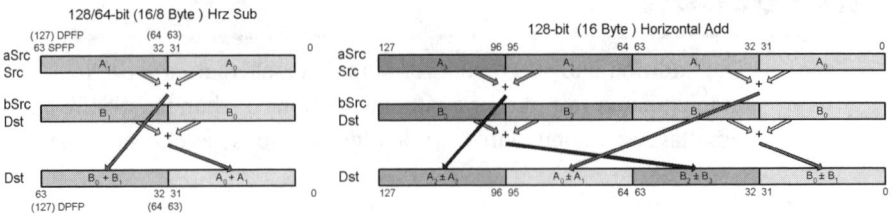

128/64-bit (16/8 Byte ) Hrz Sub      128-bit (16 Byte ) Horizontal Add

$$d_{(3)} = a_{(2)} + a_{(3)} \quad d_{(2)} = a_{(0)} + a_{(1)} \quad d_{(1)} = b_{(2)} + b_{(3)} \quad d_{(0)} = b_{(0)} + b_{(1)}$$
$$d_{(1)} = a_{(0)} + a_{(1)} \quad d_{(0)} = b_{(0)} + b_{(1)}$$

| Mnemonic | P | PII | K6 | 3D! | 3Mx+ | SSE | SSE2 | A64 | SSE3 | E64T |
|----------|---|-----|----|----|------|-----|------|-----|------|------|
| HADDPD   |   |     |    |     |      |     |      |     | ✓    | ✓    |
| HADDPS   |   |     |    |     |      |     |      |     | ✓    | ✓    |
| PFACC    |   |     |    | ✓   | ✓    |     |      | ✓   |      |      |

3DNow! pfacc    *mmxDst, mmxSrc/m64*    Single-precision    64
SSE3    haddps *xmmDst, xmmSrc/m128*    Single-precision    128
"    haddpd *xmmDst, xmmSrc/m128*    Double-precision    "

This vector instruction is a parallel operation that separately sums the odd/even pairs of the source and destination and stores the result of the *bSrc (xmmDst)* in the lower destination elements of *Dst (xmmDst)* and the result of the *aSrc (xmmSrc)* in the upper elements of *Dst (xmmDst)*.

# HSUBPS/HSUBPD/PFNACC — Vector Floating-Point Horizontal Subtraction

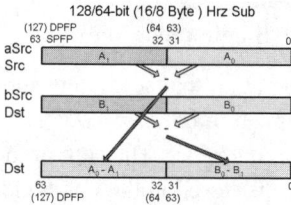

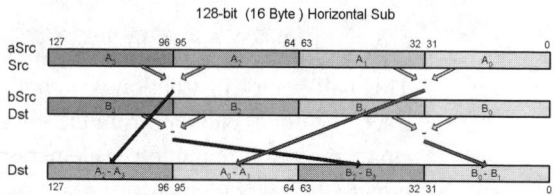

$$d_{(3)} = a_{(2)} - a_{(3)} \quad d_{(2)} = a_{(0)} - a_{(1)} \quad d_{(1)} = b_{(2)} - b_{(3)} \quad d_{(0)} = b_{(0)} - b_{(1)}$$
$$d_{(1)} = a_{(0)} - a_{(1)} \quad d_{(0)} = b_{(0)} - b_{(1)}$$

| Mnemonic | P | PII | K6 | 3D! | 3Mx+ | SSE | SSE2 | A64 | SSE3 | E64T |
|----------|---|-----|----|----|------|-----|------|-----|------|------|
| PFNACC   |   |     |    |     | ✓    |     |      | ✓   |      |      |
| HSUBPD   |   |     |    |     |      |     |      |     | ✓    | ✓    |
| HSUBPS   |   |     |    |     |      |     |      |     | ✓    | ✓    |

3Mx+    pfnacc    *mmxDst, mmxSrc/m64*    Single-precision    64
SSE3    hsubps *xmmDst, xmmSrc/m128*    Single-precision    128
"    hsubpd *xmmDst, xmmSrc/m128*    Double-precision    "

This vector instruction is a parallel operation that separately subtracts the (odd) element from the (even) element and stores the result of the *bSrc (xmmDst)* in the lower destination elements of *Dst (xmmDst)* and the result of the *aSrc (xmmSrc)* in the upper addresses of *Dst (xmmDst)*.

## PFPNACC — Vector Floating-Point Horizontal Add/Sub

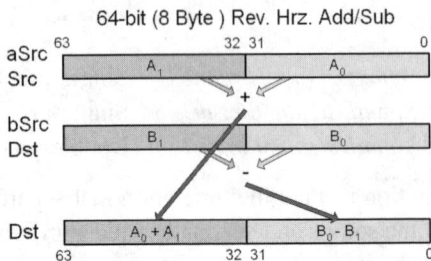

64-bit (8 Byte ) Rev. Hrz. Add/Sub

$$d_{(1)} = a_{(0)} + a_{(1)} \qquad d_{(0)} = b_{(0)} - b_{(1)}$$

| Mnemonic | P | PII | K6 | 3D! | 3Mx+ | SSE | SSE2 | A64 | SSE3 | E64T |
|----------|---|-----|----|----|------|-----|------|-----|------|------|
| PFPNACC  |   |     |    |    | ✓    |     |      | ✓   |      |      |

3Mx+   pfpnacc  *mmxDst, mmxSrc/m64*   Single-precision   64

This half-vector instruction is a parallel operation that separately subtracts the upper element from the lower element of *bSrc (mmxDst)* and stores the result in the lower element of *Dst (mmxDst)*. The sum of the upper and lower elements of *aSrc (mmxSrc)* is stored in the upper element of *Dst (mmxDst)*.

# Exercises

1. Using only Boolean logic, how could two numbers be summed?
2. If your processor had no instructions for parallel subtraction, how would you find the difference of two numbers?
3. Invert the sign of the even-numbered elements of signed 8-bit byte, 16-bit half-word, and 32-bit word of a 128-bit data value using:
   a) pseudo vector C code
   b) MMX
   c) SSE2
4. Same as problem 3 but use odd-numbered elements.
5. Invert the sign of all the elements of four packed single-precision floating-point values.

6. You have been given a 4096-byte audio sample consisting of left and right channel components with a PCM (pulse coded modulation) of unsigned 16-bit with 0x8000 as the baseline.

```
unsigned short leftStereo[1024], rightStereo[1024];
signed char Mono[???];
```

   a) How many bytes is the mixed sample?

   b) Write a mixer function to sum the two channels from stereo into mono and convert to a signed 8-bit sample.

**Project:**

You now have enough information to write an SHA-1 algorithm discussed in Chapter 5, "Bit Wrangling," for your favorite processor. Write one! HINT: Write the function code in C first.

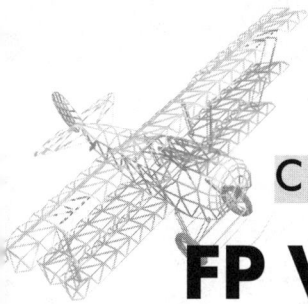

# Chapter 13

# FP Vector Multiplication and Division

There are multitudes of variations of multiplicative mnemonic manipulations. It seems almost every processor supports a slightly different scheme involving different integer word sizes, floating-point precision types, methods of rounding, with saturations, etc. Fundamentally, despite its variations, it is very similar to and uses the same methodologies as the addition detailed in the last chapter.

Notice the integer multiplication examples below. The example on the left requires more bits to contain the results of the operation and thus different methods have been implemented to reduce that value to its component size. The results of the floating-point multiplication in the other two examples follow the rules of the IEEE-754 standard for binary floating-point arithmetic. The result of a multiplication is stored with no increase in data containment size, but there is a penalty of a loss of precision.

| Integer | Floating-Point | Expanded FP |
|---|---|---|
| 3287565 | 3.28757e+006 | 3287570.0 |
| × 593 | × 593.0 | × 593.0 |
| 1949526045 | 1.94953e+009 | 1949530000.0 |

**Workbench Files:** \Bench\x86\chap13\\*project*\\*platform*

| | *project* | *platform* |
|---|---|---|
| **3D (Mul/Div)** | \vmd3d\ | \vc6 |
| **4vec (Mul/Div)** | \qvmd3d\ | \vc.net |

# Floating-Point Multiplication

## Vector Floating-Point Multiplication

Single-Precision    128-bit / 64-bit (16 / 8 Byte ) Multiplication

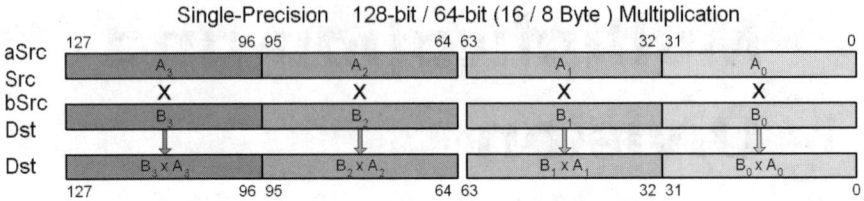

| Mnemonic | P | PII | K6 | 3D! | 3Mx+ | SSE | SSE2 | A64 | SSE3 | E64T |
|----------|---|-----|----|----|------|-----|------|-----|------|------|
| PFMUL    |   |     |    | ✓  | ✓    |     |      | ✓   |      |      |
| MULPS    |   |     |    |    |      | ✓   | ✓    | ✓   | ✓    | ✓    |

3DNow!  pfmul  *mmxDst, mmxSrc*          Single-precision   64
SSE     mulps  *xmmDst, xmmSrc/m128*     Single-precision   128

This SIMD instruction uses a 64 (128)-bit data path and so two (four) operations occur in parallel. The product is calculated for each of the Real32 single-precision floating-point elements of the multiplicand *xmmDst* and the multiplier *xmmSrc* for each block, and the result is stored in each of the original Real32 elements of the destination *xmmDst*.

(64-bit) **2×32-bit**

$$xmmDst_{(31...0)} = ( xmmDst_{(31...0)} \times xmmSrc_{(31...0)} )$$
$$xmmDst_{(63...32)} = ( xmmDst_{(63...32)} \times xmmSrc_{(63...32)} )$$
$$xmmDst_{(95...64)} = ( xmmDst_{(95...64)} \times xmmSrc_{(95...64)} )$$
$$xmmDst_{(127...96)} = ( xmmDst_{(127...96)} \times xmmSrc_{(127...96)} )$$

(128-bit) **4×32-bit**

## (Semi-Vector) DPFP Multiplication

| Mnemonic | P | PII | K6 | 3D! | 3Mx+ | SSE | SSE2 | A64 | SSE3 | E64T |
|----------|---|-----|----|----|------|-----|------|-----|------|------|
| MULPD    |   |     |    |    |      |     | ✓    | ✓   | ✓    | ✓    |

SSE2   mulpd *xmmDst, xmmSrc/m128*   Double-precision   128

This vector instruction uses a 128-bit data path and so two operations occur in parallel. The product is calculated for each of the Real64 (double-precision floating-point) pairs of the multiplicand *xmmDst* and the multiplier *xmmSrc* for each block, and the result is stored in each of the original Real64 elements of the destination *xmmDst*.

$$Dst_{(63...0)} = (Dst_{(63...0)} \times Src_{(63...0)})$$
$$Dst_{(127...64)} = (Dst_{(127...64)} \times Src_{(127...64)})$$

# SPFP Scalar Multiplication

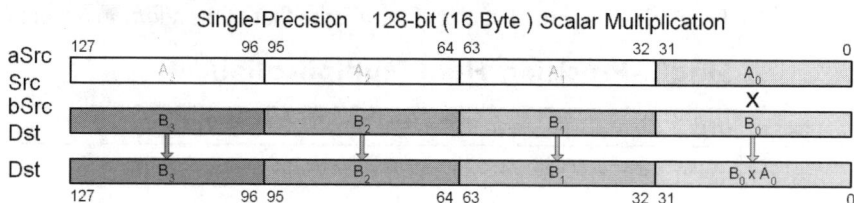

Single-Precision    128-bit (16 Byte ) Scalar Multiplication

| Mnemonic | P | PII | K6 | 3D! | 3Mx+ | SSE | SSE2 | A64 | SSE3 | E64T |
|----------|---|-----|----|----|------|-----|------|-----|------|------|
| MULSS    |   |     |    |    |      | ✓   | ✓    | ✓   | ✓    | ✓    |

SSE        mulss *xmmDst, xmmSrc/m32*        Single-precision 32

This vector instruction uses a 128-bit data path and only the first Real32 (single-precision floating-point) source *scalar* multiplier and the multiplicand *xmmDst*, and the result is stored in the original Real32 elements of the destination *xmmDst*.

$$Dst_{(31...0)} = (Dst_{(31...0)} \times Src_{(31...0)})$$
$$Dst_{(127...32)} = \text{remains unchanged.}$$

# DPFP Scalar Multiplication

| Mnemonic | P | PII | K6 | 3D! | 3Mx+ | SSE | SSE2 | A64 | SSE3 | E64T |
|----------|---|-----|----|----|------|-----|------|-----|------|------|
| MULSD    |   |     |    |    |      |     | ✓    | ✓   | ✓    | ✓    |

SSE2    mulsd *xmmDst, xmmSrc/m64*        Double-precision    64

This vector instruction uses a 128-bit data path and only the first Real64 (double-precision floating-point) source *scalar* multiplier and the multiplicand *xmmDst*, and the result is stored in the original Real64 elements of the destination *xmmDst*.

$$Dst_{(63...0)} = (Dst_{(63...0)} \times Src_{(63...0)})$$
$$Dst_{(127...64)} = \text{remains unchanged.}$$

# Vector (Float) Multiplication — ADD

Vector floating-point multiplication is one of the mathematical equations that you will tend to use the most in your video games whether as a tri or quad float vector.

# Pseudo Vec

The multiplication of vectors is similar to that of the addition of vectors.

### Single-Precision Float Multiplication

Listing 13-1: ...\chap13\fmd\Fmd.cpp

```
void vmp_FMul(float *pfD, float fA, float fB)
{
  *pfD = fA * fB;
}
```

### Single-Precision Vector Float Multiplication

Listing 13-2: ...\chap13\vmd3d\Vmd3D.cpp

```
void vmp_VecMul(vmp3DVector * const pvD,
          const vmp3DVector * const pvA,
          const vmp3DVector * const pvB)
{
  pvD->x = pvA->x * pvB->x;
  pvD->y = pvA->y * pvB->y;
  pvD->z = pvA->z * pvB->z;
}
```

### Single-Precision Quad Vector Float Multiplication

Listing 13-3: ...\chap13\qvmd3d\QVmd3D.cpp

```
void vmp_QVecMul(vmp3DQVector * const pvD,
          const vmp3DQVector * const pvA,
          const vmp3DQVector * const pvB)
{
  pvD->x = pvA->x * pvB->x;
  pvD->y = pvA->y * pvB->y;
  pvD->z = pvA->z * pvB->z;
  pvD->w = pvA->w * pvB->w;
}
```

### Single-Precision Quad Vector Float Multiplication-Add

The multiplication-add (MADD) is merely a multiplication followed by a summation. Some processors, such as AltiVec, do not support a stand-alone multiplication, some support only the multiplication-add, and some support both. But it is much more efficient to call a MADD-type instruction when appropriate, instead of separately.

Listing 13-4: ...\chap13\qvmd3d\QVmd3D.cpp

```
void vmp_QVecMAdd(vmp3DQVector * const pvD,
            const vmp3DQVector * const pvA,
            const vmp3DQVector * const pvB)
{
  pvD->x = pvA->x * pvB->x + pvC->x;
  pvD->y = pvA->y * pvB->y + pvC->y;
  pvD->z = pvA->z * pvB->z + pvC->z;
  pvD->w = pvA->w * pvB->w + pvC->w;
}
```

# Pseudo Vec (x86)

Now examine these functions closer using x86 assembly. 3DNow! supports 64-bit data so two loads must be handled simultaneously as well as two stores, but it is a simple matter of adding the two pairs of floats to each other.

```
mov   eax,vA   ; Vector A
mov   ebx,vB   ; Vector B
mov   edx,vD   ; Vector Destination
```

### vmp_VecMul   (3DNow!)

Listing 13-5: ...\chap13\vmd3d\Vmd3DX86M.asm

```
movq  mm0,[ebx]                     ; vB.xy {By Bx}
movq  mm1,[eax]                     ; vA.xy {Ay Ax}
movd  mm2,(vmp3DVector PTR [ebx]).z ; {0  Bz}
movd  mm3,(vmp3DVector PTR [eax]).z ; {0  Az}
pfmul mm1,mm0                       ; {AyBy AxBx}
pfmul mm3,mm2                       ; {  0  AzBz}
movq  [edx],mm1                     ; {AyBy AxBx}
movd  (vmp3DVector PTR [edx]).z,mm3 ; {     AzBz}
```

As you may have noticed, the vector only loaded one float instead of two, set the second to zero, calculated the product, and then wrote the three values back to memory.

## vmp_QVecMul (3DNow!)

**Listing 13-6: ...\chap13\qvmd3d\QVmd3DX86M.asm**

```
movq    mm0,[ebx+0]        ; vB.xy {By Bx}
movq    mm1,[eax+0]        ; vA.xy {Ay Ax}
movq    mm2,[ebx+8]        ; vB.zw {Bw Bz}
movq    mm3,[eax+8]        ; vA.zw {Aw Az}
pfmul   mm1,mm0            ; {AyBy AxBx}
pfmul   mm3,mm2            ; {AwBw AzBz}
movq    [edx+0],mm1        ; {AyBy AxBx}
movq    [edx+8],mm3        ; {AwBw AzBz}
```

## vmp_QVecMAdd (3DNow!)

For MADD, the addition needs to be handled separately.

**Listing 13-7: ...\chap13\qvmd3d\QVmd3DX86M.asm**

```
mov     ecx,vC             ; Vector C
movq    mm0,[ebx+0]        ; vB.xy {By Bx}
movq    mm1,[eax+0]        ; vA.xy {Ay Ax}
movq    mm4,[ecx+0]        ; vC.xy {Cy Cx}
movq    mm2,[ebx+8]        ; vB.zw {Bw Bz}
movq    mm3,[eax+8]        ; vA.zw {Aw Az}
movq    mm5,[ecx+8]        ; vC.zw {Cw Cz}

pfmul   mm1,mm0            ; {AyBy AxBx}
pfmul   mm3,mm2            ; {AwBw AzBz}
pfadd   mm1,mm4            ; {AyBy+Cy AxBx+Cx}
pfadd   mm3,mm5            ; {AwBw+Cw AzBz+Cz}

movq    [edx+0],mm1        ; {AyBy+Cy AxBx+Cx}
movq    [edx+8],mm3        ; {AwBw+Cw AzBz+Cz}
```

## vmp_VecMul (SSE)

The SSE processor in the following code snippet can load 128 bits at a time, so the entire 96-bit vector can be loaded at once, including an extra 32 bits. This introduces a problem of contamination when the 96-bit value is written to memory as 128 bits. The solution is to read those destination bits, preserve the upper 32 bits through bit masking and blending, and write the newly merged 128 bits. Keep in mind efficient memory organization and memory tail padding as discussed earlier. Data can be misaligned or aligned, but 128-bit alignment is preferable. Only aligned memory will be discussed, but for SSE keep in mind the use of MOVUPS instead of MOVAPS when memory alignment cannot be guaranteed.

### vmp_VecMul (SSE) Aligned

```
Listing 13-8: ...\chap13\vmd3d\Vmd3DX86M.asm

movaps  xmm2,[edx]                    ; vD.###w {Dw #  #  #}
movaps  xmm1,[ebx]                    ; vB.xyz# {# Bz By Bx}
movaps  xmm0,[eax]                    ; vA.xyz# {# Az Ay Ax}
andps   xmm1,OWORD PTR lomsk96        ; {0 Az Ay Ax}
andps   xmm2,OWORD PTR himsk32        ; {Dw 0  0  0}
mulps   xmm0,xmm1                     ; {## AzBz AyBy AxBx}
andps   xmm0,OWORD PTR lomsk96        ; limit -0
orps    xmm0,xmm2                     ; {Dw AzBz AyBy AxBx}
movaps  [edx],xmm0                    ; {Dw AzBz AyBy AxBx}
```

### vmp_QVecMul (SSE) Aligned

```
Listing 13-9: ...\chap13\qvmd3d\QVmd3DX86M.asm

movaps  xmm1,[ebx]                    ; vB.xyzw {Bw Bz By Bx}
movaps  xmm0,[eax]                    ; vA.xyzw {Aw Az Ay Ax}
mulps   xmm0,xmm1                     ; {AwBw AzBz AyBy AxBx}
movaps  [edx],xmm0                    ; {AwBw AzBz AyBy AxBx}
```

### vmp_QVecMAdd (SSE) Aligned

For MADD, the summation is an appended instruction as compared to the previous vector multiplication.

```
Listing 13-10: ...\chap13\qvmd3d\QVmd3DX86M.asm

movaps  xmm0,[eax]                    ; vA.xyzw {Aw Az Ay Ax}
movaps  xmm1,[ebx]                    ; vB.xyzw {Bw Bz By Bx}
movaps  xmm2,[ecx]                    ; vC.xyzw {Cw Cz Cy Cx}
mulps   xmm0,xmm1                     ; {AwBw AzBz AyBy AxBx}
addps   xmm0,xmm2                     ; {AwBw+Cw ... AxBx+Cx}
movaps  [edx],xmm0                    ; {AwBw+Cw ... AxBx+Cx}
```

# Vector Scalar Multiplication

The scalar multiplication of vectors is also a relatively simple matter for vector math instructions to handle, just like the scalar addition and subtraction of vectors. The trick is to replicate the scalar so it appears like a second vector.

# Pseudo Vec

## Single-Precision Vector Float Multiplication with Scalar

This function multiplies a scalar with each element of a vector. A scalar has multiple uses but the primary is in the use of "scaling" a vector. A scalar of one would result in the same size. Two would double the length of the vector, etc.

Listing 13-11: ...\chap13\vmd3d\Vmd3D.cpp

```
void vmp_VecScale(vmp3DVector * const pvD,
            const vmp3DVector * const pvA,
            float fScalar)
{
  pvD->x = pvA->x * fScalar;
  pvD->y = pvA->y * fScalar;
  pvD->z = pvA->z * fScalar;
}
```

## Single-Precision Quad Vector Float Multiplication with Scalar

Listing 13-12: ...\chap13\qvmd3d\QVmd3D.cpp

```
void vmp_QVecScale(vmp3DQVector * const pvD,
            const vmp3DQVector * const pvA,
            float fScalar)
{
  pvD->x = pvA->x * fScalar;
  pvD->y = pvA->y * fScalar;
  pvD->z = pvA->z * fScalar;
  pvD->w = pvA->w * fScalar;
}
```

# Pseudo Vec (x86)

```
mov     eax,vA          ; Vector A
mov     edx,vD          ; Vector destination
```

## vmp_VecScale (3DNow!)

The 32-bit scalar is unpacked into a pair and then treated similar to the vector multiplication of two vectors.

*Listing 13-13: ...\chap13\vmd3d\Vmd3DX86M.asm*

```
movd      mm0,fScalar                          ; fScalar {0 s}
punpckldq mm0,mm0                              ; {s s}
movq      mm1,[eax]                            ; vA.xy {Ay Ax}
movd      mm2,(vmp3DVector PTR [eax]).z        ; {0  Az}
pfmul     mm1,mm0                              ; {Ays Axs}
pfmul     mm2,mm0                              ; {0s  Azs}
movq      [edx],mm1                            ; {Ays Axs}
movd      (vmp3DVector PTR [edx]).z,mm2        ; {    Azs}
```

## vmp_VecScale (SSE) Aligned

The SSE version of the code is changed from a 64-bit load to a 128-bit load, but the principles remain the same.

*Listing 13-14: ...\chap13\vmd3d\Vmd3DX86M.asm*

```
pxor    xmm1,xmm1                       ; {0 0 0 0}
movss   xmm1,fScalar                    ; {0 0 0 s}
movaps  xmm2,[edx]                      ; {Dw # # #}
movaps  xmm0,[eax]                      ; vA.xyz# {# Az Ay Ax}
shufps  xmm1,xmm1,11000000b             ; 3 0 0 0 {0 s  s  s}
andps   xmm2,OWORD PTR himsk32          ; {Dw 0  0  0}

mulps   xmm0,xmm1                       ; {# Azs Ays Axs}
andps   xmm0,OWORD PTR lomsk96          ; {0 Azs Ays Axs}
orps    xmm0,xmm2                       ; {Dw Azs Ays Axs}
movaps  [edx],xmm0                      ; {Dw Azs Ays Axs}
```

## vmp_QVecScale (SSE) Aligned

*Listing 13-15: ...\chap13\qvmd3d\QVmd3DX86M.asm*

```
movss   xmm1,fScalar                    ; {0 0 0 s}
movaps  xmm0,[eax]                      ; vA.xyzw {Aw Az Ay Ax}
shufps  xmm1,xmm1,00000000b             ; 0 0 0 0 {s s s s}
mulps   xmm0,xmm1                       ; {Aws Azs Ays Axs}
movaps  [edx],xmm0                      ; {Aws Azs Ays Axs}
```

# I-VU-Q

What is the difference between a dot product and a cross product and what are their equations?

# Graphics 101 — Dot Product

A dot product, also known as an *inner product*, of two vectors is the summation of the results of the product for each of their {XYZ} elements, thus resulting in a scalar. Not to oversimplify it, but this scalar is equal to 0 if the angle made up by the two vectors are perpendicular (=90°), positive if the angle is acute (<90°), and negative if the angle is obtuse (>90°).

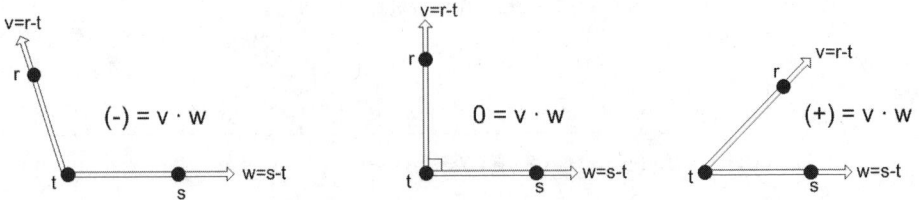

*Figure 13-1: Dot product (inner product). A positive number is an acute angle, zero is perpendicular, and negative is an obtuse angle.*

$v = \{v_1, v_2, v_3\}$ and $w = \{w_1, w_2, w_3\}$

These are vectors that produce a scalar defined by v • w when their products are combined. The dot product is represented by the following equation:

$v \bullet w = v_1 w_1 + v_2 w_2 + v_3 w_3$

The equation resolves to the following simplified form:

$D = A_x B_x + A_y B_y + A_z B_z$
$D = Ax*Bx + Ay*By + Az*Bz;$

# Pseudo Vec

So as we have learned, we first write it in a high-level language before writing it in assembly code.

### Single-Precision Dot Product

*Listing 13-16: ...\chap13\vmd3d\Vmd3D.cpp*

```
void vmp_DotProduct(float * const pfD,
        const vmp3DVector * const pvA,
        const vmp3DVector * const pvB)
{
   *pfD = pvA->x * pvB->x
        + pvA->y * pvB->y
        + pvA->z * pvB->z;
}
```

This is one of my favorite equations because it does not slice, dice, or chop, but it culls, it illuminizes, it simplifies, it cosineizes (not a real word, but you know what I mean). It is the Sledge-O-Matic!!! Well, not quite comedian Gallagher's watermelon disintegration kitchen utensil, but it does do many things and so it is just as useful.

From Figure 13-1 you will note that if the resulting scalar value is positive (+), the vectors are pointing in the same general direction. If zero (0), they are perpendicular to each other, and if negative (−), they are pointed in opposite directions.

Before explaining further it should be pointed out that to keep 3D graphic algorithms as simple as possible the three vertices for each polygon should all be ordered in the same direction. For example, by using the left-hand rule and keeping all the vertices of a visible face in a clockwise direction, such as in Figure 13-2, back face culling will result. If all visible face surfaces use this same orientation, then if the vertices occur in a counterclockwise direction they are back faced and thus pointing away and need not be drawn, saving render time.

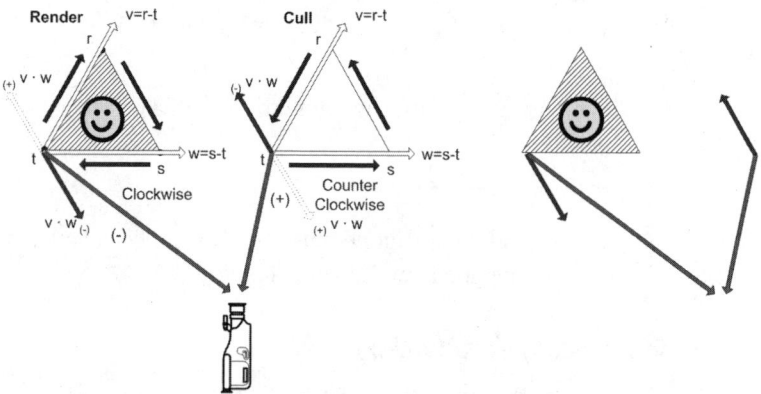

*Figure 13-2: Face culling mechanism where if the angle between the camera and the perpendicular to the face plane is obtuse, then the face is pointed away from the camera and can be culled.*

Contrarily, if polygons are arranged in a counterclockwise orientation, then the inverse occurs where a positive value is drawn and a negative value is culled. Keep in mind, however, that most software algorithms keep things in a clockwise orientation.

By calculating the dot product of the normal vector of the polygon with a vector between one of the polygon's vertices and the camera, it can be determined if the polygon is back facing and needs to be culled. A resulting positive value indicates that the face is pointed away, hence back facing and can be culled and not rendered. A negative value indicates a face oriented toward the camera and thus visible.

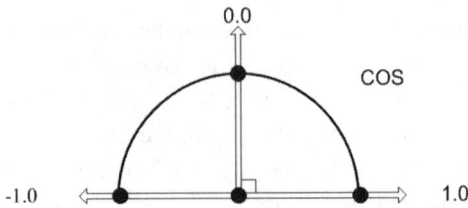

Figure 13-3: This shows the cosine of two intersecting lines.

Another use for the dot product equation is that it is also the cosine of the angle. The cosine is returned by dividing the dot product by the product of the magnitudes of the two vectors. Note that $v$ and $w$ are vectors and that $|v|$ and $|w|$ are their magnitudes.

$$\text{Cos}\,\theta = \frac{A_xB_x + A_yB_y + A_zB_z}{\sqrt{(A_x^2 + A_y^2 + A_z^2)} \times \sqrt{(B_x^2 + B_y^2 + B_z^2)}} = \frac{v \cdot w}{|v| \times |w|}$$

And using standard trigonometric formulas, such as:

$$1 = \text{Cos}^2 + \text{Sin}^2$$

...sine and other trigonometric results can be calculated.
So the good stuff is yet to come!

# Pseudo Vec (x86)

## vmp_DotProduct (3DNow!)

The 3DNow! instruction set uses the 64-bit MMX registers, but 64-bit memory alignment cannot be guaranteed. In this case, it is typically better to handle memory access as individual 32-bit floats then to unpack into 64-bit pairs, process, then save individually as 32 bit. The PFACC instruction is unique as it allows the hi/lo 32 bits to be summed with each other, within each of the vectors.

Listing 13-17: ...\chap13\vmd3d\Vmd3DX86M.asm

```
    mov   ebx,vB                          ; Vector B
    mov   eax,vA                          ; Vector A
    mov   edx,vD                          ; Vector destination

    movd  mm0,(vmp3DVector PTR [ebx]).z  ; {0 Bz}
    movd  mm1,(vmp3DVector PTR [eax]).z  ; {0 Az}
    movq  mm2,[ebx]                       ; {By Bx}
    movq  mm3,[eax]                       ; {Ay Ax}
```

```
pfmul  mm0,mm1         ; {00 BzAz}
pfmul  mm2,mm3         ; {ByAy BxAx}
pfacc  mm2,mm2         ; {ByAy+BxAx ByAy+BxAx}
pfadd  mm0,mm2         ; {ByAy+BxAx+0 ByAy+BxAx+BzAz}
movd   [edx],mm0       ; Save {ByAy+BxAx+BzAz}
```

### vmp_DotProduct (SSE) Aligned

The SSE instruction loads the 96-bit vector value using a 128-bit XMM register. The operation entails the multiplication of the {XYZ} pairs from both vectors. The data is swizzled to allow scalar additions, and then the 32-bit single-precision float scalar result is written to memory.

*Listing 13-18: ...\chap13\vmd3d\Vmd3DX86M.asm*

```
movaps xmm1,[ebx]              ; vB.xyz# {# Bz By Bx}
movaps xmm0,[eax]              ; vA.xyz# {# Az Ay Ax}
mulps  xmm0,xmm1               ; {A#B# AzBz AyBy AxBx}
movaps xmm1,xmm0
movaps xmm2,xmm0
unpckhps xmm0,xmm0             ; {A#B# A#B# AzBz AzBz}
shufps xmm1,xmm1,11100001b     ; {A#B# AzBz AxBx AyBy}
addss  xmm2,xmm0               ; {A#B# AzBz AxBx AzBz+AxBx}
addss  xmm2,xmm1               ; {A#B# AzBz AxBx AzBz+AxBx+AyBy}
movss  [edx],xmm2              ; Save {AzBz+AxBx+AyBy}
```

# Graphics 101 — Cross Product

A cross product, also known as the *outer product*, of two vectors is a third vector perpendicular to the plane of the two original vectors. The two vectors define two sides of a polygon face and their cross product points away from that face.

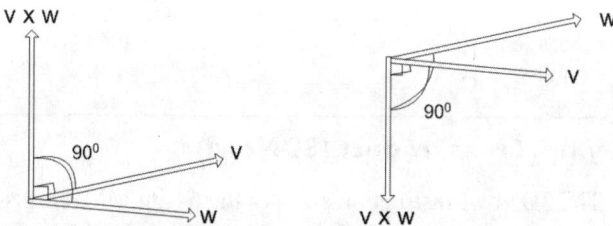

*Figure 13-4: Cross product (outer product). The perpendicular to the two vectors v and w.*

$v = \{v_1, v_2, v_3\}$ and $w = \{w_1, w_2, w_3\}$ are vectors of a plane denoted by matrix $\mathbf{R}^3$. The cross product is represented by the following equation:

The standard basis vectors are $\mathbf{i}=(1,0,0)$ $\mathbf{j}=(0,1,0)$ $\mathbf{k}=(0,0,1)$.

$$v \times w = (v_2 w_3 - v_3 w_2)\mathbf{i} - (v_1 w_3 - v_3 w_1)\mathbf{j} + (v_1 w_2 - v_2 w_1)\mathbf{k}$$

$$
\det
\begin{bmatrix}
\mathbf{i} & \mathbf{j} & \mathbf{k} \\
v_1 & v_2 & v_3 \\
w_1 & w_2 & w_3
\end{bmatrix}
\quad \text{thus} \quad
\begin{bmatrix}
v_2 w_3 - v_3 w_2 \\
v_3 w_1 - v_1 w_3 \\
v_1 w_2 - v_2 w_1
\end{bmatrix}
$$

The equation resolves to the following simplified form:

$$D_x = A_y B_z - A_z B_y \qquad \text{Dx = Ay*Bz - Az*By;}$$
$$D_y = A_z B_x - A_x B_z \qquad \text{Dy = Az*Bx - Ax*Bz;}$$
$$D_z = A_x B_y - A_y B_x \qquad \text{Dz = Ax*By - Ay*Bx;}$$

Note the following simple vector structure is actually 12 bytes, which will pose a data alignment problem for SIMD operations.

One method is to use individual single-precision floating-point calculations, of which you may already be familiar. With this in mind, examine the following simple C language function to implement it. Note the use of the temporary floats $x$, $y$ to prevent the resulting solutions of each field {x,y,z} from affecting either source *pvA* or *pvB* in the case where the destination *pvD* is also a source.

**Listing 13-19:** ...\chap13\vmd3d\Vmd3D.cpp

```
void vmp_CrossProduct(vmp3DVector* const pvD,
    const vmp3DVector* pvA, const vmp3DVector* pvB)
{
  float x, y;
        x = pvA->y * pvB->z - pvA->z * pvB->y;
        y = pvA->z * pvB->x - pvA->x * pvB->z;
  pvD->z = pvA->x * pvB->y - pvA->y * pvB->x;
  pvD->x = x;
  pvD->y = y;
}
```

## vmp_CrossProduct (3DNow!)

The 3DNow! instruction set uses the 64-bit MMX registers, but 64-bit memory alignment cannot be guaranteed. In this case it is typically better to handle memory access as individual 32-bit floats than to unpack into 64-bit pairs, process, then save individually as 32 bit. This example is kind of big so there are extra blank lines to help separate the various logic stages and it is not optimized to make it more readable.

Listing 13-20: ...\chap13\vmd3d\Vmd3DX86M.asm

```
mov     ebx,vB                              ; Vector B
mov     eax,vA                              ; Vector A
mov     edx,vD                              ; Vector destination

movd mm0,(vmp3DVector PTR [ebx]).x ; vB.x {0 Bx}
movd mm1,(vmp3DVector PTR [ebx]).y ; vB.y {0 By}
movd mm2,(vmp3DVector PTR [ebx]).z ; vB.z {0 Bz}
movd mm3,(vmp3DVector PTR [eax]).x ; vA.x {0 Ax}
movd mm4,(vmp3DVector PTR [eax]).y ; vA.y {0 Ay}
movd mm5,(vmp3DVector PTR [eax]).z ; vA.z {0 Az}

pfmul mm4,mm0                              ; vB.xy {0 AyBx}
punpckldq mm0,mm1                          ; {By Bx}

movd mm1,(vmp3DVector PTR [eax]).y ; vA.y {Ay}
movd mm6,(vmp3DVector PTR [ebx]).y ; vB.y {By}

punpckldq mm2,mm2                          ; {Bz Bz}
punpckldq mm3,mm1                          ; {Ay Ax}
punpckldq mm5,mm5                          ; {Az Az}

pfmul mm2,mm3                              ; vA.xy {BzAy BzAx}
pfmul mm5,mm0                              ; vB.xy {AzBy AzBx}
pfmul mm6,mm3                              ; vA.xy {0Ay ByAx}

movq  mm7,mm2                              ; {BzAy BzAx}
pfsub mm2,mm5                              ; {BzAy-AzBy BzAx-AzBx}

psrlq mm2,32                               ; x@ {0 BzAy-AzBy}
pfsub mm5,mm7                              ; y@ {AzBy-BzAy AzBx-BzAx}
pfsub mm6,mm4                              ; z@ {0-0 ByAx-AyBx}

movd (vmp3DVector PTR [edx]).x,mm2 ; x=AyBz-AzBy
movd (vmp3DVector PTR [edx]).y,mm5 ; y=AzBx-AxBz
movd (vmp3DVector PTR [edx]).z,mm6 ; z=AxBy-AyBx
```

If you examine it closely you will notice the operations performed within each block and how they correlate to the generic C code that was provided.

## vmp_CrossProduct (SSE) Aligned

The SSE instruction set uses the 128-bit XMM registers with MOVUPS instead of MOVAPS for unaligned memory. This function has also been unoptimized so as to make it more readable.

---

*Listing 13-21: ...\chap13\vmd3d\Vmd3DX86M.asm*

```
movaps  xmm1,[ebx]              ; vB.xyz# {# Bz By Bx}
movaps  xmm0,[eax]              ; vA.xyz# {# Az Ay Ax}
;  Crop the 4th (w) field
andps   xmm1,OWORD PTR lomsk96  ; {0 Bz By Bx}
andps   xmm0,OWORD PTR lomsk96  ; {0 Az Ay Ax}

movaps  xmm5,xmm1
movaps  xmm6,xmm0

shufps  xmm1,xmm1,11010010b     ; 3 1 0 2 {0 By Bx Bz}
shufps  xmm0,xmm0,11001001b     ; 3 0 2 1 {0 Ax Az Ay}
shufps  xmm6,xmm6,11010010b     ; 3 1 0 2 {0 Ay Ax Az}
shufps  xmm5,xmm5,11001001b     ; 3 0 2 1 {0 Bx Bz By}

movaps  xmm2,[edx]              ; Get destination {Dw # # #}
mulps   xmm1,xmm0
mulps   xmm5,xmm6
andps   xmm2,OWORD PTR himsk32  ; {Dw 0 0 0}
subps   xmm1,xmm5               ; { 0 z y x}
orps    xmm1,xmm2               ; [Dw z y x]
movups  [edx],xmm1              ; vD.wxyz {Dw z y x}
```

# Vector Floating-Point Division

$$Divisor = \frac{Quotient}{Dividend}$$

Remainder

It was discussed in a previous chapter that a difference is the summation of a term and the inverse of a second term using the additive inverse algebraic law. A division is also a play on an equation transformation: a multiplication of the dividend by the reciprocal of the divisor.

$$D = A \div B = \frac{A}{I} \div \frac{B}{I} = \frac{A}{I} \times \frac{I}{B} = \frac{A}{B}$$

Some instruction sets, such as 3DNow!, do not directly support floating-point division but do support the product of a reciprocal.

# (Vector) SPFP Division

| Mnemonic | P | PII | K6 | 3D! | 3Mx+ | SSE | SSE2 | A64 | SSE3 | E64T |
|----------|---|-----|----|----|------|-----|------|-----|------|------|
| DIVPS    |   |     |    |    |      | ✓   | ✓    | ✓   | ✓    | ✓    |

SSE     divps *xmmDst, xmmSrc/m128*     Single-precision     128

This vector instruction uses a 128-bit data path and so four operations occur in parallel. The result is calculated for each of the source Real32 (single-precision floating-point) quads of the quotient *xmmDst* and the divisor *xmmSrc* of each block, and the result is stored in each of the original Real32 elements of the destination *xmmDst*.

$$Dst_{(31...0)} = (Dst_{(31...0)} \div Src_{(31...0)})$$
$$Dst_{(63...32)} = (Dst_{(63...32)} \div Src_{(63...32)})$$
$$Dst_{(95...64)} = (Dst_{(95...64)} \div Src_{(95...64)})$$
$$Dst_{(127...96)} = (Dst_{(127...96)} \div Src_{(127...96)})$$

# (Semi-Vector) DPFP Division

| Mnemonic | P | PII | K6 | 3D! | 3Mx+ | SSE | SSE2 | A64 | SSE3 | E64T |
|----------|---|-----|----|----|------|-----|------|-----|------|------|
| DIVPD    |   |     |    |    |      |     | ✓    | ✓   | ✓    | ✓    |

SSE2     divpd *xmmDst, xmmSrc/m128*     Double-precision     128

This vector instruction uses a 128-bit data path and so two operations occur in parallel. The result is calculated for each of the source Real64 (double-precision floating-point) pairs of the quotient *xmmDst* and the divisor *xmmSrc* of each block, and the result is stored in each of the original Real64 elements of the destination *xmmDst*.

$$Dst_{(63...0)} = (Dst_{(63...0)} \div Src_{(63...0)})$$
$$Dst_{(127...64)} = (Dst_{(127...64)} \div Src_{(127...64)})$$

# SPFP Scalar Division

| Mnemonic | P | PII | K6 | 3D! | 3Mx+ | SSE | SSE2 | A64 | SSE3 | E64T |
|----------|---|-----|----|----|------|-----|------|-----|------|------|
| DIVSS    |   |     |    |    |      | ✓   | ✓    | ✓   | ✓    | ✓    |

SSE     divss *xmmDst, xmmSrc/m32*     Single-Precision     32

This scalar instruction uses a 128-bit data path but only the least significant Real32 (single-precision floating-point) elements are used — the *xmmSrc* source scalar divisor and the *xmmDst* quotient. The result is stored in the lower 32 bits of the destination *xmmDst*, leaving the upper 96 bits unaffected.

$Dst_{(31...0)} = (Dst_{(31...0)} \div Src_{(31...0)})$

$Dst_{(127...32)}$ = remains unchanged.

# DPFP Scalar Division

| Mnemonic | P | PII | K6 | 3D! | 3Mx+ | SSE | SSE2 | A64 | SSE3 | E64T |
|----------|---|-----|----|-----|------|-----|------|-----|------|------|
| DIVSD    |   |     |    |     |      |     | ✓    | ✓   | ✓    | ✓    |

SSE2    divsd *xmmDst, xmmSrc/m64*    Double-precision    64

This scalar instruction uses a 128-bit data path and only the first Real64 (double-precision floating-point) source *scalar* divisor and the quotient *xmmDst*. The result is stored in the original lower 64 bits of the destination *xmmDst*, leaving the upper 64 bits unaffected.

$Dst_{(63...0)} = (Dst_{(63...0)} \div Src_{(63...0)})$

$Dst_{(127...64)}$ = remains unchanged.

# N×SPFP Reciprocal

| Mnemonic | P | PII | K6 | 3D! | 3Mx+ | SSE | SSE2 | A64 | SSE3 | E64T |
|----------|---|-----|----|-----|------|-----|------|-----|------|------|
| RCPPS    |   |     |    |     |      | ✓   | ✓    | ✓   | ✓    | ✓    |
| RCPSS    |   |     |    |     |      | ✓   | ✓    | ✓   | ✓    | ✓    |

SSE    rcpps *xmmDst, xmmSrc/m128*    Single-precision    128
SSE    rcpss *xmmDst, xmmSrc/m32*    Single-precision    128

The RCPPS instruction uses a packed 128-bit data path and each source *xmmDst* element and divides it by each *xmmSrc* divisor, produces the reciprocal, and stores the result in destination *xmmDst*.

$Dst_{(31...0)} = (1.0 \div Src_{(31...0)})$

$Dst_{(63...32)} = (1.0 \div Src_{(63...32)})$

$Dst_{(95...64)} = (1.0 \div Src_{(95...64)})$

$Dst_{(127...96)} = (1.0 \div Src_{(127...96)})$

The RCPSS scalar instruction uses a 128-bit data path. It takes the least significant Real32 in source *xmmDst*, divides it by the least significant Real32 in *xmmSrc* divisor, produces the reciprocal, and stores the result in destination *xmmDst*.

$$Dst_{(31...0)} = (1.0 \div Src_{(31...0)})$$

# 1×SPFP Reciprocal (14-Bit)

| Mnemonic | P | PII | K6 | 3D! | 3Mx+ | SSE | SSE2 | A64 | SSE3 | E64T |
|----------|---|-----|----|----|------|-----|------|-----|------|------|
| PFRCP    |   |     |    | ✓  | ✓    |     |      | ✓   |      |      |

3DNow!    pfrcp *mmxDst, mmxSrc/m32*    Single-precision    32/64

This 3DNow! scalar instruction uses a 64-bit data path. It takes only the first Real32 (single-precision floating-point) source *scalar* divisor, produces the 14-bit reciprocal, and stores the result in both the lower 32 bits and upper 32 bits of the destination *mmxDst*.

$$Dst_{(63...32)} = Dst_{(31...0)} = (1.0 \div Src_{(31...0)})$$

To convert the result to a division it only needs to be followed up by the multiplication instruction PFMUL. This instruction would be considered a low precision division.

**Hint:**  FAST or SLOW algorithm?
Of course fast! Why would anyone even bother calling a slow algorithm or keep a slow algorithm in memory unused? In reality, this title is misleading. It really means:
*FAST* — Quicker algorithm but less accurate response.
*SLOW* — Not slow, just the standard algorithm with the best precision possible for the supported data size.
Picking and choosing an appropriate algorithm is just another level of code optimization. In a video game the standard algorithm would be used for rendering the display or another precision required event, but the fast (quick) algorithm would be used for quick processing such as pre-culling of polygons or quick distances between sprites, etc.

```
movd   mm3,fB        ; {0    B}
movd   mm0,fA        ; {0    A}
mov    edx,pfD       ; float destination
```

## vmp_FDiv (3DNow!) Fast Float Division 14-Bit Precision

A division, whether it has a 1/x or a/b orientation, is time consuming. Whenever possible, a multiplication of a reciprocal value should be used instead. If that is not possible, then the next logical method would be making a choice between an imprecise and quick calculation or a more accurate but slower calculation. The following code is for a simple 14-bit accuracy scalar division D=A÷B supported by the 3DNow! instruction set.

Note that the code has the fast precision set to 0.001f to accommodate SSE, but 0.0001f works for 3DNow! estimation.

**Listing 13-22: ...\chap13\fmd\FmdX86M.asm**

```
; Calculate reciprocal of source B then mult A
pfrcp mm1,mm3                    ; {1/B 1/B}
pfmul mm0,mm1                    ; {# A×(1/B)}
movd [edx],mm0                   ; A÷B
```

# SPFP Reciprocal (2 Stage) (24-Bit)

A fast version of the previous instruction would entail taking advantage of the two-stage vector instructions PFRCPIT1 and PFRCPIT2, in conjunction with the result of the reciprocal instruction PFRCP, to achieve a higher 24-bit precision. It uses a variation of the Newton-Raphson reciprocal square approximation.

This is an error correcting scheme to infinitely reduce the error, but typically only a single pass is used. Not to simplify it, but this typically involves calculating the product of the estimated square root, finding the difference from the original number, then adjusting by that ratio.

| Mnemonic | P | PII | K6 | 3D! | 3Mx+ | SSE | SSE2 | A64 | SSE3 | E64T |
|----------|---|-----|----|----|------|-----|------|-----|------|------|
| PFRCPIT1 |   |     |    | ✓  | ✓    |     |      | ✓   |      |      |
| PFRCPIT2 |   |     |    | ✓  | ✓    |     |      | ✓   |      |      |

First stage for 24-bit reciprocal:

3DNow!    pfrcpit1 *mmxDst, mmxSrc/m32*    Single-precision    64

Second stage for 24-bit reciprocal and/or square root:

3DNow!    pfrcpit2 *mmxDst, mmxSrc/m32*    Single-precision    64

## vmp_FDiv (3DNow!) Standard Float Division 24-Bit Precision

The following is the same as the previous scalar division algorithm but is coded for 24-bit precision. Note the addition of the PFRCPIT1 and PFRCPIT2 instructions. Note the following code is not optimized so as to make it more readable.

*Listing 13-23: ...\chap13\fmd\FmdX86M.asm*

```
; 1st calculate 14-bit accuracy
pfrcp     mm1,mm3                    ; {1/B 1/B}
; 2nd Calculate 1/sqrt() accurate to 24 bits
pfrcpit1 mm3,mm1                     ; {1st step}
pfrcpit2 mm3,mm1      ; 24 bits     ; {2nd step}

movd      mm0,fA                     ; {0 A}
pfmul     mm0,mm3                    ; {# A×(1/B)}
movd      [edx],mm0                  ; A÷B
```

### vmp_FDiv (SSE) Standard Float Division 24-Bit Precision

The SSE version merely reads the floats as scalars, divides them as scalars, and stores the scalar result.

*Listing 13-24: ...\chap13\fmd\FmdX86M.asm*

```
movss     xmm1,fB                    ; B {0 0 0 B}
movss     xmm0,fA                    ; A {0 0 0 A}
mov       eax,pfD                    ; Float destination
divss     xmm0,xmm1                  ; {0 0 0 A÷B}
movss     [edx],xmm0                 ; A÷B
```

# Pseudo Vec

The vector and quad vector operations are not much different. The scalar in essence becomes replicated into all the denominator fields and then the product of the reciprocals (division) takes place.

### Single-Precision Vector Float Scalar Division

*Listing 13-25: ...\chap13\fmd\Fmd.cpp*

```
void vmp_VecDiv(vmp3DVector * const pvD,
        const vmp3DVector * const pvA,
        float fScalar)
{
  pvD->x = pvA->x/fScalar;
  pvD->y = pvA->y/fScalar;
  pvD->z = pvA->z/fScalar;
}
```

# Pseudo Vec (x86)

Now examine these functions closer using x86 assembly. As MMX does not support floating-point only, 3DNow! and SSE can be utilized. 3DNow! supports 64-bit so two loads must be handled simultaneously. The functionality is, in essence, a reciprocal of the scalar is calculated and mirrored into each of the denominator positions, and the product is calculated with the original vector with the result stored. These examples are all quad vectors, and special consideration must be taken when dealing with three float vectors to preserve the {W} float element.

```
movd  mm2,fScalar      ; {0  s}
mov   eax,vA           ; Vector A
mov   edx,vD           ; Vector destination
```

## vmp_QVecDiv (3DNow!) Fast Quad Float Division 14-Bit Precision

*Listing 13-26: ...\chap13\qvmd3d\QVmd3DX86.asm*

```
pfrcp mm2,mm2          ; {1/s 1/s} 14-bit
movq  mm0,[eax+0]      ; vA_xy {A_y A_x}
movq  mm1,[eax+8]      ; vA_zw {A_w A_z}
pfmul mm0,mm2          ; {A_y×1/s A_x×1/s}
pfmul mm1,mm2          ; {A_w×1/s A_z×1/s}
movq  [edx+0],mm0      ; {A_y/s A_x/s}
movq  [edx+8],mm1      ; {A_w/s A_z/s}
```

## vmp_QVecDiv (3DNow!) Standard Quad Float Division 24-Bit Precision

The following code is unoptimized to make it more readable. Notice in the standard precision the second- and third-stage reciprocal instructions are used.

*Listing 13-27: ...\chap13\qvmd3d\QVmd3DX86.asm*

```
pfrcp     mm3,mm2      ; {1/s 1/s}  14-bit
punpckldq mm2,mm2      ; { s   s}
pfrcpit1  mm2,mm3      ; {1/s 1/s}
pfrcpit2  mm2,mm3

movq      mm0,[eax+0]  ; vA_xy {A_y A_x}
movq      mm1,[eax+8]  ; vA_zw {A_w A_z}

pfmul     mm0,mm2      ; {A_y × 1/s A_x × 1/s}
pfmul     mm1,mm2      ; {A_w × 1/s A_z × 1/s}
movq      [edx+0],mm0  ; {A_y/s A_x/s}
movq      [edx+8],mm1  ; {A_w/s A_z/s}
```

### vmp_QVecDiv (SSE) Standard Quad Float Division 24-Bit Precision

*Listing 13-28: ...\chap13\qvmd3d\QVmd3DX86M.asm*

```
movaps  xmm0,[eax]          ; vAxyzw {Aw Az Ay Ax}
movss   xmm1,fScalar        ; {0 0 0 s}
shufps  xmm1,xmm1,00000000b ; 0 0 0 0 {s s s s}
divps   xmm0,xmm1           ; {Aw/s Az/s Ay/s Ax/s}
movaps  [edx],xmm0          ; {Aw/s Az/s Ay/s Ax/s}
```

It is fairly simple. Similar to a scalar multiplication, the scalar is merely distributed to each of the elements of the denominator and then the division takes place. (Have you read this enough times yet?)

# Exercises

1. What is an "inner product"?
2. A cross product is known by another name. What is it?
3. What happens to a vector if a negative scalar is applied as a product?
4. What is the solution for:
   a) A B + C D, if A = 2, B = 5, C = 3, and D = 4?
   b) A = B = C = D = 0x80000000?
   c) With saturation?
   d) Without saturation?
5. What is the equation for a dot product?
6. Given the two vertices $v$: {−8, 4, −6, 4} and $w$: {8, 2, −6, 8}, resolve
   a) $v + w$
   b) $vw$
   c) $v \cdot w$
   d) $v \times w$

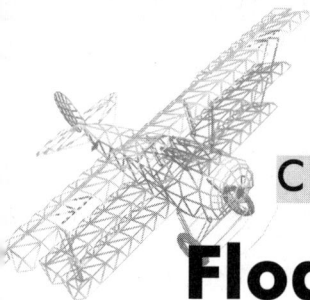

# Chapter 14

# Floating-Point Deux

Since the floating-point values have been discussed, it is now time to discuss some of the operations that can be performed with them, such as bit masking and comparisons.

Why would someone wish to generate a bit mask for a floating-point number? Due to the nature of the mantissa and exponential bits, a floating-point value can be manipulated.

**Workbench Files:** \Bench\x86\chap14\\*project*\\*platform*

|  | *project* | *platform* |
|---|---|---|
| **3D (Special)** | \vsf3d\ | \vc6 |
| **4vec (Special)** | \qvsf3d\ | \vc.net |

# SQRT — Square Root

The reciprocal and square root are two mathematical operations that have special functionality with vector processors. The division operation is typically performed by multiplying the reciprocal of the denominator by the numerator. A square root is not always just a square root; sometimes it is a reciprocal square root. So first we examine some simple forms of these.

$$y \div x = \frac{y}{1} \bullet \frac{1}{x} = \frac{y}{x} = \frac{y^1}{x^1} = y^1 \bullet x^{-1} = y^1 x^{-1}$$

$$\text{So } \frac{1}{x} = x^{-1}$$

*Equation 14-1: Reciprocal*

$$\sqrt{x} = x^{\frac{1}{2}} \frac{1}{\sqrt{x}} = x^{-\frac{1}{2}} \quad \text{so} \quad \frac{x}{\sqrt{x}} = x^{1-1/2} = x^{\frac{1}{2}} = \sqrt{x}$$

Another way to remember this is:

$$\frac{x}{\sqrt{x}} = \frac{\sqrt{x} \cdot \sqrt{x}}{\sqrt{x}} = \frac{\sqrt{x} \cdot \sqrt{x}}{\sqrt{x}} = \frac{\sqrt{x}}{1} = \sqrt{x}$$

*Equation 14-2: Square root*

The simplified form of this parallel instruction individually calculates the square root of each of the packed floating-point values, and returns the result in the destination. Some processors support the square root instruction directly, but some processors, such as the 3DNow! instruction set, actually support it indirectly through instructional stages. And some processors support it as a reciprocal square root.

So now I pose a little problem. We hopefully all know that a negative number should never be passed into a square root because computers go BOOM, as they have no idea how to deal with an identity (*i*).

$$\sqrt{-x} = i\sqrt{x}$$

With that in mind, what is wrong with a reciprocal square root? Remember your calculus and limits?

$$\sum_{x \to 0^+} \frac{1}{\sqrt{x}}$$

**Hint:** As *x* approaches zero from the right.

Okay, how about this one?

$$\sum_{x \to 0^+} \frac{1}{x}$$

Do you see it now? You cannot divide by zero, as it results in infinity and is mathematically problematic. So what has to be done is to trap for the *x* being too close to zero (as *x* approaches zero) and then substitute the value of one as the solution for the reciprocal square root.

```
y = (x < 0.0000001) ? 1.0 : (1 / sqrt(x));    // Too close to zero
```

It is not perfect but it is a solution. The number is so close to infinity that the result of its product upon another number is negligible. So in essence the result is that other number; thus the multiplicative identity comes to mind: $1 \times n = n$. But how to deal with this in vectors? Well, you just learned the trick in this chapter! Remember the packed comparison? It is just a matter of using masking and bit blending. So in the case of a reciprocal square root, the square root can be easily achieved by merely multiplying the result by the original $x$ value, thus achieving the desired square root. Recall that the square of a square root is the original value.

$$\sqrt{x} = x^{\frac{1}{2}}\frac{1}{x} = x^{-2}\frac{1}{\sqrt{x}} = x^{-\frac{1}{2}}$$

$$\sqrt{x} = \frac{x}{1} \times \frac{1}{\sqrt{x}} = x^{1-\frac{1}{2}} = x^{\frac{1}{2}}$$

vD[] = $\sqrt{}$ (vA[]);

# 1×SPFP Scalar Square Root

| Mnemonic | P | PII | K6 | 3D! | 3Mx+ | SSE | SSE2 | A64 | SSE3 | E64T |
|----------|---|-----|-----|-----|------|-----|------|-----|------|------|
| SQRTSS   |   |     |     |     |      | ✓   | ✓    | ✓   | ✓    | ✓    |

SSE     sqrtss *xmmDst, xmmSrc/m32*     Single-precision     128

This SIMD instruction is a 128-bit scalar operation that calculates the square root of only the lowest single-precision floating-point element containing the scalar *xmmSrc*. The result is stored in the lowest single-precision floating-point block at destination *xmmDst*, and the remaining bit blocks are left intact.

$Dst_{(31...0)} = sqrt(Src_{(31...0)})$
$Dst_{(127...32)} = $ remains unchanged

```
movss   xmm0,fA      ; {0 0 0  A}
sqrtss  xmm0,xmm0    ; {0 0 0 √A}
```

# 4×SPFP Square Root

| Mnemonic | P | PII | K6 | 3D! | 3Mx+ | SSE | SSE2 | A64 | SSE3 | E64T |
|----------|---|-----|-----|-----|------|-----|------|-----|------|------|
| SQRTPS   |   |     |     |     |      | ✓   | ✓    | ✓   | ✓    | ✓    |

SSE     sqrtps *xmmDst, xmmSrc/m128*     Single-precision     128

This SIMD instruction is a 128-bit parallel operation that calculates the square root of the four single-precision floating-point blocks contained within *xmmSrc*, and stores the result in the single-precision floating-point blocks at destination *xmmDst*.

$Dst_{(31...0)} = \sqrt{(Src_{(31...0)})}$

$Dst_{(63...32)} = \sqrt{(Src_{(63...32)})}$

$Dst_{(95...64)} = \sqrt{(Src_{(95...64)})}$

$Dst_{(127...96)} = \sqrt{(Src_{(127...96)})}$

# 1×DPFP Scalar Square Root

| Mnemonic | P | PII | K6 | 3D! | 3Mx+ | SSE | SSE2 | A64 | SSE3 | E64T |
|----------|---|-----|----|-----|------|-----|------|-----|------|------|
| SQRTSD   |   |     |    |     |      |     | ✓    | ✓   | ✓    | ✓    |

SSE2    sqrtsd *xmmDst, xmmSrc/m64*    Double-precision    128

This SIMD instruction is a 128-bit scalar operation that calculates the square root of only the lowest double-precision floating-point block containing the scalar *xmmSrc*, and stores the result in the lowest double-precision floating-point block at destination *xmmDst*. The remaining bit blocks are left intact.

$Dst_{(63...0)} = \sqrt{(Src_{(63...0)})}$

$Dst_{(127...64)}$ = remains unchanged

# 2×DPFP Square Root

| Mnemonic | P | PII | K6 | 3D! | 3Mx+ | SSE | SSE2 | A64 | SSE3 | E64T |
|----------|---|-----|----|-----|------|-----|------|-----|------|------|
| SQRTPD   |   |     |    |     |      |     | ✓    | ✓   | ✓    | ✓    |

SSE2    sqrtpd *xmmDst, xmmSrc/m128*    Double-precision    128

This SIMD instruction is a 128-bit parallel operation that calculates the square root of the two double-precision floating-point blocks contained within *xmmSrc*, and stores the result in the double-precision floating-point blocks at destination *xmmDst*.

$Dst_{(63...0)} = \sqrt{(Src_{(63...0)})}$

$Dst_{(127...64)} = \sqrt{(Src_{(127...64)})}$

# 1×SPFP Scalar Reciprocal Square Root (15-Bit)

| Mnemonic | P | PII | K6 | 3D! | 3Mx+ | SSE | SSE2 | A64 | SSE3 | E64T |
|----------|---|-----|----|-----|------|-----|------|-----|------|------|
| PFRSQRT  |   |     |    | ✓   | ✓    |     |      | ✓   |      |      |
| RSQRTPS  |   |     |    |     |      | ✓   | ✓    | ✓   | ✓    | ✓    |
| RSQRTSS  |   |     |    |     |      | ✓   | ✓    | ✓   | ✓    | ✓    |

| 3DNow! | pfrsqrt | *mmxDst, mmxSrc/m32* | Single-precision | 32/64 |
|--------|---------|----------------------|------------------|-------|
| SSE | rsqrtss | *xmmDst, xmmSrc/m32* | Single-precision | 32 |
| | rsqrtps | *xmmDst, xmmSrc/m128* | Single-precision | 128 |

This SIMD instruction is a 32-bit scalar operation that calculates the square root of only the lowest single-precision floating-point block containing the scalar *mmSrc,* and stores the duplicate result in the low and high single-precision floating-point blocks at destination *mmDst.*

$$Dst_{(63...32)} = Dst_{(31...0)} = \sqrt{(Src_{(31...0)})} \qquad \{\sqrt{A} \ \sqrt{A}\}$$

## Pseudo Vec

### (Float) Square Root

```
Listing 14-1: ...\chap14\fsf\Fsf.cpp

void vmp_FSqrt(float * const pfD, float fA)
{
  ASSERT_PTR4(pfD);
  ASSERT_NEG(fA);           // Watch for negative

  *pfD = sqrtf(fA);         // = √A
}
```

## Pseudo Vec (x86)

### vmp_FSqrt (3DNow!) Fast Float 15-Bit Precision

A square root is time consuming and should be omitted whenever possible. If it is indeed needed, then the next logical choice would be between an imprecise and quick calculation or a more accurate but slower calculation. The following code is for a simple 15-bit accuracy scalar square root $D = \sqrt{A}$ supported by the 3DNow! instruction set.

```
movd  mm0,fA          ; {0    fA}
mov   edx,pfD         ; float destination
```

---

*Listing 14-2: ...\chap14\fsf\FsfX86M.asm*

```
    pfrsqrt  mm1,mm0    ; {1/√fA    1/√fA}
    pfmul    mm0,mm1    ; {0/√fA   fA/√fA}
                        ; {   0      √fA}
    movd     [edx],mm0  ;          √fA
```

---

# SPFP Square Root (2 Stage) (24-Bit)

A fast version of the previous instruction would entail taking advantage of the two-stage vector instructions PFRSQIT1 and PFRCPIT2, in conjunction with the result of the square root instruction PFRSQRT, to achieve a higher 24-bit precision. It uses a variation of the Newton-Raphson reciprocal square root approximation.

| Mnemonic | P | PII | K6 | 3D! | 3Mx+ | SSE | SSE2 | A64 | SSE3 | E64T |
|---|---|---|---|---|---|---|---|---|---|---|
| PFRCPIT2 | | | | ✓ | ✓ | | | ✓ | | |
| PFRSQIT1 | | | | ✓ | ✓ | | | ✓ | | |

First stage for 24-bit reciprocal:

3DNow! pfrsqit1 *mmxDst, scalar(mmx/m32)*  Single-precision  64

Second stage for 24-bit reciprocal and/or square root (see reciprocals in Chapter 13):

3DNow! pfrcpit2 *mmxDst, scalar(mmx/m32)*  Single-precision  64

## vmp_FSqrt (3DNow!) Standard Float 24-Bit Precision

The following is the same as the previous scalar square root algorithm but is coded for 24-bit precision. Note the addition of the PFRSQIT1 and PFRCPIT2 instructions.

```
    mov      edx,pfD    ; (float) destination
```

---

*Listing 14-3: ...\chap14\fsf\FsfX86M.asm*

```
    ; 1st calculate 15-bit accuracy
    ; Calculate square root upon dot product

    pfrsqrt  mm1,mm0              ; {1/√A) 1/√A}

    ; 2nd Calculate 1/√() accurate to 24 bits

    movq     mm2,mm1             ; {1/√A 1/√A}
    pfmul    mm1,mm1             ; {1/A  1/A}
```

```
    pfrsqit1  mm1,mm0                    ; 1st step

    ; Calculate √() = 1/(1/√())  24-bit

    pfrcpit2  mm1,mm2                    ; 2nd step
    pfmul     mm0,mm1                    ; {√A √A} {A/√A A/√A}
                                         ; { A         √A}
    movd      [edx],mm0                  ;            √A
```

### vmp_FSqrt (SSE) Float Sqrt 24-Bit Precision

For SSE it is merely a scalar square root instruction.

*Listing 14-4: ...\chap14\fsf\FsfX86M.asm*

```
    movss   xmm0,fA          ;          {# # # A}
    sqrtss  xmm0,xmm0        ; SqRoot {# # # √A}
    movss   [edx],xmm0       ; Save square root
```

# Vector Square Root

*Are you nuts? Vector square roots?* What are you thinking?

Unless you have a top-of-the-line supercomputer, I would recommend you stay away from vector square roots. Instead, you will typically only need a single square root. If you really need vector-based square roots, remember that your processor can only do one at a time and your code will have to wait for it to complete before issuing a request to begin the next one. That could take almost *forever*! Well, not quite. But it is still not a great idea. Also, do not forget about preventing negative numbers from being processed by a square root. That causes exception faults!

# Pseudo Vec

### Vector Square Root

*Listing 14-5: ...\chap14\vsf3d\Vsf3D.cpp*

```cpp
void vmp_VecSqrt(vmp3DVector * const pvD,
        const vmp3DVector * const pvA)
{
  pvD->x = sqrtf(pvA->x);
  pvD->y = sqrtf(pvA->y);
  pvD->z = sqrtf(pvA->z);
}
```

### Quad Vector Square Root

*Listing 14-6: ...\chap14\qvsf3d\QVsf3D.cpp*

```
void vmp_QVecSqrt(vmp3DQVector * const pvD,
              const vmp3DQVector * const pvA)
{
  pvD->x = sqrtf(pvA->x);
  pvD->y = sqrtf(pvA->y);
  pvD->z = sqrtf(pvA->z);
  pvD->w = sqrtf(pvA->w);
}
```

Similar to an estimated reciprocal for a division, a square root some-times is available as an estimate as well. Be warned that the estimated square root is faster but has a lower precision. But if the lower precision is viable for your application, then investigate using the estimated square root instead.

# Pseudo Vec (x86)

The 3DNow! instruction set supports 64-bit so two loads must be han-dled simultaneously as well as two saves, but it is a simple matter of adding the two pairs of floats to each other.

```
mov   eax,vA    ; Vector A
mov   edx,vD    ; Vector destination
```

### vmp_QVecSqrt (3DNow!) Fast Quad Float SQRT 15-Bit Precision

*Listing 14-7: ...\chap14\qvsf3d\QVsf3DX86M.asm*

```
movq  mm0,[eax+0]                     ; vA.xy {Ay    Ax}
movd  mm6,(vmp3DQVector PTR [eax]).y ; {0     Ay}
movq  mm1,[eax+8]                     ; vA.zw {Aw    Az}
movd  mm5,(vmp3DQVector PTR [eax]).w ; {0     Aw}

  ; Calculate square root (pfrsqrt=15-bit accuracy)

pfrsqrt    mm3,mm0                    ; {1/√(Ax)  1/√(Ax)}
pfrsqrt    mm7,mm6                    ; {1/√(Ay)  1/√(Ay)}
pfrsqrt    mm2,mm1                    ; {1/√(Az)  1/√(Az)}
pfrsqrt    mm4,mm5                    ; {1/√(Aw)  1/√(Aw)}

  ; Calculate 1/√(x) accurate to 15 bits
punpckldq  mm3,mm7                    ; {1/√(Ay)  1/√(Ax)}
punpckldq  mm2,mm4                    ; {1/√(Aw)  1/√(Az)}
```

```
; {Insertion point for 24-bit precision}

pfmul       mm0,mm3     ; {Ay/√(Ay) Ax/√(Ax)}
pfmul       mm1,mm2     ; {Aw/√(Aw) Az/√(Az)}


movq        [edx+0],mm0 ; {√(Ay) √(Ax)}
movq        [edx+8],mm1 ; {√(Aw) √(Az)}
```

## vmp_QVecSqrt (3DNow!) Quad Float Sqrt 24-Bit Precision

In the previous code there is a comment in bold related to insertion for 24-bit precision. By inserting the following code the higher accuracy will be achieved. It uses the Newton-Raphson reciprocal square approximation.

*Listing 14-8: ...\chap14\qvsf3d\QVsf3DX86M.asm*

```
movq        mm6,mm3     ; {1/√(Ay) 1/√(Ax)}
movq        mm5,mm2     ; {1/√(Aw)(Aw) 1/√(Az)}
pfmul       mm3,mm3     ; {1/Ay    1/Ax}
pfmul       mm2,mm2     ; {1/Aw    1/Az}
pfrsqit1    mm3,mm0     ; xy {1st step}
pfrsqit1    mm2,mm1     ; zw
    ; Calculate √() = 1/(1/√())  24-bit
pfrcpit2    mm3,mm6     ; xy {2nd step}
pfrcpit2    mm2,mm5     ; zw
```

## vmp_QVecSqrt (SSE) Float Sqrt 24-Bit Precision

For SSE there is a 24-bit precision quad square root. For unaligned memory, substitute MOVUPS for the MOVAPS.

*Listing 14-9: ...\chap14\qvsf3d\QVsf3DX86M.asm*

```
movaps      xmm0,[eax]  ; {Aw  Az  Ay  Ax}
sqrtps      xmm0,xmm0   ; {√Aw √Az √Ay √Ax}
movaps      [edx],xmm0  ; Save square roots
```

## vmp_QVecSqrtFast (SSE) Float Sqrt Approximate

The following is a fast reciprocal square root.

*Listing 14-10: ...\chap14\qvsf3d\QVsf3DX86M.asm*

```
movaps      xmm0,[eax]  ; vA.xyzw { Aw  Az  Ay  Ax}
movaps      xmm1,xmm0
movaps      xmm2,xmm0
movaps      xmm3,xmm0


cmpps       xmm2,vTiny,5 ; >= 1's = #'s Okay
```

```
    cmpps       xmm3,vTiny,1  ; <   1's = too close to zero

      ; vD = (1 / √(vA))
    rsqrtps     xmm0,xmm0

      ; Correct for infinity due to 1/0 =  1/√(0)

    andps       xmm3,ONES      ; Preserve 1.0's for infinite
    andps       xmm0,xmm2      ; Preserve #'s too small
    orps        xmm0,xmm3      ; Blended #'s and 1.0's
    mulps       xmm0,xmm1      ; {Aw/√(Aw) ... Ax/√(Ax)}
    movaps      [edx],xmm0     ; Save Square Roots
```

# Graphics 101 — Vector Magnitude (aka 3D Pythagorean Theorem)

Ever hear that the shortest distance between two points is a straight line? The square of the hypotenuse of a right triangle is equal to the square of each of its two sides whether in 2D or 3D space. The Pythagorean equation is essentially the distance between two points, in essence the magnitude of their differences.

**Hint:** Do not use a square root unless you have to!

The first rule of a square root operation is to not use it unless you really have to as it is a time intensive mathematical operation. One method typically used for calculating the length of a line between two points whether it exists in 2D or 3D space is to use the Pythagorean equation.

### 2D Distance

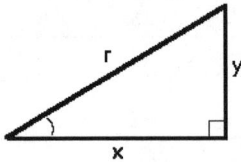

Figure 14-1: 2D right triangle representing a 2D distance

$$x^2 + y^2 = r^2$$
$$r = \sqrt{(x^2 + y^2)}$$

Code: r = sqrt(x*x + y*y);

Equation 14-3: 2D distance

## 3D Distance

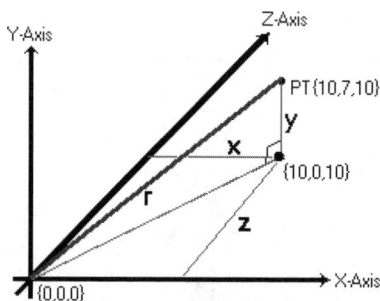

Figure 14-2: Right triangle within 3D
Cartesian coordinate system representing a
3D distance and thus its magnitude

$x^2+y^2+z^2=r^2$

$r = \sqrt{(A_x^2 + A_y^2 + A_z^2)}$

Code: r = sqrt(x*x + y*y + z*z);

Equation 14-4: 3D distance (magnitude)

**Mathematical Formula**:

| Pythagorean | $x^2+y^2=r^2$ <br> $r=\sqrt{(x^2+y^2)}$ | $x^2+y^2+z^2=r^2$ <br> $r=\sqrt{(x^2+y^2+z^2)}$ |
|---|---|---|

| 2D Distance | $d(P1,P2)=\sqrt{((x2-x1)^2+(y2-y1)^2)}$ |
|---|---|
| 3D Distance | $d(P1,P2,P3)=\sqrt{((x2-x1)^2+(y2-y1)^2+(z2-z1)^2)}$ |

$1/x = 1/0 = \infty$

So if the dot product dp $= x^2 + y^2 + z^2$ approaches zero, the value of 1/x gets closer to infinity. Once x becomes zero, the solution becomes undefined: $1/0 = \infty$. When a number is extremely close to infinity and is passed to a square root, the accuracy becomes lost. So instead of being forced to divide by zero (1/0) to represent infinity, it is instead set to a value of one (y × 1 = y); thus the original value is preserved.

The Pythagorean equation is the distance between two points, in essence, the magnitude of their differences. In a terrain-following algorithm for creature AI, the distance between each of the creatures and the main character would be compared to make an idle, run, or flee determination. The coordinates of each object are known but their distances would have to be calculated and then compared to each other as part of a solution. Let's examine a simplistic equation utilizing $r$ to represent the distance between the player and four monsters {mA through mD}:

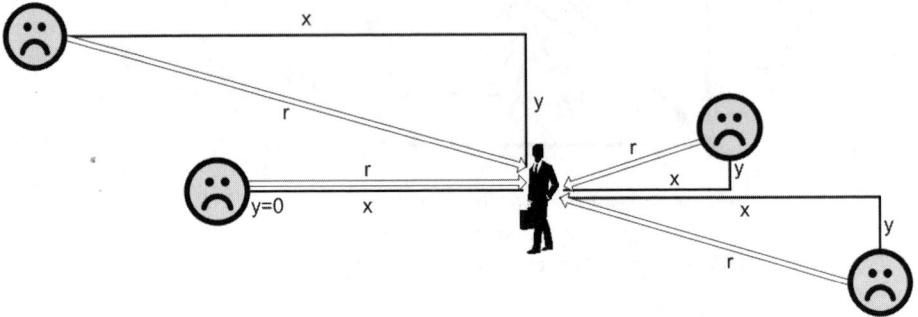

Figure 14-3: Monster to player 2D distance calculations

$$\Delta A = \text{MonsterA} = \sqrt{((mA_x \quad pA_x)^2 \quad (mA_y \quad pA_y)^2 \quad (mA_y \quad pA_y)^2)}$$
$$\Delta B = \text{MonsterB} = \sqrt{((mB_x \quad pA_x)^2 \quad (mB_y \quad pA_y)^2 \quad (mB_y \quad pA_y)^2)}$$
$$\Delta C = \text{MonsterC} = \sqrt{((mC_x \quad pA_x)^2 \quad (mC_y \quad pA_y)^2 \quad (mC_y \quad pA_y)^2)}$$
$$\Delta D = \text{MonsterD} = \sqrt{((mD_x \quad pA_x)^2 \quad (mD_y \quad pA_y)^2 \quad (mD_y \quad pA_y)^2)}$$

If you remember the algebraic law of multiplicative identity, the square root factors out of the equation, as it can be removed from both sides of the equal sign and the equation will remain in balance.

$$\text{sqrt}(\Delta A_x^2 + \Delta A_y^2 + \Delta A_z^2) =? \; \text{sqrt}(\Delta B_x^2 + \Delta B_y^2 + \Delta B_z^2)$$
$$\cancel{\text{sqrt}}(\Delta A_x^2 + \Delta A_y^2 + \Delta A_z^2) =? \; \cancel{\text{sqrt}}(\Delta B_x^2 + \Delta B_y^2 + \Delta B_z^2)$$
$$(\Delta A_x^2 + \Delta A_y^2 + \Delta A_z^2) =? \; (\Delta B_x^2 + \Delta B_y^2 + \Delta B_z^2)$$

Does this look a little similar to the sum of absolute differences operation discussed in Chapter 7? They are different by the sum of absolutes versus the sum of the squares, but they nevertheless have a similarity. The point is that there is no need to use the square root operation each time in this kind of problem. Neat, huh! It is an old trick but still an effective one.

Now supposing that it has been discovered that Monster C is the closest monster. Take the square root to calculate the distance, not forgetting to use the estimate square root version if accuracy is unnecessary.

# Pseudo Vec

*Listing 14-11: ...\chap14\vsf3d\Vsf3D.cpp*

```
void vmp_VecMagnitude(float * const pfD,
        const vmp3DVector * const pvA)
{
  *pfD=sqrtf(pvA->x * pvA->x
          + pvA->y * pvA->y
          + pvA->z * pvA->z);
}
```

# Pseudo Vec (x86)

The 3DNow! instruction set supports 64-bit so two loads and/or stores must be handled simultaneously, but the result is a simple matter of adding the two pairs of floats to each other.

```
mov   eax,vA                      ; Vector A
mov   edx,vD                      ; Vector destination
```

## vmp_VecMagnitude (3DNow!)

*Listing 14-12: ...\chap14\vsf3d\Vsf3DX86M.asm*

```
movq    mm1,[eax]                 ; {Ay     Ax}
movd    mm0,(vmp3DVector PTR [eax]).z ; {0      Az}
pfmul   mm1,mm1                   ; {AyAy  AxAx}
pfmul   mm0,mm0                   ; {0     AzAz}
pfacc   mm1,mm1                   ; {AyAy+AxAx  AyAy+AxAx}
pfadd   mm0,mm1                   ; {0+AyAy+AxAx  AzAz+AyAy+AxAx}

    ; Ignoring the upper 32 bits r= (Az)²+(Ay)²+(Ax)²
    ; Calculate square root

pfrsqrt mm1,mm0                   ; {#  1/√r}
; Calculate 1/sqrt() accurate to 24 bits
movq    mm2,mm1                   ; {#  1/√r}
pfmul   mm1,mm1                   ; {#  1/r}
pfrsqit1 mm1,mm0                  ; {1st step}
pfrcpit2 mm1,mm2                  ; {2nd step}
pfmul   mm0,mm1
movd    [edx],mm0                 ; Save distance
```

## vmp_VecMagnitude (SSE) Aligned

Replace MOVAPS with MOVUPS for unaligned memory.

Listing 14-13: ...\chap14\vsf3d\Vsf3DX86M.asm

```
movaps    xmm0,[eax]              ; {# Az Ay Ax}
mulps     xmm0,xmm0               ; {A#A# AzAz AyAy AxAx}
movaps    xmm1,xmm0
movaps    xmm2,xmm0
unpckhps  xmm0,xmm0               ; {A#A# A#A# AzAz AzAz}
shufps    xmm1,xmm1,11100001b     ; {A## Az² Ax² Ay²}

addss     xmm2,xmm0               ; {# # # Az²+Ax²}
addss     xmm2,xmm1               ; {# # # Az²+Ax²+Ay²}

; Calculate square root

sqrtss    xmm0,xmm2               ; √(Az² + Ax² + Ay²)
movss     [edx],xmm0              ; Save scalar
```

# Vector Normalize

## Pseudo Vec

Listing 14-14: ...\chap14\vsf3d\Vsf3D.cpp

```
void vmp_VecNormalize(vmp3DVector * const pvD,
              const vmp3DVector * const pvA)
{
  float fMag;

      // Magnitude = √(x² + y² + z²)
  fMag = sqrtf(pvA->x*pvA->x + pvA->y*pvA->y
                         + pvA->z*pvA->z);
  if (fMag < 0.0000001f)
    {                          // too close to zero
      pvD->x = pvA->x;
      pvD->y = pvA->y;
      pvD->z = pvA->z;
    }
  else
    {    // Ick, a division, to obtain a reciprocal!
      fMag = 1.0f / fMag;
      pvD->x = pvA->x * fMag;
      pvD->y = pvA->y * fMag;
      pvD->z = pvA->z * fMag;
    }
}
```

# Pseudo Vec (x86)

The 3DNow! processor supports 64-bit so two loads or two stores must be handled simultaneously, but it is a simple matter of adding the two pairs of floats to each other.

```
mov  eax,vA                          ; Vector A
mov  edx,vD                          ; Vector destination
```

## vmp_VecNormalize (3DNow!)

Listing 14-15: ...\chap14\vsf3d\Vsf3DX86M.asm

```
    movq  mm1,[eax]                           ; {Ay Ax}
    movd  mm0,(vmp3DVector PTR [eax]).z        ; {0  Az}
    movq  mm4,mm1                              ; {Ay Ax}
    movq  mm3,mm0                              ; {0  Az}
    pfmul mm1,mm1                              ; {AyAy AxAx}
    pfmul mm0,mm0                              ; {0      AzAz}
    pfacc mm1,mm1                              ; {AyAy+AxAx AyAy+AxAx}
    pfadd mm0,mm1                              ; {0+AyAy+AxAx AzAz+AyAy+AxAx}

    ; Calculate square root (pfrsqrt=15-bit accuracy)
    ; too close zero ...???  1.0 / 10000.0 ???

    movd  ecx,mm0
    cmp   ecx,FLOAT0001                        ; 0.0001
    jl    short zmag                           ; just set vD=vA!!!

    ; Not too close to zero, f= AzAz+AyAy+AxAx
    ; for Newton-Raphson 24-bit resolution
    pfrsqrt mm1,mm0                            ; {1/√r     1/√r}
    movq  mm2,mm1                              ; {1/√r     1/√r}
    pfmul mm1,mm1                              ; {1/r       1/r}
    pfrsqit1 mm1,mm0                           ; X2=f(x,x1) {1st step}

    ; *** mm1 = Magnitude ***
    ; Calculate sqrt() = (1/mag) 24-bit
    pfrcpit2  mm1,mm2                          ; {2nd step} {# m}
    punpckldq mm1,mm1                          ; {1/m 1/m}
    pfmul mm4,mm1                              ; {Ny Nx}= {Ay/m Ax/m}
    pfmul mm3,mm1                              ; {0 Nz}= {0/m Az/m}

zmag:                                         ; Save Resulting {x y z} Normals
    movq  [edx+0],mm4                          ; {Ny Nx}
    movd  (vmp3DVector PTR [edx]).z,mm3        ; {0  Nz}
```

## vmp_VecNormalize (SSE) Aligned

If the data is unaligned, change the MOVAPS instruction to MOVUPS.

*Listing 14-16: ...\chap14\vsf3d\Vsf3DX86M.asm*

```
movaps  xmm0,[eax]              ; {# Az Ay Ax}
movaps  xmm7,[edx]              ; {Dw # # #}
andps   xmm0,lomsk96            ; {0 Az Ay Ax}
andps   xmm7,himsk32            ; {Dw 0 0 0}
movaps  xmm6,xmm0               ; {0  Az   Ay   Ax}
mulps   xmm0,xmm0               ; {0 AzAz AyAy AxAx}
movaps  xmm1,xmm0               ; {0 AzAz AyAy AxAx}
movaps  xmm2,xmm0               ; {0 AzAz AyAy AxAx}

orps    xmm1,ONEHIGH           ; {1 Az² Ay² Ax²}
shufps  xmm1,xmm1,11001001b    ; 3021 {1 Ax² Az² Ay²}
shufps  xmm2,xmm2,11010010b    ; 3102 {0 Ay² Ax² Az²}

addps   xmm1,xmm0              ; {1+0 Az²+Ax² Ay²+Az² Ax²+Ay²}
addps   xmm1,xmm2
        ; {1+0 Ay²+Az²+Ax² Ax²+Ay²+Az² Az²+Ax²+Ay²}

  ; Too close zero?

movss   uflow,xmm1             ; r= Ay²+Az²+Ax²
cmp     uflow,FLOAT0001        ; 0.0001f
jl      short zmag             ; set vD=vA!!!

  ; Calculate square root

sqrtps  xmm0,xmm1              ; {1 √r √r √r}
divps   xmm6,xmm0              ; {0 Nz Ny Nz}

zmag:
orps    xmm7,xmm6              ; {Dw Nz Ny Nx}
movaps  [edx],xmm7             ; Save
```

**Question:** How would you upgrade the estimated precision version of the code to full 24-bit precision?

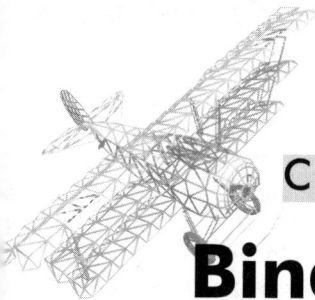

# Chapter 15

# Binary-Coded Decimal (BCD)

Converting an ASCII string to binary-coded decimal is as easy as pie (or is it a piece of cake?). In BCD, for every byte, the lower 4-bit nibble and upper 4-bit nibble each store a value from 0 to 9 (think double-digit hex only the upper six values A through F are ignored).

**Workbench Files:** \Bench\x86\chap15\\*project*\\*platform*

|  | *project* | *platform* |
|---|---|---|
| **ASE to VMP** | \ase2vmp\ | \vc6 |
| **BCD $2^N$** | \bcd\ | \vc.net |

## BCD

Table 15-1: ASCII numerical digit to hex and decimal values

| ASCII | 0 | 1 | 2 | 3 | 4 | 5 | 6 | 7 | 8 | 9 |
|---|---|---|---|---|---|---|---|---|---|---|
| **Hex** | 0x30 | 0x31 | 0x32 | 0x33 | 0x34 | 0x35 | 0x36 | 0x37 | 0x38 | 0x39 |
| **Decimal** | 48 | 49 | 50 | 51 | 52 | 53 | 54 | 55 | 56 | 57 |
| **BCD** | 0 | 1 | 2 | 3 | 4 | 5 | 6 | 7 | 8 | 9 |
| **Binary** | 0000 | 0001 | 0010 | 0011 | 0100 | 0101 | 0110 | 0111 | 1000 | 1001 |

Converting a BCD value from ASCII to a nibble is as easy as subtracting the hex value of 0x30, '0', or 48 decimal from the ASCII numerical value and get the resulting value with a range of {0...9}.

```
byte ASCIItoBCD(char c)
{
  ASSERT(('0' <= c) && (c <= '9'));

  return (byte)(c - '0');
}
```

**64-bit** **No 64-bit:** The general-purpose BCD instructions are not available in 64-bit mode.

When the 8086 processor was first manufactured the FPU was a separate optional chip (8087). There was a need for some BCD operations similar to other processors and so it was incorporated into the CPU. The 8087 had some BCD support as well. When the 64-bit processor was developed, it was decided that BCD support was not required anymore as the FPU was an alternative method.

The FPU uses the first nine bytes to support 18 BCD digits. The uppermost bit of the 10th byte indicates the value is negative if set or positive if the bit is clear.

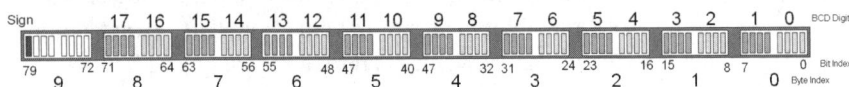

*Figure 15-1: Ten-byte BCD data storage. MSB in far left byte (byte #9) is the sign bit and the rightmost eight bytes (#8...0) contain the BCD value pairs. The 18th BCD digit resides in the upper nibble of byte #8 and the 1st BCD digit resides in the lower nibble of byte #0.*

Setting the upper nibble of a byte is merely the shifting left of a BCD digit by four bits, then logical ORing (or suming) the lower nibble.

```
byte BCDtoByte(byte lo, byte hi)
{
  return (hi << 4) | lo;
}
```

# DAA — Decimal Adjust AL (After) Addition

| Mnemonic | P | PII | K6 | 3D! | 3Mx+ | SSE | SSE2 | A64 | SSE3 | E64T |
|----------|---|-----|----|-----|------|-----|------|-----|------|------|
| DAA | ✓ | ✓ | ✓ | ✓ | ✓ | ✓ | ✓ | 32 | ✓ | 32 |

        daa                         Signed

The DAA general-purpose instruction adjusts the EFLAGS for a decimal carry after an addition.

| Flags | O.flow | Sign | Zero | Aux | Parity | Carry |
|-------|--------|------|------|-----|--------|-------|
|  | - | - | - | X | - | X |

Flags: The Aux and Carry flags are set to 1 if an addition resulted in a decimal carry in their associated 4-bit nibble; otherwise they are cleared to 0.

**No 64-bit:**   The general-purpose BCD instructions are not available in 64-bit mode.

```
        xor  eax,eax    ; Reset Carry(s)
$L1:    mov  al,[edi]   ; D = D + A
        adc  al,[esi]
        daa
        mov  [edi],al   ; Store result
        dec  esi
        dec  edi
        dec  ecx
        jne  $L1        ; Loop for n BCD bytes
```

Note that this function steps through memory in reverse byte order, which is not processor efficient. High digits are in low offset bytes, and low digits are in high offset bytes: {N...0}. So the operation must go to the end of the buffer and traverse memory backward from low-digit pairs to high-digit pairs. If not working with the FPU to handle BCD, then each nibble pair could be stored in reverse order: {0...N}. Only when they need to be displayed or printed would there be a reverse increment through memory. Note this is backward to the ordering of the FPU! The sample code uses this method.

# DAS — Decimal Adjust AL (After) Subtraction

| Mnemonic | P | PII | K6 | 3D! | 3Mx+ | SSE | SSE2 | A64 | SSE3 | E64T |
|----------|---|-----|----|----|------|-----|------|-----|------|------|
| DAS | ✓ | ✓ | ✓ | ✓ | ✓ | ✓ | ✓ | 32 | ✓ | 32 |

das                              Signed

The DAS general-purpose instruction adjusts the EFLAGS for a decimal borrow after a subtraction.

| Flags | O.flow | Sign | Zero | Aux | Parity | Carry |
|-------|--------|------|------|-----|--------|-------|
| | - | - | - | X | - | X |

Flags: The Aux and Carry flags are set to 1 if a subtraction resulted in a decimal carry set due to a borrow in their associated 4-bit nibble; otherwise they are cleared to 0.

**64-bit**  **No 64-bit:** The general-purpose BCD instructions are not available in 64-bit mode.

```
        xor  eax,eax    ; Reset Carry(s)
$L1:    mov  al,[edi]   ; D = D + A
        sbb  al,[esi]
        das
        mov  [edi],al   ; Store result
        dec  esi
        dec  edi
        dec  ecx
        jne  $L1        ; Loop for n BCD bytes
```

# AAA — ASCII Adjust (After) Addition

| Mnemonic | P | PII | K6 | 3D! | 3Mx+ | SSE | SSE2 | A64 | SSE3 | E64T |
|----------|---|-----|----|----|------|-----|------|-----|------|------|
| AAA | ✓ | ✓ | ✓ | ✓ | ✓ | ✓ | ✓ | 32 | ✓ | 32 |

aaa                                   Signed

The AAA general-purpose instruction adjusts the EFLAGS for a decimal carry. If a resulting calculation is greater than 9, then AL is set to the remainder between (0...9) and AH is incremented.

| Flags | O.flow | Sign | Zero | Aux | Parity | Carry |
|-------|--------|------|------|-----|--------|-------|
|       | - | - | - | X | - | X |

Flags: The Aux and Carry flags are set to 1 if a decimal carry resulted; otherwise they are cleared to 0.

**64-bit**  **No 64-bit:** The general-purpose BCD instructions are not available in 64-bit mode.

```
        add  al,ah
        aaa
        or   al,'0'     ; '0' + {0...9} = ASCII '0...9'
```

# AAS — ASCII Adjust AL (After) Subtraction

| Mnemonic | P | PII | K6 | 3D! | 3Mx+ | SSE | SSE2 | A64 | SSE3 | E64T |
|----------|---|-----|----|----|------|-----|------|-----|------|------|
| AAS | ✓ | ✓ | ✓ | ✓ | ✓ | ✓ | ✓ | 32 | ✓ | 32 |

aas                                   Signed

The AAS general-purpose instruction adjusts the EFLAGS depending on the results of the AL register after a multiplication operation. If a resulting calculation sets the carry indicating a borrow has occurred, then AL is set to the remainder between (0...9) and AH is decremented.

| Flags | O.flow | Sign | Zero | Aux | Parity | Carry |
|-------|--------|------|------|-----|--------|-------|
| | - | - | - | X | - | X |

Flags: The Aux and Carry flags are set to 1 if a decimal borrow resulted; otherwise they are cleared to 0.

**64-bit** **No 64-bit:** The general-purpose BCD instructions are not available in 64-bit mode.

```
sub  al,'7'
aas
or   al,'0'       ; '0' + {0...9} = ASCII '0...9'
```

# AAM — ASCII Adjust AX (After) Multiplication

| Mnemonic | P | PII | K6 | 3D! | 3Mx+ | SSE | SSE2 | A64 | SSE3 | E64T |
|----------|---|-----|-----|-----|------|-----|------|-----|------|------|
| AAM | ✓ | ✓ | ✓ | ✓ | ✓ | ✓ | ✓ | 32 | ✓ | 32 |

aam                              Signed

The AAM general-purpose instruction adjusts the EFLAGS depending on the results of the AL register after a multiplication operation.

| Flags | O.flow | Sign | Zero | Aux | Parity | Carry |
|-------|--------|------|------|-----|--------|-------|
| | - | X | X | - | X | - |

Flags: The Sign, Zero, and Parity flags are set to the resulting value in the AL register.

**64-bit** **No 64-bit:** The general-purpose BCD instructions are not available in 64-bit mode.

```
mul  al,bh
aam
```

# AAD — ASCII Adjust AX (Before) Division

| Mnemonic | P | PII | K6 | 3D! | 3Mx+ | SSE | SSE2 | A64 | SSE3 | E64T |
|---|---|---|---|---|---|---|---|---|---|---|
| AAD | ✓ | ✓ | ✓ | ✓ | ✓ | ✓ | ✓ | 32 | ✓ | 32 |

aad                                    Signed

The AAD general-purpose instruction adjusts the EFLAGS in preparation for a division operation.

| Flags | O.flow | Sign | Zero | Aux | Parity | Carry |
|---|---|---|---|---|---|---|
| | - | X | X | - | X | - |

Flags: The Sign, Zero, and Parity flags are set to the resulting value in the AL register.

**No 64-bit:** The general-purpose BCD instructions are not available in 64-bit mode.

```
and   eax,0000111100001111b
aad
```

# FBLD — FPU (BCD Load)

| Mnemonic | P | PII | K6 | 3D! | 3Mx+ | SSE | SSE2 | A64 | SSE3 | E64T |
|---|---|---|---|---|---|---|---|---|---|---|
| FBLD | ✓ | ✓ | ✓ | ✓ | ✓ | ✓ | ✓ | ✓ | ✓ | ✓ |

FPU    fbld  *source*          BCD                80

How does this all work? Well, the FPU has a single instruction that loads a BCD value and converts it to an 80-bit (10-byte) double extended precision floating-point value that it stores on the FPU stack. This can then be written back to computer memory as double-precision floating-point. Simple, fast, and minimal excess code and nothing time intensive.

Listing 15-1: ...\chap15\ase2vmp\util.cpp

```
unsigned char bcd[10];
double f;

_asm {
  fbld  tbyte ptr bcd    ; Load (80-bit) BCD
  fstp  f                ; Write 64-bit double-precision
}
```

The returned floating-point value contains the BCD number as an integer with no fractional component. For example:

```
byte bcd[10] = {0x68, 0x23, 0x45, 0x67, 0x89, 0x98, 0x87, 0x76, 0x65,
                0x80};
```

The float returned is  $-657,687,988,967,452,368.0$

At this point the decimal place needs to be adjusted to its correct position using the product of an exponential $10^{-n}$. This can be done with either a simple table lookup or a call to the function pow(10,-e), but the table lookup is faster. And *speed* is what it is all about.

# Graphics 101

All of you who start a processing tool to convert art resources or game resources into a game database and then leave to have lunch, get a soda, have a snack, go to the bathroom, pick up your kids from school, or go home, all yell, "ME!"

WOW! That was loud! It could be heard reverberating across the planet.

Those of you who have worked on games in the past, did you meet your timelines? Did you find yourself working lots of extra (*crunch*) time to meet a milestone? (We will ignore $E^3$ and the final milestones!) How often do you have to wait for a tool to complete a data conversion? Add up all that "waiting" time. What did your tally come to?

You don't really know? Here is a thought: Add a wee bit of code to your program and write the results to an accumulative log file. Then check it from time to time to see where some of that time is going.

Some people believe in optimizing the game only if there is time somewhere in the schedule. Management quite often counts the time beans and decides that getting the milestone met is much more important than early ongoing debugging or optimization. But just think of that time savings if your tools are written with optimization. Just do not tell management about it or they will think they can ship the product early.

3D rendering tools are expensive and so programmers typically do not have ready access to a live tool. They sometimes write plug-ins, but quite often they will merely write an ASCII scene exporter (ASE) file parser to import the 3D data into their tools that generate the game databases. With this method, programmers do not have to have a licensed copy of a very expensive tool sitting on their desks.

> **Hint:** Prevent artist versus programmer wars by working out who gets the burden of the day-to-day conversion of art resources for the game application before the project coding begins. Use and document it in the game design, technical design, and especially the art bible documents, and treat these as living entities and not written in stone!

This little item brings up a trivial item of artist versus programmer wars. It all comes down to who will have the task of running the tools to export and convert data into a form loaded and used by a game application. Neither typically wants the task and both consider it mundane, but it is nevertheless required. Artists need to run the tools occasionally so as to check results of their changes to art resources. Programmers occasionally need to run the tools to test changes to database designs, etc. But nobody wants to do it all the time. So my suggestion is to automate the tools and incorporate the who and what into the game design, technical design, and art bibles for the project. In that way there will be no misperception.

Let's talk about something else but related to assembly.

In this particular case, an ASE file is an ASCII export from 3D Studio MAX. How many of you have actually written a parser and have wondered where all your processing time had gone? Did you use streaming file reads to load a line at a time, or a block read to read the entire file into memory?

I personally write ASE parsers by loading the entire file into memory even when they are 20MB or larger in size. The core ASE parser code included with this book can actually parse an entire 20MB file and convert about 1.15 million floating-point values from ASCII to doubles in a few seconds. But here is where it really gets interesting!

# ASCII String to Double-Precision Float

Calling the standard C language function atof() to convert an ASCII floating-point value to single or double-precision will add significant time onto your processing time for those large ASE files.

> **Hint:** Do not use the runtime C library atof()! Use the following functionality instead. By using this single function, this book will pay for itself quickly in time savings — and that is what it is all about!

But I have good news for you. The following function will carve those hours back to something a lot more reasonable. What it does is take advantage of a little-known functionality within the floating-point unit of the 80x86 processor.

As discussed in Chapter 8, the FPU loads and handles the following data types:

- (4-byte) single-precision floating-point
- (8-byte) double-precision floating-point
- (10-byte) double extended-precision floating-point
- (10-byte) binary-coded decimal (BCD)

# ASCII to Double

Note that the following code sample expects a normal floating-point number and no exponential. The ASE files do not contain exponential, just really long ASCII floating-point numbers; thus, the reason this code traps for more than 18 digits.

Listing 15-2: ...\chap15\ase2vmp\util.cpp

```
double exptbl[] =           // -e
{
  1.0,                    0.1,
  0.01,                   0.001,
  0.0001,                 0.00001,
  0.000001,               0.0000001,
  0.00000001,             0.000000001,
  0.0000000001,           0.00000000001,
  0.000000000001,         0.0000000000001,
  0.00000000000001,       0.000000000000001,
  0.0000000000000001,     0.00000000000000001,
  0.000000000000000001
};                                    // Limit 18 places

double ASCIItoDouble(const char *pStr)
{
#ifdef CC_VMP_WIN32
  unsigned int dig[80], *pd;
  unsigned char bcd[10+2], *pb;
  double f;
  int n, e;
  const char *p;

  ASSERT_PTR(pStr);

  *(((uint32*)bcd)+0) = 0;    // Clear (12 bytes)
  *(((uint32*)bcd)+1) = 0;
  *(((uint32*)bcd)+2) = 0;    // 2 + 2 spare bytes

    // Collect negative/positive - and delimiters are pre-stripped.

  p = pStr;
  if ('-' == *p)
```

```
  {
    *(bcd+9) = 0x80;    // Set the negative bit into the BCD
    p++;
  }

    // Collect digits and remember position of decimal point

  *dig = 0;              // Prepend a leading zero
  e = n = 0;
  pd = dig+1;

  while (('0' <= *p) && (*p <= '9'))
  {
    *pd++ = (*p++ - '0');    // Collect a digit
    n++;

    // The decimal place is checked after the first digit as no
    // floating-point value should start with a decimal point.
    // Even values between 0 and 1 should have a leading zero!  0.1
    if ('.' == *p)      // Decimal place?
    {                   // Remember its position
      e = n;
      p++;
    }
  }

  // Check for a really BIG (and thus ridiculous) number

  if (n > 18)           // More than 18 digits?
  {
    return atof(pStr);
  }

  if (e)                // 0=1.0  1=0.1  2=0.01  3=0.001, etc.
  {
    e = n - e;          // Get correct exponent
  }

    // repack into BCD (preset lead zeros)
    // last to first digit

  n = (n+1)>>1;         // Start in middle of BCD buffer
  pb = bcd;             // Calc. 1st BCD character position

  while(n--)            // loop for digit pairs
  {
    pd-=2;              // Roll back to last 2 digits
    *pb++ = ((*(pd+0)<<4) | *(pd+1));  // blend two digits
  }
```

```
_asm {
  fbld   tbyte ptr bcd    ; Load (10-byte) BCD
  fstp   f                ; Write 64-bit double-precision
}


  return f * exptbl[e];                    // FASTER
//  return f * pow( 10.0, (double) -e );   // FAST
#else
  return atof(p);                          // Really SLOW
#endif
}
```

If you do not believe me about the speed, then replace all the atof() functions in your current tool with a macro to assign 0.0 and measure the difference in speed. Or better yet, embed the atof() function within this function and then do a float comparison with the precision slop factor since by now you should be very aware that you never ever compare two floating-point numbers to each other to test for equivalence unless a precision slop factor (accuracy) is utilized.

**Tip:**  One should always test optimized code (vector based or not) in conjunction with slow scalar code written in C to ensure that the code is functioning as required.

One more thing: If you insist on using atof() or sscanf(), copy the ASCII number to a scratch buffer before processing it with either of these two functions because processing them within a 20MB file dramatically increases the processing time by hours. Apparently these conversion functions scan the string until they reach the terminator, which in the case of an ASE file can be a few megabytes away instead of a few bytes.

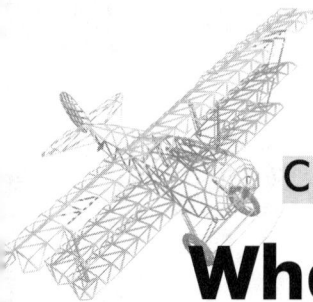

# Chapter 16

# What CPUID?

There are multiple manufacturers all making different models of the 80x86 type microprocessors. Some are variations of the Intel processors and are highly specialized, but most are not. They are clones of the Intel processor family but with their own designs that require alternate optimization methods. Most of these manufacturers have technical manuals usually available in a PDF format that can be downloaded from the Internet and used for all your custom optimization needs. If the project you're coding for uses custom hardware, then you are probably using a custom processor such as National Semiconductor's NS486SXF under an operating system such as pSOS. When you are designing code for a specific processor, your code can be highly optimized and tuned accordingly.

When the hardware you are writing code for is a little more generic, the programmer needs a method to identify the exact model of processor that the code is running on. Each manufacturer has written a sample CPU code detection algorithm that uses the CPUID instruction. This is great, but these code samples are not exactly compatible with each other. Since it is ridiculous to write code that encapsulates all of these samples I have written this chapter to help you. You can find all sorts of variations of the following program on the Internet, but the following is designed to be expandable and versatile.

Most of these Intel processors are deviations of each other but if we take a closer look at their "family type" we will note a pattern of 80(x)86, where the x represents a family number. A 3 would be the 80386, etc. So using this family type number we can actually group the processor into a category of functionality, as each "group" actually has its individual subset of instructions that it could execute.

Other manufacturers have second sourced various models of the 80x86 processor line. Intel and AMD are the primary manufacturers, but other manufacturers have brought to market their modified or less expensive versions of these same processors.

**Workbench Files:** \Bench\x86\chap03\*project*\*platform*

|  | *project* | *platform* |
|---|---|---|
| **CPU ID** | **\cpuid\** | \vc6 |
|  |  | \vc.net |

# CPUID

| Mnemonic | P | PII | K6 | 3D! | 3Mx+ | SSE | SSE2 | A64 | SSE3 | E64T |
|---|---|---|---|---|---|---|---|---|---|---|
| CPUID | ✓ | ✓ | ✓ | ✓ | ✓ | ✓ | ✓ | ✓ | ✓ | ✓ |

cpuid

This instruction uses the value stored in the EAX register as a function identifier and returns the related requested information in the various associated registers.

With the release of the Pentium chip, Intel instituted the CPUID instruction, which gives detailed information of the capabilities of the individual processor. This was also introduced into the re-release of the Intel 80486 processor. AMD has implemented it in all models since the Am486. This makes it easier to identify the capabilities of the CPU being tested.

Before trying to use this instruction, bit #21 of the EFLAGS/RFLAGS must be tested to see if it is writable. If it is, the CPUID instruction exists and therefore can be called. The application code uses mainly the PUSHFD/PUSHFQ and POPFD/POPFQ instructions to manipulate the EFLAGS/RFLAGS register.

```
        pushfd                  ; push EFLAGS register
        pop     eax             ; pop those flags into EAX
        xor     eax,EFLAGS_ID   ; flip ID bit#21 in EFLAGS
        push    eax             ; push modified flags on stack
        popfd                   ; pop flags back into EFLAGS
        pushfd                  ; Push resulting EFLAGS on stack
        pop     ecx             ; pop those flags into ECX
        xor     eax,ecx         ; See if bit stayed flipped
        jz      $nope           ; Jump if bit not flipped

; If here then bit flipped so CPUID exists
        cpuid
```

At a very minimum, all CPUs that support the CPUID instruction support both functions #0 and #1.

| **Flags** | O.flow | Sign | Zero | Aux | Parity | Carry |
|-----------|--------|------|------|-----|--------|-------|
|           | -      | -    | -    | -   | -      | -     |

Flags: None are altered by this opcode.

| Function | Returned Data |
|----------|---------------|
| EAX=0 | EAX = The highest CPUID function number this CPU can handle. The Intel Pentium and 486 return a 1 in EAX. The Pentium Pro returns a 2 in EAX. The EBX, EDX, ECX registers contain a text identifier.<br><br>            ebx   edx   ecx<br>Amd      = Auth, enti, cAMD<br>Centaur = Cent, aurH, auls<br>Cyrix   = Cyri, xIns, tead<br>Intel   = Genu, ineI, ntel |
| EAX=1 | EAX = Version Information.<br>  Bits 0...3 – Stepping ID<br>  Bits 4...7 – Model<br>  Bits 8...11 – Generation / family<br>  Bits 12...15 – Reserved<br>  Bits 16...19 – Extended model<br>  Bits 20...27 – Extended family<br>  Bits 28...31 – Reserved.<br>EBX =<br>  Bits 0...7 – Brand Index<br>  Bits 8...15 – CLFLUSH line size<br>  Bits 16...23 – (**Intel**) # of logical processors<br>              (**AMD**) Reserved<br>  Bits 24...31 – Processor's initial local APIC ID<br>ECX = (**Intel**) Feature info. (**AMD**) Reserved<br>EDX= Feature info |
| **Intel** EAX=2 | EAX, EBX, ECX, EDX = Cache and TLB information |
| **Intel** EAX=3 | EAX, EBX, ECX, EDX = Reserved |

| Function | Returned Data |
|---|---|
| **Intel** EAX=4 | EAX = <br> Bits 0...4 – Cache type <br> Bits 5...7 – Cache level <br> Bit 8 – Self-initializing cache <br> Bit 9 – Fully associative cache <br> Bits 10...13 – Reserved <br> Bits 14-25 – Number of threads sharing cache <br> Bits 26...31 – Number of processor cores on the die <br> EBX = <br> Bits 0...11  L = System coherency line size <br> Bits 12...21  P = Physical line partitions <br> Bits 22...31  W = Ways of associativity <br> ECX = 0...31 Number of sets <br> EDX = Reserved |
| **Intel** EAX=5 | EAX = <br> Bits 0...15 – Smallest monitor-line byte size <br> Bits 16...31 – Reserved <br> EBX, ECX, EDX = Reserved |

| **AMD, Cyrix, and WinChip** <br> EAX= <br> 80000000h | If string identifier with function #0 matches for AMD, Cyrix, or WinChip, test for this function. If a non-zero value is returned in EAX, an extended function set is supported, just like function #0.  The EAX register contains the highest extended function that the CPU can handle. |
|---|---|
| **Intel** <br> EAX= <br> 80000000h | EAX = Maximum input value for extended CPUIDs <br> EBX, ECX, EDX = Reserved |

| **AMD, Cyrix, and WinChip** <br> EAX= <br> 80000001h | See the Intel – Standard CPUID ECX-Feature Flags section. <br> EAX = Processor signature <br> EBX, ECX = Reserved <br> See the AMD – Extended #1 CPUID EDX-Feature Flags section. |
|---|---|
| **Intel** <br> EAX= <br> 80000001h | Extended processor signature and extended feature bits. <br> See the Intel – Extended #1 CPUID EDX-Feature Flags section. |

| AMD, Cyrix, WinChip, and Intel<br><br>EAX =<br>80000002h<br>80000003h<br>80000004h | EAX, EBX, ECX, EDX = 4 * 4 * 3 = 48 byte text string |
|---|---|

| AMD<br>EAX =<br>80000005h | TLB and L1 cache information |
|---|---|
| Intel<br>EAX =<br>80000005h | EAX, EBX, ECX, EDX = Reserved |

| AMD, Cyrix, WinChip, and Intel<br><br>EAX =<br>80000006h | L2 Cache bits<br>ECX =<br>    Bits 0...7 – Cache line size<br>    Bits 8...11 – Lines per tag<br>    Bits 12...15 – L2 Associativity<br>    Bits 16...31 – Number of 1K cache blocks<br>EAX, EBX, EDX = Reserved |
|---|---|

| AMD<br>EAX =<br>80000007h | EDX = Advanced power management<br>EAX, EBX, ECX = Reserved |
|---|---|
| Intel<br>EAX =<br>80000007h | EAX, EBX, ECX, EDX = Reserved |

| AMD, Intel<br>EAX =<br>80000008h | EAX =<br>    Bits 0...7 – Physical address bits<br>    Bits 8...15 – Virtual address bits<br>    Bits 16...31 – Reserved<br>EBX, ECX, EDX = Reserved |
|---|---|

The initial CPUID call gives us the manufacturer ID string.

```
Intel:   db     "GenuineIntel"

         mov    eax,0            ; Function #0
         cpuid

         cmp    ebx,dword ptr Intel
         jne    $Nope            ; Jump if not a match
         cmp    edx,dword ptr Intel+4
         jne    $Nope            ; Jump if not a match
         cmp    ecx,dword ptr Intel+8
         jne    $Nope            ; Jump if not a match

; We have a match!!! (If an Intel chip!)
```

# Standard CPUID EDX-Feature Flags

```
; CPUID (EDX= flags)  <<< Command EAX=1
```

| CPUIDFLG_ | Code | Bit | Flag Descriptions |
|---|---|---|---|
| FPU | 000000001h | 0 | Floating-point support |
| VME | 000000002h | 1 | Virtual Mode Extensions |
| DE | 000000004h | 2 | Debugging Extensions |
| PSE | 000000008h | 3 | Page Size Extension |
| TSC | 000000010h | 4 | RDTSC supported |
| MSR | 000000020h | 5 | RDMSR and WRMSR |
| PAE | 000000040h | 6 | Physical Address Extensions |
| MCE | 000000080h | 7 | Machine Check Exception |
| CX8 | 000000100h | 8 | CMPXCHG8B supported |
| APIC | 000000200h | 9 | Advanced Programmable Interrupt Controller |
| --- | 000000400h | 10 | Reserved |
| SEP | 000000800h | 11 | SYSCALL, SYSRET enable |
| MTRR | 000004000h | 12 | Memory-type Range Reg |
| PGE | 000002000h | 13 | Page Global Enable |
| MCA | 000004000h | 14 | Machine Check Architecture |
| CMOV | 000008000h | 15 | CMOV supported |
| PAT | 000010000h | 16 | Page Attribute Table |
| PSE | 000020000h | 17 | 36-bit Page-Size Extensions |
| PSN | 000040000h | 18 | (Intel) Processor Serial # (AMD) Reserved |
| CLFLUSH | 000080000h | 19 | CLFlush enabled |
| --- | 000100000h | 20 | Reserved |
| DS | 000200000h | 21 | (Intel) Debug Store (AMD) Reserved |

| CPUIDFLG_ | Code | Bit | Flag Descriptions |
|---|---|---|---|
| ACPI | 000400000h | 22 | (Intel) Thermal Monitor<br>(AMD) Reserved |
| MMX | 000800000h | 23 | MMX supported |
| FXSR | 001000000h | 24 | Fast floating-point save and load |
| SSE | 002000000h | 25 | SSE supported |
| SSE2 | 004000000h | 26 | SSE2 supported |
| SS | 008000000h | 27 | (Intel) Self Snoop<br>(AMD) Reserved |
| HTT | 010000000h | 28 | (Intel) HTT (HyperThread)<br>(AMD) Reserved |
| TM | 020000000h | 29 | (Intel) Thermal Monitor<br>(AMD) Reserved |
| --- | 040000000h | 30 | Reserved |
| PBE | 080000000h | 31 | (Intel) Pending Break<br>(AMD) Reserved |

# Intel — Standard CPUID ECX-Feature Flags

```
; CPUID (ECX= flags)  <<< Command EAX=1
```

| CPUIDFLG_ | Code | Bit | Flag Descriptions |
|---|---|---|---|
| SSE3 | 000000001h | 0 | SSE3 supported |
| --- | 00000000xh | 1, 2 | Reserved |
| MONITOR | 000000008h | 3 | MONITOR,WAIT supported |
| DS_CPL | 000000010h | 4 | CPL Qualified Debug Store |
| --- | 0000000x0h | 5, 6 | Reserved |
| EIST | 000000080h | 7 | Enhanced Intel SpeedStep |
| TM2 | 000000100h | 8 | Thermal Monitor 2 |
| --- | 000000200h | 9 | Reserved |
| CID | 000000400h | 10 | Context ID |
| --- | 00000xx00h | 11-13 | Reserved |
| xTPR | 000004000h | 14 | Send Task Priority Messages |
| --- | | 15-31 | Reserved |

## Intel — Extended #1 CPUID EDX-Feature Flags

; CPUID (**EDX**= flags)  <<< Command EAX=8000:0001h

| CPUIDFLG_ | Code | Bit | Flag Descriptions |
|---|---|---|---|
| --- | | 0-28 | Reserved |
| VME | 020000000h | 29 | EM64T supported |
| --- | | 30-31 | Reserved |

## AMD — Extended #1 CPUID EDX-Feature Flags

; CPUID (**EDX**= flags)  <<< Command EAX= 8000:0001h

| AMD_EFLG | Code | Bit | Flag Descriptions |
|---|---|---|---|
| FPU | 000000001h | 0 | Floating Point support |
| VME | 000000002h | 1 | Virtual Mode Extensions |
| DE | 000000004h | 2 | Debugging Extensions |
| PSE | 000000008h | 3 | Page Size Extension |
| TSC | 000000010h | 4 | RDTSC supported |
| MSR | 000000020h | 5 | RDMSR and WRMSR |
| PAE | 000000040h | 6 | Physical Address Extensions |
| MCE | 000000080h | 7 | Machine Check Exception |
| CX8 | 000000100h | 8 | CMPXCHG8B supported |
| APIC | 000000200h | 9 | Advanced Programmable Interrupt Controller |
| --- | 000000400h | 10 | Reserved |
| SEP | 000000800h | 11 | SYSCALL, SYSRET enabled |
| MTRR | 000004000h | 12 | Memory-type Range Reg |
| PGE | 000002000h | 13 | Global Page Extension |
| MCA | 000004000h | 14 | Machine Check Architecture |
| CMOV | 000008000h | 15 | CMOV supported |
| PAT | 000010000h | 16 | Page Attribute Table |
| PSE | 000020000h | 17 | Page-Size Extensions |
| --- | 0000x0000h | 18, 19 | Reserved |
| NEPP | 000100000h | 20 | No-Execute Page Protection |
| --- | 000200000h | 21 | Reserved |
| MMXEXT | 000400000h | 22 | MMX Extensions supported |
| MMX | 000800000h | 23 | MMX supported |
| FXSAVE | 001000000h | 24 | FXSAVE, FXRSTOR enable |
| FFXSAVE | 002000000h | 25 | Fast FXSAVE, FXRSTOR |

| AMD_EFLG | Code | Bit | Flag Descriptions |
|---|---|---|---|
| --- | | 26, 28 | Reserved |
| EM64T | 020000000h | 29 | EM64T / AMD64 (long) |
| 3DNOWX | 040000000h | 30 | 3DNow! MMX+ supported |
| 3DNOW | 080000000h | 31 | 3DNow! supported |

# PIII Serial License

Intel created a feature for the PIII processor in the original SSE instruction set, but due to a political uproar as an infringement upon privacy it was removed in successive processors. In some respects it was a good thing to be able to track a particular computer, such as a violator of an online gaming network. An exact machine could be banned due to its fingerprint. However, others felt that people would lose their anonymity while on the Internet.

```
mov eax,1
cpuid

test  edx,CPUIDFLG_PSN
jz  $xit

   ; CPUID serial number is supported and enabled!

push eax
mov eax,3
cpuid
pop  eax

   ; eax:edx:ecx = 96-bit serial number in capitalized hex digits.
   ;               XXXX-XXXX-XXXX-XXXX-XXXX-XXXX
$xit:
```

# Sample CPU Detection Code

There are a lot of features in the CPUID, but most of them are not needed for what we are doing here. I have documented some of what this instruction does (a lot more than what I normally need), but I strongly recommend that if you are truly interested in this instruction that you download the manufacturer's technical manuals.

Most programs being written these days are primarily written for a Protected Mode environment and so we only need to deal with, at a minimum, the first processor capable of truly running in Protected

Mode — the 386 processor. (The 80286 does not count!) This CPU detection algorithm detects the model, manufacturer, and capabilities, and sets flags as such. As we really only deal with 32-bit modes in this book, we do not bother detecting for an 8086, 80186, or an 80286. We do, however, detect for a 386 or above. In our algorithm we use the following CPU IDs.

This instruction has been enhanced since I wrote *Vector Game Math Processors* as newer instructions have been added to the processor. It has been used throughout the book, but let us examine it a bit closer.

```
;       CPU Detect - definition IDs


CPU_386           = 3      ; 80386
CPU_486           = 4      ; 80486
CPU_PENTIUM       = 5      ; P5 (Pentium)
CPU_PENTIUM_PRO   = 6      ; Pentium Pro
CPU_PII           = 6      ; PII
```

Prior to the Pentium processor, a computer system would optionally have a floating-point chip, which contained a FPU. In the case of CPUs, no functionality is lost as one upgrades to a more advanced processor; they are all downward compatible. This is not the case with the FPU. Some functionality was lost; so if writing any floating-point instructions, you should know which FPU you are coding for. Some external FP chips did not exactly match the processor but were compatible.

```
; Legacy CPUs and compatible FPU coprocessors
;                  CPU_086       NONE, FPU_087
;                  CPU_186       NONE, FPU_087
;                  CPU_286       NONE, FPU_287
;                  CPU_386       NONE, FPU_287, FPU_387
;                  CPU_486       NONE, FPU_387, FPU_487

;       FPU Detect - definition IDs

FPU_NONE      =   0           ; No FPU chip
FPU_087       =   1           ; 8087
FPU_287       =   2           ; 80287
FPU_387       =   3           ; 80387
FPU_487       =   CPU_486
FPU_PENTIUM   =   CPU_PENTIUM
FPU_PII       =   CPU_PII
```

The various manufacturers implemented the same functionality as Intel but recently have begun to do their own. Due to this, unions and intersections can be drawn, and so we use individual flags to indicate CPU capability.

## x86 CPU Detect — Bit Flags

```
typedef enum
{
    CPUBITS_FPU        = 0x0001, // FPU flag
    CPUBITS_MMX        = 0x0002, // MMX flag
    CPUBITS_3DNOW      = 0x0004, // 3DNow! flag
    CPUBITS_FXSR       = 0x0008, // Fast FP Store
    CPUBITS_SSE        = 0x0010, // SSE
    CPUBITS_SSE2       = 0x0020, // SSE (Ext 2)
    CPUBITS_3DNOW_MMX  = 0x0040, // 3DNow! (MMX Ext)
    CPUBITS_3DNOW_EXT  = 0x0080, // 3DNow! (Ext)
    CPUBITS_3DNOW_SSE  = 0x0100, // 3DNow! Professional
    CPUBITS_HTT        = 0x0200, // Hyperthreading Tech
    CPUBITS_SSE3       = 0x0400, // Prescott NI
    CPUBITS_EM64T      = 0x0800, // EM64T supported
    CPUBITS_AMD64      = 0x1000, // AMD Long Mode
} CPUBITS;
```

Each manufacturer has its own unique optimization methods and so we get a vendor name.

## x86 CPU Detect — Vendors

**Listing 16-1: ...\inc???\CpuAsm.h**

```
typedef enum
{
    CPUVEN_UNKNOWN   = 0, // Unknown
    CPUVEN_INTEL     = 1, // Intel
    CPUVEN_AMD       = 2, // AMD
    CPUVEN_CYRIX     = 3, // Cyrix
    CPUVEN_CENTAUR   = 4, // IDT Centaur (WinChip)
    CPUVEN_NATIONAL  = 5, // National Semiconductor
    CPUVEN_UMC       = 6, // UMC
    CPUVEN_NEXGEN    = 7, // NexGen
    CPUVEN_RISE      = 8, // Rise
    CPUVEN_TRANSMETA = 9  // Transmeta
} CPUVEN;
```

We use the following data structure to reference the extracted CPU information.

## Cpu Detect — Information

```
typedef struct CpuInfoType
{
    uint   nCpuId;   // CPU type identifier
    uint   nFpuId;   // floating-point Unit ID
    uint   nBits;    // Feature bits
    uint   nMfg;     // Manufacturer
    byte   nProcCnt; // # of logical processors
    byte   pad[3];
```

```
} CpuInfo;
CpuInfo struct 4
        nCpuId   dd      0  ; CPU type identifier
        nFpuId   dd      0  ; Floating-point unit identifier
        nBits    dd      0  ; Feature bits
        nMfg     dd      0  ; Manufacturer
        nProcCnt db      0  ; # of logical processors
        pad      db      0,0,0
CpuInfo ends
```

This book's CPU detection uses the following data structure for finding matching vendor information. Each microprocessor that supports the CPUID instruction has encoded a 12-byte text string identifying the manufacturer.

```
;       Vendor Data Structure

VENDOR STRUCT   4
        vname   BYTE      '------------'
        Id      DWORD     CPUVEN_UNKNOWN
VENDOR ENDS

VENDOR { "AMD ISBETTER", CPUVEN_AMD }       ; AMD Proto
VENDOR { "AuthenticAMD", CPUVEN_AMD }       ; AMD
VENDOR { "CyrixInstead", CPUVEN_CYRIX }     ; Cyrix & IBM
VENDOR { "GenuineIntel", CPUVEN_INTEL }     ; Intel
VENDOR { "CentaurHauls", CPUVEN_CENTAUR }   ; Centaur
VENDOR { "UMC UMC UMC ", CPUVEN_UMC }       ; UMC (retired)
VENDOR { "NexGenDriver", CPUVEN_NEXGEN }    ; NexGen (retired)
VENDOR { "RiseRiseRise", CPUVEN_RISE }      ; Rise
VENDOR { "GenuineTMx86", CPUVEN_TRANSMETA } ; Transmeta
```

---

**Listing 16-2: ...\RootApp.cpp**

```cpp
#include "CpuAsm.h"                  // CPU module

    CpuInfo cinfo;
    char szBuf[ CPU_SZBUF_MAX ];

    CpuDetect( &cinfo );             // Detect CPU

    cout << "\nCPU Detection Code Snippet\n\n";
            // Fills in buffer 'szBuf' with CPU information!
    cout << CpuInfoStr( szBuf, &cinfo ) << endl;

    CpuSetup( &cinfo );              // Now set up function pointers
```

---

This is an example of what gets filled into the ASCII buffer with a call to the function CpuInfoStr().

```
"CpuId:15 'INTEL' FPU MMX FXSR SSE SSE2 SSE3 HTT"
```

That took care of the initial detection code. Now comes the fun part — function mapping. Every function you write should have a set of slower default code written in a high-level language such as C. This is really very simple. First there are the private definitions:

```
void FmdSetup(const CpuInfo * const pcinfo);

void vmp_FMulGeneric(float * const pfD, float fA, float fB);
void vmp_FMulAsm3DNow(float * const pfD, float fA, float fB);
void vmp_FMulAsmSSE(float * const pfD, float fA, float fB);

void vmp_FDivGeneric(float * const pfD, float fA, float fB);
void vmp_FDivAsm3DNow(float * const pfD, float fA, float fB);
void vmp_FDivAsmSSE(float * const pfD, float fA, float fB);

void vmp_FDivFastAsm3DNow(float * const pfD, float fA, float fB);
void vmp_FDivFastAsmSSE(float * const pfD, float fA, float fB);
```

Then there are the public application definitions:

```
// Multiplication
typedef void (*vmp_FMulProc)(float * const pfD, float fA, float fB);
extern vmp_FMulProc vmp_FMul;

// Division
typedef void (*vmp_FDivProc)(float * const pfD, float fA, float fB);
extern vmp_FDivProc vmp_FDiv;
extern vmp_FDivProc vmp_FDivFast;
```

There are the generic as well as processor-based functions such as:

```
// Multiplication

void vmp_FMulGeneric(float * const pfD, float fA, float fB)
{
    ASSERT_PTR4(pfD);

    *pfD = fA * fB;
}
```

The initialization code assigns the appropriate processor-based function to the public function pointer:

```
void CpuSetup(const CpuInfo * const pcinfo)
{
    ASSERT_PTR4(pcinfo);

    if (CPUBITS_SSE & pcinfo->nBits)
      {
        vmp_FMul =            vmp_FMulAsmSSE;
        vmp_FDiv =            vmp_FDivAsmSSE;
        vmp_FDivFast =        vmp_FDivFastAsmSSE; // ***FAST***
      }
```

```
else if (CPUBITS_3DNOW & pcinfo->nBits)
  {
    vmp_FMul =              vmp_FMulAsm3DNow;
    vmp_FDiv =              vmp_FDivAsm3DNow;
    vmp_FDivFast =          vmp_FDivFastAsm3DNow;    //***FAST***
  }

else
  {
    vmp_FMul =              vmp_FMulGeneric;
    vmp_FDiv =              vmp_FDivGeneric;
    vmp_FDivFast =          vmp_FDivGeneric;
  }
}
```

You will probably need to play with the mapping until you get used to it. You could use case statements, function table lookups, or other methods, but due to similarity of processor types I find the conditional branching with Boolean logic seems to work best.

What is supplied should be thought of as a starting point. It should be included with most applications, even those that do not use any custom assembly code, as it will compile a breakdown of the computer that ran the application. With custom assembly code, it is the building block of writing cross processor code. There is one more bit of "diagnostic" information that you can use — the processor speed. It can give you an idea of why your application is not running well. (Sometimes processors do not run at their marked speed either through misconfiguration or overheating.) This is discussed in Chapter 18, "System."

The listed information can be obtained by using the included function CpuDetect(); however, from your point of view, who manufactured the CPU is not nearly as important as to the bits CPUBITS listed above! Each of those bits being set indicates the existence of the associated functionality. Your program would merely check the bit and correlate the correct set of code. If the processor sets the CPUBITS_3DNOW bit, then it would need to vector to the 3DNow!-based algorithm. If the CPUBITS_SSE bit is set, then it would vector to that set of code. Keep in mind that when I first started writing this book neither existed on the same CPU, but while I was writing it, AMD came out with 3DNow! Professional. This is a union of the two superset families (excluding the SSE3) for which there is also a CPU bit definition. However, that can easily change in the future. My recommendation would be to rate their priority from highest to lowest performance in the initialization logic of your program based upon your applications' criteria.

# Chapter 17

# PC I/O

All computers have to have some form of input or output in their execution. This will be one of the following:

- Neither input nor output — A box that does not do anything!
- Input only — Those status reports for your manager that never get read.
- Output only — Always talking but never thinking!
- Input *and* output — A (hopefully) *useful computer*

This chapter discusses one method needed to allow for the input and output of data. There is usually a BIOS or software library that you can use that encapsulates the hardware known as the BSP (board support package), but if you are programming an application that requires direct port access, read on! For example, the communications API in Win32 does not give you time stamps or error status on each character received and some communication protocols require it.

Cameras typically input to a computer using memory in graphic frame grabbers just as a graphic display outputs using memory in graphic frame buffers, but the I/O (input/output) port is another method one can use to communicate with a computer. Network cards, serial communications, computer mouse, display controller on a graphics card, keyboard, etc., all use an input port, a "doorway," to get information into or out of a computer.

For example, pressing a key to type this document caused the little computer chip in my keyboard to decode the row and column of the keyboard matrix it was scanning, convert it to the corresponding value representing that scan code, and send it out that little wire or infrared port from my keyboard to my computer. There it arrived in an input port, causing an interrupt and letting my computer know there was something waiting to be read. Interested? Well, read on!

# IN — Input from Port

IN *operand*

| Mnemonic | P | PII | K6 | 3D! | 3Mx+ | SSE | SSE2 | A64 | SSE3 | E64T |
|----------|---|-----|----|-----|------|-----|------|-----|------|------|
| IN | ✓ | ✓ | ✓ | ✓ | ✓ | ✓ | ✓ | ✓ | ✓ | ✓ |

in    *AL/AX/EAX/RAX, #8*       (Un)signed
in    *AL/AX/EAX/RAX, DX*

This instruction inputs an 8-, 16-, 32-, or 64-bit value from the specified 8-bit port (0…255), or an 8-, 16-, 32-, or 64-bit value from the 16-bit port (0…65535) specified by the DX register.

| Flags | O.flow | Sign | Zero | Aux | Parity | Carry |
|-------|--------|------|------|-----|--------|-------|
| | - | - | - | - | - | - |

Flags: None are affected by this opcode.

## Vertical Sync

When working a legacy VGA graphics display there is sometimes a need to synchronize your code to the VBlank (vertical blank). An example would be using DirectX under Win95. If we have animation running at a frame rate in a dual frame environment, there is no clean way to wait for the VBlank on frames that do not need to flip because it is too easy to miss them as DirectX only waits for the leading edge of the VBlank. Note that in a multithreaded environment there is a chance that we could get preempted by another thread, causing us to miss the VBlank. We could also be preempted just after detecting it, causing us to miss it entirely.

```
VGA_STATUS   = 03dah      ; VGA Status address
VSYNC_MASK   = 00001000b  ; VSync bit

        mov     edx,VGA_STATUS
        mov     ah,VSYNC_MASK

Loop:   in      al,dx       ; Get VGA status
        test    al,ah       ; Is VSync bit set?
        jz      Loop        ; Jump if not
```

# OUT — Output to Port

OUT *operand*

| Mnemonic | P | PII | K6 | 3D! | 3Mx+ | SSE | SSE2 | A64 | SSE3 | E64T |
|----------|---|-----|-----|-----|------|-----|------|-----|------|------|
| OUT | ✓ | ✓ | ✓ | ✓ | ✓ | ✓ | ✓ | ✓ | ✓ | ✓ |

out    #8, *AL/AX/EAX/RAX*        (Un)signed
out    *DX, AL/AX/EAX/RAX*

This instruction outputs an 8-, 16-, 32-, or 64-bit value to the specified
8-bit port (0…255), or an 8-, 16-, 32-, or 64-bit value to the 16-bit port
(0…65535) specified by the DX register.

| **Flags** | O.flow | Sign | Zero | Aux | Parity | Carry |
|-----------|--------|------|------|-----|--------|-------|
|           | - | - | - | - | - | - |

Flags: None are affected by this opcode.

The following two functions are snippets from the examples later in this
chapter.

```
;   Initialize the parallel port
;
;   void PPortInit(void)

PPortInit proc  near
        mov     edx,PPort       ; Get base address
        add     edx,iPIO_DCR    ; Add offset
        in      al,dx           ; Get control bits

        or      al,iPIO_DCR_DIR ; Set direction bit to tristate
                                ; For bidirectional access
        out     dx,al           ; Do it!
        ret
PPortInit endp



;   Serial Out  ah=char

Sout    proc    near
        mov     edx,ComAdr
        add     edx,5

$S1:    in      al,dx           ; Get status
        test    al,00100000b    ; Twx holding register empty
        jz      $S1             ; Jump if still has character

        mov     al,ah           ; Get character
```

```
        mov    edx,ComAdr
        out    dx,al
        ret
Sout    endp
```

# INSx — Input from Port to String

| Mnemonic | P | PII | K6 | 3D! | 3Mx+ | SSE | SSE2 | A64 | SSE3 | E64T |
|----------|---|-----|----|-----|------|-----|------|-----|------|------|
| INSB | ✓ | ✓ | ✓ | ✓ | ✓ | ✓ | ✓ | ✓ | ✓ | ✓ |

| | | |
|---|---|---|
| insb | (Un)signed | 8 |
| insw | | 16 |
| insd | | 32 |
| ins   byte ptr es:[edi], dx | | 8 |
| ins   word ptr es:[edi], dx | | 16 |
| ins   dword ptr es:[edi], dx | | 32 |

This instruction inputs an 8-, 16-, or 32-bit value from the specified 16-bit port (0...65535), copies it to the destination string referenced by ES:[EDI], and advances the EDI register based upon the setting of the Direction flag and the data size. It is similar to a STOSx instruction except that the data is read from the port instead of the AL/AX/EAX register and both are written (stored) to the string. This is actually a DMA transfer from an input port but is really only efficient if trying to move more than 64 bytes.

| Flags | O.flow | Sign | Zero | Aux | Parity | Carry |
|-------|--------|------|------|-----|--------|-------|
| | - | - | - | - | - | - |

Flags: None are affected by this opcode.

# OUTSx — Output String to Port

| Mnemonic | P | PII | K6 | 3D! | 3Mx+ | SSE | SSE2 | A64 | SSE3 | E64T |
|----------|---|-----|----|-----|------|-----|------|-----|------|------|
| OUTSB | ✓ | ✓ | ✓ | ✓ | ✓ | ✓ | ✓ | ✓ | ✓ | ✓ |

| | | |
|---|---|---|
| outsb | (Un)signed | 8 |
| outsw | | 16 |
| outsd | | 32 |

| | |
|---|---|
| outs   dx, byte ptr ds:[esi] | 8 |
| outs   dx, word ptr ds:[esi] | 16 |
| outs   dx, dword ptr ds:[esi] | 32 |

This instruction outputs an 8-, 16-, or 32-bit value from the source string referenced by DS:[ESI], copies it to the 16-bit port (0…65535), and advances the ESI register based upon the settings of the Direction flag and the data size. It is similar to a LODSx instruction as data is read (loaded) from a string but with the exception that the data is written to the port instead of AL/AX/EAX register. This is actually a DMA transfer to an output port but is really only efficient if trying to move more than 64 bytes.

| **Flags** | O.flow | Sign | Zero | Aux | Parity | Carry |
|---|---|---|---|---|---|---|
| | - | - | - | - | - | - |

Flags: None are affected by this opcode.

A UART (universal asynchronous receiver/transmitter) these days has a FIFO (first in, first out) buffer typically 16 bytes in length. You could send this in a variety of ways. If you know the FIFO is empty, you can have some sort of unrolled loop:

```
i=0
REPEAT   16
         mov     al,[esi+i]
         out     dx,al
i=i+1
ENDM
         add     esi,16
```

…or use a string function:

```
         mov     ecx,16
rep      outsb                    ; outs dx,byte ptr [esi]
```

…keeping in mind the >=64 repeat needed to be efficient. Because of this, the unrolled loop is better.

# Serial/Parallel Port for IBM PC

To get information about the serial and parallel ports of your PC, visit the National Semiconductor web site at www.national.com and download the following PDF data sheets.

■   16550 UART — At the time of this printing this was the PC16550D, which is a UART (universal asynchronous receiver/ transmitter) used for serial communications.

■   NS486SXF processor — This is a 486 embedded processor, but we're really only interested in two sections: "3.4.2 The IEEE 1284 Bi-directional Parallel Port" and "3.4.5 The Serial UART Port."

**Hint:**  Do not print the entire manual for the 80486 as it is a very *big* manual! And yes, I know. 486? But the manual describes peripheral components compatible with the standard PC computer.

Both of these are excellent references for all the I/O information necessary for communicating directly with the serial and parallel ports on your PC.

## Parallel Port

Normally you do not need to access this port, but what if you have a specialized application that is not communicating with a printer but something else, like a parallel communications device or a dongle (hasp). What if your PC is in reality an embedded system where it runs a display in a Gazebo and as such has no mouse or standard keyboard, but merely a couple of buttons for advancing through a slide presentation. It just powers up and runs an advertisement or is a slot machine using a NLX motherboard or some other embedded device, not necessarily a PC. What if it can be signaled through communications to play something else? What if this same device needs a watchdog to know it failed or dip switches for some kind of addressing or feature selection just by setting some switches? Maybe it drives an LCD (liquid crystal display). (Remember, no keyboard or maybe it drives one directly in parallel.) Or maybe you are just itching to build some hardware to plug into your computer.

Datel used to manufacture a special parallel interface card for the PC. This was designed to connect via a parallel cable to a Game Shark made by InterAct and allowed a PC to be able to connect to various consoles. Hackers built software drivers and tools that allowed them to develop games for some of those consoles such as the old Sony Playstation.

## Parallel Port Dip Switches

Our little experiment lets us tinker with reading dip switches plugged into the parallel port. You can buy an eight-bank dip switch at your local Radio Shack store (part #275-1301).

The PC parallel port specifications state that:

| | DB25P | Description |
|---|---|---|
| ⇔ | 2 | DO |
| ⇔ | 3 | DI |
| ⇔ | 4 | D2 |
| ⇔ | 5 | D3 |
| ⇔ | 6 | D4 |
| ⇔ | 7 | D5 |
| ⇔ | 8 | D6 |
| | 9 | D7 |
| | 18-25 | GND |

| | DB25P | Description |
|---|---|---|
| ⇐ | 1 | ~Strobe |
| ⇒ | 10 | ~ACK |
| ⇒ | 11 | ~BUSY |
| ⇒ | 12 | PE |
| ⇒ | 13 | SLCT |
| ⇐ | 14 | ~AUTOFEED XT |
| ⇒ | 15 | ~ERROR |
| ⇐ | 16 | ~INIT |
| ⇐ | 17 | ~SLCT IN |

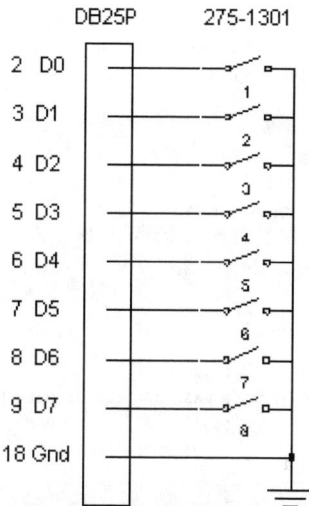

*Figure 17-1: Parallel port to octal switch*

First we need to initialize the port that we will consider LPT1, which uses a base address of 378h. We should note that the typical parallel port is set up to be unidirectional and not bidirectional, which means that we normally can only write to the data lines, not read from them. In our initialization function we set the bit, which causes our eight data bits to tri-state, thus making them bidirectional.

Parallel Port Base Address

| LPTI | LPT2 |
|---|---|
| 378h | 278h |

**Note:** Old monochrome cards used 3BCh for their parallel port.

```
iPIO_DCR        = 2                ; Device control register

iPIO_DCR_DIR  = 00100000b      ; 20h = direction bit

PPort   dd      378h           ; Using LPT1 for base address


;  Initialize the parallel port
;
;  void PPortInit(void)

PPortInit proc   near
        mov     edx,PPort      ; Get base address
        add     edx,iPIO_DCR   ; Add offset
        in      al,dx          ; Get control bits

        or      al,iPIO_DCR_DIR ; Set direction bit to tri-state
                               ; For bidirectional access
        out     dx,al          ; Do it!
        ret
PPortInit endp


;  Read switches from the parallel port
;  Note: Only lower 8 bits will be set, upper bits clear
;
;  uint32 PPortRead(void)

PPortRead proc   near
        xor     eax,eax        ; eax=0
        mov     edx,PPort      ; base address is data port
        in      al,dx          ; get 8 bits from port
        ret                    ; return value in EAX
PPortRead endp
```

Lets look at the C code calling our parallel port functions:

```
uint32 n;

PPortInit();
n = PPortRead();

printf("switches =0x%x", n);
```

You will note that the logic is inverted so when a switch is off, thus leaving the circuit open, a logical 1 is produced, but if the switch is on, thus closing the circuit and shorting the input to ground, a logic 0 occurs. You can think of this as upside-down binary. To solve for this just insert the following:

```
PPortRead proc  near
        xor     eax,eax             ; eax=0
        mov     edx,PPort           ; base address is data port
        in      al,dx               ; get 8 bits from port
        xor     eax,000000ffh       ; Flip switch bits
        ret                         ; return value in EAX
PPortRead endp
```

The second XOR just before the RET will flip the switch bits so off=0 and on=1. This will help make life simpler.

I need to mention that there is one little problem with the circuit. Although the specifications of the data port consider the tri-state (float) condition to be a logical 1 until pulled to ground, some computers float with voltage a little low so they are not considered a logical 1. And as such the switches are thought of as always closed. The parallel port has no (+5v) source and as such one of two things need to be done: an external one supplied (battery, etc.) or one leached off all the other control signals, creating a pseudo 5-volt supply. Those signals would obviously have to have their output signals in a high state. That voltage would then need to be connected in series to a pull-up resistor attached to one side of each of the switch terminals, thus giving them a logical high signal. The other switch terminal is connected to ground, so when the switch is closed it pulls the signal low.

# Serial Port

DOS had a BIOS function that allowed you to print a TTY message to the output device. But what if you are running an embedded operating system like pSOS or running under Win32? The printf() and TTY functions do not really go anywhere, especially if you are running a full-screen DirectX application. Well, you could always do a kind of printf() out the serial port to a smart terminal. Did you know you could pick up old PS/2 computers from places like Goodwill for $9-$50 still in running condition and looking in pretty good shape? I call them throw-away computers. When running an old DOS version of ProComm, they work great. When they break, you throw them away! The lap-link cable to connect your two computers will probably cost you more than the computer. To reduce my desk footprint I use a very small 9" VGA monochrome monitor and a very small 83-key keyboard. Unfortunately, they are not as cheap. I use a logging library that I recreate for every company I work for. In it I do a single log write and it can optionally go to a disk file, a Notepad window, and/or a particular serial port at a specified baud rate. In Win32 I use the CommAPI so it'll work in all the Win32 platforms, but the following will only work in Win95, DOS, or Linux.

Of course, other operating systems such as embedded systems that allow Real Mode or security access to the I/O ports and interrupts, will work as well. To simplify it I have hard-coded the base address and IRQ information to COM1, but it is really a snap to do a table lookup during the initialization function to set things up and save the actual information needed for the send function.

The PC serial port specifications state that:

| | DB9S | DB25S | Description |
|---|---|---|---|
| ⇒ | 1 | 8 | CD (Carrier Detect) |
| ⇒ | 2 | 3 | RCV (Receive Data) |
| ⇐ | 3 | 2 | TWX (Transmit Data) |
| ⇐ | 4 | 20 | DTR (Data Terminal Ready) |
| | 5 | 7 | GND |
| ⇒ | 6 | 6 | DSR (Data Set Ready) |
| ⇐ | 7 | 4 | RTS (Request To Send) |
| ⇒ | 8 | 5 | CTS (Clear To Send) |
| ⇒ | 9 | 22 | RI (Ring Indicator) |

Serial Port Table

| | COM1 | COM2 | COM3 | COM4 | COM5 | COM6 |
|---|---|---|---|---|---|---|
| BaseAddr | 3F8h | 2F8h | 3E8h | 2E8h | 368h | 268h |
| IRQ Interrupt | 0Ch | 0Bh | 0Ch | 0Bh | 0Ch | 0Bh |
| IRQ Mask | 0EFh | 0F7h | 0EFh | 0F7h | 0EFh | 0F7h |

```
INTMSK      = 21h              ; Mask register port #

ComAdr  dd   3f8h
ComIO   db   0ch
ComMask db   0efh

OldMask db   0              ; Old interrupt mask


; bool ComInit(uint nBaud);

ComInit proc    near
        push    ebp
        mov     ebp,esp
        push    ebx
```

```
; Disable 8259 interrupt for IRQ

        in      al,INTMSK       ; Get IRQ bits
        mov     ah,ComMask      ; Clear interrupt bit
        mov     OldMask,al      ; Save them
        not     ah              ; Flip mask into strip
        or      al,ah           ; Disable bit
        out     INTMSK,al       ; Set IRQ bits

; Disable UART interrupts

        mov     edx,ComAdr      ; Port address
        inc     edx             ; (+1) .IER - Interrupt Enable
        mov     eax,0           ; disable UART interrupt bits
        out     dx,al           ; Disable UART interrupts

; Disable all handshaking

        add     edx,3           ; (+4)
        out     dx,al           ; Disable all handshaking

; Set up for appropriate protocol

        dec     edx             ; (+3) .LCR - Line Control
        in      al,dx           ; Get Line Control
        or      al,10000000b    ; Set Divisor Latch Access
        out     dx,al

; Calculate baud rate divisor

        mov     ecx,[ebp+8]
        mov     edx,0
        mov     eax,1843200/16
        div     ecx

; Write baud rate

        mov     edx,ComAdr      ; Port address
        out     dx,al
        inc     edx             ; (+1)
        mov     al,ah
        out     dx,al

; Bits per char and parity

        mov     al,00000011b    ; 8 bits no parity
        add     edx,2           ; (+3) .LCR
        out     dx,al
```

```
; Set handshaking lines

        inc     edx                 ; (+4) .MCR
        mov     al,00001111b
        out     dx,al

        mov     eax,1               ; Success
        pop     ebx
        pop     ebp
        ret
ComInit endp


; Serial Out   ah=char

Sout    proc    near
        mov     edx,ComAdr
        add     edx,5

$S1:    in      al,dx               ; Get status
        test    al,00100000b        ; Twx Holding Register Empty
        jz      $S1                 ; Jump if still has character

        mov     al,ah               ; Get character
        mov     edx,ComAdr
        out     dx,al
        ret
Sout    endp


; void ComStr(byte *pStr);
;
; Write String

ComStr  proc    near
        push    ebp
        mov     ebp,esp

        mov     ecx,[ebp+arg1]      ; Get string pointer

        mov     ah,[ecx]            ; Get a character
        inc     ecx
        test    ah,ah
        jz      $xit                ; string terminator?

$1:     call    Sout                ; Write a character

        mov     ah,[ecx]            ; Get a character
        inc     ecx
        test    ah,ah               ; string terminator?
        jnz     $1                  ; jump if not
```

```
$xit:   pop     ebp
        ret
ComStr  endp
```

Let's look at the C code calling our serial port functions:

```
ComInit(19200);
ComStr("The quick brown fox\n\r");
```

Since the port number is hard coded to simplify this example, the code is initialized but only the baud rate can be set. Thereafter, zero delimited character strings are written to that serial port through the call to the ComStr() function. In this elementary form, very simple.

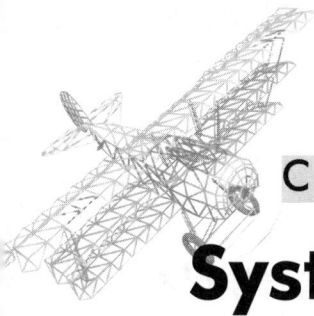

# Chapter 18

# System

## System "Lite"

There are other instructions available in your processor, but they have very little to no relationship to your application code. As mentioned at the beginning of this book, there are basically three types of instructions. (Note that I am oversimplifying here!) They are general-purpose, floating-point, and system instructions. The existence of these later instructions has to do with writing system level, thus operating system, code. They are not typically accessible or needed by those programmers writing non-operating system code. As this book is not targeted for that market, there is no need to make the standard application programmer wade through it. But as some of you may just cry foul, I have included a very light overview of these instructions. Besides, there are some tidbits in here for all of you!

Chapter 3, "Processor Differential Insight," as well as Chapter 16, "What CPUID?" gave some background on the processor. We shall now continue with that information. Some of what is included here is not necessarily just for system programmers as some features of the 80x86 are system related but are accessible from the application level. Note the System "Lite" part? Keep in mind that this is a superficial overview. If you need an in-depth explanation, please refer to documentation direct from the manufacturer.

# System Timing Instructions

## RDPMC — Read Performance — Monitoring Counters

| Mnemonic | P | PII | K6 | 3D! | 3Mx+ | SSE | SSE2 | A64 | SSE3 | E64T |
|----------|---|-----|----|-----|------|-----|------|-----|------|------|
| RDPMC | ✓ | ✓ | ✓ | ✓ | ✓ | ✓ | ✓ | ✓ | ✓ | ✓ |

rdpmc

This instruction loads the 40-bit performance monitoring counter indexed by ECX into the EDX:EAX register pair. For 64-bit mode, RDX[0...31]:RAX[0...31]=[RCX]. This instruction is accessible from any layer inclusive of the application layer only if the PCE flag in CR4 is set. When the flag is clear, this instruction can only be run from privilege level 0.

## RDTSC — Read Time-Stamp Counter

| Mnemonic | P | PII | K6 | 3D! | 3Mx+ | SSE | SSE2 | A64 | SSE3 | E64T |
|----------|---|-----|----|-----|------|-----|------|-----|------|------|
| RDTSC | ✓ | ✓ | ✓ | ✓ | ✓ | ✓ | ✓ | ✓ | ✓ | ✓ |

rdtsc

This system instruction reads the 64-bit time-stamp counter and loads the value into the EDX:EAX registers. The counter is incremented every clock cycle and is cleared (reset) to zero upon the processor being reset. This instruction is accessible from any layer inclusive of the application layer unless the TSD flag in CR4 is set. So far while running under Win32 the flag has been clear as a default, thus allowing an application to access this instruction.

```
;        void CpuDelaySet(void)

        public  CpuDelaySet
CpuDelaySet     proc    near
        rdtsc                           ; Read time-stamp counter

        mov     tclkl,eax               ; Save low 32 bits
        mov     tclkh,edx               ; Save high 32 bits
        ret
CpuDelaySet     endp
```

```
; long int CpuDelayCalc(void)
;
; This function is called after IClkSet() to get the
; elapsed interval in clock cycles.
;
; Note: On a 400MHz computer, only reading the lower 32 bits
; gives a maximum 10 second sampling before rollover.

        public  CpuDelayCalc
CpuDelayCalc proc    near
        rdtsc                           ; Read time-stamp counter

        sub     eax,tclkl
        sbb     edx,tclkh               ; edx:eax = total elapsed interval

        ret                             ; return edx:eax = 64 bits of info.
CpuDelayCalc endp
```

These two functions can be used for time trials while optimizing code. Due to multithreaded environments, another thread or interrupt can steal your time slice while you are trying to do time analysis on a bit of code. You could divide the number of loops into the total delay to get an average loop delay count. What I like to do is run a benchmark of executing the same code a few thousand times, ignoring the effects the prefetch has on these times or the fact the Nth time around the data is already sitting in memory. One time I took the governor off an MPEG decoder so it would run full speed, allowing code to be optimized so that it would run faster and faster.

# Calculating Processor Speed

The following code snippet can be included within your own code for determining computer speed. The computer quite often is not running at the speed you may think. I had a weird problem in an application running on my laptop and it did not make any sense until I wrote this code. Even then I thought it had a bug until I realized the laptop had a thermal problem and dropped its computer speed by 50% or more so as to run cooler. Clients running your application may have some weird problems or be misinformed of their machines' capabilities, and this code can give you or customer support representatives more debugging insight.

```
typedef struct SpeedDataType
{
    uint tSpeed;
    uint tSpeedState;
    uint nCnt;
    uint wTimerID;
```

```
} SpeedData;


// Win32 Timer - Calculate CPU Speed

void CALLBACK SpeedCalcTimer(UINT wTimerID, UINT msg, DWORD dwUser,
                            DWORD dw1, DWORD dw2)
{
    SpeedData *sp = (SpeedData *)dwUser;

    if (sp->wTimerID != wTimerID)  // Is this our timer ID?
    {
        return;
    }

    switch(sp->tSpeedState)
    {
    case 2:                           // 2nd tick (avg of the two intervals)
        sp->tSpeed = (CpuDelayCalc() + sp->tSpeed) >> 1;
        sp->nCnt++;
        CpuDelaySet();
        break;

    case 1:                           // 1st tick
        sp->tSpeed = CpuDelayCalc();
        sp->nCnt++;

        // Allow flow through!

    case 0:                           // Starting tick
        CpuDelaySet();
        sp->tSpeedState++;
        break;

    default:
        break;
    }
}


// Be VERY careful when this is called, as your OS may not like it!

uint SpeedCalc(void)
{
    TIMECAPS tc;
    uint wTimerRes, nCnt;
    SpeedData sd;

    wTimerRes = 1;

// Set the timer resolution for the multimedia timer
    if (TIMERR_NOERROR == timeGetDevCaps(&tc, sizeof(TIMECAPS)))
    {
```

```
        wTimerRes = min(max(tc.wPeriodMin, 1), tc.wPeriodMax);
        timeBeginPeriod(wTimerRes);         // 1ms resolution
    }

    sd.nCnt = sd.tSpeed = sd.tSpeedState = 0;

    sd.wTimerID = timeSetEvent(1, wTimerRes, SpeedCalcTimer,
        (DWORD)&sd, TIME_PERIODIC | TIME_KILL_SYNCHRONOUS);

    if (sd.wTimerID)                // If we were given a TimerId
    {                               // (Should not fail!)
        do {
            nCnt = sd.nCnt;
            Sleep(10);              // Sleep 10ms

            if (sd.nCnt > 100)      // Cycle 100 times
            {
                timeKillEvent(sd.wTimerID);
                return sd.tSpeed/1000;
            }
        } while (nCnt != sd.nCnt);  // If the same, the timer failed!

        timeKillEvent(sd.wTimerID);
    }
// Didn't work? Try it the really not-so-accurate way!

    CpuDelaySet();
    Sleep(10);
    return CpuDelayCalc()/10000;
}
```

# 80x86 Architecture

The Intel and AMD processors have similar functional architecture. Different processors have different numbers of caches, on chip cache, off chip cache, different speeds, different instruction sets, different methods of pipelining instructions. All this book is interested in is helping you, the application programmer, make your code go fast by writing it in assembly. You have no control over what flavor of processor the user of your application chooses to run their applications on. (Of course you could program your application to check these parameters and refuse to run on a system you do not like! But that would be evil!)

```
        test    ebx,ebx
        mov     ecx,ebx
        mov     esi,ebx
        mov     edi,ebx
        test    ebx,ebx
```

The use of full registers (such as in the above 32-bit code snippet in Protected Mode) allows instructions to be able to be executed on the same clock.

Partial stalls occur if a short version of a register is written to and then immediately followed by a larger version. For example:

```
mov al,9
add bx,ax   ; clock stall

mov al,9
add ebx,eax ; clock stall

mov ax,9
add ebx,ax  ; clock stall
```

The AL register will cause the next instruction to have a partial stall if it contains a large form such as AX, EAX, or RAX and if it is being written. This is like being at a red signal light in your car and when the light turns green you slam down on the accelerator; your car will sputter, spit a little, hesitate (stall), and then finally accelerate.

# CPU Status Registers (32-Bit EFLAGS/64-Bit RFLAGS)

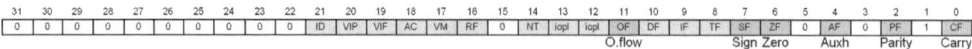

| 31 | 30 | 29 | 28 | 27 | 26 | 25 | 24 | 23 | 22 | 21 | 20 | 19 | 18 | 17 | 16 | 15 | 14 | 13 | 12 | 11 | 10 | 9 | 8 | 7 | 6 | 5 | 4 | 3 | 2 | 1 | 0 |
|---|---|---|---|---|---|---|---|---|---|---|---|---|---|---|---|---|---|---|---|---|---|---|---|---|---|---|---|---|---|---|---|
| 0 | 0 | 0 | 0 | 0 | 0 | 0 | 0 | 0 | 0 | ID | VIP | VIF | AC | VM | RF | 0 | NT | iopl | iopl | OF | DF | IF | TF | SF | ZF | 0 | AF | 0 | PF | 1 | CF |

O.flow (OF); Sign Zero (SF ZF); Auxh (AF); Parity (PF); Carry (CF)

*Figure 18-1: CPU status register*

| EFLAG | Code | Bit | Flag Descriptions |
|---|---|---|---|
| EFLAGS_CF | 000000001h | 0 | Carry |
| | 000000002h | 1 | 1 |
| EFLAGS_PF | 000000004h | 2 | Parity |
| | 000000008h | 3 | 0 |
| EFLAGS_AF | 000000010h | 4 | Auxiliary Carry |
| | 000000020h | 5 | 0 |
| EFLAGS_ZF | 000000040h | 6 | Zero |
| EFLAGS_SF | 000000080h | 7 | Sign |
| EFLAGS_TF | 000000100h | 8 | Trap |
| EFLAGS_IF | 000000200h | 9 | Interrupt Enable |
| EFLAGS_DF | 000000400h | 10 | Direction |
| EFLAGS_OF | 000000800h | 11 | Overflow |
| EFLAGS_IOPL | 000003000h | 12, 13 | I/O Privilege Level |
| EFLAGS_NT | 000004000h | 14 | Nested Task |

| EFLAG | Code | Bit | Flag Descriptions |
|---|---|---|---|
| | 000010000h | 15 | 0 |
| EFLAGS_RF | 000010000h | 16 | Resume |
| EFLAGS_VM | 000020000h | 17 | Virtual-8086 Mode |
| EFLAGS_AC | 000040000h | 18 | Alignment Check |
| EFLAGS_VIF | 000080000h | 19 | Virtual Interrupt |
| EFLAGS_VIP | 000100000h | 20 | Virtual Interrupt Pending |
| EFLAGS_ID | 000200000h | 21 | CPUID |
| | | 23...31 | 0 |

And in 64-bit mode the upper 32 bits of the RFLAGS register (0:EFLAGS):

| | | 32...63 | RFLAG (extra) bits |
|---|---|---|---|

# Protection Rings

The 386 and above have layers of protection referred to as protection rings.

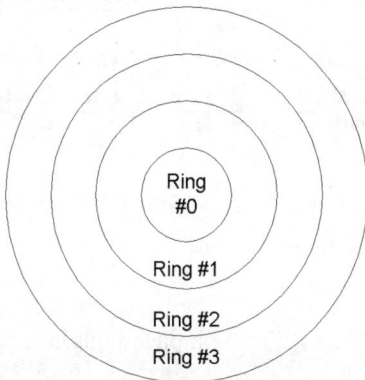

*Figure 18-2: Protection rings*

The inner ring #0 contains the operating system kernel. The two middle rings (#1 and #2) contain the operating system services (device drivers), and the outer ring #3 is where the application (user code) resides. The ring numbers are also referred to as privilege levels with 0 being the highest and 3 being the lowest.

An application can access functions in the other rings by means of a gate. The SYSCALL and SYSENTER functions are two methods. This is a protection system to protect the inner rings from the outer. You know, to keep the riffraff out! Any attempt to access an inner ring without going through a gate will cause a general protection fault.

# Control Registers

There are four control registers {CR0, CR2, CR3, CR4} that control system level operations. Note that CR1 is reserved.

Table 18-1: Control register 0 (CR0) extensions

| CR0 | Code | Bit | Flag Descriptions |
|---|---|---|---|
| CR0_PE | 000000001h | 0 | Protection Enable |
| CR0_MP | 000000002h | 1 | Monitor Coprocessor |
| CR0_EM | 000000004h | 2 | Emulation |
| CR0_TS | 000000008h | 3 | Task Switched |
| CR0_ET | 000000010h | 4 | Extension Type |
| CR0_NE | 000000020h | 5 | Numeric Error |
|  |  | 6...15 |  |
| CR0_WP | 000010000h | 16 | Write Protected |
|  |  | 17 |  |
| CR0_AM | 000040000h | 18 | Alignment Mask |
|  |  | 19...28 |  |
| CR0_NW | 020000000h | 29 | Not Write-Through |
| CR0_CD | 040000000h | 30 | Cache Disable |
| CR0_PG | 080000000h | 31 | Paging |

And in 64-bit mode the upper 32 bits of the CR0 register (0:CR0):

|  |  | 32...63 |  |
|---|---|---|---|

Control register 2 (CR2) is a 32/64-bit page fault linear address.

Table 18-2: Control register 3 (CR3) extensions

| CR3 | Code | Bit | Flag Descriptions |
|---|---|---|---|
|  |  | 0...2 |  |
| CR3_PWT | 000000008h | 3 | Page Writes Transparent |
| CR3_PCD | 000000010h | 4 | Page Cache Disable |
| Page Dir.Base |  | 12...31 |  |

And in 64-bit mode the upper 32 bits of the CR3 register (0:CR3):

|  |  | 32...63 | CR3 (extra) bits |
|---|---|---|---|

*Table 18-3: Control register 4 (CR4) extensions*

| CR4 | Code | Bit | Flag Descriptions |
|---|---|---|---|
| CR4_VME | 000000001h | 0 | Virtual-8086 Mode Ext. |
| CR4_PVI | 000000002h | 1 | Protected Virtual Int. |
| CR4_TSD | 000000004h | 2 | Time Stamp Disable |
| CR4_DE | 000000008h | 3 | Debugging Extensions |
| CR4_PSE | 000000010h | 4 | Page Size Extension |
| CR4_PAE | 000000020h | 5 | Physical Address Ext. |
| CR4_MCE | 000000040h | 6 | Machine Check Enable |
| CR4_PGE | 000000080h | 7 | Global Page Enable |
| CR4_PCE | 000000100h | 8 | RDPMC Enabled |
| CR4_OSFXSR | 000000200h | 9 | FXSAVE, FXRSTOR |
| CF4_OSXMMEXCPT | 000000400h | 10 | Unmasked SIMD FP Exception |

And in 64-bit mode the upper 32 bits of the CR4 register (0:CR4):

| | | | |
|---|---|---|---|
| | | 32...63 | CR4 (extra) bits |

## (TPR) Task Priority Registers — (CR8)

*Table 18-4: Control register 8 (CR8) extensions. This is new for EM64T.*

| CR8 | Code | Bit | Flag Descriptions |
|---|---|---|---|
| CR8_APSC | | 0...3 | Arbitration Priority Sub-class |
| CR8_AP | | 4...7 | Arbitration Priority |
| | | 8...63 | CR4 (extra bits) |

# Debug Registers

There are eight debug registers: {DR0, DR1, DR2, DR3, DR4, DR5, DR6, DR7}. Knowing them is unimportant as you are most likely using a debugger to develop your application, not building a debugger. These are privileged resources and only accessible at the system level to set up and monitor the breakpoints {0...3}.

# Cache Manipulation

Several mechanisms have been put into place to squeeze optimal throughput from the processors. One method of cache manipulation discussed in Chapter 10, "Branching," is Intel's hint as to the prediction of logic flow through branches counter to the static prediction logic. Another mechanism is a hint to the processor about cache behavior so as to give the processor insight into how a particular piece of code is utilizing memory access. Here is a brief review of some terms that have already been discussed:

- Temporal data — Memory that requires multiple accesses and therefore needs to be loaded into a cache for better throughput.

- Non-temporal hint — A hint (an indicator) to the processor that memory only requires a single access (one shot). This would be similar to copying a block of memory or performing a calculation, but the result is not going to be needed for a while so there is no need to write it into the cache. Thus, the memory access has no need to read and load cache, and therefore the code can be faster.

For speed and efficiency, when memory is accessed for read or write a cache line containing that data (whose length is dependent upon manufacturer and version) is copied from system memory to high-speed cache memory. The processor performs read/write operations on the cache memory. When a cache line is invalidated, the write back of that cache line to system memory occurs. In a multiprocessor system, this occurs frequently due to non-sharing of internal caches. The second stage of writing the cache line back to system memory is called a "write back."

## Cache Sizes

Different processors have different cache sizes for data and for code. These are dependent upon processor model, manufacturer, etc., as shown below:

| CPU | L1 Cache (Data /Code) | L2 Cache |
|---|---|---|
| Celeron | 16Kb / 16Kb | 256Kb |
| Pentium 4 | 8Kb / 12K$\mu$ops | 512Kb |
| Athlon XP | 64Kb / 64Kb | 256Kb |
| Duron | 64Kb / 64Kb | 64Kb |
| Pentium M | 32Kb / 32Kb | 1024Kb |
| Xeon | | 512Kb |

Depending on your code and level of optimization, the size of the cache may be of importance. For the purposes of this book, however, it is being ignored, as that topic is more suitable for a book very specifically targeting heavy-duty optimization. This book, however, is interested in the cache line size as that is more along the lightweight optimization that has been touched on from time to time. It should be noted that AMD uses a minimum size of 32 bytes.

## Cache Line Sizes

The (code/data) cache line size determines how many instruction/data bytes can be preloaded.

| Intel | Cache Line Size |
|---|---|
| PIII | 32 |
| Pentium M | 64 |
| P4 | 64 |
| Xeon | 64 |

| AMD | Cache Line Size |
|---|---|
| Athlon | 64 |
| Opteron | 64 |

The cache line size can be obtained by using the CPUID instruction with EAX set to 1. The following calculation will give you the actual cache line size.

```
mov    eax,1
cpuid

and    ebx,00000FF00h
shr    ebx,8-3              ; ebx = size of cache line
```

## PREFETCH$_x$ — Prefetch Data into Caches

| Mnemonic | P | PII | K6 | 3D! | 3Mx+ | SSE | SSE2 | A64 | SSE3 | E64T |
|---|---|---|---|---|---|---|---|---|---|---|
| PREFETCH | | | | ✓ | ✓ | | | ✓ | | |
| PREFETCHNTA | | | | | ✓ | ✓ | ✓ | ✓ | ✓ | ✓ |
| PREFETCHT0 | | | | | ✓ | ✓ | ✓ | ✓ | ✓ | ✓ |
| PREFETCHT1 | | | | | ✓ | ✓ | ✓ | ✓ | ✓ | ✓ |
| PREFETCHT2 | | | | | ✓ | ✓ | ✓ | ✓ | ✓ | ✓ |
| PREFETCHW | | | | ✓ | ✓ | | | ✓ | | |

| | | |
|---|---|---|
| 3DNow! | prefetch | *mSrc8* |
| | prefetchw | *mSrc8* |
| SSE | prefetcht0 | *mSrc8* |
| | prefetcht1 | *mSrc8* |

prefetcht2     *mSrc8*
prefetchnta    *mSrc8*

The PREFETCHNTA instruction performs a non-temporal hint to the processor with respect to all the caches, to load from system memory *mSrc8* into the first-level cache for a PIII or a second-level cache for a P4 or Xeon processor.

The PREFETCHT0 instruction performs a temporal hint to the processor to load from system memory *mSrc8* into the first- or second-level cache for a PIII, or a second-level cache for a P4 or Xeon processor.

The PREFETCHT1 instruction performs a temporal hint to the processor with respect to the first-level cache to load from system memory *mSrc8* into the second-level cache for PIII, P4, or Xeon processor.

The PREFETCHT2 instruction performs a temporal hint to the processor with respect to the second-level cache to load from system memory *mSrc8* into the first-level cache for PIII or the second-level cache for P4 or Xeon processor.

If data is already loaded at the same or higher cache, then no operation is performed.

AMD processors alias PREFETCHT1 and PREFETCHT2 instructions to the PREFETCHT0 instructions, so they all have the PREFETCHT0 functionality.

The 3DNow! PREFETCH instruction loads a cache line into the L1 data cache from the *mSrc8*.

The 3DNow! PREFETCHW instruction loads a cache line into the L1 data cache from the *mSrc8* but sets a hint indicating that it is for write operations.

# LFENCE — Load Fence

| Mnemonic | P | PII | K6 | 3D! | 3Mx+ | SSE | SSE2 | A64 | SSE3 | E64T |
|----------|---|-----|-----|-----|------|-----|------|-----|------|------|
| LFENCE   |   |     |    |     |      |     | ✓    | ✓   | ✓    | ✓    |

lfence

This instruction is similar to the MFENCE instruction, but it acts as a barrier between memory load instructions issued before and after the LFENCE and MFENCE instructions.

# SFENCE — Store Fence

| Mnemonic | P | PII | K6 | 3D! | 3Mx+ | SSE | SSE2 | A64 | SSE3 | E64T |
|----------|---|-----|----|-----|------|-----|------|-----|------|------|
| SFENCE | | | | | ✓ | ✓ | ✓ | ✓ | ✓ | ✓ |

sfence

This instruction is similar to the instruction MFENCE but it acts as a barrier between memory save instructions issued before and after the SFENCE or MFENCE instructions.

# MFENCE — Memory Fence

| Mnemonic | P | PII | K6 | 3D! | 3Mx+ | SSE | SSE2 | A64 | SSE3 | E64T |
|----------|---|-----|----|-----|------|-----|------|-----|------|------|
| MFENCE | | | | | | | ✓ | ✓ | ✓ | ✓ |

mfence

This instruction is a barrier (fence) to isolate system memory to and from cache memory operations that occur before and after this instruction.

# CLFLUSH — Flush Cache Line

| Mnemonic | P | PII | K6 | 3D! | 3Mx+ | SSE | SSE2 | A64 | SSE3 | E64T |
|----------|---|-----|----|-----|------|-----|------|-----|------|------|
| CLFLUSH | | | | | | | ✓ | ✓ | ✓ | ✓ |

clflush *mSrc8*

This instruction invalidates the cache line (code or data) containing the linear address specified by *mSrc8*. If the line is dirty — that is, different from the system memory in the process of being written to — it is written back to system memory. This instruction is ordered by the MFENCE instruction. Check CPUID bit #19 (CLFSH) to see if this instruction is available.

## INVD — Invalidate Cache (WO/Writeback)

| Mnemonic | P | PII | K6 | 3D! | 3Mx+ | SSE | SSE2 | A64 | SSE3 | E64T |
|---|---|---|---|---|---|---|---|---|---|---|
| INVD | ✓ | ✓ | ✓ | ✓ | ✓ | ✓ | ✓ | ✓ | ✓ | ✓ |

invd

This instruction invalidates the internal caches without waiting for write back of modified cache lines and initiates bus cycles for external caches to flush. This is similar to WBINVD but without a write back.

**No App (Sys Only):** This is only accessible from Real Mode or Privilege Level 0.

## WBINVD — Write Back and Invalidate Cache

| Mnemonic | P | PII | K6 | 3D! | 3Mx+ | SSE | SSE2 | A64 | SSE3 | E64T |
|---|---|---|---|---|---|---|---|---|---|---|
| WBINVD | ✓ | ✓ | ✓ | ✓ | ✓ | ✓ | ✓ | ✓ | ✓ | ✓ |

wbinvd

This instruction writes back all the modified cache lines, then invalidates the internal caches, and initiate bus cycles for external caches to flush. This is similar to INVD but with a write back.

**No App (Sys Only):** This is only accessible from Real Mode or Privilege Level 0.

# System Instructions

The scope of system instructions are not covered in this book. Refer to the Intel and AMD specific documentation for full specifications. They are considered OS/System instructions and as such will not be discussed in this book. Some are accessible by the application layer at the low privilege level but are not part of the general application development process. They are only referenced here for informational purposes and to ensure this book lists all instructions available at the time of its publication.

# ARPL — Adjust Requested Privilege Level

| Mnemonic | P | PII | K6 | 3D! | 3Mx+ | SSE | SSE2 | A64 | SSE3 | E64T |
|----------|---|-----|-----|-----|------|-----|------|-----|------|------|
| ARPL | ✓ | ✓ | ✓ | ✓ | ✓ | ✓ | ✓ | 32 | ✓ | 32 |

arpl  *rmDst16, rSrc16*

This system instruction adjusts the RPL (Request Privilege Level) by comparing the segment selector of *rSrc* with *rmDst*. If *rSrc* > *rmDst*, then set the Zero flag; otherwise clear (reset) it. This instruction can be accessed by an application.

**No 64-bit:**  The ARPL system instruction is not supported in 64-bit mode!

# BOUND — Check Array Index For Bounding Error

| Mnemonic | P | PII | K6 | 3D! | 3Mx+ | SSE | SSE2 | A64 | SSE3 | E64T |
|----------|---|-----|-----|-----|------|-----|------|-----|------|------|
| BOUND | ✓ | ✓ | ✓ | ✓ | ✓ | ✓ | ✓ | 32 | ✓ | 32 |

bound   *rSrcA16, mSrcB16* ∧ *16*
bound   *rSrcA32, mSrcB32* ∧ *32*

This system instruction checks if the array index *rSrcA* is within the bounds of the array specified by *mSrcB*. A #BR (Bounds Range) exception is triggered if it is not inclusive.

**No 64-bit:**  The BOUND system instruction is not available in 64-bit mode.

# CLTS — Clear Task Switch Flag

| Mnemonic | P | PII | K6 | 3D! | 3Mx+ | SSE | SSE2 | A64 | SSE3 | E64T |
|----------|---|-----|-----|-----|------|-----|------|-----|------|------|
| CLTS | ✓ | ✓ | ✓ | ✓ | ✓ | ✓ | ✓ | ✓ | ✓ | ✓ |

clts

This system instruction clears the task switch flag TS Bit #3 of CR0 (CR0_TS). The operating system sets this flag every time a task switch occurs and this flag is used to clear it. It is used in conjunction with the synchronization of the task switch with the FPU.

**Not Applications (System Only)** **No App (Sys Only):**   This is only accessible from Real Mode or Privilege Level 0.

# HLT — Halt Processor

| Mnemonic | P | PII | K6 | 3D! | 3Mx+ | SSE | SSE2 | A64 | SSE3 | E64T |
|----------|---|-----|-----|-----|------|-----|------|-----|------|------|
| HLT | ✓ | ✓ | ✓ | ✓ | ✓ | ✓ | ✓ | ✓ | ✓ | ✓ |

hlt

This is a system instruction that stops the processor and puts it into a halt state.

**Not Applications (System Only)** **No App (Sys Only):**   This is only accessible from Real Mode or Privilege Level 0.

# UD2 — Undefined Instruction

| Mnemonic | P | PII | K6 | 3D! | 3Mx+ | SSE | SSE2 | A64 | SSE3 | E64T |
|----------|---|-----|-----|-----|------|-----|------|-----|------|------|
| UD2 | ✓ | ✓ | ✓ | ✓ | ✓ | ✓ | ✓ | ✓ | ✓ | ✓ |

ud2

UD2 is an undefined instruction and guaranteed to throw an opcode exception in all modes.

# INVLPG — Invalidate TLB

| Mnemonic | P | PII | K6 | 3D! | 3Mx+ | SSE | SSE2 | A64 | SSE3 | E64T |
|----------|---|-----|-----|-----|------|-----|------|-----|------|------|
| INVLPG | ✓ | ✓ | ✓ | ✓ | ✓ | ✓ | ✓ | ✓ | ✓ | ✓ |

invlpg *mSrc*

This instruction invalidates the TLB (Translation Lookaside Buffer) page referenced by *mSrc*.

**Not Applications (System Only)** **No App (Sys Only):**   This is only accessible from Real Mode or Privilege Level 0.

# LAR — Load Access Rights

| Mnemonic | P | PII | K6 | 3D! | 3Mx+ | SSE | SSE2 | A64 | SSE3 | E64T |
|----------|---|-----|-----|-----|------|-----|------|-----|------|------|
| LAR | ✓ | ✓ | ✓ | ✓ | ✓ | ✓ | ✓ | ✓ | ✓ | ✓ |

    lar    *rDst16, rmSrc16*
    lar    *rDst32, rmSrc32*
    lar    *rDst64, rmSrc64*

This system instruction copies the access rights from the segment descriptor referenced by the source *rmSrc*, stores them in the destination *rDst*, and sets the zero flag. This instruction can only be called from Protected Mode.

# LOCK — Assert Lock # Signal Prefix

| Mnemonic | P | PII | K6 | 3D! | 3Mx+ | SSE | SSE2 | A64 | SSE3 | E64T |
|----------|---|-----|-----|-----|------|-----|------|-----|------|------|
| LOCK | ✓ | ✓ | | | | ✓ | ✓ | ✓ | ✓ | ✓ |

    lock

This system instruction is a code prefix to turn the trailing instruction into an atomic instruction. In a multiprocessor environment it ensures that the processor using the lock has exclusive access to memory shared with the other processor.

   This instruction can only be used with the following instructions and only when they are performing a write operation to memory: ADD, ADC, AND, BTC, BTR, BTS, CMPSCHG, CMPXCHG8B, DEC, INC, NEG, NOT, OR, SBB, SUB, XADD, XCHG.

   This instruction works best with a read-modify-write operation such as the BTS instruction.

# LSL — Load Segment Limit

| Mnemonic | P | PII | K6 | 3D! | 3Mx+ | SSE | SSE2 | A64 | SSE3 | E64T |
|----------|---|-----|-----|-----|------|-----|------|-----|------|------|
| LSL | ✓ | ✓ | ✓ | ✓ | ✓ | ✓ | ✓ | ✓ | ✓ | ✓ |

    lsl    *rDst16, rmSrc16*
    lsl    *rDst32, rmSrc32*
    lsl    *rDst64, rmSrc64*

This system instruction copies the segment descriptor referenced by the source *rmSrc* to the destination *rDst*.

# MOV — Move To/From Control Registers

| Mnemonic | P | PII | K6 | 3D! | 3Mx+ | SSE | SSE2 | A64 | SSE3 | E64T |
|---|---|---|---|---|---|---|---|---|---|---|
| MOV CR | ✓ | ✓ | ✓ | ✓ | ✓ | ✓ | ✓ | ✓ | ✓ | ✓ |

```
mov   cr{0...4}, r32                          32
mov   r32, cr{0...4}
```

This system instruction copies memory from the control register to a general-purpose register or from a general-purpose register to a control register.

**Not Applications (System Only)** **No App (Sys Only):** This is only accessible from Privilege Level 0.

# MOV — Move To/From Debug Registers

| Mnemonic | P | PII | K6 | 3D! | 3Mx+ | SSE | SSE2 | A64 | SSE3 | E64T |
|---|---|---|---|---|---|---|---|---|---|---|
| MOV DR | ✓ | ✓ | ✓ | ✓ | ✓ | ✓ | ✓ | ✓ | ✓ | ✓ |

```
mov   r32, dr{0...7}                          32
mov   dr{0...7}, r32
```

This system instruction copies memory from the debug register to a general-purpose register or from a general-purpose register to a debug register.

**Not Applications (System Only)** **No App (Sys Only):** This is only accessible from Real Mode or Privilege Level 0.

# STMXCSR — Save MXCSR Register State

| Mnemonic | P | PII | K6 | 3D! | 3Mx+ | SSE | SSE2 | A64 | SSE3 | E64T |
|---|---|---|---|---|---|---|---|---|---|---|
| STMXCSR | | | | | | ✓ | ✓ | ✓ | ✓ | ✓ |

```
stmxcsr  mDst32
```

This system instruction saves the MXCSR control and status register to the destination *mDst32*. The complement to this instruction is LDMXCSR.

# LDMXCSR — Load MXCSR Register State

| Mnemonic | P | PII | K6 | 3D! | 3Mx+ | SSE | SSE2 | A64 | SSE3 | E64T |
|----------|---|-----|-----|-----|------|-----|------|-----|------|------|
| LDMXCSR  |   |     |     |     |      | ✓   | ✓    | ✓   | ✓    | ✓    |

     ldmxcsr *mSrc32*

This system instruction loads the MXCSR control and status register from the source *mSrc32*. The complement of this instruction is STMXCSR.

     The default value is 00001F80h.

# SGDT/SIDT — Save Global/Interrupt Descriptor Table

| Mnemonic | P | PII | K6 | 3D! | 3Mx+ | SSE | SSE2 | A64 | SSE3 | E64T |
|----------|---|-----|-----|-----|------|-----|------|-----|------|------|
| SGDT     | ✓ | ✓   | ✓   | ✓   | ✓    | ✓   | ✓    | ✓   | ✓    | ✓    |
| SIDT     | ✓ | ✓   | ✓   | ✓   | ✓    | ✓   | ✓    | ✓   | ✓    | ✓    |

     sgdt *m*
     sidt *m*

The SGDT system instruction copies the Global Descriptor Table Register (GDTR) to the destination. The complement of this instruction is LGDT.

     The SIDT system instruction copies the Interrupt Descriptor Table Register (IDTR) to the destination. The complement of this instruction is LIDT.

# LGDT/LIDT — Load Global/Interrupt Descriptor Table

| Mnemonic | P | PII | K6 | 3D! | 3Mx+ | SSE | SSE2 | A64 | SSE3 | E64T |
|----------|---|-----|-----|-----|------|-----|------|-----|------|------|
| LGDT     | ✓ | ✓   | ✓   | ✓   | ✓    | ✓   | ✓    | ✓   | ✓    | ✓    |
| LIDT     | ✓ | ✓   | ✓   | ✓   | ✓    | ✓   | ✓    | ✓   | ✓    | ✓    |

$$lgdt \quad mSrc16 \wedge (32/64)$$
$$lidt \quad mSrc16 \wedge (32/64)$$

The LGDT system instruction loads the source *mSrc16* into the Global Descriptor Table Register (GDTR).

The LIDT system instruction loads the source *mSrc16* into the Interrupt Descriptor Table Register (IDTR).

**No App (Sys Only):**  This is only accessible from Real Mode or Privilege Level 0.

# SLDT — Save Local Descriptor Table

| Mnemonic | P | PII | K6 | 3D! | 3Mx+ | SSE | SSE2 | A64 | SSE3 | E64T |
|----------|---|-----|----|----|------|-----|------|-----|------|------|
| SLDT | ✓ | ✓ | ✓ | ✓ | ✓ | ✓ | ✓ | ✓ | ✓ | ✓ |

sldt    *rmDst16*

This system instruction copies the segment selector from the Local Descriptor Table Register (LDTR) to the destination *rmDst16*.

# LLDT — Load Local Descriptor Table

| Mnemonic | P | PII | K6 | 3D! | 3Mx+ | SSE | SSE2 | A64 | SSE3 | E64T |
|----------|---|-----|----|----|------|-----|------|-----|------|------|
| LLDT | ✓ | ✓ | ✓ | ✓ | ✓ | ✓ | ✓ | ✓ | ✓ | ✓ |

lldt    *rmSrc16*

This system instruction loads the source *rmSrc16* into the segment selector element of the Local Descriptor Table Register (LDTR). This instruction is only available in Protected Mode.

# SMSW — Save Machine Status Word

| Mnemonic | P | PII | K6 | 3D! | 3Mx+ | SSE | SSE2 | A64 | SSE3 | E64T |
|----------|---|-----|----|----|------|-----|------|-----|------|------|
| SMSW | ✓ | ✓ | ✓ | ✓ | ✓ | ✓ | ✓ | ✓ | ✓ | ✓ |

smsw    *rmDst16*

This system instruction copies the lower 16 bits of control register CR0 into the destination *rmDst16*.

# LMSW — Load Machine Status Word

| Mnemonic | P | PII | K6 | 3D! | 3Mx+ | SSE | SSE2 | A64 | SSE3 | E64T |
|----------|---|-----|----|----|------|-----|------|-----|------|------|
| LMSW | ✓ | ✓ | ✓ | ✓ | ✓ | ✓ | ✓ | ✓ | ✓ | ✓ |

lmsw *rmSrc16*

This system instruction loads the lower four bits of the source *rmSrc16* and overwrites the lower four bits of the control register CR0.

**No App (Sys Only):**   This is only accessible from Real Mode or Privilege Level 0.

# STR — Save Task Register

| Mnemonic | P | PII | K6 | 3D! | 3Mx+ | SSE | SSE2 | A64 | SSE3 | E64T |
|----------|---|-----|----|----|------|-----|------|-----|------|------|
| STR | ✓ | ✓ | ✓ | ✓ | ✓ | ✓ | ✓ | ✓ | ✓ | ✓ |

str *rmDst16*

This system instruction reads the task register and saves the segment selector value into the 16-bit destination *rmDst16*. The register gets the upper 16 bits cleared to zero in the upper bits of the 32-bit form.

```
str ax              ; actually stores 0000:AX into EAX
```

# LTR — Load Task Register

| Mnemonic | P | PII | K6 | 3D! | 3Mx+ | SSE | SSE2 | A64 | SSE3 | E64T |
|----------|---|-----|----|----|------|-----|------|-----|------|------|
| LTR | ✓ | ✓ | ✓ | ✓ | ✓ | ✓ | ✓ | ✓ | ✓ | ✓ |

ltr *rmSrc16*

This system instruction sets the task register with the segment selector stored in the 16-bit source *rmSrc16*.

**No App (Sys Only):**   This is only accessible from Real Mode or Privilege Level 0.

# RDMSR — Read from Model Specific Register

| Mnemonic | P | PII | K6 | 3D! | 3Mx+ | SSE | SSE2 | A64 | SSE3 | E64T |
|---|---|---|---|---|---|---|---|---|---|---|
| RDMSR | ✓ | ✓ | ✓ | ✓ | ✓ | ✓ | ✓ | ✓ | ✓ | ✓ |

rdmsr

This is a system instruction that may only be run in Privilege Level 0. The Model Specific Register (MSR) indexed by ECX is loaded into the EDX:EAX register pair.

**Not Applications (System Only)**   **No App (Sys Only):**   This is only accessible from Real Mode or Privilege Level 0.

# WRMSR — Write to Model Specific Register

| Mnemonic | P | PII | K6 | 3D! | 3Mx+ | SSE | SSE2 | A64 | SSE3 | E64T |
|---|---|---|---|---|---|---|---|---|---|---|
| WRMSR | ✓ | ✓ | ✓ | ✓ | ✓ | ✓ | ✓ | ✓ | ✓ | ✓ |

wrmsr

This system instruction writes the 64-bit value in EDX:EAX to the Model Specific Register specified by the ECX register. In 64-bit mode the lower 32 bits of each 64-bit register RDX[0..31]:[RAX[0...31] form the 64-bit value that is written to the MSR specified by the RCX register.

    MSR[ecx] = edx:eax

**Not Applications (System Only)**   **No App (Sys Only):**   This is only accessible from Real Mode or Privilege Level 0.

# SWAPGS — Swap GS Base Register

| Mnemonic | P | PII | K6 | 3D! | 3Mx+ | SSE | SSE2 | A64 | SSE3 | E64T |
|---|---|---|---|---|---|---|---|---|---|---|
| SWAPGS | | | | | | | | 64 | | 64 |

swapgs

This system instruction swaps the GS register value with the value in the MSR address C0000102H.

**No App (Sys Only):** This is only accessible from Real Mode or Privilege Level 0.

# SYSCALL — 64-Bit Fast System Call

| Mnemonic | P | PII | K6 | 3D! | 3Mx+ | SSE | SSE2 | A64 | SSE3 | E64T |
|----------|---|-----|-----|-----|------|-----|------|-----|------|------|
| SYSCALL  |   |     | ✓   | ✓   | ✓    |     |      | ✓   |      | 64   |

syscall

This instruction is a fast 64-bit system call to privilege level 0. It allows code at the lower privilege levels to call code within Privilege Level 0.

# SYSRET — Fast Return from 64-Bit Fast System Call

| Mnemonic | P | PII | K6 | 3D! | 3Mx+ | SSE | SSE2 | A64 | SSE3 | E64T |
|----------|---|-----|-----|-----|------|-----|------|-----|------|------|
| SYSRET   |   |     | ✓   | ✓   | ✓    |     |      | ✓   |      | 64   |

sysret

This instruction is a return from a fast 64-bit system call. It is a complement to SYSCALL.

# SYSENTER — Fast System Call

| Mnemonic | P | PII | K6 | 3D! | 3Mx+ | SSE | SSE2 | A64 | SSE3 | E64T |
|----------|---|-----|-----|-----|------|-----|------|-----|------|------|
| SYSENTER |   |     |     |     |      | ✓   | ✓    |     | ✓    | ✓    |

sysenter

This instruction is a fast system call to Privilege Level 0. It allows code at the lower privilege levels to call code within Privilege Level 0.

# SYSEXIT — Fast Return from Fast System Call

| Mnemonic | P | PII | K6 | 3D! | 3Mx+ | SSE | SSE2 | A64 | SSE3 | E64T |
|----------|---|-----|-----|-----|------|-----|------|-----|------|------|
| SYSEXIT  |   |     |     |     |      | ✓   | ✓    |     | ✓    | ✓    |

sysexit

This instruction is a return from a fast system call. It is a complement to SYSENTER.

# RSM — Resume from System Management Mode

| Mnemonic | P | PII | K6 | 3D! | 3Mx+ | SSE | SSE2 | A64 | SSE3 | E64T |
|----------|---|-----|-----|-----|------|-----|------|-----|------|------|
| RSM | ✓ | ✓ | ✓ | ✓ | ✓ | ✓ | ✓ | ✓ | ✓ | ✓ |

```
rsm
```

This system instruction returns control from the System Management Mode (SMM) back to the operating system or the application that was interrupted by the SMM interrupt.

# VERR/VERW — Verify Segment for Reading

| Mnemonic | P | PII | K6 | 3D! | 3Mx+ | SSE | SSE2 | A64 | SSE3 | E64T |
|----------|---|-----|-----|-----|------|-----|------|-----|------|------|
| VERR | ✓ | ✓ | ✓ | ✓ | ✓ | ✓ | ✓ | ✓ | ✓ | ✓ |
| VERW | ✓ | ✓ | ✓ | ✓ | ✓ | ✓ | ✓ | ✓ | ✓ | ✓ |

```
verr  rm16
verw  rm16

mov  ax,cs
verr ax
verw ax
```

These instructions verify whether the specified segment/selector CS, DS, ES, FS, or GS is VERR (readable) or VERW (writeable) and sets the zero flag to 1 if yes or resets (clears) the zero flag if no. Code segments are never verified as writeable. The stack segment-selector (SS) is not an allowed register. These instructions are not available in Real Mode.

# LDS/LES/LFS/LGS/LSS — Load Far Pointer

| Mnemonic | P | PII | K6 | 3D! | 3Mx+ | SSE | SSE2 | A64 | SSE3 | E64T |
|----------|---|-----|----|-----|------|-----|------|-----|------|------|
| LDS | ✓ | ✓ | ✓ | ✓ | ✓ | ✓ | ✓ | ✓ | ✓ | ✓ |
| LES | ✓ | ✓ | ✓ | ✓ | ✓ | ✓ | ✓ | ✓ | ✓ | ✓ |
| LFS | ✓ | ✓ | ✓ | ✓ | ✓ | ✓ | ✓ | ✓ | ✓ | ✓ |
| LGS | ✓ | ✓ | ✓ | ✓ | ✓ | ✓ | ✓ | ✓ | ✓ | ✓ |
| LSS | ✓ | ✓ | ✓ | ✓ | ✓ | ✓ | ✓ | ✓ | ✓ | ✓ |

| | | | |
|---|---|---|---|
| lds | *r32Dst, mSrc(16:32)* | Protected Mode | 48 |
| lds | *r16Dst, mSrc(16:16)* | Real Mode | 32 |
| les | *r32Dst, mSrc(16:32)* | Protected Mode | 48 |
| les | *r16Dst, mSrc(16:16)* | Real Mode | 32 |
| lfs | *r64Dst, mSrc(16:64)* | 64-bit Mode | 80 |
| lfs | *r32Dst, mSrc(16:32)* | 64-bit, Protected Mode | 48 |
| lfs | *r16Dst, mSrc(16:16)* | 64-bit, Real Mode | 32 |
| lgs | *r64Dst, mSrc(16:64)* | 64-bit Mode | 80 |
| lgs | *r32Dst, mSrc(16:32)* | 64-bit, Protected Mode | 48 |
| lgs | *r16Dst, mSrc(16:16)* | 64-bit, Real Mode | 32 |
| lss | *r64Dst, mSrc(16:64)* | 64-bit Mode | 80 |
| lss | *r32Dst, mSrc(16:32)* | 64-bit, Protected Mode | 48 |
| lss | *r16Dst, mSrc(16:16)* | 64-bit, Real Mode | 32 |

This is a special memory pointer instruction that moves a memory address into a register pair with a specified pointer value. The form you use is determined by the (64-bit/Protected/Real) mode your code is for.

| Flags | O.flow | Sign | Zero | Aux | Parity | Carry |
|-------|--------|------|------|-----|--------|-------|
| | - | - | - | - | - | - |

Flags: None are altered by this opcode.

**64-bit**

**No 64-bit:** The general-purpose instructions LDS and LES are not supported in 64-bit mode.

Protected Mode Win95 programmers do not need to get at the VGA, but if you have an old monochrome adapter plugged into your system this will be handy using Microsoft's secret (unpublished) selector {013fh}, which gets you access to every linear address on your machine {013fh:00000000...0fffffffh}. This became the data selector for Win 95B and is a Bounds Error for Win32 and Win64 developers.

```
monoadr dd      0b0000h
monosel dw      013fh

        mov     edi,monoadr
        mov     es,monosel
```

or

```
        les     FWORD PTR monoadr
```

Of course, that pointer is used in a function such as:

```
        mov     es:[edi],eax
        add     edi,4
```

Saving that pointer back to the address:

```
        mov     monoadr,edi
        mov     monosel,es
```

That was fine and dandy, but the following is a quicker method even though it takes a little organization and is very easy to make a mistake due to its length.

```
monobase FWORD  013f000b0000h

        les     edi,monobase
```

The declaration has too many zeros and is a lil' too darn long, don't you think! It almost looks like binary. Loading that address into the pointer is very quick, but trying to save the pointer back to the address isn't so slick and it seems a little murky to me.

```
        mov     DWORD PTR monobase,edi
        mov     WORD PTR monobase+4,es
```

An alternate method would be using a data structure such as follows:

```
;       Protected Mode address (Far)
PMADR   STRUC
        adr     dd      ?       ; PM Address
        sel     dw      ?       ; PM Segment (Selector)
PMADR   ends

monobase PMADR  {000b0000h,013fh} ; Monochrome Base Address
```

And to actually get the pointer:

```
        les     edi,FWORD PTR monobase
```

Save the pointer back:

```
        mov     monobase.adr,edi
        mov     monobase.sel,es
```

Now, doesn't that look much cleaner? Assembly coding can get convoluted enough without creating one's own confusion. Now for those Real Mode programmers, a touch of VGA nostalgia:

```
vgaseg  dw      0a000h

mov     di,0
mov     es,vgaseg
```

The following code snippet is similar to the previous 32-bit version but scaled down for 16-bit. Using the same techniques:

```
;       Real Mode address (Far)
RMADR   STRUC
        off     dw      ?       ; Real Mode Offset
        rseg    dw      ?       ; Real Mode Segment
RMADR   ends

vgabase RMADR   {0,0a000h}      ; VGA Base Address

les     di,vgabase
```

And using that pointer:

```
mov     es:[di],ax
add     di,2
```

# Hyperthreading Instructions

The scope of hyperthreading instructions is not covered in this book. Refer to the Intel-specific documentation for full specifications. They are considered OS/System instructions and as such will not be discussed in this book. They are accessible by the application layer at the low privilege level but are not part of the general application development process. They are only referenced here for informational purposes.

## MONITOR — Monitor

| Mnemonic | P | PII | K6 | 3D! | 3Mx+ | SSE | SSE2 | A64 | SSE3 | E64T |
|----------|---|-----|----|----|------|-----|------|-----|------|------|
| MONITOR  |   |     |    |    |      |     |      |     | ✓    | ✓    |

```
monitor
```

This system instruction sets up a hardware monitor using an address stored in the EAX register and arms the monitor. Registers ECX and

EDX contain information to be sent to the monitor. This is accessible at any privilege level unless the MONITOR flag in the CPUID is not set, indicating the processor does not support this instruction. This instruction is used in conjunction with the instruction MWAIT.

## MWAIT — Wait

| Mnemonic | P | PII | K6 | 3D! | 3Mx+ | SSE | SSE2 | A64 | SSE3 | E64T |
|----------|---|-----|----|----|------|-----|------|-----|------|------|
| MWAIT    |   |     |    |    |      |     |      |     | ✓    | ✓    |

mwait

This system instruction is similar to a NOP but works in conjunction with the MONITOR instruction for signaling to a hardware monitor. It is a hint to the processor that it is okay to stop instruction execution until a monitor related event. MONITOR can be used by itself, but if MWAIT is used, only one MWAIT instruction follows a MONITOR instruction (especially in a loop).

# Chapter 19

# Gfx 'R' Asm

This is one of two chapters that are probably the reason you bought this book. You are probably working with a graphics library and then ran into a little bind in which there did not seem to be a software library function available with that special needed functionality. Your schedules are sliding, nerves are wrecked, and paranoia is beginning to set in as you believe that your project lead or manager is beginning to doubt your abilities and that pink slip is only about a week away. Out of desperation you have escaped to your refuge, that favorite technical bookstore that has rescued you so many times in the past. You find lots of graphics books but not what you are looking for. There are a few assembly books that you have seen over the years, but they have always been targeted for beginners, but you have bought them anyway for your personal library as another resource book. (I have always been impressed with someone who has multiple large bookcases with multitudes of dog-eared books in their office. There is a fine art to making brand new books look well used.) And then you see this book. You flip through it and this chapter catches your gleaming eye and then you whisper in euphoria to yourself, "This book will save my butt!" At that point you look around and see everyone in the bookstore staring at you as you skulk toward the sales clerk.

Of course, there are other code samples in my *Vector Game Math Processors* book so do not forget to buy that book as well.

For those of you C programmers out there, this chapter is very similar to those heavily used functions memset() and memcpy(). They are used in almost every application for a large variety of purposes, but their behavior typically is not that useful or fast enough in the clearing or blitting of graphic images. Some of you are probably thinking "Why isn't this guy using the hardware blitter on a graphics card?" Well, in some cases, the blitter is hidden from you in the bowels of drivers such as Direct Draw but that's all it is, a blitter — a hardware device designed to move video card memory to video card memory and you only have 64 to 256 MB to play with. Okay, okay, that is much better than a couple years ago when you only had 2 to 8 MB. What we are trying to do here

**459**

is learn the optimal method of moving memory around the computer system and from system memory to video memory. Also, just where did those images come from? Whose file format, and what compression type? How did they get loaded? Where do you get the driver, etc? There is also more to life than displaying video games! What about streaming media such as MPEG-4 and DivX, video analysis, scientific research, speech recognition, stereoscopic vision, etc.? The list is endless and new reasons are being invented all the time. Now that I am off my soapbox we can continue.

# Setting Memory

If you happen to be constructing 8-bit images, then the memset() function can work pretty well for you as the transparency value can be anywhere from 0 to 255. If working in 16-, 24-, or 32-bit colors this function is only useful if the transparency color that you are trying to set just happens to be 0; if it is any other value, you have a serious problem. You have put together a C function to do the task but even though this function is not called that often, its speed is not up to your needs.

Your older 32-bit C libraries typically have the following library function for clearing a block of memory:

```
; void *memset(void *pMem, int val, uint nCnt)
;
; Note: if nCnt is set to 0 then no bytes will be set!

        public  memset
memset  proc    near
        push    ebp
        mov     ebp,esp
        push    edi

        mov     ecx,[ebp+arg3]      ; nCnt
        mov     edi,[ebp+arg1]      ; pMem
        mov     eax,[ebp+arg2]      ; val

        // Insert one of the following example code here!

$xit:   mov     eax,[ebp+arg1]      ; Return pointer
        pop     edi
        pop     ebp
        ret
memset  endp
```

---

✖ **Warning:** The following loop is really inefficient code except when used on the old 8086 processors.

```
        test    ecx,ecx
        jz      $xit

$L0:    stosb
        loop    $L0
```

That code is relatively small but pretty inefficient as it is using the repeating string function to write a series of 8-bit bytes. The payoff on Pentium processors only comes with a repeat of 64 or more.

```
    rep stosb
```

With a repeat factor of less than 64, use the following. Note that in using the ES:[EDI], the ES: IS the default and so we do not really need to put it in the code.

```
        test    ecx,ecx
        jz      $xit            ; jump if len of 0

$L1:    mov     es:[edi],al     ; set a byte
        inc     edi
        dec     ecx
        jne     $L1
```

An alternate method that is a lot more efficient than those listed above is to divide our total number of bytes into the number of 4-byte blocks, then loop on that, not forgetting to handle the remainders.

```
        test    ecx,ecx
        jz      $xit            ; jump if len of 0

; The speed of writing 1 byte is the same as writing 4 bytes
; properly aligned so we build a 32-bit value to write (al = val)

        mov     ah,al
        mov     edx,eax
        shl     eax,16
        mov     ax,dx           ; eax=replicated byte x4

        mov     edx,ecx         ; Get # of bytes to set
        shr     edx,2           ; n = n ÷ 4
        jz      $L2             ; Jump if 1..3 bytes

; edx = # of 32-bit writes

$L1:    mov     [edi],eax       ; set 4 bytes
        add     edi,4           ; advance pointer by 4 bytes
        dec     edx
        jne     $L1             ; Loop for DWORDS
```

```
        ; Remainders (1..3) bytes

$L2:    and     ecx,00000011b     ; Mask remainder bits (0..3)
        jz      $L4               ; Jump if no remainders

;           1 to 3 bytes to set

$L3:    mov     [edi],al          ; set 1 byte
        inc     edi               ; advance pointer by 1 byte
        dec     ecx
        jne     $L3               ; Loop for 1's

$L4:
```

There are more sophisticated methods that you can employ but this is a good start.

For optimal performance all data reads and writes must be on a 32-bit boundary. In a copy situation, if the source and destination are misaligned, there is not much that can be done about it. But in the case of setting memory that is misaligned, it is a snap to fix it.

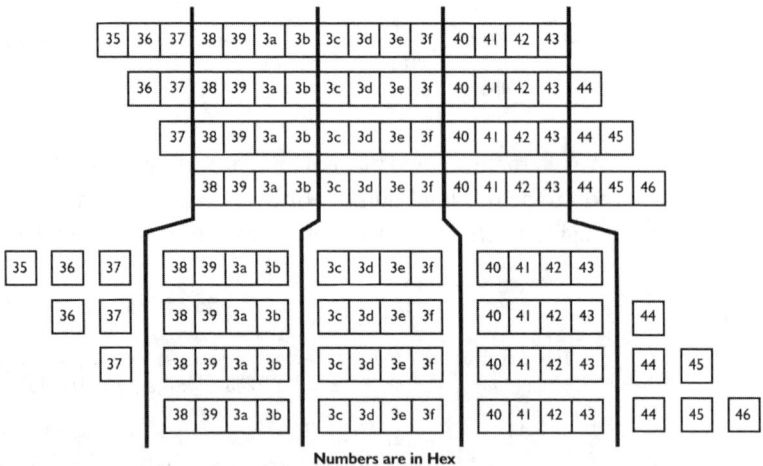

**Numbers are in Hex**

*Figure 19-1: Imagine these four differently aligned memory strands as eels. We pull out our sushi knife and finely chop off their heads into little 8-bit (1-byte) chunks, chop off the tails into 8-bit (1-byte) chunks, and then coarsely chop the bodies into larger 32-bit (4-byte) chunks, and serve raw.*

The first three memory strands had their heads misaligned, but the fourth was aligned properly. On the other hand, the tails of the last three were misaligned and the first one was aligned properly. Now that they're sliced and diced, their midsections are all properly aligned for best data handling.

The latest C runtime libraries use something a lot more elaborate such as the following function:

```
; void *memset(void *pMem, int val, uint nCnt)
;
; Note: if nCnt is set to 0 then no bytes will be set!

        public  memset
memset  proc    near

$BSHFT  =       2                   ; Shift count
$BCNT   =       4                   ; Byte count

        push    ebp
        mov     ebp,esp
```

```
; Unlike the code above, flow does not have to fall through
; if a size of 0 was passed, and so we need to test for it.
; The lines are adjusted to help prevent a stall.

        mov     ecx,[ebp+arg3]      ; nCnt
        push    edi
```

```
; Older programmers will say hey, why didn't you 'OR ecx,ecx'
; but this is a read/write function that will cost you
; time for the write. The 'TEST ecx,ecx' is a read only!

        test    ecx,ecx
        push    ebx
        jz      $Xit                ; jump if size is 0


        mov     edi,[ebp+arg1]      ; pMem
```

```
; If the size is (1...3) bytes long, then handle as tail bytes

        test    ecx,NOT ($BCNT-1)
        mov     eax,[ebp+arg2]      ; val
        jz      $Tail
```

```
; If already aligned on a (n mod 3)==0 boundary

        mov     edx,edi
        and     edx,($BCNT-1)
        jz      $SetD
```

```
; The memory attempting to be set may not be properly aligned on
; a 4-byte boundary and thus if the block is 4 bytes in size or
; greater, then the 32-bit writes will have clock penalties on
; each write and so first adjust to be properly aligned.
```

```
        sub     edx,$BCNT
        add     ecx,edx             ; Reduce # of bytes to set

$Lead:  mov     [edi],al            ; Set a byte
        inc     edi
        inc     edx
        jne     $Lead               ; Loop for those {1..3} bytes

; The speed of writing 1 byte is the same as writing 4 bytes
; properly aligned so build a 32-bit value to write  (al = val)

$SetD : mov     ah,al
        mov     edx,eax
        shl     eax,16
        mov     ax,dx               ; eax=replicated byte ×4

; Now we set the bytes four at a time

        mov     edx,ecx
        shr     edx,$BSHFT          ; (n÷4) = # of 32-bit writes

$SetD1: mov     [edi],eax
        add     edi,$BCNT
        dec     edx
        jne     $SetD1

        and     ecx,($BCNT-1)
        jz      $Xit                ; jump if size is 0

; Write any trailing bytes

$Tail:  mov     [edi],al            ; set a byte
        inc     edi
        dec     ecx
        jne     $Tail               ; loop for trailing bytes

$Xit:   pop     ebx
        pop     edi
        mov     eax,[ebp+arg1]      ; Return destination pointer
        pop     ebp
        ret
memset  endp
```

As you can see, that simple memory set function became a lot bigger, but its execution speed became a lot quicker. With very short lengths of bytes to set, such as sizes of fewer than four bytes, this code is actually slower but it quickly gains in speed as the memory lengths increase in size, especially if aligned on 4-byte boundaries. For an extra efficiency on a size of 256 bytes or more, using the STOSD instruction would be best.

**Note:** You should use the string functions such as STOSD *only* if the repeat factor is 64 or more.

These numbers aren't exactly right as this function has not been tuned for its optimal timing yet, but I leave that to you. Besides, what would be the fun in it if I gave you all the answers? As versatile as the MMX instruction set is, the linear setting or copying of memory is no more efficient than the integer instructions. In fact, a STOSD/MOVSD string set/copy with a repeat of 64 or more is actually faster than the equivalent MMX instructions on legacy processors. This would also leave the XMM register for math related solutions. It turns out that we are actually pumping data very close to or at the bus speed. For experimental purposes and to have some MMX practice, one alternative would be the use of the MMX instruction MOVQ in the $SetD section of the code so eight bytes would be written at one time.

Alter the $BSHFT and $BCNT to the new values:

```
$BSHFT  =        3               ; Shift count ×8=(1<<3)
$BCNT   =        8               ; Byte count

; Run lookup table replicates an 8-bit byte into a 64-bit qword.
; It saves a lot of shifting and ORing and only costs
; 256x8 = 2048 bytes and 1 time cycle.
;
; 00000000h,00000000h,01010101h,01010101h,02020202h,02020202h,
;   etc.

Replicate64 label  DWORD
        .XLIST
    foo     =        0
    REPEAT           256
            DD       foo,foo
            foo      =    foo + 01010101h
    ENDM
        .LIST


$SetD : lea        eax,Replicate64[eax*8]
        movq       mm7,[eax]

        mov        edx,ecx
        shr        edx,$BSHFT        ; (n÷8) = # of 64-bit writes

$SetD1: movq       [edi],mm7
        add        edi,$BCNT
        dec        edx
        jne        $SetD1
```

And call at the appropriate time only if your CPU thread has floating-point operations to handle:

```
Emms
```

**Note:** I recommend the use of the ZeroMemory() function instead. It saves passing an extra argument value of 0, or the time to replicate the single byte to four bytes.

# Copying Memory

A few years ago I was working on a project that was required to run on a 386 processor but typically ran on a 486 and had this little squirrely problem. One of the in-house computer systems that I tested the application on ran the code extremely slowly. I spent quite a while on it and when doing some benchmark testing to isolate the problem I found that the memory copy algorithm, which was used to blit graphical sprites onto the screen, was the culprit. Sprites could appear on screen with any kind of data alignment as they moved horizontally across the screen. Upon deeper investigation I found that this computer system was running DOS like all the others but in this particular case, it was running on an AMD 386SX processor. AMD usually has pretty good processors but I was intrigued and so I ordered and received their AM386 data book unique to that model processor. Upon reading the book I found out to my horror that this processor had a little zinger. As it is a 32-bit processor with a 16-bit bus, if your source and destination pointers are not properly aligned, then a single 32-bit memory access has an additional eight clock penalty for that misaligned access. And so we come to my next rule.

**Hint:** Write your assembly to be CPU model and manufacturer specific!

That little problem required the need to detect not only the exact manufacturer but also the model of processor and must route function calls to special code to handle each. In most cases the code could be shared, but some isolated instances required the special code. The following is an older style of the C function memcpy().

```
; void *memcpy(void *pDst, const void *pSrc, uint nSize)
;
; Note: if nSize is set to 0 then no bytes will be copied!
```

```
        public  memcpy
memcpy  proc    near
        push    ebp
        mov     ebp,esp
        push    esi
        push    edi

        mov     esi,[ebp+arg1]          ; pSrc
        mov     edi,[ebp+arg2]          ; pDst
        mov     ecx,[ebp+arg3]          ; nSize

        // Insert one of the following example code here!

        mov     eax,[ebp+arg1]          ; Return pointer
        pop     edi
        pop     esi
        pop     ebp
        ret
memcpy  endp
```

✖ **Warning:**  This loop is really inefficient code except when used on the old 8086 processors.

```
$L0:    movsb
        loop    $L0
```

The following code is relatively small but pretty inefficient as it is using the repeating string function to write a series of 8-bit bytes. The payoff on a Pentium only comes with a repeat of 64 or more.

```
        rep movsb
```

With a repeat factor of less than 64 use the following. Note that we do not need to put the DS: or the ES: AS the default for the ESI source register is DS, and the default for the EDI destination register is ES.

```
$L1:    mov     al,[esi]        ; al,ds:[esi]
        mov     [edi],al        ; es:[edi],al
        inc     esi
        inc     edi
        dec     ecx
        jne     $L1
```

In the above example we actually get a dependency penalty as we set the AL register but have to wait before we can actually execute the next instruction. If we adjust the function as follows, we no longer have that problem. You will note that the "inc esi" line was moved up to separate the AL, and the AL register.

```
$L1:    mov     al,ds:[esi]
        inc     esi                     ; removes dependency penalty
        mov     es:[edi],al
```

```
        inc     edi
        dec     ecx
        jne     $L1
```

Another method that is a lot more efficient than those listed above uses the same techniques we learned for setting memory. We divide our total number of bytes into the number of 4-byte blocks, then loop on that, not forgetting to handle the remainders. We handle the dependency penalty at $L1 in the same way.

```
        mov     edx,ecx         ; Get # of bytes to set
        shr     edx,2           ; n = n ÷ 4
        jz      $L2             ; Jump if 1..3 bytes

    ;   DWORDS (uint32)

$L1:    mov     eax,[esi]       ; 1µOP read 32 bits
        add     esi,4
        mov     [edi],eax       ; 2µOP write 32 bits
        add     edi,4
        dec     edx
        jne     $L1             ; Loop for DWORDS

    ;   Remainders

$L2:    and     ecx,00000011b   ; Mask remainder bits (0..3)
        jz      $L4             ; Jump if no remainders

    ;   1 to 3 bytes to set

$L3:    mov     al,[esi]
        inc     esi
        mov     [edi],al
        inc     edi
        dec     ecx
        jne     $L3             ; Loop for 1's

$L4:
```

This following method is significantly faster as it moves eight bytes at a time instead of four. There is no dependency penalty since the register being set is not being used immediately.

```
        mov     ecx,[ebp+arg3]  ; nSize
        shr     ecx,3           ; n = n ÷ 8
        jz      $L2             ; Jump if 1..7 bytes

    ;   QWORDS (uint64)

$L1:    mov     eax,[esi]       ; 1µOP read 32 bits
        mov     edx,[esi+4]     ; read next 32 bits
        mov     [edi],eax       ; 2µOP write 32 bits
```

```
          mov      [edi+4],edx        ; write next 32 bits
          add      esi,8
          add      edi,8
          dec      ecx
          jne      $L1                ; Loop for QWORDS

;         Remainders

$L2:      mov      ecx,[ebp+arg3]     ; nSize
          and      ecx,00000111b      ; Mask remainder bits (0..7)
          jz       $L4                ; Jump if no remainders

;         1 to 7 bytes to set

$L3:      mov      al,[esi]           ; read a byte
          inc      esi
          mov      [edi],al           ; write byte
          inc      edi
          dec      ecx
          jne      $L3                ; Loop for 1's

$L4:
```

This code is just about as fast as a copy using MMX. An example would be to replace $L1 with the following code:

```
$L1:      movq     mm7,[esi]          ; read 64 bits
          add      esi,8
          movq     [edi],mm7          ; write 64 bits
          add      edi,8
          dec      ecx
          jne      $L1                ; Loop for QWORDS
```

There are more sophisticated methods that you can employ, but this is a good start.

It is important for memory to be aligned, as a problem occurs when the source and/or destination are misaligned. Memory movement (copy) functions should try to reorient source and destination pointers. Unfortunately, if one is not lucky enough that the source and destination are either both properly aligned or they are misaligned exactly the same:

```
If ((pSrc AND 00000000111b) == (pDst AND 00000000111b))
```

...then adjust them. If their logically AND'ed values are 0, no adjustment is needed. If the alignment is the same, adjust by 1's to get into the alignment position. If both are out of alignment, obtain a speed increase by putting at least one of them into alignment (preferably the destination):

```
            mov     edx,edi          ; At least align destination!
            and     edx,0000111b
            jz      $Mid             ; Jump if properly aligned

            ; Remove misaligned bytes

            add     edx,0ffffffffch  ; -3

$lead:      mov     al,[esi]         ; read byte
            inc     esi
            mov     [edi],al         ; write byte
            inc     edi
            dec     ecx              ; reduce total to move
            inc     edx              ; increment to 0
            jne     $lead            ; loop for lead bytes

$Mid:
```

For the actual memory movement operation there are various techniques that can be used, each with its own benefit or drawback.

The best method is a preventative one. If the memory you're dealing with is for video images, then not only should the (width mod 8) equal a remainder of zero but the source and destination pointers should also be properly aligned. In this way, there is no problem of clock penalties for each memory access and no extra and possibly futile effort trying to align them.

In 8-bit images, moving (blitting) sprite memory can be difficult as sprites will always be misaligned. In 32-bit images where one pixel is 32 bits, alignment is a snap, as every pixel is properly aligned.

```
#ifdef __cplusplus
extern "C" void gfxCopyBlit8x8Asm(byte *pDst, byte *pSrc,
        uint nStride, uint nWidth, uint nHeight);
#endif


    // Comment this line out for 'C' code

#define USE_ASM_COPYBLIT_8X8

    // 8-bit to 8-bit Copy Blit
    //
    // This function is pre-clipped to copy an 8-bit color
    // pixel from the buffer pointed to by the source
    // pointer to an identical sized destination buffer.

#ifdef USE_ASM_COPYBLIT_8X8
#define CopyBlit8x8  CopyBlit8x8Asm
#else
void CopyBlit8x8(byte *pDst, byte *pSrc, uint nStride,
        uint nWidth, uint nHeight)
```

```
{
    // If width is the stride then copy entire image
    if (nWidth == nStride)
    {
        memcpy(pDst, pSrc, nStride * nHeight);
    }
    else
    {   // Copy image 1 scanline at a time.
        do {
            memcpy(pDst, pSrc, nWidth);

            pSrc += nStride;      // Source stride adjustment
            pDst += nStride;      // Destination Stride adj.
        } while(--nHeight);       // Loop for height
    }
}
#endif
```

As you probably noted, there is extra logic checking if width and stride
are the same. If so, then unroll the loop to make the code even more
efficient.

**Goal:** Try to write the listed function in assembly optimized for your processor.
Or multiple processors.

# Speed Freak

The code size would increase but using a vector table such as follows
would allow you to unroll your (remainder) loops. With normal code,
four states would be required but for MMX all eight would be best.

```
        mov     eax,ecx         ; Get Width
        and     eax,0000111b
        jmp     $SetTbl[eax*4]

; At bottom of assembly source file insert the vector table so
; it doesn't interfere with your memory caches.

        Align 16
$SetTbl: dd      $SetQ           ; (n mod 8) = 0
         dd      $Set1           ; (n mod 4) = 1
         dd      $Set2           ; (n mod 4) = 2
         dd      $Set3           ; (n mod 4) = 3
         dd      $SetD           ; (n mod 4) = 0
         dd      $Set1'          ; (n mod 4) = 1
         dd      $Set2           ; (n mod 4) = 2
         dd      $Set3           ; (n mod 4) = 3
```

# Graphics 101 — Frame Buffer

When dealing with graphic images there are various parameters defining its geometry.

- **memptr** — The base pointer to a coordinate within the image related to its physical memory address.

- **bits per pixel** — The number of bits per pixel used to represent the image. Typically 1/4/8/16/24/32-bit but pretty much only 8- to 32-bit are used these days.

- **width** — The width of the image in pixels.

- **height** — The height of the image in pixels.

- **stride** — The number of bytes used to represent the start of one row of pixels to the start of another. It should be noted that there may be extra bytes beyond the last visible pixel and the start of the row of pixels. For example, in Figure 19-2 the 640-pixel scanline has an overage of 384 bytes. That means when you write that 640th pixel you need to add 384 to get to the start of the next scanline (640+384=1024).

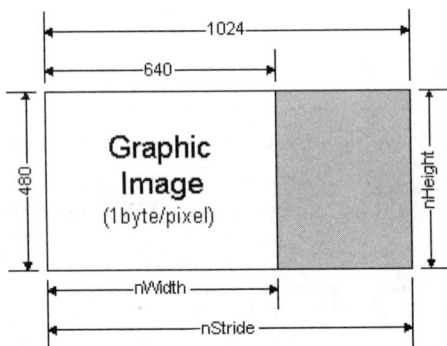

*Figure 19-2: Bitmap dimension information*

So now let's use this information in some real code.

```
#ifdef __cplusplus
extern "C" void gfxClrAsm(byte *pDst, uint nStride,
  uint nWidth, uint nHeight);
#endif
```

```
//  Comment this line out for C code
```

```
#define USE_ASM_GFXCLR

    //  Graphics Clear
    //
    //  This is a pre-clipped function used to clear a bitmap
    //  pointed to by the destination pointer.
    //  Note: This can be used to clear 8/16/24/32-bit pixels.

#ifdef USE_ASM_GFXCLR
#define gfxClr  gfxClrAsm
#else

void gfxClr(byte *pDst, uint nStride, uint nWidth, uint nHeight)
{
    do {
        memset(pDst, 0, nWidth);
        pDst += nStride;
    } while (--nHeight);
}
#endif
```

**Project:**

Using what you've learned, try to write the C function above in assembly optimized for your processor.

```
void gfxClrAsm(byte *pDst, uint nStride, uint nWidth, uint nHeight);
```

# Graphics 101 — Blit

There are different methods one can choose to blit or bit field copy a graphics image, including a pure blit where the image is merely copied pixel by pixel or a transparent copy such as detailed here.

A transparent pixel is referred to by a variety of names, including transparent, color key, skip color, invisible color, and non-displayed pixel. This is a pixel containing no image color data that allows the color of the pixel directly underneath it to be displayed. It is typically set to an unusual color that helps the artists and programmers easily identify it in relation to the rest of the colors.

If you watch the news you see this process every day compliments of the weatherman. He is shot on a green screen, being careful not to wear a color similar to the *color key*, so the electronics will make him appear in front of an image such as a map and that composite image is transmitted to your television. If he wore the same shade of color as the color key, in the middle of his chest he would appear to have a big hole where you would be able to see through his body.

When using film, moviemakers shoot models or actors on a blue screen, as the color of blue is actually clear on the film negative. Over-simplifying this explanation, the non-clear areas would be converted into a mask and the images would be cut into a composite typically using a matte backdrop.

When using digitized graphics in a computer, movie/game makers shoot actors on a green screen and digitally map the images into a single image using some sort of backdrop.

Your transparency color can be any color. I typically pick a dark shade of blue. For instance, in an RGB range of (0 to 255) {red:0, green:0, blue:108}. This allows me to differentiate between the color of black and transparency and still have the transparent color dark enough so as not to detract from the art. When I am nearly done with the image and almost ready to test it for any stray transparent pixels, I set them to a bright purple {red:255, green:0, blue:255} as that particular color of bright purple is not usually found in my art images and it really stands out. It does not matter what color you use as long as the image does not contain that particular color.

In a 2D graphics application, there is typically a need to composite images and so this leads to how to handle a transparent blit.

A few years ago, I taught a College for Kids program during the summer titled "The Art of Computer/Video Game Design." For that class, I had put together a small program that reinforced the need for computer games to have foreign language support. This particular game was called "Monster Punch." A language would be selected and then various living fruit with their eyes moving around would drop down from the top of the screen and pass through the opening out of view at the bottom of the screen. After all the fruit had fallen, the display would snap to a view of a blender, at which point all the fruit would be blended, while screaming, into monster punch where the blender comes alive, à la "Monster Punch!" (Okay, maybe I am a little warped, but you should have been able to figure that out by now!)

The following sections use Monster Punch to demonstrate blitting.

## Copy Blit

The following sprite imagery is that of a copy blit, where a rectangular image is copied to the destination and overwrites any overlapped pixel.

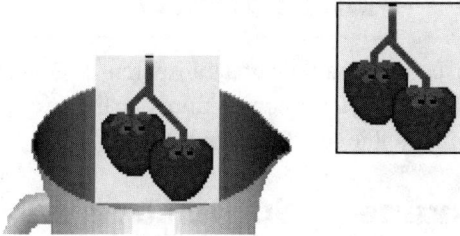

*Figure 19-3: Monster Punch — Copy blit of strawberry image on the right into the blender on the left.*

Using efficiently optimized code, up to eight bytes at a time can be copied with 64-bit access, which corresponds to simultaneously writing eight 8-bit pixels, or four 16-bit pixels, or almost three 24-bit pixels, or only two 32-bit pixels. With 128-bit, up to 16 bytes can be accessed, thus 16 8-bit pixels, or eight 16-bit pixels, or slightly over five 24-bit pixels, or only four 32-bit pixels.

## Transparent Blit

As the following sprite image portrays, all pixels from the source that match the transparent color are not copied, thus causing the sprite to be seamlessly pasted into the background.

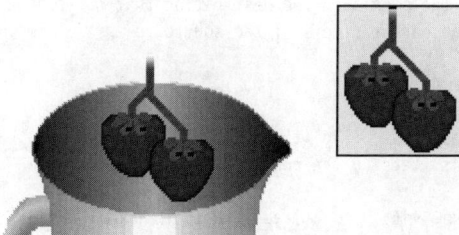

*Figure 19-4: Monster Punch — Transparent blit of strawberry image on the right into the blender on the left.*

Normally when dealing with transparencies, only one pixel at a time can be tested to detect if it is transparent or not and so wind up introducing inefficiencies such as branch mispredictions, but that is where the sample in the following section comes in handy.

# Graphics 101 — Blit (MMX)

The following code is a sample of a transparent blit, where a scanline of a count of ECX 8-bit bytes is copied from one graphic source row [ESI] to a destination graphic row [EDI] one pixel at a time.

## Graphics Engine — Sprite Layered

This eight 8-bit transparent pixel copy uses MMX code. Note that there is only one branch loop every eighth pixel.

```
tcolor qword 03f3f3f3f3f3f3f3fh ; 03fh = transparent pixel

; esi=source  edi=destination  ecx=# of qwords

        movq    mm7,tcolor    ; Get replicated transparency

$TO: movq    mm5,[esi]    ; Get 8 source pixels
     movq    mm4,[edi]    ; Get background
     movq    mm6,mm5      ; Copy 8 source pixels

; Compare each pixel's color to transparency color and if
; a match, set each pixel in the mask to FF else 00!

        pcmpeqb mm5,mm7      ; Create masks for transparency

        add     esi,8        ; Adjust source pointer

;    Only keep the pixels in the destination that correspond
;    to the transparent pixels of the source!

        pand    mm4,mm5

; Using the same mask, flip it, then AND it with the
; source pixels, keeping the non-transparent pixels.

        pandn   mm5,mm6      ; erase transparent pixels

; Or the destination pixels with the source pixels.

        por     mm4,mm5      ; blend 8 pixels into art
        movq    [edi],mm4    ; Save new background

        add     edi,8        ; Adjust destination pointer
        dec     ecx          ; any pixels left?
        jne     $TO          ; Loop for eight 8-bit pixels
```

There is no transparency testing or branching, only the masking and blending of data, which makes the process of a transparent blit much faster. These two different blits (copy, transparent) are typically designed for a graphic environment such as in Figure 19-5 where the background seen on the right is kept in a separate buffer like wallpaper.

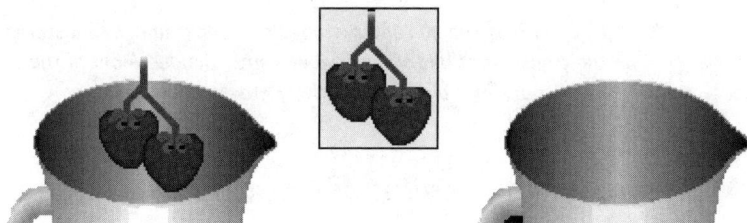

*Figure 19-5: Transparent copy blit of strawberry sprite and blender image background to achieve composite result of both.*

The background is CopyBlit to the working surface as seen on the left, and the sprite image is Transparent Blit in front of it. When the sprite image is animated, the area being changed is "erased" from the working surface by a rectangular CopyBlit of that area from the background to the working surface and then the update sprite image has a rectangular area Transparent Blit in front. This is a layered approach typically used in a video game that has a number of animated objects moving around the display.

## Graphics Engine — Sprite Overlay

Another graphic sprite environment method is where the area under the sprite is remembered in a buffer attached to the sprite before the sprite image is Transparent Blit. This operation typically occurs simultaneously to reduce the amount of calculation work.

This is typically called an "overlay" method used by Windows and some sprite engines. The drawback to this method is that overlapping of sprites needs to be minimized because erasing one requires all the other intersecting sprites visible above that sprite to be erased. The list of sprites needs to be traversed to find out which sprites intersect the area and need to be erased and repainted by replacing the image under each intersecting sprite in the image buffer with the corresponding original background image. The list of sprites then needs to be traversed again, this time drawing the sprites back into the scene.

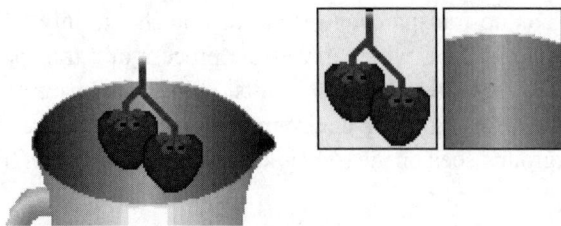

*Figure 19-6: The blit of a rectangular blender image to a storage buffer, then the transparent blit of a strawberry into blender. A blit of the saved blender image back into blender effectively erases the strawberry.*

```
tcolor qword 03f3f3f3f3f3f3f3fh ; 03fh = transparent pixel

; esi=source  edi=destination  ebx=buffer  ecx=# of qwords

        movq    mm7,tcolor      ; Get replicated transparency

$T0: movq     mm5,[esi]        ; Get 8 source pixels
     movq     mm4,[edi]        ; Get 8 background pixels
     movq     mm6,mm5          ; Copy 8 source pixels

; Compare each pixel's color to transparency color and if
; a match, set each pixel in the mask to FF, else 00!

        pcmpeqb mm5,mm7         ; Create masks for transparency
        movq    [ebx],mm4       ; Save BGnd in buffer

; Only keep the pixels in the destination that correspond
; to the transparent pixels of the source!

        pand    mm4,mm5

; Using the same mask, flip it then AND it with the
; source pixels, keeping the non-transparent pixels.

        pandn   mm5,mm6         ; erase transparent pixels

; Or the destination pixels with the source pixels.

        add     ebx,8           ; Adjust buffer pointer
        por     mm4,mm5         ; Blend 8 pixels into art
        add     esi,8           ; Adjust source pointer
        movq    [edi],mm4       ; Save new background
        add     edi,8           ; Adjust destination pointer

        dec     ecx             ; Any pixels left?
        jne     $T0             ; Loop for eight 8-bit pixels
```

# Graphics 101 — Clipping Blit

*Figure 19-7: 2D bitmap on left with 2-bit clipping plane on right*

The same trick of using inverse logic can be used for expanding image clipping planes.

In the image on the left, no matter how it's encoded (8/16/24/32 bits), only a single bit in the clipping plane image on the right would be needed to represent a single pixel. If black=0 and white=1, then a sprite object could appear to pass in front of the fence as well as behind it but in front of the distant background. This could be done in a variety of ways. One would be to use masks where both the sprite pixel and the background pixel are masked so only one has a non-zero value. The resulting color is written to the destination buffer.

```
; esi = sprite image pointer
; ebx = clipping plane
; ebp = background image pointer
; edi = destination image buffer pointer

        mov    edx,[ebx]      ; Get clipping plane
        mov    ch,32          ; 32 pixels at a time

$L1:    mov    al,[esi]       ; Source sprite image
        inc    esi            ; Next sprite pixel pointer
        mov    cl,[ebp]       ; Source background image
        inc    ebp            ; Next src background pixel

        test   al,tcolor      ; transparent color
        je     $T1            ; Jump if transparent pixel

        shr    edx,1          ; Get a masking bit into carry
        setnc  ah             ; 1=background 0=foreground
        dec    ah             ; 00=background ff=foreground
        and    cl,ah          ; ff=keep bgnd 00=kill it
        not    ah             ; Flip masking bits
        and    al,ah          ; ff=keep sprite 00=kill it
        or     cl,al          ; (XOR type) Blend pixels
```

```
$T1:    mov    [edi],cl        ; Save new pixel to destination
        inc    edi             ; Next dst working pixel
        dec    ch              ; 1 less pixel in run
        jnz    $L1             ; Loop
```

# Chapter 20

# MASM vs. NASM vs. TASM vs. WASM

This chapter reminds me of the old *Batman and Robin* show where in a fight scene we see sound effect words flash on screen such as "OOF," "KABONG," "ZING," "MASM," "ZOT," "TASM," "ZANG," "WASM," and "POW." These, by an amazing coincidence, are the war cry of the assembly language programmer. Wars have started for far less than trying to get one of these programmers to use a different C/C++ compiler or assembler. At one company I spent almost two years writing a good portion of the application core libraries and all the documentation for their SDK that allowed internal and external programmers to write online computer games using dedicated game servers. For the last year and a half there I worked on their Win32 Network API SDK (not to be confused with Microsoft's GameSDK). For the first four months there I wrote the DOS SDK, which uses 16-bit and various forms of 32-bit Extended DOS. It was a mix and match of C/C++ compilers, assemblers, linkers, and DOS extenders. It seemed every company had their own flavor. They had gotten used to their favorite combination and nothing was better! So every now and then I had to create libraries for that new flavor to entice new clients. Some of the code I currently write also uses the High C/C++ compiler with MASM or Pharlap's 386ASM. I do not use it these days, but there is also the Watcom C/C++ with their WASM Assembler. Occasionally on software I write today, I get inquiries if my libraries are compatible with the Borland TASM Assembler. I have used all of these and a few others, and to date my favorite is MASM by Microsoft.

There is a form of assembly that we should not forget: in-line assembly. Some people swear by it. I, on the other hand, swear at it! I rarely use it and only for some specific type of data conversion that I need to be fast without the penalty of a stack call to call a pure assembly function. It is akin to programming with one arm tied behind one's back. A lot of macro assembler functions are not available.

I have read book reviews in which advocates of non-MASM assemblers indicate a book could have been a lot better if the author had used TASM instead of MASM. Again, a personal bias! Although I have a few apprehensions about MASM, I have a personal bias for it. In writing this book I have tried to appease the critics by keeping the examples as generic as possible, and if this was not good enough for you, "☹ RASPBERRIES! ☺ " MASM is only available separately by download but it's built into the Visual C++ 6 and VC .NET compilers.

You should always use the latest and greatest version of your favorite assembler because if you do not, your version could have bugs (I find them all the time) or be too old to support some of the newer instructions. Back when MMX first came out I had to use the IAMMX.INC by Intel with the MASM as a workaround just to support MMX instructions. Since then it has been built into MASM. Now for SSE3 support you need to either get the latest VC .NET or download the ia_pni.inc file to get assembly instruction macro emulation. With one other company's assembler I had to hand-code the opcodes to make sure I had the appropriate JMP instruction. There was a bug and the jump instruction that I had coded in assembly code was not the jump instruction being encoded into machine code. A bug was being introduced into compiled code because of a bug in the assembler itself!

With the latest instruction sets there seem to be two assemblers at the forefront with recently introduced assembly instructions: MASM and NASM. No matter whose assembler you're using, I use the following as placeholders for the arguments being passed into the example code used in this book:

```
arg1    equ    8          ; Argument #1
arg2    equ    (arg1+4)   ; Argument #2
arg3    equ    (arg2+4)   ; Argument #3
arg4    equ    (arg3+4)   ; Argument #4
arg5    equ    (arg4+4)   ; Argument #5
arg6    equ    (arg5+4)   ; Argument #6
arg7    equ    (arg6+4)   ; Argument #7
arg8    equ    (arg7+4)   ; Argument #8


; void unzip(byte *pRaw, byte *pZip, uint nWidth);

        public unzip
unzip   proc   near
        push   ebp
        mov    ebp,esp
        push   ebx
        push   esi
```

```
        push    edi

        mov     esi,[ebp+arg1]   ; pRaw
        mov     edi,[ebp+arg2]   ; pZip
        mov     ecx,[ebp+arg3]   ; nWidth

    ;
    ;
    ;

        pop     edi
        pop     esi
        pop     ebx
        pop     ebp
        ret
unzip   endp
```

You will note that I used arg1 instead of 8 as shown below:

```
        mov     eax,[ebp+8]
```

As an alternative to the arg1 you could use a define to make the argument name make more sense.

```
pRaw = arg1
    mov     eax,[ebp+pRaw]
```

The following information is a brief overview and you should refer to your assembler's documentation for specific information.

# MASM — Microsoft Macro Assembler

When using Macro Assembler by Microsoft you should use the latest and greatest version because of the extended instruction sets. However, to use those new instructions you need to turn on functionality.

When using this assembler, the first thing you need to do is activate the appropriate CPU target by using one of the following assembler directives depending on what processor will be executing that section of code. There are several of these directives such as .386, .486, .586, etc. If the target is for an embedded 486, then obviously the .586 directive would not be used, as instructions would be allowed that the 486 would not understand. When you write your code for a single processor you can merely set the appropriate directive(s) at the top of the file, but quite often a single file will contain sets of code unique to individual processors.

■  .686 — This allows Model 6 type x86 code to be assembled. The next line actually allows MMX instructions to be assembled. You can pretty much have this directive as most processors being released these days support MMX. You do need to make sure that the code is only going to be executed by one of those processors, however.

The directives not only target processors but certain instruction sets, and so care must be used when setting the appropriate directives.

- .MMX — An alternate method is to set the supported instruction sets such as this directive for enabling MMX code.

- .K3D — This is the directive for the 3DNow! instruction set. As you do not want an Intel processor trying to execute one of these instructions, only insert this above 3DNow! instruction code. These are also order dependent and so this must occur after the .MMX directive.

- .XMM — Use this if you are using any SSE-based instructions requiring XMM registers.

There are other legacy declarations such as .387, .286, .386, .386P, .486, .486P, etc. The suffix "P" indicates an enabling of privileged instructions.

For more information, see http://msdn2.microsoft.com/library/afzk3475(en-us,vs.80).aspx.

Here is a sample file that you should be able to drop into a Win32 application in conjunction with the Visual C++ compiler:

```
        TITLE zipX86M.asm — My x86 (MASM) Assembly
        PAGE    53,160
;       This module is designed to Blah Blah Blah!
;
;       Created - 20 May 98 - J.Leiterman
;       Tabs = 8

        .686
        .MMX
        .K3D
        .model flat, C

        .data
        ALIGN 4
foo     dd      0                       ; Data value

zipX86M SEGMENT USE32 PUBLIC 'CODE'

;
; void unzip(byte *pRaw, byte *pZip, uint nWidth);
;
```

Chapter 20: MASM vs. NASM vs. TASM vs. WASM

**485**

```
            align     16
    unzip   PROC C PUBLIC USES ebx esi edi pRaw:PTR, pZip:PTR,
               nWidth:DWORD

            mov       esi,pRaw
            mov       edi,pZip
            mov       ecx,nWidth
            ;
            ;
            ;
            ret
    unzip   endp

zipX86M  ends
         end
```

The function is declared PUBLIC, meaning it's global in definition and can therefore be accessed by functions in other files.

```
    unzip   PROC C PUBLIC USES ebx esi edi pRaw:PTR, pZip:PTR,
               nWidth:DWORD
```

For convenience, you can specify the registers to push onto the stack and in what order. The RET instruction is actually a macro when used within this PROC, and therefore the registers are popped automatically in a reverse order wherever a RET instruction is encountered. The coup de grâce? No more pesky code like:

```
  mov   esi,[ebp+arg1]              ; pRaw
```

Instead, you just use:

```
  mov   esi,pRaw
```

The assembler expands the PROC macro and takes care of everything for you, making your code a little more readable.

You will notice that I used the default data segment (.data) as this is a flat memory model, but I declared a 32-bit Protected Mode code segment. The reasoning is that I tend to group my assembly files using an object-oriented approach and as such all my decompression functions/procedures would reside within this segment. Other assembly code related to other functionality would be contained in a different file with a different segment name. They can occur with the same segment name but they wouldn't appear very organized, especially in the application address/data map.

```
zipX86M  SEGMENT USE32 PUBLIC 'CODE'
:
:
zipX86M  ends
```

Since segments are being mentioned I am going to give you a snapshot
of segments back in the days of DOS and DOS extenders. Code and
data was differentiated by 16-bit code/data versus 32-bit code/data
addressing. The following is a snippet of code from those days.

```
;     Segment Ordering Sequence

      INN_CODE32   segment para USE32 'CODE'
      INN_CODE32   ends
      _TEXT        segment
      _TEXT        ends
      INN_DATA32   segment para USE32 'DATA'
      INN_DATA32   ends

      DGROUP       GROUP INN_DATA32
      CGROUP       GROUP _TEXT
      CGROUP       GROUP INN_CODE32
```

We also must not forget the (end) signal to the assembler that it has
reached the end of the file:

```
End
```

I personally think this is just a carryover from the good old days of
much simpler assemblers. With the advent of macros such as the following, you can turn on or off various sections of code and not just the
bottom portion of your file:

```
if  0
else
endif
```

Visual C++ has never really had a peaceful coexistence with its own
MASM Assembler. In the early days of around version 3.x you had to
assemble your files using batch files or external make files and only link
the *.obj files into your project files. Microsoft has fortunately made
this a little simpler, but in my opinion it still seems shortsighted. My
assumption is that they would prefer you to use either inline assembly
or none at all. (But I've been known to be wrong before!)

The first thing you need to do is add the MASM hooks into your
version 5.0 or above Visual C++ environment. Select the Tools|Options
menu item, and then select the Directories tab. Set the following to the
path of your MASM installation:

```
Executable Files:  c:\masm\bin
                   c:\masm\binr
   Include Files:  c:\masm\include
```

With your project loaded in your FileView tab, just right-click on the
project files folder, and select the pop-up menu item Add Files to

Project. The Insert Files into Project dialog box will be displayed. That dialog seems to support almost every file type known except for assembly! What you need to do is select the All Files (\*.\*) option, select the assembly file you desire, and then press the OK button.

Now that the file occurs in your list of files in your project, right-click on that file and select the Settings item from the pop-up menu. In the Commands edit box insert the following:

```
ml @MyGame.amk ..\util\unzipx86.asm
```

This will execute the assembler using the option switches defined in the MyGame.amk file. In the Outputs edit box insert the following:

```
unzipx86.obj
```

Then press the OK button.

To make my life simpler I use a file, such as the following, that I refer to as my assembly make file. I clone it from project to project, as you'll never know when you'll need to tweak it.

```
File: MYGAME.AMK
       /L../util
       /c
       /coff
       /Cp
       /Fl
       /Fm
       /FR
       /Sg
       /Zd
       /Zi
```

For those of you who would prefer to use in-line assembly or just plain don't have an assembler, you can do the same thing with the following from within your C/C++ code.

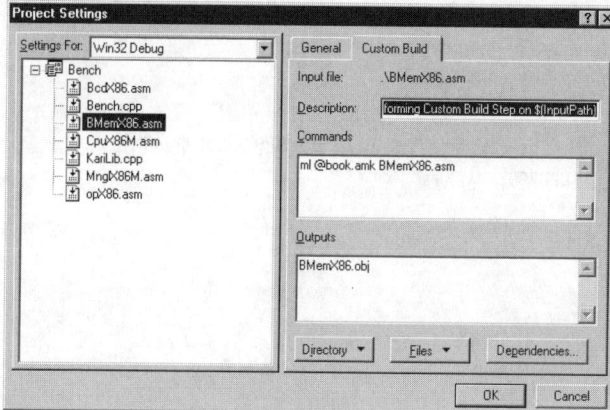

Figure 20-1:
VC6
assembler
configuration
display

```
void unzip(byte *pRaw, byte *pZip, uint nWidth)
{
    _asm {
        mov     esi,pRaw
        mov     edi,pZip
        mov     ecx,nWidth

    };
}
```

You should be very careful if you mix C/C++ and in-line assembly code unless you push the registers to save them. Setting a breakpoint at the beginning of your function and then examining the source code during run time can help point out any register use conflicts.

MASM is my favorite macro assembler as it has an excellent macro expansion ability. Not only can new instructions be incorporated by use of macros but the predefined macro expansion can be taken to advantage as they are C like. In some cases, I find it better than C. In fact, in-line assembly sucks! (Another technical term!) (Note: I only said in some cases!) The following are some of the highlights. For details, read the technical manuals. For example, the MASM toolset has the following manuals:

- Environment and Tools
- Programmers Guide
- Reference

In the following charts, notice the C method on the left and the MASM method on the right.

Defines are pretty similar; however, enums do not exist and so must be emulated with a standard equate.

| C | MASM |
|---|---|
| `#define FOO  3` | `FOO = 3` |
| `typedef enum` | |
| `{` | |
| `    CPUVEN_UNKNOWN = 0,` | `CPUVEN_UNKNOWN = 0` |
| `} CPUVEN;` | |

MASM can contain a structure definition just like C:

| C | MASM |
|---|---|
| ```typedef struct CpuInfoType {``` | ```CpuInfo struct 4``` |
| ```    uint   nCpuId;  // CPU Id``` | ```    nCpuId dd 0   ; CPU Id``` |
| ```    uint   nFpuId;  // FPU Id``` | ```    nFpuId dd 0   ; FPU Id``` |
| ```    uint   nBits;   // Feature``` | ```    nBits  dd 0   ; Feature``` |
| ```    uint   nMfg;    // Mfg``` | ```    nMfg   dd 0   ; Mfg.``` |
| ```    uint16 SerialNum[6];``` | ```    SerialNum dw 0,0,0,0,0,0``` |
| ```    uint   nSpeed;  // Speed``` | ```    nSpeed dd 0   ; Speed``` |
| ```} CpuInfo;``` | ```CpuInfo ends``` |

In C there is no looping macro expansion; there is only one-shot (a definition gets expanded). However, some special macro functionality is available when using a MACRO assembler.

# REPEAT

MASM supports the repeat declaration when used in conjunction with a local temporary argument.

```
i = 0
   REPEAT 5
mov [i + ebx],eax
i = i + 4
   ENDM
```

The i is temporary and expands the code. For this example, the REPEAT macro is replicated five times and adds 4 (the size of the write) onto every iteration. So the code is unrolled:

```
mov [0 + ebx],eax
mov [4 + ebx],eax
mov [8 + ebx],eax
mov [12 + ebx],eax
mov [16 + ebx],eax
```

# WHILE

MASM also supports a while loop.

```
i = 0
   WHILE i LE 20   ; <
mov [i + ebx],eax
i = i + 4
   ENDM
```

This is essentially similar code. The example was a simple loop, but while loops are typically used in loops of more complexity.

## FOR

MASM also supports a for loop.

```
    FOR  arg, <1,3,5,7,9,11,13,17,19,23>
  out dx,arg
    ENDM
```

As mentioned, these are examples of MASM related code. Those assemble-time loops are something not available to a C compiler. Other items are available including access to data/code segment specification and all assembly instructions, while inline assembly has only a limited set of instructions available. The macro assembler allows code/data intermixed, while a C compiler does not. The IF-ELSE-ENDIF conditionals are also available, along with other features available in a standard C compiler.

# Compiler Intrinsics

The more recent Visual C++ and Intel compilers support a method of programming in assembly language referred to as *intrinsics*. This is where the functionality of SIMD instructions has been wrapped within C wrappers and compiled into code as inline code. Let us examine the following example:

```
void test(float *c, float a, float b)
{
   *c = a + b;
}
```

Not to oversimplify the power of using intrinsics to get code up and running quickly, the following code uses intrinsics in conjunction with (_m128) XMM registers with SSE single-precision floating-point instructions. Note that it looks more complicated, but I chose a simple scalar expression to resolve.

```
#include <xmmintrin.h>

void test(float *c, float a, float b)
{
   __m128 ta, tb;

   ta = _mm_load_ps(&a);
   tb = _mm_load_ps(&b);
```

```
    ta = _mm_add_ps(ta, tb);
    _mm_store_ps(c, ta);
}
```

But underneath in the pure assembly code generated by the compiler
this breaks down to something similar to the following:

```
push    ebx
mov     ebx,esp
sub     esp,8
and     esp,0FFFFFFF0h    ; 16-byte align stack
add     esp,4
push    ebp
mov     ebp,dword ptr [ebx+4]
mov     dword ptr [esp+4],ebp
mov     ebp,esp
sub     esp,98h
push    esi
push    edi
  ; __m128 ta, tb
  ; ta = _mm_load_ps(&a);
lea     eax,[ebx+0Ch]
movaps  xmm0,xmmword ptr [eax]
movaps  xmmword ptr [ebp-30h],xmm0
movaps  xmm0,xmmword ptr [ebp-30h]
movaps  xmmword ptr [ebp-10h],xmm0
  ; tb = _mm_load_ps(&b);
lea     eax,[ebx+10h]
movaps  xmm0,xmmword ptr [eax]
movaps  xmmword ptr [ebp-40h],xmm0
movaps  xmm0,xmmword ptr [ebp-40h]
movaps  xmmword ptr [ebp-20h],xmm0
  ; ta = _mm_add_ps(ta, tb);
movaps  xmm0,xmmword ptr [ebp-20h]
movaps  xmm1,xmmword ptr [ebp-10h]
addps   xmm1,xmm0
movaps  xmmword ptr [ebp-50h],xmm1
movaps  xmm0,xmmword ptr [ebp-50h]
movaps  xmmword ptr [ebp-10h],xmm0
  ; _mm_store_ps(c, ta);
movaps  xmm0,xmmword ptr [ebp-10h]
mov     eax,dword ptr [ebx+8]
movaps  xmmword ptr [eax],xmm0

pop     edi
pop     esi
mov     esp,ebp
pop     ebp
mov     esp,ebx
pop     ebx
ret
```

# Chapter 21

# Debugging Functions

Debugging code written for vector processors can be either complicated or very simple, depending on your toolset. The first item to remember is to have a good IDE (integrated development environment). With this and the proper processor package, the packed data vector registers can be immediately dumped and examined to verify the data is as expected.

**Workbench Files:** \Bench\x86\chap21\*project*\*platform*

|  | *project* | *platform* |
|---|---|---|
| **Debugging** | **\vecbug\** | \vc6 |
|  |  | \vc.net |

# Guidelines of Assembly Development

I do not want to bog you down or lecture to you as I have done enough of that already, but here are some suggestions for developing assembly code:

- Always write your functions in C first.
- Vectorize it in C if possible.
- *Debug* the C. Single step it.
- Lock the code. There should be little to no (preferably no) changes later.
- If code is not fast enough, then and only then start your assembly.
- Single step the assembly.
- Compare output of C to output of assembly. Do them both! Their outputs *must* match.
- Keep the C code in a safe place.

It never fails. You may be in the middle of optimizing some assembly code and management comes by for a demo. If you still have the C code, you can switch over to it; it runs slower but you are still able to run the demo.

If your code deals with arrays of numbers or a series of like numbers, then orient your C code in groups of four for single-precision floating-point numbers, etc. The idea is 128-bit data. Read *Vector Game Math Processors* for more information on this topic.

Debug your C code! Every loop, every variable. Make sure it works exactly as you think it does. This is important when you go to benchmark its results with the assembly code.

Locking your function means that it is done. There is (hopefully) absolutely no reason ever to make any more changes to it.

Maybe your optimized C code is fast enough for your needs. It takes time to write assembly code and get it working correctly. Also, you will want to phase in your assembly code. From within your C code, call the assembly function (at least initially during development). This allows you to generate two sets of results and compare them. This also allows you to handle the aligned memory algorithm first before moving on to the misaligned version, etc. One by one, you phase them in. Eventually you actually vector the assembly code instead of the C code. You keep the C code as a fallback position, plus it gives you a starting point if the function is changed in a major way.

# Visual C++

If using Visual C++ version 7 or higher, then your compiler has already been updated with the latest and greatest processor information, but if you're using Visual C++ version 6 you need to download and install the service packs from http://msdn.microsoft.com/vstudio/downloads/updates/sp/vs6/sp5/default.asp.

You will also need the processor packs if you are running service pack 4, available at http://msdn.microsoft.com/vstudio/downloads/ppack/Beta/download.asp.

If you are using a version older than Visual C++ version 6 you will need to rely heavily on functions that you can call to dump the contents of your registers.

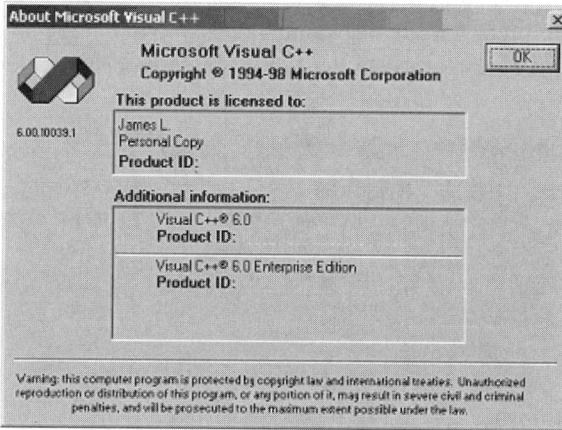

Figure 21-1: About Visual C++ version 6.0

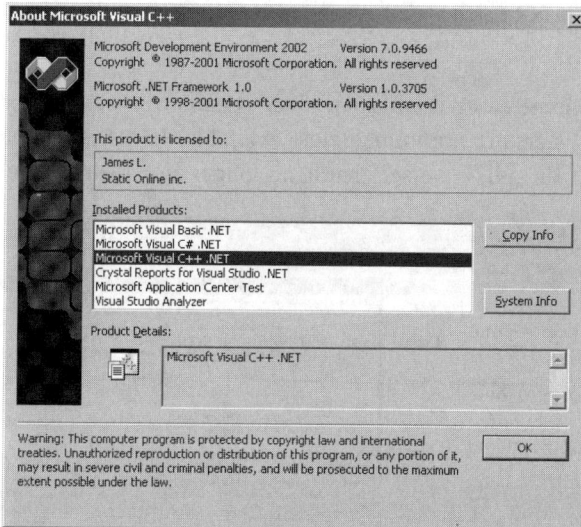

Figure 21-2: About Visual C++ .NET version 7.0

You can find out what version of compiler you are using by choosing the About option from the Help menu. In your particular case, your Product ID number will be displayed. For this example, I have erased my numbers from the figures for security.

As you will note in the following Visual C++ dump for an x86 type processor under VC6, only MMX — not XMM — registers are supported in this example. Since this is from a run using a 3DNow! processor, there is a dump of the MMX registers in hex (MM#) as well as floating-point, denoted by (MM##) in upper and lower 32-bit

single-precision floating-point values. MM00 in the bottom portion of
Figure 21-3 represents the lower single-precision value of the MM0
register.

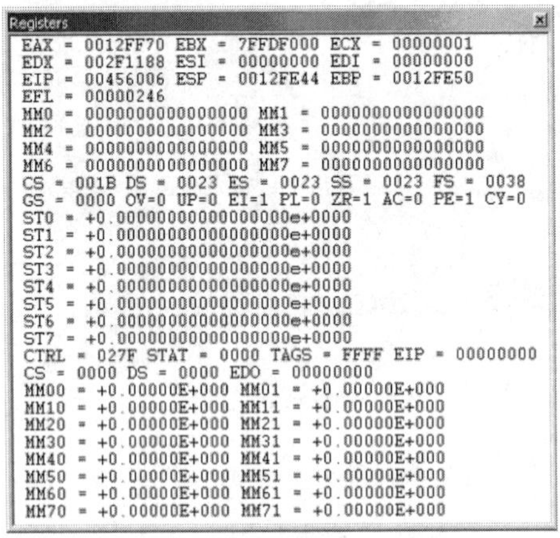

Figure 21-3: Register dump from Visual C++ 6.0 (3DNow! extensions)

In some cases, such as an older version of the compiler, the extended
registers are not immediately available. In the newer version, such as
the VC .NET toolset, that is no longer an issue. As you may notice in

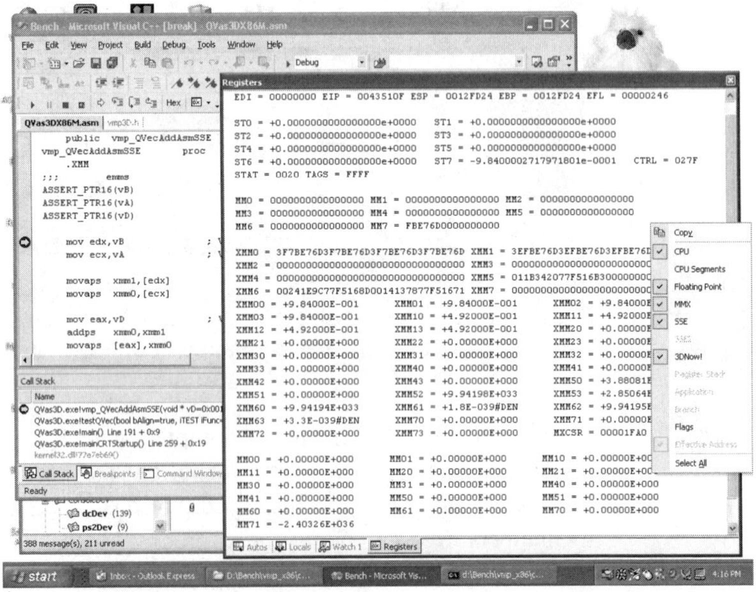

Figure 21-4: Register dump from Visual C++ .NET version 7.0 (3DNow!
professional extensions). Note the 3DNow! and SSE supported registers as well
as the extra pop-up menu of register type selections that you can choose from.
The enabled selections are based upon the processor type running on the
computer that is being debugged.

Figure 21-4, selective dumps of the other registers have been made available. Using at least version 7 of the compiler allows the active register sets to be enabled and thus viewed in the window.

The one thing that you will really need while developing assembly code is a second monitor. This is because you will need lots of screen real estate for all the various windows that you will need for debugging your assembly code.

Since we are talking here about Win32 code, whether it is targeted for the Xbox or PC platforms, then you are most likely dealing with Direct3D or the less likely OpenGL. If it is Direct3D, then it is in your best interest to install the debug versions of the DirectX dynamic-link libraries (DLLs). They will run slower but if something weird happens they will give you more information as to the type of failure. And remember that your application will run that much faster on a retail version of the DLLs.

> **Tip:** Another handy debugging tool for vectors is the use of multi-colored pens. Using multiple colors on graph paper can produce layered results, giving depth and helping make complex problems easier to understand.

The biggest help in developing vector-based applications above all is the symbolic debugger. The program counter can be followed throughout the code and the general-purpose and SIMD registers monitored. The changes to memory as the results are written can be observed.

# Tuning and Optimization

There are multiple programs on the market for tuning and optimizing your application. The two most popular performance monitoring applications are the VTune program by Intel for use with Intel's chips, available at http://developer.intel.com/software/products/eval, and the AMD Code Analyst for use with AMD's chips, available at http://www.amd.com.

These programs allow you to balance your pipelining and monitor the overall performance of your application and make recommendations as to how to balance your code to make it as tight as possible. By setting up monitoring zones indicated by start and stop markers, the application can be benchmark between those zones.

# Exception Handling — AKA: Dang that 1.#QNAN

Part of code development is dealing with exceptions. In Chapter 2, "Coding Standards," aligning memory and using assertions were the primary topics. Using misaligned memory with an instruction that requires alignment will generate an exception. The floating-point chapter (Chapter 8) mentioned how a divide by zero or square root of –N should be avoided. Exceptions are in reality interrupts that vector the processor to special handling code when a situation occurs, but despite being an interrupt it is directly related to debugging an application and so they are being discussed here instead of Chapter 10, "Branching." Let us examine this a bit closer.

## Exceptions

There are two types of exceptions in the 80x86 processor: hardware and software. The hardware exception has a maskable and non-maskable type. The software exception has three subtypes: fault, trap, and abort.

### Hardware Exception

■ Nonmaskable — Signaled by a NMI (nonmaskable interrupt) and cannot be ignored.

■ Maskable — Signaled by a INTR but can be ignored by clearing the Interrupt flag in EFLAGS with the instruction CLI.

### Software Exception

■ Fault — A detectable error before it occurs, but the program is restartable.

■ Trap — An error is trapped after it occurs, but the application is not restartable.

■ Abort — An error trapped after it occurs, but the program may need to be terminated.

Almost every instruction that the 80x86 uses has an association with an exception. Some have been mentioned, but if they had been thoroughly documented this book would be at least twice its size. So general rules apply, such as the divide by zero, using privileged instructions from a non-privileged protection layer, trying to use bad floating-point values, protection violations, and internal machine faults. Even a breakpoint that is set and triggered during debugging is an exception. Each exception is indicated by a "#" followed by a two-letter ID encapsulating an optional error code in parentheses: #GP(fault#). For example, #GP(0) is a general-protection fault with an error code of zero. The following is a list of exceptions.

*Table 21-1: 80x86 exception types*

| Vector | Type | Err | Description |
|--------|------|-----|-------------|
| 0 | Fault | | #DE ÷0 Divide by zero. DIV and iDIV |
| 1 | Fault/ Trap | | #DB Debug (reserved for Intel use only) |
| 2 | TRAP | | NMI (non-maskable interrupt) |
| 3 | Trap | | #BP Breakpoint. INT 3 |
| 4 | Trap | | #OF Overflow. INTO |
| 5 | Fault | | #BR Bound. BOUND |
| 6 | Fault | | #UD Invalid opcode. UD2 or reserved |
| 7 | Fault | | #NM Device n/a. FPU, WAIT/FWAIT |
| 8 | Abort | ✓ | #DF Double fault. Any exception generating instruction or NMI or INTR |
| 9 | Abort | | --- Coprocessor segment overrun. FPU |
| 10 | Fault | ✓ | #TS Invalid TSS. Task switch or TSS access |
| 11 | Fault | ✓ | #NP Segment not present. Load segment register |
| 12 | Fault | ✓ | #SS Stack-segment fault. Stack operation |
| 13 | Fault | ✓ | #GP General-protection. Memory reference |
| 14 | Fault | ✓ | #PF Page fault. Memory reference |
| 15 | Trap | | --- Reserved |
| 16 | Fault | | #MF FPU error. FPU or WAIT/FWAIT |
| 17-31 | | | Reserved |
| 32-255 | | | Maskable interrupts and INT # vectors |

When an exception occurs, an interrupt is generated and the instruction pointer is immediately redirected to the special handler associated with the interrupt slot in the Interrupt Descriptor Table (IDT). Each slot in the table is a gate to layer #0. As shown in Table 21-1, there are up to 256 interrupts, of which 32 are reserved for exceptions and interrupts. Note that some are actually unused and reserved for the future.

## FPU Versus MMX

If you are trying to develop code that contains FPU versus MMX, especially if using a 3DNow! processor, do yourself a favor and first debug under SSE for floating-point and/or SSE2 for integer. SSE will not have to go through the dreaded EMMS switch so there is no need for vmp_SIMDEntry() or vmp_SIMDExit(); although technically they are the same thing. Do your 3DNow! debugging last. If you encounter a floating-point value with a value of 1.#QNAN, this is sometimes due to the result of a missing switch between FPU and MMX.

Throughout this book I have been oversimplifying, using merely vmp_SIMDEntry() and vmp_SIMDExit() to block off sections of code, but it is actually more complicated than that as you truly need to differentiate between MMX and FPU. But remember, MMX can be floating-point on an AMD or integer or logical bit for all x86 processors. In this book, I did not use them on every function call like most books tell you to do. Instead, I used them between blocks of code but in essence, for some processors such as SSE I overused them. Having multiple flavors of SIMD that can stub out helps to lighten your code even more so.

# Print Output

"To *printf* or not to *printf*, that is the question!" Well, not to butcher Shakespeare, but sometimes the old ASCII text output is an excellent method of tracking down obscure bugs. This is not meant to displace the use of full-blown symbolic debuggers, but sometimes the old fashioned *printf* is better.

Note that I said *sometimes*!

This is where things get interesting! (I keep saying that in this book, do I not!) With the C++ cout IOStream class it would have to be overloaded and the output rerouted to your own device. The printf function is a little harder to capture although the standard output could be reassigned. Some platforms such as Win32 do not use printf. Instead they use a string output function such as OutputDebugString(). What I like to do is create a thin abstraction layer (whether it be written in C++ or C) of log functions that route to one or more specified output devices. This is set up for two types of output: Debug, which is not shipped with the game, and Release, which is. So, for example:

```
LogWrite()
LogRDWrite()
```

They are both similar to the functionality of printf() except they do not return a count of bytes written. The LogWrite() function is a debug version that gets stubbed to nothing in a release build. LogRDWrite() is compiled for both a release and debug skew and gets shipped with the code. This helps to simplify the job of customer support when something really bad happens. There are other functions in the log module, but these two are at the core and they in essence would call printf() and/or OutputDebugString(), etc. The idea is that your cross-platform application would call the log functions and be abstracted for the individual platform.

When I develop Win32 applications I frequently route this output to one or all of the following: the function OutputDebugString(), a Notepad window, a text file, a high-speed serial port with hardware handshake, and a TCP/IP communications setup for data collection on another computer. I do something similar for other embedded platforms. With a smart terminal there, I can back scroll through live memory dumps to track behaviors.

One of the methods I frequently use with this type of diagnostics is to set threshold values to enable the trigger, which in effect allows the capture and printing of select data. This helps to minimize being inundated with massive amounts of data that hinders rather than helps detect problems.

As a superset of this functionality, the following functions are generated for even more detailed information on a generic basis.

For platforms that do not offer you the advantage of an IDE or if you need to track problems and history dumps of memory or registers, then some of the following functions should come in handy.

# Float Array Print

This function prints a memory dump of a list of single-precision floats (four per line of printed text).

*Listing 21-1: ...\chap20\vecBug\vecBug.cpp*
```
void vmp_FloatPrint(const float * pf, uint nCnt)
{
  unsigned int n;
  int i;
```

```
    ASSERT_PTR4(pf);
    ASSERT_ZERO(nCnt);

    vmp_SIMDEntry();

    do {
      i = (--nCnt >= 4) ? 3 : (nCnt & 3);
      nCnt -= i;

      printf("%8.8x ", pf);

      do {
        printf("%lf ", (double)(*pf));
        pf++;
      } while (i-- > 0);

      printf("\n");
    } while (nCnt);

    vmp_SIMDExit();
}
```

Once a float array function is in place, creating other dependent functions such as the following is a snap. Also, by creating a debug versus release version, the debug would be the function type definitions and the release would be empty macros, thus stubbing the code to non-existence similar to the following:

```
#ifdef USE_LOG
void vmp_FloatPrint(const float * pf, uint nCnt);
#else
#define vmp_FloatPrint(pf, nCnt)    // stub
#endif
```

The same would need to be implemented in the logging header file for any other logging function that would need to be stubbed in a release build.

## Vector Print

*Listing 21-2:* ...\chap20\vecBug\vecBug.cpp

```
void vmp_VecPrint(const vmp3DVector *pVec)
{
  vmp_FloatPrint((float *)pVec, 3);
}
```

# Quad Vector Print

*Listing 21-3: ...\chap20\vecBug\vecBug.cpp*

```
void vmp_QVecPrint(const vmp3DQVector *pVec)
{
  vmp_FloatPrint((float *)pVec, 4);
}
```

# Quaternion Print

*Listing 21-4: ...\chap20\vecBug\vecBug.cpp*

```
void vmp_QuatPrint(const vmpQuat *pVec)
{
  vmp_FloatPrint((float *)pVec, 4);
}
```

# Matrix Print

This function dumps a single-precision floating-point matrix. It expands single-precision to double-precision to help minimize any problems of ASCII exponential representations.

*Listing 21-5: ...\chap20\vecBug\vecBug.cpp*

```
void vmp_MatrixPrint(const vmp3DMatrix Mx)
{
  ASSERT_PTR4(Mx);

  vmp_SIMDEntry();

  printf("%8.8x ", Mx);          // Print address
  printf("%lf %lf %lf %lf\n",  (double)Mx[0][0],
      (double)Mx[0][1], (double)Mx[0][2], (double)Mx[0][3]);
  printf("          %lf %lf %lf %lf\n",  (double)Mx[1][0],
      (double)Mx[1][1], (double)Mx[1][2], (double)Mx[1][3]);
  printf("          %lf %lf %lf %lf\n",  (double)Mx[2][0],
      (double)Mx[2][1], (double)Mx[2][2], (double)Mx[2][3]);
  printf("          %lf %lf %lf %lf\n\n",  (double)Mx[3][0],
      (double)Mx[3][1], (double)Mx[3][2], (double)Mx[3][3]);

  vmp_SIMDExit();
}
```

# Memory Dump

There is nothing sweeter than a memory dump similar to the old DOS debug.exe program. A combination of address, hex data, and ASCII equivalents is dumped on an up to 16-byte ASCII string. Even when you have a memory dump window within your IDE it can typically only handle one dump at a time. If you are trying to track a nasty little problem or to verify proper functionality, sometimes a print trail is far superior. So with this in mind, the following should be a handy little tool for your development cycle.

**Listing 21-6: ...\chap20\vecBug\vecBug.cpp**

```
void vmp_LogMem(const void * const vp, uint size)
{
  uint  x, y, run, tail, col, n;
  char *p, buf[256];
  byte *mp;

  ASSERT_PTR(vp);
  ASSERT_ZERO(size);

  mp = (byte *) vp;

  run = 16;
  col = tail = 0;

    // For all lines

  for (y = 0; y < size;)
  {
    if (size-y < run)
    {
      run = size-y;        // Display only requested!
      n = 16 - run;        // trailing places
      tail = n * 3;        // trailing spaces
      tail += ((n+3) >> 2);  // column separators
    }
                           // Print address
    p = buf + sprintf(buf, "%8.8x ", mp);

      // Hex values

    for (x = 0; x < run; x++)
    {
      p += sprintf(p, " %2.2x", *(mp+x));

      if ((++col % 4) == 0)
      {
        *p++ = ' ';
      }
```

```
        }

            //  Any trailing spaces ?

        while (tail--)
        {
          *p++ = ' ';
        }

            //  ASCII chars

        for (x = 0; x < run; x++)
        {
          if ((0x20 <= *mp) && (*mp <= 0x7f))
          {
            *p++ = *mp++;
          }
          else
          {
            *p++ = '.';
            mp++;
          }
        }

        *p++ = '\r';
        *p++ = '\n';
        *p = 0;
        printf(buf);

        y += run;
        run = 16;
        tail = col = 0;
        }

    printf("\r\n");
}
```

# Test Jigs

One sometimes needs data to load vector algorithms during testing. These functions may seem downright silly but they do come in handy from time to time.

## Matrix Test Fill

The following function does just that. It fills a matrix with a sequential set of single-precision floating-point whole numbers. This helps to keep the floating-point stored in memory in a recognizable form when just doing a memory dump.

---

*Listing 21-7: ...\chap20\vecBug\vecBug.cpp*

```
void vmp_MatrixTestFill(vmp3DMatrix Mx)
{
  uint n;
  float *pF, f;

  f = 0.0f;              // Starting value of 0.0f
  pF = (float *)Mx;
  n = 16;

  do {
    *pF = f;
    f += 1.0f;           // Advance value by 1.0f
    pF++;
  } while (--n);
}
```

---

# Matrix Splat

This function splats (replicates) a single-precision floating-point value into all sixteen elements of a matrix.

---

*Listing 21-8: ...\chap20\vecBug\vecBug.cpp*

```
void vmp_MatrixSplat(vmp3DMatrix Mx, float f)
{
  uint n;
  float *pF;

  pF = (float *)Mx;
  n = 16;

  do {
    *pF = f;
    pF++;
  } while (--n);
}
```

---

There are other functions and test jigs for use in the debugging of vector code that are available for purchase from middleware providers. They are also something to be developed from your imagination.

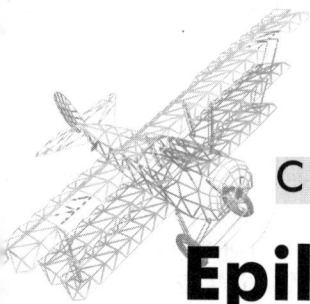

# Chapter 22
# Epilogue

If you actually read this entire book and haven't skipped around here and there, you should have found a diverse spectrum of topics related to computer processing using all the flavors of the x86 instruction set, from general-purpose instructions up through SSE3, AMD64, and EM64T, such as the terrible penalty (and hidden problems) of not having your data properly aligned, how to detect problems early in your development cycle, and the importance of using assertions and constant declarations within your code. Okay, I did not go overboard on the concept of const but you can find that in any good C++ programming book.

Also contained within were answers to some of the most often asked questions that are typically encountered in a job interview and my insight into that and other topics of game or embedded development. The companion files, available at www.wordware.com/files/8086 and www.leiterman.com/books.html, contain practical problems and solutions despite the fact that they are not heavily optimized and algorithmically tuned.

The principles found throughout this book can be applied to your project to make it that much better. There have been programming tricks as well as other foundational elements for you to use to build upon and enhance your knowledge. I hope you have found this book to be informative, that it has taught you at least one new item, and has been a value for your dollars. Please feel free to contact me and let me know your opinion about what you would like to see in any future revision.

I am sorry the code included with this book is not heavily optimized but as mentioned at the beginning, "optimized code is difficult to understand!" An unmentioned reason for not doing so is greed! There is gold in them thar hills! Companies make money writing heavily optimized—thus very, very fast—algorithms. You too can possibly make lots of money from the comfort of your home writing optimized libraries targeted for a specific processor. In fact, consider any algorithms you find in this book that you need in your code a homework assignment of optimization.

I hope this book was as pleasant for you to read as it was fun for me to research and write. In the process of writing this book I too learned a few new things, and that is what it is all about! I also hope you were not too irritated with seeing similarities (okay 80x86 targeted and refined copies) of some of the chapters found in my vector book. But that shouldn't stop you from buying a copy of my vector book! After all, this book is actually the prequel to that book!

Please send an email to books@leiterman.com to register your email address as a purchaser of this book. Insert the word "Register" into the Subject field and in the message section, list your processors of interest and any other comment. I can add you to an update notification list to let you know when additional code samples or chapter supplements are available for download. Or you can just make a comment about this book. For additional information or related links, check out the associated web site at http://www.leiterman.com/books.html.

Oh, and one last item. Buy my brother's books as well. He has a large family too and can use some extra income! What books you ask? Rewind the book and read the preface!

Happy bit twiddling!

# Data Structure Definitions

When dealing with three-dimensional transformation, data structures are needed to contain the data type. The data structures listed here are discussed in terms of this book.

### Integer 2D Point

This is mostly used within a 2D game but has uses within a 3D game. It is used for specifying a starting point within a bitmap image with the origin {0,0} located in the upper-left corner. This is primarily used as the starting point of a texture within a bitmap image. It is also used in relationship to the anchor point of a font baseline so as where to position it within an image or two-triangle quad polygon tile.

```
typedef struct iPosType
{
   int    x;
   int    y;
} iPos;
```

### Integer 2D Size

Normally bitmaps range from 0 to w–1 for width and 0 to h–1 for height and are never negative. With that in mind, only unsigned arguments are used.

```
typedef struct iSizeType
{
   uint   w;        // Width
   uint   h;        // Height
} iSize;
```

### *Integer Rectangle*

Some rectangle structures are designed with a field definition such as {x1,y1,x2,y2}, but any movement has to be translated with the modification of four coordinates. With the following structure {x,y,w,h}, only the two fields {x,y} need to be modified.

```
typedef struct iRectType
{
  int   x;      // X coord.
  int   y;      // Y coord.
  uint  w;      // Width
  uint  h;      // Height
} iRect;
```

### *3D Vector (Integer)*

```
typedef struct iVector3DType
{
  int   x;
  int   y;
  int   z;
} iVector3D;
```

### *3D Quad Vector (Integer)*

```
typedef struct iQVector3DType
{
  int   x;
  int   y;
  int   z;
  int   w;
} iQVector3D;
```

### *3D Vector (Floating Point)*

```
typedef struct vmp3DVector
{
  float x;
  float y;
  float z;
} vmp3DVector;


vmp3DVector point = {0.0, 0.0, 0.0};
vmp3DVector vector = {1.0, 2.0, 3.0};
```

### 3D Quad Vector (Floating Point)

```
typedef struct vmp3DQVector
{
  float x;
  float y;
  float z;
  float w;
} vmp3DQVector;


vmp3DQVector point = {0.0, 0.0, 0.0, 0.0};
vmp3DQVector vector = {1.0, 2.0, 3.0, 0.0};
```

### Quaternion (Single-precision Floating-point)

```
typedef struct vmpQuat
{
  float x;
  float y;
  float z;
  float w;
} vmpQuat;
```

# Mnemonics

The following is the supported mnemonic lookup table per processor. They have been divided into revisions of Intel and AMD. Sub-instruction types are indented and the root mnemonic has a shaded background.

| | Intel |
|---|---|
| P | Pentium |
| PII | Pentium II |
| SSE | SSE (Katmai NI) |
| SSE2 | SSE2 |
| SSE3 | SSE3 (Prescott NI) |
| EM64T | 64-bit memory |

| | AMD |
|---|---|
| K6 | K6 |
| 3D! | 3DNow! |
| 3Mx+ | 3DNow! & MMX Ext. |
| A64 | AMD64 |

Legend:
| | |
|---|---|
| ✓ | Mnemonic supported |
| 32 | 32-bit support only |
| 64 | 64-bit support only |

| Mnemonic | Page# | P | PII | K6 | 3D! | 3Mx+ | SSE | SSE2 | A64 | SSE3 | E64T |
|---|---|---|---|---|---|---|---|---|---|---|---|
| AAA | 394 | ✓ | ✓ | ✓ | ✓ | ✓ | ✓ | ✓ | 32 | ✓ | 32 |
| AAD | 396 | ✓ | ✓ | ✓ | ✓ | ✓ | ✓ | ✓ | 32 | ✓ | 32 |
| AAM | 395 | ✓ | ✓ | ✓ | ✓ | ✓ | ✓ | ✓ | 32 | ✓ | 32 |
| AAS | 394 | ✓ | ✓ | ✓ | ✓ | ✓ | ✓ | ✓ | 32 | ✓ | 32 |
| ADC | 176 | ✓ | ✓ | ✓ | ✓ | ✓ | ✓ | ✓ | ✓ | ✓ | ✓ |
| ADD | 176 | ✓ | ✓ | ✓ | ✓ | ✓ | ✓ | ✓ | ✓ | ✓ | ✓ |
| ADDPD | 83 | | | | | | | ✓ | ✓ | ✓ | ✓ |
| ADDPS | 83 | | | | | | ✓ | ✓ | ✓ | ✓ | ✓ |
| ADDSD | 335 | | | | | | | ✓ | ✓ | ✓ | ✓ |
| ADDSS | 335 | | | | | | ✓ | ✓ | ✓ | ✓ | ✓ |
| ADDSUBPD | 346 | | | | | | | | | ✓ | ✓ |
| ADDSUBPS | 346 | | | | | | | | | ✓ | ✓ |
| AND | 83 | ✓ | ✓ | ✓ | ✓ | ✓ | ✓ | ✓ | ✓ | ✓ | ✓ |
| ANDNPD | 99 | | | | | | | ✓ | ✓ | ✓ | ✓ |
| ANDNPS | 99 | | | | | | ✓ | ✓ | ✓ | ✓ | ✓ |

| Mnemonic | Page# | P | PII | K6 | 3D! | 3Mx+ | SSE | SSE2 | A64 | SSE3 | E64T |
|---|---|---|---|---|---|---|---|---|---|---|---|
| ANDPD | 83 | | | | | | | ✓ | ✓ | ✓ | ✓ |
| ANDPS | 83 | | | | | | ✓ | ✓ | ✓ | ✓ | ✓ |
| ARPL | 445 | ✓ | ✓ | ✓ | ✓ | ✓ | ✓ | ✓ | 32 | ✓ | 32 |
| BOUND | 445 | ✓ | ✓ | ✓ | ✓ | ✓ | ✓ | ✓ | 32 | ✓ | 32 |
| BSF | 122 | ✓ | ✓ | ✓ | ✓ | ✓ | ✓ | ✓ | ✓ | ✓ | ✓ |
| BSR | 122 | ✓ | ✓ | ✓ | ✓ | ✓ | ✓ | ✓ | ✓ | ✓ | ✓ |
| BSWAP | 133 | ✓ | ✓ | ✓ | ✓ | ✓ | ✓ | ✓ | ✓ | ✓ | ✓ |
| BT | 255 | ✓ | ✓ | ✓ | ✓ | ✓ | ✓ | ✓ | ✓ | ✓ | ✓ |
| BTC | 255 | ✓ | ✓ | ✓ | ✓ | ✓ | ✓ | ✓ | ✓ | ✓ | ✓ |
| BTR | 256 | ✓ | ✓ | ✓ | ✓ | ✓ | ✓ | ✓ | ✓ | ✓ | ✓ |
| BTS | 257 | ✓ | ✓ | ✓ | ✓ | ✓ | ✓ | ✓ | ✓ | ✓ | ✓ |
| CALL | 311 | ✓ | ✓ | ✓ | ✓ | ✓ | ✓ | ✓ | ✓ | ✓ | ✓ |
| CBW | 156 | ✓ | ✓ | ✓ | ✓ | ✓ | ✓ | ✓ | ✓ | ✓ | ✓ |
| CDQ | 160 | ✓ | ✓ | ✓ | ✓ | ✓ | ✓ | ✓ | ✓ | ✓ | ✓ |
| CDQE | 156 | | | | | | | ✓ | | | ✓ |
| CLC | 53 | ✓ | ✓ | ✓ | ✓ | ✓ | ✓ | ✓ | ✓ | ✓ | ✓ |
| CLD | 77 | ✓ | ✓ | ✓ | ✓ | ✓ | ✓ | ✓ | ✓ | ✓ | ✓ |
| CLFLUSH | 443 | | | | | | | ✓ | ✓ | ✓ | ✓ |
| CLI | 320 | ✓ | ✓ | ✓ | ✓ | ✓ | ✓ | ✓ | ✓ | ✓ | ✓ |
| CLTS | 445 | ✓ | ✓ | ✓ | ✓ | ✓ | ✓ | ✓ | ✓ | ✓ | ✓ |
| CMC | 54 | ✓ | ✓ | ✓ | ✓ | ✓ | ✓ | ✓ | ✓ | ✓ | ✓ |
| CMOVcc | | | | | | | | | | | |
| CMOVA | 271 | ✓ | ✓ | | | | ✓ | ✓ | ✓ | ✓ | ✓ |
| CMOVAE | 271 | ✓ | ✓ | | | | ✓ | ✓ | ✓ | ✓ | ✓ |
| CMOVB | 271 | ✓ | ✓ | | | | ✓ | ✓ | ✓ | ✓ | ✓ |
| CMOVBE | 271 | ✓ | ✓ | | | | ✓ | ✓ | ✓ | ✓ | ✓ |
| CMOVC | 271 | ✓ | ✓ | | | | ✓ | ✓ | ✓ | ✓ | ✓ |
| CMOVE | 271 | ✓ | ✓ | | | | ✓ | ✓ | ✓ | ✓ | ✓ |
| CMOVG | 271 | ✓ | ✓ | | | | ✓ | ✓ | ✓ | ✓ | ✓ |
| CMOVGE | 271 | ✓ | ✓ | | | | ✓ | ✓ | ✓ | ✓ | ✓ |
| CMOVL | 271 | ✓ | ✓ | | | | ✓ | ✓ | ✓ | ✓ | ✓ |
| CMOVLE | 271 | ✓ | ✓ | | | | ✓ | ✓ | ✓ | ✓ | ✓ |
| CMOVNA | 271 | ✓ | ✓ | | | | ✓ | ✓ | ✓ | ✓ | ✓ |
| CMOVNAE | 271 | ✓ | ✓ | | | | ✓ | ✓ | ✓ | ✓ | ✓ |
| CMOVNB | 271 | ✓ | ✓ | | | | ✓ | ✓ | ✓ | ✓ | ✓ |
| CMOVNBE | 271 | ✓ | ✓ | | | | ✓ | ✓ | ✓ | ✓ | ✓ |
| CMOVNC | 271 | ✓ | ✓ | | | | ✓ | ✓ | ✓ | ✓ | ✓ |
| CMOVNE | 271 | ✓ | ✓ | | | | ✓ | ✓ | ✓ | ✓ | ✓ |
| CMOVNG | 271 | ✓ | ✓ | | | | ✓ | ✓ | ✓ | ✓ | ✓ |
| CMOVNGE | 271 | ✓ | ✓ | | | | ✓ | ✓ | ✓ | ✓ | ✓ |

| Mnemonic | Page# | P | PII | K6 | 3D! | 3Mx+ | SSE | SSE2 | A64 | SSE3 | E64T |
|---|---|---|---|---|---|---|---|---|---|---|---|
| CMOVNL | 271 | ✓ | ✓ | | | | ✓ | ✓ | ✓ | ✓ | ✓ |
| CMOVNLE | 271 | ✓ | ✓ | | | | ✓ | ✓ | ✓ | ✓ | ✓ |
| CMOVNO | 271 | ✓ | ✓ | | | | ✓ | ✓ | ✓ | ✓ | ✓ |
| CMOVNP | 271 | ✓ | ✓ | | | | ✓ | ✓ | ✓ | ✓ | ✓ |
| CMOVNS | 271 | ✓ | ✓ | | | | ✓ | ✓ | ✓ | ✓ | ✓ |
| CMOVNZ | 271 | ✓ | ✓ | | | | ✓ | ✓ | ✓ | ✓ | ✓ |
| CMOVO | 271 | ✓ | ✓ | | | | ✓ | ✓ | ✓ | ✓ | ✓ |
| CMOVP | 271 | ✓ | ✓ | | | | ✓ | ✓ | ✓ | ✓ | ✓ |
| CMOVPE | 271 | ✓ | ✓ | | | | ✓ | ✓ | ✓ | ✓ | ✓ |
| CMOVPO | 271 | ✓ | ✓ | | | | ✓ | ✓ | ✓ | ✓ | ✓ |
| CMOVS | 271 | ✓ | ✓ | | | | ✓ | ✓ | ✓ | ✓ | ✓ |
| CMOVZ | 271 | ✓ | ✓ | | | | ✓ | ✓ | ✓ | ✓ | ✓ |
| CMP | 260 | ✓ | ✓ | ✓ | ✓ | ✓ | ✓ | ✓ | ✓ | ✓ | ✓ |
| CMPPD | 265 | | | | | | | ✓ | ✓ | ✓ | ✓ |
| CMPPS | 265 | | | | | | ✓ | ✓ | ✓ | ✓ | ✓ |
| CMPS | 263 | ✓ | ✓ | ✓ | ✓ | ✓ | ✓ | ✓ | ✓ | ✓ | ✓ |
| CMPSB | 263 | ✓ | ✓ | ✓ | ✓ | ✓ | ✓ | ✓ | ✓ | ✓ | ✓ |
| CMPSD | 263 | ✓ | ✓ | ✓ | ✓ | ✓ | ✓ | ✓ | ✓ | ✓ | ✓ |
| CMPSQ | 263 | | | | | | | | | | ✓ |
| CMPSW | 263 | ✓ | ✓ | ✓ | ✓ | ✓ | ✓ | ✓ | ✓ | ✓ | ✓ |
| CMPSD | 265 | | | | | | | ✓ | ✓ | ✓ | ✓ |
| CMPSS | 265 | | | | | | ✓ | ✓ | ✓ | ✓ | ✓ |
| CMPXCHG | 272 | ✓ | ✓ | ✓ | ✓ | ✓ | ✓ | ✓ | ✓ | ✓ | ✓ |
| CMPXCHG8B | 272 | ✓ | ✓ | ✓ | ✓ | ✓ | ✓ | ✓ | ✓ | ✓ | ✓ |
| CMPXCHG16B | 273 | | | | | | | | | | 64 |
| COMISD | 261 | | | | | | | ✓ | ✓ | ✓ | ✓ |
| COMISS | 261 | | | | | | ✓ | ✓ | ✓ | ✓ | ✓ |
| CPUID | 404 | ✓ | ✓ | ✓ | ✓ | ✓ | ✓ | ✓ | ✓ | ✓ | ✓ |
| CQO | 160 | | | | | | | | 64 | | 64 |
| CVTDQ2PD | 167 | | | | | | | ✓ | ✓ | ✓ | ✓ |
| CVTDQ2PS | 165 | | | | | | | ✓ | ✓ | ✓ | ✓ |
| CVTPD2DQ | 168 | | | | | | | ✓ | ✓ | ✓ | ✓ |
| CVTPD2PI | 169 | | | | | | | ✓ | ✓ | ✓ | ✓ |
| CVTPD2PS | 168 | | | | | | | ✓ | ✓ | ✓ | ✓ |
| CVTPI2PD | 170 | | | | | | | ✓ | ✓ | ✓ | ✓ |
| CVTPI2PS | 166 | | | | | | ✓ | ✓ | ✓ | ✓ | ✓ |
| CVTPS2DQ | 165 | | | | | | | ✓ | ✓ | ✓ | ✓ |
| CVTPS2PD | 169 | | | | | | | ✓ | ✓ | ✓ | ✓ |
| CVTPS2PI | 166 | | | | | | ✓ | ✓ | ✓ | ✓ | ✓ |
| CVTSD2SI | 171 | | | | | | | ✓ | ✓ | ✓ | ✓ |

| Mnemonic | Page# | P | PII | K6 | 3D! | 3Mx+ | SSE | SSE2 | A64 | SSE3 | E64T |
|---|---|---|---|---|---|---|---|---|---|---|---|
| CVTSD2SS | 172 | | | | | | | ✓ | ✓ | ✓ | ✓ |
| CVTSI2SD | 171 | | | | | | | ✓ | ✓ | ✓ | ✓ |
| CVTSI2SS | 167 | | | | | | ✓ | ✓ | ✓ | ✓ | ✓ |
| CVTSS2SD | 172 | | | | | | | ✓ | ✓ | ✓ | ✓ |
| CVTSS2SI | 170 | | | | | | ✓ | ✓ | ✓ | ✓ | ✓ |
| CVTTPD2DQ | 168 | | | | | | | ✓ | ✓ | ✓ | ✓ |
| CVTTPD2PI | 169 | | | | | | | ✓ | ✓ | ✓ | ✓ |
| CVTTPS2DQ | 165 | | | | | | | ✓ | ✓ | ✓ | ✓ |
| CVTTPS2PI | 166 | | | | | | ✓ | ✓ | ✓ | ✓ | ✓ |
| CVTTSD2SI | 171 | | | | | | | ✓ | ✓ | ✓ | ✓ |
| CVTTSS2SI | 170 | | | | | | ✓ | ✓ | ✓ | ✓ | ✓ |
| CWD | 160 | ✓ | ✓ | ✓ | ✓ | ✓ | ✓ | ✓ | ✓ | ✓ | ✓ |
| CWDE | 156 | ✓ | ✓ | ✓ | ✓ | ✓ | ✓ | ✓ | ✓ | ✓ | ✓ |
| DAA | 392 | ✓ | ✓ | ✓ | ✓ | ✓ | ✓ | ✓ | 32 | ✓ | 32 |
| DAS | 373 | ✓ | ✓ | ✓ | ✓ | ✓ | ✓ | ✓ | 32 | ✓ | 32 |
| DEC | 181 | ✓ | ✓ | ✓ | ✓ | ✓ | ✓ | ✓ | 32 | ✓ | 32 |
| DIV | 204 | ✓ | ✓ | ✓ | ✓ | ✓ | ✓ | ✓ | ✓ | ✓ | ✓ |
| DIVPD | 367 | | | | | | | ✓ | ✓ | ✓ | ✓ |
| DIVPS | 367 | | | | | | ✓ | ✓ | ✓ | ✓ | ✓ |
| DIVSD | 368 | | | | | | | ✓ | ✓ | ✓ | ✓ |
| DIVSS | 367 | | | | | | ✓ | ✓ | ✓ | ✓ | ✓ |
| EMMS | 58 | | ✓ | ✓ | ✓ | ✓ | ✓ | ✓ | ✓ | ✓ | ✓ |
| ENTER | 310 | ✓ | ✓ | ✓ | ✓ | ✓ | ✓ | ✓ | ✓ | ✓ | ✓ |
| F2XM1 | 226 | ✓ | ✓ | ✓ | ✓ | ✓ | ✓ | ✓ | ✓ | ✓ | ✓ |
| FABS | 221 | ✓ | ✓ | ✓ | ✓ | ✓ | ✓ | ✓ | ✓ | ✓ | ✓ |
| FADD | 221 | ✓ | ✓ | ✓ | ✓ | ✓ | ✓ | ✓ | ✓ | ✓ | ✓ |
| FADDP | 221 | ✓ | ✓ | ✓ | ✓ | ✓ | ✓ | ✓ | ✓ | ✓ | ✓ |
| FBLD | 236 | ✓ | ✓ | ✓ | ✓ | ✓ | ✓ | ✓ | ✓ | ✓ | ✓ |
| FBSTP | 236 | ✓ | ✓ | ✓ | ✓ | ✓ | ✓ | ✓ | ✓ | ✓ | ✓ |
| FCHS | 221 | ✓ | ✓ | ✓ | ✓ | ✓ | ✓ | ✓ | ✓ | ✓ | ✓ |
| FCLEX | 245 | ✓ | ✓ | ✓ | ✓ | ✓ | ✓ | ✓ | ✓ | ✓ | ✓ |
| FCMOVcc | | | | | | | | | | | |
| FCMOVB | 234 | ✓ | ✓ | ✓ | ✓ | ✓ | ✓ | ✓ | ✓ | ✓ | ✓ |
| FCMOVBE | 234 | ✓ | ✓ | ✓ | ✓ | ✓ | ✓ | ✓ | ✓ | ✓ | ✓ |
| FCMOVE | 234 | ✓ | ✓ | ✓ | ✓ | ✓ | ✓ | ✓ | ✓ | ✓ | ✓ |
| FCMOVNB | 234 | ✓ | ✓ | ✓ | ✓ | ✓ | ✓ | ✓ | ✓ | ✓ | ✓ |
| FCMOVNBE | 234 | ✓ | ✓ | ✓ | ✓ | ✓ | ✓ | ✓ | ✓ | ✓ | ✓ |
| FCMOVNE | 234 | ✓ | ✓ | ✓ | ✓ | ✓ | ✓ | ✓ | ✓ | ✓ | ✓ |
| FCMOVNU | 234 | ✓ | ✓ | ✓ | ✓ | ✓ | ✓ | ✓ | ✓ | ✓ | ✓ |
| FCMOVU | 234 | ✓ | ✓ | ✓ | ✓ | ✓ | ✓ | ✓ | ✓ | ✓ | ✓ |

| Mnemonic | Page# | P | PII | K6 | 3D! | 3Mx+ | SSE | SSE2 | A64 | SSE3 | E64T |
|---|---|---|---|---|---|---|---|---|---|---|---|
| FCOM | 231 | ✓ | ✓ | ✓ | ✓ | ✓ | ✓ | ✓ | ✓ | ✓ | ✓ |
| FCOMI | 233 | ✓ | ✓ | ✓ | ✓ | ✓ | ✓ | ✓ | ✓ | ✓ | ✓ |
| FCOMIP | 233 | ✓ | ✓ | ✓ | ✓ | ✓ | ✓ | ✓ | ✓ | ✓ | ✓ |
| FCOMP | 231 | ✓ | ✓ | ✓ | ✓ | ✓ | ✓ | ✓ | ✓ | ✓ | ✓ |
| FCOMPP | 231 | ✓ | ✓ | ✓ | ✓ | ✓ | ✓ | ✓ | ✓ | ✓ | ✓ |
| FCOS | 242 | ✓ | ✓ | ✓ | ✓ | ✓ | ✓ | ✓ | ✓ | ✓ | ✓ |
| FDECSTP | 219 | ✓ | ✓ | ✓ | ✓ | ✓ | ✓ | ✓ | ✓ | ✓ | ✓ |
| FDIV | 224 | ✓ | ✓ | ✓ | ✓ | ✓ | ✓ | ✓ | ✓ | ✓ | ✓ |
| FDIVP | 224 | ✓ | ✓ | ✓ | ✓ | ✓ | ✓ | ✓ | ✓ | ✓ | ✓ |
| FDIVR | 224 | ✓ | ✓ | ✓ | ✓ | ✓ | ✓ | ✓ | ✓ | ✓ | ✓ |
| FDIVRP | 224 | ✓ | ✓ | ✓ | ✓ | ✓ | ✓ | ✓ | ✓ | ✓ | ✓ |
| FEMMS | 58 | | | | ✓ | ✓ | | | ✓ | | |
| FFREE | 246 | ✓ | ✓ | ✓ | ✓ | ✓ | ✓ | ✓ | ✓ | ✓ | ✓ |
| FIADD | 231 | ✓ | ✓ | ✓ | ✓ | ✓ | ✓ | ✓ | ✓ | ✓ | ✓ |
| FICOM | 233 | ✓ | ✓ | ✓ | ✓ | ✓ | ✓ | ✓ | ✓ | ✓ | ✓ |
| FICOMP | 233 | ✓ | ✓ | ✓ | ✓ | ✓ | ✓ | ✓ | ✓ | ✓ | ✓ |
| FIDIV | 224 | ✓ | ✓ | ✓ | ✓ | ✓ | ✓ | ✓ | ✓ | ✓ | ✓ |
| FIDIVR | 224 | ✓ | ✓ | ✓ | ✓ | ✓ | ✓ | ✓ | ✓ | ✓ | ✓ |
| FILD | 217 | ✓ | ✓ | ✓ | ✓ | ✓ | ✓ | ✓ | ✓ | ✓ | ✓ |
| FIMUL | 223 | ✓ | ✓ | ✓ | ✓ | ✓ | ✓ | ✓ | ✓ | ✓ | ✓ |
| FINCSTP | 219 | ✓ | ✓ | ✓ | ✓ | ✓ | ✓ | ✓ | ✓ | ✓ | ✓ |
| FINIT | 245 | ✓ | ✓ | ✓ | ✓ | ✓ | ✓ | ✓ | ✓ | ✓ | ✓ |
| FIST | 217 | ✓ | ✓ | ✓ | ✓ | ✓ | ✓ | ✓ | ✓ | ✓ | ✓ |
| FISTP | 217 | ✓ | ✓ | ✓ | ✓ | ✓ | ✓ | ✓ | ✓ | ✓ | ✓ |
| FISTTP | 217 | | | | | | | | | ✓ | ✓ |
| FISUB | 222 | ✓ | ✓ | ✓ | ✓ | ✓ | ✓ | ✓ | ✓ | ✓ | ✓ |
| FISUBR | 223 | ✓ | ✓ | ✓ | ✓ | ✓ | ✓ | ✓ | ✓ | ✓ | ✓ |
| FLD | 214 | ✓ | ✓ | ✓ | ✓ | ✓ | ✓ | ✓ | ✓ | ✓ | ✓ |
| FLD1 | 218 | ✓ | ✓ | ✓ | ✓ | ✓ | ✓ | ✓ | ✓ | ✓ | ✓ |
| FLDCW | 248 | ✓ | ✓ | ✓ | ✓ | ✓ | ✓ | ✓ | ✓ | ✓ | ✓ |
| FLDENV | 248 | ✓ | ✓ | ✓ | ✓ | ✓ | ✓ | ✓ | ✓ | ✓ | ✓ |
| FLDL2E | 218 | ✓ | ✓ | ✓ | ✓ | ✓ | ✓ | ✓ | ✓ | ✓ | ✓ |
| FLDL2T | 218 | ✓ | ✓ | ✓ | ✓ | ✓ | ✓ | ✓ | ✓ | ✓ | ✓ |
| FLDLG2 | 218 | ✓ | ✓ | ✓ | ✓ | ✓ | ✓ | ✓ | ✓ | ✓ | ✓ |
| FLDLN2 | 218 | ✓ | ✓ | ✓ | ✓ | ✓ | ✓ | ✓ | ✓ | ✓ | ✓ |
| FLDPI | 218 | ✓ | ✓ | ✓ | ✓ | ✓ | ✓ | ✓ | ✓ | ✓ | ✓ |
| FLDZ | 218 | ✓ | ✓ | ✓ | ✓ | ✓ | ✓ | ✓ | ✓ | ✓ | ✓ |
| FMUL | 223 | ✓ | ✓ | ✓ | ✓ | ✓ | ✓ | ✓ | ✓ | ✓ | ✓ |
| FMULP | 223 | ✓ | ✓ | ✓ | ✓ | ✓ | ✓ | ✓ | ✓ | ✓ | ✓ |
| FNCLEX | 245 | ✓ | ✓ | ✓ | ✓ | ✓ | ✓ | ✓ | ✓ | ✓ | ✓ |

| Mnemonic | Page# | P | PII | K6 | 3D! | 3Mx+ | SSE | SSE2 | A64 | SSE3 | E64T |
|----------|-------|---|-----|----|----|------|-----|------|-----|------|------|
| FNINIT | 245 | ✓ | ✓ | ✓ | ✓ | ✓ | ✓ | ✓ | ✓ | ✓ | ✓ |
| FNOP | 220 | ✓ | ✓ | ✓ | ✓ | ✓ | ✓ | ✓ | ✓ | ✓ | ✓ |
| FNSAVE | 246 | ✓ | ✓ | ✓ | ✓ | ✓ | ✓ | ✓ | ✓ | ✓ | ✓ |
| FNSTCW | 248 | ✓ | ✓ | ✓ | ✓ | ✓ | ✓ | ✓ | ✓ | ✓ | ✓ |
| FNSTENV | 247 | ✓ | ✓ | ✓ | ✓ | ✓ | ✓ | ✓ | ✓ | ✓ | ✓ |
| FNSTSW | 249 | ✓ | ✓ | ✓ | ✓ | ✓ | ✓ | ✓ | ✓ | ✓ | ✓ |
| FPATAN | 237 | ✓ | ✓ | ✓ | ✓ | ✓ | ✓ | ✓ | ✓ | ✓ | ✓ |
| FPREM | 225 | ✓ | ✓ | ✓ | ✓ | ✓ | ✓ | ✓ | ✓ | ✓ | ✓ |
| FPREM1 | 225 | ✓ | ✓ | ✓ | ✓ | ✓ | ✓ | ✓ | ✓ | ✓ | ✓ |
| FPTAN | 237 | ✓ | ✓ | ✓ | ✓ | ✓ | ✓ | ✓ | ✓ | ✓ | ✓ |
| FRNDINT | 226 | ✓ | ✓ | ✓ | ✓ | ✓ | ✓ | ✓ | ✓ | ✓ | ✓ |
| FRSTOR | 246 | ✓ | ✓ | ✓ | ✓ | ✓ | ✓ | ✓ | ✓ | ✓ | ✓ |
| FSAVE | 246 | ✓ | ✓ | ✓ | ✓ | ✓ | ✓ | ✓ | ✓ | ✓ | ✓ |
| FSCALE | 226 | ✓ | ✓ | ✓ | ✓ | ✓ | ✓ | ✓ | ✓ | ✓ | ✓ |
| FSIN | 242 | ✓ | ✓ | ✓ | ✓ | ✓ | ✓ | ✓ | ✓ | ✓ | ✓ |
| FSINCOS | 242 | ✓ | ✓ | ✓ | ✓ | ✓ | ✓ | ✓ | ✓ | ✓ | ✓ |
| FSQRT | 226 | ✓ | ✓ | ✓ | ✓ | ✓ | ✓ | ✓ | ✓ | ✓ | ✓ |
| FST | 217 | ✓ | ✓ | ✓ | ✓ | ✓ | ✓ | ✓ | ✓ | ✓ | ✓ |
| FSTCW | 248 | ✓ | ✓ | ✓ | ✓ | ✓ | ✓ | ✓ | ✓ | ✓ | ✓ |
| FSTENV | 247 | ✓ | ✓ | ✓ | ✓ | ✓ | ✓ | ✓ | ✓ | ✓ | ✓ |
| FSTP | 217 | ✓ | ✓ | ✓ | ✓ | ✓ | ✓ | ✓ | ✓ | ✓ | ✓ |
| FSTSW | 249 | ✓ | ✓ | ✓ | ✓ | ✓ | ✓ | ✓ | ✓ | ✓ | ✓ |
| FSUB | 222 | ✓ | ✓ | ✓ | ✓ | ✓ | ✓ | ✓ | ✓ | ✓ | ✓ |
| FSUBP | 222 | ✓ | ✓ | ✓ | ✓ | ✓ | ✓ | ✓ | ✓ | ✓ | ✓ |
| FSUBR | 223 | ✓ | ✓ | ✓ | ✓ | ✓ | ✓ | ✓ | ✓ | ✓ | ✓ |
| FSUBRP | 223 | ✓ | ✓ | ✓ | ✓ | ✓ | ✓ | ✓ | ✓ | ✓ | ✓ |
| FTST | 231 | ✓ | ✓ | ✓ | ✓ | ✓ | ✓ | ✓ | ✓ | ✓ | ✓ |
| FUCOM | 232 | ✓ | ✓ | ✓ | ✓ | ✓ | ✓ | ✓ | ✓ | ✓ | ✓ |
| FUCOMI | 233 | ✓ | ✓ | ✓ | ✓ | ✓ | ✓ | ✓ | ✓ | ✓ | ✓ |
| FUCOMIP | 233 | ✓ | ✓ | ✓ | ✓ | ✓ | ✓ | ✓ | ✓ | ✓ | ✓ |
| FUCOMP | 232 | ✓ | ✓ | ✓ | ✓ | ✓ | ✓ | ✓ | ✓ | ✓ | ✓ |
| FUCOMPP | 232 | ✓ | ✓ | ✓ | ✓ | ✓ | ✓ | ✓ | ✓ | ✓ | ✓ |
| FWAIT | 220 | ✓ | ✓ | ✓ | ✓ | ✓ | ✓ | ✓ | ✓ | ✓ | ✓ |
| FXAM | 235 | ✓ | ✓ | ✓ | ✓ | ✓ | ✓ | ✓ | ✓ | ✓ | ✓ |
| FXCH | 218 | ✓ | ✓ | ✓ | ✓ | ✓ | ✓ | ✓ | ✓ | ✓ | ✓ |
| FXRSTOR | 247 | | | | | | ✓ | ✓ | ✓ | ✓ | ✓ |
| FXSAVE | 247 | ✓ | ✓ | ✓ | ✓ | ✓ | ✓ | ✓ | ✓ | ✓ | ✓ |
| FXTRACT | 227 | ✓ | ✓ | ✓ | ✓ | ✓ | ✓ | ✓ | ✓ | ✓ | ✓ |
| FYL2X | 227 | ✓ | ✓ | ✓ | ✓ | ✓ | ✓ | ✓ | ✓ | ✓ | ✓ |
| FYL2XP1 | 227 | ✓ | ✓ | ✓ | ✓ | ✓ | ✓ | ✓ | ✓ | ✓ | ✓ |

| Mnemonic | Page# | P | PII | K6 | 3D! | 3Mx+ | SSE | SSE2 | A64 | SSE3 | E64T |
|----------|-------|---|-----|----|----|------|-----|------|-----|------|------|
| HADDPD | 346 | | | | | | | | | ✓ | ✓ |
| HADDPS | 346 | | | | | | | | | ✓ | ✓ |
| HLT | 446 | ✓ | ✓ | ✓ | ✓ | ✓ | ✓ | ✓ | ✓ | ✓ | ✓ |
| HSUBPD | 347 | | | | | | | | | ✓ | ✓ |
| HSUBPS | 347 | | | | | | | | | ✓ | ✓ |
| IDIV | 205 | ✓ | ✓ | ✓ | ✓ | ✓ | ✓ | ✓ | ✓ | ✓ | ✓ |
| IMUL | 195 | ✓ | ✓ | ✓ | ✓ | ✓ | ✓ | ✓ | ✓ | ✓ | ✓ |
| IN | 418 | ✓ | ✓ | ✓ | ✓ | ✓ | ✓ | ✓ | ✓ | ✓ | ✓ |
| INC | 177 | ✓ | ✓ | ✓ | ✓ | ✓ | ✓ | ✓ | 32 | ✓ | 32 |
| INS | 420 | ✓ | ✓ | ✓ | ✓ | ✓ | ✓ | ✓ | ✓ | ✓ | ✓ |
| INSB | 420 | ✓ | ✓ | ✓ | ✓ | ✓ | ✓ | ✓ | ✓ | ✓ | ✓ |
| INSD | 420 | ✓ | ✓ | ✓ | ✓ | ✓ | ✓ | ✓ | ✓ | ✓ | ✓ |
| INSW | 420 | ✓ | ✓ | ✓ | ✓ | ✓ | ✓ | ✓ | ✓ | ✓ | ✓ |
| INT | 318 | ✓ | ✓ | ✓ | ✓ | ✓ | ✓ | ✓ | ✓ | ✓ | ✓ |
| INT n | 318 | ✓ | ✓ | ✓ | ✓ | ✓ | ✓ | ✓ | ✓ | ✓ | ✓ |
| INTO | 318 | ✓ | ✓ | ✓ | ✓ | ✓ | ✓ | ✓ | 32 | ✓ | 32 |
| INVD | 444 | ✓ | ✓ | ✓ | ✓ | ✓ | ✓ | ✓ | ✓ | ✓ | ✓ |
| INVLPG | 446 | ✓ | ✓ | ✓ | ✓ | ✓ | ✓ | ✓ | ✓ | ✓ | ✓ |
| IRET | 320 | ✓ | ✓ | ✓ | ✓ | ✓ | ✓ | ✓ | ✓ | ✓ | ✓ |
| IRETD | 320 | ✓ | ✓ | ✓ | ✓ | ✓ | ✓ | ✓ | ✓ | ✓ | ✓ |
| IRETQ | 320 | | | | | | | | 64 | | 64 |
| Jcc | | | | | | | | | | | |
| JA | 291 | ✓ | ✓ | ✓ | ✓ | ✓ | ✓ | ✓ | ✓ | ✓ | ✓ |
| JAE | 291 | ✓ | ✓ | ✓ | ✓ | ✓ | ✓ | ✓ | ✓ | ✓ | ✓ |
| JB | 291 | ✓ | ✓ | ✓ | ✓ | ✓ | ✓ | ✓ | ✓ | ✓ | ✓ |
| JBE | 291 | ✓ | ✓ | ✓ | ✓ | ✓ | ✓ | ✓ | ✓ | ✓ | ✓ |
| JC | 291 | ✓ | ✓ | ✓ | ✓ | ✓ | ✓ | ✓ | ✓ | ✓ | ✓ |
| JE | 291 | ✓ | ✓ | ✓ | ✓ | ✓ | ✓ | ✓ | ✓ | ✓ | ✓ |
| JG | 291 | ✓ | ✓ | ✓ | ✓ | ✓ | ✓ | ✓ | ✓ | ✓ | ✓ |
| JGE | 291 | ✓ | ✓ | ✓ | ✓ | ✓ | ✓ | ✓ | ✓ | ✓ | ✓ |
| JL | 291 | ✓ | ✓ | ✓ | ✓ | ✓ | ✓ | ✓ | ✓ | ✓ | ✓ |
| JLE | 291 | ✓ | ✓ | ✓ | ✓ | ✓ | ✓ | ✓ | ✓ | ✓ | ✓ |
| JNA | 291 | ✓ | ✓ | ✓ | ✓ | ✓ | ✓ | ✓ | ✓ | ✓ | ✓ |
| JNAE | 291 | ✓ | ✓ | ✓ | ✓ | ✓ | ✓ | ✓ | ✓ | ✓ | ✓ |
| JNB | 291 | ✓ | ✓ | ✓ | ✓ | ✓ | ✓ | ✓ | ✓ | ✓ | ✓ |
| JNBE | 291 | ✓ | ✓ | ✓ | ✓ | ✓ | ✓ | ✓ | ✓ | ✓ | ✓ |
| JNC | 291 | ✓ | ✓ | ✓ | ✓ | ✓ | ✓ | ✓ | ✓ | ✓ | ✓ |
| JNE | 291 | ✓ | ✓ | ✓ | ✓ | ✓ | ✓ | ✓ | ✓ | ✓ | ✓ |
| JNG | 291 | ✓ | ✓ | ✓ | ✓ | ✓ | ✓ | ✓ | ✓ | ✓ | ✓ |
| JNGE | 291 | ✓ | ✓ | ✓ | ✓ | ✓ | ✓ | ✓ | ✓ | ✓ | ✓ |

| Mnemonic | Page# | P | PII | K6 | 3D! | 3Mx+ | SSE | SSE2 | A64 | SSE3 | E64T |
|---|---|---|---|---|---|---|---|---|---|---|---|
| JNL | 291 | ✓ | ✓ | ✓ | ✓ | ✓ | ✓ | ✓ | ✓ | ✓ | ✓ |
| JNLE | 291 | ✓ | ✓ | ✓ | ✓ | ✓ | ✓ | ✓ | ✓ | ✓ | ✓ |
| JNO | 291 | ✓ | ✓ | ✓ | ✓ | ✓ | ✓ | ✓ | ✓ | ✓ | ✓ |
| JNP | 291 | ✓ | ✓ | ✓ | ✓ | ✓ | ✓ | ✓ | ✓ | ✓ | ✓ |
| JNS | 291 | ✓ | ✓ | ✓ | ✓ | ✓ | ✓ | ✓ | ✓ | ✓ | ✓ |
| JNZ | 291 | ✓ | ✓ | ✓ | ✓ | ✓ | ✓ | ✓ | ✓ | ✓ | ✓ |
| JO | 291 | ✓ | ✓ | ✓ | ✓ | ✓ | ✓ | ✓ | ✓ | ✓ | ✓ |
| JP | 291 | ✓ | ✓ | ✓ | ✓ | ✓ | ✓ | ✓ | ✓ | ✓ | ✓ |
| JPE | 291 | ✓ | ✓ | ✓ | ✓ | ✓ | ✓ | ✓ | ✓ | ✓ | ✓ |
| JPO | 291 | ✓ | ✓ | ✓ | ✓ | ✓ | ✓ | ✓ | ✓ | ✓ | ✓ |
| JS | 291 | ✓ | ✓ | ✓ | ✓ | ✓ | ✓ | ✓ | ✓ | ✓ | ✓ |
| JZ | 291 | ✓ | ✓ | ✓ | ✓ | ✓ | ✓ | ✓ | ✓ | ✓ | ✓ |
| JCXZ | 303 | ✓ | ✓ | ✓ | ✓ | ✓ | ✓ | ✓ | 32 | ✓ | ✓ |
| JECXZ | 303 | ✓ | ✓ | ✓ | ✓ | ✓ | ✓ | ✓ | 32 | ✓ | ✓ |
| JMP | 287 | ✓ | ✓ | ✓ | ✓ | ✓ | ✓ | ✓ | ✓ | ✓ | ✓ |
| JRCXZ | 303 | | | | | | | | 64 | | ? |
| LAHF | 50 | ✓ | ✓ | ✓ | ✓ | ✓ | ✓ | ✓ | 32 | ✓ | 32 |
| LAR | 447 | ✓ | ✓ | ✓ | ✓ | ✓ | ✓ | ✓ | ✓ | ✓ | ✓ |
| LDDQU | 62 | | | | | | | | | ✓ | ✓ |
| LDMXCSR | 449 | | | | | | ✓ | ✓ | ✓ | ✓ | ✓ |
| LDS | 455 | ✓ | ✓ | ✓ | ✓ | ✓ | ✓ | ✓ | ✓ | ✓ | ✓ |
| LEA | 70 | ✓ | ✓ | ✓ | ✓ | ✓ | ✓ | ✓ | ✓ | ✓ | ✓ |
| LEAVE | 310 | ✓ | ✓ | ✓ | ✓ | ✓ | ✓ | ✓ | ✓ | ✓ | ✓ |
| LES | 455 | ✓ | ✓ | ✓ | ✓ | ✓ | ✓ | ✓ | ✓ | ✓ | ✓ |
| LFENCE | 442 | | | | | | ✓ | ✓ | ✓ | ✓ | ✓ |
| LFS | 455 | ✓ | ✓ | ✓ | ✓ | ✓ | ✓ | ✓ | ✓ | ✓ | ✓ |
| LGDT | 449 | ✓ | ✓ | ✓ | ✓ | ✓ | ✓ | ✓ | ✓ | ✓ | ✓ |
| LGS | 455 | ✓ | ✓ | ✓ | ✓ | ✓ | ✓ | ✓ | ✓ | ✓ | ✓ |
| LIDT | 449 | ✓ | ✓ | ✓ | ✓ | ✓ | ✓ | ✓ | ✓ | ✓ | ✓ |
| LLDT | 450 | ✓ | ✓ | ✓ | ✓ | ✓ | ✓ | ✓ | ✓ | ✓ | ✓ |
| LMSW | 451 | ✓ | ✓ | ✓ | ✓ | ✓ | ✓ | ✓ | ✓ | ✓ | ✓ |
| LOCK | 447 | ✓ | ✓ | | | ✓ | ✓ | ✓ | ✓ | ✓ | ✓ |
| LODS | 73 | ✓ | ✓ | ✓ | ✓ | ✓ | ✓ | ✓ | ✓ | ✓ | ✓ |
| LODSB | 73 | ✓ | ✓ | ✓ | ✓ | ✓ | ✓ | ✓ | ✓ | ✓ | ✓ |
| LODSD | 73 | ✓ | ✓ | ✓ | ✓ | ✓ | ✓ | ✓ | ✓ | ✓ | ✓ |
| LODSQ | 73 | | | | | | | | 64 | | 64 |
| LODSW | 73 | ✓ | ✓ | ✓ | ✓ | ✓ | ✓ | ✓ | ✓ | ✓ | ✓ |
| LOOP | 305 | ✓ | ✓ | ✓ | ✓ | ✓ | ✓ | ✓ | ✓ | ✓ | ✓ |
| LOOPcc | | | | | | | | | | | |
| LOOPE | 304 | ✓ | ✓ | ✓ | ✓ | ✓ | ✓ | ✓ | ✓ | ✓ | ✓ |

| Mnemonic | Page# | P | PII | K6 | 3D! | 3Mx+ | SSE | SSE2 | A64 | SSE3 | E64T |
|---|---|---|---|---|---|---|---|---|---|---|---|
| LOOPNE | 304 | ✓ | ✓ | ✓ | ✓ | ✓ | ✓ | ✓ | ✓ | ✓ | ✓ |
| LOOPNZ | 304 | ✓ | ✓ | ✓ | ✓ | ✓ | ✓ | ✓ | ✓ | ✓ | ✓ |
| LOOPZ | 304 | ✓ | ✓ | ✓ | ✓ | ✓ | ✓ | ✓ | ✓ | ✓ | ✓ |
| LSL | 447 | ✓ | ✓ | ✓ | ✓ | ✓ | ✓ | ✓ | ✓ | ✓ | ✓ |
| LSS | 455 | ✓ | ✓ | ✓ | ✓ | ✓ | ✓ | ✓ | ✓ | ✓ | ✓ |
| LTR | 451 | ✓ | ✓ | ✓ | ✓ | ✓ | ✓ | ✓ | ✓ | ✓ | ✓ |
| MASKMOVDQU | 80 | | | | | | | ✓ | ✓ | ✓ | ✓ |
| MASKMOVQ | 80 | | | | ✓ | ✓ | ✓ | ✓ | ✓ | ✓ | ✓ |
| MAXPD | 286 | | | | | | | ✓ | ✓ | ✓ | ✓ |
| MAXPS | 285 | | | | | | ✓ | ✓ | ✓ | ✓ | ✓ |
| MAXSD | 286 | | | | | | | ✓ | ✓ | ✓ | ✓ |
| MAXSS | 286 | | | | | | ✓ | ✓ | ✓ | ✓ | ✓ |
| MFENCE | 443 | | | | | | | ✓ | ✓ | ✓ | ✓ |
| MINPD | 282 | | | | | | | ✓ | ✓ | ✓ | ✓ |
| MINPS | 281 | | | | | | ✓ | ✓ | ✓ | ✓ | ✓ |
| MINSD | 282 | | | | | | | ✓ | ✓ | ✓ | ✓ |
| MINSS | 281 | | | | | | ✓ | ✓ | ✓ | ✓ | ✓ |
| MONITOR | 457 | | | | | | | | | ✓ | ✓ |
| MOV | 62 | ✓ | ✓ | ✓ | ✓ | ✓ | ✓ | ✓ | ✓ | ✓ | ✓ |
| MOV CR | 448 | ✓ | ✓ | ✓ | ✓ | ✓ | ✓ | ✓ | ✓ | ✓ | ✓ |
| MOV DR | 448 | ✓ | ✓ | ✓ | ✓ | ✓ | ✓ | ✓ | ✓ | ✓ | ✓ |
| MOVAPD | 62 | | | | | | | ✓ | ✓ | ✓ | ✓ |
| MOVAPS | 62 | | | | | | ✓ | ✓ | ✓ | ✓ | ✓ |
| MOVD | 62 | ✓ | ✓ | ✓ | ✓ | ✓ | ✓ | ✓ | ✓ | ✓ | ✓ |
| MOVDDUP | 154 | | | | | | | | | ✓ | ✓ |
| MOVDQ2Q | 141 | | | | | | | ✓ | ✓ | ✓ | ✓ |
| MOVDQA | 62 | | | | | | | ✓ | ✓ | ✓ | ✓ |
| MOVDQU | 62 | | | | | | | ✓ | ✓ | ✓ | ✓ |
| MOVHLPS | 144 | | | | | | ✓ | ✓ | ✓ | ✓ | ✓ |
| MOVHPD | 147 | | | | | | | ✓ | ✓ | ✓ | ✓ |
| MOVHPS | 143 | | | | | | ✓ | ✓ | ✓ | ✓ | ✓ |
| MOVLHPS | 143 | | | | | | ✓ | ✓ | ✓ | ✓ | ✓ |
| MOVLPD | 146 | | | | | | | ✓ | ✓ | ✓ | ✓ |
| MOVLPS | 142 | | | | | | ✓ | ✓ | ✓ | ✓ | ✓ |
| MOVMSKPD | 269 | | | | | | | ✓ | ✓ | ✓ | ✓ |
| MOVMSKPS | 269 | | | | | | ✓ | ✓ | ✓ | ✓ | ✓ |
| MOVNTDQ | 78 | | | | | | | ✓ | ✓ | ✓ | ✓ |
| MOVNTI | 78 | | | | | | | ✓ | ✓ | ✓ | ✓ |
| MOVNTPD | 79 | | | | | | | ✓ | ✓ | ✓ | ✓ |
| MOVNTPS | 79 | | | | | | ✓ | ✓ | ✓ | ✓ | ✓ |

| Mnemonic | Page# | P | PII | K6 | 3D! | 3Mx+ | SSE | SSE2 | A64 | SSE3 | E64T |
|---|---|---|---|---|---|---|---|---|---|---|---|
| MOVNTQ | 78 | | | | | ✓ | ✓ | ✓ | ✓ | ✓ | ✓ |
| MOVQ | 61 | | | ✓ | ✓ | ✓ | ✓ | ✓ | ✓ | ✓ | ✓ |
| MOVQ2DQ | 141 | | | | | | | ✓ | ✓ | ✓ | ✓ |
| MOVS | 76 | ✓ | ✓ | ✓ | ✓ | ✓ | ✓ | ✓ | ✓ | ✓ | ✓ |
| MOVSB | 76 | ✓ | ✓ | ✓ | ✓ | ✓ | ✓ | ✓ | ✓ | ✓ | ✓ |
| MOVSD | 76 | ✓ | ✓ | ✓ | ✓ | ✓ | ✓ | ✓ | ✓ | ✓ | ✓ |
| MOVSQ | 76 | | | | | | | | 64 | | 64 |
| MOVSW | 76 | ✓ | ✓ | ✓ | ✓ | ✓ | ✓ | ✓ | ✓ | ✓ | ✓ |
| MOVSD | 145 | | | | | | | ✓ | ✓ | ✓ | ✓ |
| MOVSHDUP | 154 | | | | | | | | | ✓ | ✓ |
| MOVSLDUP | 153 | | | | | | | | | ✓ | ✓ |
| MOVSS | 140 | | | | | | ✓ | ✓ | ✓ | ✓ | ✓ |
| MOVSX | 157 | ✓ | ✓ | ✓ | ✓ | ✓ | ✓ | ✓ | ✓ | ✓ | ✓ |
| MOVSXD | 157 | | | | | | | | 64 | | 64 |
| MOVUPD | 62 | | | | | | | ✓ | ✓ | ✓ | ✓ |
| MOVUPS | 62 | | | | | | ✓ | ✓ | ✓ | ✓ | ✓ |
| MOVZX | 158 | ✓ | ✓ | ✓ | ✓ | ✓ | ✓ | ✓ | ✓ | ✓ | ✓ |
| MUL | 194 | ✓ | ✓ | ✓ | ✓ | ✓ | ✓ | ✓ | ✓ | ✓ | ✓ |
| MULPD | 352 | | | | | | | ✓ | ✓ | ✓ | ✓ |
| MULPS | 352 | | | | | | ✓ | ✓ | ✓ | ✓ | ✓ |
| MULSD | 353 | | | | | | | ✓ | ✓ | ✓ | ✓ |
| MULSS | 353 | | | | | | ✓ | ✓ | ✓ | ✓ | ✓ |
| MWAIT | 458 | | | | | | | | | ✓ | ✓ |
| NEG | 93 | ✓ | ✓ | ✓ | ✓ | ✓ | ✓ | ✓ | ✓ | ✓ | ✓ |
| NOP | 54 | ✓ | ✓ | ✓ | ✓ | ✓ | ✓ | ✓ | ✓ | ✓ | ✓ |
| NOT | 92 | ✓ | ✓ | ✓ | ✓ | ✓ | ✓ | ✓ | ✓ | ✓ | ✓ |
| OR | 88 | ✓ | ✓ | ✓ | ✓ | ✓ | ✓ | ✓ | ✓ | ✓ | ✓ |
| ORPD | 88 | | | | | | | ✓ | ✓ | ✓ | ✓ |
| ORPS | 88 | | | | | | ✓ | ✓ | ✓ | ✓ | ✓ |
| OUT | 419 | ✓ | ✓ | ✓ | ✓ | ✓ | ✓ | ✓ | ✓ | ✓ | ✓ |
| OUTS | 420 | ✓ | ✓ | ✓ | ✓ | ✓ | ✓ | ✓ | ✓ | ✓ | ✓ |
| OUTSB | 420 | ✓ | ✓ | ✓ | ✓ | ✓ | ✓ | ✓ | ✓ | ✓ | ✓ |
| OUTSD | 420 | ✓ | ✓ | ✓ | ✓ | ✓ | ✓ | ✓ | ✓ | ✓ | ✓ |
| OUTSW | 420 | ✓ | ✓ | ✓ | ✓ | ✓ | ✓ | ✓ | ✓ | ✓ | ✓ |
| PACKSSDW | 163 | | ✓ | ✓ | ✓ | ✓ | ✓ | ✓ | ✓ | ✓ | ✓ |
| PACKSSWB | 162 | | ✓ | ✓ | ✓ | ✓ | ✓ | ✓ | ✓ | ✓ | ✓ |
| PACKUSWB | 162 | | ✓ | ✓ | ✓ | ✓ | ✓ | ✓ | ✓ | ✓ | ✓ |
| PADDB | 184 | | ✓ | ✓ | ✓ | ✓ | ✓ | ✓ | ✓ | ✓ | ✓ |
| PADDD | 184 | | ✓ | ✓ | ✓ | ✓ | ✓ | ✓ | ✓ | ✓ | ✓ |
| PADDQ | 184 | | | | | | | ✓ | ✓ | ✓ | ✓ |

| Mnemonic | Page# | P | PII | K6 | 3D! | 3Mx+ | SSE | SSE2 | A64 | SSE3 | E64T |
|---|---|---|---|---|---|---|---|---|---|---|---|
| PADDSB | 186 | | ✓ | ✓ | ✓ | ✓ | ✓ | ✓ | ✓ | ✓ | ✓ |
| PADDSW | 186 | | ✓ | ✓ | ✓ | ✓ | ✓ | ✓ | ✓ | ✓ | ✓ |
| PADDUSB | 186 | | ✓ | ✓ | ✓ | ✓ | ✓ | ✓ | ✓ | ✓ | ✓ |
| PADDUSW | 186 | | ✓ | ✓ | ✓ | ✓ | ✓ | ✓ | ✓ | ✓ | ✓ |
| PADDW | 184 | | ✓ | ✓ | ✓ | ✓ | ✓ | ✓ | ✓ | ✓ | ✓ |
| PAND | 83 | | ✓ | ✓ | ✓ | ✓ | ✓ | ✓ | ✓ | ✓ | ✓ |
| PANDN | 99 | | ✓ | ✓ | ✓ | ✓ | ✓ | ✓ | ✓ | ✓ | ✓ |
| PAUSE | 299 | | | | | | | ✓ | ✓ | ✓ | ✓ |
| PAVGB | 191 | | | | | ✓ | ✓ | ✓ | ✓ | ✓ | ✓ |
| PAVGUSB | 191 | | | | ✓ | ✓ | | | ✓ | | |
| PAVGW | 192 | | | | | ✓ | ✓ | ✓ | ✓ | ✓ | ✓ |
| PCMPEQB | 265 | ✓ | ✓ | ✓ | ✓ | ✓ | ✓ | ✓ | ✓ | ✓ | ✓ |
| PCMPEQD | 265 | ✓ | ✓ | ✓ | ✓ | ✓ | ✓ | ✓ | ✓ | ✓ | ✓ |
| PCMPEQW | 265 | ✓ | ✓ | ✓ | ✓ | ✓ | ✓ | ✓ | ✓ | ✓ | ✓ |
| PCMPGTB | 266 | ✓ | ✓ | ✓ | ✓ | ✓ | ✓ | ✓ | ✓ | ✓ | ✓ |
| PCMPGTD | 266 | ✓ | ✓ | ✓ | ✓ | ✓ | ✓ | ✓ | ✓ | ✓ | ✓ |
| PCMPGTW | 266 | ✓ | ✓ | ✓ | ✓ | ✓ | ✓ | ✓ | ✓ | ✓ | ✓ |
| PEXTRW | 161 | | | | | ✓ | ✓ | ✓ | ✓ | ✓ | ✓ |
| PF2ID | 166 | | | | ✓ | ✓ | | | ✓ | | |
| PF2IW | 166 | | | | | ✓ | | | ✓ | | |
| PFACC | 346 | | | | ✓ | ✓ | | | ✓ | | |
| PFADD | 334 | | | | ✓ | ✓ | | | ✓ | | |
| PFCMPEQ | 265 | | | | ✓ | ✓ | | | ✓ | | |
| PFCMPGE | 266 | | | | ✓ | ✓ | | | ✓ | | |
| PFCMPGT | 266 | | | | ✓ | ✓ | | | ✓ | | |
| PFMAX | 285 | | | | ✓ | ✓ | | | ✓ | | |
| PFMIN | 281 | | | | ✓ | ✓ | | | ✓ | | |
| PFMUL | 352 | | | | ✓ | ✓ | | | ✓ | | |
| PFNACC | 347 | | | | | ✓ | | | ✓ | | |
| PFPNACC | 348 | | | | | ✓ | | | ✓ | | |
| PFRCP | 369 | | | | ✓ | ✓ | | | ✓ | | |
| PFRCPIT1 | 370 | | | | ✓ | ✓ | | | ✓ | | |
| PFRCPIT2 | 370 | | | | ✓ | ✓ | | | ✓ | | |
| PFRSQIT1 | 380 | | | | ✓ | ✓ | | | ✓ | | |
| PFRSQRT | 379 | | | | ✓ | ✓ | | | ✓ | | |
| PFSUB | 336 | | | | ✓ | ✓ | | | ✓ | | |
| PFSUBR | 338 | | | | ✓ | ✓ | | | ✓ | | |
| PI2FD | 166 | | | | ✓ | ✓ | | | ✓ | | |
| PI2FW | 164 | | | | | ✓ | | | ✓ | | |
| PINSRW | 149 | | | | | ✓ | ✓ | ✓ | ✓ | ✓ | ✓ |

| Mnemonic | Page# | P | PII | K6 | 3D! | 3Mx+ | SSE | SSE2 | A64 | SSE3 | E64T |
|---|---|---|---|---|---|---|---|---|---|---|---|
| PMADDWD | 202 | | ✓ | ✓ | ✓ | ✓ | ✓ | ✓ | ✓ | ✓ | ✓ |
| PMAXSW | 284 | | | | | ✓ | ✓ | ✓ | ✓ | ✓ | ✓ |
| PMAXUB | 283 | | | | | ✓ | ✓ | ✓ | ✓ | ✓ | ✓ |
| PMINSW | 280 | | | | | ✓ | ✓ | ✓ | ✓ | ✓ | ✓ |
| PMINUB | 279 | | | | | ✓ | ✓ | ✓ | ✓ | ✓ | ✓ |
| PMOVMSKB | 268 | | | | | ✓ | ✓ | ✓ | ✓ | ✓ | ✓ |
| PMULHRW | 199 | | | | ✓ | ✓ | | | ✓ | | |
| PMULHUW | 198 | | | | | ✓ | ✓ | ✓ | ✓ | ✓ | ✓ |
| PMULHW | 198 | | ✓ | ✓ | ✓ | ✓ | ✓ | ✓ | ✓ | ✓ | ✓ |
| PMULLW | 197 | | ✓ | ✓ | ✓ | ✓ | ✓ | ✓ | ✓ | ✓ | ✓ |
| PMULUDQ | 201 | | | | | | | ✓ | ✓ | ✓ | ✓ |
| POP | 307 | ✓ | ✓ | ✓ | ✓ | ✓ | ✓ | ✓ | ✓ | ✓ | ✓ |
| POPA | 309 | ✓ | ✓ | ✓ | ✓ | ✓ | ✓ | ✓ | ✓ | ✓ | 32 |
| POPAD | 309 | ✓ | ✓ | ✓ | ✓ | ✓ | ✓ | ✓ | ✓ | ✓ | 32 |
| POPF | 52 | ✓ | ✓ | ✓ | ✓ | ✓ | ✓ | ✓ | ✓ | ✓ | ✓ |
| POPFD | 52 | ✓ | ✓ | ✓ | ✓ | ✓ | ✓ | ✓ | 32 | ✓ | 32 |
| POPFQ | 52 | | | | | | | | 64 | | 64 |
| POR | 88 | | ✓ | ✓ | ✓ | ✓ | ✓ | ✓ | ✓ | ✓ | ✓ |
| PREFETCH | 441 | | | | ✓ | ✓ | | | ✓ | | |
| PREFETCHNTA | 441 | | | | | ✓ | ✓ | ✓ | ✓ | ✓ | ✓ |
| PREFETCHT0 | 441 | | | | | ✓ | ✓ | ✓ | ✓ | ✓ | ✓ |
| PREFETCHT1 | 441 | | | | | ✓ | ✓ | ✓ | ✓ | ✓ | ✓ |
| PREFETCHT2 | 441 | | | | | ✓ | ✓ | ✓ | ✓ | ✓ | ✓ |
| PREFETCHW | 441 | | | | ✓ | ✓ | | | ✓ | | |
| PSADBW | 193 | | | | | ✓ | ✓ | ✓ | ✓ | ✓ | ✓ |
| PSHUFD | 152 | | | | | | | ✓ | ✓ | ✓ | ✓ |
| PSHUFHW | 151 | | | | | | | ✓ | ✓ | ✓ | ✓ |
| PSHUFLW | 151 | | | | | | | ✓ | ✓ | ✓ | ✓ |
| PSHUFW | 150 | | | | | ✓ | ✓ | ✓ | ✓ | ✓ | ✓ |
| PSLLD | 106 | | ✓ | ✓ | ✓ | ✓ | ✓ | ✓ | ✓ | ✓ | ✓ |
| PSLLDQ | 106 | | | | | | | ✓ | ✓ | ✓ | ✓ |
| PSLLQ | 106 | | ✓ | ✓ | ✓ | ✓ | ✓ | ✓ | ✓ | ✓ | ✓ |
| PSLLW | 106 | | ✓ | ✓ | ✓ | ✓ | ✓ | ✓ | ✓ | ✓ | ✓ |
| PSRAD | 116 | | ✓ | ✓ | ✓ | ✓ | ✓ | ✓ | ✓ | ✓ | ✓ |
| PSRAW | 116 | | ✓ | ✓ | ✓ | ✓ | ✓ | ✓ | ✓ | ✓ | ✓ |
| PSRLD | 113 | | ✓ | ✓ | ✓ | ✓ | ✓ | ✓ | ✓ | ✓ | ✓ |
| PSRLDQ | 113 | | | | | | | ✓ | ✓ | ✓ | ✓ |
| PSRLQ | 113 | | ✓ | ✓ | ✓ | ✓ | ✓ | ✓ | ✓ | ✓ | ✓ |
| PSRLW | 113 | | ✓ | ✓ | ✓ | ✓ | ✓ | ✓ | ✓ | ✓ | ✓ |
| PSUBB | 187 | | ✓ | ✓ | ✓ | ✓ | ✓ | ✓ | ✓ | ✓ | ✓ |

| Mnemonic | Page# | P | PII | K6 | 3D! | 3Mx+ | SSE | SSE2 | A64 | SSE3 | E64T |
|---|---|---|---|---|---|---|---|---|---|---|---|
| PSUBD | 187 | | ✓ | ✓ | ✓ | ✓ | ✓ | ✓ | ✓ | ✓ | ✓ |
| PSUBQ | 187 | | | | | | | ✓ | ✓ | ✓ | ✓ |
| PSUBSB | 188 | | ✓ | ✓ | ✓ | ✓ | ✓ | ✓ | ✓ | ✓ | ✓ |
| PSUBSW | 188 | | ✓ | ✓ | ✓ | ✓ | ✓ | ✓ | ✓ | ✓ | ✓ |
| PSUBUSB | 188 | | ✓ | ✓ | ✓ | ✓ | ✓ | ✓ | ✓ | ✓ | ✓ |
| PSUBUSW | 188 | | ✓ | ✓ | ✓ | ✓ | ✓ | ✓ | ✓ | ✓ | ✓ |
| PSUBW | 187 | | ✓ | ✓ | ✓ | ✓ | ✓ | ✓ | ✓ | ✓ | ✓ |
| PSWAPD | 135 | | | | | ✓ | | ✓ | | | |
| PUNPCKHBW | 137 | | ✓ | ✓ | ✓ | ✓ | ✓ | ✓ | ✓ | ✓ | ✓ |
| PUNPCKHDQ | 139 | | ✓ | ✓ | ✓ | ✓ | ✓ | ✓ | ✓ | ✓ | ✓ |
| PUNPCKHQDQ | 148 | | | | | | | ✓ | ✓ | ✓ | ✓ |
| PUNPCKHWD | 138 | | ✓ | ✓ | ✓ | ✓ | ✓ | ✓ | ✓ | ✓ | ✓ |
| PUNPCKLBW | 136 | | ✓ | ✓ | ✓ | ✓ | ✓ | ✓ | ✓ | ✓ | ✓ |
| PUNPCKLDQ | 139 | | ✓ | ✓ | ✓ | ✓ | ✓ | ✓ | ✓ | ✓ | ✓ |
| PUNPCKLQDQ | 147 | | | | | | | ✓ | ✓ | ✓ | ✓ |
| PUNPCKLWD | 137 | | ✓ | ✓ | ✓ | ✓ | ✓ | ✓ | ✓ | ✓ | ✓ |
| PUSH | 307 | ✓ | ✓ | ✓ | ✓ | ✓ | ✓ | ✓ | ✓ | ✓ | ✓ |
| PUSHA | 309 | ✓ | ✓ | ✓ | ✓ | ✓ | ✓ | ✓ | ✓ | ✓ | 32 |
| PUSHAD | 309 | ✓ | ✓ | ✓ | ✓ | ✓ | ✓ | ✓ | ✓ | ✓ | 32 |
| PUSHF | 51 | ✓ | ✓ | ✓ | ✓ | ✓ | ✓ | ✓ | ✓ | ✓ | ✓ |
| PUSHFD | 51 | ✓ | ✓ | ✓ | ✓ | ✓ | ✓ | ✓ | 32 | ✓ | 32 |
| PUSHFQ | 51 | | | | | | | | 64 | | 64 |
| PXOR | 90 | | ✓ | ✓ | ✓ | ✓ | ✓ | ✓ | ✓ | ✓ | ✓ |
| RCL | 118 | ✓ | ✓ | ✓ | ✓ | ✓ | ✓ | ✓ | ✓ | ✓ | ✓ |
| RCPPS | 368 | | | | | | ✓ | ✓ | ✓ | ✓ | ✓ |
| RCPSS | 368 | | | | | | ✓ | ✓ | ✓ | ✓ | ✓ |
| RCR | 121 | ✓ | ✓ | ✓ | ✓ | ✓ | ✓ | ✓ | ✓ | ✓ | ✓ |
| RDMSR | 452 | ✓ | ✓ | ✓ | ✓ | ✓ | ✓ | ✓ | ✓ | ✓ | ✓ |
| RDPMC | 432 | ✓ | ✓ | ✓ | ✓ | ✓ | ✓ | ✓ | ✓ | ✓ | ✓ |
| RDTSC | 432 | ✓ | ✓ | ✓ | ✓ | ✓ | ✓ | ✓ | ✓ | ✓ | ✓ |
| REP | 75 | ✓ | ✓ | ✓ | ✓ | ✓ | ✓ | ✓ | ✓ | ✓ | ✓ |
| REPE | 75 | ✓ | ✓ | ✓ | ✓ | ✓ | ✓ | ✓ | ✓ | ✓ | ✓ |
| REPNE | 75 | ✓ | ✓ | ✓ | ✓ | ✓ | ✓ | ✓ | ✓ | ✓ | ✓ |
| REPNZ | 75 | ✓ | ✓ | ✓ | ✓ | ✓ | ✓ | ✓ | ✓ | ✓ | ✓ |
| REPZ | 75 | ✓ | ✓ | ✓ | ✓ | ✓ | ✓ | ✓ | ✓ | ✓ | ✓ |
| RET | 313 | ✓ | ✓ | ✓ | ✓ | ✓ | ✓ | ✓ | ✓ | ✓ | ✓ |
| RETF | 313 | ✓ | ✓ | ✓ | ✓ | ✓ | ✓ | ✓ | ✓ | ✓ | ✓ |
| ROL | 117 | ✓ | ✓ | ✓ | ✓ | ✓ | ✓ | ✓ | ✓ | ✓ | ✓ |
| ROR | 120 | ✓ | ✓ | ✓ | ✓ | ✓ | ✓ | ✓ | ✓ | ✓ | ✓ |
| RSM | 454 | ✓ | ✓ | ✓ | ✓ | ✓ | ✓ | ✓ | ✓ | ✓ | ✓ |

| Mnemonic | Page# | P | PII | K6 | 3D! | 3Mx+ | SSE | SSE2 | A64 | SSE3 | E64T |
|---|---|---|---|---|---|---|---|---|---|---|---|
| RSQRTPS | 379 | | | | | | ✓ | ✓ | ✓ | ✓ | ✓ |
| RSQRTSS | 379 | | | | | | ✓ | ✓ | ✓ | ✓ | ✓ |
| SAHF | 51 | ✓ | ✓ | ✓ | ✓ | ✓ | ✓ | ✓ | 32 | ✓ | 32 |
| SAL | 104 | ✓ | ✓ | ✓ | ✓ | ✓ | ✓ | ✓ | ✓ | ✓ | ✓ |
| SAR | 114 | ✓ | ✓ | ✓ | ✓ | ✓ | ✓ | ✓ | ✓ | ✓ | ✓ |
| SBB | 180 | ✓ | ✓ | ✓ | ✓ | ✓ | ✓ | ✓ | ✓ | ✓ | ✓ |
| SCAS | 269 | ✓ | ✓ | ✓ | ✓ | ✓ | ✓ | ✓ | ✓ | ✓ | ✓ |
| SCASB | 269 | ✓ | ✓ | ✓ | ✓ | ✓ | ✓ | ✓ | ✓ | ✓ | ✓ |
| SCASD | 269 | ✓ | ✓ | ✓ | ✓ | ✓ | ✓ | ✓ | ✓ | ✓ | ✓ |
| SCASQ | 269 | | | | | | | | 64 | | 64 |
| SCASW | 269 | ✓ | ✓ | ✓ | ✓ | ✓ | ✓ | ✓ | ✓ | ✓ | ✓ |
| SETcc | | | | | | | | | | | |
| SETA | 259 | ✓ | ✓ | ✓ | ✓ | ✓ | ✓ | ✓ | ✓ | ✓ | ✓ |
| SETAE | 259 | ✓ | ✓ | ✓ | ✓ | ✓ | ✓ | ✓ | ✓ | ✓ | ✓ |
| SETB | 259 | ✓ | ✓ | ✓ | ✓ | ✓ | ✓ | ✓ | ✓ | ✓ | ✓ |
| SETBE | 259 | ✓ | ✓ | ✓ | ✓ | ✓ | ✓ | ✓ | ✓ | ✓ | ✓ |
| SETC | 259 | ✓ | ✓ | ✓ | ✓ | ✓ | ✓ | ✓ | ✓ | ✓ | ✓ |
| SETE | 259 | ✓ | ✓ | ✓ | ✓ | ✓ | ✓ | ✓ | ✓ | ✓ | ✓ |
| SETG | 259 | ✓ | ✓ | ✓ | ✓ | ✓ | ✓ | ✓ | ✓ | ✓ | ✓ |
| SETGE | 259 | ✓ | ✓ | ✓ | ✓ | ✓ | ✓ | ✓ | ✓ | ✓ | ✓ |
| SETL | 259 | ✓ | ✓ | ✓ | ✓ | ✓ | ✓ | ✓ | ✓ | ✓ | ✓ |
| SETLE | 259 | ✓ | ✓ | ✓ | ✓ | ✓ | ✓ | ✓ | ✓ | ✓ | ✓ |
| SETNA | 259 | ✓ | ✓ | ✓ | ✓ | ✓ | ✓ | ✓ | ✓ | ✓ | ✓ |
| SETNAE | 259 | ✓ | ✓ | ✓ | ✓ | ✓ | ✓ | ✓ | ✓ | ✓ | ✓ |
| SETNB | 259 | ✓ | ✓ | ✓ | ✓ | ✓ | ✓ | ✓ | ✓ | ✓ | ✓ |
| SETNBE | 259 | ✓ | ✓ | ✓ | ✓ | ✓ | ✓ | ✓ | ✓ | ✓ | ✓ |
| SETNC | 259 | ✓ | ✓ | ✓ | ✓ | ✓ | ✓ | ✓ | ✓ | ✓ | ✓ |
| SETNE | 259 | ✓ | ✓ | ✓ | ✓ | ✓ | ✓ | ✓ | ✓ | ✓ | ✓ |
| SETNG | 259 | ✓ | ✓ | ✓ | ✓ | ✓ | ✓ | ✓ | ✓ | ✓ | ✓ |
| SETNGE | 259 | ✓ | ✓ | ✓ | ✓ | ✓ | ✓ | ✓ | ✓ | ✓ | ✓ |
| SETNL | 259 | ✓ | ✓ | ✓ | ✓ | ✓ | ✓ | ✓ | ✓ | ✓ | ✓ |
| SETNLE | 259 | ✓ | ✓ | ✓ | ✓ | ✓ | ✓ | ✓ | ✓ | ✓ | ✓ |
| SETNO | 259 | ✓ | ✓ | ✓ | ✓ | ✓ | ✓ | ✓ | ✓ | ✓ | ✓ |
| SETNP | 259 | ✓ | ✓ | ✓ | ✓ | ✓ | ✓ | ✓ | ✓ | ✓ | ✓ |
| SETNS | 259 | ✓ | ✓ | ✓ | ✓ | ✓ | ✓ | ✓ | ✓ | ✓ | ✓ |
| SETNZ | 259 | ✓ | ✓ | ✓ | ✓ | ✓ | ✓ | ✓ | ✓ | ✓ | ✓ |
| SETO | 259 | ✓ | ✓ | ✓ | ✓ | ✓ | ✓ | ✓ | ✓ | ✓ | ✓ |
| SETP | 259 | ✓ | ✓ | ✓ | ✓ | ✓ | ✓ | ✓ | ✓ | ✓ | ✓ |
| SETPE | 259 | ✓ | ✓ | ✓ | ✓ | ✓ | ✓ | ✓ | ✓ | ✓ | ✓ |
| SETPO | 259 | ✓ | ✓ | ✓ | ✓ | ✓ | ✓ | ✓ | ✓ | ✓ | ✓ |

| Mnemonic | Page# | P | PII | K6 | 3D! | 3Mx+ | SSE | SSE2 | A64 | SSE3 | E64T |
|---|---|---|---|---|---|---|---|---|---|---|---|
| SETS | 259 | ✓ | ✓ | ✓ | ✓ | ✓ | ✓ | ✓ | ✓ | ✓ | ✓ |
| SETZ | 259 | ✓ | ✓ | ✓ | ✓ | ✓ | ✓ | ✓ | ✓ | ✓ | ✓ |
| SFENCE | 443 | | | | | ✓ | ✓ | ✓ | ✓ | ✓ | ✓ |
| SGDT | 443 | ✓ | ✓ | ✓ | ✓ | ✓ | ✓ | ✓ | ✓ | ✓ | ✓ |
| SHL | 104 | ✓ | ✓ | ✓ | ✓ | ✓ | ✓ | ✓ | ✓ | ✓ | ✓ |
| SHLD | 105 | ✓ | ✓ | ✓ | ✓ | ✓ | ✓ | ✓ | ✓ | ✓ | ✓ |
| SHR | 110 | ✓ | ✓ | ✓ | ✓ | ✓ | ✓ | ✓ | ✓ | ✓ | ✓ |
| SHRD | 111 | ✓ | ✓ | ✓ | ✓ | ✓ | ✓ | ✓ | ✓ | ✓ | ✓ |
| SHUFPD | 155 | | | | | | | ✓ | ✓ | ✓ | ✓ |
| SHUFPS | 153 | | | | | | ✓ | ✓ | ✓ | ✓ | ✓ |
| SIDT | 449 | ✓ | ✓ | ✓ | ✓ | ✓ | ✓ | ✓ | ✓ | ✓ | ✓ |
| SLDT | 450 | ✓ | ✓ | ✓ | ✓ | ✓ | ✓ | ✓ | ✓ | ✓ | ✓ |
| SMSW | 450 | ✓ | ✓ | ✓ | ✓ | ✓ | ✓ | ✓ | ✓ | ✓ | ✓ |
| SQRTPD | 378 | | | | | | | ✓ | ✓ | ✓ | ✓ |
| SQRTPS | 377 | | | | | | ✓ | ✓ | ✓ | ✓ | ✓ |
| SQRTSD | 378 | | | | | | | ✓ | ✓ | ✓ | ✓ |
| SQRTSS | 377 | | | | | | ✓ | ✓ | ✓ | ✓ | ✓ |
| STC | 54 | ✓ | ✓ | ✓ | ✓ | ✓ | ✓ | ✓ | ✓ | ✓ | ✓ |
| STD | 77 | ✓ | ✓ | ✓ | ✓ | ✓ | ✓ | ✓ | ✓ | ✓ | ✓ |
| STI | 320 | ✓ | ✓ | ✓ | ✓ | ✓ | ✓ | ✓ | ✓ | ✓ | ✓ |
| STMXCSR | 448 | | | | | | ✓ | ✓ | ✓ | ✓ | ✓ |
| STOS | 75 | ✓ | ✓ | ✓ | ✓ | ✓ | ✓ | ✓ | ✓ | ✓ | ✓ |
| STOSB | 75 | ✓ | ✓ | ✓ | ✓ | ✓ | ✓ | ✓ | ✓ | ✓ | ✓ |
| STOSD | 75 | ✓ | ✓ | ✓ | ✓ | ✓ | ✓ | ✓ | ✓ | ✓ | ✓ |
| STOSQ | 75 | | | | | | | | 64 | | 64 |
| STOSW | 75 | ✓ | ✓ | ✓ | ✓ | ✓ | ✓ | ✓ | ✓ | ✓ | ✓ |
| STR | 451 | ✓ | ✓ | ✓ | ✓ | ✓ | ✓ | ✓ | ✓ | ✓ | ✓ |
| SUB | 180 | ✓ | ✓ | ✓ | ✓ | ✓ | ✓ | ✓ | ✓ | ✓ | ✓ |
| SUBPD | 336 | | | | | | | ✓ | ✓ | ✓ | ✓ |
| SUBPS | 336 | | | | | | ✓ | ✓ | ✓ | ✓ | ✓ |
| SUBSD | 337 | | | | | | | ✓ | ✓ | ✓ | ✓ |
| SUBSS | 337 | | | | | | ✓ | ✓ | ✓ | ✓ | ✓ |
| SWAPGS | 452 | | | | | | | | 64 | | 64 |
| SYSCALL | 453 | | | ✓ | ✓ | ✓ | | | ✓ | | 64 |
| SYSENTER | 453 | | | | | | ✓ | ✓ | | ✓ | ✓ |
| SYSEXIT | 453 | | | | | | ✓ | ✓ | | ✓ | ✓ |
| SYSRET | 453 | | | ✓ | ✓ | ✓ | | | ✓ | | 64 |
| TEST | 254 | ✓ | ✓ | ✓ | ✓ | ✓ | ✓ | ✓ | ✓ | ✓ | ✓ |
| UCOMISD | 262 | | | | | | | ✓ | ✓ | ✓ | ✓ |
| UCOMISS | 262 | | | | | | ✓ | ✓ | ✓ | ✓ | ✓ |

| Mnemonic | Page# | P | PII | K6 | 3D! | 3Mx+ | SSE | SSE2 | A64 | SSE3 | E64T |
|----------|-------|---|-----|----|----|------|-----|------|-----|------|------|
| UD2 | 446 | ✓ | ✓ | ✓ | ✓ | ✓ | ✓ | ✓ | ✓ | ✓ | ✓ |
| UNPCKHPD | 148 | | | | | | | ✓ | ✓ | ✓ | ✓ |
| UNPCKHPS | 139 | | | | | | ✓ | ✓ | ✓ | ✓ | ✓ |
| UNPCKLPD | 148 | | | | | | | ✓ | ✓ | ✓ | ✓ |
| UNPCKLPS | 139 | | | | | | ✓ | ✓ | ✓ | ✓ | ✓ |
| VERR | 454 | ✓ | ✓ | ✓ | ✓ | ✓ | ✓ | ✓ | ✓ | ✓ | ✓ |
| VERW | 454 | ✓ | ✓ | ✓ | ✓ | ✓ | ✓ | ✓ | ✓ | ✓ | ✓ |
| WAIT | 220 | ✓ | ✓ | ✓ | ✓ | ✓ | ✓ | ✓ | ✓ | ✓ | ✓ |
| WBINVD | 444 | ✓ | ✓ | ✓ | ✓ | ✓ | ✓ | ✓ | ✓ | ✓ | ✓ |
| WRMSR | 452 | ✓ | ✓ | ✓ | ✓ | ✓ | ✓ | ✓ | ✓ | ✓ | ✓ |
| XADD | 179 | ✓ | ✓ | ✓ | ✓ | ✓ | ✓ | ✓ | ✓ | ✓ | ✓ |
| XCHG | 66 | ✓ | ✓ | ✓ | ✓ | ✓ | ✓ | ✓ | ✓ | ✓ | ✓ |
| XLAT | 71 | ✓ | ✓ | ✓ | ✓ | ✓ | ✓ | ✓ | ✓ | ✓ | ✓ |
| XLATB | 71 | ✓ | ✓ | ✓ | ✓ | ✓ | ✓ | ✓ | ✓ | ✓ | ✓ |
| XOR | 90 | ✓ | ✓ | ✓ | ✓ | ✓ | ✓ | ✓ | ✓ | ✓ | ✓ |
| XORPD | 90 | | | | | | | ✓ | ✓ | ✓ | ✓ |
| XORPS | 90 | | | | | | ✓ | ✓ | ✓ | ✓ | ✓ |

# Reg/Mem Mapping

This appendix maps the addressing methods for memory load/save, jump table lookup, and call table lookup.

The same kind of memory reference that is used to access a memory table or array can also be used to access a jump vector. Almost any register can be used alone, in a pair addition, and with an optional base address and/or scale factor of {2, 4, or 8}, but you will note that there are some limitations in regard to the ESP register.

(Real Mode — Near or far is same opcodes)
(Protected Mode — Near or far is same opcodes)

```
jmp ...
jmp NearAdrPtr[...]
```

| eax | ebx | ecx | edx | esp | ebp | esi | edi |
|-----|-----|-----|-----|-----|-----|-----|-----|
| ax  | bx  | cx  | dx  | sp  | bp  | si  | di  |

(Real Mode — Near or far is same opcodes)
(Protected Mode — Near or far is same opcodes)

```
jmp word ptr [...]
jmp dword ptr [...]
jmp fword ptr [...]
jmp NearAdrPtr[...]
```

| eax | ebx | ecx | edx | esp | ebp | esi | edi |
|-----|-----|-----|-----|-----|-----|-----|-----|

| eax+eax | eax+ebx | eax+ecx | eax+edx | eax+esp | eax+ebp | eax+esi | eax+edi |
|---------|---------|---------|---------|---------|---------|---------|---------|
| ebx+eax | ebx+ebx | ebx+ecx | ebx+edx | ebx+esp | ebx+ebp | ebx+esi | ebx+edi |
| ecx+eax | ecx+ebx | ecx+ecx | ecx+edx | ecx+esp | ecx+ebp | ecx+esi | ecx+edi |
| edx+eax | edx+ebx | edx+ecx | edx+edx | edx+esp | edx+ebp | edx+esi | edx+edi |
| esp+eax | esp+ebx | esp+ecx | esp+edx | -       | esp+ebp | esp+esi | esp+edi |
| ebp+eax | ebp+ebx | ebp+ecx | ebp+edx | ebp+esp | ebp+ebp | ebp+esi | ebp+edi |
| esi+eax | esi+ebx | esi+ecx | esi+edx | esi+esp | esi+ebp | esi+esi | esi+edi |
| edi+eax | edi+ebx | edi+ecx | edi+edx | edi+esp | edi+ebp | edi+esi | edi+edi |

| | | | | | | | |
|---|---|---|---|---|---|---|---|
| eax*2 | ebx*2 | ecx*2 | edx*2 | - | ebp*2 | esi*2 | edi*2 |
| eax+eax*2 | eax+ebx*2 | eax+ecx*2 | eax+edx*2 | - | eax+ebp*2 | eax+esi*2 | eax+edi*2 |
| ebx+eax*2 | ebx+ebx*2 | ebx+ecx*2 | ebx+edx*2 | - | ebx+ebp*2 | ebx+esi*2 | ebx+edi*2 |
| ecx+eax*2 | ecx+ebx*2 | ecx+ecx*2 | ecx+edx*2 | - | ecx+ebp*2 | ecx+esi*2 | ecx+edi*2 |
| edx+eax*2 | edx+ebx*2 | edx+ecx*2 | edx+edx*2 | - | edx+ebp*2 | edx+esi*2 | edx+edi*2 |
| esp+eax*2 | esp+ebx*2 | esp+ecx*2 | esp+edx*2 | - | esp+ebp*2 | esp+esi*2 | esp+edi*2 |
| ebp+eax*2 | ebp+ebx*2 | ebp+ecx*2 | ebp+edx*2 | - | ebp+ebp*2 | ebp+esi*2 | ebp+edi*2 |
| esi+eax*2 | esi+ebx*2 | esi+ecx*2 | esi+edx*2 | - | esi+ebp*2 | esi+esi*2 | esi+edi*2 |
| edi+eax*2 | edi+ebx*2 | edi+ecx*2 | edi+edx*2 | - | edi+ebp*2 | edi+esi*2 | edi+edi*2 |

| | | | | | | | |
|---|---|---|---|---|---|---|---|
| eax*4 | ebx*4 | ecx*4 | edx*4 | - | ebp*4 | esi*4 | edi*4 |
| eax+eax*4 | eax+ebx*4 | eax+ecx*4 | eax+edx*4 | - | eax+ebp*4 | eax+esi*4 | eax+edi*4 |
| ebx+eax*4 | ebx+ebx*4 | ebx+ecx*4 | ebx+edx*4 | - | ebx+ebp*4 | ebx+esi*4 | ebx+edi*4 |
| ecx+eax*4 | ecx+ebx*4 | ecx+ecx*4 | ecx+edx*4 | - | ecx+ebp*4 | ecx+esi*4 | ecx+edi*4 |
| edx+eax*4 | edx+ebx*4 | edx+ecx*4 | edx+edx*4 | - | edx+ebp*4 | edx+esi*4 | edx+edi*4 |
| esp+eax*4 | esp+ebx*4 | esp+ecx*4 | esp+edx*4 | - | esp+ebp*4 | esp+esi*4 | esp+edi*4 |
| ebp+eax*4 | ebp+ebx*4 | ebp+ecx*4 | ebp+edx*4 | - | ebp+ebp*4 | ebp+esi*4 | ebp+edi*4 |
| esi+eax*4 | esi+ebx*4 | esi+ecx*4 | esi+edx*4 | - | esi+ebp*4 | esi+esi*4 | esi+edi*4 |
| edi+eax*4 | edi+ebx*4 | edi+ecx*4 | edi+edx*4 | - | edi+ebp*4 | edi+esi*4 | edi+edi*4 |

| | | | | | | | |
|---|---|---|---|---|---|---|---|
| eax*8 | ebx*8 | ecx*8 | edx*8 | - | ebp*8 | esi*8 | edi*8 |
| eax+eax*8 | eax+ebx*8 | eax+ecx*8 | eax+edx*8 | - | eax+ebp*8 | eax+esi*8 | eax+edi*8 |
| ebx+eax*8 | ebx+ebx*8 | ebx+ecx*8 | ebx+edx*8 | - | ebx+ebp*8 | ebx+esi*8 | ebx+edi*8 |
| ecx+eax*8 | ecx+ebx*8 | ecx+ecx*8 | ecx+edx*8 | - | ecx+ebp*8 | ecx+esi*8 | ecx+edi*8 |
| edx+eax*8 | edx+ebx*8 | edx+ecx*8 | edx+edx*8 | - | edx+ebp*8 | edx+esi*8 | edx+edi*8 |
| esp+eax*8 | esp+ebx*8 | esp+ecx*8 | esp+edx*8 | - | esp+ebp*8 | esp+esi*8 | esp+edi*8 |
| ebp+eax*8 | ebp+ebx*8 | ebp+ecx*8 | ebp+edx*8 | - | ebp+ebp*8 | ebp+esi*8 | ebp+edi*8 |
| esi+eax*8 | esi+ebx*8 | esi+ecx*8 | esi+edx*8 | - | esi+ebp*8 | esi+esi*8 | esi+edi*8 |
| edi+eax*8 | edi+ebx*8 | edi+ecx*8 | edi+edx*8 | - | edi+ebp*8 | edi+esi*8 | edi+edi*8 |

# Glossary

**#** — a number

**absolute address** — A fixed address within an application's code space.

**AI** — Artificial intelligence. Computer simulation of human behavior and intelligence.

**alpha channel** — A field within an RGBW (red, green, blue, alpha) color value representing the level of opacity and/or transparency.

**ALU** — Algorithmic Logic Unit

**AMD64** — AMD's 64-bit based processor family. Superset of their 32-bit processors.

**AoS** — Array of Structures {XYZW}[4]

**ASCII** — American Standard Code for Information Interchange. A 7-bit numerical representation used to represent control characters and the standard English language character set.

**ASE** — ASCII Scene Exporter (3D Studio MAX). Application Specific Extension (MIPS-3D)

**BCD** — Binary-coded decimal notation

**bi-endian** — A byte ordering of either big-endian or little-endian supported by a processor.

| (Byte) | 0 | 1 | 2 | 3 | |
|---|---|---|---|---|---|
| 0x1A2B3C4D | 1A | 2B | 3C | 4D | Big |
| | 4D | 3C | 2B | 1A | Little |

Note that the byte is endianless; that is, whether it is big-endian or little-endian, the MSB (most significant bit) is bit #7 and the LSB (least significant bit) is bit #0.

**big-endian** — The byte ordering typically used by large mainframes. For purposes of this book, that would include the EE, VU, PowerPC-AltiVec, and PowerPC-Gekko processors.

| | 0 | 1 | 2 | 3 |
|---|---|---|---|---|
| 0x1A2B3C4D | 1A | 2B | 3C | 4D |

**blit** — The process of transferring one or more blocks of data. The etymology of the word is Bacon, Lettuce, and Interactive Tomato.

**branch prediction** — A methodology used by a processor to predict at a conditional jump whether an instruction branch will be taken or not.

**BSP** — Board Support Package

**BTB** — Branch Target Buffer

**CD** — Compact Disc (storage capacity 540MB to 700MB)

**CODEC** — Compression/decompression

**compiler** — A software tool that converts symbolic source code into object code

**coprocessor** — A secondary processor that adds enhanced functionality to a primary processor

**CPU** — Central Processor Unit

**culling** — A process of reducing the number of polygons needed to be passed to the rendering engine

**DOS** — Disk operating system

**double extended-precision** — An extra long format (80-bit) storage of floating-point data

**double-precision** — A long format (64-bit) storage of floating-point data

**DSP** — Digital Signal Processing

**DV** — Digital Video

**DVD** — Digital Versatile Disk (storage capacity 17 GB)

**EM64T** — Extended Memory 64 Technology. A superset of the IA32 (Intel architecture) used by Xeon and advanced P4 processors.

**EULA** — End user license agreement

**FIFO** — First in, first out

**fixed-point** — A number in which the decimal point is fixed to a number of places

**flat memory** — An address space that appears to be one contiguous block of memory. This can be made up of RAM or virtual memory.

**floating-point** — A number in which the decimal point is floating and thus can be in any position. But it is typically stored in a sign, exponent, and mantissa components.

**FPU** — Floating-point unit

**GCC** — GNU C Compiler

**GDTR** — Global Descriptor Table Register

**GNU** — Gnu is not UNIX

**GPU** — Graphics processor unit

**GRDB** — Game Relational Data Base

**IA32** — Intel architecture 32-bit

**IA64** — Intel architecture 64-bit

**IDE** — Integrated development environment

**IDTR** — Interrupt Descriptor Table Register

**IEEE** — Institute of Electrical and Electronics Engineers

**indexed address** — An indexed element of an array of items. This is made up of the result of a base address summed with the product of the index and the size of the element (D = Base + index × element_size).

**IP** — Instruction pointer

**JPEG** — Joint Photographic Experts Group

**LCD** — Liquid crystal display

**little-endian** — The byte ordering used by most modern computers. For purposes of this book that would include the x86 and MIPS processor. A MIPS processor can be configured for big-endian but for game consoles it is used in a little-endian configuration.

| | 0 | 1 | 2 | 3 |
|---|---|---|---|---|
| 0x1A2B3C4D | 4D | 3C | 2B | 1A |

**LSB** — Least significant bit. The related bit depends upon the endian orientation.

**MBCS** — Multi-Byte Character System

**MIPS** — Million Instructions Per Second. See the References section for MIPS organization.

**MMX** — Multimedia Extensions

**MPEG** — Motion Picture Experts Group

**MSB** — Most significant bit. The related bit depends upon the endian orientation.

**MSR** — Model Specific Register

**non-temporal hint** — A hint (an indicator) to the processor that memory only requires a single access (one shot). This would be similar to copying a block of memory or performing a calculation but the result is not going to be needed for a while so there is no need to write it into the cache. Thus the memory access has no need to read and load cache, and therefore the code can be faster.

**open source** — A standard of the Open Source Initiative (OSI) that makes available the source code of a computer program free of charge to the general public

**PCM** — Pulse Coded Modulation

**polygon** — In the context of 3D rendering, a graphical primitive within a closed plane consisting of a three-sided (triangle) or four-sided (quadrilateral) representing a face typically covered by a texture.

**QNaN** — Quiet Not a Number

**relative address** — A delta address from a fixed address within an application

**RGB** — Red Green Blue

**RPL** — Request Privilege Level

**RPN** — Reverse Polish Notation

**SBCS** — Single Byte Character System

**scalar** — A single operation performed on a single data element
$D = A + B$

**scalar processor** — A processor that can perform only one instruction on one data element at a time

**SIMD** — Single Instruction Multiple Data. A computer instruction that performs the same instruction in parallel for a series of isolated packed data blocks.

**single-precision floating-point** — A standard format (32-bit) storage of floating-point data

**SMM** — System Management Mode

**SNaN** — Signaled Not a Number

**SoA** — Structure of Arrays

**squirrely** — A term I use in an attempt to explain the behavior of a piece of code

**superscalar processor** — A processor that performs similarly to a scalar processor but can handle multiple data operations simultaneously

**temporal data** — Memory that requires multiple accesses and therefore needs to be loaded into a cache for better throughput

**texture** — A 2D image that is mapped upon a 3D wireframe polygon to represent its surface

**TLB** — Translation Lookaside Buffer

**VBlank** — Vertical Blank

**vector** — (1) A pointer to code or data typically used in a table (vector table); (2) A one-dimensional array; (3) A line defined by a starting and ending points.

**vector processor** — A processor that performs an instruction on an entire array of data in a single step. See: scalar processor and superscalar processor.

**vertex** — The intersection of two vectors used to define a corner of a polygon, for example, three corners of a triangle or eight corners of a cube.

**vertex normal** — A direction vector perpendicular to the plane intersecting the three vertices of a triangle

**VSync** — Vertical Sync

**VU** — Vector Units

**x86** — An abbreviation for the 80x86 processor family inclusive of all its processors: 8086, 80186, 80286, 80386, 80486, Pentium, PII, PIII, P4, Xeon, K5, K6, Athlon, Duron, Opteron, etc.

**w-buffer** — A rectangular representation of the image buffer used to store the distance of each pixel in the image from the camera. The range of possible Z values is linearly distributed between the camera and a point in 3D space depicted as infinity. The distances from the camera are finer in resolution than those closer to infinity, allowing for a more refined depth of view.

**z-buffer** — A rectangular representation of the image buffer used to store the distance of each pixel in the image from the camera. The range of possible Z values is uniformly distributed between the camera and a point in 3D space depicted as infinity.

# Alignment Macros

```
#define ALIGN2(len)  ((len+1) & ~1)    // round up to 16 bits
#define ALIGN4(len)  ((len+3) & ~3)    // round up to 32 bits
#define ALIGN8(len)  ((len+7) & ~7)    // round up to 64 bits
#define ALIGN16(len) ((len+15) & ~15)  // round up to 128 bits
#define ALIGN32(len) ((len+31) & ~31)  // round up to 128 bits

#define ALIGN2048(len) ((len + 2047) & ~2047)
                                       // round up to 1 CD sector
```

# Algebraic Laws Used in This Book

| | | |
|---|---|---|
| *Additive Identity* | $n + 0 = 0 + n = n$ | |
| *Multiplicative Identity* | $n1 = 1n = n$ | |

| | |
|---|---|
| *Additive Inverse* | $a - b = a + (-b)$ |

| | |
|---|---|
| *Commutative Law of Addition* | $a + b = b + a$ |
| *Commutative Law of Multiplication* | $ab = ba$ |

| | | |
|---|---|---|
| *Distributive* | $a(b+c) = ab+ac$ | $(b+c)/a = b/a + c/a$ |

# References

AMD (Advanced Micro Devices)
http://www.amd.com

Intel
http://www.intel.com

Millennium Copyright Act
http://www.loc.gov/copyright/legislation/dmca.pdf

## ASE File Format

3ds max ASCII Scene Exporter description
http://www.solosnake.fsnet.co.uk/main/ase.htm

## Game Development Links

Online community for game developers of all levels
http://www.gamedev.net

Gamasutra — game developers
http://www.gamasutra.com

GDC — Game Developers Conference
http://www.gdconf.com

Game developer magazine
http://www.gdmag.com

Game development magazine
http://www.gignews.com

Game development search engine
http://www.game-developer.com

JPEG (Joint Photographic Experts Group)
http://www.jpeg.org

## MPEG

MPEG (Motion Picture Experts Group)
http://www.mpeg.org

Project Mayo — Open DivX
http://www.projectmayo.com

*MPEG-2*. John Watkinson. Butterworth-Heinemann, 1998. ISBN: 02405015-102.

*MPEG Video Compression Standard*. Joan L. Mitchell, Didier J. Legall, William B. Pennebaker, and Chad E. Fogg, editors. Chapman & Hall Publications, 1996. ISBN: 0412087715.

## SHA-1

Secure Hash Algorithm

### Personal Computer

IBM personal computer
http://www-1.ibm.com/ibm/history/catalog/itemdetail_57.html

Charlie Chaplin IBM promotion
http://www.multimania.com/myibm/pub_chaplin.htm

# Index

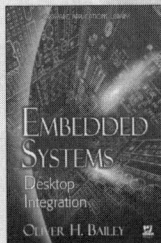

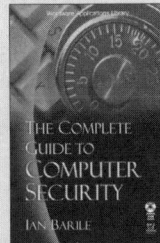